The Management of Strategy in the Marketplace

Ernest R. Cadotte
University of Tennessee

Harry J. Bruce
CEO
Illinois Central Railroad

D0166128

Contributing Authors

Harry J. Bruce
CEO Illinois Central Railroad

Ernest R. Cadotte
University of Tennessee

Sarah F. Gardial
University of Tennessee

Dominique Garval
Reims Management School

Kenneth C. Gilbert
University of Tennessee

Jacquelyn DeMatteo Jacobs
University of Tennessee

John T. Mentzer
University of Tennessee

James M. Reeve
Deloitte and Touche Professor of Accounting
University of Tennessee

Joyce E. A. Russell
University of Maryland

Ivan Slimák
Volkswagen Transmission (Shanghai) Co.

James W. Wansley
University of Tennessee

Robert B. Woodruff
Proffitt's, Inc. Professor of Marketing
University of Tennessee

THOMSON

SOUTH-WESTERN

Australia · Canada · Mexico · Singapore · Spain · United Kingdom · United States

THOMSON

SOUTH-WESTERN

The Management of Strategy in the Marketplace

Ernest R. Cadotte, Harry J. Bruce, Sarah F. Gardial, Dominique Garval, Kenneth C. Gilbert, Jacquelyn DeMatteo Jacobs, John T. Mentzer, James M. Reeve, Joyce E. A. Russell, Ivan Slimák, James W. Wansley, and Robert B. Woodruff

Editor-in-Chief:
Jack W. Calhoun

Vice President/Team Director:
Michael P. Roche

Executive Editor:
John Szilagyi

Developmental Editor:
Judith O'Neill

Marketing Manager:
Rob Bloom

Production Editor:
Emily S. Gross

Manufacturing Coordinator:
Diane Lohman

Compositor:
Pre-Press Company, Inc.

Printer:
Edwards Brothers
Ann Arbor, MI

Design Project Manager:
Christy Carr

Internal Designer:
Christy Carr

Cover Designer:
Christy Carr

Cover Photograph:
© PhotoDisc

Cover Illustration:
Christy Carr

Media Developmental Editor:
Kristen Meere

Media Production Editor:
Karen L. Schaffer

Library of Congress Cataloging-in-Publication Data

The management of strategy in the marketplace /
edited by Ernest R. Cadotte, Harry J. Bruce ;
contributing authors, Harry J. Bruce . . . [et al.].
  p. cm.
 Includes bibliographical references.
 ISBN 0-324-17575-2
 1. Industrial management. 2. Business
planning. 3. Marketing—Management.
 4. Self-directed work teams. 5. Leadership.
 6. Personnel management. I. Cadotte,
Ernest R. II. Bruce, Harry J. (Harry
James)
  HD30.4 M3615 2003
  658—dc21   2002008820

Dedication

This book and the Marketplace simulation are dedicated to my loving wife, Bonnie, and to my wonderful children, Joseph, Katie and John, who have always given me their enthusiastic support and encouragement.

—Ernie Cadotte

This book is dedicated to my children Robert, Stacy, and Beth and in loving memory of their Mother Vivienne and their Brother Jay.

—Harry Bruce

About the Authors

Ernest R. Cadotte

Ernest R. Cadotte is a professor of marketing at the University of Tennessee, where he teaches courses in integrated business management and market opportunity analysis. He holds a Ph.D. in marketing and logistics from Ohio State University, an M.B.A. in management science from the University of Colorado, and a B.S. in psychology from Michigan State University. His research interests include breakthrough work in customer satisfaction, channel management, market opportunity analysis, and psychological measurement. As a consultant, he developed a market analysis program for technology transfers at Oak Ridge National Laboratory and has advised a number of technology-based businesses. While at the University of Tennessee, Dr. Cadotte developed *Marketplace,* an integrated business simulation, with the goals of breaking business disciplines out of their own silos and of making business education more holistic. Used around the world in more than 100 universities and in numerous corporate training programs, *Marketplace* delivers top-quality management education to a broad and growing audience. He has published widely in the academic press, including *Journal of Marketing Research, Journal of Marketing, Research in Marketing,* and *Cornell Quarterly.*

Harry J. Bruce

Harry J. Bruce retired in 1990 after serving as chairman and chief executive officer of the Illinois Central Railroad. His retirement culminated a 35-year career that began when he joined the United States Steel Corporation as Assistant to the Director of Transport Research. He moved on to become Vice President of Marketing for the Spector Freight System, Assistant Vice President of Plant Operations at the Joseph Schlitz Brewing Company and Vice President of Marketing at the Western Pacific Railroad. Holder of a B.S. in transportation and industrial engineering from Kent State University and an M.S. in transportation economics from the University of Tennessee School of Business, Mr. Bruce also attended the Harvard Business School Advanced Management Program. He has held teaching positions at Duquesne University, the University of Pittsburgh, and Florida Atlantic University. He has published over 50 articles appearing in international business and academic journals and three texts: *How to Apply Statistics to Physical Distribution* (Chilton), *Distribution and Transportation Handbook* (Cahners), and Chapter 25, "Physical Distribution," in *Handbook of Modern Marketing,* 2nd ed. (McGraw-Hill). He also is the lead author, with Russel K. Hirst and Michael L. Keane, of *A Short Guide to Business Writing* (Prentice Hall). In 1988, Mr. Bruce became a fellow of the International Academy of Management. Following his retirement, Mr. Bruce was elected non-executive chairman of Roman Adhesives. He has also served as a director on several boards .

Lisa Dragoni

Lisa Dragoni is a Ph.D. Candidate in Organizational Behavior at the University of Maryland. She holds an M.A. in Public Policy and Women's Studies from George Washington University and a B.A. in Business Administration from Franklin and Marshall College. Prior to pursuing her Ph.D., she served as a consultant to public- and private-sector organizations on human resource management issues. She has delivered training to over 6,000 employees, managers, and executives in the areas of Equal Employment Opportunity, workforce diversity, teambuilding, and supervisory skill development. Examples of her consulting engagements include conducting large-scale organizational assessments, identifying future human resource needs, and leading strategic planning sessions to enact change within organizations. Her practical experience has inspired her current research interests of employee learning and development, leadership in innovative environments, and managerial development.

Sarah F. Gardial

Sarah Fisher Gardial is Assistant Dean in charge of the full-time M.B.A. program and an Associate Professor in the Department of Marketing, Logistics, and Transportation at the University of Tennessee. She earned her undergraduate and M.B.A. degrees in Marketing from the University of Arkansas, and her Ph.D. in Marketing from the University of Houston. Her primary expertise and research interests are in the areas of customer value and satisfaction, the decision processes of customers and consumers, consumer information processing, and buyer-seller relationships. With Bob Woodruff, she is the co-author of *Know Your Customer: New Perspectives on Customer Value and Satisfaction*. She has also written numerous articles for journal publications and conferences.

Dominique Garval

Dominique Garval graduated with a Civil Engineering Diploma from INSA Lyon and started his professional career as a field engineer with Becthel Corporation in San Francisco. He then moved on to work as a Sales Engineer for Universal Oil Products / Johnson Div. in Europe and Africa. After obtaining his Master of Sciences in Petroleum Engineering from the University of Texas at Austin, he was recruited by Phillips Petroleum where he worked as a Production Engineer in Texas and as a Marine Superintendent in the Gulf of Guinea. He subsequently followed the INSEAD M.B.A. program, after which he joined StratX, a management training firm, as a Managing Partner in charge of European Operations. At StratX, he delivered numerous management training seminars for blue chip companies in Europe, the United States and Japan. He is now Professor of Marketing at the Reims Management School and pursues his management training activities for large European and American companies. His academic interests revolve around Marketing Strategy, Strategic Management and the Management of Services. He is also in charge of RMS Center for Action Based Learning, the objective of which is to develop and foster action-based learning and multidisciplinary pedagogical approaches. During his time at RMS, he also obtained a DEA from the University of Lille.

Kenneth C. Gilbert

Kenneth C. Gilbert is a Professor in the Management Department at the University of Tennessee. He is a lead faculty member and previous chairman of the Management Science Program within the College of Business.

Dr. Gilbert's research and consulting interests are focused in the areas of production management systems, inventory control systems, supply chain integration, and lean manufacturing. He has worked with numerous organizations, including PepsiCo, Inc. and Georgia Pacific. He serves as a member of the University of Tennessee's MBA and Executive MBA core faculty teams, and he played a key role in developing the content for both programs. He has also taught in the Executive Development Programs of Ashridge Management College, England, and in Germany and Taiwan. He is the recipient of the University of Tennessee's prestigious Keally Award for Outstanding Teaching.

Dr. Gilbert received his M.S. in Mathematics and his Ph.D. in Management Science from the University of Tennessee.

Jacquelyn DeMatteo Jacobs

Jacquelyn DeMatteo Jacobs is an Adjunct Professor in the Management Department at the University of Tennessee, Knoxville, where she teaches both undergraduates and graduate students in the Professional MBA program. Her primary areas of research and applied work include compensation, work teams, performance appraisal, justice in the workplace, and employee relocation. She has published articles in several journals, including *Research in Organizational Behavior*, *Journal of Vocational Behavior*, *Journal of Organizational Behavior*, *American Compensation Association Journal*, *Training Research Journal*, and *Leadership Quarterly*, and she has presented research at numerous professional conferences. She is a member of the American Psychological Association, the Society for Industrial and Organizational Psychology, and the Academy of Management. She has consulted with a variety of organizations, including Eastman Chemical, Bryce Corporation, the Tennessee Assessment Center, and the University of Tennessee's Management Development Center. She received her Ph.D. in industrial/organizational psychology from the University of Tennessee, her M.A. in psychology from the American University, and her B.S. in psychology from Penn State.

John T. Mentzer

Dr. John T. (Tom) Mentzer is the Harry J. and Vivienne R. Bruce Chair of Excellence in Business Policy in the Department of Marketing, Logistics, and Transportation at the University of Tennessee. He has written more than 160 papers and articles and five books. Dr. Mentzer was recognized in 1996 as one of the five most prolific authors in the *Journal of the Academy of Marketing Science,* and in 1999 as the most prolific author in the *Journal of Business Logistics*. His research has focused on the contribution of marketing and logistics to customer satisfaction and strategic advantage; the application of computer decision models to marketing, logistics, and forecasting; and the management of the sales forecasting function. He serves on the editorial review boards of five journals and as occasional reviewer for six others. He presently serves on the Executive Committee and is Immediate Past President of the Council of Logistics Management. He was formerly President of the Academy of Marketing Science and is a Distinguished Fellow of the Academy of Marketing Science—a distinction granted to less than 20 scholars worldwide. Dr. Mentzer has conducted numerous programs and workshops for various segments of the business and government communities. He has served as a consultant for over 70 corporations and government agencies, is on the boards of directors of several corporations, and previously worked for General Motors Corporation.

James M. Reeve

Jim Reeve joined the faculty of the University of Tennessee in 1980 after completing his MBA from Drake University and Ph.D. from Oklahoma State University. At the University of Tennessee Dr. Reeve is a member of the MBA and EMBA core faculty and is on the MACC business core team. He is also a member of the Lean Enterprise Institute faculty. Dr. Reeve's research interests are in the areas of performance management, the lean enterprise, cost management, and information management. He has published over 35 articles in academic and professional journals, including the *Journal of Cost Management*, *Journal of Management Accounting Research*, *Accounting Review*, *Management Accounting*, and *Accounting Horizons*. In addition, Dr. Reeve has co-authored six books, including the market-leading *Accounting* (South-Western Publishing). He has consulted or provided training around the world for a wide variety of organizations, including Boeing, Procter and Gamble, Eaton Corporation, Freddie Mac, AMOCO, Lockheed Martin, Coca-Cola, and Philips Consumer Electronics.

Joyce E. A. Russell

Dr. Joyce E. A. Russell is a licensed industrial and organizational psychologist and has over 20 years of experience consulting with both private and public sector organizations. Her expertise is primarily in the areas of leadership and management development, negotiation tactics, training, career development, work teams, and change management. Some of her clients have included: Lockheed Martin Energy Systems, Marriott, Oak Ridge National Laboratory, Frito-Lay, Quaker Oats, M&M Mars, ALCOA, Boeing Corporation, Tennessee Valley Authority, and the State of Tennessee. She is the Distinguished Teaching Professor of Management and Organization in the Robert H. Smith School of Business at the University of Maryland. Since joining the Maryland faculty, she has consistently been honored for being an outstanding teacher (Top 15%). In 2001, she was named the University of Maryland's

Outstanding Faculty Advisor, and, in 2000, she was awarded the Allen J. Krowe Award for teaching excellence. She has also been on faculty at the University of Tennessee, where she taught in the Executive MBA, MBA, doctoral, and undergraduate programs and received numerous teaching and research awards, including the *Chancellor's Award for Excellence in Team Development and Team Teaching* for her work with the integrated MBA curriculum. Dr. Russell has published widely and currently serves as associate editor for the *Journal of Vocational Behavior* and is on the editorial boards of the *Journal of Applied Psychology*, *Human Resource Management Review*, and *Performance Improvement Quarterly*. She is an active member of the Academy of Management, American Psychological Association, American Society for Training and Development, Society for Industrial & Organizational Psychology, and the Society for Human Resource Management. She received her Ph.D. and M.A. degrees in Industrial & Organizational Psychology from the University of Akron and her B.A. degree in psychology/business from Loyola College in Maryland. She resides in her native state of Maryland with her family. She enjoys traveling, photography, sports, and cheering her favorite teams to victory!

Ivan Slimák

Ivan Slimák is a Senior Quality Assurance Manager of Volkswagen Transmission (Shanghai) Co. Ltd. in China, where he has been the management team member since establishing the new Chinese-German joint venture company. His industrial experience also includes the job as Senior Manager of Quality Process Technology for Powertrain at the headquarters of Volkswagen Group in Germany, where he was responsible for benchmarking development of process improvement quality standards and quality techniques for all Volkswagen Group powertrain and foundry plants worldwide. He was also Senior Manager of Quality Strategy and Quality Audits of Volkswagen brand Skoda Auto in Czech Republic. During his years in the car industry he has been working in cross-cultural projects in Europe, Asia, and North America as well, where he gained on-the-job experience of building, training, and leading new teams.

Before joining the car industry in 1992 he was working as a Senior Assistant Professor in Quality Management and Engineering Metrology at the Technical University Kosice and also as a consultant in quality management. He holds a Ph.D. in mechanical engineering technology from the Technical University Kosice, Slovak Republic.

James W. Wansley

Dr. James W. Wansley, Ph.D., C.F.A. is the head of the finance department at the University of Tennessee. He also holds the Clayton Homes Chair of Excellence in Finance. He is the former Director of the Financial Institutions Center at the University of Tennessee. He previously served on the finance faculty at Louisiana State University. Dr. Wansley earned his B.A. from Emory University, his M.B.A. from the University of Georgia, and his Ph.D. from the University of South Carolina. He is the author of more than two dozen publications and research papers that have appeared in journals, including: *Journal of Financial and Quantitative Analysis*, *Journal of Banking and Finance*, *Financial Management*, *The Financial Review, Journal of Financial Research,* and *Journal of Business Finance and Accounting*. His research has focused on the market for corporate control, especially the method of payment used in acquisitions, corporate financial policies, and bank capital issues.

Dr. Wansley serves as an associate editor for the *Journal of Financial Research, The Financial Review*, and *Survey and Synthesis*. He is currently trustee of the Eastern Finance Association and has served formerly as President and Vice President of the Eastern Finance Association; President, Vice President and member of the executive board of the Southern Finance Association; and President and Vice President of the Financial Management Association.

Dr. Wansley teaches regularly at the Graduate School of Banking of the South and the Southeastern School of Banking. He has been a finalist for the Ross Outstanding Teaching Award presented by the College of Business for senior faculty. In 1994 he was the recipient of the Hoechst-Celanese Award for Research and Teaching, and in 1999 he received the Bank of America Faculty Leader Medal Award in the College of Business. He currently is working as a consultant with several bank holding companies in the area of compliance and investment policies, and is an advisor for a regional money management firm. He is a member of the board of directors of Vinyl Corners, Inc. He is the founding President of the Knoxville chapter of Chartered Financial Analysts and holds the Chartered Financial Analysts designation. Dr. Wansley speaks nationally on stock selection and mutual funds for the American Association of Individual Investors.

Robert B. Woodruff

Robert B. Woodruff is Proffitt's, Inc. Professor of Marketing and Department Head for the Department of Marketing, Logistics and Transportation at the University of Tennessee. His research concerns customer value and satisfaction, market opportunity analysis, and marketing strategy issues. He has published five books and authored more than 40 journal articles and conference papers. His work has appeared in the *Journal of Marketing*, *Journal of Marketing Research*, *Journal of Consumer Research*, *Journal of the Academy of Marketing Science*, and *Journal of Consumer Satisfaction, Dissatisfaction and Complaining Behavior*. He is active in professional associations, and currently, he is a member of the Board of Governors for the Academy of Marketing Science. He also serves on the editorial review boards of the *Journal of the Academy of Marketing Science* and *Journal of Strategic Marketing*. Through consulting, learning, and research partnerships, he has worked with more than two dozen companies in consumer, industrial, product, and service industries.

Brief Contents

Contents

Preface

The genesis of this book and its accompanying simulation (an optional add-on for instructors who wish to incorporate a "virtual practice field" in their courses) grew out of the integrative MBA program pioneered at the University of Tennessee in the early 1990s. At that time, we conducted an assessment of our program and those of several peer institutions around the country. Students, alumni, recruiters, executives, educators, and administrators all participated. The findings were consistent and unequivocal: although the graduates of our program were well trained in the "science" of management, they lacked a certain set of intangibles. So we asked our "customers," beyond the acquisition of expert knowledge in eight or nine subject silos ranging from finance to marketing to strategy to accounting, what does it take to be an effective manager? The answer came back loud and clear: an integrated perspective of business, interpersonal skills, the ability to work in teams, and experience in leadership. Up until then, it was apparent, we had overtrained in some areas and undertrained in other critical areas. So we went to work to develop a program that explicitly promotes interdisciplinary thinking and interpersonal development.

A team of faculty from across the business school was pulled together to redesign the MBA program, with the goal of creating a curriculum that developed leadership, teamwork, interpersonal skills, and an integrative perspective, along with substantive knowledge in each of the core business functions. After a year in design and two more years of purposeful adjustment in the classroom, we accomplished our goal. And with this success, we went on to create an integrative Executive MBA, Physicians EMBA, EMBA in Taiwan, Professional MBA, and, more recently, a newly burnished undergraduate curriculum, all patterned after the same design principles.

One of the real benefits of our working together to build a new MBA curriculum without silos was the elimination of much of the silo thinking present in our own departments. Another extension of our drive to achieve cross-disciplinary learning in the redesign of our MBA program is this textbook—*The Management of Strategy in the Marketplace*. Key faculty and industry practitioners—experts in leadership, governance, quality control, and strategy—joined forces to create this integrative approach to the business school curriculum. Contributing authors asked themselves, What should students learn if they could master just a handful of critical issues within their disciplines? What, in essence, does every manager need to know? The resulting set of concepts, viewpoints, principles, tools, and ways of thinking are clearly represented in each chapter of this book. Together with the optional online business simulation that accompanies it—*Global Corporate Management in the Marketplace*—the two provide the competence and confidence that students need to be effective, responsive, and competitive in their ensuing careers.

Target Audience

In a sense, this textbook encapsulates the core of the business school curriculum and provides an overview of what is typically taught in the first year of most MBA programs. As such, it is an ideal resource for the student who, about to start an MBA, is looking for a leg up. It is also an ideal compendium for the second-year MBA student who wants to review and integrate many of the key principles delivered in the first-year MBA core. At the undergraduate level, *The Management of Strategy in the Marketplace* delivers a truly integrative capstone experience. And, among practitioners who haven't yet made the commitment to go to graduate school yet nonetheless need training now in many of the core elements of an MBA education, *The Management of Strategy in the Marketplace* definitely fills a void.

Powerful Pedagogy

As a carefully winnowed compendium of deep, reliable information on how to conduct a business, this textbook can make a valuable contribution to the lifelong learning of any business student. But our desire to validate learning through application is why a strategy simulation—*Global Corporate Management in the Marketplace*—is an available counterpart to this book; in combination, the two constitute a powerful pedagogy for learning. In short, the textbook lays the foundation and the simulation provides the practice: First understand and then apply. This intensive pedagogy—the complementary fusion of theory and practice—has effectively honed the abilities of many in the military, musical, and competitive arenas. When applied to business training, the same rigorous mental and physical exercises that so benefit high-skill military personnel and elite athletes can also train the mind and actions of business decisionmakers, engendering an instinctive ability to act and react as professionals.

Organization of Text

Mature organizations are very complex and, consequently, difficult to understand without hours of investment in analysis and conjecture. But, regardless of their complexity, organizations do not spring up in full form overnight. They evolve in response to changing conditions, yet their evolution more or less follows a logical course. By modeling the evolutionary path of a new venture, students more readily understand why firms do the things they do and why they structure their operations as they do than when asked to look at an existing firm in cross-section. Thus this textbook and its accompanying simulation are laid out according to the lifecycle of a new firm. Our organizational strategy is to present students with ideas, ways of thinking, and tools as they logically become relevant to an evolving firm.

Part One of the text presents the fundamentals of how to lead and organize the business team. Part Two focuses on the startup phase of a business, including market opportunity analysis, strategic planning, creation of customer value, and financial accounting. Part Three addresses the issue of how to grow a business via the use of outside capital and the role of boards of directors in expanding firms. Part Four discusses the tools of business and how businesses can continually improve their performance through the management of the team, production processes, profits, the supply chain, and human resources.

The chronology of decisions and actions in *Global Corporate Management* mirrors the composition and arrangement of material in this textbook. As simulation play progresses from one decision period to the next, players are faced with an evolving set of issues and decisions. The textbook provides what players need to know in order to deal competently with these issues and decisions. We call this "just in time" learning. If students are handed a tool when they are in need of that particular tool, they will appreciate its relevance and be more receptive to incorporating it into their natural thought processes.

Part One: Before You Start in Business

The managing partners of any new business need first to organize themselves before they start up a business. The guidance on leadership **(Chapter 1)** and on forming a business team **(Chapter 2)** is crucial. Chapter 1 on leadership provides a compelling review of what it takes to be a leader. Leadership is all about self-discipline and initiative. It does not come by accident; it is attained via purposeful study and hard work. Chapter 2 on group dynamics and teamwork lays out the process by which teams are formed and how they can evolve into effective organizational units. It also offers a number of worthwhile prescriptions for developing successful business teams.

Part Two: Getting Started in Business

Before expending any resources on a new business venture, managers must understand the business opportunity ahead of them and have a strategy for attacking it.

Even good ideas come to bad ends if not properly pursued. The focus in Part Two is on how to approach a business opportunity. What is the strategy for success? The strategic planning process **(Chapter 3)** explains how to develop a game plan for creating and managing a business. In the next five chapters, we drill into the mechanics of developing a strategy for creating and serving demand. First, we present a model for evaluating a market opportunity **(Chapter 4)**. Next, we zero in on understanding customer value **(Chapter 5)**. We then put the focus on exploiting the market's many response functions with a perspective on marketing strategy **(Chapter 6)**. In **Chapter 7**, we introduce Quality Function Deployment, a great tool for aligning product features with the benefits desired by the target market. In **Chapter 8**, we review how to track and thus manage business performance, putting the focus on measuring wealth (balance sheet), measuring the change in wealth (income statement), and measuring the change in cash (statement of cash flows).

Part Three: Expanding the Business

Many new ventures reach a point where the business opportunity is greater than the capital available to exploit it. Any business can grow slowly using the profits from current operations, but restricting growth in this fashion can severely affect the ability to remain competitive or create wealth for its owners. Thus many startup firms seek outside funding in the form of new equity investment.

The venture capital community is a frequent source for new funding among entrepreneurial firms. But to attract this money, venture capitalists require a plan. In Part Three we begin by discussing how to prepare a business plan for venture capitalists **(Chapter 9)**. Next, we explore the sources of funding, the management of financial resources, and firm valuation, always a key ingredient in venture capital negotiations **(Chapter 10)**.

Once a firm obtains outside funding, it is generally expected that the firm takes on a professional Board of Directors that has serious oversight responsibility. Part Three concludes with an in-depth review of the role of the Board of Directors **(Chapter 11)**, a highly relevant discussion of the Board's fiduciary responsibility in light of the Enron collapse.

Part Four: Skillful Adjustment and Continuous Improvement

As General George C. Patton observed during World War II, a strategy rarely survives the test of battle intact. Constant adjustment is imperative as new information comes to light and events unfold in unexpected ways. Similarly, customers, channel partners, or rival firms will not always respond as assumed. To succeed, business managers must become skillful adjusters. They must (1) monitor customer satisfaction and consumer behavior, the competitive landscape, and the internal operations of the firm; (2) discover opportunities for improvement; then (3) skillfully adjust strategy and tactics in order to realize the overarching goals set for the firm. Part Four is designed to provide the perspective and tools to manage a firm to excellence. The chapters in this part could be presented in any order: as a firm grows towards maturity, everything is important.

We begin Part Four by offering guidelines on how to manage a team to excellence **(Chapter 12)**. We stress the need for self-diagnosis as a necessary prerequisite to high performance. Next, we carefully lay out the process for continuously improving the quality of the firm's operations and processes and, thereby, the reliability of the products it produces **(Chapter 13)**. In **Chapter 14** we extend this line of thinking by focusing attention on how to create a lean manufacturing operation that is responsive to the market. Next we shift attention to the mental and financial discipline of profit management **(Chapter 15)**. A particularly useful tool, Activity-Based Costing, is explored. The goal is to discover the profitability of every business activity so that a firm's strategy and tactics can be adjusted to take advantage of profit winners and to revitalize or cut profit losers. We wrap up our presentation of process improvement by discussing supply chain management and the concept of logistics leverage **(Chapter 16).** Numerous examples of how to improve a firm's logistical operations up and down the sales channel are discussed. Finally, we complete Part Four with a thoughtful review of the human resource needs of a young organization and how they evolve over time **(Chapter 17).** Additional properties on how to recruit, maintain, and motivate the people who create the wealth for a firm's owners are analyzed.

"This integrated text and simulation is the best of the newest breed of high level approaches to teaching strategy: conceptual, engaging and tied to how 'real world' decisions are made. Kudos to Ernest Cadotte and Harry Bruce for this path-breaking work."

John Rau
Chief Executive Officer, Chicago Title and Trust Company
former Chief Executive Officer, LaSalle National Bank
former Dean, School of Business, Indiana University

"The latest management knowledge presented by scholars, successful also as global practitioners, is unique. The student can readily identify the author's concern for applicability and for results. The publication of The Management of Strategy *in the Marketplace is more refined towards these concerns."*

Dr. Pedro Nueno
IESE University, Barcelona
Chairman, Academic Council, China/Europe International
Business School (Shanghai)

"It has only been in the last decade or so that business texts have recognized the importance of leadership. In most cases, the subject of leadership has been treated with a cursory brush. I am pleased to see attention given the subject and related chapters on teamwork in The Management of Strategy *in the Marketplace. Recent tragic events elevate the study of leadership from that of important to imperative."*

James M. Denny
Vice Chairman
Sears, Roebuck and Company

"This new book embodies a fresh and compelling approach in the quest to divine the formula for management success. It contains an intriguing combination of how-to-advice coupled with thoughtful dissertations on subjects of overarching importance."

Richard J. L. Senior
Chairman, President, and Chief Executive Officer
Morgan Industries

"A comprehensive and invaluable text for all students of management whether currently enrolled in degree programs or work-a-day practitioners desiring to sharpen the focus of their thinking."

Roger E. Birk
former Chairman
Merrill Lynch

Acknowledgments

Harry Bruce and I would like to acknowledge the tremendous support of all those who have helped to prepare *The Management of Strategy in the Marketplace*. First, we would like to thank our co-authors. They have done an absolutely wonderful job of selecting material that is highly relevant to today's manager and of communicating it in a concise and interesting style.

Next, we would like to thank Michael Keene, who edited each chapter and provided many valuable suggestions to improve flow and delivery of the disciplinary material. He was ably assisted by Jill Krase and Fritz Plous.

Our friends at South-Western have also been very helpful in preparing the final product. John Szilagyi, Executive Editor, had the foresight to publish the text and to put the publisher's resources behind our work. Judy O'Neill, Developmental Editor, has been the tough but pleasant taskmaster. She has worked hard with everyone to make sure the project stayed on schedule and provided lots of good ideas to improve the text and link it to the simulation. Emily Gross and Robert Caceres also lent their expertise to the preparation of the manuscript. They provided the final edit and executed the layout of the book, which was designed by Christy Carr.

We would also like to thank the reviewers who provided valuable feedback and encouragement. In particular, we would like to thank:

Roger E. Birk
Chairman, Merrill Lynch

James M. Denny
Vice Chairman and Chief Financial Officer
Sears, Roebuck and Company

Gerald H. Graham
R. P. Clinton Distinguished Professor of Management
Wichita State University

Douglas Hagestad
Adjunct Professor of Marketing
Northwestern University

Pedro Nueno
Professor IESE, Barcelona
Vice Chancellor, International Academy of Management
Member of the Board, Chairman
Academic Council, China Europe International Business School (Shanghai)

John Rau
CEO, LaSalle National Bank
CEO, Chicago Title and Trust Company
Dean, School of Business, Indiana University

Michael D. Santoro
Assistant Professor of Management
Lehigh University

Richard L. Senior
Chairman, President, and Chief Executive Officer
Morgan Industries

Marketplace

Marketplace simulations have been the focus of my work for more than a dozen years. My goal has been to create world-class business training tools. With the creative help and thoughtful work of many individuals, the goal has been achieved. *Global Corporate Management* represents the pinnacle of our development efforts.

Dean Jan Williams and C. Warren Neel (former Dean) deserve special thanks for their generous investment in the *Marketplace* development program over the years. I am thankful that, in spite of the many competing demands for funding, both Jan and Warren invested in this wonderful educational venture.

I want to thank all of my co-authors for their contributions to the learning experience. They identified the critical areas in their disciplines that needed to be addressed in *Marketplace*. They patiently explained the nuances of decisions to be made and their linkages with the other parts of the business. They are the source of the great richness in this edition of *Marketplace*.

I would also like to thank the development team that turned ideas into action, including Peter Matis, Jozef Briss, Peter Kolciter, and Martin Klima. Peter Matis served as the courseware coordinator and had the primary responsibility for development. Without Peter's "magic," *Marketplace* would not have achieved its full potential. Peter Kolciter and Jozef Briss were instrumental in programming the screens from which *Marketplace* players work. Martin Klima designed the user interface and graphical content for students and instructors. He added his artistic touch to make the Web interface more interesting, fun, pleasant, and easier to work with. In addition, Maria Vaskova, Yvette Fragile, and Sean Mullins were very helpful in preparing the textual content that guides players through the decision-making process.

Global Corporate Management in the Marketplace was born on the Web. It benefited greatly from the faculty who had the courage to experiment with it, including John Nicholls (Florida International University), Ron Decker (University of Wisconsin—Eau Claire), Ira Dollich (Florida International University), Barnett Greenberg (Florida International University), Bruce Behn (University of Tennessee), Nittaya Wongtada (National Institute of Development Administration, Thailand), Charlotte Lehman (University of Tennessee), Geoff Stewart (University of Oklahoma), Melinda Jones (University of Tennessee), Juan Florin (Bryant College), Marian Kapuscinski (Krakow School of Management and Banking), Ken Gehert (University of Arizona), Stanley Shapiro (Simon Fraser University), Alfred Hawkins (Rockhurst College), Jean Walker (University of Houston-Clear Lake), Steve Meckley (Jackson Community College), and Carol Decker (Lincoln Memorial University).

Over the years, I have found that beta testers are a special breed. These faculty are willing to take risks and put in extra work in their quest for a better learning experience for their students. The *Marketplace* experience is much improved for their thoughtful suggestions.

The *Marketplace* Processing Center at Innovative Learning Solutions, Inc., also deserves special thanks. Martin Klima was the leading designer for the creation of the automated system for processing simulation games and works closely with faculty on intensive simulation exercises. Jan Simicka is a superb Web master and skillfully manages the Web infrastructure on which *Marketplace* runs. Sean Mullins manages the day-to-day play of *Marketplace* for thousands of students and manages to keep everyone happy. Jeanine Schmierbach works with faculty to arrange games and makes sure the trains run on time, and Maria Vaskova helps to service new customers. They often work long after closing hours to ensure that the games run smoothly. The entire ILS team does a great job. Faculty and students are always complimentary of the proficient and friendly support of Sean, Jano, Martin, Jeanine, and Maria. I would also like to thank the thousands of students who were the first to experience this great adventure. They took all the difficulties in stride. They told me what they liked and did not like. Many of the best ideas came from these students. It is my hope that they have gained as much from *Marketplace* as I have gained from them.

All of these people have helped to make the integrated *Marketplace* simulation and this textbook a reality. Their wonderful talents have made an enormous difference. To each of you I say, "Thank you for a job well done."

Most of all, I would like to thank my wife, Bonnie, and my children, Joseph, Kate, and John. Joseph is the Writing Center Administrator and Web Master at the College of Architecture and Urban Planning at the University of Washington. Joseph was my first alpha tester and helped me with the early refinements of the simulation. Kate, a recent graduate of the University of Tennessee, has been my longest-running (and best) alpha tester. Her thoughtful questions, comments, and suggestions have helped me to create a more meaningful exercise. Together Kate and Joseph thankfully discovered software bugs and interface problems before the software was handed off to beta testers and their students. Of course my youngest, John, has always been my pleasant distraction. He has helped me to keep my work in perspective.

Bonnie was my sounding board for all of the ideas that went into this simulation. She gave me good counsel and encouragement throughout this endeavor. Thankfully, my family was very patient with the many hours that I have spent developing and refining *Marketplace*.

Ernie Cadotte
University of Tennessee

Ernest R. Cadotte
University of Tennessee

Overview

This text and its accompanying simulation—*Global Corporate Management in the Marketplace*—is a rigorous training regimen designed to develop business leadership and management skills. It promotes strategic thinking and team dynamics through a rare combination of strategic business instruction and compelling market challenges within a true-to-life simulated environment. There are five hallmarks to its learning methodology:

1. In-depth treatment of all functional areas of business.
2. Heavy emphasis on the interconnectedness of business disciplines.
3. Continual application of strategic planning and execution skills.
4. Repetitive practice of business fundamentals.
5. Ongoing opportunities to demonstrate leadership, teamwork, and interpersonal skills.

Essential to the training regimen is the integration of this textbook and the *Marketplace* business simulation. The textbook lays out an intellectual foundation that will prepare you to compete in the real marketplace. The simulation provides a living case through which you will gain hands-on experience in business management. In short, the textbook provides the theory; the simulation provides the practice. The two together represent a powerful and ambitious learning methodology that is personally relevant and, we hope, highly motivating. At the very least, the type of experiential learning epitomized by *Marketplace* provokes a slew of benefits.

- Facilitates the learning of important business concepts, principles, tools, and ways of thinking.
- Enhances your understanding of the linkages among the functional areas of business.
- Promotes better decision making by helping you see how your decisions can affect the performance of others and the organization as a whole.
- Develops strategic planning and execution skills within a rapidly changing environment.
- Crystallizes the financial implications of your business decisions by linking them to cash flows and bottom line performance.
- Instills financial accountability and the simultaneous need to deliver customer value.
- Internalizes how important it is to use market data and competitive signals to adjust the strategic plan and more tightly focus business tactics.
- Excites the competitive spirit and the drive to excel in the market.
- Builds confidence through knowledge and experience.

WHAT IS *MARKETPLACE*?

Marketplace is a powerful yet entertaining way to learn how to compete in a fast-paced market where customers are demanding and the competition is working hard to take away your business. It is not only a motivational learning experience but also a transformational one.

Working in teams of four to five, you and your teammates build an entrepreneurial firm, experiment with strategies, compete with other participants in a virtual business world filled with tactical detail, and struggle with business fundamentals and the interplay among marketing, manufacturing, logistics, human resources, finance, accounting, and team management. You take control of an enterprise and manage its operations through several decision cycles. Repeatedly, you must analyze a situation, plan a strategy to improve it, and then execute that strategy out into the future. You face great uncertainty both from the outside environment and from your own decisions. Incrementally, you learn to skillfully adjust your strategy as you discover the nature of real-life decisions, conflicts, trade-offs, and potential outcomes.

LEARNING STRATEGY

Time is compressed and the business cycle is accelerated; then you are immersed in the management of business. Rather than start you and your team in the middle of a story (with a mature firm), *Marketplace* mimics a new venture situation. Your firm expands its operations and takes on new tasks and responsibilities over eight or more decision rounds representing a two- to three-year period of compressed time. You will evaluate the market opportunity, choose a business strategy, evaluate tactical options, and enter a series of decisions with profitability in mind. Your decisions are then weighed against the decisions of your competitors in the *Marketplace* simulator. Results are quickly fed back to you, and the next round of decision making begins.

How do you adjust your strategy to become a stronger competitor? By studying end-user opinions, smart competitive moves, and your own operational and financial data. As your business grows, the simulation gradually but purposefully introduces new issues that you must master. As you will discover, each quarter, or decision period, has a dominant activity and a set of decisions that pull you through the business life cycle, from start-up to development, to growth, and ultimately to near maturity. As you work through this cycle, *Marketplace* phases in content relevant to the current period. Corresponding readings in this textbook and in the simulation's help files isolate the nature of the decisions being faced, the issues to be dealt with, linkages with other decisions, and the trade-offs to be considered.

By design, the simulation requires that each quarter's activities build upon prior content so that there is considerable opportunity to learn which actions drive performance up or down. By design, the simulation repeatedly challenges your skill in cash-flow planning, value creation in product design, production scheduling, supply chain management, employee motivation, profitability analysis, and strategic planning and management. The repetitive nature of the exercise works in your favor.

By design, the simulation makes competition key. The competitive excitement of the game is infectious. Winning requires that your team know more and acts faster than the competition. Knowing that the competition is also working hard to win will catch you and all other players in an upward spiral of excellence. We see it all the time.

MARKETPLACE ENVIRONMENT

The *Marketplace* environment has four major components: the game scenario, market segmentation, determinants of demand, and tactical decisions.

Game Scenario

When you enter *Marketplace,* you will be starting up a new manufacturing company in the nascent international microcomputer industry. To keep the scenario simple, you will assume that the microcomputer industry is in the introductory stage of its product life cycle; that is, there is no industry history, and there are no established competitors. In fact, you and your classmates will become the PC industry. Furthermore, all competitors, including your own firm, will start the game with exactly the same resources and knowledge of the market.

You will compete in 20 international markets (see **Exhibit 1**), where needs and wants vary by country/region. Market potential and operating costs will be affected by changing exchange rates and tariffs. These, in turn, will be affected by international politics and the global economy.

All players will sell through company-owned sales channels in major metropolitan markets located around the world or over the Internet. Your target market will be the business sector. You will not sell to the home market; you will not sell through retail stores. Rather, your business strategy will be tightly focused on direct sales to business customers.

To generate sales, your salespeople will search out customers by calling on business offices within their geographic markets. In addition, each sales office will have a showroom where potential customers can stop by to inspect equipment and learn about its use.

Your products ship from a factory warehouse to regional break-bulk centers and on to individual customers within the region. If the product is not available at the time of the order, the customer is lost. Beware of the disgruntled customer. He will tell other potential customers of his dissatisfaction and thus adversely affect demand in the next quarter. End users are represented in the simulation by a computer algorithm that emulates the decision-making process of individual business users.

Market Segmentation

Five market segments constitute the *Marketplace* PC market: Cost Cutter, Innovator, Mercedes, Workhorse, and Traveler.

- The *Cost Cutter* segment is a large segment that looks for a very easy-to-use computer for very basic office applications. The segment is very price sensitive.

- The *Workhorse* segment is the largest group of customers. They want a PC for a variety of office workers to use. It should have substantial capability and flexibility, although not top of the line. Ease of use is more important than high performance. It should also be modestly priced.

- The *Innovator* segment is a small segment that uses a computer for large computational problems (engineering, accounting, inventory management). The segment wants the latest technology and will pay a small premium for this high performance.

- The *Mercedes* segment is looking for a high-performance computer to use in sophisticated engineering and manufacturing applications. Mercedes customers are willing to pay substantially more for high performance. At the start of the exercise, Mercedes customers are not in the market for PCs. They prefer mainframes and minicomputers. It is not likely that Mercedes customers will be willing to buy until some time in the second year when new computer technology is introduced.

- The *Traveler* segment wants a practical computer to use on the road. Traveler customers are executives and salespeople who travel a great deal. This segment is moderately price sensitive.

These five segments are portrayed in **Exhibit 2**. The circles are positioned to indicate the price and performance require-

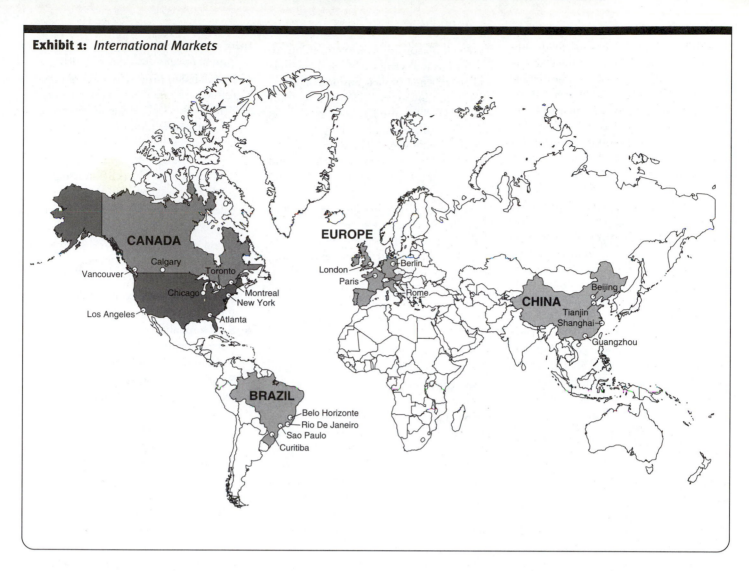

ments of each segment. The size of the segment is portrayed by the size of the circle.

As you might expect, each segment has different needs and wants, and each requires a different market strategy to appeal to it. Each segment will respond to different advertising messages and be selective in the media it reads or watches. Expect a certain amount of crossover between segments. However, as competing teams begin to design brands that are better targeted to individual segment needs, less crossover should occur. The size of each segment is expected to vary by geographic area.

Determinants of Demand

Several factors determine the rate at which potential customers become active buyers in a market. Total demand in any quarter will be determined by (1) the market's sales potential, (2) the seasonal and economic conditions of the global economy, and (3) the nature and extent of competition.

Market Potential

Sales will depend upon the number and composition of potential buyers in each geographic market. Markets with a larger population base will almost always yield more potential customers. Their distribution across different segments, however, will depend upon the unique characteristics of the region, including its industrial base, geography, climate, and the current state of its economy.

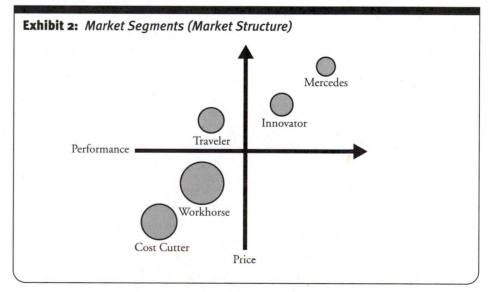

Exhibit 2: *Market Segments (Market Structure)*

Economic Conditions

You will find that total demand follows the natural swings of the international economy, including seasonal, cyclical, and long-term business trends. In terms of seasonality, the fall, or fourth, quarter of the calendar year usually has the highest sales potential due to end-of-year buying among industrial firms and holiday-season buying among consumers. The first quarter of the year (winter) is a decent sales period, but sales are usually down relative to the fall peak. The slowest sales period is during the second quarter (spring) of the year. Sales pick up again during the summer and reach their peak in the fall. At this time, the overall economy is experiencing a slow upward growth trend. International economic conditions and the political climate between countries also deserve careful scrutiny. These evolving conditions are reported in the industry newsletter and affect potential demand, exchange rates, and tariffs. They, in turn, affect business opportunities and costs throughout the world.

Competition

In *Marketplace*, demand does not exist for the taking. Demand is zero at the outset of the game. You and the other competitors must create the market. You must (1) discover where your customers are and locate a sales channel there; (2) sell brands that customers want and at a price they are willing to pay; (3) inform and persuade customers to buy through advertising; and (4) hire salespeople to go out and find customers and persuade them to buy.

Many students make a fundamental error in their assumptions regarding market potential. They think that if the market potential is 10,000 units, then demand will be 10,000 units. All they have to do is hire one or two salespeople and take orders. *No demand exists until it is created.* To sell more units, your team must skillfully improve its sales channel, brands, prices, ads, and advertising. If no teams target a segment, then there will be little demand in that segment. If several teams target a segment, then demand can be several times greater than the potential demand.

In short, you are a *market maker,* not a *market taker.* Total industry demand is a function of the collective decisions of all the competitors in the marketplace. As such, it can be much more or much less than the reported potential demand. It all depends on how smart and aggressive the players become.

Tactical Decisions

As a manufacturing firm, your ability to earn profits is determined by the magnitude and effectiveness of your business decisions relative to those of your competitors. Your decisions will fall into five areas: marketing, manufacturing, supply chain, human resources, and finance. The simulation provides you the relevant market research and accounting data to manage the organization effectively.

In one respect or another, all decisions affect your competitiveness. Obviously, your marketing decisions (brand design, pricing, sales channel management, and advertising) will impact your ability to generate sales. Your hiring policies, training techniques, and motivational tactics will influence the productivity of your employees. Your manufacturing and supply chain decisions will influence cost of goods sold and the reliability of your product and, hence, prices and profits.

Your financial options are affected by the outside world and your performance in the areas listed. Your financial decisions will affect your tactical options and the rate at which you can successfully grow the company. Cash flow will be your major consideration. In the early quarters, you will discover that cash inflows from sales will be insufficient to grow the business. New products, sales outlets, factory capacity, and employees require up-front investments that result in revenues only in later quarters. Thus, you must manage your sources of capital (revenue, equity, and debt) relative to your uses of capital over the life of your firm.

Marketing research and accounting are information tools. They are designed to help you to evaluate your market, operational, and financial performance. Used properly, they will also help you discern how to improve your decision making and, thus, your performance in the market.

Teamwork, interpersonal skills, and leadership come into play throughout the exercise and can become a major source of competitive advantage. In terms of teamwork, the complexity of the simulation requires a division of tasks and a coordination of work among the team members. Interpersonal skills come into play as you and your teammates debate the many tactical options and trade-offs. To win the day, good listening and persuasion must be coupled with sound business thought, and leadership is required not only to sort through many conflicting indicators but also to channel the competitive energies of the team.

Your *marketing* decisions include:

1. Brand design (from a long list of brand features, you must select components that satisfy target market needs and simultaneously minimize production and changeover costs).

2. Research and development (you may upgrade your products by investing in R&D to create new features).

3. Sales channel (you choose from 20 geographic markets and Internet channels).

4. Brand selection (you must decide which brands to carry in each market and their sales emphasis).

5. Pricing (you must set retail prices and the use of price rebates).

6. Sales force allocation (you must hire salespeople for each office and assign them to the various segments).

7. Sales force support (you can stimulate selling efforts through training programs, demonstration kits, sales contests, cash bonuses, and free gifts).

8. Advertising copy design (you must decide what benefits to feature in an ad and what their relative priority is).

9. Media placement (you must decide how often to run each advertisement in the media available for communicating to your target audience).

Your *human resource* decisions include:

1. Hiring policies (you compete for a limited number of employees, and thus the quantity and quality of your personnel and their productivity are directly affected).

2. Incentive programs (to retain good employees, your incentive programs must be competitive).

3. Corporate policies (from time to time, various issues will arise among your employees, and how you handle these issues will set precedents and policy that can affect employee morale and productivity).

Your *manufacturing and supply chain* decisions include:

1. Plant location (you are limited to one factory and must choose the site from five different locations, each of which has different manufacturing and distribution costs).

2. Plant capacity (you must build a factory in anticipation of future sales and adjust the daily operating capacity).

3. Production planning and inventory control (you must develop a production schedule that will meet demand but not lead to unnecessary inventory and cash flow requirements).

4. Quality control (you must determine how much unwanted variation is in your production line, identify the sources of variation, and develop an action plan to bring it into control).

5. Supply chain (as your business matures, you may wish to outsource part of your production operation and coordinate distribution activities with channel partners).

Your *finance* decisions include:

1. Cash flow management (you must balance your cash outflows with your cash inflows).

2. Sources of capital (you can draw upon debt capital—short-term bank loans and long-term notes—or equity capital—common stock and preferred stock).

3. Money market (you can place your excess cash in an interest-bearing account).

All decisions are tied into the balance sheet, income statement, and cash flow statement so that the business team can immediately see how its decisions impact the various accounts and the firm's profitability. Every team is financially constrained so that it must carefully manage receipts and disbursements and must project cash flow requirements several quarters into the future.

Market research can also be purchased in order to learn about your potential customers, the market's reaction to your decisions, and the market decisions of your competitors.

PLAY OF THE GAME

Marketplace allows you to run a business for eight or more quarters of play. In this section, we introduce you to the chronology of events in the simulation, the financing conditions that you will face, and the rate at which events will unfold. See **Exhibit 3** for a list of quarterly activities.

Chronology of Events

The chronology of events has been scripted to follow the normal life cycle of a start-up business. You will start slowly and then grow the company as you gain experience and resources. During the first four quarters, you are financially constrained from

expanding too quickly before you have developed a feel for the market.

Quarter 1: Organize the Company

In Q1, you organize your team and assign corporate responsibilities. You also name the company and contract for a survey of potential customers.

Quarter 2: Set Up Shop

In Q2, the survey arrives, providing information on benefits sought, buying patterns, demographic characteristics, buying intentions, and market size. You analyze these data and decide on your overall business strategy, including corporate goals, target markets, and strategic direction. You must also make several tactical decisions, focusing on brand design, plant location, production capacity, and sales office location.

Quarter 3: Go to Test Market

In Q3, your team test-markets its marketing strategy, including brands, prices, ad copy, media campaigns, and sales staffing. The team works through its employee hiring policies and production planning process for the first time and schedules production for the quarter. You contract market research so that you can discover customer reactions to your marketing decisions and what the competition has done. Finally, you need to forecast market demand and simulate your production operation given your supply chain decisions. *Marketplace* prepares pro forma financial statements (cash-flow and income statements and a balance sheet). The pro forma statements will help you to evaluate the potential financial outcome of your first quarter of total business operation. You may need to adjust your tactics if the projections are not favorable.

Quarter 4: Skillful Adjustment

In Q4, you receive the market research data that you commissioned during the test market. You also have manufacturing and accounting data from your first quarter of sales. With these data in hand, you evaluate your performance and may adjust your firm's strategy and tactics. With one quarter's worth of market experience, your performance should improve substantially in Q4.

Quarter 5: Invest in the Future

Q5 begins with a review of marketing, human resource, manufacturing, and accounting data from your second quarter of test marketing. In Q5, you have the

opportunity to substantially expand your position in the market by investing in research and development, new sales outlets, factory capacity, logistics, and employee recruitment and retention programs. You also have the opportunity to seek outside funding from venture capitalists.

To obtain this funding, your team must prepare a one-year business plan in which you assess market opportunity, review your performance to date, and lay out your strategy for your second year in business. This plan must include coordinated marketing, manufacturing, human resource, and financial strategies. The business plan must also include a tactical plan that includes the sequencing and timing of events to achieve the firm's goals. Finally, the plan must include both historical financial statements (Q1 to Q4) and pro forma statements for the second year (Q5 to Q8).

Quarter 6 and Beyond: Expand and Improve the Business

The major emphasis in Q6 and beyond is on improving your marketing, manufacturing, human resource, and financial performance through careful monitoring and continuous improvement. You also face new competitive threats as other firms introduce new technology, more reliable products, better prices, and more advertising, and as they expand into new segments and geographic markets. During this time, the team also has the opportunity to explore new relationships through cross licensing technology and outsourcing of supply.

Final Quarter: Submit Report to Board

At the conclusion of the exercise, your team prepares a report to the board. In it, you (1) highlight the key features of the business plan that were presented to the venture capitalists; (2) assess your business strategy and performance during the second year (compare actions taken against the business plan; discuss departures from the business plan, justification, and outcome; and review significant events that affected the company and market); (3) assess your current situation and the market (what are your firm's strengths and weaknesses?); and (4) summarize how you have prepared your firm to compete in the future.

Financing

Initial capitalization for your company is $4,000,000. The assumption is that you and your teammates make investments in

Exhibit 3: *Sequence of Simulation Activities*

Quarter 1: Organize team to do the job

Focus on process of working as a team to achieve goals
    assess team members' skills, personalities, and work styles
    set organizational and personal goals to organize the work
    determine how to manage the organization
    establish leadership
Order market survey of end user market
Sell stock to executive team

Quarter 2: Evaluate Market Opportunities, set up operations, and prepare for test market

Analyze market opportunities—evaluate segments, geographic markets and potential competition
Develop strategy direction—corporate goals, target segments, competitive style
Create customer value—design initial brands for test market
    match components to benefits desired (quality function deployment–QFD)
    evaluate impact of different components on changeover costs and scale economies
Set up manufacturing operations—evaluate financial trade-offs
    compare regional cost differences of labor and distribution on plant location
    evaluate economy and liquidity of different capacity investments
Human resources
    Establish salary ranges and benefit packages for employees
    Initiate recruitment of employees
Select test markets—set up sales channel

Quarter 3: Go to market to test strategy and market assumptions

Marketing strategy—evaluate tactical options and choose marketing mix
    pricing and price promotions
    sales force management—number employed, training, incentives
    advertising—ad copy design, media selection, ad frequency
Manufacturing—plan production and inventory levels
    Forecast total demand across brands
    Establish operating capacity
    Set target and replenishment points for pull manufacturing
Human resources—hire employees from available pool
Market research—budget collection of information

Quarter 4: Evaluate test market performance and revise strategy, become a learning organization

Evaluate performance
    financial performance—financial statements, ratios, industry norms
    manufacturing performance—cost of goods, inventory, stockouts, reliability
    market performance—customer satisfaction with brand designs, prices, advertising, sales force

    competitor tactics—segments targeted, selection of marketing tactics
Human resources—recruit additional employees to fill needs due to expansion
Revise marketing and manufacturing tactics as needed and continue test marketing

Quarter 5: Seek external funding—prepare business plan, negotiate equity investment

Evaluate performance—financial, marketing, manufacturing, competitive, and human resources
Develop business plan to achieve major growth over next 12 months
    goals—marketing, financial, and ownership
    marketing strategy
    manufacturing and supply chain strategy
    human resource strategy
    financial strategy
    tactical pert chart (show tactics over time)
    pro forma cash-flow statement, income statement and balance sheet
    size of equity request, number of shares offered and share price
Present business plan to venture capitalists and negotiate equity investment
Begin roll out of business plan

Quarter 6: Monitor, improve, and execute

Evaluate team—self-assessment of roles played, contributions made, and adjustments needed
Evaluate performance—financial, marketing, and competitive
Skillfully adjust strategy
    marketing—make incremental changes in tactics
        use activity-based costing to evaluate profitability of brands, sales channels
        conduct demand analysis to estimate brand, price, advertising, sales force elasticities
        invest in R&D for new technology
    manufacturing—work on
        quality improvements with statistical process control
        demand-driven production scheduling
        capacity utilization by reducing changeover time and costs
        reducing pipeline whiplash by managing market stimulation activities
        supply chain—outsourcing production, coordination with channel partners
    human resources—dealing with the strains of growth and the uncertainty of labor supply
    project cash flows and adjust strategy within financial capability

$1,000,000 increments, over four quarters in the first year. Thus, your team will own 100 percent of the company during the first year.

The firm is authorized to issue 150,000 shares of stock. Forty thousand shares of stock are issued to the executive team in exchange for your $4,000,000 investment. Initial stock value is $100 per share.

Your firm will need to make substantial investments in research and development, supply chain improvements, plant capacity, sales channel expansion, and human resources. These investments can be accomplished only by expanding the capital structure to bring on additional investors and take on debt.

The first source of funding that you should consider is the venture capital community. You are free to sell an additional $5,000,000 in stock. Total equity funding is limited to $9,000,000. To obtain this additional funding, your executive team presents a business plan to a group of venture capitalists, who then become your board of directors.

The venture capitalists are expecting your pitch for outside capital. The financial request should include how much of the company you are willing to sell for the requested investment. This factor is usually determined by the number of shares of stock offered for sale and the proposed stock price. You may offer either common stock or preferred stock. The venture capitalists may want to negotiate the size of the investment, number of shares to be purchased, and stock price. Their negotiations will depend upon what you are offering and their assessment of the team's performance to date, the soundness of the business plan, and the firm's profit potential.

In addition to equity capital, you may also borrow money from the *Marketplace* bank or go to the bond market. The bank can extend a line of credit equal to one and one-half times the firm's equity position in the previous quarter; that is, bank loan capacity = 1.5 × (Common stock + Preferred stock + Retained earnings in previous quarter).

You can also take out a long-term loan from the bond market. The financial institutions in *Marketplace* accept a greater debt-to-equity ratio than the bank, but at a higher interest rate (approximately two percentage points higher). Your long-term debt capacity will be equal to two times the firm's equity position in the previous quarter.

Your debt capacity changes over the course of the simulation. During Q1 through Q4, you have no debt capacity. Until your firm establishes itself in the market, no financial institution will lend. With the successful conclusion of your first year in business, your firm gains access to the debt market. Your debt capacity will probably be at its greatest in Q5. It will probably decline in Q6 and Q7 as you incur many start-up expenses and as your retained earnings turn increasingly negative. It will not substantially improve until after your investments in new business development come online and begin to generate new profits.

If your firm ends a quarter with a negative cash position, the bank will contact a loan shark to obtain an emergency loan. The loan shark will lend you the money to cover the checks that otherwise would have bounced due to insufficient funds. The loan shark is not your friend. He requires repayment in the next quarter, charges an exorbitant interest rate, and takes an equity position in the company. To pay off the emergency loan, expenditures must be curtailed, revenue increased, and/or a conventional loan must be obtained.

The emergency loan interest rate is a sliding scale that begins at 10 percent per quarter and may go as high as 25 percent per quarter. In addition, for each $100 that the loan shark places in your checking account, he will take one share of stock in your firm at zero cost. The issuing of stock causes a dilution of your share of the company and thus of your stock value.

Pace of Play

Like most new ventures, your company must start from scratch with very little knowledge of the market. However, the play of the game is structured to help you move along the learning curve. (See Exhibit 3.) You move into the market slowly by forming a team and conducting a market survey (Q1). The pace picks up in Q2 with the addition of brand design, sales office, and manufacturing. By Q3, you are running at almost full speed with the addition of advertising, sales management, human resource, and production decisions.

Q2 and Q3 are very tense quarters because you must make important market decisions with no experience and little knowledge. Anxiety drops in Q4 with the information you receive from the Q3 test market. You are able to revise your strategy in an intelligent way and find noticeable improvement in Q4 test market results.

Q5 is the most difficult, challenging, and time-consuming quarter because you must prepare a business plan, estimate funding requirements, and negotiate equity funding. Q6 is a comparatively quiet quarter. Preparation of the business plan makes the day-to-day decisions easier. You know your market, where you are going, and how you are going to get there. During the lull in Q6, we will introduce you to the process of continuous improvement in team management, marketing, manufacturing, supply chain, and finance.

Starting in Q7, you will begin to be surprised by your competition. You will learn that the competition is much smarter than you thought. Events will force you to become a "skillful adjuster." The balance of the exercise is primarily skillful adjustment. The workload is manageable, and it is fun to pit your skills against those of formidable opponents.

PERFORMANCE MEASUREMENT

A balanced scorecard will be used to measure your firm's performance, drawing on the work of Kaplan and Norton.[1] Their guidance on how to set objectives and measure performance has spurred many real-world firms to maximize long-term viability. A team's performance will be based upon its total business performance: its financial performance, market effectiveness, marketing performance, investments in the firm's future, human resource management, asset management, and creation of wealth. The simulation's *total business performance* indicator is a quantitative measure of the team's ability to effectively manage firm resources. It considers both the historical performance of the firm as well as how well the firm is positioned to compete in the future and, as such, measures the action potential of the firm.

The most important measure is the team's financial performance and, thus, its ability to create wealth for investors. However, a focus on current profits causes many executives to stress the present at the expense of the future. The long-term viability of the firm requires that the team excel at managing not only the firm's profitability but also its marketing activities, production operations, human resources, cash, and financial resources. The management team must also invest in the future. These investments might depress current financial

1 Robert Kaplan and David Norton, *The Balanced Scorecard* (Boston: Harvard Business School Press, 1996).

performance, but they are vital to creating new products, markets, human capital and manufacturing capabilities.

In short, top managers must be good at managing all aspects of the firm. The balanced scorecard puts this perspective into practice. It focuses attention on multiple performance measures and multiple decision areas. None can be ignored or downplayed. The best managers are strong in all areas measured.

The simulation computes total business performance multiplying eight indicators. This model underscores the importance of all measures: any strength or weakness has a multiple effect on the final outcome, the action potential of the firm. Your final evaluation will be based upon your team's average performance during the last four quarters of play.

Total business performance =

Financial performance ×

Market performance ×

Marketing effectiveness ×

Investments in the firm's future ×

Human resource management ×

Asset management ×

Manufacturing productivity ×

Creation of wealth

Here is how the individual performance indicators are measured:

Financial performance measures how well the executive team has been able to create profits for its shareholders. It is computed by dividing net operating profit from current operations by the number of shares of stock issued, yielding operating profit per share.

Market performance is a measure of how well your firm is able to create and fulfill demand in its target segments. Demand creation is measured by the firm's average market share in its primary and secondary target segments. Customer fulfillment is measured as the proportion of orders filled. Market performance is the product of these two numbers. Thus, the firm is penalized if it overstimulates demand, leading to customer dissatisfaction and wasted marketing expenditures.

Marketing effectiveness is a measure of how well your executive team has satisfied the needs of your customers. Your primary and secondary target segments evaluate the quality of your brands and ads, and the satisfaction scores are averaged to obtain a measure of your marketing effectiveness.

Investments in the firm's future reflects the willingness of the executive team to spend current revenues on future business opportunities. It is measured by computing the proportion of current revenues spent on activities that have a long-term payback, such as research and development, factory improvements, and training programs for employees.

Human resource management is a measure of your executive team's ability to recruit, compensate, motivate, and satisfy the firm's employees. Human resource management is measured by computing employee satisfaction and productivity. Employee satisfaction is directly affected by your compensation package and your handling of policies, issues, and problems that arise over the course of the exercise. Productivity is related to the units produced per employee in your factory.

Asset management is a measure of the executive team's ability to use the firm's assets to create sales revenue. Total sales are divided by total assets to yield asset turnover (ATO). To discourage the buildup of excess inventories (which would increase demand fulfillment), ATO is adjusted downward based upon the percent of production that remains in inventory at the end of the quarter.

Manufacturing productivity measures your executive team's ability to create reliable products efficiently. Efficiency is measured as the percent of scheduled capacity that is ultimately used to produce products. Efficiency is negatively affected by the scheduling of what turns out to be unneeded production capacity and by the amount of production time lost due to brand changeover. When too much capacity is scheduled, workers must be laid off rather than be used to build excessive inventory. High changeover times are the result of brand diversity (marketing's desire to have a wide assortment of brands) and the failure to make improvements in the time required to change the production line from one brand to another. Reliability is measured through the eyes of your customers and reflects product defects and warranty claims, all correctable. Manufacturing productivity is the product of the efficiency and reliability measures.

Creation of wealth is a measure of how well your executive team has been able to add wealth to the initial investments of the stockholders. Creation of wealth is measured by dividing the net equity of the firm

(Retained earnings + Common and Preferred stock) by the total investments of the stockholders (Common + Preferred stock). Retained earnings represent the sum of all profits from the inception of the firm.

PROCESSING TEAM DECISIONS

Exhibit 4 portrays the key components of *Marketplace*. As portrayed in Exhibit 4, each team employs the *decision template* to review options and make decisions at three levels. First, it makes a series of decisions that help to create demand, including brand design, sales channel, sales force management, brand selection, pricing, ad copy design, and media planning. Second, the team makes plant management and supply chain decisions (plant location, fixed capacity, operating capacity, production scheduling, outsourcing, inventory control, and statistical process control) that indirectly affect sales through cost of goods sold (prices) and product reliability (perceived product quality). Finally, each team makes financial (equity versus debt) and human resource decisions (types of employees, salaries, motivational techniques, and training) that affect the firm's ability to grow and create wealth.

The *Parameter Set-Up Program* (PSUP) specifies the unique characteristics of each game scenario. Through it, simulation designers can create and modify all aspects of your competitive world, including the number of firms, the decisions to be made, and the needs and wants of the end user market. The *Demand Generator*, a mathematical program that employs the game parameters, emulates how real end users make decisions when faced with an assortment of market offers (products, prices, promotions, and distribution).

When you have completed your decisions for any quarter, they are transferred to the market Demand Generator. The decisions of your competitors are also transferred, along with the parameters specified for your game. The Demand Generator computes market demand based upon your decisions, your competitors' decisions, and the nature of the market as modeled by PSUP.

The primary role of the Demand Generator is to allocate demand among the various market offerings. Although the computations are very complex, the basic algorithm, or procedure, is fairly simple.

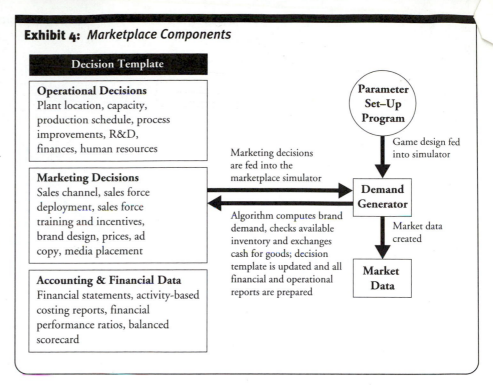

Exhibit 4: *Marketplace Components*

Decision Template

Operational Decisions
Plant location, capacity, production schedule, process improvements, R&D, finances, human resources

Marketing Decisions
Sales channel, sales force deployment, sales force training and incentives, brand design, prices, ad copy, media placement

Accounting & Financial Data
Financial statements, activity-based costing reports, financial performance ratios, balanced scorecard

Parameter Set–Up Program

Game design fed into simulator

Marketing decisions are fed into the marketplace simulator

Demand Generator

Algorithm computes brand demand, checks available inventory and exchanges cash for goods; decision template is updated and all financial and operational reports are prepared

Market data created

Market Data

Basically, the Demand Generator reviews all your decisions and assigns points to them based upon their relevance to the market. For example, if you choose a brand feature that is of limited value to a particular segment, you would receive a small number of points. If you select a feature that offers great value to that segment, you would receive substantially more points. Similarly, if you offer technical support for your brand, assign it a high sales priority for your salespeople and promote it heavily through advertising, then it will accumulate even more points.

The objective is to accumulate as many points as possible for each brand. The computer compares the number of points a brand has accumulated to the number accumulated by competing brands. Demand will then be allocated among the available brands based upon which brand has the greatest appeal (points). It is important to note that different segments will place different weights (points) on each decision you make. As a result, a marketing plan designed for one segment may have little appeal to another segment.

After demand has been computed by brand and by market area, it is deducted from the available inventory. If there is sufficient inventory, then the appropriate cash is added to the balance sheet. If not, then sales are lost, potential customers become unhappy, and future sales are affected. All of this is accomplished by transferring the demand files from the Demand Generator to the decision template, and then updating the template to the next quarter of play. During the update process, your financial statements are closed for the quarter, an assortment of accounting and operational information is prepared, and all other business decisions are executed as specified.

The final component of *Marketplace* is the *market research module*. It is designed to select and retrieve market information from the Demand Generator according to your market research requests. For example, you may wish to know your competitors' advertising decisions, sales office decisions, or the market's reaction to your ad copy or retail prices. Some of the information is free; other information may be purchased.

CORRESPONDENCE TO THE REAL WORLD

There are no other firms in the market except those participating in the simulation. Your instructor will specify the number of firms, usually four to eight, and determine the composition of each team.

Although *Marketplace* parallels real market conditions in a number of significant ways, any simulated environment is clearly a simplification. Still, *Marketplace* constitutes the world within which you must learn to compete, and, make no mistake about it, your competitors are very real.

A word of caution: Do not assume that the *Marketplace* world behaves exactly like the real world. If you have much specialized knowledge about the real-world PC industry, you may become frustrated that the simulation does not behave in exactly the same manner. First, remember that *Marketplace* is a simplification of the real world. Second, the *Marketplace* PC world is in its infancy, whereas the actual industry is not. Third, the members of your class are essentially entrepreneurs with little experience in working together or within this industry. Finally, your instructor may intentionally alter market parameters from class to class to keep each new class on its toes. All four conditions guarantee that differences will exist. The best assumption to make is that *Marketplace* is a microcosm unto itself.

In terms of your knowledge of the real world, then, you should use it only as background information to help in your *initial* planning and decision making. The important lesson is not in knowing the "right" answer but in being able to *adapt* to what the market wants. To bring this factor home, consider a situation where you are forced to change jobs. If you had to move from the microcomputer business to compact disc players, to tennis rackets, to dishwashers, to printing presses, you would find that the "right" answers would change accordingly. Every market is unique, and you must learn to adapt to each one.

Finally, keep in mind that no amount of research ever gives you the "right" answer in the real world. Every time you participate in a new product introduction, you will find that you misjudged, misunderstood, or overlooked some aspect of what the customer wants. At times, the customer may even appear to be illogical. That is the customer's prerogative. Your job is to respond to the expressed needs and wants of the customer. The "right" answer, the "reasonable" response, and the "logical" conclusion are determined by the market—not by what we think they should be.

EVOLUTION OF THE MARKET AND YOUR COMPANY

Let's review what you are likely to experience during the play of the game.

Product Life Cycle

You will find that the market will evolve along the lines of the product life cycle. **Exhibit 5** indicates where your firm is like-

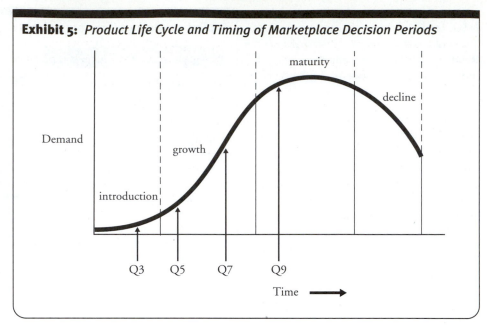

Exhibit 5: *Product Life Cycle and Timing of Marketplace Decision Periods*

ly to be in the product life cycle at different times over the course of this (simulated) two-year exercise.

At the outset, initial brand designs, advertising, media plans, distribution, and pricing will be lacking in some respect. During this introductory period (Q3 and Q4), sales will be slow as most customers sit on the sidelines awaiting better offers. As the industry gains experience, decisions will be refined and the market will begin to expand. The rate of growth will depend upon how fast the industry adapts to the expressed needs of the market and how aggressively it pursues the market (Q5 and Q6).

Strong market growth will come as new technology is introduced, prices come down, advertising goes up, and distribution becomes more widespread (Q7 and Q8). The new technology will push early brand designs into the decline stage of the product life cycle. The size of the market pie is growing, although the shares of that pie will change in response to the resourcefulness and aggressiveness of each competitor.

Maturity enters the picture when the markets become highly segmented and each market niche is successfully served by a highly focused brand design, advertising campaign, price, and distribution system (Q9 to Q12). Most customers will have entered the market at this stage, and a large share of the sales will represent replacement purchases. Without further stimulation, the market may even decline to what represents a steady state of replacement purchases.

At maturity, competition is very stiff. All of the competitors have access to full mar-

ket knowledge. They should know what represents a good brand design, a good price, a good ad, a good media plan, and good distribution. Market share becomes very important because it drives up production volumes to allow greater economies of scale. Market share is achieved through heavy advertising, good distribution, and low prices.

Interestingly, the industry's movement along the product life cycle occurs naturally in the *Marketplace* game. No formula or equation forces the game along the product life cycle. The market takes on a life of its own once it is set in motion. The rate of growth, pattern of growth, and ultimate size of the market depend upon the market savvy and aggressiveness of the players in the game.

Company Evolution

The Hay Group, a management consultancy specializing in people, performance, and work, has studied the strategic decision-making processes of many organizations over their development lives. They have found that the decision-making process evolves as a company progresses through four phases of business development, including emergence, development, maturity, and liquidation. Thus, the decision-making process of an emerging organization will vary considerably from that of a mature organization. The significance of these findings is that your fledgling organization will also experience similar changes as it progresses through its own life cycle.

During the first four quarters of play, your firm will be in the *emergence* phase of business development. Some of the characteristics you will observe in your organization include the lack of formalized goals, the limited availability of information to make decisions, informal planning and control (rigid organizational structure has not been established), the need for strong leadership and someone to take charge, and a need (willingness) to accept unaccustomed risks. You will also find that your anxiety level will be at an all-time high because you are faced with new responsibilities in an unknown environment. This phase is a risk-filled, high-pressure time for you and your executive team.

During the second year of business, your firm will probably be in the *developmental* phase of business growth. The experiences of the first year will help you to understand your environment and what it takes to succeed. Some of the characteristics you will observe in your organization include a high degree of delegation to individual executives (you will become more comfortable with each others' decisions and realize that you personally cannot participate in every decision), the formation of marketing and business goals and of an ability to measure performance, an ability to assess the implications of market events and react to them, a gradual shift toward less risky decision making, and a broader perspective on one's area of responsibility and what can be done to further the growth of the firm.

Near the start of the third year of business (Q9 or Q10), the firm will begin to move into the *mature* phase of business development. By this time, you are seasoned executives in a market that is well known to you. Some of the characteristics you will observe in your organization include a high degree of clarity in decision making due to both experience and the availability of good information, an increasing orientation toward financial goals over market goals, more stability in decision making due to a more predictable market, and a more conservative posture on the decisions made.

It is possible that by the end of the third year (Q12), the industry could experience a shakeout with one or two firms being liquidated. We have no experience with *liquidation*, but have observed firms that would be likely candidates if the simulation were to continue.

The Hay Group's analysis of organizational development is valuable because it demonstrates that your organizational experiences are not unique. The anxiety you will experience during the emergence phase is to be expected because so little is known about your business, market, executive team, and even yourself. The growth in confidence and decision-making prowess you will experience during the developmental phase are natural developments of having gained experience within your organization and in the market in which you compete. By the time your firm enters the mature phase of business, you will become a seasoned veteran who knows what it takes to succeed. Your confidence level will be high, and you will look forward to the competition in the market. While not every organization or individual will follow these patterns, it is surprising how many do.

TEXTBOOK + SIMULATION: INTEGRATED SET

The structure of this textbook unfolds in tandem with the play of the game, according to the life cycle of a new business. The textbook presents you with ideas, ways of thinking, and tools as they become relevant to your advancing play. If you are handed a tool when you need that particular tool, it requires far less effort to appreciate its relevance, and you will be much more receptive to incorporating it into your natural thought processes.

The textbook, however, is intended to provide you more than written cues on how to proceed through the simulation exercise. *It is written at a higher level than that and represents the work of a team of multidisciplinary academics and practitioners.* Each contributing author was asked to identify a handful of critical issues within her or his particular discipline. And so we asked ourselves if students could master only a few things during their capstone experience of strategic management, what should they learn? We then encapsulated these important viewpoints and principles within our respective chapters.

Fundamental concepts and principles of each business discipline are built into the play of *Marketplace*. The more of these concepts and principles you can draw upon, the greater the likelihood of your success; but do not simply rely upon your recall. Be resourceful. Use this text. Then, when it is time to decide whether your firm should issue debt, you will know, for instance, that debt has both a leverage benefit *and* a bankruptcy risk and plan accordingly.

For your benefit, Part 1 presents the fundamentals on how to lead and organize a business. Part 2 focuses on the startup phase of your business: How to lay a foundation for a successful enterprise via market analysis, strategic planning, creation of customer value, and financial accounting. Part 3 prepares you to raise additional funding and deal with a board of directors. Part 4 focuses on the tools of business and how you can continuously improve your performance via management of the team, manufacturing and supply chain processes, profits, and human resources.

MENTAL DISCIPLINE OF *MARKETPLACE*

Marketplace requires mastery of the fundamentals not only within each individual functional area of business but also of the important linkages among them. **Exhibit 6** portrays the integrative challenge that awaits you. Do not panic. At the highest level of play, you move through the strategic planning process, performing an environmental analysis, establishing a business strategy, and adjusting to the simulation's performance measurement system. Once formulated, your high-level strategy will flow into the rest of the organization. You will develop an integrated mental picture that lets you zoom down from the highest organizational level to the managerial details in each functional area. For the moment, we will leave you with this picture of the conceptual challenges of *Marketplace*. Keep it in mind as you begin your preparations to compete.

Marketplace Vantage Points

Remember over the course of this exercise that important trade-offs exist not only within each functional decision area but also among them.

From a *management* perspective, you will develop your leadership and team management skills. You will recruit an executive team, assess skills and work styles, divide corporate responsibilities, assign tasks, coordinate business decisions, and manage the team to excellence. You will also learn about managing your human capital and the challenges in recruiting, motivating, and retaining a workforce that can satisfy all of the many stakeholders that you must serve.

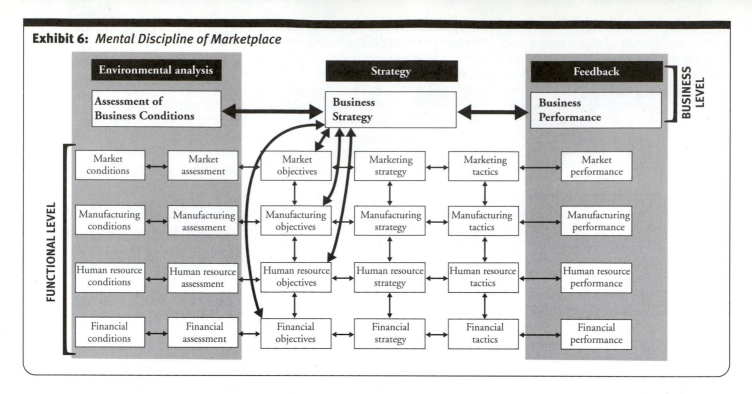

Exhibit 6: *Mental Discipline of Marketplace*

From *accounting*, you will develop a deep understanding of financial record keeping, including balance sheets, income statements, and cash-flow statements, and the way in which the three are interlinked and affected by your business decisions. Your accounting skills will help you not only to understand your past but also to project your future by way of pro forma financial planning. You will also learn about activity-based costing and how it can be used to evaluate the profitability of your brands and sales channels.

From *finance*, you will learn to assess the financial performance of your firm by using an assortment of financial tools, including financial ratio analysis (liquidity, activity, leverage, and profitability), return on equity (ROE), decomposition, common size statements, and indexing. You will also learn to use capital budgeting techniques and come to understand the advantages and disadvantages of alternate sources of capital (debt versus equity).

From *manufacturing and supply chain management*, you will learn about flexible manufacturing and how to balance the economies of scale of large production runs against their large-inventory carrying costs and cash-flow requirements. You will see how brand design decisions affect the changeover time and costs on the production line, which in turn affect your effective operating capacity. You will also learn how marketing decisions that are designed to

stimulate demand can cause drastic swings in your production operation (called *pipeline whiplash*). You will learn how unwanted variation in your production line affects product reliability and, hence, customer service costs, company image, and demand. You will be given the opportunity to apply statistical process control techniques in order to bring this variation into control and improve reliability, and you will learn about the benefits and challenges of outsourcing production to a third party.

From *economics*, you will learn to deal with seasonal, trend, and cyclical determinants of demand and the nature of competition under an oligopolistic and/or a monopolistic industry structure. You must also deal with international trade issues and how international politics can affect business opportunities. Furthermore, you will also discover the relevance of the concept of elasticity as it is applied to prices, advertising, sales force, and brand performance. Knowledge of these elasticities will help you decide how much more or less to do in order to obtain the desired changes in demand and costs.

From *marketing*, you will have the opportunity to conduct a market opportunity analysis (MOA) and develop a market strategy. From your MOA, you will learn about customer value and the differences among attributes, consequences, and values. Your market strategy will be concerned with selecting target markets, designing

brands, setting prices, developing advertising campaigns, and managing your sales channel. You will have the opportunity to apply quality functional deployment (QFD) as you attempt to match your market offer (brand features, service, price) to the needs and values of the customer. You will also learn how important it is to continuously adjust your strategy in response to customer impressions and competitive tactics, and thus you will learn the importance of market research.

You will learn a great deal about the *strategic planning process*. You will repeatedly analyze the situation, establish your objectives, develop your strategy, evaluate your tactical options, and make your tactical decisions. As new information comes in, you will learn to skillfully adjust your tactics in order to achieve the stated goals of the firm.

Finally, you will learn to use an *assortment of tools* to help you maintain control of the firm and channel its resources toward productive ends. The balanced scorecard will become your primary mechanism for checking performance relative to goals. As time passes, you may find that your market or financial performance falls short of your goals. As a consequence, it will become necessary to adjust individual tactics (such as price, brand design, and production) or the entire strategy in order to realize these objectives. Control of your business program must become a very conscious effort on your part. You must study the market, evaluate performance relative to your objectives, and adjust your strategy accordingly.

Marketplace Forces

Participation in *Marketplace* requires that you work toward success while four forces buffet you (see **Exhibit 7**): the customer, the competition, the cash flow, and your colleagues. At times, you will feel pushed in several directions. The challenge is to manage these energies toward productive ends.

The *customer* represents the opportunity. The customer has needs and wants that must be satisfied, even if they do not always seem logical. The customer is always the boss. The way to make money for your business is to satisfy the customer by responding to his or her needs. If you fail to recognize this requirement, you will be left behind.

You must also never lose sight of your *competition*. Competition is the perennial threat to your success. *Marketplace* is a zero-sum game in which the competition's gain is your loss and vice versa. If you are fortunate to be number 1 for a time, you cannot afford to rest. Those behind you will study your moves and emulate your successful tactics. They will also try to find your weaknesses, perhaps before you do, and develop tactics to take advantage of them. They will be highly motivated to do so. By being number 2 or 3 in the market, they may be more motivated than you are.

Marketplace should teach you the importance of *cash flow* in business management. Cash flow is the major constraint with which you must deal. With enough money, you could probably realize all of your objectives, but you will never have enough. Whether you are a brand manager, a product category manager, a division manager, or the president of your firm, you will find there is never enough money. There is always competition for money because there are more good ideas than there is money to fund them. Moreover, some businesspeople will purposely give you less money than you want to force you to be creative and to challenge your resourcefulness to accomplish your objectives. They want you to stretch, to extend yourself, perhaps to reach higher than you would have considered otherwise.

Your *colleagues* are your most important asset. Great things can be accomplished by working together. At the same time, your

Exhibit 7: *Market Forces Buffeting Players*

greatest challenges will also be interpersonal. To manage other forces in the market, you must first harness the energies within your own team.

All of us whose work is represented in this book hope that you will learn to manage even as *Marketplace* forces swirl around you. Never forget that the customer is always the opportunity and the boss; the competition is always the threat; cash flow is always the constraint; and your colleagues are always your means to success.

PART 1

Before You Start in Business

Chapter 1

Harry J. Bruce
CEO
Illinois Central Railroad

Leaders and Leadership
How They Emerged from History and How
They Emerge within Today's Organizations

"I sit here all day trying to persuade people to do things they ought to have sense enough to do without my persuading them. . . . That's all the powers of the presidency amount to."

Harry Truman

Less than a generation ago, the subject of leadership rarely arose in discussions about how to run a business or in books on business management. Leadership was widely assumed to apply only to military affairs or statecraft.

Today that situation is almost totally reversed. The business departments of the nation's bookstores are well stocked with books on executive leadership, and the shelves are amply replenished with fresh titles each publishing season. Leadership courses, leadership workshops, leadership seminars, and even leadership wilderness retreats are offered to senior business executives by a wide range of universities, colleges, and professional associations. The more advanced graduate schools of business are even beginning to include a few elective courses in leadership in their MBA curricula.

For all of leadership's newfound popularity, however, the bulk of the contemporary literature on this topic still fails to come to grips with two issues essential to a full understanding—and a competent exercise—of leadership.

The first issue is what I call *leadership without portfolio*—that is, the exercise of leadership by persons well below the senior executive ranks, usually with little formal authority, and often with no specific assignment. The second issue is *power* as a component of effective leadership. Only a small minority of today's academic researchers seem to be facing the controversial issue of power, while the popular authors appear to be ignoring it almost totally. Any treatment of leadership that ignores either of these elusive elements is likely to leave business students unprepared for some of the most serious challenges and opportunities they are likely to encounter in the workplace.

The intent of this chapter, then, is twofold: first, to introduce the concept of *leadership without portfolio* into your preparation as future business managers; second, to reawaken an appreciation of the importance of power in the actual work that managers do.

LEARNING LEADERSHIP
Where It Is Taught and Where It Is Not

What the Business Schools Do Not Tell You about Leadership

Two decades ago the School of Business Administration at Northwestern University changed its name to the J. L. Kellogg School of Management. Kellogg graduates began receiving Master of Management degrees, and the old degree title, Master of Business Administration, was dropped.

That particular change in business school nomenclature, along with similar changes that followed at other institutions, acknowledged a simple but often ignored truth of organizational dynamics—*administrators do not manage*; that is, they do not make policy. The most an administrator can do is take a policy made by a manager and, literally, administer it to subordinates who apply the policy in carrying out their work. An administrator is a sort of organizational bellhop, someone who totes ideas and policies from those who originated them to those who need to implement them. *Administrators do not run businesses. Managers do.*

About three quarters of a century elapsed between the emergence of management as a subject of scientific research and the adoption of the word "management" as an element in business school names. Even after management made the transition from

BEST-USE CORRELATIONS

Before you spend a single dollar, euro, or yen, your team must organize itself and decide who will lead it. In *Marketplace*, as in the real world, a business cannot reach its maximum potential without good leadership. Thus the first chapter in this book, corresponding to your first quarter of simulation play, focuses on leadership and on taking the first steps in getting your start-up launched.

Cultivate the Characteristics of a Good Leader

Chapter 1 provides a compelling review of what it takes to be a good leader. The *Marketplace* environment gives you plenty of room to put chapter principles and your own leadership skills to the test. Be advised leaders earn the willingness of others to follow by showing (1) concern for the task and (2) consideration for the people involved in the task.

Leadership without Portfolio

Leadership without portfolio, a concept introduced in Chapter 1, is particularly relevant to *Marketplace* play because no one person on your team is given the authority to lead. In *Marketplace*, lack of formal authority to lead should not limit anyone's ability to lead.

Rotate Leadership

In *Marketplace*, natural breaks in the play of the game allow team members to rotate in and out of the leadership position. The first opportunity to lead occurs during the startup phase of the business, Q1 through Q4; the second, during the preparation of the business plan and during negotiations with venture capitalists, Q5; the third, during the growth phase of the business, Q5 through Q8; the fourth, during the preparation and presentation of a report to the Board of Directors, which occurs at the end of simulation play.

a researcher's curiosity to the core of the business school curriculum, it still took 50 years before institutional names began to reflect the change. As veteran management consultant, author, and teacher Peter F. Drucker points out,

> Management as a discipline . . . was first dimly perceived around the time of the First World War. It did not emerge until the Second World War and then did so primarily in the United States. Since then it has been the fastest-growing new function, and the study of it the fastest-growing new discipline. No function in history has emerged as quickly as has management in the past 50 or 60 years, and surely none has had such worldwide sweep in such a short period.[1]

Ironically, now that the word "management" at long last is finding a place over the doors of the nation's business schools, an even newer concept—leadership—is knocking on those same doors and asking for admission. Business school researchers say they are now learning how to identify and analyze business leadership, and the top business schools claim they are even beginning to teach it.

Will "leadership studies" become the next great advance in the way future business executives are trained for the decision-making role? Are we on the brink of understanding as much about leadership as we know—or claim we know—about management?

While exciting things are happening, some restraint is probably in order. One reason is that the vocabulary of leadership is still under discussion, with a multitude of academic and popular researchers still debating what exactly it is that leaders do and what those activities should be called. Leadership studies are still a long way from where managerial studies stood in 1916, when French industrialist and business writer Henri Fayol declared that the four functions of management are to plan, organize, coordinate, and control.[2] Fayol's nomenclature was adopted widely in the world of business and in business schools. No such agreement on nomenclature currently prevails in the study of leadership.

Another reason is that academic research into business leadership is still quite young, and formal instruction in leadership skills and behavior for MBA candidates is even younger, with only a few of the leading schools offering specific courses in leadership. Stanford University's Graduate School of Business, which introduced the subject

of leadership into the MBA curriculum during the late 1980s with a series of lectures by author and retired executive John Gardner, has now begun offering a formal course, Learning to Lead. The new course is not required, however, and enrollment is restricted to those currently holding jobs while attending classes. The Harvard Business School offers one mandatory leadership course, Leadership and Organizational Behavior, in the first year of its MBA curriculum. Students with a strong interest in the subject may pursue it further in several elective courses.

At most business schools, however, the academic study of leadership receives only token representation in the curriculum, while practical training in leadership behavior, skills, and attitudes is usually absent altogether. Most MBA programs still deal with leadership in cursory fashion—usually in a brief, more or less obligatory chapter buried deep in a textbook, or in an occasional guest lecture by a visiting CEO. As a rule, U.S. business schools devote nowhere near as much attention to developing leadership skills as they do to teaching number crunching, marketing, or strategic planning. While students may be exposed to certain kinds of thinking and theorizing *about* leadership, they are not systemically trained to *exercise* leadership the same way they are taught to use other business school skills.

The gap between the teaching of leadership and the teaching of more commonly accepted business skills is not hypothetical. It has been documented by Indiana University Professor Paul J. Gordon and St. John's University Professor Larry W. Boone in an unpublished research paper presented to the International Academy of Management at its December 9, 1994, meeting in Philadelphia. In a nationwide survey of deans of collegiate schools of business, the two scholars asked, "Regarding each of the business programs offered by your school, what relative emphasis (expressed as a percentage) is placed on each of the following 12 educational objectives?"

The responses to the lengthy questionnaire were statistically significant and instructive. Core competencies, such as accounting, economics, finance, marketing, law, and management, received a number-1 ranking in both undergraduate and graduate programs (38.7 percent and 36.0 percent, respectively).

When asked to rank the other 11 possible objectives of a business school education, the deans scored leadership skills ninth in undergraduate programs and seventh in graduate programs, with relative emphases of 4.1 percent and 5.8 percent, respectively.[3]

Interestingly, when the deans were queried about the course material included in nondegree programs, such as advanced management courses for senior executives, leadership rose to third place in the total 12-factor analysis. This appears to confirm the widespread existence of a misguided belief that leadership studies are best saved for the latter stages of a managerial career.

The late William Oncken, Jr., sharpened the focus of this ongoing debate in 1984 when he wrote:

> Textbooks in organizational development consistently declare that managerial leadership begins at the top, but they just as consistently don't specify where the top is. The impression is therefore conveyed, whether intentionally or not, that effective managerial leadership is not possible at lower organizational levels if it is not already being practiced at the higher levels.[4]

Oncken gives additional illumination with a humorous medical metaphor: Picture yourself on an operating table about to have your appendix removed under a local anesthetic. Just before the doctor has opened your abdomen, the electricity goes off, and the room is plunged into darkness. You hear the doctor saying through the gloom to the nurse, "Well, that does it! If top management doesn't do *its* job, we can't do *ours.* Guess we'll just have to leave the patient as is while we sit it out in the coffee shop until the lights come on. Let's go." Before they could leave, you would be screaming, "Is there a pro in the house?"

What is a pro? A doctor who knows what to do if and when the lights go out—no matter whose job it was to see that they didn't. In management you often do not find out who the pros are until the lights go out. Leadership, at your level, begins with you.[5]

Leadership Can Be Learned

The omission of leadership studies from the business school curricula is puzzling. We know something about what leadership is, and we know some ways to teach it—at least to those who have shown some basic aptitude for it. The U.S. armed services continually conduct research into the nature of leadership, and they regularly recycle both

their academic research results and the battlefield experience of their personnel into the training of future officers and noncoms. Courses in leadership theory and programs offering practical training in leadership behavior are a standard part of the curriculum, not only at the three service academies but also in the Officer Candidate Schools (OCS) and Reserve Officer Training Corps (ROTC) programs. The military would not consider a future officer's preparation complete if the candidate had acquired proficiency only in such technical specialties as gunnery, engineering, aeronautics, or navigation. The ability to lead is considered essential, and all future officers are specifically trained to fill leadership roles.

Yet MBAs, who typically enter their first jobs with two years more college credit than the military officer, still join the business world with virtually no formal leadership training or experience. Instead, they are expected to pick up their leadership techniques and develop their leadership abilities as best they can on the job.

Can leadership be taught and learned as a discipline, or is it simply an innate talent that will manifest itself inevitably in those who have it and will never appear in those who do not, no matter how intensely they are trained? Yes, leadership is a talent, and as such it will be distributed unevenly among the population. But there is no reason to believe that leadership *potential* will inevitably ripen into full leadership without some sort of formal education and training. The curriculum of the military academies is premised on that assumption. It is also premised on the idea that those who select themselves for leadership development and who are screened for leadership potential will benefit the most and experience the greatest development of that potential once they get appropriate training and discipline.

All of which is to say the obvious: Leadership can be taught, but only to those who have the innate ability and desire to learn it.

There is a less obvious corollary to this statement, however: Leadership not only *can* be taught to certain people but also *needs* to be taught. If not properly cultivated and restrained, leadership ability—particularly when coupled with strong ambition—can run out of control, destroying careers, institutions, and reputations. We will see a sobering example of untrained and unrestrained business leadership at the end of this chapter.

How the Service Academies Teach Leadership

What makes it possible for the U.S. military to teach leadership to people in their teens and early twenties? Students enrolled in the nation's service academies do not just pick up leadership by observing and modeling the behavior of their superiors on the parade ground or the gunnery range; they study it—formally and rigorously, in theory and practice—in each of the four years of undergraduate work leading up to commissioning. Cadets or midshipmen entering a service academy today can expect to:

- Study theories of leadership in textbooks and training manuals and discuss leadership concepts in class.
- Read, analyze, and discuss biographies of well-known leaders.
- Undergo repeated psychological testing to identify leadership potential and track its development.
- Undergo practical training designed to develop leadership attitudes and skills, including teamwork, communications, self-reflection and self-correction, and both giving and receiving counseling.

For more than a decade, the Department of Defense as well as the individual armed services have funded research at some of the nation's top universities in an effort to better understand the dynamics of leadership and to improve the leadership training of future officers. In addition to exploiting the latest breakthroughs in formal behavioral studies, the academies have opened their classrooms to the burgeoning collection of popular leadership literature.[6]

Col. George B. Forsythe, the director of undergraduate studies in the Department of Behavioral Sciences and Leadership Studies at West Point, says that academic research, popular self-help literature, and biographies of great military, political, and business leaders all seem to point in the same direction: Leadership development begins with self-development, including introspection, reflection, self-monitoring, and self-correction through the development of sound habits. These personal attitudes and behaviors, once they are refined and developed through repeated practice, enable the student to build outward from an understanding of self to an understanding of others. The resulting feel for how one's own attitudes and behavior influence others can be parlayed into powerful leadership. The ability to develop oneself through self-observation—and then move on to observing and developing others—can now be taught as a skill. "A lot of the work being done today in adult development suggests that how well you do in problem solving has to do with how well you take perspective on yourself and your situation in the world," Col. Forsythe says.[7] The armed forces now train their future officers to do exactly that.

Forsythe's counterpart in leadership studies at the U.S. Naval Academy, Marine Corps Col. Paul Roush, agrees with this approach. "The first thing a leader has to know is himself," he says. "You have to understand yourself and become personally effective before you can begin learning to understand others and become organizationally effective."[8]

Because the Academy's midshipmen, who carry a full schedule of tough engineering courses and sleep only about five hours a night, do not have the time to learn about themselves through conventional forms of introspection, the Academy's leadership curriculum accelerates their acquisition of self-knowledge with some tools that have emerged from several decades of research.

The Myers-Briggs Type Indicator, a widely used psychological assessment tool, helps midshipmen recognize the psychological type to which they belong and their preferred modes of mental functioning. At the beginning of the freshman year, they learn whether they are predominantly right-brain intuitives or left-brain analytical types, whether they are predominantly extroverted or introverted, and whether their interactions with others are primarily oriented toward thinking or feeling, judging or perceiving.[9] They learn that leadership ability is found among members of all the types, and they undergo leadership-development exercises that do the best job of developing their strengths and overcoming their weaknesses.

The latter is a particularly important benefit of armed services leadership training. Lacking an explicit program of leadership development, many individuals with leadership potential will follow the path of least resistance, using and developing the leadership skills in which they already feel confident while ignoring weak or underdeveloped areas. Leadership training for military officers, by contrast, helps each future leader to identify his weak points so they can be overcome or at least offset or minimized.

As they progress through their four years of study, midshipmen retake the Myers-Briggs in a more complex and sophisticated format known as the Expanded Analysis. The results of this follow-up test deepen their self-knowledge and provide senior midshipmen with insights that help them guide the younger midshipmen's development. As midshipmen rise to upper-class ranks, they in turn become counselors to the classes following them. The entire experience—counseling and being counseled repeatedly using a rolling set of psychological test results—gives the midshipmen a priceless resource for developing their abilities to lead others. Col. Roush explains:

> Counseling is a critical part of what we do here. It's organized so that the upper class works with the plebes to set up goals and develop systems of getting feedback. What it does is provide a way to take what you learn in a classroom and then do something with it. It might be a simple goal like wearing the uniform properly, or running a mile and a half in a specific time, or achieving a certain level of performance in an academic subject. You and your senior-class counselor work out the goal together and then monitor your progress toward it.[10]

The armed services focus intensely on understanding the personal attitudes and behaviors required for leadership, and they work hard to devise classroom studies and training exercises that will develop 18-year-old plebes—freshmen Army and Air Force cadets and Navy midshipmen—into budding leaders by the time they reach the age of 22.[11]

What would happen if future business managers were trained to become leaders as explicitly and purposefully as military officers? Would the leadership-training exercises of the military travel well to academia?

One person who should know is Col. John Kirchenstein. He retired in 1978 after a 35-year career in the U.S. Army and joined the School of Business at the University of Tennessee, Knoxville, where he is now assistant to the dean.

"My definition of leadership is to get someone to do something cheerfully that they really don't want to do—such as charging up a hill against a dug-in enemy," says Col. Kirchenstein.[12] Col. Kirchenstein insists that business situations call for leadership very similar to what works in the military and that the leadership-training programs used in the armed services are

sorely needed by the business schools. Col. Kirchenstein continues:

> I would train the [MBA] students in group activities the way military officer candidates are [trained]. I would have them role-play as members of teams solving various management problems and scenarios. I would have them assemble teams of, say, five people to solve a particular business problem. And I'd rotate the leadership position on the team so everyone could have a chance to be the boss. Then I would grade the whole team—not the individual players—on its performance. The absence of this path in the business school curricula of today is detrimental to one's aspiring to become a "master" of business.[13]

Leaving MBA Students Out of the Loop

What the MBA schools do not teach about leadership is disturbing. Even more disturbing, however, is what they do teach. Apparently, most MBA candidates in U.S. business schools are left with the impression that they will not even need to exercise leadership until they have reached the peak of the corporate pyramid. The business world itself has long been aware that leadership emerges and develops even at the lowest and most obscure levels of the corporate pyramid. My own career, like that of many others, contradicts the notion that leadership happens only "at the top."

I was fortunate enough to receive leadership training during the early 1950s, when my superiors in the U.S. Army plucked me out of the ranks for aptitude testing, identified me as having leadership potential, and sent me to Officer Candidate School.

When I left the Army and joined the United States Steel Corporation as a 28-year-old staff assistant, I put my leadership training to work immediately, much as would a second lieutenant in the Army, where leadership is expected from all officers regardless of rank.

Later in my career, acting as a senior executive, I made it a priority to identify leaders at the lower levels of the organization and to encourage them in developing their leadership abilities on behalf of the company. Most effective CEOs do the same. Leadership is not something senior managers reserve for themselves; if they are worth their salaries, they are identifying, promoting, training, and encouraging leadership among their subordinates at all levels of the organization. One of the ways they do this is by watching for those subordinates who exercise what I call "leadership without portfolio."

Open any textbook of case studies used in a typical MBA program and examine the cast of decision makers. Almost without exception, those who appear in the cases occupy positions at the highest level of the corporation—the office of the chairman and chief executive officer, the president, and the senior vice presidents. "Here and only here," the case studies seem to say, "is where the leaders are found. Here and only here is where organizational leadership takes place." All leadership is depicted as originating at the top and cascading downward through the organization. Viewers of the televised management course *Taking the Lead* are left with this impression when the narrator announces in the first episode:

> Occupying the top rungs on the organizational ladder are the senior-level managers, the vice presidents, presidents, CEOs, in short, those charged with the responsibility not only of managing, but of leading, of charting the long-range course of the organization as a whole.[14]

No wonder MBA students get so little exposure to leadership training. The business schools assume it will be years before their graduates will be required to use it. This is precisely the point Bill Oncken was making in 1984.

Fortunately for the young MBA candidate interested in developing as a leader, the local bookstore and the public library have a wide selection of self-help books on leadership and personal development. Warren Bennis and Burt Nanus's *Leaders: The Strategies for Taking Charge,* Phillip Crosby's *Running Things,* Stephen R. Covey's bestselling *The Seven Habits of Highly Effective People,* and *The Leadership Challenge* by James M. Kouzes and Barry G. Posner represent just a small sample of recent publications that offer real value to students who want to learn more about leadership and are seeking ways to develop their own leadership potential.

Even these books, however, are not addressed to MBA students; their authors seem to assume that only a senior manager would be interested in the subject of leadership, or that only a senior manager—or entrepreneur—would be in a position to benefit from leadership training and use it to improve his or her effectiveness on the job. The business schools appear to be saving these texts for older executives who return to school for advanced studies. Per-

haps they assume that leadership studies and leadership training would only be wasted on MBA candidates.

Secret of "Leadership without Portfolio"

Contrary to what the case studies suggest, there is good news for the young MBA recipient heading out into the corporate world. If you have leadership ability, you can find a way to use it at any level of a business organization—even in your first job, even if you have no formal authority, even if you work in an organization that insists on a crisp distinction between the roles of manager and leader. Ronald A. Heifetz, a psychiatrist who directs the Leadership Education Project at Harvard University's John F. Kennedy School of Government, writes:

> Rather than define leadership either as a position of authority in a social structure or as a personal set of characteristics, we may find it a great deal more useful to define leadership as an *activity.* This allows for leadership from multiple positions in a social structure. A president and a clerk can both lead.[15]

There are those leaders who have the authority and responsibility to command. And then there are others who lead without this portfolio of formal authority. When a subordinate exercises *leadership without portfolio* successfully, superiors take notice. "If this individual could accomplish this much *without* authority," they reason, "just think what he or she could do *with* a little authority."

At this point the fledgling leader is awarded a promotion, a new title, and a measure of formal power to command some of the organization's resources. By dispensing this kind of recognition, the organization signals it is now willing to share some of its authority with a person who has demonstrated an ability to use it constructively and responsibly. *Leadership without portfolio* has earned its just reward: a portfolio.

How early in a person's life can leadership activity emerge? Warren Bennis, who began studying the phenomenon of leadership at MIT in the 1950s and now is Distinguished Professor of Business at the University of Southern California, says his first encounter with leadership occurred in childhood, when he observed a critical difference between his older twin brothers.

"When we were growing up, one of my brothers was the archetypal natural leader, able to talk his teenage peers into doing

things that parents never dreamed of, including ditching school for long periods of time," Bennis writes. "My other brother was the exact opposite, an innate follower without power, or even voice, within the group."[16]

What really piqued Bennis's curiosity about that early experience was that his two brothers were identical twins, "alike in almost everything but their ability to lead."[17] His fascination with the difference in their personalities was one of the factors that drove him to make the study of leadership his life's work.

I call this type of leadership *leadership without portfolio* because when it occurs in an organization, it can spring up at even the earliest stages of a career, with or without the blessing of higher authority, irrespective of title or formal position in the organization, and usually without a formally prescribed job assignment or set of duties.[18] The term is roughly analogous to the British expression "minister without portfolio," defined by the dictionary as "a member of a ministry who is not appointed to any specific department in a government."[19] Historically, prime ministers or monarchs appointed ministers without portfolio when confronted with some sort of nonroutine problem requiring an original solution by a person with a get-things-done reputation.

Even in cases where formal authority has been conferred on an individual, those who exemplify real leadership typically exceed their authority, exploring new areas of achievement and probing for new possibilities that they were not specifically authorized to undertake. This kind of leadership is acknowledged to exist even in the military, where lines of authority are rigidly structured and officers are given not just authority but also command.

The purpose of the rest of this chapter is to supply you with what even the best MBA programs still leave out—practical information on how to develop your own leadership potential right from your first day on the job by exercising *leadership without portfolio.*

LOCUS OF LEADERSHIP

Why Leaders Are Found at the Bottom As Well As the Top of the Organization, and Why Leadership Appears at the Beginning, As Well As the Peak, of a Career

Why do the textbook authors fail to advise young MBAs that they can begin a career of leadership in their very first entry-level position? Probably because they confuse leadership with authority, the formal power that legitimizes the behavior of those in the organization.

But leadership and authority are not the same. Leadership can occur separately from authority, and in individuals with strong leadership ability, leadership usually manifests itself well before the individual has had the chance to acquire formal authority. Leadership is an attribute (Heifetz would say an "activity") of individuals; authority is an attribute of organizations. Authority is conferred by organizations upon those individuals who have earned it through displaying leadership. "Leadership is the process of influencing others in order to accomplish the organization's goals," says West Point's Col. Forsythe. "Most people would say it comes from some power above and beyond formal authority.[20]

The idea of leadership as an activity that emerges from some source other than the organizational chart is implicit in the title of John P. Kotter's 1985 monograph, *Power and Influence: Beyond Formal Authority.*[21] Kotter notes that recent trends have drawn so many new players and new functions into the business environment that traditional lines of corporate authority are stretched too thin and too far to connect all the participants effectively. The result, he says, is a growing number of "power gaps," which can be filled only by the efforts of individuals exercising leadership functions without conventional forms of authorization. These trends are making people more and more dependent on government officials, technical experts, key subordinates, other departments in their firms, key customers, important suppliers, major unions, the business press, and so forth without automatically giving them additional ways to control these groups. As a result, they are turning individual contributor and management jobs into leadership jobs—jobs in which there is a sizable gap between the power one needs to get the job done well and the power that automatically comes with the job.[22]

Almost all of us can recall at least one person in our lives who displayed leadership in ways not specifically conferred by authority. Consultant and former CEO Phillip Crosby says he "began to recognize that some people could lead and others couldn't" when he was still in grammar school in Wheeling, West Virginia. "The principal would walk into the room, and in

a few moments everyone was involved in something she had suggested," Crosby writes in his book *Running Things.* "There were no obvious commands or finger pointings—it all seemed sort of spontaneous. We fell in happily and participated. Very few of the teachers could make it happen that way; they needed to rely on authority, and that didn't always work."[23]

Both the teachers and the principal had formal authority to run a classroom; the authority was conferred by the state along with the teacher's certificate to anyone who had passed the required teacher's college courses. But while the state could confer authority, it could not bestow leadership. It was up to each individual teacher to bring her own leadership abilities to the job. Evidently, Crosby's principal was one of the few who did. No doubt that is why she was promoted to principal.

Crosby says he noticed the distinction between leadership and authority again during his World War II naval service, when he served under two successive skippers aboard the same vessel. Both had the authority that went with their rank, but only one turned out to be a leader. He writes:

> I was on a ship that was an absolute joy. We loved every minute of it, the commodore kept pointing out our performance to the others in the squadron, and I seriously toyed with the idea of a naval career. Then a new captain arrived. Suddenly, everything changed. It became a dismal place to live and work. Nothing was appreciated, nothing was ever right. We were guilty until proven innocent and then suspected of being devious at that. It was a terrible experience.[24]

Why the discrepancy? If the Navy can't make a man a leader, who or what can? If gold bars can't confer leadership, where *does* it come from? What, exactly, is this thing called "leadership," and why does it so often spring up in places where it has no formal authorization to exist—*leadership without portfolio?*

What Leaders Do

Leaders Go First So Others May Follow

What exactly is it that leaders do? What does it mean to be a leader? The dictionary defines "lead" as "to go first; to be in advance . . . to take the directing or principal part." A "leader" is "one who leads . . . a guiding or directing head, as of an army, movement, political group."[25]

Leadership starts people moving. Movement is going to take place; more than one person is involved; one of those people will make the move earlier than the others and, in doing so, will ease or expedite the movement of those who are to follow. This movement is in some sense difficult; many of those involved feel reluctant to undertake it; and the movement is unlikely to take place unless one of the group initiates the process and helps the others to realize that they can do it too.

The existence of followers is implicit in the definition of leader and helps distinguish leadership from a related but still separate concept—initiative. The dictionary defines initiative as "the ability to think and act without being urged."[26] Leaders have this ability, of course, but so do many other people who are not leaders. Self-employed people display initiative when setting their own deadlines and completing projects on schedule without prompting. But if a self-employed person works alone, this initiative functions in a vacuum. It does not influence, much less inspire, organize, or coordinate the work of others. But when a leader moves, others move with the leader and because of the leader.

Today, of course, leaders do not literally lead people geographically from one place to another, like Moses leading the Israelites to the Promised Land. The movements that modern leaders initiate are metaphorical. Leaders now initiate change.

Leaders Build Organizations

In the business world, however, there is more to leading than simply setting an example that others follow through imitation. Leading is not the same as pioneering or serving as an example for others to follow. A pioneer is someone who does something for the first time; those who follow a pioneer merely repeat what the pioneer did (e.g., establish a homestead on the American frontier). A person who serves as a role model or exemplar performs much the same function: People watch the model in action and then say to themselves, "If that person can do that, I can too." They then model the behavior of the person who set the example.

Those who follow a leader in business, however, do not simply repeat what the leader did. While the followers of a business leader pursue the same organizational *goal* as the leader, they reach the goal by performing widely differing *tasks and assignments*, to which they bring a widely differing range of skills, aptitudes, training and experience. While effective business leaders usually have something of the pioneer or role model in them, it is not their pioneering or role modeling alone that makes them leaders. It is their ability to articulate a goal that will inspire collaborative effort, plus their ability to create and run an *organization* in which individuals of differing abilities and temperaments each contribute to the attainment of the goal.[27]

To do this, leaders focus intently on the needs and sensibilities of their followers. They observe and listen closely for cues as to what approaches will win the followers' support for the leader's ideas, projects, and methods. Good leaders seem to have a talent for sensing which approaches will work on different types of people—and in which situations.

But talent alone is not sufficient for the task of bonding with followers, enlisting their support, and then coordinating the multitude of personalities, abilities, tasks, and timetables that characterize a modern business organization. Leaders have to work at getting to know their followers, and they have to work just as hard at assigning them the appropriate tasks.

Pulitzer Prize-winning author Garry Wills writes:

> The leader needs to understand his followers far more than they need to understand him. This is the time-consuming aspect of leadership. It explains why great thinkers and artists are rarely leaders of others as opposed to influences on them. The scientist absorbed in the solution of a problem does not have the energy or patience to understand the needs of a number of other people who might be marshaled to deal with the problem.[28]

The leader has to understand something else as well—the importance of the correct fit between the leader and the situation. The biographical record of great historic figures, as well as the growing body of empirical evidence from academic studies of organizational behavior, makes it clear that there is no such thing as a universal leader type.[29] The military has long recognized that a general who displays brilliant tactical leadership on the battlefield does not necessarily make an equally brilliant strategist when promoted to the general staff. Coincidentally, the business world is replete with anecdotal, journalistic, and academic evidence of entrepreneurial executives who proved to be highly gifted in the leadership skills needed to pilot a company through the start-up and lift-off stage of growth but seemed to run out of leadership tricks—and even interest—when their companies had to enter the corporate phase of the growth trajectory. One of the things leaders must do, therefore, is know themselves well enough to make sure they place themselves in the appropriate leadership situations so that their abilities are not squandered.

Real Origins of Leadership

In his 1938 book, *The Functions of the Executive*, New Jersey Bell Telephone Company President Chester I. Barnard set forth a radical idea that still ignites controversy among some academic students of organizational behavior. Barnard claimed that the ultimate source of authority resides not within the individual who carries authority, or even with the organization that conferred it upon him—what he called the *authority of position*—but with the subordinate individuals on whom authority is supposed to act. Those who successfully wield authority, Barnard wrote, are able to do so because their subordinates concede them that privilege.

"[I]t is obvious that some men have superior ability," Barnard says. "Their knowledge and understanding regardless of position command respect." When followers detect this ability, Barnard writes, they tacitly agree to allow themselves to be led by the person who has it. "This," he says, "is the *authority of leadership*."[30]

If we are to believe Barnard, then, the authority embodied in leadership represents something of a paradox: It becomes effective only when a signal from the top down meets an appropriate response from the bottom up. The leader more or less gets permission to be leader from the people being led.

Fifty-five years after Barnard wrote those words, James M. Kouzes and Barry Z. Posner echoed them in *Credibility: How Leaders Gain and Lose It, Why People Demand It*. "Loyalty," they write, "is not something a boss can demand. It is something the people—the constituency—choose to grant to a leader who has earned it. The people's choice is based not upon authority, but upon the leader's perceived capacity to serve a need."[31]

One of my favorite authorities on this voluntary relationship between the leader and her followers is the late Louis B. Lundborg, developer of the VISA card and eventually chairman of the Bank of America. Toward the end of his career, Lundborg contributed a column called "Executive Survival Kit" to *Industry Week* magazine. In one of those columns he wrote: "In the most bare-bones definition, a leader is one whom others will follow willingly and voluntarily. That rules out tyrants, bullies, autocrats, and all those others who use coercive power to impose their wills on others."[32]

Lundborg identifies eight personal qualities that enable leaders to elicit this voluntary cooperation. He says people will follow the person who they feel:

- Knows where he's going.
- Knows how to get there.
- Has courage and persistence—will not run away or back down from danger, opposition, or discouragement.
- Can be believed.
- Can be trusted not to sell their cause out for his personal advantage.
- Makes the mission seem important, exciting, and possible to accomplish.
- Makes them feel capable of performing their role.[33]

Lundborg also says "a true leader has one quality that may not have to come into play very often, but that quickly identifies him when it does":

> If things have gone wrong in the company because people under an executive's command have made mistakes or performed badly, he might try to clear his skirts by criticizing those subordinates—to the board of directors, to investors, to the press. But the real leader does not hide behind others. He says one way or another: "I was responsible for what these people were doing, and I knew what they were doing" (or "I should have known what they were doing"), so don't blame them—blame me.[34]

Finally, Lundborg distinguishes the true leader from another type he calls the "driver," or "take-charge guy." Like the leader, the driver "gets the job done." But only the leader, he says, gets the job done while building morale—an organizational intangible that Lundborg considers essential. "Even in ordinary circumstances, good morale can have a tonic effect, and a measurable effect on productivity," he writes. "But when survival is threatened—in a company or a country—morale is more than a tonic; it is a lifesaver."[35]

The question is how leaders do this. What strengths and abilities do they project to win this kind of implicit permission from their followers, particularly when the leaders are at the start of their careers and have little formal authority from the organization?

To answer those questions we first have to understand where the idea of leadership came from and what kind of circumstances brought it into existence.

LOGIC OF LEADERSHIP

How the Human Race Gradually Switched from Hereditary Rulers to Chosen Leaders to Ensure Competent Management of Governments, Armies, and Businesses

Mortimer Adler, the former University of Chicago chancellor who compiled and edited the *Great Books of the Western World* series, says he deliberately left leadership off his list of the 102 Great Ideas because the great thinkers of classical Greece and Rome were not strongly attracted to it as a subject for discussion and philosophizing. For them, leadership just did not add up to the kind of full-fledged idea or concept they found in Truth, Virtue, Duty, or Beauty. Adler's publisher, Peter Norton, chairman of Encyclopedia Britannica, Inc., says, "leadership, as we understand it, is very much a 20th-century word."[36]

The late Ralph Stogdill made a similar observation in his massive *Handbook of Leadership,* now edited by his former student, Bernard M. Bass:

Leadership appears to be a rather sophisticated concept. Words meaning head of state, military commander, princess, proconsul, chief, or king are the only ones found in many languages to differentiate the ruler from other members of society. A preoccupation with leadership as opposed to headship based on inheritance, usurpation, or appointment occurs predominantly in countries with an Anglo-Saxon heritage. The *Oxford English Dictionary* (1933) notes the appearance of the word "leader" as early as the year 1300. However, the word "leadership" did not appear until the first half of the nineteenth century in writings about political influence and control of the British parliament.[37]

The idea of leadership, in other words, had to evolve historically—away from the ancient hereditary authority of kings and toward a more rational system in which authority is awarded only to those who first display some sort of proven ability to persuade others to follow them. The ancient custom of passing on the kingdom to the eldest son of the previous king did not always result in the selection of a strong, wise, or able ruler. Statesmen began looking for a way to identify ability wherever it occurred, spontaneously, with or without lineage or authority dictated by custom. Military men sensed a similar need to change the way they selected the leaders of their armies. They realized that officers who made it to the top through cunning, politicking, or ruthless eliminating of rivals did not necessarily have the ability to train, develop, rally, and inspire troops to victory on the battlefield.

Despite the failure of Plato and Aristotle to concern themselves with leadership in the ancient world, we have evidence of at least one example of it in the figure of Pericles (495–429 B.C.), the legendary soldier-statesman who presided over the Golden Age in which Athens rose to become the military, economic, and cultural center of Mediterranean civilization.

It is no mystery why 5th-century Athens should have produced one of the first—if not *the* first—personalities that a modern student of organizational dynamics would recognize as a leader, rather than a ruler, monarch, tyrant, or dictator. Athens was a democracy—the first democracy of which we have record. All freeborn adult males in the city-state—about 60,000 of them—were the sole source of legitimate power. The Athenians would not follow a leader they themselves had not freely chosen, and they would not permit their leaders to carry out a program—including a military campaign—unless it was first approved by this assembly of citizens. As Yale University historian Dr. Donald Kagan points out in his recently published study of the Peloponnesian War:

The sovereign in Athens, which made all decisions on policy—foreign and domestic, military and civil—was the assembly. All male citizens were eligible to attend, vote, make proposals, and debate. The assembly met no fewer than forty times a year in the open air, overlooking the marketplace beside the Acropolis. . . . This was the body that had to approve treaties of peace and declarations of war. Whatever strategic decisions were taken had to be proposed, discussed, and debated in the open before thousands of people, a majority of whom must approve every detail of every action. For any expedition, the assembly voted on its target and purpose, the number and specific nature of ships and men, the funds to be spent, the commanders to lead the forces, and the specific instructions to those commanders. The Council of Five Hundred, chosen by lot from the Athenian citizenry, prepared bills for the assembly's consideration but was totally subordinate to the larger body.[38]

In fact, says Kagan, the Athenians were so democratic that even their military leaders had to stand for election annually.

The most important offices in the Athenian state, among the few filled by election rather than by lottery, were those of the ten generals. Because they commanded divisions of the Athenian Army and fleets of ships in battle they had to be military men; because they needed to be elected for a one-year term, and could be reelected without limit, they had to be politicians. In the fifth century, most generals had skills in both directions, although some were stronger in one direction than the other. These men could and did impose military discipline on campaign, but they were not very potent in the city. At least ten times a year, there were formal opportunities for them to face complaints against their conduct in office, and at the end of their terms they had to make full accountings of their behaviors in office, military and financial. On each occasion they were subject to trial if accused and serious punishment if convicted.[39]

In such an intensely democratic environment, where both civil and military figures were held to standards of accountability far more severe than our own, and where any sort of dictatorial tendencies were instantly detected and quashed, only someone exhibiting genuine leadership could be expected to attract the loyalty and support of the people and to maintain it over a sufficient span of time to build enduring institutions of civilization.

Without using a term such as "leadership without portfolio," Kagan shows how—in a democratic environment—an individual with no particular title or authority can emerge into the public consciousness and win sufficient support to become the people's *de facto* leader.

[T]he assembly was the government. Sometimes, however, a general would gain so much political support and influence as to become the leader of the

Athenians *in fact, if not in law* (emphasis added). Such was Cimon for the seventeen years between 479 and 462, when he appears to have been elected general each year, to have led every important expedition, and to have persuaded the Athenian assembly to support his policies at home and abroad. After the departure of Cimon, Pericles achieved similar success over an even longer period.[40]

As the *Encyclopedia Britannica* says of Pericles, "His integrity, ability and experience enabled him to dominate the assembly and impose his will alike in domestic and foreign policy. He inspired the citizens with his unqualified loyalty to Athens and with his ambitions for its future."[41]

In Pericles, Kagan finds all the traits and behaviors of the democratically chosen leader in full flower. With only a token amount of military force at his disposal, subject to almost weekly scrutiny in the assembly, and vulnerable to recall in each annual election, Pericles nevertheless managed to remain as leader of the Athenians almost continually over the 32 years from 461 B.C. until his death in 429 B.C. Under his leadership, Athenian civilization produced masterpieces of architecture, navigation, mathematics, commerce, art, literature, drama, and philosophy that are still studied and appreciated 2,500 years later. The Athenians were under no compulsion to undertake such tasks. As Kagan makes clear, they followed Pericles voluntarily because his vision, integrity, and credibility—as well as his responsible use of the power with which they had entrusted him—inspired them to pursue the grandeur that he was the first to imagine and communicate.

> Pericles was one of those rare people who place their own stamp on their time. An Athenian aristocrat, he first became a democratic political reformer, and then the leader of the Athenian democracy. He personally commanded armies and navies, negotiated treaties, selected the sculptors and architects who beautified the Acropolis, and counted among his friends and associates the leading artists, poets, philosophers, and historians of his age. It is hard to think of any political leader who ever had so direct and versatile a role in guiding the life of his people. For three decades . . . he seems to have been general each year, to have assisted the election of some of his associates, to have conducted those campaigns he thought necessary, and to have gained the support of the Athenians for his

domestic and foreign policies. It is important to note, however, that he never had any greater formal powers than the other generals and never tried to alter the constitution. He was still subject to the scrutiny provided for in the constitution and required a vote in the open and uncontrolled assembly to take any action. He did not always get what he wanted and, on some occasions, his enemies persuaded the assembly to act against his wishes, but an accurate description of the Athenian democracy . . . was that it was a democracy led by its first citizen. Pericles was influential not because of any hidden power or the control of armed force, for he had none. The Athenians followed his lead because of his reputation for intelligence, wisdom, ability, honesty, and patriotism; because of his remarkable talents as a public speaker; and because of the success and popularity of his policies and leadership. Thucydides introduces him into his history as "Pericles son of Xanthippus, the leading man in Athens at that time and the ablest in speech and action."[42]

Two elements in Kagan's treatment of Pericles merit particular attention. The first is his observation that "Pericles was influential not because of any hidden power or the control of armed force, for he had none." This comes very close to suggesting that even in his position at the center of the Athenian democracy, Pericles was without substantial portfolio. He led not because he had a lofty title, wore a splendid robe, occupied luxurious quarters or controlled armed men, but because his vision, honesty, and record for accomplishment persuaded growing numbers of Athenians to follow him voluntarily.

The second noteworthy element in Kagan's treatment of Pericles, however, is what *is not* there: Kagan calls Pericles a "great leader," crediting him for "the popularity of his policies and leadership." He says of Pericles that "the Athenians followed his lead," and he creates in his portrait of Pericles a virtual textbook example of a real leader in action. The theme of leadership runs like a golden thread through Kagan's entire treatment of the great Athenian. Yet the words "lead," "leadership," and "leader" are not listed in the index of Kagan's otherwise exhaustive, absorbing, and often dramatic 573-page book.

This is a phenomenon we must expect to encounter repeatedly in trying to raise our consciousness of leadership. While the idea of leadership is important, it is also *elusive.* Like particle physicists recording

the passage of electrons through a cloud chamber, we notice not the thing itself, but the effects it leaves in its wake. Or, to use another laboratory analogy, identifying and describing leadership is like identifying and describing a biological specimen under a microscope. When we first look down the barrel of the scope, we do not see anything unless we have some idea of what to look for. Only after we adjust the lenses—sometimes repeatedly—does the subject of our inquiry come into focus.

Examples of leadership are available in an increasingly broad and diverse spectrum of publications. One of the best, however, can be found in one of the world's oldest printed (and hand-inscribed) texts, the New Testament. My appreciation of this story recently was sharpened after I heard it retold as a lesson in leadership by Dr. Joe Stowell, president of Chicago's world-renowned Moody Bible Institute. Like any dedicated Christian, Dr. Stowell acknowledges Jesus as Redeemer and Savior. But as the chief executive officer of an admired and successful organization, he sees Jesus as well in the role of leader.

Dr. Stowell calls his version of the story "Staying on Mission." He adapted it from John 21:3–17. Jesus, the leader of a developing religious movement, has been grooming a senior staff in his organization, the Disciples. They have been following his lead, learning his message, repeating his Parables, understanding his vision, and helping develop a formal plan to propagate the new faith among an ever-widening circle of potential believers. This is a tight group, a loyal staff made up of second-level leaders, any one of whom should be able to step forward and take over the top leadership position should anything happen to the incumbent.

Suddenly all hell breaks loose. Treachery, divisiveness, suspicion, rejection, and denial rip through the organization. The leader's worthiness to head a growing religious movement has come into question. Demoralized for the first time by doubt, the senior staff wavers. As loyalty falters, some of the team begin carrying false reports to the civil authorities, hoping to curry favor with the powerful to assure favorable treatment for themselves should the new religious movement fail (many a chief executive can relate to this scenario).

The situation deteriorates. The leader, Jesus, is arrested, tried, and put to death. Leaderless now, the senior staff crumbles.

Peter, supposedly the strongest and most qualified second-in-command, drops the ball. Instead of pulling the team together and reestablishing leadership, he says, "Well, that's it. We never realized those doctrines could get us in so much trouble. Let's just file for moral bankruptcy and return to our old ways and our old jobs." In effect, he and the other team members go off message, off calling, and off mission. They are in business for themselves now, not for the Cause. The once-focused team is now little more than a gang, a group held together more by their mutual need for massed strength than by any conviction of what to use it for. They pile into their frail boats and head out for what they know best, fishing with their old boss, Peter. They fish all night but catch nothing.

As dawn breaks, they see and hear a figure on the shore calling out, "Hey fellas, how's the fishing?"

"No good!" they answer.

"Well, throw your nets on the other side of the boat and see what happens," cries the figure.

They comply, and this time the nets are filled to bursting.

Peter swims to shore to greet the visitor. He discovers the man is Jesus. He has lit a small fire and cooks up a mess of fish. (As an aside, Dr. Stowell observes that this event was the "Last Breakfast.")

Jesus puts his arm around Peter's shoulder, looks him straight in the eye, and says "What's the problem? Didn't you and the others on the team understand my vision?"

"Oh, yes," says Peter.

"Then why are you out fishing instead of carrying my message throughout the land to all who need to hear it? Why isn't the organization moving forward? I want you to get back on vision, back on mission, and back on plan."

The rest, as they say, is history. Clearly, great religious movements have developed over the ages because strong-willed, dynamic people of immense conviction persisted in carrying a simple but powerful message out to the masses of the spiritually starved. Different in philosophy or theology though they may be, these leaders have a common bond: They possess a clear vision of where they want to go and what they expect to achieve. They understand their goal clearly and can articulate clearly to their followers both the mission and the means by which it will be accomplished. They have developed a plan, a testament of purpose that directs the processes of the organization in an orderly flow toward their final goal.

Connection of Leadership and Power: An Embarrassment of Riches

Why do we have such trouble focusing on leadership, even when we sense very strongly that it is present among us and that we need it? We have such trouble because leadership is—among others things—about *power*, a word that stirs deeply ambivalent feelings in the politically correct, antiauthoritarian American psyche that developed in the wake of the Vietnamese War, the Watergate scandal, and other abuses of power. Because leadership is about power, many people today find it embarrassing.

Consult some of the recent best-sellers on leadership, particularly the self-help guides to business leadership, and you will discover an amazing absence: Despite thousands of words about leaders and leadership, there is almost no discussion—or even mention—of power.

Some of the top leadership books, including Michael Maccoby's *The Leader*, Charles C. Manz's *Superleadership: Leading Others to Lead Themselves*, and Burt Nanus's *The Leader's Edge*, do not even list "power" as an entry in the index.[43] The most unintentionally amusing example of such an omission occurs in John P. Kotter's otherwise useful and informative 1985 book, *Power and Influence: Beyond Formal Authority. Power* is missing from the index, even though it is the first word in the title. Nor is *power* actually defined in Kotter's book. It is not even discussed until Chapter 7, where it makes its entry as part of the term "power base."

This reluctance to come to grips with the question of organizational power appears to be endemic in much of the current popular leadership literature. In several recent books, the word *power* appears only as the root of the New Age buzzword "empowerment" (with little or no explanation of why the new version is good while its antecedent is bad). No general theory of power is introduced, and no relationship between power and leadership is suggested. Power seems to be almost as big a taboo in leadership books of the 1990s as sex was in books about marriage prior to the mid-50s.

"Power is America's last dirty word," writes Rosabeth Moss Kanter. "It is easier to talk about money—and much easier to talk about sex—than it is to talk about power."[44]

Yet just as marriage cannot be discussed realistically without mentioning sex, leadership cannot be studied effectively without reference to power. Effective leaders must deal in power because it is both their stock in trade and the raw material out of which they craft their accomplishments. Leaders attract and pool the personal power of many individuals and put it to work.

So what is the big problem with power? The answer is simply that power, like the money that people entrust to capitalists, is subject to abuse. When such abuses are exposed, as they are very dramatically in today's hyperbolic media, many people begin to confuse the abuse of power with power itself. All power—and all who wield power—then become suspect. A person who seeks and uses power without apology is regarded as something of an embarrassment, regardless of the ends toward which the power is directed.

Kagan writes:

> To many in the modern world, *power* has an unpleasant ring. It seems to imply the ability to impose one's will upon another, usually by the use of force. Power is felt inherently to be bad. That, however, is an unduly restricted understanding. In itself, power is neutral. It is the capacity to bring about desired ends, and these may be good or bad. It is also the capacity to resist the demands and compulsions of others. In this latter sense, power is essential for the achievement and preservation of freedom. In the Kingdom of Heaven, we are led to believe, human beings will not require power, but in the world in which we all live, it is essential, and the struggle for it inevitable.[45]

One academic who has not tried to avoid the issue of power in his research and writing is Jeffrey Pfeffer, professor of Organizational Behavior in the Graduate School of Business at Stanford University. Professor Pfeffer forthrightly titled his 1992 monograph *Managing with Power: Politics and Influence in Organizations*, and the index to his 389-page work lists "power" repeatedly—with eight entries under "Power and performance," four under "Power dynamics," six under "Power in organizations," and 15 under "Sources of power."

"That we are ambivalent about power is undeniable," Pfeffer writes. "It is as if we know that power and politics exist, and we even grudgingly admit that they are necessary to individual success, but we nevertheless don't like them."[46]

The reasons for that ambivalence, Pfeffer says, are multiple. First, the American educational system trains youngsters to become strong individual contributors—stars, if you will—but slights the importance of managing one's ego and joining in collaborative efforts that can be led only by the powerful. Second, American culture confuses ends with means, leaving many people unable to distinguish between power and the ends to which it can be directed. The untutored mind can easily be led to believe that power and the abuse of power are the same thing ("the same strategies and processes that may produce outcomes we desire can also be used to produce results that we consider undesirable").[47]

Finally, Pfeffer even indicts the New Age movement for blinding people to the simple truth that without power (including its acquisition, manipulation, and direction through politics), organizational effort yields no results.

> [O]rganizations, particularly large ones, are like governments in that they are fundamentally political entities. To understand them, one needs to understand organizational politics; just as to understand governments, one needs to understand governmental politics. Ours is an era in which people tend to shy away from this task. As I browse through bookstores, I am struck by the incursion of "New Age" thinking, even in the business sections. New Age can be defined, I suppose, in many ways, but what strikes me about it are two elements: (1) self-absorption and self-focus, which looks toward the individual in isolation; and (2) a belief that conflict is largely the result of misunderstanding, and if people only had more communication, more tolerance, and more patience, many (or all) social problems would disappear. These themes appear in books on topics ranging from making marriages work to making organizations work. A focus on individual self-actualization is useful, but a focus on sheer self-reliance is not likely to encourage one to try to get things done with and through other people—to be a manager or a leader. . . . One can be quite content, quite happy, quite fulfilled as an organizational hermit; but one's influence is limited and the potential to accomplish great things, which requires interdependent action, is almost extinguished.[48]

Kagan's and Pfeffer's readings of the contemporary American response to power are something I can confirm from personal experience. In the six years since I began teaching graduate courses in business, I have noticed a curious phenomenon in the lecture hall. Whenever I refer to power as one of the concerns of business leaders, several of the students visibly wince. The mere mention of power seems offensive to them. They seem disappointed that it keeps turning up like a bad penny. They make me feel like some kind of bull in the china shop who does not realize that power is out of fashion now, as if we had all agreed to put powerseeking behind us and move into some kind of postpower era of enlightened self-interest.

The truth is that there is no postpower era, because nothing has been discovered that can take the place of power as a fuel for organizational effort. Power, like matter and energy, may change its form but cannot go out of existence. Kagan, too, feels that we needlessly endanger ourselves when we let our fear of the abuse of power prejudice us against the very notion of power itself. When he was interviewed on the Cable News Network's *Charlie Rose Show,* he told the host:

> In the first place, I'm convinced it's all about power, and that's a naughty word in the minds of most people. It shouldn't be. It's a neutral word. Power is something everybody needs. Power is the ability to do what you want and the ability to prevent somebody else from imposing his will on you.[49]

What Kagan is trying to do here is to relegitimize a venerable concept often misunderstood or dismissed in modern politically correct America. It is the idea of power as morally neutral, an objective force of nature like fire or electricity that is neither good nor bad in itself but can be directed to good or bad ends by the human beings who use it.

Is fire good or bad? As posed, the question is meaningless, because fire is simply a natural phenomenon. If it is out of control and burns down my house, it is bad. If it is under control in my furnace and keeps my house heated to 70 degrees Fahrenheit, it is good. The only question is whether the phenomenon of combustion is being managed and directed for appropriate ends—human good.

As with fire, so with power. In the competent hands of a humane individual who understands both its upside and downside, power can be an indispensable force for human good. But to be effective as a leader, such an individual must be realistic about power. She must not have a knee-jerk disdain for it; rather, she must genuinely want it, must have the ability to acquire it, must have a respect for both its useful and its dangerous properties, and must have skill in using it. No matter how humane or decent the ends to which power may be directed, somebody must first *take it* (i.e., persuade many others to give up a share of their individual power and place it in the collective savings pool under the control of a leader who can apply it where needed for solving collective problems). Kagan told Charlie Rose:

> I'm talking about leaders. . . . The individual human beings who are making the decisions are extraordinarily important, and the differences between them are essential. So I would hope that out of this thing there would emerge pictures of important individuals performing in their role as decision makers.[50]

Kagan feels that Britain's wartime Prime Minister Winston Churchill exemplified this ideal of a democratically chosen leader whose followers agreed to commit their individual power to him because they felt he would manage it judiciously and deploy it effectively to ends they felt were necessary:

> Winston Churchill is a truly amazing man. It's not that he was right all the time, because he sure as hell wasn't right all the time. But as a matter of fact, he was right in the critical moment . . . when he finally gained power after it looked like it was almost too late, he had this marvelous capacity to say, "Okay, let's forget all that now. Let's all get together. Let's work together for the common cause." And he was able to do that and hold them together throughout that terrible war.[51]

" . . . *when he finally gained power.*" This is the connection between leadership and power. The leader is able to lead not only because he understands his followers and makes his vision theirs, but because he first acknowledges the reality of power, moves resolutely to take it when the possibility opens to him, and masters the dynamics of applying it on behalf of his followers' interests. He doesn't lose precious time in philosophical doubts about whether power is good or bad. If he's good, if his followers are convinced he's good, and if all are convinced their cause is good, all can be confident that the power they share will be directed by the leader toward good ends.

Although Kagan's ideas about power developed out of his research into statecraft, politics, and warfare, I find them equally applicable to business—as well as to government, the armed forces, and non-profit institutions. Because it is needed everywhere, leadership exists everywhere (though never, apparently, in adequate amounts). Leadership is not a substitute for power or some New Age successor to power; it is a more effective and humane way of exercising power.

Yet even when leadership is present, it often goes unnoticed. This is perhaps due to its association with power, from which so many contemporary Americans wish to avert their eyes. Another reason is that so much leadership is conducted in a way we have not been trained to recognize—*without portfolio.*

Leadership without portfolio, then, is not an isolated or accidental phenomenon; it is an integral part of the way leaders develop, emerge, win recognition, and begin to acquire power and authority based on ability rather than accident of birth, ritualized succession, or brazen usurpation. There most certainly is a logic to leadership. Leadership is not just a set of abilities that certain individuals display; it is also an organizing principle, a newer and more logical way to make sure authority is given only to those who have shown they can use it wisely and effectively.

Just knowing that leadership can operate *without a portfolio* is a valuable lesson for anyone entering a business career and feeling the first stirrings of leadership potential. But how do you know whether what you are feeling *is* leadership potential? What is it that actually makes someone a leader?

Bennis and the "Four Competencies"

Since the late 1950s, a small group of researchers, many of them trained in the Systems Thinking and Organizational Learning Program at MIT's Sloan School of Management, has been asking those very questions. Warren Bennis is one of them. He says leaders display what he calls the "four competencies of leadership." Bennis defines those competencies as *management of attention, management of meaning, management of trust,* and *management of self.* (*Note:* The following discussion of Bennis's four competencies is a paraphrase of material found on pages 78–95 of *An Invented Life.*)

Management of attention, Bennis's term for what other writers often call "vision," is evident in the way leaders draw others to them, hold their attention, and inspire them.

"I cannot exaggerate this difference," Bennis told a Chicago *Tribune* reporter.

"It's as if they're drawing people to them, but it's not necessarily the quality we think of as charisma. It's a kind of laser-beam intensity they get when talking about their vision. When they're talking about something else they can be as boring as the next person."[52]

Bennis says leaders are able to manage other people's attention because they project a strong conviction both that they know what needs to happen next and that it *can* happen. Leaders use this sense of conviction to captivate others and involve them in the project. When followers sense that a leader has a vision as well as a plan for achieving it, they experience a rallying effect that focuses their efforts on the leader's goal and maintains that focus over the long term.

The techniques the leader uses to manage other people's attention can vary depending on the leader's personality and the situation: Leaders may inspire, charm, cajole, flatter, manipulate, listen carefully, urge, even threaten or humiliate in an effort to focus their followers' attention. Seasoned leaders skillfully employ several techniques in turn as necessary. But it is not the techniques that make the leader; it is the leader's vision and the leader's conviction that the vision can be achieved. The techniques are best understood as tools that leaders use to involve followers in their vision and communicate to them the leader's feelings of excitement and urgency.

Bennis says leaders exert a similar captivating effect through the *management of meaning,* perhaps a more precise expression for what so many other writers mean when they tell us that leaders are "good communicators." *Management of meaning,* Bennis says, means leaders project a sense that they understand the real underlying patterns that make apparently unrelated elements form a coherent, understandable whole. Bennis says that when leaders discover meanings and communicate them to their followers, the followers respond with another burst of organized energy, enthusiasm, and focus.

Bennis finds Ronald Reagan an exemplar of this *management of meaning:*

The reason is that Reagan uses metaphors with which people can identify. In his first budget message, for example, Reagan described a trillion dollars by comparing it to piling up dollar bills beside the Empire State Building. . . . In contrast, President Carter was boring.

Carter was one of our best-informed presidents; he had more facts at his fingertips than almost any other president. But he never made the meaning come through the facts. . . . An assistant secretary of commerce appointed by Carter . . . told me that after four years in his administration, she still did not know what Jimmy Carter stood for. She said that working for him was like looking through the wrong side of a tapestry; the scene was blurry and indistinct.[53]

Bennis's *management of trust* means that the leader can be trusted to adhere to a constant theme or motif. Bennis says even though leaders may have to adjust some aspects of their approach periodically in response to changing conditions, they continue to project to their followers a strong signal that they remain true to certain underlying principles, even if those principles are not always articulated. Bennis also calls this trait *constancy* and says followers find it assuring and empowering. When people sense they can trust a leader to remain constant in his or her loyalty to a principle, they will follow that person because they know they will not be betrayed. He writes:

When I talked to the board members or staffs of these leaders, I heard certain phrases again and again: "Whether you like it or not, you always know where he's coming from, what he stands for." In fact, a recent study showed that people would much rather follow individuals they can count on, even when they disagree with their viewpoint, than people they agree with who shift positions frequently.[54]

There's another, much older word for what Bennis is describing here—integrity. He feels this quality is largely responsible for the stunning successes of former British Prime Minister Margaret Thatcher. Many disagreed with her, but no one ever seemed to be puzzled about what she stood for.

Bennis's fourth leadership competency, *management of self,* shows up in the works of other students of leadership as well. Bennis defines it as "knowing one's skills and deploying them effectively. . . . Leaders know themselves; they know their strengths and nurture them."

Management of self, Bennis suggests, is not the same as self-confidence, which sometimes appears in people who have nothing in particular to be confident about—a form without content. Real leaders, he says, have real abilities and know what they are. Because they know and trust these abilities, they do not lose momentum by engaging in pointless soul-searching or agonizing when they make a mistake. They pause just long enough to learn from the experience, and then move ahead again. As one leader told him, "A mistake is just another way of doing things." This ability, too, builds trust in followers. Just as they feel secure in committing to a leader who knows and sticks to principles, so too do they feel secure in the hands of someone who knows and sticks with his strengths.

The leadership attitudes and behaviors identified by Bennis and his colleagues in decades of formal academic studies are echoed in the anecdotal recollections of those who have worked alongside acknowledged leaders. For example, when former Michigan Governor and American Motors Chairman George Romney died in the summer of 1995, media interviews with his former associates revealed that Romney had captivated them with the very same traits described by Bennis. He had a clear and unflinching conviction, even in the 1950s, that Americans needed and wanted smaller, more fuel-efficient cars. He communicated that conviction eloquently and tirelessly. And he communicated it so clearly and unequivocally that no one ever doubted his sincerity or confused his conviction with a mere opinion.

"You always knew what he stood for," a former colleague told Detroit *News-Free Press* columnist James V. Higgins.[55] John Conde, one of AMC's former public relations executives, recalled that Romney's great talent was for "getting people fired up." "Romney was pretty good at getting attention called to himself," Conde told Higgins. "He was a great communicator. I never saw anybody who knew how to make the dealers as enthusiastic as he did."[56]

Another anecdote that throws some light on the nature of leadership is told by senior *Business Week* writer John A. Byrne in his 1993 book, *The Whiz Kids*. Byrne's book tells how ten World War II Army Air Corps statisticians led by the legendary Col. "Tex" Thornton sold themselves in a package deal at war's end to young Henry Ford II, who had just assumed the presidency of the Ford Motor Company from his aging grandfather, Henry Ford. The Whiz Kids, whose advanced number-crunching techniques helped rescue Ford from two decades of bad management, included not only Thornton (who went on to form Litton Industries), but also Robert S. McNamara (chosen by President John F. Kennedy to become Secretary of Defense), and Arjay Miller (who became president of Ford and then dean of the Graduate School of Business at Stanford University).

As Byrne makes clear, however, it was Thornton's leadership, not his technical skills or even his intelligence, that made the package deal happen. While all of the Whiz Kids were brilliant—their pioneering wartime statistical work had given the Army Air Corps unprecedented control over its planes, personnel, and equipment—it was Thornton who held the group together throughout the four-year war, and it was Thornton who held it together after the war and proposed the daring idea of offering themselves and their skills as a group to a single employer. In the ultimate display of chutzpah, Thornton sent a cold-canvass telegram to Henry Ford asking for an interview. (He got it, and the Whiz Kids got hired.)

No one was surprised, therefore, when after Ford agreed to hire the ten men, company psychologists who administered a battery of tests to the Whiz Kids found objective evidence that Thornton was their leader, even though his intellectual gifts were inferior to those of the other team members.

> It was revealing to Ford . . . to look over the results of Tex's exams. The tests showed him to be dead last in mental ability and among the lower half of the group in knowledge. Tex, though, topped the others in outstanding leadership qualities. The evaluator noted that the results showed "exceptional understanding of human nature and ability to evaluate others" as well as the "presence of strong motivation and drive."[57]

Four "Competencies" or Seven "Habits"?

In *The Seven Habits of Highly Effective People*, management consultant and educator Stephen R. Covey does not specifically set out to address the issue of leadership.[58] But since leaders are among the highly effective, it is worth looking at Covey's Seven Habits to see how they apply to leaders.

Covey divides his Seven Habits into chronological groups. The first group consists of three habits that make up what Covey calls "private victory." These habits are something similar to Bennis's *management of self.* They are character-building habits, self-mastery exercises designed to strengthen the individual so she can act independently.

Independence is not an end in itself in Covey's scheme, however; it is the precursor of *inter*dependence—the ability to interact effectively with others, particularly in the world of work. Covey says the three habits making up private victory must be in place before an individual can go on to become highly effective in an organizational setting. Covey identifies the habits leading to private victory as:

- **Be proactive.** Effective people do not wait to react to developments or to be told what to do. They exercise initiative and originality because they have cultivated a highly developed sense of being responsible. They do not engage in blaming or excuse-making and see themselves as conditioned more by their own will and judgment than by the environment.

- **Begin with the end in mind.** Effective people first develop a strong vision of how something ought to be before they act. They have a strong ability to visualize the final or ideal form in which an idea will be realized. They virtually see a picture of what they want to create.

- **Put first things first.** Effective people get things done without wasting time because they have cultivated the ability to see the order in which things have to happen. Because they set priorities and schedule their activities correctly, they rarely have to go back and repeat a step in a process.

Once these three habits of private victory are firmly in place, Covey says, the individual can proceed to develop the three habits of "public victory," or organizational effectiveness:

- **Think win–win.** Just as a poorly performing athlete will tend to beat himself before his opponent can, so too can a business lose out to a rival because the competitive drives of its employees are being pitted against one another in an endless series of internecine power struggles and turf battles. Highly effective managers overcome this organizational centrifugal force by deliberately working to build trust and cooperation. They focus people on the broad-based enduring gains that emerge from collaboration rather than the short-term advantages that accrue from political infighting. They make sure their organizations compete with the competition, not with themselves or their customers.

- **Seek first to understand . . . then to be understood.** Highly effective people diagnose before they prescribe. Although they have powerful knowledge and skills, they take the time to ask plenty of questions and do the required research before they apply their skills to the treatment of a problem. Covey calls this approach "the mark of all true professionals" and "the key to effective interpersonal communication."

- **Synergize.** Effective people know how to combine elements in a way that makes the whole add up to more than the sum of the parts. They get people with different viewpoints together to work on a problem. They detect relationships between ideas that appear to be unrelated. They even combine the elements of their own psyches synergistically, using "both the intuitive, creative, and visual right brain and the analytical, logical, and verbal left brain" so that "the whole brain is working."[59]

Covey's seventh habit, *sharpen the saw,* is a kind of self-administered continuing education program. Highly effective people periodically revisit their three private and three public habits and work at sharpening them. They never consider any of the habits supporting their effectiveness as finished.

Although Bennis and Covey use different nomenclature and differ in the number of categories they set up, their schemes have much in common. In particular, they both focus on the power of a coherent, well-thought-out and well-articulated *vision* to inspire and motivate others. So does almost every other writer on leadership. Whether you call it *management of attention, vision,* or *begin with the end in mind,* the effect seems to be the same. Before leaders begin a project, they are able to visualize the form and dimensions of the final outcome. They know how things are supposed to be. They know what they want to create. They know and trust their own ability to establish an orderly sequence of steps that will make the vision real. And because they know these things, they are able to communicate the vision—and the excitement associated with it—to the followers who must help the leader turn vision into reality.

Notice, too, that neither Bennis nor Covey says anything about formal authority being essential to the leadership process. Neither does the dictionary. All three sources tacitly acknowledge the possibility of *leadership without portfolio.*

STAMINA AND PERSISTENCE
Leadership's Overlooked Foundations?

Which qualities and attributes most accurately mark a leader? According to Pulitzer Prize-winning historian and author Garry Wills, one of the most common leadership traits is plain old physical stamina—the bodily strength and staying power to keep going at a task that wears others down.

It may seem a prosaic thing to say that a leader needs great physical stamina. When people talk of a leader's qualities, they prefer to mention such things as vision, self-confidence, "charisma" or such. But great students of leadership, from Machiavelli to Clausewitz, have said that physical endurance ranks very high among the requisites.

It is easy to see why. The best brain, the greatest charm, is useless if a person's energies are zapped after long spells of effort. A general must have his wits about him even after sleepless nights. Classical authors knew this when they praised Caesar and Mark Antony for their ability to make clear-eyed decisions when their own aides were brain dead from continued trials.[60]

Where does the leader's physical endurance come from? Is it inborn? Is it acquired? Does it develop as some sort of by-product of leadership?

This question fascinated Dr. Mihaly Csikszentmihalyi, the Hungarian-born director of the University of Chicago Department of Psychology. In his book *Flow: The Psychology of Optimal Experience,* Dr. Csikszentmihalyi documented a mental phenomenon that gives some people an apparently inexhaustible supply of energy and an almost uncanny ability to find the easiest and fastest way to accomplish a task. The phenomenon is called "flow" because people who experience it in their work do not feel themselves to be engaged in an effort against resistance; rather, they feel carried forward toward their goal as if on a current of "deep but effortless involvement."[61]

Some of these people will tell you, "I know I'm doing hard work, but I don't feel as if I've ever really done a day's work in my life." They really love what they are doing. They love it and they do not want to quit. They have so much focus that they engage in very little wasted effort, so there is no cause for fatigue. They do not seem to have this split consciousness that most people do in their work—the kind that tells you, "I want to do this job but I also wish I were somewhere else."[62]

Dr. Csikszentmihalyi, however, does not identify flow solely with leaders. He says it is found in virtually all of those whom Stephen Covey identifies as "highly effective people." He has identified the flow phenomenon in corporate executives, small-business proprietors, artists, musicians, and even farmers. One of his subjects was a welder in a railroad-car factory on the south side of Chicago who continually dazzled his colleagues and superiors with his seemingly effortless output of fast, high-quality work. The welder found every aspect of his work fascinating, was totally absorbed in it, and even had the ability to make the work more exciting to his less-inspired co-workers. Yet for all his output, he would leave the plant at the end of the day almost as fresh as when he arrived. His stamina seemed to be a product of his fascination and focus, not the cause of it. Dr. Csikszentmihalyi says that in his research for his latest book, he found the same level of flow in the CEO of a major Italian insurance company. The man was 84 years old!

While stamina is normally defined as a physical attribute, it has a mental equivalent in perseverance, another trait of leaders and other high achievers. The dictionary defines *to persevere* as "to persist in any business or enterprise undertaken; to pursue steadily any design or course once begun; to be steadfast in purpose."[63]

Leaders, in other words, are among the few who just do not give up. A classic example is Winston Churchill, who endured not just public displeasure, but something close to official disgrace for his bungled military strategizing in World War I. Despite nearly 20 years of political banishment—and despite devastating episodes of depression he called "black dog"—Churchill persisted in learning the lessons of European history and warning his fellow Britons of the growing threat to their country. He succeeded only at the last hour, serving his nation—and probably saving it—as its wartime prime minister. Rejected in favor of a Socialist at war's end, he battled his way back into power in 1951 at the age of 77 and served until a stroke disabled him at the age of 81.

An even more amazing demonstration of perseverance in the face of seemingly insuperable obstacles is that of Abraham Lincoln. Like Churchill, he suffered periodic bouts of debilitating depression. But the number of personal and professional reverses Lincoln encountered seems to be even greater than what Churchill endured. Moreover, Lincoln lacked the family wealth and social status that kept Churchill afloat even when his professional fortunes were in limbo. Unlike Churchill, Lincoln had to earn a living in a preindustrial, frontier economy. Lincoln triumphed in the end, of course, but the scale of his stamina and perseverance becomes apparent only when we review his depressingly lackluster résumé and total up the failures he endured virtually every other year before he finally was elected President. Consider these failures (and some successes) and the ages at which he experienced them:

Failed in business—22

Defeated for state legislature—23

Again failed in business—24

Elected to legislature—25

Sweetheart died—26

Had a nervous breakdown—27

Defeated for speaker—29

Defeated for elector—31

Defeated for Congress—34

Elected to Congress—37

Defeated for Congress—39

Defeated for Senate—46

Defeated for Vice President—47

Defeated for Senate—49

Elected President of the United States—51

If Lincoln and Churchill seem too lofty to serve as personal role models, consider a more approachable figure.

In the Depression year of 1930, this 40-year-old man in Corbin, Kentucky, was struggling to support his wife and three children.[64] Driven by a strong work ethic, he had earned his own living since the age of 12 when his stepfather literally kicked him out of the house. Yet despite his persistence, nothing he did seemed to work out for long. During the 1920s he had lost three good jobs in disputes with superiors. Finally realizing that he could succeed only if he worked for himself, he started a business that furnished acetylene-gas lighting systems for farms, only to see the venture fail when Delco developed a superior system that used electricity. He took a job selling tires but was laid off when the company had to downsize during the Depression. He opened his own business again, this time a tiny service station in Nicholasville, Kentucky, but he lost all his money when the hardscrabble farmers who

patronized it could not pay for the gasoline he had sold them on credit.

Still unwilling to quit, he started yet another filling station, but this time with a difference. His new business was located in Corbin, a small town, but an important stop for tourists navigating U.S. 25 between Detroit and Cleveland in the North and Atlanta and Miami in the South. This strategic repositioning brought in trade that might otherwise have been missed.

The other breakthrough was his realization not only that he was good at selling to people, but also that he liked to take care of them—especially to cook for them. To the service station he added a tiny, scrupulously clean dining room in which he served delicious recipes he had learned from his mother. Famished tourists fed up with the roadside greasy spoons of the day quickly spread the word about the crisply managed little gas station-café in Corbin, and the business thrived. Within a few years, it had become a larger filling station, a larger restaurant, and a motel. In 1935 Gov. Ruby Lafoon named the 45-year-old entrepreneur a Kentucky Colonel for his contributions to the state's economy and reputation, and in 1939 the oasis at Corbin won one of the coveted spots in Duncan Hines's *Adventures in Good Eating*.

Business sagged somewhat when gasoline rationing crimped the nation's motoring habit during World War II, but at war's end the business grew again, and by the early 1950s the restaurant had expanded to 142 tables. It appeared that all the striving had finally had paid off.

But fate has a way of kicking its favorites. In the mid-50s the federal government announced that due to traffic congestion in Corbin's bustling downtown, U.S. Route 25 would be rerouted around the city core on a new bypass. Ironically, the booming food-and-lodging business that had fueled much of Corbin's traffic congestion was about to be stranded. The restaurateur had to sell his property at auction to cover his debts. At the age of 66 he was forced to start all over again.

And start over he did, though all he had left was a monthly Social Security check of $105 and his customers' favorite recipe—a specially spiced version of fried chicken steamed in a pressure cooker to reduce cooking time. Taking the recipe and a pressure cooker on the road, he served the dish to restaurateurs and offered to franchise it

to them by packaging and shipping them his specially flavored flour for breading the chicken. Unable to afford the price of a motel room, the former motel owner slept in his car during his grueling sales trips.

One by one, restaurateurs signed up to serve the famous recipe. By 1960, there were 400 franchisees in the United States and Canada. In 1964, with his format a nationwide fast-food hit, the 74-year-old owner sold his business for $2 million and a lifetime job promoting the business through broadcast commercials and personal appearances. He continued working and growing richer until his death in 1980 at the age of 90.

In case you haven't guessed, the persevering restaurateur was the legendary Colonel Harland Sanders. His company, Kentucky Fried Chicken, now a division of PepsiCo, Inc., is approaching $8 billion in annual sales. Like Lincoln and Churchill, the Colonel kept trying and trying even when old age and common sense would seem to argue otherwise. Clearly he had perseverance, and he probably had stamina as well.

As Wills concludes: "It is not the stuff of inspirational literature, but it gets the job done."[65]

Making Sense out of the Leadership Trend

It is exciting and encouraging to see the question of leadership finally being addressed by so many business writers, retired CEOs, academics, and military thinkers. American business has had a rough time in the last two decades and needs all the leadership it can get. Fresh ideas may be arriving just in time.

However, there is also a downside to this excitement. The first signs of a shallow trendiness have already begun showing up in our fascination with leadership. A whole series of leadership books, ranging from serious academic studies to the breeziest pop psychology self-instruction guides, has poured from the publishers' presses in the last decade. Each source offers its own inventory of leadership attributes. If you find Bennis's "four competencies of leadership" or Covey's "Seven Habits" too demanding, you can embrace the "ten ingredients" being touted by California sales executive Danny Cox or the "thirteen heroic strategies" worked out by New York consultant Emmett C. Murphy.[66] Even the professional football coaches are joining in with leadership sound bites for the desperate executive. Here's one forgettable goody: "I think goal-setting is overrated."[67]

Alternatively, you can dispense with the contemporary leadership literature altogether and join the neoclassicists who claim to have rediscovered the secrets of leadership in the writings of the ancients. During the early 1980s, when U.S. business and industry first began waking up to the threat of Japan's growing economic power, Miyamoto Musashi's *The Book of Five Rings*, dating from 1645, was republished and touted as the true samurai source of Japan's modern industrial effectiveness. Other advocates of Eastern wisdom cited *The Art of War*, a 2,000-year-old treatise by the Chinese general Sun Tzu. "Absorb this book and you can throw out all those contemporary books about management leadership," enthused a reviewer for *Newsweek*.[68] Meanwhile, the more conventional observers of leadership continued to uphold the heroes of the more familiar Western tradition—Julius Caesar subduing the Gauls in 52 B.C. or Alexander the Great pursuing Darius the Persian across the Middle East between 335 and 330 B.C.

To those students who wish to review the careers and study the strategies of these shoguns and emperors, I say "enjoy." Before attempting to apply their strategies in a modern setting, however, please keep in mind that the heroic leaders of ancient and medieval times enjoyed at least one advantage not available to today's business leaders, *with or without portfolio*: They could enforce their orders with draconian punishments up to and including death. History tells us that when Alexander conquered Thebes in 335 B.C., he burned down every house in the city, killed 6,000 people, and sold the remainder into slavery. These actions make moot the question as to whether Alexander's leadership abilities made people follow him "willingly and voluntarily." Clearly, the lessons in leadership left to us by ancient leaders need to be taken with a grain of salt.

The student of leadership probably should employ another grain of salt in evaluating leadership courses, leadership workshops, leadership seminars, and even leadership wilderness retreats now proliferating in lush variety as Americans become more concerned about who is in charge of their business and governmental organizations. "Being picked for a sexy new leadership training program sure beats working," notes *Inc.* magazine columnist J. Case. But Case also warns his readers not to expect too much from "all sorts of nutty training programs" to which big firms send their managers in hopes of turning them into leaders.

"In one such program, teams from General Foods Corporation found themselves trying to build rafts and sail down a river, first under nit-picking managerial inspection and then on their own," Case writes. "Which rafts sank and which ones floated? No, you tell me."[69]

Case wrote that column in 1987. Since then the leadership-training trend has swollen in size and taken on dubious features that have left much of the field looking like a cross between a cult and a racket. In 1992 the trend even picked up a federal subsidy in the form of something called the Dwight D. Eisenhower Leadership Development Program—an amendment to the Higher Education Act that offered $10 million in grants to colleges and universities able to convince the U.S. Department of Education that they could teach leadership.

Fortunately for people who take leadership seriously, when DOE bureaucrats assembled an academic jury to judge the grant applications, one of the jurors turned out to be the skeptical and insightful Dr. Benjamin DeMott, Mellon Professor of Humanities at Amherst College, who immediately blew the whistle on the scam in a *Harper's* magazine article titled "Choice Academic Pork."

DeMott branded the federal leadership grants a "fiasco," a "turkey," and "a contender, arguably, for the title of worst-conceived taxpayer-financed program in the history of the republic." The day he spent judging grant proposals with 18 other academics, DeMott said, introduced him to "the leadership-studies cult, a . . . perfect specimen of late-twentieth-century academic avarice and a precise depth-gauge of some recent professorial descents into pap, cant, and jargon."

> In some respects the leadership cult resembles a real culture. It possesses a distinct language. It honors heroes and texts comparatively unknown to the general public. It consistently defines past and present reality on its own terms. And it displays a strong determination to enlarge the spheres of its influence.[70]

DeMott said that as he and his fellow academics reviewed the proposals from a variety of institutions seeking federal leadership grants, the panel members grew "noisy and irritable." A letter of greeting from the federal bureaucrats had implied that the meeting would address such questions as "What is the definition of leadership? How and why does one teach leadership? To whom should leadership be taught? When and where?"

"You tell us," DeMott retorted when he realized that neither the organizers nor the grant applicants were facing those issues. In fact, the grant applications were so poorly worded and spelled, so lacking in scholarly rigor, and so burdened with the jargon of pop psychology that DeMott and his fellow jurors gloomily began to suspect that the grant program was little more than a scheme to funnel federal funds to second-rate academics. None of the grant proposals showed any real grasp of what leadership was or how it could be formally taught. At last, one juror exploded in frustration:

> This is bullshit. . . . Nobody can teach this stuff. You can't have a curriculum. All you can do is some hands-on out in the community. Identify people and go out and do something, for Christ's sake.[71]

Viewed in context, the wacky, federally financed "leadership-development program" in which DeMott found himself ensnared may be just one more in a growing list of trends that regularly sweep through the business community on the wings of the great American media machine. I'm old enough to remember when Philip Crosby first sold International Telephone & Telegraph Chairman Harold Geneen on his zero-defects concept. I can also remember T-groups, Theory X and Theory Y, the Peter Principle, management by objectives, sensitivity training, and a host of other fads touted as solutions to making organizations more productive and managers more effective.

Some of these trends succeeded in bringing about change—at least for a time. Others seem to have disappeared as quickly and mysteriously as they came. Let's be careful about the way we approach leadership. It is a subject we have only begun to study. It is also a subject far too important to be trivialized in a bumper-sticker cliché like "Managers do things right; leaders do the right things." Such shallow reductionism only reinforces the suspicion that much of today's alleged interest in leadership really represents a thinly disguised attempt to pussyfoot around the question of power in the accomplishment of organized work.

Leadership is tacitly posited as a substitute for power or as a successor to power, rather than an enlightened way of using power.

Dr. DeMott was right to resist the siren song of this new-and-improved power-free leadership. So was the skeptical and sardonic columnist J. Case. Both recognized that what they saw being offered as leadership was not the classic leadership of a Pericles, a Churchill, or a MacArthur, but only a pathetic latter-day shadow—"Leadership Lite."

Simplified Leadership Scheme

I find a great deal of merit in the leadership traits and elements worked out by Bennis and Covey. Because they overlap, and because students need a simple, practical, and easy-to-remember scheme to help them develop their leadership skills on the job, however, I also feel a need to combine the best of Bennis and Covey and then distill the result down to a small number of salient factors on which the student of leadership can focus.

Covey is right on target when he lists *proactivity and an eager display of initiative* as essential qualities of a budding leader. For a second factor, I like Bennis's *management of attention.* On close inspection vision turns out to be very similar to Covey's *begin with the end in mind.* Leaders have the capacity to see the design, shape, and configuration of the objective. This is what other writers mean when they talk about how subordinates grant leadership power to those they sense have the capacity to see where the organization will be going and why it ought to go there in the first place.

For a practical and simple way to schematize and memorize complex material, it is hard to beat the old Rule of Three. The human mind just naturally seems to embrace ideas that are broken down into three related components, particularly if the components can be alliterated—reduced to three words that all begin with the same sound. The Rule of Three causes the mind to elbow aside any elements that add up to a greater number. In distilling Bennis, Covey, and other leadership writers down to a simple, alliterative Rule of Three scheme, I arrived at the following elements of leadership: recognition, response, and renewal.

Recognition

Every writer on leadership mentions this one, because anyone who understands human motivation realizes that members of an organization are more likely to follow a superior who recognizes their performance.

This recognition cannot be expressed adequately in monetary or other material gratification. All of us like to hear the simple words, "Well done." This is the psychic income that nourishes the ego and satisfies our appetite for approval. People with leadership ability quickly learn that approval and recognition of good performance win follower loyalty.

Another, more subtle reason that a willingness to recognize good performance is such a powerful leadership lever. Most members of an organization immediately grasp a willingness to share credit as the sign of a strong, secure personality that they can trust and rely upon. Comedy writer Alan Zweibel, a longtime friend and colleague of the late "Saturday Night Live" star Gilda Radner, told interviewer Larry King that other performers loved working with Radner because she never hogged the limelight as so many show business people do. She gave her fellow performers the "space" to shine before the public. People wanted to work with Radner because they knew her efforts would help them do their best. A similar observation was made two generations earlier by associates of Jack Benny. They recalled that on most of the radio comedy shows of the 30s and 40s, the writers always wrote their funniest lines for the star to deliver. Benny did not accept this practice. If a supporting player's line got a terrific laugh during rehearsal, Benny never followed the standard show-biz procedure of having it rewritten for himself. The result was that the top stars in the industry were always eager to work with him because he made them look good.

Response

Response is the continuous feedback of information that nourishes organizational effectiveness the way the circulation of the blood nourishes the body. Good leaders listen and talk to everyone in their circle—subordinates, superiors, customers, vendors, and peers within the organization. They collect, channel, funnel, and distribute information in whatever way seems to make the work flow more easily and effectively, keeping the boss informed about details of the unit's operation while keeping all members of the unit current on the needs, wants, and observations of management.

Keeping yourself and your organization informed may seem too mundane to qualify as a leadership strength, but it works. Organizations thrive on accurate information—and shrivel without it. Becoming an effective two-way communicator is one of the quickest ways to win recognition as somebody who can get things done.

Renewal

Covey talks of *sharpening the saw.* Other observers of organizational behavior talk of periodic re-education and updating of skills. Tom Peters suggests that you "'re-pot' yourself every 10 years."[72]

All are excellent admonitions, but they still skirt a sensitive issue that can be almost too tricky to talk about with your colleagues in the workplace. I refer to nothing less than the ugly truth that Henry David Thoreau disclosed when he wrote, "The mass of men lead lives of quiet desperation."[73] Although Thoreau made his famous statement in *Walden* in 1854, when America was still an agrarian society, it is just as relevant in today's industrial and postindustrial economy. Perhaps even more so, for today many jobs in management and the skilled professions provide people with such a high level of material security that they are loath to risk a change in their status or activity for fear of losing some material advantage.

People who keep their eyes and ears open in a typical modern corporation will soon encounter people—some of them at very lofty levels in the organization, including even the CEO—who have begun to grow sterile from having exhausted the personal-growth potential of their job. Remember that even the most exciting and challenging jobs have a shelf life. When that shelf life comes to an end, it is time to move on to another position, usually with a different employer.

The management writers are correct when they say we should sharpen our saws, go back to school and get that extra degree, or perhaps drop out of the corporation entirely and start that entrepreneurial business we have always dreamed about.

But sometimes renewal can go forward without such radical measures. Taking that vacation—and making sure those under your direction take theirs—is a simple way to make sure you and your colleagues periodically regain perspective. Short sabbaticals, temporary transfers to other departments, and refresher courses, including courses in subjects outside your specialty, can be useful as well. But most important is your willingness to engage in serious self-reflection and self-monitoring to make sure you do not slip into denial when the first wispy shudders of discontent, boredom, or burnout begin to manifest themselves. As the armed services have learned in their efforts to train future officers, self-monitoring and self-reflection are essential to leadership. There is no more important subject upon which a leader can reflect than the possibility that this job might be leading to quiet desperation. When that sensation comes, do not ignore it. Face it, reflect, and act. As long as you do not hide from the problem, you are almost certain to make a correct career move.

While you are reflecting on whether your own personal growth is coming to a halt, take a look around and see whether the same syndrome is afflicting any of your colleagues or superiors. In poorly led organizations, less than optimal performance is not only tolerated but also sometimes secretly welcomed by insecure superiors who fear the emergence of competence and initiative. In these low-performance workplace cultures, a display of leadership—particularly *leadership without portfolio*—is viewed as a threat by entrenched superiors trying to protect their jobs.

The typical business student would be surprised at how many organizations actually enshrine mediocrity in their managerial ranks. Mediocre people are attracted to one another and help one another maintain their positions in an organization through a kind of mutual blackmail. They say to each other, in effect, "I won't tell anybody how mediocre you are if you don't tell anybody how mediocre I am." Thus, mediocre subordinates are attracted to a mediocre superior and serve him loyally because they know that the culture he enforces will protect them against the challenges and demands of a high-performance workplace. The superior, in turn, can rest assured that no subordinate will engage in the kind of competent or innovative behavior that would call attention to the boss's own lack of performance. Each party has a vested interest in maintaining the mediocrity of the other.

Fortunately, it is easy to tell if you are in such a workplace. The sense of futility and fatigue in the environment is almost palpable. Suggestions for action are ignored. Innovations are stifled. Every manager seems empowered to say no, but nobody in the organization has the authority to say yes. Expressions such as "we don't do it that way here" or "nobody ever asked that question before" are the standard answer to proposed innovations.

If you seem to be in such a work environment, resist the urge to go into denial. Your intuitions are probably correct. Examine your surroundings—and yourself—honestly. If you find that your employer is enforcing a culture of mediocrity, get out before you find you have become a part of it.

Leadership and Core Competency

Much of the popular literature on leadership focuses on leadership "traits" or leadership "behavior," as if the correct mix of these attributes were all that were necessary for a person to be recognized as a leader. My own observations and experience, however, suggest that there may be one other element—not exactly a leadership trait, but perhaps a catalyst—that enables leadership traits to take effect. It is that simple piece of professional property known as *core competency*.

The fact is, nobody is a leader in a vacuum. You have to be a leader *at* something. Even the lowest-level leaders without portfolio start out with some basic skill or with a mastery of some core discipline that assures others of their ability. An entry-level management trainee comes to the first employer having mastered the fundamentals of at least one complex discipline—perhaps industrial engineering, accounting, law, or computer science. Once an individual demonstrates a core competency in the workplace, it becomes much easier for that individual to project leadership ability and have it acknowledged by others.

LESSONS IN LEADERSHIP
Eight Examples of Leadership in the Workplace

Discussions and definitions of leadership behavior will always abound, but the real definition of leadership is in the doing—the activities and results of those who lead. In the end, nothing helps us understand leadership like the chance to observe a leader in action. This is why, in addition to their studies of leadership theory and their training in leadership behavior, midshipmen at the U.S. Naval Academy must read about the lives of leaders and identify the attitudes and actions that gave their leadership its real-world form.

Most examples of leaders in action show us well-known soldiers and statesmen over the course of their entire professional lives. The following nine examples are much shorter and are specifically tailored for use by students preparing to enter business. Each example has been selected to show leadership in a corporate context.[74] Each has been selected to show a lower-level manager, often at a very early phase of his or her career, in a specific situation in which he or she demonstrated *leadership without portfolio*.

Although the examples of leadership set forth in the following profiles are instructive and in some cases inspiring, readers should keep in mind that these cases are not intended to portray any of the subjects as a total leader personality or as some sort of leader for all seasons. Most case histories reveal leadership to be episodic, even ephemeral; the leadership touch can come and go mysteriously, depending on, among other things, the individual's stage of development and the opportunities he encounters. An individual may, as Lee Iacocca did, toil for years in a routine job before displaying a burst of leadership that catches the eyes of superiors and sends that person on an upward trajectory. Or an individual may display dazzling leadership in one job only to lose the magic in another. After John Sculley moved from PepsiCo to Apple Computer, he never quite regained the leadership touch he had developed in the soft-drink business.

Some of the variables that seem to influence the development of leadership are luck, timing, and the willingness to persevere in a company or industry one cares about deeply until one's moment comes. In addition to a gift for leadership, training in leadership, and an appetite for leadership, the potential leader must sense how to get into the right place and stay there until the right time. Bill Knight, for example, was fortunate to have chosen the railroad industry at a time when it had a strong need for his particular abilities. It was a business he loved and felt strongly about, and his devotion almost certainly helped to bring out leadership abilities that might not have ripened in a different environment. Lee Iacocca has said repeatedly that he loves automobiles and the automobile business. It seems hard to believe he would have displayed the same kind of leadership he manifested at Ford and Chrysler in an industry that did not provide him the mystique he found in making and selling cars. A similar mix of luck, timing, and personal inclination may also have been a factor in the perfect match between World War II veteran Harry Gray and fledgling defense contractor Litton Industries when they met in the early 1950s. Litton was entering its corporate buildup phase just as Gray was entering his own personal and professional buildup phase. Gray came to Litton with the precise mix of battlefield savvy and business experience the fledgling company needed.

Why a particular individual becomes a leader in a particular time and place will probably always remain something of a mystery. The following profiles, therefore, are nothing more than what they purport to be: individual lessons in leadership. They do not add up to a general theory.

1. DIANE M. BETTI

"I couldn't stand it; I had to do it another way."

Diane M. Betti has recently been promoted to Vice President and General Manager for quality and six sigma in General Electric Company's Medical Systems Information Technology Division (Milwaukee, Wisconsin). Prior to this, she was the global sourcing manager for the same division, in which position she led more than 100 employees in six locations worldwide as head of the company's Americas Sourcing team. How did she manage to rise so high on the corporate ladder? Her B.S. in accounting from Boston College and MBA in finance from Babson College only partially account for her success. Many managers can boast of equal or superior academic credentials yet have not risen as far or contributed as much as Betti. What makes her different?

It could be *leadership without portfolio*, something Betti displayed back in the mid-1980s—well before she had ever heard the expression. But to understand what she did and why it was so daring, you have to ask yourself a number of questions about today's business environment: How did U.S. industry make the transition from managing by paper to managing by computer? Did it "just happen"? Was it some sort of "natural evolution"? Was it a workplace technique that "emerged" as computer manufacturers and software developers approached businesses with new products and new ways of getting things done?

All of those things no doubt happened, but they still cannot explain how modern business made the transition to the automated workplace we know today. To really understand how the conversion took place, you have to understand *leadership without portfolio* as it was exercised by young managers who saw the potential of the new technology—but had to fight to get it accepted in the workplace.

Diane Betti was one of them. In 1985, at the age of 31, after working as a financial analyst for Fram Corporation, Burroughs Corporation, and the automotive division of the Boeing Company, Betti was named to her first management job, the highly responsible and demanding position of Manager of Cost Control for the B-1B supersonic bomber that the Boeing Company's North American Aircraft Division was building for the U.S. Air Force. The job required that Betti maintain a "Big-Picture" perspective and a fixation on detail at the same time, a balancing act for which few people—even the most intelligent and industrious—are suited. She and her 40 direct reports faced the daunting task of tracking the true purchasing costs of all of the parts and supplies needed to build the giant bomber and then writing up their findings every three months in a report for top management.

"My team and I would spend four weeks, 10 to 12 hours per day, six days a week to capture, analyze, and estimate the total cost of the material of the B-1B," Betti said. "We would manually capture every Purchase Order that had been established and interface with hundreds of buyers to evaluate what changes in costs had occurred in each of the POs during the quarter. Then our team would summarize the year-to-date and the full-year estimate of the costs."[75]

One of the elements that made this task so daunting was that it was essentially manual. Computerized spreadsheets capable of embracing the full range of parts and supplies needed to assemble the bomber were not yet commercially available.

"We would manually fill out 20 pages of 14-column spreadsheets (41 lines, each representing a different cost element) and attempt to summarize the information for review by management so we could understand the impact of each cost change on the total program," Betti said. "Remember: Our goal was to bring this program in on schedule and under cost."

Betti found herself increasingly frustrated by the huge amount of manual work the process required and the low level of accuracy that resulted.

"This process was arduous and thankless, and because it was manual, it was not particularly accurate," she said. "In no way did it approach the accuracy of the Six Sigma process that is now becoming routine. It was fraught with errors, and it was time-consuming. By the time we had completed the reporting there was little time for analysis or validation of the data. I went through one iteration after another. I spent a lot of hours, and my people spent a lot of hours, and as we used up those hours we had to decide whether to hit the numbers or hit the deadline. The best that I could do was inform management of 'approximate' changes."

But when Betti began discussing "another way," she met resistance or incomprehension from employees spouting the typical line: "But we've always done it that way!"

"My group leader told me that was how we had done it for the first six quarters of the program and it was good enough for the rest of the program," she said. Besides, management had not demanded any improvements, so why fix something the front office thought was working?

Betti bristled at that attitude. The first feeble rays of *leadership without portfolio* had begun to illuminate her thinking.

"I told my group leader that because I didn't have a better alternative for the current quarterly estimate that I would do it the old-fashioned way one more time. But I also told them that when the time arrived for the next quarter's review, I would have an alternative."

Making good on that promise was not easy in an era when the first personal computers had just begun to find acceptance in the workplace and little was available in the way of custom software. Like legions of would-be innovators before her, Betti found that it is hard to innovate without the necessary resources, and hard to command the necessary resources without authority from top management.

"In a rapid ramp-up environment there are few 'free' resources for those who want to introduce change into the workplace," Betti said. "In 1985 there were few personal computers in our organization. Information Technology had most of them, and even they only had six. And there was a significant wait for any programming changes."

Betti simply commandeered the resources she needed, including time out of her personal schedule. Betti had neither the authority nor a mandate to do what she was doing. In true *leadership without portfolio* fashion, she just did it because she saw what needed to be done and could not wait for a commercial solution to "emerge."

"Five days a week I finished my 10-hour day and went upstairs to the IT Department and worked at night for another four," she said. "On Saturdays and Sundays I spent 10 hours each. No one asked me to do it, and I didn't tell anybody I was doing it—except for the request for time from IT, since I was using their computers. I wrote a computer program in Lotus 1-2-3 to summarize the costs and write summary and exception reporting for management review and cost containment for the program."

This was not an easy task in the early days of the personal computer and the Lotus spreadsheet.

"With only 256K of RAM, and the huge volume of data that had to be entered, I had to break the programming into six segments per report and spread it across the six PCs," Betti said. "At night I would have all the computers working at once, printing, saving, and crunching numbers. To eliminate repetitive operations I programmed macros that consolidated like functions under a single keystroke for each of the three reports I had designed. Each report was obtained by running ⅙ of the data on each of the six PCs. In six weeks I had a great new process!"

What resulted was a breakthrough, a demonstrably better way of collecting, processing, and analyzing the huge amount of data making up the B-1B purchasing process. Upper management, along with the skeptical members of Betti's own department, now understood that a better way was possible and that it could deliver meaningful results.

"The next quarter was significantly different," Betti said. "We still had to do the manual review with each of the hundred buyers, since they had no computerized input to our process. But now there was time to ensure accuracy of data, and also to do some analysis. Each member of my team filled out a form. I would then input the data into an entry section on my reports.

"With only 10 hours needed to go from data input to report generation, we now had three reports plus adequate time to analyze

them," Betti said. "Instead of just reporting data, we now had the luxury of understanding it so we could put it to practical use. The data we had collected, organized, and analyzed had been transformed into information that helped us make mid-course corrections that reduced the cost of purchasing materials for the B-1B. It was this new ability to get out ahead of the curve and anticipate changes that gave us dramatic new power to control costs. Ultimately, we were able to bring about a 35 percent reduction in our departmental head count, a 50 percent reduction in cycle time, and over $300,000 in savings per year."

2. HARRY J. BRUCE
"How could I contribute anything?"

In many ways I was typical of the young men who began their careers in corporate America during the Cold War days of the late 1950s. After leaving the U.S. Army and finishing college, I joined the United States Steel Corporation in Pittsburgh as a trainee in January 1959. After an eight-week course in the fundamentals of steelmaking, I was assigned to the office of the vice president of transportation. I had none of the formal authority or insignia of rank that I'd recently enjoyed as an Army officer. My uniform with its bars and brass hung in the closet at home. I went off to work in the standard corporate gray flannel suit.

In fact, it would be disingenuous to pretend that I embarked on this new job brimming with confidence about my prospects for the future. The truth was, I had serious doubts about the decision I had just made. Instead of envisioning the new worlds I was about to conquer, I wondered silently just what a person of my background could bring to a company like U.S. Steel, which at that time was considered one of the largest and most successful corporations in the industrialized world and seemingly had all the answers. How could I contribute anything to a company that already dominated its industry, an integrated industrial giant that knew everything there was to know about mining the raw materials, making them into steel, and selling and shipping the final product to thousands of customers?

Fortunately, I still retained one souvenir from my Army days—my leadership training and the urge to put it to good use.

I was fortunate in another regard. My immediate superior was Dr. Gayton Ger-

mane, a Stanford University professor on a three-year sabbatical. Neither of us had a clear mandate from top management, so we decided to search for ways to improve the flow of raw steelmaking materials. The next three years served as a classic example of how much leadership a person can exercise *without portfolio,* especially when the boss enthusiastically endorses creativity.

In his book, *The Common Denominator of Success,* E. M. Gray writes, "The successful person has the habit of doing things failures don't like to do."[76] That's a more-or-less accurate description of how I began my career at U.S. Steel. I looked for transportation problems that were not being solved, transportation opportunities that had been overlooked, and transportation projects that had not been managed well or had suffered from inadequate follow-up.

And I found plenty. The first was a program for automating the movement of materials within steel mills by using radio-controlled off-highway vehicles and rail cars. Westinghouse Air Brake Company had made a presentation on the subject to U.S. Steel executives, but something about the presentation was off the mark, and the idea was not being pursued. Picking up the dropped threads, I spent three weeks analyzing the steel-making process to determine where automation was logical. Then I detailed my findings in a report illustrated with charcoal sketches prepared by my wife. The sketches showed how ingot molds, coke-transfer cars, and ore trains could be moved from point to point within a steel mill under the control of a central monitor.

This time both U.S. Steel and Westinghouse became enthusiastic, the project recovered its momentum, and a booklet was issued under the title: *The Future of Automated Movement Control in the Iron and Steel Industry.* As a result of the recommendations in the booklet, a prototype automated transporter for use in steel mills was built and tested.

Because I had virtually no formal authority to do what I did in that first job, and because nobody ever ordered me to do it, my accomplishment represented a true example of *leadership without portfolio.* I exercised my own initiative, organized my own project, and carried someone else's incomplete original idea through to a satisfying result. Because the logic of leadership was in operation, my successful management of the project triggered a favorable response from my superiors. News of my accomplishment percolated up the chain of command, and a small measure of recognition and authority came back down.

After forty years playing a variety of leadership roles, I can now share with students methods that helped me. First and foremost, I learned the most important step in getting a job done was in the recognition of a problem. Once I recognized and focused on the problem, I usually could think of someone who could work it out better than I could.

---

3. JOHN SCULLEY
"I was given neither an assignment nor an office."

Launching a career by exercising *leadership without portfolio* is not unusual. Students would be surprised how many executives can report a similar experience at the start of their careers. John Sculley, the Pepsi-Cola marketing mastermind who made a highly publicized switch to the CEO position at Apple Computer in 1983, recalls just this type of episode in his 1987 book, *Odyssey*.

Sculley writes that when he left an advertising agency job to join Pepsi in 1967 as that company's first MBA, his new employers actually had no job ready for him; the position of manager of product development in the marketing department failed to open up as scheduled, and Sculley was shunted across Park Avenue to vegetate in the market-research department for what turned out to be nine months before his predecessor finally left. "I was given neither an assignment nor an office," he writes.[77]

What at first appeared to be a dead end actually turned out to be the runway from which Sculley launched the most amazing career in the history of the soft-drink industry. What Sculley found was a market-research department sitting on years and years of highly meaningful research into consumer preferences, none of which the marketing department had ever used. Sculley decided to make himself master of this potentially valuable but long-ignored material.

> I was disillusioned but determined to take advantage of my time. So I would arrive each day, find a place to sit, and begin to sift through every research file I could find. I just sat there all day and read every piece of paper the research department had on file. Most of it was related to consumer behavior. What became clear was that I was in an essen-

tially meaningless department. Little of its work was utilized by the higher-ups. The researchers went off and researched, then the sales and marketing staff went off and made their own decisions, independent of each other.[78]

When the post for new product development finally opened up, Sculley was in the catbird seat. He knew more about consumer preferences than anyone else in the company. His nine months of poring over research files, combined with his six-month training program delivering soft drinks and snack foods for bottlers in Pittsburgh and Phoenix, had given him the knowledge and confidence to launch successful new products, and he shortly brought out his first one. "It was an incredibly exciting idea, and it became very successful," he writes. Sculley's display of *leadership without portfolio* had turned nine months of would-be exile into the start of a successful career in the highly competitive food and beverage industry.

---

4. BILL KNIGHT (1929–1996)
"Everyone trusted and followed him."

Leadership is not displayed only by those destined to reach the CEO level. I have found leadership ability in a variety of people at different levels of the organization chart, including a number who never intended to try for the top position. One of them was Bill Knight, a man I got to know at the Illinois Central Railroad.

Throughout the time I knew him, Bill Knight held the title of engineering superintendent in Memphis, Tennessee. He was responsible for the maintenance and safety of all the railroad's track and bridges between Memphis and New Orleans, including branch lines that radiated west to Baton Rouge and southeast to Gulfport, Mississippi, and Mobile, Alabama.

Despite the name "engineering" in his title, Bill had never been to engineering school. He almost certainly would have made an excellent engineer if he had had the opportunity. But Bill was from rural Mississippi, where few families had the money to send a child to college in 1945, the year 16-year old Bill hired on at the railroad.

Despite Bill's lack of formal education, it was immediately apparent to his superiors and subordinates alike that he was a natural leader. He had several hundred men under his jurisdiction, most of them track laborers and their supervisors, and it was always a

delight to see him interact with his crews. They genuinely respected and esteemed him and took satisfaction in knowing they were doing the job the way he wanted it done.

One reason for this loyalty may have been that Bill did not use the tough-guy approach typical of officials in his position. The old-time railroad track bosses often maintained control by verbally chewing their subordinates up and spitting them out, and sometimes by getting physical as well. Bill did not need to use that approach because he had something better—an ability to lead.

A major component of Bill's ability was his encyclopedic knowledge of his job. In addition to having a strong natural grasp of engineering problems, he had invested large amounts of time in getting to know and understand the parts of the railroad under his jurisdiction. He worked incessantly and asked questions wherever he went, absorbing details until he seemed to know every classification yard, every length of rail, every tie, and every spike in the hundreds of miles of line entrusted to his care. What Bill Knight exemplified in his style of leadership was a core competency so vast that it amounted to virtual mastery of his subject. Subordinates and superiors alike were awed by his knowledge and came to depend upon it.

Perhaps more important to his effectiveness as a leader, we all understood that Bill *cared deeply* about the safety and effectiveness of the railroad plant and about the success of the railroad company. Because he radiated this kind of concern, everyone trusted him and everyone followed him. He may not have had a CEO's vision of what the railroad needed to become, but he had a vision of how a well-maintained main line should look, and he communicated his vision effortlessly to the people who had to keep that line in shape. Bill regularly murdered the King's English, but nobody ever mistook his meaning. He was a natural communicator who used his attitude as well as words to get his meaning across, and he always knew what he wanted.

All of Bill's leadership skills became apparent to me within a short time after I first joined him on a track-inspection trip. But I did not understand the full extent of his abilities until the day I realized he had virtually read my mind.

It happened in the mid-1980s when we were vigorously pursuing a program of downsizing the railroad, which had grown over the years through a series of poorly planned mergers and acquisitions into nearly 10,000 miles of tangled, sprawling main and branch lines that seemingly led to everywhere and nowhere and had been losing money for two decades. We eventually sold much of this trackage to local short-line and regional railroad entrepreneurs, who operated it much more successfully than the IC could have. But some of the trackage was totally unneeded and would never have attracted a buyer. For example, the railroad owned three different main lines between Memphis and Jackson. There was no way all of them could be operated profitably, so we were greatly relieved when the Interstate Commerce Commission gave us permission to abandon one of the redundant routes. That meant we could take up the rail and ties and reuse them at points on the railroad where they were better needed.

But recycling unused materials was not the only reason to dismantle the extra Memphis-Jackson line quickly. Under the law, if a railroad abandons a route and another company wants to operate it, the new operator gets to run its trains over the rail that is in place.

Shortly after the ICC gave us permission to abandon, I casually mentioned to Bill Knight, "You know, we ought to get out there and pull that track up pretty soon before somebody else decides to use it."

Without a word, Bill took my offhand remark for an order. Without telling me, he ordered a crew and equipment into operation, and that same night, in the middle of a prolonged and violent thunderstorm, his men dismantled seven miles of track in rural Mississippi. Part of the work took place just across the road from a small-town diner, where the patrons peered through the plate-glass windows in astonishment at the scene that appeared intermittently before them whenever lightning flashes interrupted the darkness. One of them became alarmed and called the state police.

The next morning the governor of Mississippi called me and asked, "Mr. Bruce, what the _____ were your people doing out there?" After my explanation reassured him that we had ICC permission to take up the track, he replied, "Mr. Bruce, if you're going to do that sort of thing again, would you please not do it in a blinding thunderstorm?"

Bill Knight was not totally *without portfolio* when he pulled up that track. It was one of his duties as engineering superinten-dent. But in deciding to do the job immediately, and in knowing his crews would agree to do the job for him in darkness and rain, he was a true leader. Only someone thoroughly trusted by both his subordinates and his superiors can undertake such extraordinary action.

---

5. LEE IACOCCA
"I came up with a better plan."

Everyone who follows American business now knows the story of Lee Iacocca, the brilliant developer of the Ford Mustang who in the early 1980s went on to save the moribund Chrysler Corporation from what all the experts said was certain extinction.

Most of those who recognize Iacocca's name and achievements, however, know them only secondhand—from media coverage of the high spots of his career. A much more complete catalogue that includes numerous low spots is available to readers of his 1984 autobiography, *Iacocca*. A careful reading of that book shows that Iacocca's 1964 success with the Mustang and his 1983 turnaround at Chrysler actually were foreshadowed as early as 1956, when he was a lowly assistant district sales manager in Ford's badly floundering Philadelphia district. In that capacity, Iacocca used *leadership without portfolio* not only to turn around his district's dreadful performance but also to launch his own spectacular climb to the top of the U.S. auto business.

"While sales of 1956 Fords were poor everywhere, our district was the weakest in the country," says Iacocca. After a futile effort to turn the 1956 Ford's new safety features into a selling point, he says, "I came up with another—and, I hoped, better—plan. I decided that any customer who bought a new 1956 Ford should be able to do so for a modest down payment of 20 percent, followed by three years of monthly payments of $56. This was a payment schedule that almost anyone could afford, and I hoped that it would stimulate sales in our district. I called my idea '56 for 56.'"

"At that time, financing for new cars was just coming into its own," Iacocca says. "'56 for 56' took off like a rocket. Within a period of only three months, the Philadelphia district moved from last place in the country all the way to first. In Dearborn, Robert S. McNamara, vice president in charge of the Ford Division—he would become secretary of defense in the Kennedy administration—admired the plan so much that he made it part of the company's national marketing strategy. He later estimated it was responsible for selling 75,000 extra cars.

"And so, after ten years of preparation, I became an overnight success." Iacocca says. "Suddenly, I was known and even talked about in national headquarters. I had toiled in the pits for a good decade, but now I had a big break. My future looked a lot brighter. As a reward, I was promoted to district manager of Washington, D.C."[79]

But there was more. Before Iacocca and his wife could move into their new house in suburban Washington, he was promoted again and brought to headquarters in Dearborn to be national truck marketing manager. Within a year he was put in charge of car marketing, and in March 1960, he took over both functions, setting the stage for the legendary and highly profitable Mustang project of 1962–64.

Why was Iacocca's "56 for 56" payment plan an example of *leadership without portfolio*? Iacocca barely hints at the reason when he writes, "At that time, financing for new cars was just coming into its own." According to a retired Fortune 500 CEO who was an executive at Ford headquarters during the mid-50s, Iacocca actually had no authority to design the financing package that ignited his career climb. Most customers who financed the purchase of a car in the mid-50s did so through a bank, not through a dealer.

"Iacocca was one of 35 district sales managers, and it was unheard of at that time for a district sales manager to get involved in financing," the Ford veteran said. "The district sales manager never messed around with the financing of a product. Any change in that area originated at corporate headquarters."[80]

Considering that Iacocca was only an *assistant* district sales manager, his decision to originate a new financing policy at the bottom rather than the top of the organization, and with no prior review from headquarters, appears considerably more risky than he suggests in his book. It fully merits being called *leadership without portfolio*. (What it would have been called if it had failed is anybody's guess.)

---

6. RAY TOWER
"My disclosure was met with total apathy."

As the retired President/Chief Operating Officer of Chicago-based FMC Corporation, Ray Tower has enjoyed—and earned—all the power, perquisites, authority, and status that go with the office.

But it was not always that way. In 1955, as a 30-year-old eastern district sales manager for one of the company's chemical divisions, Tower had little power and little authority, and his first effort to get himself more was rebuffed by his superiors. FMC, or Food Machinery and Chemical Corporation as it was known then, was a typical 1950s American corporation—rigid, stratified and, by today's lean-and-mean standards, probably overstaffed as well. As Tower tells it, "To place my position in perspective, the chain of command was chairman, president, executive vice-president/division general manager, vice-president/marketing, general sales manager, and then me. At that time there were four chemical divisions and about 16 machinery divisions."[81]

Soon after assuming his job, Tower realized his department was missing something—a formal training program for the new salesmen it was hiring. The only preparation the salesmen were given for their jobs was shadowing (i.e., traveling for several weeks with an experienced salesman and learning to "do what I do, say what I say").

"I suggested to the general sales manager and the VP of marketing that we should create a sales training program for our division and the other chemical divisions as well," Tower says. "They didn't buy the idea at all and discouraged me from pursuing it any further."

For many—perhaps most—young executives, a bright idea like Tower's would have died right there. But not for someone exercising *leadership without portfolio*. "I felt so strongly about the need for such a program," Tower says, "that I devised one on my own and put it into effect in my division. I also told my bosses that I had done so. My disclosure was met with total apathy."

But not for long.

"Some months later, the general sales manager burst into my office, saying, 'Give me a copy of that sales training program that you told me about.' I handed him my manual, and he took it and left hurriedly without explanation."

Some time later the reason for all the excitement became clear: Corporate management had suddenly become interested in training programs. Headquarters was conducting a thorough review—actually an audit—of all training programs used in all of the divisions.

"Rather than admit that they had no such programs," Tower says, "our staff appropriated mine and passed it off at the corporate level as a division-wide operation. Later, the same general sales manager who had twice discouraged my efforts to initiate a sales program sheepishly admitted that the corporate people had told him 'our' sales training program was one of the best submitted for review. In fact, our staff was complimented highly for its forward thinking."

Ray Tower's recollection of an early career triumph merits several observations.

First, the unexpected and resounding vindication of Tower's effort to *lead without portfolio*, while gratifying, is not typical. Young people seeking to exercise such leadership should be advised that many such efforts do not succeed—at least not on the first try—and that even when success occurs, appreciation can be slow to develop.

Second, an often unappreciated feature of *leadership without portfolio* is that the followers are as likely to come from the leaders' superiors as from their subordinates. While Tower was leading the sales force under him toward better training, he was leading the company's top managers to a better appreciation of formal training for salesmen and ultimately to a change in the corporate policy on training. Perhaps we should say of leaders that they are not so much found at the top as at the center.

Finally, while an episode of leadership activity is relatively easy to narrate in retrospect, there can still be a good deal of mystery about just why it worked. Leaders often are strongly but unconsciously intuitive about possibilities for change and often time their moves to gain maximal leverage on what others in the organization are not yet thinking—but are about to think. Heifetz says effective leaders have a sensitivity about when an issue is ripening to a state in which it can safely be brought up for discussion, and the best leaders know how to pace and sequence this ripening process. They orchestrate an issue so they can jump aboard the wave just as it is building to a crest.[82] Did Ray Tower unconsciously realize that top management at FMC was beginning to grow dissatisfied with the company's sales training efforts? Did he sniff a change in the corporate atmosphere that his immediate superiors had missed? Did a strong intuition, finely honed by sales and managerial experience, signal to him that sales training was an idea whose time was about to come?

In business, as in acting or comedy, timing can be everything. Everything, that is, except making your boss look good. And Ray Tower got that right, too.

---

7. GAIL MCGOVERN
"Staff for great performance and staff for chemistry."

Leadership without portfolio often means getting things done even when nobody knows what *should* be done. That's what Gail McGovern did at AT&T Corporation in 1992, when she put together a team that solved a problem the "experts" had called hopeless.

The problem AT&T faced was the potential erosion of one of its most lucrative lines of business: the toll-free 800 numbers the company had originated in the 1960s. Under a Federal Communications Commission ruling scheduled to take effect May 1, 1993, business customers using AT&T 800 service would be able to switch their accounts to discount long-distance carriers, such as MCI or Sprint, and take their old 800 numbers with them.

This was a radical and—for AT&T—dangerous departure from conventional practice. Although telephone deregulation had ended AT&T's long-distance monopoly in 1984, the 800 business had effectively been sheltered by an FCC rule prohibiting "portability" of 800 numbers from one carrier to another. AT&T customers who switched their toll-free business to a discount carrier had to get a new 800 number, a move that threatened to confuse and alienate customers trying to contact the business over its toll-free line. A new number also could sock the subscriber with heavy one-time costs for new stationery, business cards, brochures, display advertising, and broadcast commercials, all of which would have to reflect the switchover. As long as 800 customers faced those costs and risks, AT&T's business was safe from lower-priced competitors. New businesses setting up their first toll-free line might go with a discounter, but established businesses in AT&T's portfolio would find it too costly to switch.

Now all of that was about to change, and the penalty to AT&T promised to be steep. As the originator of 800 service during the comfortable days of monopoly, AT&T had a 20-year head start on its competitors, who were not legitimized until 1984. That head start had left AT&T with by far the largest portfolio of 800 customers—tens of millions, in fact—but it also had left AT&T with the most to lose. Industry experts said 800 service was just a commodity, a look-alike product always vulnerable to competition from the lowest-cost supplier. Nor could AT&T join the discounters in price-cutting. As the original universal long-distance provider, it had the largest embedded infrastructure base and hence the highest costs. AT&T had to be seen as a premium provider meriting higher rates or face the loss of its business.

"Internal AT&T analysts had concluded the telephone giant would lose 10 percentage points of market share in toll-free business once customers got 'portability' in May 1993," noted the *Wall Street Journal*. "[T]op executives were resigned to losing a huge block of customers."[83] McGovern, the 39-year-old director of Outbound Networking Services, was not resigned. She sensed that the endangered 800 service might still be rescued from the deregulated discounters, and she wanted to try. She did not know exactly how the rescue could be effected, but a leader is not necessarily a person who has all the answers. A leader is a person who can inspire a *team* to come up with answers and get it to work.

And McGovern had a record for doing just that. Holder of a B.A. in theoretical mathematics from Johns Hopkins and an M.B.A. from Columbia, she had risen rapidly through the ranks after joining the Bell Telephone Company of Pennsylvania as a computer programmer in 1974. By 1980, she was district manager for long-range systems planning at then parent AT&T's headquarters in Basking Ridge, N.J., and over the next 12 years she earned six more promotions. With a tremendous drive to solve difficult problems and a strong record for assembling and managing successful problem-solving teams, McGovern clearly had the marks of a leader.

Perhaps most important, she had the will to tackle problems that others dismissed as hopeless. The last characteristic is strongly associated with *leadership without portfolio*, and with her promotion to Vice President-AT&T 800 and Business Application Services in January 1992, McGovern got her chance to show how *leadership without portfolio* can work.

Her first job was to assemble a team. It was a task she relished and understood well.

"One of my fundamentals is: Staff for great performance and staff for chemistry," she said. "Find people with a wide diversity of thought who enjoy learning from one another. Each 800 team member in a key position was a leader in his or her own right. When that happened, even the people who were responsible for technology started coming up with good marketing ideas, and the people in marketing started seeing the possibilities in technology."[84]

The team quickly grasped something that previous discussions of the problem had missed: AT&T was having trouble figuring out how to protect its 800 business because it did not really understand what the business was. The company's management needed to have a clearer understanding of what toll-free telephone lines meant to the businesses that used them.

At the team's request, the McCann-Erickson advertising agency interviewed 3000 businesses that used 800 service—AT&T's and the competition's. But the agency did not ask those customers to fill out a questionnaire. Instead, the interviewers showed the customers a series of dummy television commercials for the toll-free services of all three major carriers and then asked their opinions.

The interviews revealed something no one at AT&T had suspected: If customers were shown an appropriately structured and dramatized commercial, they began to develop suspicions about the reliability of the toll-free services of AT&T's Johnny-come-lately competitors.

"The interview showed that when AT&T talked about the reliability of its 800 service, the people believed it much more than when we discussed any other attribute of AT&T and much more than what any of the competitors' commercials attributed to their companies," McGovern said. "They showed that when we talked about reliability they believed us, but they did not believe the competitors' commercials when they talked about reliability."

Acting on what the team had discovered, AT&T began blitzing prime-time television with commercials that brought to life the importance of reliability to users of 800 numbers. One commercial featured a dramatized interview with a merchandise-catalogue executive whose company stood to lose thousands of dollars worth of orders for every minute its toll-free customer-order line was out of service. Another focused on a factory manager who had to shut down a production line when a supplier's disabled 800 line made it impossible to order a vital spare part. Each commercial concluded with a cut to the darkened interior of an AT&T dispatching center and an electronic map of AT&T's vast network of land lines, satellite links, and microwave stations. The authoritative voiceover assured viewers that regardless of technological glitches or natural disasters, AT&T's redundant capacity so far exceeded that of its competitors that no customer's 800 line would ever be down for more than a few seconds. Every company using AT&T service would remain in touch with its customers 24 hours a day.

Not content just to salvage AT&T's 800 business, the campaign reached out to businesses using AT&T's competitors, telling them their 800 numbers would soon be portable into the AT&T system, where they would find higher reliability. AT&T's vast embedded base of transmission lines had been transformed from a high-cost millstone into a competitive edge.

"We showed them that customers held hostage on an inferior network now had the freedom to migrate to AT&T," McGovern recalled. "We ran commercials with Aretha Franklin belting out 'FREE-DOM!'"

The discovery of the previously unsuspected "reliability issue," along with the commercials developed to exploit the issue, proved a huge success—and not just with 800 customers who saw the commercials on TV.

"When we brought these results back to our team it really gave them something to rally around," McGovern said. "The news really raised morale. We told all our people, 'The customers really want reliability.' And we changed all our advertising to stress reliability.

"At that point it really became fun," she said. "We did spreadsheet analyses to show what businesses lost with each missed call. It became a rallying point for the team."

Acting on what they now understood about the importance of reliability, AT&T's top executives began advising their golfing partners to move their companies' 800 numbers from discount carriers to AT&T. McGovern's team also designed an incentive program to reward salespeople who persuaded Sprint and MCI customers to switch their 800 numbers to AT&T. The impact on sales effort and creativity was like the kick from an afterburner.

"An employee in Minneapolis sat down with the Yellow Pages from all over the country and photocopied 19,000 vanity numbers—800 numbers that spelled something," McGovern said. "We ran a computer check to see which numbers weren't ours and then started contacting those that belonged to the competition. That employee won a free trip for two on the *Q.E.2.* We held a sales rally at headquarters on the night before portability started, and when her voice was piped into the auditorium she got a three-minute standing ovation."

The business results generated by McGovern's team exceeded all expectations. "They said we'd lose 10 share points the first year," she said. "We lost two points, and since then our 800 business has been growing 20% a year. We just landed the Internal Revenue Service account. Their call volume is phenomenal."

McGovern's leadership in the 800 portability crisis was acknowledged by her superiors when, later in 1993, she was promoted to Vice President-Strategic Planning for the Communication Services Group. In the next two years she received three more promotions, the latest being Executive Vice President-Consumer and Small Business Division.

"They say if you take a job no one else likes you'll propel your career," she said. "I personally enjoy the challenge of attacking unsolved problems. It's not just about winning the final reward. It's about the process of getting to a solution. You've got to enjoy walking into a room where different personalities are disagreeing about what to do and there's no sense of direction, and you start to help those people act as a team and start developing a way of solving the problem. I always liked that.

"I wish I could say the ideas are mine," McGovern concluded, "but the ad agency was incredibly creative and the team members just kept coming up with fresh ideas."

The mysterious interaction between a *leader without portfolio* and the followers who produce the results hardly could be better described.

8. HARRY GRAY

"What the hell do you know about electronics?"

Harry Jack Gray, who retired as Chairman, President, and Chief Executive Officer of United Technologies Corporation in 1985, exemplifies the concept of *leadership with-out portfolio.* As is typical of this type of leader, however, his exercise of *leadership without portfolio* remains virtually invisible because it manifested itself largely in the early and more obscure phases of his amazingly successful career. But while the latter stages of Gray's career are impressive, they are not necessarily instructive in showing us how—while still young—he began his rapid and decisive ascent to the pinnacle of corporate power.

Born in Georgia in 1919 and orphaned at an early age, Gray graduated from the University of Illinois in 1941 and joined the U.S. Army. He was promoted to captain at the age of 24 and commanded an infantry company that performed with distinction in the grimmest single campaign endured by U.S. forces in the European Theater, the Battle of the Bulge in December 1944. The Army awarded him both the Bronze Star for valor and the Silver Star for his achievements at the Battle of the Bulge as well as Normandy.

On his discharge in 1946, Gray returned to his *alma mater* and in 1947 was awarded a master's degree. He moved to Chicago and became sales manager of a dealership specializing in heavy-duty trucks and related industrial equipment. By giving him the opportunity to work on large-scale technical projects, this job helped Gray to hone his analytical skills, including a rare ability to see the implications beyond the facts. From 1950 to 1951 he worked in a sales position with another employer before moving to the job where he first displayed *leadership without portfolio.*

It happened after Gray joined Greyvan Lines, a Greyhound Corporation subsidiary specializing in household-goods moving. As executive vice president, Gray noticed that the company was assessing warehouse charges based on how many square feet of floor space a customer's goods occupied. Yet the operative figure, as he saw it, should have been cubic capacity. If Greyvan were to begin costing and charging based on three dimensions instead of two, he reasoned, revenues would improve dramatically.

Like so many cases of *leadership without portfolio,* Gray's approach represented a fresh rethinking of a conventional, unquestioned practice that had become so endemic to an entire industry that only an outsider—and a very self-confident one at that—could grasp its fundamental absurdity.

Management accepted Gray's suggestion that its schedule of warehouse charges be recomputed based on cubic capacity, and Greyvan's bottom line began improving immediately.

Unfortunately, Gray's did not. When he approached his boss, Orville Caesar, with a request that his innovation be recognized with additional compensation in the form of a stock option, Caesar rebuffed him.

Gray promptly resigned. Although still a young man, he was experienced enough to understand that further advances in his career were unlikely unless he was part of an organization that recognized and rewarded leadership. Gray's perception that profits lay hidden in the distinction between floor space and cubage, along with his advocacy of a new schedule of charges reflecting that distinction, represented the performance of a task he had assigned himself rather than a job his superiors had designed for him. Risk taking, innovative thinking, and ambition clearly were part of his persona, along with a tidy share of courage already demonstrated in the way he led his men against stiff Wehrmacht resistance in wartime Belgium. His next employer had to be congenial to a man of his temperament. With no particular employer or job in mind, but with his heart full of confidence in his skills and his willingness to take risks, Harry Gray left Chicago and headed for the West Coast.

Although his original plan had been to settle in San Francisco, Gray soon realized that California's best job market in the Korean War era lay among the fast-growing aerospace and defense industries that had sprung up in the Los Angeles basin. Among the most exciting was Litton Industries, a tiny start-up venture headed by "Tex" Thornton, organizer of the legendary "Whiz Kids" who had redesigned—and shaken up—the managerial system at the Ford Motor Company.

Gray's first interview with Thornton was so spirited that it came to the brink of confrontation. Thorton's interview style was to downplay a candidate's previous accomplishments in order to buy the applicant at the cheapest possible price. It was not the best approach to use on Gray, who knew his worth and was not eager to have it trashed by someone unfamiliar with his record.

"We're an electronics firm," snarled Thornton. "What the hell do you know about electronics, anyway?"

Gray bristled as he shot back, "More than you knew about cars when you went to work for Henry Ford."

Thornton backed down and Gray was hired. His assignment was to help the fledgling company publicize itself. He was to interview the engineers and executives, learn about the new technologies they were developing, and then write news releases and stories about Litton's advanced products and get the publicity placed in a variety of media. Trained in journalism, but with a strong subspecialty in engineering, Gray had good story sense that enabled him to turn dry technical reports into exciting stories about the way high technology was revolutionizing the nation's armed forces.

If Gray had done nothing more than fulfill that assignment, he no doubt would have enjoyed a gratifying and well-paid career at Litton. Fortunately, he brought more to the task than a combination of engineering and story sense. He brought *leadership without portfolio*. As he talked with the engineers in their labs and drafting rooms, Gray began to venture beyond his original assignment, obtruding himself into areas such as product design, testing, marketing, finance, and logistics.

Why, he asked, were certain products being developed in the first place? Where had the ideas come from? How did the company know whether markets for these products existed? Which executives or engineers were sponsoring the projects? In response to what kinds of pressures and opportunities was the company acting? What were the chances the products would work? If they did work, could they be manufactured and sold at a profit? What about the competition? Were they working on similar products?

Gray became particularly intrigued when Litton engineers announced plans to develop a battlefield X-ray machine to be used by the Army's MASH units in Europe and Korea. If successful, the device held great promise; wounded personnel could be examined and treated with less delay if they did not have to be evacuated from the immediate battle area to be X-rayed. But as Gray began interrogating the engineers, he realized the device carried a significant downside risk as well.

Because the device derived its energy from radioactive thulium instead of electricity, Gray inquired whether it could generate enough current to take X-ray photos repeatedly. Nobody knew.

"Better check it out first," Gray advised. The engineers returned with calculations showing that thulium, with a half-life of six months, would be able to power the machines for only about three months at a time, after which an expensive and cumbersome "refueling" procedure would have to be conducted under unpredictable battlefield conditions. Gray recommended the project be scrapped.

Gray's display of *leadership without portfolio* was not universally welcomed at first. "What makes you think you know what the military needs?" asked Thornton, who felt his connections in the Pentagon made him an authority on defense contracting.

"You may know some generals, but you don't know the battlefield arena," Gray replied.

Again, Thornton backed down. His business instincts overcame his ego once he realized that Litton's veteran of the Battle of the Bulge and Normandy knew what he was talking about. The X-ray project underwent an agonizing reappraisal and was dropped when it became clear that the device could not be developed in a practical or profitable way.

Harry Gray had found his niche. He had become a "corporate proctologist," one of those rare critics who have the nerve—and the skills—to peer into the dark recesses of the product-development process that most executives prefer to avoid. He asked dangerous questions, probed tender areas, and risked bruising powerful egos in order to learn the truth about what the company was doing.

It is not a task that every critic can get away with. Fortunately, Gray had the poise, diplomacy, and people skills to perform his investigatory review and oversight functions without making too many enemies. He knew how to disagree without being disagreeable. Thornton soon realized that Gray's abilities were saving Litton millions of dollars in potentially wasted effort while helping to identify the best projects in the conceptual stage and keep them solidly on track—from the development phase, through testing and prototype rollout, to serial production. When Gray joined Litton in 1954, the company was losing money on sales of $100,000 a year. When he left in 1971 to join United Aircraft (later United Technologies), Litton was profitable, annual revenues were $2 billion, and Harry Gray had risen to the rank of senior vice president.

THE LIMITATIONS OF LEADERSHIP

Why Leadership Alone Is Not Enough

What is required is that we unite with others in order that all may complement and aid one another through holding together. But such holding together requires a central figure around whom others unite. To become a center of influence holding people together is a grave matter and fraught with great responsibility. It requires greatness of spirit, consistency, and strength. Therefore let him who wishes to gather others about him ask himself whether he is equal to the undertaking, for anyone attempting the task without a real calling for it only makes the confusion worse than if no union at all had taken place.

— *I Ching (Book of Changes)*, c. 500 B.C.[85]

The latest crop of leadership books offers many useful insights into the nature of leadership, the identification of leaders, and the development of their skills. If these books do nothing more than show us examples of real business leaders in action, they will have served a very useful purpose.

The popular enthusiasm for leadership studies and leadership training carries within it a potential for excess—an overemphasis on leadership at the expense of less glamorous organizational skills such as core competency—and perhaps at the expense of such indispensable personal traits as character and judgment, which can play a serious role in determining whether leadership will be effective. Some of the leadership advocates seem to be overpromising, as if leadership were a sort of universal solvent that makes other attributes irrelevant. The pop-psych writers seem particularly infatuated with the concept of the leader and the leader's vision, to the virtual exclusion of such banal but essential details as whether the leader has a business plan or even an appointment calendar. At the same time, all but a small minority of very serious leadership analysts seem uninterested in the potentially troublesome relationship between leadership and power.

Ask the average person to name a great leader and the typical response will be a statesman or military commander. Churchill is a common response of Americans familiar with modern history. MacArthur would be another. Those whose sense of leadership reaches deeper into history might volunteer more ancient names: Elizabeth I, Charlemagne, Suleiman the Magnificent.

Others will unfurl the honor roll of business titans who began emerging with the Industrial Revolution. "What about Rockefeller?" they might say. "The petroleum empire he built is bigger than ever and central to our modern mobile existence. What about Andrew Carnegie and J.P. Morgan and Henry Ford and Alfred P. Sloan? What about Steve Jobs and Bill

Gates and Lou Gerstner? These people forever changed the way we live."

Nobody would argue with any of those choices. All of them had a leader's vision, and each of them was able to translate that vision into reality by building, inspiring, and managing an organization.

But there is another kind of leader that nobody likes to talk about: a Hitler, a Stalin, a Milosevic. Actually, people do like to talk about them, but most of us are reluctant to admit those people are successful leaders. Whatever we may think of them, however, and despite our disapproval of the goals they pursued or the means they employed, they too were leaders. Each had a vision, and each had the persuasive powers and organizational skills to inspire millions to join them in making it real. They represent the dark side of leadership. They remind us that leadership can be a toxic substance if it has no moral anchor.

The world of business leadership has its problem children too, but their regimes rarely end in bloodshed and mayhem. Bankruptcy, wasted capital, broken promises, lost jobs, and ruined careers are a more typical legacy. Business seems to be different from statecraft and warfare in at least one essential way: It has a built-in self-correcting feature that tends to limit the damage and remove the malefactor. As business leaders fail, boards, shareholders, creditors, and even the media take action. Errors and overreaching committed by careless business leaders usually trip them up and expose them before they can cause the kind of damage wreaked by a well-armed tyrant with access to all the powers of a nation-state.

The "self-correcting" component found in business may even extend to the errant leader himself. Unlike tyrannical warlords and dictators, who typically go down in flames without ever realizing the nature of their excesses, a failed business leader occasionally may come to his senses. In the case of Chris Whittle, cited later, we will actually see a failed leader recover from his excesses, regain his psychological balance, and develop the necessary resources of character to reapply his leadership skills successfully.

First, however, let's look at a failed leader who did not make it.

"Chain-Saw Al" Dunlap: The Moonbeam Who Wrecked Sunbeam

In 1994, Albert J. Dunlap began making history as the new CEO of Philadelphia-based Scott Paper Company. His ruthless cost cutting, which included the elimination of thousands of jobs, brought millions of formerly wasted dollars to the bottom line. It also earned him the nickname "Chain-Saw Al" in the business media, which loved his tough-guy attitude and his seemingly bottomless stock of outrageous and quotable opinions. After less than two years at Scott, Dunlap left when the company merged with Green Bay, Wisconsin–based Kimberly-Clark Corporation. He published his memoirs, *Mean Business*, and his flinty opinions became even more popular on the talk-show circuit. "Most CEOs are ridiculously overpaid," he wrote in his best-selling bio, "but I deserved the $100 million I took away when Scott merged with Kimberly-Clark."

The media ate it up, and so did corporate America. Both love a tough guy, and both love simplistic solutions. "Chain-Saw Al" supplied both. In his next job, as CEO of troubled appliance maker Sunbeam Corporation, Dunlap seemingly did the impossible by attracting even more media attention than he had at Scott, firing thousands of workers and claiming that his methods were turning the company around on a dime.

At first he seemed to be right. The numbers said Sunbeam's fortunes were rebounding. Then, in 1998, after less than two years at Sunbeam, Dunlap was fired after the company's board and the Securities and Exchange Commission alleged he had committed fraud. Income had been inflated by booking merchandise as "sold" when in fact it had merely been advanced to dealers who had never ordered it. Sales that should have been recorded in a later quarter had been telescoped into the previous quarter. The books had not been debited when merchandise was returned unsold. Critical expenses went unrecorded. Worse, the nonexistent "profits" had been used to justify big bonuses paid to Dunlap. *Mean Business* slid off the best-seller lists, and the invitations to appear on talk shows ceased. Sunbeam filed for Chapter 11 bankruptcy and withheld Dunlap's bonus. Dunlap, who has not had a job since, sued for its restoration.

But the story was not over. On July 16, 2001, *New York Times* reporter Floyd Norris revealed that Sunbeam was not the first company at which Dunlap had issued inflated profit statements while failing to report expenses.[86] According to a pair of lawsuits unearthed from the National Archives, when Dunlap headed Nitec Paper Corporation of Niagara Falls, New York, in 1976, he was awarded a bonus for producing an annual profit of $5 million. After Dunlap was fired for what the *Times* called his "grating" management style, an auditing team from Arthur Young & Company found he actually left Nitec with a $5.5 million loss. Nitec filed for bankruptcy in 1982. Amazingly, Dunlap's term at Nitec never appeared in his résumé, and neither Spencer Stuart, the blue-ribbon headhunter firm that recruited him for the CEO post at Scott, nor Korn-Ferry International, which recruited him for the Sunbeam job, ever asked him about the gaps in his employment history. In addition to missing his firing from Nitec, both firms also overlooked Dunlap's dismissal from the job he held just prior to Nitec, as CEO of Max Phillips & Son, a paper mill in Eau Claire, Wisconsin. Court records show he was fired from that job because he "had neglected his duties and spoken so disparagingly of his boss that he hurt the company's business."

The Dunlap revelations of 2001 sent a major shock through the pricey executive-recruiting industry. Spokesmen at Korn-Ferry and SpencerStuart were hard pressed to explain how their researchers managed to miss Dunlap's long record of fraud, firings, and personality problems.

But the most puzzling aspect of the Dunlap case went unremarked by the *Times*. According to the thumbnail vita that accompanied the article, Dunlap, born in Hoboken, New Jersey, in 1937, was a 1960 graduate of the U.S. Military Academy! Apparently, even West Point's vaunted leadership training cannot catch all the misfits.

Management consultant Peter J. Drucker has described a type he calls the "counterfeit executive," an individual who knows how to wear the right suit, flash the right smile, bandy the latest business buzzwords, and get into the right clubs. From head to toe he looks and sounds exactly like a successful executive. The only problem is his record; on examination he turns out to have no skill in managing businesses successfully. His sole skill set is his ability to do a good executive impression. When his board finally discharges him, he simply moves on and fools a new headhunter firm and a new board of directors. "Chain-Saw Al" Dunlap sounds like a textbook example of Drucker's "counterfeit executive," with one important new wrinkle: He had a remarkable talent for using the media to enhance his image—until the auditors and the press caught up with him.

Leadership Comeback: The Fall and Rise of Chris Whittle

The October 31, 1994, issue of *The New Yorker* contains a sobering feature article that ought to call a number of our assumptions about leadership into question. "Grand Illusion," by Pulitzer Prize-winning *Wall Street Journal* reporter James B. Stewart, tells the story of the rise and fall of Chris Whittle, the young publishing genius from East Tennessee who rocketed to fame during the 1970s when he and his partner, Phillip Moffitt, rescued the moribund *Esquire* magazine and turned it into a highly profitable bible for "the new American man" of the 1980s.

A decade later, after he and Moffitt sold *Esquire* for $30 million, Whittle struck out on his own and created the Channel One television network that cabled daily newscasts (and commercials) into public schools. His growing empire also included the Medical News Network, an interactive TV service for physicians' offices, and *Special Report,* a wall-mounted, illustrated monthly medical newspaper that appeared in doctors' waiting rooms. Hailed as a visionary with almost magical powers of persuasion, Whittle signed Time, Inc. in 1988 as a $40 million partner in his company, an investment Time, Inc. and successor Time-Warner ultimately ran up to $185 million. In 1992, in need of additional financing, Whittle sold a $175 million stake in Whittle Communications to the Dutch conglomerate Philips Electronics. At about the same time, he announced the most audacious coup of his career. As business and academic circles marveled, Whittle revealed that he had hired Yale University President Benno Schmidt to run the Edison Project, a new business designed to build, manage, and operate a nationwide network of privately funded, for-profit elementary schools that would outperform—and eventually replace—the public schools.

Yet by the summer of 1994, Stewart reports, Whittle Communications was in forced liquidation, its vast assets largely dissipated and its financial backers groping to account for the whereabouts of their investment capital. Only when a consortium of lenders led by the Bank of New York demanded an accounting did it become apparent that Whittle's corporate empire had been overstating its revenues and underreporting its obligations, perhaps for years. Whittle's board of directors did the right thing under the circumstances. They removed him from his post as CEO.

What happened?

It is not enough to dismiss Whittle as a charlatan. His admirers and his detractors agree that he had terrific energy and persistence, vast intelligence, genuine vision, and a superb ability to communicate his vision to others and motivate them to work with him to achieve it. People not only believed him but also joined him when he announced that he wanted to create an electronic network that could put news of the latest medical discoveries into doctors' offices. They willingly invested their careers or their money with him as he planned a cable TV service to bring current events into grade school classrooms. His plans for a privately owned and managed high-performance/low-cost school system galvanized some of the nation's brightest minds into joining his organization. And while bright minds pledged him their efforts, two legendary corporations put hundreds of millions of dollars in equity into his companies. Several top banks extended him a $150 million line of credit. None of this would have happened if Whittle had not displayed at least some of the elements of leadership. Selling skills alone could not have done it.

For all his leadership ability, it seems that Whittle fell prey to the classic ego hazard of the leader: He began believing in the legend of his own infallibility, assuming he could do no wrong, as if everything done by a leader were predestined to be right. He began treating leadership as if it were some kind of shortcut to success, rather than what it really is—a slow, careful, and painstaking process of nurturing and building an organization to perform a mission with excellence.

In hindsight, those who worked for Whittle or had invested with him should have seen the signs. Immediately after receiving the first $40 million capital infusion from Time, Inc., Whittle bought and renovated a 16-acre estate in Long Island's exclusive Hamptons for his personal use. At the same time he bought and redecorated a $12-million Manhattan townhouse and leased two corporate jets, which he often used for personal trips, at an annual cost of $8 million.

Most astonishing of all, he erected a corporate headquarters campus of four-story colonial-style buildings in Knoxville, even though the bulk of the company's employees and operations were in New York and Los Angeles, and Knoxville itself had a surplus of first-class office space available at fire-sale prices due to the savings-and-loan crash.

But that was not the end of the story. Instead of following the usual CEO-discharge script by either fading away quietly or staging a guerilla campaign of lawsuits and press releases in an effort to get back into power, Whittle entered into a period of serious self-examination and reflection in an effort to understand the nature of his mistakes and correct them. When you hear him talking about it, you can understand why so few people do it.

"I've never been through anything so painful," he says today. "It was pretty rough."[87]

Whittle says he got through his ordeal by sticking with a pair of tried-and-true self-management strategies.

"The first was that I took the blame myself," he says. "It's been a trait of mine since I was very young—and I don't know where this came from—but when trouble comes I don't look for other people to blame. Also, ever since the age of 30 I've seen a therapist twice a week. I've had this 'coach' for a long time. It really helped during the stress."

By focusing on his own errors and using a professional therapist as a guide, Whittle was able to pinpoint where he went wrong and why. It turned out to be the old story of the successful leader who overreaches himself because he assumes he cannot be wrong.

"From 1970 to about 1990 I had 20 very good years in the publishing and media businesses," Whittle says. "I started a company from scratch in 1970, and it grew and began making profits in 1974. I was viewed as very successful.

"Then, in the early 90s, I began to transform what had largely been a print company into an electronic publishing company," he says. "We placed three big bets. Channel One was the first. Today it's in 12,000 middle and high schools—40% of the middle and high schools in the country. Medical News Network was next. It placed the latest medical news directly on the doctor's desk. Number three was Edison.

"Basically, what happened was that I became overcommitted," Whittle says. "Therein lies the story. It was not wise to place those three bets simultaneously."

Starting up three large pioneering ventures demanded more of Whittle's time and attention than any of his previous businesses. Publishing news and information over two electronic networks turned out to be very different from publishing magazines, and making Edison into a profit-making player and a quality leader in the education industry was entirely distinct from advertising to students. The learning curve for his three new businesses was far steeper than anything Whittle had ever encountered before, yet it was not until the board fired him that he was able to step back and admit he had been struggling ever more intensely over a period of more than two years.

Why did it take so long for Whittle to acknowledge that he had been overwhelmed by his creations?

"When you've had a 20-year run and most of the things you've tried have gone right, you can easily come to believe that all of the things you do will go right," he says. "And that's not real. Just because you know how to do all these things doesn't mean you're infallible. I had always succeeded, so I thought I always would succeed."

Whittle's willingness to acknowledge and learn from his mistakes marked him as an unusual leader, and probably as a leader due for a comeback. But even a veteran expert on business leadership hardly would have anticipated the way he would do it—by exercising *leadership without portfolio* at an age when most successful executives no longer find it necessary.

"My board fired me in 1994," Whittle says. "So I said, 'O.K., guys, I'm not CEO any more, and I'm not getting paid, but I'm not going to stop working.'"

How could Whittle do that? Because he was the majority shareholder in Whittle Communications, he could not be barred from the premises. So every day he came in to work at no salary. To make sure he would succeed this time he deliberately avoided the error he knew had brought him down the last time: trying to accomplish too much. He focused on only one business— the Edison Project—and he focused on only one aspect of that business—raising capital.

"What I really did was return to what had originally made me successful: tremendous focus, persistence, and not being spread too thin," Whittle says. "I just came in every morning and raised money for the Edison project. Medical News did not work out, so to cover its debt I had closed it and

sold Channel One. I focused totally on Edison and even resisted the board's urging that we go into other businesses.

"I think most people would have just left, turned the page, and gone on to the next chapter," Whittle says. "The reason I stayed was Edison. It was the most important idea I'd ever had."

And he is still polishing that idea, as Edison gradually closes in on its goal of being a profitable company. On February 20, 2001, *The Wall Street Journal* reported that Edison had 113 schools under management, 40 percent of them with unionized employees, and was under consideration to take over 11 distressed school districts in Pennsylvania. It also noted that Whittle is chief executive of Edison. He's back in the front office and getting paid again.[88]

"I took my lumps just like everybody else," Whittle says of his ordeal. "We made mistakes trying to do too much, and we paid for it. Then we went back to work.

"Periodically, good leaders get themselves in trouble by thinking they're better than they are," he adds. "The recovery from that is to go back to the fundamentals. There are examples of leaders who have done that. I hope I am one. But the tale is not yet told."

"The heart that's been broken and mended is stronger than the heart that's never been broken at all," runs an old saying meant to console maidens betrayed in amour.

Perhaps the same might be said of leadership. Is it possible that the strongest and most reliable leader of all could be the one whose leadership skills have been wounded, treated, and—over time—healed?

Perhaps that too is a tale not yet told.

CONCLUSION

A properly designed, constructed, and programmed machine will perform its functions with impressive accuracy. Because of the limitations inherent in all devices and in the materials from which they are made, that machine will from time to time break down and fail. But the trained technician can repair or rebuild the machine, or even replace it with a better one. The task for which the machine was designed will continue to be performed.

Leadership is infinitely more complex. Fortunately, people are not monotonous, robotlike, task-performing devices. That's what makes the leader's job so exciting and

so frustrating. The human beings who make up organizations bring with them into the workplace all the unpredictable vagaries that mortal existence can bestow. They come with their cultural, racial, ethnic, religious, and family backgrounds. They come with their unique personal histories. They come with their strengths, weaknesses, talents, passions, aversions, personalities, health, intelligence, and language. They come with their prejudices and biases, some cultural, some personal. And each comes in one of two packages—male or female.

This is the material—literally, the human resources—with which the leader must have the capacity to work. Unlike the inanimate machine which this same human species has created, humans themselves are dynamic, organic, living creatures that make the leader's job complex and difficult.

The activities of leadership in working with human beings are in one sense like the game of golf: It is not how well you manage your best shots, but how well you manage the relentless succession of misplaced drives and bad lies, most of them caused by your own ineptitude.[89] If golf is not your game, pick another sport, because the principle is the same. Every serious baseball fan realizes that, while home runs can be spectacular crowd pleasers, most games are won by the team that does a consistent job of cranking out base hits and limiting its errors. In football, the spectacular pass completions and 40-yard touchdown runs drive the crowd wild, but it is the slow and frustrating accretion of yardage, first down by first down, that puts teams in position to score repeatedly and go on to win championships.

Such is the daily life of leaders, because leaders come to the party with the same complex mixture of vague and ill-defined personal baggage as followers. Unlike the followers, however, the leaders must give shape and definition to their own attributes before trying to manage the attributes of the others. They must carry on their own struggles and those of their organizations simultaneously.

For some students, this business of leadership may prove dark and daunting. But those willing to take up the challenge are promised the most exciting and fulfilling experience of all time.

1. Peter F. Drucker, "The Age of Social Transformation," *The Atlantic Monthly*, November 1994, p. 72.

2. Henry Mintzberg, "The Manager's Job: Folklore and Fact," *Harvard Business Review* (March–April 1990): 163.

3. Paul J. Gordon and Larry W. Boone, "Educating the Educators: B-School Faculty Development Practices Relating to Institutional Mission per 1991 AACSB Accreditation Standards." (Presented at the International Academy of Management, "A New Paradigm for 21st-Century Enterprise," Wharton School of the University of Pennsylvania, December 9, 1994.)

4. William Oncken, Jr., *Managing Management Time* (Englewood Cliffs, NJ: Prentice Hall, 1984): 60–61.

5. Ibid.

6. Paul Roush, Col., USMC, United States Naval Academy, telephone interview, August 9, 1994.

7. George B. Forsythe, Col., United States Military Academy, telephone interview, July 20, 1994.

8. Roush, telephone interview.

9. An excellent layperson's introduction to the Myers-Briggs test can be found in Maj. Gen. Perry M. Smith, *Taking Charge: A Practical Guide for Leaders* (Washington, DC: National Defense University Press, 1986): 85–86.

10. Roush, telephone interview.

11. Forsythe, telephone interview.

12. Personal letter to Harry J. Bruce, October 17, 1994.

13. John Kirchenstein, Col., telephone interview, November 4, 1994.

14. *Taking the Lead: The Management Revolution*, Episode 101, "Management at Work: The Managerial World" (Pasadena, CA: INTELECOM Intelligent Communications, 1993).

15. Ronald A. Heifetz, *Leadership without Easy Answers* (Cambridge, MA: The Belknap Press of Harvard University Press, 1994): 20.

16. Warren Bennis, *An Invented Life: Reflections on Leadership and Change* (Reading, MA: Addison-Wesley, 1993): xiii.

17. Ibid.

18. In John P. Kotter's *The Leadership Factor* (New York: The Free Press, 1988), he recognizes the same distinction when he establishes two categories of leadership: "leadership with a capital 'L,'" which is the classic type emanating from the chief executive officer, and "leadership with a lower case 'l,'" the less conspicuous type active at lower levels in the organization. Kotter insists that both deserve to be acknowledged as leadership because both display the two earmarks of leadership he identifies in many empirical studies: vision combined with a well-managed organization that successfully implements the vision. "In other words, the effective leadership of a project team located ten layers below the CEO in a large corporation and the effective leadership of the overall corporation by the CEO both seem to share some fundamentals in common: a good vision and strategy backed up by sufficient teamwork and motivation" (p. 19).

19. *Random House Dictionary of the English Language*, unabridged ed. (New York: Random House, 1967): 913.

20. Forsythe, interview.

21. John P. Kotter, *Power and Influence: Beyond Formal Authority* (New York: The Free Press, 1985).

22. Ibid., 26.

23. Phillip Crosby, *Running Things* (New York: McGraw-Hill, 1986): ix.

24. Ibid., xi.

25. *The Random House Dictionary of the English Language,* unabridged ed. (New York: Random House, 1967): 814.

26. *Webster's New World Dictionary of the American Language*, 2d college ed. (New York: New World Dictionaries/Simon & Schuster, 1984): 725.

27. Kotter, in *Leadership,* comes to virtually the same conclusion. Based on his and Paul Lawrence's 1972 study of 20 big-city mayors, plus more recent work by Bennis, Levinson and the Center for Creative Leadership, Kotter writes (p. 20): "Effective Leadership in Complex Organizations" consists essentially of two fundamental activities: "Creating an Agenda for Change" and "Building a Strong Implementation Network."

28. Garry Wills, "What Makes a Good Leader?" *The Atlantic Monthly,* April 1994, p. 69.

29. Cf. Kotter, *Leadership*, 29.

30. Chester I. Barnard, *The Functions of the Executive,* 30th anniv. ed. (Cambridge, MA: Harvard University Press, 1979): 173.

31. James M. Kouzes and Barry Z. Posner, *Credibility: How Leaders Gain and Lose It, Why People Demand It* (San Francisco: Jossey-Bass, 1993): 9.

32. Louis B. Lundborg, *The Art of Being an Executive* (New York: The Free Press, 1981): 85. Cf. Kotter, *Leadership*: "[Leadership is] a process of moving a group (or groups) of people in some direction through (mostly) non-coercive means" (p. 16); and "'Good' leadership moves people in a direction that is genuinely in their real long-term best interests. It does not march people off a cliff. It does not waste their scarce resources. It does not build up the dark side of their human nature. In this sense, one could say Adolf Hitler displayed strong leadership at times, but not effective leadership" (p. 17).

33. Ibid., 86.

34. Ibid., 87.

35. Ibid.

36. Letter to Ralph Gilbert, September 20, 1994.

37. Ralph Stogdill and Bernard M. Bass, *Manual of Leadership: A Survey of Theory and Research* (New York: The Free Press, 1981): 7.

38. Donald Kagan, *On the Origins of War and the Preservation of Peace* (New York: Doubleday, 1995): 25–26.

39. Ibid., 26.

40. Ibid.

41. *Encyclopedia Britannica,* vol. 7 (Chicago: Encyclopedia Britannica, Inc., 1966): 609.

42. Kagan, *Origins,* 27.

43. It should be pointed out in fairness, however, that Nanus and his collaborator Warren Bennis earlier noted the absence of the power issue in contemporary leadership literature and addressed that absence in a manner remarkably forceful for academics: "However, there is something missing," they wrote. "POWER, the basic energy to initiate and sustain action translating intention to reality, the quality without which leaders cannot lead . . . power is at once the most necessary and the most distrusted element exigent to human progress . . . power is the basic energy needed to initiate and sustain action, or, to put it another way, the capacity to translate intention into reality and sustain it." Warren Bennis and Burt Nanus, *Leaders: The Strategies for Taking Charge* (New York: Harper & Row, 1985): 15–17.

44. Rosabeth Moss Kanter, "Power Failure in Management Circuits," *Harvard Business Review* (July/August 1979): 65.

45. Kagan, *Origins,* 6.

46. Jeffrey Pfeffer, *Managing with Power: Politics and Influence in Organizations* (Boston: Harvard Business School Press, 1992): 15.

47. Ibid.

48. Ibid., 8–9.

49. *The Charlie Rose Show,* January 13, 1995, Transcript No. 1291, 1.

50. Ibid., 5.

51. Ibid.

52. Stevenson Swanson, "Leading question: What kind of people do others follow?" *Chicago Tribune,* November 29, 1984, p. 1.

53. Bennis, *Life,* 140.

54. Ibid., 82.

55. James V. Higgins, "Romney: Iacocca of His Day," *Detroit News-Free Press,* July 28, 1995, p. 2A.

56. Ibid.

57. John A. Byrne, *The Whiz Kids* (New York: Currency Doubleday, 1993): 98.

58. Stephen R. Covey, *The Seven Habits of Highly Effective People* (New York: Simon & Schuster, 1989).

59. Ibid., 275.

60. Garry Wills, "Gingrich's Energy Helped Ideas Pay Off," *Chicago Sun-Times,* January 7, 1996, p. 32.

61. Mihaly Csikszentmihalyi, *Flow: The Psychology of Optimal Experience* (New York: Harper & Row, 1990): 49.

62. Mihaly Csikszentmihalyi, telephone interview, February 26, 1996.

63. *Webster's New Twentieth Century Dictionary of the English Language,* unabridged, 2nd ed. (New York: Prentice Hall, 1983): 1337.

64. All information on this subject appears in "Colonel Sanders: From Corbin to the World," *Bucket* magazine, 22, no. 1, 1980, pp. 3–7.

65. Wills, "Gingrich's Energy."

66. Emmett C. Murphy, with Michael Snell, *The Genius of Sitting Bull: 13 Heroic Strategies for Today's Business Leaders* (Englewood Cliffs, NJ: Prentice Hall, 1993).

67. Don Shula and Ken Blanchard, *Everyone's a Coach* (New York: HarperBusiness, 1995).

68. Sun Tzu, *The Art of War,* trans. Thomas Cleary (Boston: Shambala, 1991): back cover.

69. J. Case, "Desperately Seeking Leadership," *Inc.,* December 1987, pp. 20, 22.

70. Benjamin DeMott, "Choice Academic Pork: Inside the Leadership Studies Racket," *Harper's,* December 1993, pp. 61–62.

71. Ibid.

72. "Tom Peters on Excellence: Want Success? Step Right up and Try Your Luck," *San Jose Mercury News,* April 1, 1991.

73. Henry David Thoreau, *Walden* (New York: Barnes & Noble, 1993): 7.

74. The material making up these examples of leadership came from a variety of sources. Bill Knight was personally known to the author. Material on John Sculley came from his 1987 autobiography, *Odyssey,* co-authored with John A. Byrne and conversations the author and Sculley had in Hong Kong April 2002. Harry Gray's recollections of his work at Greyvan Lines and Litton Industries and Ray Tower's recollections of his work at FMC Corporation were related by these sources in personal interviews with the author. Information on Diane Betti and Gail McGovern came from correspondence and interviews between these sources and the author. The material on Lee Iacocca's first career successes at Ford is from his 1987 autobiography, *Iacocca,* co-authored with William Novak.

75. Interview with author, August 8, 2001.

76. E. M. Gray, "The Common Denominator of Success," in Covey, 148–49.

77. John Sculley, with John A. Byrne, *Odyssey* (New York: Harper & Row, 1987): 13.

78. Ibid.

79. Lee Iacocca, with William Novak, *Iacocca* (New York: Bantam Books, 1984): 39–40.

80. Personal communication. Source requested anonymity.

81. Personal communication.

82. See Heifitz, *Leadership,* 116, 117, 129, 168, 170, 207, 208.

83. Joseph B. White and Carol Hymowitz, "Watershed Generation of Women Executives Is Rising to the Top," *Wall Street Journal,* February 10, 1997, p. A6.

84. Telephone interview, April 22, 1997.

85. Richard Wilhelm and Cary F. Baynes, trans., *I Ching (Book of Changes),* 3d ed., Bollingen Series XIX (Princeton, NJ: Princeton University Press, 1990): 36.

86. Floyd Norris, "An Executive's Missing Years: Papering over Past Problems," *New York Times*, National Edition, July 16, 2001, 1.

87. Telephone interview with author, August 12, 2001.

88. Daniel Golden, "For-Profit School Managers Discover Teachers' Unions Can Be Allies," *Wall Street Journal,* February 20, 2001, p. B1.

89. For this sobering but useful insight, I am grateful to Lou Biago, golf professional, Lake Toxaway Country Club, N.C.

Chapter 2

Joyce E. A. Russell
University of Maryland

Jacquelyn DeMatteo Jacobs
University of Tennessee

Group Dynamics, Processes, and Teamwork

"No matter what your business, teams are the wave of the future."
Jerry Junkins, CEO Texas Instruments[1]

We are working under increased pressure, with more effort, for longer hours, with fewer resources than we need. We are trying to cope with huge changes in structure, technology, business demands, and competition. Everyone wants results yesterday. The effect is that stress levels for us are dangerously high and not consistent with the rewards provided. Our strategies must reflect the needs, goals, and aspirations of the business, and so must our teams.[2]

OVERVIEW

Most everyone has been a member of a team, either at work or in school. Many people have experienced both positive and negative experiences when working in teams. Why are some teams more successful than others? This chapter addresses some of the factors related to group processes and teamwork. The intent is to help you understand the dynamics of groups and how to address some of the issues that teams face.

Today's organizations increasingly use work groups and teams as primary work units.[3] For example, the Miller Brewing Company found that using self-directed, cross-functional teams at its Trenton, Ohio, brewery resulted in a 30 percent increase in productivity compared to its other plants.[4] By 1996, it was estimated that 47 percent of Fortune 1,000 firms used self-managed teams with at least some employees.[5] The move toward work teams has come about due to a larger paradigm shift involving the redesign of organizations, the alteration of labor contracts, and the changing demographics of the workforce.

Organizations today exist in highly complex and turbulent environments. The need to compete in a global marketplace with rapid technological advances has required

Learning Objectives

After reading this chapter, you should be able to:

1. Define various types of teams as well as characteristics of effective teams and activities performed by self-managed teams.

2. Understand the increasing importance of teams for today's changing organizations and their effectiveness.

3. Describe the stages of group development.

4. Understand the initial steps in building effective teams, including planning initial team meetings, setting goals, creating a mission, clarifying roles, examining the characteristics of effective team members, determining the size of the team, and understanding the ability, personality characteristics, and preferences of team members.

5. Explain how teams can make more effective decisions.

6. Understand common problems with teams and how to manage conflict effectively in teams.

7. Describe the role of leadership in teams.

firms to question the way they have traditionally done business and to place increasing emphasis on quality improvements. This has necessitated breaking down vertical and horizontal boundaries to facilitate lateral, cross-functional collaboration. To improve

processes and enhance quality, organizations have become flatter, more information based, and organized around teams. This trend is expected to continue in the future.[6]

Self-directed teams were not used in the United States until the mid-1960s and early 1970s, with their introduction into a few companies such as Procter & Gamble Company and the Gaines dog food plant in Topeka, Kansas.[7] It was not until the 1980s, however, that self-directed teams really caught on. By the 1990s, 26 percent of the organizations in North America were experimenting with self-directed teams.[8] Today, large manufacturing firms such as Xerox Corporation, Cadillac, Milliken & Co., Best Foods, Cummins Engine, Ford, Chrysler, Motorola, Boeing, Monsanto, General Electric Company, IBM Corporation, Corning, Digital Equipment Corporation, Colgate-Palmolive Company, and TRW are only a few firms using teams. Smaller firms such as Johnsonville Foods and Lake Superior Paper Industries, as well as white-collar and service firms such as AT&T and AAL, have also been employing teams.[9]

It is projected that rapid growth in the use of teams will occur. Some of the common settings where teams have been used have included pet food plants, parts manufacturing, paint manufacturing, coal mines, auto manufacturing, supply warehouses, paper mills, hospitals, financial offices, insurance offices, and government organizations.[10] In addition, teams will be used not only to organize work in manufacturing facilities but also in service industries and white-collar jobs. For example, teams are used in American Transtech, with all major lease-processing functions represented on each team. At Ravenswood Aluminum, a privately owned company, the customer service department is organized into teams. In addition, at Corning and Texas Instruments, the management information systems and accounting departments have reorganized into teams.

The reliance on teams in businesses has encouraged researchers and practitioners to identify ways to enhance teamwork. In this chapter, we will discuss the critical issues that influence the effectiveness of teams.

DEFINITIONS AND TYPES OF TEAM

Defining a Team and Effective Team Characteristics

A **team** has been defined as "a small number of people (approximately 2 to 25) with complementary skills who are committed to a common purpose, performance goals, and approach for which they hold themselves mutually accountable."[11] Generally, an average of about 5 to 8 members seems effective for managing many team activities. The basic characteristics of a team are depicted in **Exhibit 2.1**. The vertices of the triangle indicate what teams deliver (performance results, collective work products, personal growth), and the sides and center describe the elements that make it happen (skills, accountability, commitment).

Members of high-performance teams are deeply committed to their purpose, goals, and approach. They are very committed to one another and understand that they need to focus on collective work products, personal growth, and performance results. One way to determine whether a group is functioning as a "team" and possesses the basic characteristics of a team is to complete the assessment found in Appendix 2.A.

Another set of characteristics that is critical for a team to possess includes the following:[12]

- **Themes and identity.** A team should have a set of themes that indicate its purpose. The themes, which can be illustrated through logos, T-shirts, songs, or special codes, enable the team members to rally around their identity.

- **Enthusiasm and energy level.** Based on the interactions among members, the team should have a high level of energy and enthusiasm for what it is doing. Outsiders should be able to sense the excitement among the team members.

- **Event-driven histories.** Teams often experience success and failure stories that serve to push them forward.

- **Personal commitment.** Members on the team care about one another and are committed to each other and to the team.

- **Performance results.** High-performance teams often outperform expectations for the team and outperform other groups of individuals who are not organized into teams.

Work Groups and Teams

Not all work groups are teams. In fact, some work groups never become teams. In some cases, individuals share ideas and learn from one another, but they are not working toward a common goal. **Exhibit 2.2** illustrates the differences between a working group and a team. A work group

Exhibit 2.1: Basic Characteristics of a Team

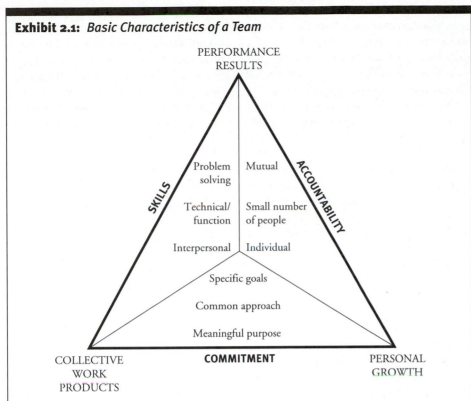

Source: Reprinted by permission of Harvard Business School Press. From *The Wisdom of Teams: Creating the High-Performance Organization* by J.R. Katzenbach and D.K. Smith. Boston, MA 1993, p. 8. Copyright © 1993 by McKinsey & Company, Inc., all rights reserved.

becomes a team when the following occurs:[13]

- Leadership becomes a shared activity.
- Accountability shifts from strictly individual to both individual and collective.
- The group develops its own purpose or mission.
- Problem solving becomes a way of life, not a part-time activity.
- Effectiveness is measured by the group's collective outcomes and products.

Types of Teams

There is no such thing as a typical team. Different organizations give birth to teams of various sorts, and teams within an organization may be at different points on the empowerment continuum at any given time.[14]

There are a number of different types of teams. Four general types of work teams include advice, production, project, and action teams.[15]

- **Advice teams** (e.g., committees, advisory councils, employee involvement groups, quality circles) are created to broaden the information base for managerial decisions. They tend to have a low degree of technical specialization and low levels of

coordination. Also, their work cycles can be brief or long.

- **Production teams** (e.g., assembly teams, manufacturing crews, mining teams, flight attendant crews) are responsible for performing day-to-day operations. While they may not require extensive technical specialization, they do require high coordination with other work units. Their work cycles are often repeated continuously.
- **Project teams** (e.g., engineering teams, task forces, research groups, architect

teams) may require high technical specialization and high coordination if they are cross functional, since they involve creative problem solving and using specialized expertise. Their work cycles usually differ for each new project.

- **Action teams** (e.g., surgery teams, cockpit crews, military squads, sports teams) may require high technical specialization and high coordination. Their work cycles are often brief, yet can be repeated, and require extended training.

Self-Managed Team Activities

Team activities and responsibilities can range from traditional work groups, where managers have control of the group's structure, staffing, and task procedures (*manager-led team*), to *semiautonomous* work groups, to *self-managed teams*. Work teams grow more empowered as they increase ownership of their processes. That ownership grows from production activities (doing the job) to production control (coordinating the job) to leadership (group support and team governance).[16] For example, at Whole Foods Markets, the largest natural-foods grocer in the United States, the 43 stores are all autonomous profit centers consisting of 10 self-managed teams including produce, grocery, prepared foods, and others.[17]

Groups are classified as follows:

Traditional: Work groups

Semiautonomous: Work groups

Self-managed: Teams

One definition of a self-managed or self-directed team is as follows:

A **self-directed team (SDT)** is a group of employees who have day-to-day

Exhibit 2.2: Differences between a Work Group and a Team

Work Group	Team
Strong, clearly focused leader	Shared leadership roles
Individual accountability	Individual and mutual accountability
The group's purpose is the same as the broader organization mission	The team has a unique, specific team purpose that the team itself delivers
Individual work products (rely on the sum of individuals' best work)	Collective work products (require joint effort)
Measures its effectiveness indirectly by its influence on others (e.g., firm's financial performance)	Measures performance directly by assessing collective work products
Discusses, decides, and delegates	Discusses, decides, and does real work together

Source: Adapted and reprinted by permission of Harvard Business School Press. From *The Wisdom of Teams: Creating the High-Performance Organization* by J.R. Katzenbach and D.K. Smith. Boston, MA 1993, p. 214. Copyright © 1993 by McKinsey & Company, Inc., all rights reserved.

responsibility for managing themselves and what work they do. Members of self-directed teams typically handle job assignments, plan and schedule work, make production-related decisions, and take action on problems. Employees on SDTs work with a minimum of direct supervision.[18]

Self-managed team activities include many of the activities noted below:

- Set their own work schedules and plan their own work.
- Allocate task responsibilities among team members.
- Coordinate work among team members.
- Coordinate work with other teams or departments.
- Determine their own training needs; acquire needed training.
- Engage in multiskilling and job rotation (i.e., learning many jobs or skills).
- Set their own production quotas or performance targets.
- Deal directly with external customers.
- Conduct performance appraisals of team members and provide feedback to each other.
- Directly deal with their vendors or suppliers.
- Purchase their own equipment or services.
- Do their own budgeting.
- Recruit, select, and hire their own team members.
- Discipline and fire team members as the need arises.
- Inspect their own work.
- Change the nature of their work to improve quality (i.e., plan, control, and improve their own work processes).

In a survey of U.S. organizations with 100 or more employees, for those with self-managed teams, the activities performed by more than half of the firms included setting their own work schedules (72 percent), training (65 percent), setting production quotas or performance targets (57 percent), and dealing directly with external customers (58 percent).[19] In most cases, autonomy is a high priority for a self-managed team since it empowers members with additional responsibilities. They may possess autonomy in determining the method to use in doing their work, scheduling their work, or deciding on what performance criteria to use in evaluating their work. At the Saturn plant in Tennessee, team members have been involved in selecting the firm's advertising agency and in choosing the suppliers of some electronic components. This is impressive, since union autoworkers have typically not been involved in decisions regarding purchasing and installing equipment.[20]

A number of teams have been involved in their own training, whether it is technical training or team building. There are also many examples of teams engaging in multiskilling. In a number of automotive plants (e.g., Toyota in Kentucky, Subaru-Isuzu in Indiana, Saturn in Tennessee), every team member learns all the assembly tasks for which the team is responsible. In a service organization, Aid Association for Lutherans (AAL, a fraternal society that operates a large insurance business), team members can learn 20 different service-related jobs necessary to meet the needs of their customers. Similarly, at IDS Financial Services, team members handle a variety of jobs, including establishing business accounts, performing changes in account ownership, and redeeming mutual fund shares.[21]

Although very little research has been conducted on the relative effectiveness of various types of teams, one review indicated that employing self-managed teams had a positive impact on productivity and specific attitudes relating to self-management, such as perceptions of responsibility and control. However, no impact was detected for general attitudes such as job satisfaction and organizational commitment, absenteeism, or turnover.[22] In another report, AAL used self-directed work teams, and in one year the company increased productivity by 20 percent, cut case-processing time by 75 percent, and reduced staffing by 10 percent, while handling 10 percent more transactions.[23]

In most reports, self-directed teams have shown successes. For example, some companies employing SDTs such as General Foods, General Motors Corporation, Cummins Engine Company, and Procter & Gamble have reported increases in quality, lower absenteeism and turnover, and reductions in operating and support costs.[24] In addition, the Digital Electronic Corporation plant in Enfield used teams whose members were trained in each step of the building process and a skill-based pay system rewarded members. As a result, the plant has been cited as one of the most successful examples of self-directed teams.[25] The Fort Wayne, Indiana, Edy's Grand Ice Cream Company is completely run by self-managed teams. A typical business unit team consists of four or five people who are responsible for making certain types of ice cream and responsible for everything from sanitation checks to team member training and development. They also have a pay-for-skills compensation program that rewards employees for improving their skills and abilities.[26]

Virtual Teams

You have probably worked in some **virtual teams** where your teamwork is done via phone or email instead or face-to-face. There is a variety of types of virtual teams. For example, some teams have members who are located in the same building while other teams have members who are across international borders. What makes them virtual teams is that they are networked together through technology. See **Exhibit 2.3** for some of the differences between conventional teams and virtual teams.[27]

While they do not have the benefits of face-to-face interaction, virtual teams bring tremendous flexibility to an organization. This is especially true if they are ad hoc teams that are formed to work on certain projects and can be readily changed as customer demands change.

Exhibit 2.3: *Conventional versus Virtual Teams*

Conventional Team	Virtual Team
Same place, same time zone	Different place, often different time zone
Accessible most of the time	Need to preplan access
Regular face-to-face communication	Sporadic face-to-face interaction
Lots of informal networking	Rare informal networking
Free access to supervision and help	Limited access to help and supervision
More time and less pressure to complete tasks	Less time and more pressure to get things done within tight work schedules
Team players are less conscious of how they communicate	They must be very aware of how they communicate and plan for it

REASONS FOR USING TEAMS

Today, both employers and employees recognize the benefits associated with using work teams in organizations. For employers, having flexible, self-disciplined, multiskilled work teams enables firms to better meet their competitive organizational goals. For employees, working in teams provides them with a sense of empowerment as they are able to participate in their jobs and decision making, to learn different job skills, and to feel a greater sense of commitment to their jobs. In fact, self-directed team members have been shown to score higher than their counterparts in innovation, information sharing, employee involvement, and task significance.[28]

Senior managers have given several reasons why their organizations have adopted teams. They are listed below by the percentage of repondents:[29]

Quality, 38%

Productivity, 22%

Reduced operating costs, 17%

Job satisfaction, 12%

Restructuring, 5%

Other, 6%

Essentially, employers have changed to teams due to their increasing interest in improved quality, productivity, and service. In addition, teams offer greater flexibility and responsiveness to customers and the marketplace as well as faster responses to technological changes. Work teams are often designed as cells that can readily be reorganized to be in alignment with shifting demands from the marketplace. Organizations have also reduced costs by eliminating many managerial positions and levels, requiring them to place more decision-making authority in the hands of employees. Employees who cite participation in decision making and challenging work as more important job factors to them than pay view this quite favorably.[30]

EFFECTIVENESS OF TEAMS

I see us moving toward a team-oriented, multiskilled environment in which the team takes on many of the supervisor's and trainer's tasks. If you combine that with some sort of gain sharing, you probably will have a much more productive plant with higher employee satisfaction and commitment.

—Robert Hass, CEO, Levi Strauss[31]

When used effectively, teams have been shown to have numerous benefits such as these:[32]

• Increased productivity

• Improved quality

• Greater focus on task problems

• Enhanced employee quality of work life and job satisfaction

• Reduced costs

• Reduced turnover and absenteeism

• Reduced conflict

• Increased development of members for organizational work

• Improved creativity (e.g., out-of-the-box thinking) and innovation

• Better organizational adaptability and flexibility

For example, Citibank used teams and substantially improved customer satisfaction and service in 11 key areas. Dun & Bradstreet cut its turnaround on report generation from seven to three days. Similarly, Dana Corporation's Minneapolis, Minnesota, valve plant trimmed customer lead time from six months to six weeks.[33] AT&T's Richmond, Virginia operator service increased service quality by 12 percent.[34] At General Electric, significant operating improvements were made in quality, flexibility, and speed, and GE achieved a 30 percent decrease in backlogs within the first year. At Hewlett-Packard, teams were used in the analytic products and the medical product areas to help the divisions become higher-margin businesses. At Weyerhaeuser, the Roundwood team showed an increase in delivery performance from 85 to 95 percent with significant increases in quality and profitability.[35]

Other examples reveal similar positive findings with teams. Shenandoah Life Insurance Company in Roanoke, Virginia, reduced staffing needs, yielding a savings of $200,000 per year, while the volume of work handled increased by 33 percent.[36] Westinghouse Furniture Systems increased productivity by 74 percent in three years.[37] Federal Express Corporation cut service errors by 13 percent.[38] Volvo Corporation's Kalmar facility reduced defects by 90 percent.[39] Corning's new specialty cellular ceramics plant decreased defect rates from 1,800 parts per million to 9 parts per million.[40]

Some evidence suggests that teams are "turning companies around." Motorola relied heavily on teams to surpass its Japanese competition in producing the lightest, smallest, and highest-quality cellular phones. Specifically, between 1988 and 1990, the GEG leadership team saw profits move from $25 million to $60 million, and return on assets increased from 6.5 percent to 16.5 percent. At Kodak, the Zebra team turned around a failing business, trimmed its inventory, and cut its missed delivery rate in half. At DH&S, teams reversed a 10-year trend in declining real profitability and went from last to first in new accounts won. At Prudential, the leadership team showed a consistent performance improvement over a five-year period. Also, 3M used teams to meet the company's goal of producing half of each year's revenues from the previous five years' innovations.[41] At Klear Knit, an apparel manufacturer, when employees got involved in making production decisions and quality improvement suggestions, the firm reduced its reject rate to zero percent. Other apparel manufacturers, including Russel Corporation and Oxford Industries, have adopted similar changes.[42]

Teams have also been used successfully outside the business sector. For example, in the Girl Scouts, a team in the innovation center greatly increased minority girls' involvement in the program. Also, in a New York City partnership, the founding team greatly improved cooperation between the public and private sector, with innovative programs for creating jobs and reducing crime. In PBS–featured schools, faculty and student teams were able to report a dramatic increase in attendance, grades, test scores, and college admissions among disadvantaged children. Even in military operations, teams have been used successfully. For instance, in Desert Storm, the log cell team was responsible for expeditiously moving hundreds of thousands of individuals and supplies back to the United States in record time.[43]

While these statistics are impressive, it is important to note that many of the successes reported by organizations cannot be attributed solely to the use of self-directed teams. Many of these firms also reorganized their work flows, increased their training, brought in new technologies, and implemented new production and quality processes. Thus, probably several factors, in addition to teamwork, were responsible for each organization's success.[44] Also, despite the benefits of teamwork, not all organizations that have adopted teams have been as successful. Sealed Air's Totowa team noted only marginal improvements in productivity. Likewise, at Duchess Day School, the faculty/staff teams did not make substantial improvements in the counseling they provided to students.[45] For this reason, it is important to understand the factors that contribute to the success and failure of teams. Moreover, it is critical to understand how to design and manage work teams so that individuals can work more effectively in teams. As the management consultants Katzenbach and Smith note, based on hundreds of interviews with people working in teams, "Many people simply do not apply what they already know about teams in any disciplined way, and thereby miss the team performance potential before them."[46]

HOW TEAMS DEVELOP

The road to self-directed teams is littered with landmines. . . . Even the wary are liable to find the process uncomfortable, confusing, and excruciatingly slow.[47]

It is very important to understand the different stages *of group development* a team goes through, the obstacles members may experience, and how to manage the transitions effectively. Understanding how a team develops over time can help team members to better understand and anticipate the problems and issues they may face during the team's development. Teams can be successful during the transition stages they experience. For example, the Gaines dog food plant in Topeka, Kansas experienced many difficulties, yet the plant operated for nearly four years without a lost time accident and realized savings of millions of dollars annually.[48]

Stages of Group Development

It is believed that all groups pass through a series of predictable stages in their development. One of the earliest theories of group development was developed by Tuckman[49] and is still widely used today. Tuckman's model outlines four major stages of group development, including *forming, storming, norming,* and *performing*. In addition, occasionally a final stage, *adjourning,* takes place. This model describes the changes in group structure and task behavior at each stage.

Forming

When you first join a group, you will experience a *forming stage*. As members get to know one another, they may have some uncertainty about the group's purpose,

structure, and leadership. Members may be excited and proud to be on the team but may also be suspicious or fearful about the job ahead.[50] Members introduce themselves to others, and they may try to find out how the group feels about them (i.e., whether they are liked and accepted or not). They may test the waters to determine which types of behavior are acceptable. For example, an individual may miss a meeting or arrive late because he is unsure of how the group feels about attendance and punctuality. Generally, members have a number of initial concerns when placed in a team. These include concerns about their roles, what they are going to get out of the team, what others expect of them, if others have hidden agendas, how they should behave, how things should be done, and what level of performance is necessary.[51]

Productivity is typically low or moderate during the forming stage, since members spend more time understanding their roles and each other than working toward task accomplishment. The forming stage is complete when members have started to think of themselves as part of a group.

Storming

Most groups go through a *storming stage* once they start working on projects. Do not be alarmed if this happens to your team. While it may be the most difficult phase for the team, you can get through this period successfully. Why do groups storm? Generally, there may be struggles over leadership, or members may resist the control that the group imposes on individuality. For example, a member may resent being told by the team to turn in her work a week in advance. Consequently, the member may refuse to turn in the work until the last possible moment. In the storming phase, there may also be power struggles or conflict over leadership issues, such as who will control the group. Team members may express concerns over the excessive work and establish unrealistic goals. Sometimes, team members are individuals with high individual needs for achievement or those with minimal experience working in groups. What they may discover is that several of the team members, including themselves, may want to be the leader of the group. As such, there may be conflict over who is really in charge. The storming phase is near completion when there is a relatively clear understanding of leadership within the group.[52] For example, one member may assume the role

of task leader while another may perform the activities of a social leader. Another possibility is that the team may decide to rotate who is the leader for each project.

Norming

The third stage is one in which close relationships develop, and the group demonstrates cohesiveness and a sense of group identity. Members may have feelings of accepting their membership into the team, relief that everything is going to work out, or a new ability to express criticism constructively.[53] The *norming stage* is complete when the group has assimilated a common set of expectations of what defines "good team member behavior" (i.e., rules, standards or *norms*). Norms are shared attitudes, opinions, feelings, or actions among two or more people that guide their social behavior.[54] Often, norms are unwritten rules that may not even be discussed openly, yet they have a powerful effect on members' behavior. Norms are often established by the first few group meetings. In fact, some are even developed within the first few minutes of a team's meeting, such as whether it is appropriate to come in late to a meeting or what the dress code should be for the meeting. Norms tend to be enforced by team members when they help the group survive, simplify behavioral expectations, help individuals avoid embarrassing situations, and clarify the group's central values or mission.[55]

It is important for teams to discuss and agree upon the norms to which they want to adhere. At Intel Corporation, teams have a norm of constructive confrontation whereby members are allowed to challenge others in a productive manner rather than simply avoiding conflict.[56] Some examples of rules or norms established by a team may include the following:

- Attendance at all meetings is mandatory unless members inform others in advance of a conflict.
- Meetings start and end on time.
- Members come prepared for all meetings (having completed all assignments or projects).
- Outsiders must be approved before they are allowed to attend meetings.
- An agenda is prepared and followed in each meeting. Topics that go beyond the time limit are renegotiated to see whether the team is willing to continue discussing the topic or is ready to postpone it until another meeting.

- Members brainstorm solutions to problems and critique suggestions only after all ideas have been placed on the table.
- Everyone has an opportunity to participate in discussions, and members use active listening techniques and refrain from interrupting one another.
- Members minimize or abstain from allowing outside interruptions in the meeting (e.g., phone calls, visits).
- Members maintain confidentiality of what is discussed in team meetings.
- Members are open to giving and receiving honest feedback.
- Roles for a timekeeper and meeting facilitator are rotated for meetings.

Performing

When the team reaches the fourth stage, *performing*, it is fully functional and the group's energy has shifted from interpersonal issues to the job of getting the task done. Members have feelings of satisfaction at the team's progress and have greater insights into each other's strengths and weaknesses. Some say that the team has "jelled" since members are focused on their goals and performance without being disrupted by minor setbacks.

Adjourning

In later research, it was shown that a final stage called *adjourning* might exist. This represents a termination phase in which the group's energy is devoted to wrapping up the group's activities and preparing for the group's breakup.[57] For example, the team may plan a social event to "say goodbye" to each other and thank each other for the experience. Generally, teams that have been more cohesive (i.e., feel closer and have enjoyed working together) and productive will plan final get-togethers. They may even continue to meet socially long after their work together has ended. On the other hand, teams that were dysfunctional and did not get along usually disband relatively quickly without any final social activities.

This model of group development described is one of many models that have been proposed by researchers. While other theories of group development exist, it is important to point out that most models assume a progression through stages that resemble the stages put forth by Tuckman. In addition, the movement through the stages is not always as clear cut as described in the model. In some cases, two stages can be going on simultaneously (e.g., forming and norming), or there may be occasions when a group actually regresses to previous stages (e.g., a group that has reached the performing stage may revisit the storming stage). The point is that while the sequence or timing of the stages may vary, most groups typically experience the major hurdles associated with the stages. An understanding of these stages can help a team better understand the problems and issues that they may face during their development.

GETTING STARTED: TEAM BUILDING

A persistent barrier to effective cross-functional teamwork is the failure of people to work well together in groups. Many people in the workplace are poorly prepared to function as team players. . . . Few people take courses in group dynamics; few are naturally endowed with group process skills.[58]

A 1995 survey of 134 separate project teams in 88 companies in the United States found that many of the firms did a poor job of building effective teams. They did not have good systems in place to evaluate team member performance or reward teams, and they did not give good training or emphasis on project management skills and team goal setting.[59] If a firm spends the time to design the teams, then they are more likely to be successful. For example, customer-service teams at Xerox that were well designed (i.e., monitored their own performance, managed their own strategies and goals) were more effective than were poorly designed teams according to customers and supervisors.[60]

In building a team, the primary focus should be on assessing the task components (e.g., is it a creativity task or problem-solving task), the people components (e.g., how many people should be included and what type of experiences should they have), and the relationships among the people (e.g., what level of cohesion is needed). **Exhibit 2.4** illustrates some of the key questions to ask when building a team.[61]

For teams to be successful, there are a number of activities the team should complete in the early stages. The team members should create a mission statement to reflect their unique identity and establish goals to achieve their stated mission. They should determine the roles and responsibilities of various members on the team and examine their goals and plans for the first few meetings. In addition, the team may also want to consider factors such as the size of the team and the ability, preferences, and personality characteristics of its members. Periodically, the team should review all of these issues in order to

---

Exhibit 2.4: *Key Questions to Ask When Building a Team*

Phase I: Task Analysis
- What work needs to be performed?
- How much authority does the group have to manage its own work?
- What is the focus of work the group will do?
- What is the degree of interdependence among team members?
- Does there exist only one correct solution, or is the task more subjective?
- Are team members' interests aligned or competitive?

Phase 2: People
- How many people should be on the team?
- Who is ideally suited to do the work?
- What technical, task, management, and interpersonal skills are required?
- What types of diversity are optimal in the team?

Phase 3: Relationships
- How do team members socialize with each other?
- What roles are implicitly negotiated among team members?
- What norms are conducive or harmful for the group?
- Is cohesion among team members important?
- How is trust developed, threatened, and rebuilt among team members?

Source: L. L. Thompson, *Making the Team: A Guide for Managers* (Upper Saddle River, NJ: Prentice Hall, 2000): 61. Reprinted by permission of Pearson Education, Inc.

make improvements. In this section, we will offer tips for teams that are getting started on their teambuilding endeavors.

Conducting Initial Team Meetings

In the first few team meetings, the group should focus on building relationships between members, establishing their educational goals, and starting to work toward the desired project goals.[62] It may require several meetings to accomplish these objectives. As such, the team should engage in the following practices:[63]

- **Get to know each other.** Take some time to learn a little about each other's backgrounds, work experiences, work styles, preferences, interests, and career goals.

- **Learn to work as a team.** Try to find ways to maximize each other's strengths.

- **Work out decision-making issues and processes.** Determine how the group will arrive at decisions and the types of decisions the team will use (e.g., consensus, majority vote, unanimity).

- **Determine support services and logistical issues.** Determine how the team will get any needed support (e.g., copying, supplies) and how the team will manage communication and logistics (e.g., e-mail, voice mail, which types of computers and software will be used).

- **Set meeting ground rules.** These might include attendance, promptness, preparation, assignments, participation, listening skills, interruptions, meeting places and times, breaks, rotation of leadership or various roles, using agendas, having a timekeeper.

It is also important that team members spend some off-hours together in an informal atmosphere (e.g., meals, socials, events). This is a good way for teammates to get to know one another better. Personal time invested in informal team gatherings is critical to developing camaraderie that can pull the team together during tough times.[64]

Establishing Goals

The first thing you have to have is a common goal. And everyone must have a clear understanding of the goal. Finally, everyone must keep on the same track toward that goal.
—Gary Jobson, crew tactician on three America's Cup teams[65]

Good teams always have common goals. When you find that goals of certain members differ from the team's, then the team will usually do poorly.
—Red Auerbach, Boston Celtics president[66]

In the initial meetings, the team should determine what their *educational goals* are (i.e., what do they need to learn about). For instance, they may need to gain more skills in marketing or accounting or finance in order to complete their assignment. They may need background in the scientific approach (e.g., information-gathering or data analysis tools) or the quality movement.

The team should also try to outline their *project goals*. This means they need to understand the assignment and process, identify any needed resources, and develop a plan to complete their project. If possible, members may want to get a manager to review the goals they have established to ensure that they are on track.

It is important that the team identify its long-term goals and specific objectives. Often this is done by defining subtasks and establishing timetables.[67] Articulating goals enables the team to keep focused on the most important activities rather than getting sidetracked on less critical activities. It also ensures that the team will emphasize goals that will be consistent with the organization's strategic plan. For example, if a firm has established customer service as an important priority, then the team may develop some goals to help meet this organizational objective.

Teams must take their broad directives or objectives and translate them into specific and measurable performance goals. For example, a specific goal may be to respond to all customers within 24 hours.[68] The specific goals also enable the team to have small wins (i.e., early successes) that are critical for building team members' commitment. Goals also help the team to track its progress and hold itself accountable for performance.

Teams without goals will have difficulty being successful. At Rexam Custom in North Carolina, when teams were first started they were a failure; one reason was that they were very large teams that did not have clear goals and objectives. At team meetings they discussed so many different topics that it was difficult for the teams to be focused and get anything accomplished. Once the company identified the lack of goals in the teams, they were able to successfully turn around the teams to be more successful.[69]

Creating a Team Mission and Identity (The Team Charter)

Each team should create a team charter to clarify its purpose and to provide a clear

definition of the team's role and expectations. A team mission or charter will do the following:[70]

- Clarify what the team is expected to do.
- Focus the energies and activities of team members; set the tone.
- Provide a basis for setting goals and making decisions.
- Help team members visualize their potential.
- Communicate the team's purpose to others.

A number of elements should be written into the charter. The purpose for the team should be described (i.e., why the team is necessary). The key customers or those who will use the products or services provided by the team should be identified. The key result areas should be included to define what the team is expected to accomplish. These may consist of measurable goals or objectives by which the team can plan and monitor its progress. Guiding principles or the team's operating beliefs and values should be described. Some common principles used with teams are "All team members own the meeting and its results," "We are more committed to decisions that we participate in making," and "Our goal is to know and serve our customer better than anyone else." Time frames should also be included to indicate the time commitments required by the team (i.e., major deadlines, hours necessary to accomplish team objectives).

When you think of all the good teams of the past, like the old Steelers, the old Raiders, the Forty-Niners, they all had identity. We will have an identity in Atlanta.
—Jerry Glanville, head coach, Atlanta Falcons[71]

For creating and using a team charter, several guidelines have been offered:[72]

1. Prior to the team meeting, members should prepare their own views of the key elements that should be included in the charter.

2. In the team meeting, all members should offer their views. Brainstorming can be used to enable members to build off each other's ideas.

3. In the team meeting, create a rough draft of the charter. Focus on capturing the main themes rather than worrying about the details of the language (i.e., actual writing).

4. Give each member a copy of the initial draft to review.

5. Meet again as a team to finalize the charter.

6. Once the charter is finalized, distribute a copy to each member.

7. Periodically review and update the charter over time.

In sports, it's called tradition, in business it's called corporate culture, but they both refer to the same thing. A sports team may have a tradition of being tough, hardworking, committed, disciplined, winning. A business organization may have a corporate culture that makes it professional, energetic, ethical, reliable, innovative, and efficient. Your team's tradition or corporate culture determines your reputation and establishes your identity.

—Don Martin[73]

Clarifying Roles in Teams

Football has goals that are clearly defined. At the end of the field is a goal line. Why do we call it a goal line? Because eleven people on the offensive team huddle for a single purpose—to move the ball across it. Everyone has a specific task to do—the quarterback, the wide receiver, each lineman; every player knows exactly what his assignment is.

—Jim Tunney, NFL referee[74]

Clarifying team members' **roles** and responsibilities is essential for a team just starting out. It can also be helpful when a team reorganizes, begins a new project, shifts individual responsibilities, or sets new priorities.[75] To define team members' roles and responsibilities, the following steps should be followed:

1. **Analyze the work to be done by the team.** Review the team's charter and discuss the key projects and activities necessary for the team to accomplish in order to reach its objectives.

2. **Identify strengths and weaknesses of the team's work.** Organize the work into major areas of responsibility.

3. **Define the common activities for which all members are responsible.**

4. **Define individual roles and responsibilities.** To do this, identify team members' strengths, talents, and expertise. The goal is to match individuals' strengths with various work areas of responsibility. Prepare an individual role description for each person on the team.

5. **Create a plan for learning the activities of others on the team.** Decide on the degree to which members should learn each other's tasks and effective methods for learning (e.g., on-the-job training, providing job descriptions).

6. **Periodically review team members' roles and responsibilities.**

For a team to be successful and accomplish its goals, both task and maintenance roles need to be performed.[76]

- **Task roles** enable the work group to define, clarify, and pursue a common purpose. These roles keep the group on the project at hand.

- **Maintenance roles** foster supportive and constructive interpersonal relationships. These roles keep the group together.

Exhibit 2.5 depicts the various task and maintenance roles members can play in a team. Teams should conduct periodic assessments to see which roles each individual member is playing. This would help the team better understand the team's processes. An example of one instrument that can be used in this assessment is found in **Appendix 2.B**. In this measure, brief definitions of the task and maintenance roles are provided.

Sometimes team members may disregard the maintenance roles, believing that only the task roles are critical. This can be a problem if the team is made up of members from various cultures who differentially weight the various roles. For example, members from Japan or Asian countries may place more weight on maintenance roles, especially harmonizer and compromiser roles.[77] If the other team members downplay the significance of maintenance roles, these members may feel they are not able to make a valuable contribution to the team. This is unfortunate since both types of roles are essential to the success of a team.

Champy recently gave an example of how a team enables members to play various roles. He notes:

> Rick Zaffarano of Hannaford Brothers is director of Warehouse Operations. He redistributed authority in the warehouse among seven teams (of 20 workers each) and two mentors or coaches. Each team has an informal leader called an operations coordinator. The teams work because they each have their own internal monitors. Each team has a team coordinator and a "Star Point" who is the coordinator on a specific work function. For example, the operations Star Point makes sure the team has its schedules; the safety Star Point discusses ways to improve the physical environment. They rotate the positions so that they can always bring in fresh ideas.[78]

It is important that all members know what all other members' responsibilities are. As stated by Dr. Ken Carson, chief of

---

Exhibit 2.5: *Roles Performed by Team Members*

Task Roles	Maintenance Roles
Initiator	Encourager
Information seeker	Gatekeeper
Information giver	Compromiser
Coordinator	Harmonizer
Evaluator	Energizer
Challenger	Processor
Completer	Standard setter

Source: R. Glaser, *Team Communication Inventory* (King of Prussia, PA: Organization Design & Development, Inc., 1993).

---

pediatric neurosurgery at Johns Hopkins Medical School, Baltimore, Maryland, "That's a crucial part of teamwork: Not just playing your role but knowing what everybody else's role is, too. That way you know where everybody fits into the whole equation."[79]

Examining Characteristics Required of Team Members

Team members should possess certain characteristics if they are to carry out the diverse activities of a self-managed team. These critical team member dimensions are described in **Exhibit 2.6**. It should be noted that as the team takes on more self-directed activities, the weighting of some of the dimensions may change, but the actual dimensions will not change.

Determining the Size of the Team

How many members should be on a team? Does **team size** affect the group's performance? Research reveals that the effects of a group's size on its performance depend on the group's goal or task. For example, it has been shown that groups need to be large enough to accomplish their work but small enough to avoid difficulties in communication and social loafing.[80] Most researchers agree that the most effective groups include between 5 and 11 members and have an odd number of members.[81] For group decision-making tasks (e.g., NASA's Moon Survival Simulation) often groups of about five members are ideal.[82] An odd number of members is recommended if decisions are to be made by majority vote. In many cases, however, using majority vote is not as effective for the long-term survival of the group as is

Exhibit 2.6: Critical Team Member Dimensions

Dimension	Importance to Team
Ability to learn	Multiskilling/job rotation
Analysis or problem identification	Team solves its own problems
Attention to detail	Focus on continuous improvement
Influence	Persuades others inside and outside the organization
Initiative	Emphasis on continual improvement
Job fit (motivation to work in an empowered setting)	Job satisfaction, reduction of turnover, team "owns" decisions
Judgment or problem solution	Quality, productivity, team issues
Oral communication	Presents ideas to others
Planning and organizing (work management)	Team determines work/production scheduling
Teamwork (cooperation)	Team members work with others on their own work team and on other teams
Technical/professional proficiency	Job rotation/multiskilling
Tolerance for stress	Handles ambiguity/stress related to new demands and roles
Training and coaching	Team members teach and train each other
Work standards	Quality/productivity focus

Source: R. S. Wellins, W. C. Byham, and J. M. Wilson, *Empowered Teams: Creating Self-Directed Work Groups That Improve Quality, Productivity, and Participation* (San Francisco, CA: Jossey-Bass, 1991): 61.

using consensus decision making or requiring unanimous decisions.[83]

There are no hard-and-fast rules about team size. It depends on the group's objective. If the objective is to generate creative ideas, encourage participation, socialize new members, engage in training, or communicate policies, then groups larger than five could be justified. However, as group size increases, the group leader often becomes more directive and member satisfaction declines slightly.[84] Often, managers err on the side of making teams too large, and the members have troubles coordinating their work.[85] Some research has also found that group decision quality has been negatively related to group size. That is, the larger the group, the more likely members talk about frivolous topics, have difficulty focusing, and make poorer decisions. In addition, it is harder to have equal participation by all members if the team gets to be too large.[86]

Typically, the average size of work teams ranges from 6 to 12 people. For example, Schreiber Foods, a large cheese processor in Arizona, has 7 people on each team. Monogram Credit Corporation uses 10 to 12 people on its white-collar teams. Similarly, General Electric's aircraft engine plant in Vermont has 12 to 14 people on each of its teams.[87]

Examining the Ability of Team Members

Research has consistently shown that greater **ability** among group members leads to better group performance.[88] Groups composed of all high-ability members perform better than the sum of their abilities would predict.[89] In other words, having high-ability members together inspires team members to achieve even higher performance than would be predicted or expected. Thus, if it is important to maximize the performance of the best groups, then employers should concentrate the talent or high-ability performers in the same team.[90] If, however, the objective is to improve the performance of all work groups or to train and develop new talent, then the talent or ability should be dispersed evenly to the various teams.

If individuals are assigned to a team and they have no control over who has been selected to the team, then it is important for members to develop as much talent as possible. If individuals build their own personal strengths, they are essentially building the reservoir of the team. Individuals who come to the team with fewer skills must develop competencies in critical areas for the team to be successful. The types of skills

that should be assessed in forming a team include technical or functional expertise, task-management or leadership skills (planning and coordinating work), and interpersonal skills (objectivity, listening, encouraging).

If there's an occupation or activity that promotes itself as a team sport, it's auto racing. Most of the others don't come close. It's the chain theory of teamwork. Everybody who prepares for the race (e.g., machinists, fabricators, mechanics) must be of equal strength. Everybody's got to be on par.

—Chuck Sprague, team manager for Penske Racing, NASCAR[91]

Understanding Members' Personalities and Preferences

Are there certain types of people who work more effectively in teams? The research has explored this question for decades, and the general conclusion is that there is no one trait or personality characteristic that can be used to predict whether an individual will be an effective team member. Certain characteristics of individuals, however, may increase their chances for success in teams.

Collectivism vs. Individualism and Preference for Teamwork

Given the need to foster cooperation and information sharing in team-based environments, researchers have suggested that individuals with a "collectivistic" orientation may be better suited for a team environment than those who are "individualistic." **Collectivism** is characterized by an orientation toward group goals, attachment to and identification with the groups, and concern for group members.[92] In contrast, **individualism** is characterized by a preference for autonomous work and working alone.[93] Furthermore, collectivists tend to be motivated by group goals, whereas individualists are motivated by individual goals. Recent research has shown that as the proportion of team members with a collectivistic orientation increased on a team, cooperation was enhanced, leading to higher team performance.[94]

A variable that has recently been examined for its role in understanding team composition is **preference for teamwork.** It has been shown that individuals who prefer to work in teams are more satisfied working in a group.[95] Some individuals, however, are resistant to working in teams despite the success of teams in organizations. They may be resistant to moving beyond individual roles and responsibilities. For example, you may feel quite comfortable with your own responsibilities, yet you may not want to take responsibility for others or have them assume responsibility for you. Also, you may have confidence in your own abilities yet be somewhat skeptical about the skills and abilities of others. In order to assess your preferences for teamwork and those of your teammates, you may want to complete the instrument in **Appendix 2.C.**

Myers-Briggs Type Indicator (MBTI)

Numerous personality instruments have been used to examine characteristics of individuals who would be successful in teams. One instrument commonly employed to assist teammates in better understanding themselves and each other is the **Myers-Briggs Type Indicator (MBTI).** The MBTI was developed by Katharine Briggs and her daughter Isabel Briggs Myers and is based on Carl Jung's work on psychological types. For a more thorough background on the MBTI, the reader is referred to several sources.[96] Briefly, the MBTI measures an individual's preferences along four scales:

How a person is energized: extroversion (E), introversion (I)

What a person pays attention to: sensing (S), intuitive (N)

How a person makes decisions: thinking (T), feeling (F)

The lifestyle a person adopts: judging (J), perceiving (P)

Extroverts draw their energy from the outside world of people, activities, or things, while introverts prefer to get their energy from the internal world of ideas or impressions. Sensing types prefer to take in information through the five senses (i.e., what is real and practical). They emphasize the present, while intuitive types go beyond the five senses and use a sixth sense or insight and inspiration. They focus on the future possibilities. Thinking types prefer to make decisions in a logical, objective way, outlining the pros and cons of alternatives. Feeling types make decisions in a more personal way, relying on their values. Judging types like life to be planned, organized, and structured. They enjoy completing tasks (i.e., the joy of closure). Perceiving types like life to be spontaneous and flexible; thus, they stay open to possibilities (i.e., the joy of processing).

Taken together, an individual has a four-letter type reflecting his or her preferences (e.g., ENTJ, ISFP). There are 16 possible types, each of which has its own strengths and potential problem areas. The value of using the MBTI for teams is that it enables members to better understand their own styles and those of others; specifically, how individuals communicate with each other, lead and influence one another, and contribute to the team. An MBTI team profile will also reveal the similarities and differences among teammates on the MBTI, how they may irritate one another, and their potential sources of conflict. The objective is to enable the team to anticipate and better manage any potential trouble spots. Some of the benefits of the MBTI for teams include the following:[97]

- Reducing unproductive work.
- Identifying areas of strength and possible areas of weakness.
- Clarifying team behavior.
- Matching specific assignments with team members.
- Helping members better manage conflict.
- Helping members see that using different perspectives and methods can lead to effective problem solving.

Some of the research conducted using the MBTI and teams has revealed the following:[98]

- The more similar the types on a team, the sooner the team members will understand one another and reach decisions.
- Groups with different types may take longer to reach decisions, but they might reach better decisions because more viewpoints are covered.
- Leadership roles may shift as the tasks require the skills of different types on the team.
- Team members who are opposite on all four preferences (e.g., ENFP vs. ISTJ) may have special problems understanding each other. Members who share two preferences from each of the opposites may be "translators." For example, a person who is an ESFJ or INTP can better relate to both people.
- A person who is the only one of a particular type may be seen as "different" from the others (e.g., the only feeling type in a team of all thinking types).
- Teams that capitalize on the differing styles of the group members may experience less conflict over the long term.

USING TEAMS TO MAKE DECISIONS
Advantages and Disadvantages

Using groups, relative to individuals, to make decisions has some advantages as well as disadvantages. For example, groups have a greater pool of knowledge and expertise. This enables different perspectives to be brought into discussions. Groups also allow underlying rationales for viewpoints to be articulated, and thus everyone's understanding can be enhanced. In addition, team members often have better acceptance of a final decision if everyone was involved in making the decision. Groups also enable less experienced members to receive some training from other members.

There are, however, some disadvantages with having groups be responsible for making decisions. Members may feel social pressure to keep quiet about divergent opinions for fear of being seen as "rocking the boat" and not conforming. In addition, a few individuals may dominate the group. Members may forget that their primary goal is to make a good decision and get consumed with winning the point or argument. *Groupthink* can occur, where the group unanimously decides on a course of action without thinking through all of the possibilities.[99] In addition, groups may be less efficient than individuals at making decisions since it requires more time to make decisions when groups are used.

Types of Team Decisions

Teams can make decisions using a variety of approaches, including *autocratic, democratic, consensus,* and *unanimous.* When an **autocratic decision** is made, the leader, one individual, or a small subgroup typically makes the decision. *Democratic* decisions made take place by voting. The alternative with the most votes becomes the team's decision. **Consensus decisions** indicate that all members are committed to support the decision. Everyone may not agree that it is the best possible decision, yet everyone agrees to support the decision. In making a consensus decision, members should feel comfortable that by supporting the decision they are not compromising their ethics, values, or interests. **Unanimous decisions** refer to situations where everyone on the team agrees that the best possible decision has been made.

While it would be smoother for team processes if unanimous decisions were reached, it is unlikely that members will frequently agree on the same strategy as the best decision. Thus, consensus decision making is often recommended for teams. In some situations, however, it would be better to use another style of decision making. For example, a crisis situation in a team may call for immediate action. One or more members may go ahead and make a quick autocratic decision. In addition, the team may learn that the decision is beyond its scope, and an autocratic decision by management is necessary.

Making Decisions by Consensus

Reaching a consensus decision means that the team has arrived at a decision that all members can support. It reflects the thinking of all group members. It does not mean that it is a unanimous decision, a majority opinion, or that everyone is totally satisfied. If consensus decision making is to be used, members should follow these steps and tips:[100]

1. Members should state the purpose of the decision and the alternatives available.

2. Members should gather any additional information critical to making the decision.

3. Members should individually prepare their own thoughts on the decision prior to meeting as a team. Everyone should do his homework, and be prepared to explain his position.

4. Each member should express her thoughts about the decision in the team meeting.

5. Members should stay focused on the purpose of the decision.

6. Each member should carefully listen to the views expressed by others and make sure all views are understood.

7. Members should make sure that everyone has been heard and that all points have been considered.

8. Members should expect conflict and differences of opinions and not be afraid to address conflict. Confront ideas and issues, not people.

9. Members should avoid the urge to wrap things up too soon; otherwise, the team may have overlooked some issues or facts.

10. The decision made should be one that everyone agrees to support (not everyone may agree it is the best decision, but all agree to support the decision). Mem-

bers should agree with the decision only if they feel they can support it.

11. Everyone takes ownership for the decision and assists in its implementation.

Without a structured format in place, group decision making can be a frustrating experience for many people. Asking a team to make a decision sometimes results in conflict, wasted time, and decisions that are made without the full consensus of all team members. Frequently, groups have trouble reaching consensus. To assist them, there are several **problem-solving techniques** to use. These include brainstorming, multivoting, the nominal group technique, and the Delphi technique and are described next.

Brainstorming

Brainstorming is a technique in which group members present alternatives without regard to issues of feasibility or practicality. It is used primarily to help groups generate as broad a range of options as possible for solving problems.[101] To employ the brainstorming procedure, the following steps should be used:

1. The group meets and indicates the problem.

2. Each member silently writes down or thinks about his ideas for addressing the problem. Members are encouraged to write down or come up with as many creative ideas as possible, no matter how strange. Quantity of ideas is encouraged.

3. The team writes all ideas on a board. Members are encouraged to come up with new ideas after seeing those on the board (i.e., piggybacking or hitchhiking on ideas). At this point, ideas should not be evaluated or criticized. This is critical since members want to make sure to first get all the ideas written down. Sometimes an idea that initially seems "crazy" might be the best idea.

4. After all ideas have been written down, in the same session or in a later session, the members critique and evaluate the alternatives.

In a successful brainstorming session, ideas flow freely and there is no censorship of ideas. This technique is well suited for simple, well-defined problems and tends to encourage enthusiasm from team members. Moreover, brainstorming prevents members from feeling helpless about the range of possibilities in a given situation. Unfortunately, the brainstorming method is not without problems. Research has shown that the quality of ideas generated

from brainstorming may be a function of the characteristics of the group members rather than the brainstorming process itself. Similarly, asking group members to generate as many ideas as possible may not result in ideas of better quality than simply asking individuals to come up with high-quality ideas in the first place. In addition, brainstorming is more effective when the group faces the task of generating ideas rather than selecting alternatives.[102] In other words, brainstorming has limited usefulness and is not appropriate for all types of group decisions. Another problem is that individuals sometimes feel inhibited and/or uncomfortable when proposing ideas or offering suggestions. In addition, when group members interact, they may succumb to social pressure pushing them toward conformity.[103] Finally, dominating group members may prevent the involvement of all group members in the decision-making process. For brainstorming to work effectively, it is critical that all members feel free to share all the ideas they have without being critiqued until all the ideas are posted.

Multivoting

Suppose a group believes that it has numerous ideas based on some earlier brainstorming, yet it has only a limited amount of time to discuss them. This may be a good time to use **multivoting.** It is a way to select the most important or popular items from a list for discussion purposes. The steps are as follows:[104]

1. Generate a list of items and number each one.

2. Combine similar items if the group agrees they are the same. Renumber items if necessary.

3. Have each member pick one-third of the items she wishes to discuss. Members should write down the numbers of items they chose.

4. Tally all votes (e.g., "Who picked item number 1, 2, 3" and so on). A written ballot can be conducted if there is a need for secrecy.

5. Reduce the list by eliminating the items with the smallest number of votes. Three rules of thumb: if the group has 5 or fewer members, cross off items with only one to two votes. If the group has 6 to 15 members, cross off items with three or fewer votes. If the group has more than 15 members, eliminate items with four or fewer votes.

6. Repeat steps 3 to 6 after renumbering all remaining items. Continue using this procedure until only a few items remain for discussion. The other items can be tabled for future discussions.

Nominal Group Technique

Nominal group technique (NGT) is used for generating ideas as well as evaluating and selecting solutions. It is especially useful for new teams or highly controversial issues. The format is as follows:[105]

1. The group gets together to discuss a problem or issue.

2. Group members each silently write down their ideas.

3. Taking turns, each person offers one idea from his list; all ideas are recorded on a board. Ideas are not discussed at this point.

4. After all ideas are written down, the group discusses them by offering support or critiques.

5. Each person anonymously votes for her top three choices, which are weighted (1st choice = 3 points; 2nd choice = 2 points; 3rd choice = 1 point).

6. A group member adds the votes to determine the group's choice.

7. If desired, the group can discuss the top choices and take a second vote.

The NGT represents a more structured approach to group decision making. There are several advantages of this approach. For example, it allows the group to work together but does not restrict independent thinking. In addition, the nominal group technique allows a large number of ideas or alternatives to be reduced and evaluated relatively quickly. In addition, it avoids some of the problems inherent in interacting groups (e.g., dominating or overbearing members).[106]

Delphi Technique

The **Delphi technique** is a group process that anonymously generates ideas or judgments from physically dispersed group members.[107] Members' ideas are collected from survey questionnaires rather than face-to-face discussions. This is a useful technique when face-to-face discussions are not possible or when the group has trouble communicating (due to groupthink, dominating members, conflict, etc).[108] The procedure is as follows:

1. A member or leader identifies the issue to examine.

2. Someone develops a questionnaire to solicit ideas from members.

3. Members are each sent a questionnaire and return them completed to the developer.

4. The developer summarizes the responses and sends feedback to each member.

5. Each member is asked to review the feedback, prioritize the issues being considered, and return the survey.

The Delphi technique is similar to the NGT with the exception that it does not require actual physical interaction between group members. This makes the Delphi technique ideal for situations in which group members are unable to meet face-to-face but the decision warrants the input of others. For example, it might be ideal for virtual teams. It is also useful when poor communication or conflict may impair the group decision-making process, when there is the potential for groupthink to occur, and when group heterogeneity must be preserved. This method also prevents the undue influence of a dominating group member.[109]

As with the other methods of group decision making, the Delphi method has some problems. It is extremely time consuming and relatively expensive when compared with other group decision-making practices. As a result, it is not a viable option when a quick decision is necessary. Moreover, groups using this method may not generate the rich array of alternatives that interacting groups or nominal groups often generate. Nevertheless, the Delphi technique is well suited for novel or unusual problems since it encourages unrestricted sharing of the expertise of group members.[110]

Improving a Team's Decision-Making Process

Recent research has found that the group's interaction process can contribute to successful decision making. Unfortunately, not all groups are characterized by effective decision making. In fact, in many cases, groups often end up succumbing to conformity pressure, groupthink, and the inability to reach a decision in a timely manner. Research has found that groups with higher-quality decision making exhibit the following characteristics:[111]

• **Timely decisions.** More effective teams make decisions during critical "windows of opportunity."

• **Presence of vigilance.** Teams have a careful, thoughtful, and systematic discussion of the pros and cons of various alternatives. Decisions are precise and well thought out.

• **Frequent second-guessing.** Retrospective questioning or challenging of questionable information is encouraged.

• **Accurate information processing.** The rejection of faulty information and acceptance of valid information takes place.

• **Absence of improbable fantasy chains.** Interactions between group members are characterized by realistic scenarios.

• **Commitment by members.** Members are willing to support and implement the decision.

As compared to individual decision making, group decision making has the potential to result in more accurate, creative, and acceptable solutions. Group decision making also tends to be more time consuming, more influenced by conformity pressure, and more likely to result in decreased accountability. As members work in their teams, they may want to consider experimenting with the structured group decision-making methods suggested here.

COMMON PROBLEMS WITH TEAMS

All teams experience some difficulties when trying to work together and make decisions. The more successful teams are those whose members can identify their problems and work to resolve them. Some of the most common problems that occur when team members are trying to make decisions are described in **Exhibit 2.7**. Some strategies for addressing those problems are also offered.[112]

Understanding Conflict in Teams

One of the biggest problems with teams is conflict. The role of conflict in groups has been debated over the years. Traditionally, conflict was viewed as a negative event that should be completely avoided. It was believed that conflict was a sign of malfunctioning and a problem to be overcome by a group. More recently, however, the presence of conflict has been seen as an inevitable consequence of group interaction. The most current thinking about conflict is that a moderate amount of conflict can actually prevent a group from becoming apathetic, static, and unresponsive to needs for change.[113] In other words, some conflict may be functional and play a role in keeping a group self-critical, creative, and innovative. In general, when conflict is too low, the

Floundering

Definition: Teams may have trouble getting started on a project (i.e., they have false starts, directionless discussions). They may have difficulty moving on or completing a project. They may delay unnecessarily or postpone decisions. The team may be unclear or overwhelmed by its task. It may be that members are not yet comfortable with each other to engage in real decision making.

Recommendation: Have the group review its mission statement to make sure it is clear to everyone. Have each person discuss what is needed for the group to be able to move to the next step (e.g., data, knowledge, assurances, support, feelings). Reserve time at the meeting to discuss how the team is proceeding.

Overbearing Participants

Definition: This occurs when a team member exercises a disproportionate amount of influence on the group. Usually, the member has an authority position or some valued expertise which can be beneficial to the group. If, however, the person discourages discussions in an area or uses technical jargon to indicate that he/she is the only person capable of speaking on the topic, then this inhibits the team's meeting.

Recommendation: A team member should talk to the person outside of the team meeting to get their cooperation. Members should reinforce the idea that no topic is too sacred to discuss.

Dominating Participants

Definition: Some team members do a lot of the talking, whether they have expertise or not. As a result, they may inhibit the group from making progress. In addition, other members may feel inhibited from speaking up or may avoid attending the meetings.

Recommendation: Members can use the nominal group technique so that all members have equal participation. Members can practice gate keeping (e.g., "We've already heard from you Bill, let's hear from someone else").

Reluctant Participants

Definition: This occurs when one or more members in the team rarely speak. They may feel shy or they may enjoy listening and processing what the group is saying. Problems develop in the group when there are no built-in mechanisms that encourage the more introverted members to speak up and the more extroverted members to listen.

Recommendation: Members can act as gatekeepers and encourage participation from everyone (e.g., "Lynn, we haven't heard from you in a while, what do you think about this decision?"). Tasks could also be broken up into individual assignments so that all members would have to report on their findings.

Unquestioned Acceptance of Opinions as Facts

Definition: Sometimes a member expresses an opinion in such an assertive, confident tone that other members believe it is factual. This can lead the group to make faulty conclusions if no one is willing to question the person.

Recommendation: Ask the person for their facts or data (e.g., "Larry, what data do you have to back up your statement?"). The team should agree to use the scientific approach in their discussions.

Rush to Accomplishment

Definition: Most teams will have at least one member who is impatient or very action- or closure-oriented. He/she will want to make the decision quickly, and will push others (e.g., "Come on you guys, can't you make a decision, we already have all the information we need, what are you waiting for"). The person may display impatience through their verbal and nonverbal behaviors (e.g., toe or finger tapping). The problem is that the team may make a quick decision without considering all of the pertinent facts.

Recommendation: One person can use constructive feedback to confront the rusher to let him/her know how the behavior is affecting the group. The team should also reinforce its commitment to making sound, thorough decisions.

Attribution

Definition: One member may attribute the motives of another team member without checking for the facts. For example, Matt may say "Tasha is late because she doesn't care about the team." In fact, Tasha may be meeting with a supervisor to collect more details for the team.

Recommendation: Team members should avoid making attributions for others' behaviors. Instead, they should rely on actual data. They should also check out attributions made by one another ("Matt, what evidence do you have for saying that Tasha doesn't care about the team?").

Discounts and "Plops"

Definition: Sometimes, a member may make a comment in the group, and no one responds (i.e., the statement "plops"). Another possibility is that someone discounts or ridicules the person's idea ("Maria, where did you come up with that strange idea?") This can be a serious problem for teams since eventually the discounted member will quit offering ideas or may stop coming to meetings.

Recommendation: A team member could use constructive feedback to say something to a person who frequently discounts, puts down or ignores team members. In addition, during the meeting, it is critical that members support the discounted person ("Wait a minute everybody, Maria was offering her idea. Maria, I'd appreciate it if you could share your idea again."). Make sure all team members are trained in active listening skills and offer refresher training as needed.

Wanderlust: Digression and Tangents

Definition: The team may experience unfocused conversations or straying from the topic. One member tells a story that reminds another person of another story, and the meeting gets off track.

Recommendation: Post the group's written agenda with timetables. Have someone serve as a timekeeper to keep the group on track.

Feuding Members

Definition: Sometimes members fight with each other because of personality clashes or differences of opinions. Members may be pushed to take sides, which can be very disruptive for the team.

Recommendation: Use a facilitator to get the parties to discuss their arguments outside of the team's meeting. Encourage them to seek agreement or a compromise ("If Jie agrees to _____, then Taka will _____.").

Source: P. R. Scholtes, *The Team Handbook: How to Use Teams to Improve Quality* (Madison, WI: Joiner Associates, 1988): 6-36 to 6-45. Portions of these materials are copyrighted by Oriel Incorporated, formerly Joiner Associates, and are used here with permission. Further reproductions are prohibited without written consent of Oriel Incorporated 1-800-669-8326.

group may become apathetic. When conflict is too high, the group may be too stressed to be effective. Both of these cases illustrate **dysfunctional conflict.** When the level of conflict is moderate, however, the conflict is functional, and the group can reach its highest level of performance.

> The struggle of "me versus we" is no stranger to team members. You can expect occasional conflict between your selfish interests and what's best for the team. Sooner or later, everyone comes up against a situation where he or she must decide whether to "look out for old #1," or to make personal sacrifices for the greater good of the group. . . . For example, will you pass the ball or go for the shot yourself?. . . These choices get really tough at times. Sometimes, there's a lot at stake—prestige, power, or maybe money. . . . And how about when nobody on the team is watching? Will you take all the credit for success and dodge the blame for mistakes? Even if your teammates aren't watching, word sure gets around. People figure out in a hurry just how much you can be trusted to protect the team. If you "sell out" the group to your selfish interests, how can you expect your teammates to be there when you need them? Personal sacrifice is part of the price you pay for membership in the group.[114]

Dysfunctional Conflict in Teams

There are many different types of dysfunctional conflict in a team setting. Some of the more common forms of conflict are listed next.[115] Typically, conflicts arise due to differences among people in personalities, work styles, backgrounds, expectations, standards, work-related goals, communication styles, and performance problems (e.g., social loafing or free riders).

Forms of Dysfunctional Conflict

- **Personal conflict.** An individual member is experiencing his own personal conflict that may or may not be related to the team, yet his performance is suffering as a result of the conflict. For example, suppose Dan is in the middle of a breakup with his wife Alanna. The stress he feels in his personal life may bleed over into his team performance. Perhaps he spends a lot of time in team meetings sharing his grief with his teammates, or perhaps he has trouble getting his work done on time because he cannot sleep or concentrate. Dan's personal troubles may stress the team.

- **Conflict between two team members.** One common form of conflict found in

teams is due to personality clashes between team members. Suppose Jose and Jamal are constantly arguing, or else they are ignoring each other because they are angry with each other. The team may experience some splintering such that some members side with Jose and others side with Jamal. As a result, the team loses its esprit de corps. It becomes very difficult for the team to get its work done when members are fighting with one another.

- **Individual member conflict with the entire team.** An individual team member can experience conflict with the entire team or with several members. For example, perhaps Vijay feels isolated from the entire team. He believes that members do not value his input because when he makes suggestions, he feels they ignore his ideas. When he turns in written assignments, they never use his sections of the papers, or else they totally rewrite his parts. He has tried to "connect" with his teammates by hanging out with them, but they have very different likes and dislikes. The team suffers as a result.

- **Team conflict with one member.** The majority of the team experiences some conflict with one member. For instance, four of the five members of the team are trying to get rid of one person (Chaodong) because they believe she is not doing enough work. They may be distressed with her because they believe that she is not taking the team's work seriously. Maybe she turns in assignments late, does not show up for meetings, gets defensive when members critique her work, and storms out of meetings when things are not going her way. This conflict causes considerable stress for the team.

- **Conflict between two teams.** It is very common in organizations for conflict to exist between two teams. For example, a sales group and a production group may be arguing over timeliness of getting products to customers. When teams are competing for scarce resources, conflict between them can be very intense. For instance, suppose several teams are competing to win a competitive game. In the push to win, one team may sabotage the efforts of another team by not revealing critical information given to them by the game's administrator. Conflict between teams can be very destructive for an organization if the teams engage in unethical, illegal, or sabotaging activities.

- **Team conflict with one person outside the team.** The team as a whole may be experiencing conflict with an outsider. For example, team members may decide that they do not care for the attitudes and restrictions imposed by the attorney working in the organization's legal department. Maybe they think he has little credibility or expertise. So they decide to ignore the legal mandates. This could be very damaging for the firm.

Conflict Management Styles

It is important not only to understand the nature of conflict but also to understand how individuals in teams manage conflict. The manner in which individuals resolve conflict can have long-term implications for the success of the team. Individuals tend to handle conflict in patterned ways referred to as *styles*. There is no single best style, and each method of handling conflict has its strengths and limitations. Some of the more common methods for handling conflict include avoiding, dominating or forcing, obliging or accommodating, compromising, and integrating or collaborating.[116] The five styles vary in their degree of concern for others and their concern for self as depicted in **Exhibit 2.8.**

- The **avoiding strategy** involves low concern for self and for the other party. It consists of either passive withdrawal from the problem, active suppression of the issue, sidestepping or passing the buck. This style would be most beneficial if a

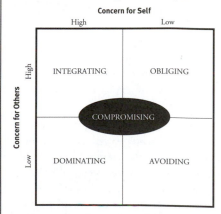

Exhibit 2.8: *Model of Conflict Management Styles*

Concern for Self

	High	Low
High	INTEGRATING	OBLIGING
	COMPROMISING	
Low	DOMINATING	AVOIDING

Concern for Others

Source: M. A. Rahim and N. R. Magner, "Confirmatory factor analysis of the styles of handling interpersonal conflict; First-order facto model and its invariance across groups," *Journal of Applied Psychology,* 80 (1995): 122–132. Copyright © 1995 by the American Psychological Association. Adapted with permission.

...rary separation would give the ...members time to "cool off." While ...s an effective *temporary* solution, team members will still have to address their issues at some point.

- The **dominating or forcing strategy** involves high concern for self and low concern for the other party.[117] It may mean the use of "I win, you lose" tactics. Specifically, an individual using this style forces her view on others and typically ignores the needs of the other party in an attempt to resolve the conflict. It is a useful approach, however, when a deadline is near or an unpopular solution must be implemented. One member might press his viewpoint in order to get the project completed. While an effective strategy occasionally, it should not be the sole method by which team members resolve conflict.

- The **obliging strategy** involves low concern for self and high concern for the other party. It may mean playing down any differences while emphasizing the similarities between the conflicting sides. An accommodating person neglects her own concerns to satisfy the concerns of the other party. One team member might accommodate or give in to the team's wishes, and this could be beneficial. If a person always accommodates, however, he might eventually build up some resentment toward the team. Thus, this approach might be good to use periodically, but it should not be the only method used by the team to manage conflict.

- The **compromising or accommodating strategy** is characterized by a moderate concern for self and others. It involves a give-and-take approach in which each party is required to give up something of value. Generally, good decisions can be made; however the *best* decision may not be reached if members quickly make a decision without explaining their underlying views and interests.

- Individuals using an **integrating or collaborating strategy** confront the issue and cooperatively attempt to identify the problem, generate and weigh alternative solutions, and select a solution. It is useful for situations that are complex and characterized by misunderstandings. It involves a high concern for self and for the other party. Openness, exchange of information, and examination of differences are emphasized. It is very time consuming since it involves trying to reach the best decision for all sides.[118]

It is important for teams to periodically assess the conflict management style each member uses. One instrument for doing this can be found in **Appendix 2.D**.

Resolving Dysfunctional Conflict in Teams

Resolving dysfunctional conflict in a timely and effective manner is the key to preventing further disruptions of the team's progress. To resolve the conflict, it is important to engage in the following practices:[119]

- **Acknowledge that the conflict exists.** All members should share a commitment to individually recognize conflict situations and jointly work toward solutions. If members adopt an avoidance approach and act as if nothing is wrong, the team will suffer since the underlying tension exists.

- **Review the nature of the conflict.** Examine the degree to which the conflict is getting in the way of reaching team goals. Reach some consensus on how serious the conflict is in terms of interfering with the attainment of the team's goals.

- **Collect information to understand all views.** While members may not agree with the different issues, they should be open minded enough to bring all views out into the open.

- **Attack the issues, not the people.** It is important to channel hostility and anger into more productive activities such as problem solving and action planning.

- **Develop an action plan.** Outline a plan to indicate what each person will do to resolve the conflict. Each person should understand the plan, agree to it, and sign off on it.

For the team to be successful in handling its own conflict, it should make sure that the process for handling the conflict is effective. Some important "do nots" when resolving conflict include these:[120]

- Do not force people to choose between sides and individuals.

- Sometimes a neutral third party may be helpful to resolve the team's conflict. Do not automatically go to the third party, however, without first trying to work it out yourself.

- Be careful not to sweep the conflict under the rug and hope it will go away on its own. Typically, the conflict will emerge later in a bigger way.

- Do not take turns determining who should win various conflicts. In other words, one side should not give in simply because it is its turn to lose the conflict,

knowing that it will "win" the next round. This strategy does not allow the team to make the best decisions.

- Do not allow hallway or parking lot commentary. Encourage team members to discuss all issues in the meeting. One problem occurs when members do not say everything in the meeting but talk afterwards with some team members to complain about the others. The team may continue to splinter as a result of these side conversations.

LEADERSHIP ISSUES WITH TEAMS

Effective team leaders realize that they neither know all the answers nor can succeed without the other members of the team.[121]

Some teams have a leader who has been either selected by the team or assigned by management. Many team leaders mistakenly believe that they have to direct and control all of the activities of their members for the team to be effective. On the contrary, the Chinese philosopher Lao-Tzu described team leadership in the following way:

> As for the best leaders, people do not notice their existence. The next best leaders—the people honor and praise. The next best—the people fear; and the last—the people hate. When the best leader's work is done, the people say, "We did it ourselves."[122]

Sometimes the most effective leadership in teams is called **self-leadership.** That is, it is the process whereby leaders lead others to lead themselves. The underlying assumption is the belief by leaders that their subordinates can effectively perform the critical leadership functions for themselves and that the most appropriate job of the leader is to "teach and encourage others to lead themselves."[123] To move a team to "self-leadership," a leader should engage in the following activities:[124]

- Encourage self-reinforcement by getting team members to praise each other for good work and good results.

- Encourage self-observation and evaluation by teaching team members to judge how well they are doing.

- Encourage self-expectation by enabling team members to expect high performance from themselves and the team.

- Encourage **goal setting** by having the team set its own performance goals and objectives.

- Encourage rehearsal by getting team members to think about and practice new tasks.

- Encourage self-criticism by encouraging team members to be critical of their own poor performance.

Responsibilities of Team Leaders

Leaders may actually wear three hats in team-based organizations, including administrator, coach, and adviser. The administrator helps the team meet its objectives through goal setting, problem solving, and other group processes. The coach focuses on helping the team develop as it matures. The adviser provides the team with the necessary technical support.[125] Essentially, leadership responsibilities change over time such that it is a shift away from control and toward coaching. For example, at Chrysler, leaders have assumed the role of coaches and champions of teams. Over time, the leaders have reevaluated themselves and their relationship to the teams that they sponsor.[126] What can a leader do for good team leadership? Some important attributes are described here:[127]

1. **Keep the purpose, goals, and approach relevant and meaningful.** Help the team members clarify and commit to their mission, goals, and approach. Allow them to discuss the goals so that they can become more strongly committed to final goals. Demonstrate patience and silence when the team members discuss specifics of the team's purpose and goals. Do not feel the need to force a solution before its time.

2. **Unleash energy and enthusiasm.** Create a motivating vision of a possible future for the team. Leaders should work to build the commitment and confidence of each individual as well as the team as a whole. Provide positive, constructive reinforcement while avoiding intimidation. Using intimidation tactics may cause members to avoid taking risks.

3. **Strengthen the mix and level of skills.** Leaders make sure that they have a team with all of the necessary technical, functional, problem-solving, decision-making, interpersonal, and teamwork skills. To get these skills, the leader encourages members to take advantage of opportunities for growth and development. They also continually stretch members by altering their roles and assignments.

4. **Understand the environment and needs of customers, and manage relationships with outsiders.** The leader should be a business analyzer and understand the environment surrounding the team. Leaders should work with customers to understand their desires and expectations of the products and services so that they can share this information with the team. The leader must also manage many of the team's contacts and relationships with outsiders.

5. **Remove obstacles.** Team leaders must be able to intercede for the team when outside obstacles get in the way. They should break down barriers that limit the ability of the team to innovate and improve its performance.

6. **Coach others, and create developmental opportunities for others.** The leader should coach others and develop them to their fullest potential through training, mentoring, and providing personal support. Leaders must be able to provide performance opportunities and challenges to members of the team and not keep all of the best assignments for themselves.

7. **Do real work.** Team leaders, like every other member, must contribute in whatever way the team needs. Leaders do not delegate all of the "grunt" assignments or nasty jobs to others. They should be prepared to pitch in as needed.

8. **Be a role model.** A leader should be a role model for effective interpersonal communication and teamwork and should set an example of the espoused values of the team.

Skills Required of Team Leaders

The team leader should possess a number of important **skills or attributes,** some of which are noted in **Exhibit 2.9.** For the team to be successful, the leader's attitudes and behaviors should be monitored. One tool that can be used to assess the effectiveness of the leader's role is found in **Appendix 2.E.**

SUMMARY

Teams have become increasingly more popular as a powerful way to organize work so that the needs of both employees and employer are better met. Employees gain more autonomy and participation in work that directly affects them. Employers report more effectiveness in terms of productivity, quality, and efficiency by using teams. It is expected that teams will continue to grow in popularity in the United States and abroad. For example, Volvo Corporation in Sweden

> **Exhibit 2.9:** *Skills Required of Team Leaders*
>
> Ability to learn
> Analysis
> Business planning
> Collaboration
> Communication (oral and written)
> Delegation of authority and responsibility
> Developing organizational talent
> Follow-up
> Individual leadership or influence
> Initiative
> Judgment
> Maximizing performance
> Meeting leadership
> Motivation to empower others
> Operational planning
> Organizational fit (compatibility of personal and organizational values)
> Rapport building
> Work standards
>
> Source: R. S. Wellins, W. C. Byham, and J. M. Wilson, *Empowered Teams: Creating Self-Directed Work Groups That Improve Quality, Productivity, and Participation* (San Francisco, CA: Jossey-Bass, 1991): 132–133.

was one of the first team experiences. It has been followed by Berkel in Germany, Ebthoner A.G. in Switzerland, NCR Corporation in Scotland, and Intel Corporation in Singapore.[128] The continued prevalence of teams necessitates an understanding of the factors related to team effectiveness.

As noted in this chapter, numerous variables are associated with the effectiveness of teams. Members should understand what is involved in getting started with teams, including creating a team mission, establishing goals, clarifying roles, and conducting initial team meetings. Members should also understand the characteristics required of team members and how issues of size, ability, and personality characteristics may impact on the team's processes and performance. Furthermore, members should be skilled in the strategies to use to improve the group's decisions as well as manage any dysfunctional conflict or leadership concerns. While the information presented in this chapter presents a good foundation for teambuilding, it will be important for a team to continually monitor and measure its progress. Tips for continuous improvement and becoming a high-performance team are provided in a later chapter.

1. B. Dumaine, "Who Needs a Boss?" *Fortune,* May 7, 1990, pp. 52–55, 58, 60.

2. A. M. Barratt, "Future Teams and Implications," in *Kaizen Strategies for Improving Team Performance,* ed. M. Colenso (London: Prentice-Hall, 2000): 202–203.

3. B. Dumaine, "The Trouble with Teams," *Fortune,* 1994: 86–90. See also R. A. Guzzo and G. P. Shea, "Group Performance and Intergroup Relations in Organizations," in *Handbook of Industrial and Organizational Psychology,* 2d ed., vol. 3, ed. M. D. Dunnette and L. M. Hough (Palo Alto, CA: Consulting Psychologists Press, 1992): 269–313; and E. E. Lawler, S. Mohrman, and G. Ledford, *Employee Involvement and Total Quality Management: Practices* and *Results in Fortune 1000 Companies* (San Francisco, CA: Jossey-Bass, 1992).

4. C. Parnell, "Teamwork: Not a New Idea, but It's Transforming the Workplace," *Executive Speeches* 12, no. 3 (1998): 35–40.

5. S. G. Cohen, G. E. Ledford, Jr., and G. M. Spreitzer, "A Predictive Model of Self-Managing Work Team Effectiveness," *Human Relations* 49 (1996): 643–676.

6. P. F. Drucker, "The Coming of the New Organization," *Harvard Business Review* (January–February 1998): 47.

7. L. D. Ketchum, "How Redesigned Plants Really Work," *National Productivity Review* 3 (1984): 246–254. See also R. S. Wellins, W. C. Byham, and J. M. Wilson, *Empowered Teams: Creating Self-Directed Work Groups That Improve Quality, Productivity, and Participation* (San Francisco, CA: Jossey-Bass, 1991).

8. B. S. Moskal, "The Wizards of Buick City," *Industry Week,* May 7, 1991, pp. 22–28. See also Wellins et al., *Empowered.*

9. G. L. Stewart, C. C. Manz, and H. P. Sims, Jr., *Team Work and Group Dynamics* (New York, NY: John Wiley & Sons, 1999). See also G. M. Bounds, G. H. Dobbins, and O. S. Fowler, *Management: A Total Quality Perspective* (Cincinnati, OH: South-Western College Publishing, 1995); and Wellins et al., *Empowered.*

10. Wellins et al., *Empowered.* See also Stewart et al., *Team Work.*

11. J. R. Katzenbach and D. K. Smith, *The Wisdom of Teams: Creating the High-Performance Organization* (Boston, MA: Harvard Business School Press, 1993).

12. Ibid., 105–107.

13. Ibid., 214.

14. Wellins et al., *Empowered,* 43.

15. E. Sundstrom, K. P. DeMeuse, and D. Futrell, "Work Teams," *American Psychologist* 45, 1990: 120–133.

16. Wellins et al., *Empowered.*

17. C. Fishman, "Whole Foods Is All Teams," *Fastcompany* 2 (1996): 103.

18. Wellins et al, *Empowered,* 238.

19. P. Froiland, "The Teaming of America," *Training Magazine,* October 1993, 58–59.

20. S. C. Gwynne, "The Right Stuff," *Time,* October 29, 1990, pp. 74–84. See also Wellins et al., *Empowered.*

21. Wellins et al., *Empowered.*

22. P. S. Goodman, R. Devadas, and T. L. G. Hughson, "Groups and Productivity: Analyzing the Effectiveness of Self-Managing Teams," in *Productivity in Organizations,* ed. J. P. Campbell and R. J. Campbell (San Francisco, CA: Jossey Bass, 1990): 295–327.

23. J. Hoerr, "Work Teams Can Rev Up Paper Pushers Too," *Business Week,* November 28, 1988, pp. 68–69; "The Cultural Revolution at A. O. Smith," *Business Week,* May 29, 1989, pp. 66–68; "The Payoff from Teamwork," *Business Week,* July 10, 1989, pp. 56–62; and J. Hoerr and M. A. Pollack, "Management Discovers the Human Side of Automation," *Business Week,* September 29, 1986, pp. 74–77.

24. R. E. Walton, "From Control to Commitment in the Workplace," *Harvard Business Review* (March–April, 1985): 77–84.

25. B. H. Proctor, "A Sociotechnical Work-Design System at Digital Enfield: Utilizing Untapped Resources," *National Productivity Review* (Summer 1986): 262–270.

26. Bounds et al., *Management.* See also T. B. Kirker, "Edy's Grand Ice Cream," *Industry Week,* October 18, 1993, 29–32.

27. R. Hersowitz, "The Virtual Team," in *Kaizen Strategies for Improving Team Performance,* ed. M. Colenso (London: Prentice-Hall, 2000).

28. Wellins et al., *Empowered.*

29. R. S. Wellins, J. M. Wilson, A. J. Katz, P. Laughlin, and C. R. Day, "Self-Directed Teams: A Study of Current Practice." Survey report (Pittsburgh, PA: Development Dimensions International, Association for Quality and Participation, and Industry Week, 1990).

30. "What Workers Want: The Gap in Management's Perception," *Behavioral Sciences Newsletter* (June 27, 1988): 1.

31. R. Howard, "Values Make the Company," *Harvard Business Review* (September–October, 1990): 132–145.

32. A. Bernstein, "The Difference Japanese Management Makes," *Business Week,* July 14, 1986, p. 48.

33. J. H. Sheridan, "America's Best Plants," *Industry Week,* October 1990, pp. 27–64.

34. M. Wesner and C. Egan, "Self-Managed Teams in Operator Services," Paper presented at the International Conference on Self-Managed Work Teams, Denton, TX, September 1990.

35. Katzenbach and Smith, 45.

36. C. O'Dell, "Team Play, Team Pay: New Ways of Keeping Score," *Across the Board* (November 1989): 38–45.

37. J. Hoerr, "Getting Man and Machine to Live Happily Ever After," *Business Week,* April 20, 1987, pp. 61–62.

38. B. Dumaine, "Who Needs a Boss?" *Fortune,* May 7, 1990, pp. 52–55, 58, 60.

39. M. Patinkin, "Gamble on Assembly Teams Pays Off," *Pittsburgh Press,* 1987, pp. B6–B7.

40. J. H. Sheridan, "America's Best Plants," *Industry Week,* October 1990, pp. 27–64.

41. Katzenbach and Smith, *Wisdom.*

42. C. Glickman, "Klear Knit Brings Back the Sewing Circle," *The Charlotte Observer,* March 19, 1990, pp. 1D, 14D.

43. Katzenbach and Smith, *Wisdom.*

44. Wellins et al., *Empowered.*

45. Katzenbach and Smith, *Wisdom.*

46. Ibid., 2.

47. C. Lee, "Beyond Teamwork," *Training,* June, 1990, pp. 25–32.

48. R. E. Walton, "Work Innovations at Topeka: After Six Years," *The Journal of Applied Behavioral Science* 13 no. 3 (1979): 422–433.

49. B. W. Tuckman, "Developmental Sequence in Small Groups," *Psychological Bulletin* 63 (1965): 384–389. See also C. J. G. Gersick, "Time and Transition in Work Teams: Toward a New Model of Group Development," *Academy of Management Journal* 31 (1988): 9–41; C. J. G. Gersick, "Making Time: Predictable Transitions in Task Groups," *Academy of Management Journal* 32 (1989): 274–309; and L. N. Jewell and J. Reitz, *Group Effectiveness in Organizations* (Glenview, IL: Scott Foresman, 1981).

50. P. R. Scholtes, *The Team Handbook: How to Use Teams to Improve Quality* (Madison, WI: Joiner Associates, 1988).

51. N. Foster, "Setting Up the Team: Preconditions for Success," in *Kaizen Strategies for Improving Team Performance,* ed. M. Colenso (London: Prentice-Hall, 2000).

52. S. P. Robbins, *Essentials of Organizational Behavior,* 3d ed. (Englewood Cliffs, NJ: Prentice Hall, 1992).

53. Scholtes, *Team Handbook.*

54. R. R. Blake, and J. S. Mouton, *The Managerial Grid III: The Key to Leadership Excellence,* 3d ed. (Houston, TX: Gulf Publishing Company, 1985).

55. D. C. Feldman, "The Development and Eenforcement of Group Norms," *Academy of Management Review* 9 (1984): 47–53. See also R. Kreitner and A. Kinicki, *Organizational Behavior,* 3d ed. (Homewood, IL: Irwin, 1995).

56. L. Thompson, *Making the Team: A Guide for Managers* (Upper Saddle River, NJ: Prentice-Hall, 2000).

57. B. W. Tuckman and M. Jensen, "Stages of Small-Group Development Revisited," *Group and Organization Studies* 2 (1977): 419–427.

58. G. M. Parker, "Cross-Functional Collaboration," *Training and Development Journal* 48, no. 10 (1994): 49–53.

59. D. D. Tippett and J. F. Peters, "Team Building and Project Management: How Are We Doing?" *Project Management Journal* 26, no, 4 (1995): 29–37.

60. R. Wageman Study: Critical F for Creating Superb Self-Managing Teams at Xerox," *Compensation & Benefits Review* 29, no. 5 (1997): 31–41.

61. Thompson, *Making*.

62. Scholtes, *Team Handbook*.

63. Ibid.

64. P. Pritchett, *The Team Member Handbook for Teamwork* (Dallas, TX: Pritchett & Associates, Inc., 1992).

65. Pritchett, 38.

66. D. Martin, *Teamthink: Using the Sports Connection to Develop, Motivate, and Manage a Winning Business Team* (New York: Penguin Books, 1993).

67. Bounds et al., *Management*.

68. Katzenbach and Smith, *Wisdom*.

69. S. Pope. "The Power of Guidelines, Structure, and Clear Goals," *Journal for Quality and Participation* 19, no. 7 (1996): 56–60.

70. K. Fisher, S. Rayner, and W. Belgard, *Tips for Teams: A Ready Reference for Solving Common Team Problems* (New York: McGraw-Hill, 1995).

71. Martin, *Teamthink*, 22.

72. Fisher et al., *Tips*.

73. Martin, *Teamthink*, 22.

74. Ibid.

75. Fisher et al., *Tips*.

76. K. D. Benne and P. Sheats, "Functional Roles of Group Members," *Journal of Social Issues* (Spring 1948): 41–49.

77. A. Zander, "The Value of Belonging to a Group in Japan," *Small Group Behavior* (February 1983): 7–8.

78. J. Champy, *Reengineering Management: The Mandate for New Leadership* (New York: Harper Collins Publishers, 1995): 118.

79. Pritchett, *The Team*.

80. B. Latane, K. Williams, and S. Harkins, "Many Hands Make Light the Work: The Causes and Consequences of Social Loafing," *Journal of Personality and Social Psychology* 37 (1979): 822–832.

81. Katzenbach and Smith, *Wisdom*.

82. P. Yetton, and P. Bottger, "The Relationships among Group Size, Member Ability, Social Decision Schemes, and Performance," *Organizational Behavior and Human Performance* (October 1983): 145–159.

83. L. L. Thompson, E. A. Mannix, and M. H. Bazerman, "Group Negotiation, Effects of Decision Rule, Agenda, and Aspiration," *Journal of Personality and Social Psychology* 54 (1988): 86–95.

84. B. Mullen, C. Symons, L. T. Hu, and E. Salas, "Group Size, Leadership Behavior, and Subordinate Satisfaction," *The Journal of General Psychology* (April 1989): 155–169.

85. M. Cini, R. L. Moreland, and J. M. Levine, "Group Staffing Levels and Responses to Prospective and New Members," *Journal of Personality and Social Psychology* 65 (1993): 723–734. See also Thompson, *Making*.

86. J. H. Davis, "Some Compelling Intuitions about Group Consensus Decisions, Theoretical and Empirical Research, and Interpersonal Aggregation Phenomena: Selected Examples, 1950–1990," *Organizational Behavior and Human Decision Processes* 52 (1992): 3–38.

87. Wellins et al., *Empowered*.

88. G. W. Hill, "Group versus Individual Performance: Are N=1 Heads Better Than One?" *Psychological Bulletin* 91 (1982): 517–539.

89. A. Tziner and D. Eden, "Effects of Crew Composition on Crew Performance: Does the Whole Equal S sum of Its Parts?" *Journal of Applied Psychology* 70 (1985): 85–93.

90. R. Saavedra, C. P. Earley, and L. Van Dyne, "Complex Interdependence in Task-Performing Groups," *Journal of Applied Psychology* 78 (1993): 61–72. See also Kreitner and Kinicki, *Organizational*.

91. Pritchett, *The Team*.

92. H. C. Triandis, R. Bontempo, M. J. Villareal, M. Asai, and N. Lucca, "Individualism and Collectivism: Cross-Cultural Perspectives on Self-Ingroup Relationships," *Journal of Personality and Social Psychology* 54 (1988): 323–338.

93. J. A. Wagner and M. K. Moch, "Individualism-Collectivism: Concept and Measure," *Group and Organization Studies* 11 (1986): 280–304. See also J. A. Wagner, "Studies of Individualism-Collectivism: Effects on Cooperation in Groups," *Academy of Management Journal* 38 (1995): 152–172.

94. L. T. Eby and G. H. Dobbins, "An Individual and Group Analysis of Preference for Working in Teams," Paper presented at the 10th annual meeting of the Society for Industrial and Organizational Psychology, Orlando, Florida, May 1995.

95. M. A. Campion, G. J. Medsker, and A. C. Higgs, "Relations between Work Group Characteristics and Effectiveness: Implications for Designing Effective Work Groups," *Personnel Psychology* 46 (1993): 823–850.

96. S. K. Hirsh, MBTI *Team Building Program* (Palo Alto, CA: Consulting Psychologists Press, 1992). See also S. K. Hirsh and J. M. Kummerow, *Introduction to Type in Organizations* 2d ed. (Palo Alto, CA: Consulting Psychologists Press, 1990); and O. Kroeger and J. M. Thuesen, *Type Talk at Work* (New York: Bantam Doubleday Dell Publishing, 1992).

97. Ibid.

98. M. H. McCaulley, "How Individual Differences Affect Health Care Teams," *Health Team News* 1, no. 8 (1975): 1–4.

99. L. L. Janis, *Groupthink*, 2d ed. (Boston, MA: Houghton Mifflin, 1982): 9.

100. Scholtes, *Team Handbook*. See also Fisher et al., *Tips*.

101. A. F. Osborn, Applied Imagination: Principles and Procedures of Creative Thinking, 3d ed. (New York, NY: Scribners, 1979).

102. Kreitner and Kinicki, *Organizational*.

103. Robbins, *Essentials*.

104. Scholtes, *Team Handbook*, 2–40.

105. A. L. Delbecq, A. H. Van de Ven, and D. H. Gustafson, *Group Techniques for Program Planning: A Guide to Nominal Group and Delphi Processes* (Glenview, IL: Scott, Foresman, 1975). See also Scholtes, *Team Handbook*.

106. Bounds et al., *Management*.

107. N. C. Dalkey, D. L. Rourke, R. Lewis, and D. Snyder, *Studies in the Quality of Life: Delphi and Decision Making* (Lexington, MA: Lexington Books: D.C. Heath & Co., 1972).

108. Kreitner & Kinicki, *Organizational*.

109. Robbins, *Essentials*.

110. Griffin, *Management*, 4th ed. (Princeton, NJ: Houghton Mifflin Company, 1993). See also Robbins, *Essentials*

111. Fisher et al., *Tips*.. See also R. Y. Hirokawa, "Why Informed Groups Make Faulty Decisions: An Investigation of Possible Interaction-Based Explanations," *Small Group Behavior* 18 (1987): 3–29.

112. Scholtes, *Team Handbook*, 6-36 to 6-45.

113. Robbins, *Essentials*.

114. Pritchett, *The Team*, 26.

115. Fisher et al., *Tips*.

116. M. A. Rahim and N. R. Magner, "Confirmatory Factor Analysis of the Styles of Handling Interpersonal Conflict: First-Order Factor Model and Its Invariance across Groups," *Journal of Applied Psychology* 80 (1995): 122–132.

117. Ibid.

118. Kreitner & Kinicki, *Organizational*.

119. Fisher et al., *Tips*.

120. Ibid.

121. Katzenbach and Smith, *Wisdom*, 86.

122. Ibid., 148.

123. C. C. Manz and H. P. Sims, "Leading Workers to Lead Themselves: The External Leadership of Self-Managing Teams. *Administrative Science Quarterly* 32 (1987): 106–128.

124. C. C. Manz and H. P. Sims, *Superleadership: Leading Others to Lead Themselves* (Englewood Cliffs, NJ: Prentice-Hall, 1989).

125. H. R. Jessup, "New Roles in Team Leadership," *Training and Development Journal* 44, no. 11 (1990): 79–83.

126. Bounds et al., *Management*.

127. Fisher et al., *Tips*. See also J. R. Katzenbach and D. K. Smith, *The Wisdom of Teams: Creating the High-Performance Organization*.

128. Wellins et al., *Empowered*.

ASSESSMENT OF TEAM BASICS

Instructions:

To determine how effectively your group functions as a team, each team member should respond to the following questions individually. After all team members have completed the instrument, compare your responses. Your answers should help you diagnose your team's strengths and problem areas. Based on your findings, you may want to make some modifications in the team's characteristics (e.g., size, skills, purpose, goals, working approach, accountability). Refer back to Figure 2-2 in the chapter for more details. Using the scale below, circle one response for each item.

SD	D	N	A	SA
Strongly Disagree	Disagree	Neither	Agree	Strongly Agree

Size

1. We can convene easily and frequently	SD	D	N	A	SA
2. We can communicate easily and frequently	SD	D	N	A	SA
3. Our discussions are open and interactive	SD	D	N	A	SA
4. Everyone understands the others' roles and skills	SD	D	N	A	SA
5. We need more people to achieve our goals	SD	D	N	A	SA
6. Subgroups are possible or necessary	SD	D	N	A	SA

Levels of Complementary Skills

7. All three categories of skills (technical/functional, problem solving, interpersonal) are either actually or potentially represented across team members	SD	D	N	A	SA
8. Each member has potential in all three categories to advance his/her skills to the level required	SD	D	N	A	SA
9. Some critical skill areas are missing on our team	SD	D	N	A	SA
10. Members are, individually and collectively, willing to spend the time to help themselves and others learn and develop skills	SD	D	N	A	SA
11. New skills can be introduced as needed	SD	D	N	A	SA

Meaningful Purpose

12. The team's purpose constitutes a broader, deeper aspiration than just near-term goals	SD	D	N	A	SA
13. We have a "team" purpose, as opposed to just one individual's purpose (e.g., the leader's)	SD	D	N	A	SA
14. All members understand and articulate the purpose the same way	SD	D	N	A	SA
15. Members define the purpose vigorously in discussion with outsiders	SD	D	N	A	SA
16. Members frequently refer to the purpose and explore its implications	SD	D	N	A	SA
17. Our purpose contains themes that are meaningful	SD	D	N	A	SA
18. We feel our purpose is important	SD	D	N	A	SA

Specific Goals

19. We have "team," rather than individuals' goals	SD	D	N	A	SA
20. Our goals are clear, simple, and measurable	SD	D	N	A	SA
21. Our goals are realistic as well as ambitious	SD	D	N	A	SA
22. Our goals allow for small wins along the way	SD	D	N	A	SA
23. Our goals call for a concrete set of team products	SD	D	N	A	SA
24. The relative importance and priority of our goals are clear to all members	SD	D	N	A	SA

25. All members agree with the goals, their relative importance, and the way in which their achievement will be measured   SD   D   N   A   SA

26. All members articulate the goals in the same way   SD   D   N   A   SA

Clear Working Approach

27. Our approach is concrete, clear, and really understood and agreed to by everybody   SD   D   N   A   SA

28. Our approach will result in achievement of the objectives   SD   D   N   A   SA

29. Our approach will capitalize on and enhance the skills of all members   SD   D   N   A   SA

30. Our approach requires all members to contribute similar amounts of real work   SD   D   N   A   SA

31. Our approach provides for open interaction, fact-based problem solving, and results-based evaluation   SD   D   N   A   SA

32. Our approach allows modifications over time   SD   D   N   A   SA

33. Fresh input and perspectives are sought and added   SD   D   N   A   SA

Sense of Mutual Accountability

34. Members are individually and jointly accountable for the team's goals, approach, and products   SD   D   N   A   SA

35. Progress can be measured against specific goals   SD   D   N   A   SA

36. Members feel responsible for all measures   SD   D   N   A   SA

37. Members are clear on what they are individually vs. jointly responsible for   SD   D   N   A   SA

Source: Adapted and reprinted by permission of Harvard Business School Press. From *The Wisdom of Teams: Creating the Performance-Performance Organization* by J.R. Katzenbach and D.K. Smith. Boston, MA 1993, pp. 62–64. Copyright © 1993 by McKinsey & Company, Inc., all rights reserved.

ROLES PERFORMED BY TEAM MEMBERS

Instructions:

Team members can serve a number of different roles on a team. Some of these roles are called **task roles** and are helpful in facilitating group problem solving and decision making. Other roles are referred to as **group building** or **maintenance roles** and include all of the team member behaviors needed to facilitate the development of a group into a team. For your group, you may want to have a discussion regarding who plays which roles on the team. To do this, read each role description. In the space provided, indicate who on your team fulfills that role. Note that several people can play the same role on a team, and that each person can play several roles on your team. After all team members have completed the assessment, share your findings with each other in a team discussion.

Initiator: helps the group get started with the task, suggests new approaches to solving problems, keeps the team supplied with new ideas and fresh insights

Team members serving this role:

Information Giver: offers his/her own interpretation of facts stated by others, provides the team with information relevant to the problem as it is needed in an understandable and productive way

Team members serving this role:

Information Seeker: asks for facts, obtains information from members during discussions, asks questions of individuals to solicit input, increases the participation of team members

Team members serving this role:

Evaluator: focuses on the quality of the team's outputs by comparing them to both formal and informal standards, offers judgments about the quality of the team's work

Team members serving this role:

Challenger: assumes the role of devil's advocate, examines ideas critically and questions the assumptions and data that led to the idea, asks members to explain their reasoning, suggests that different alternatives be considered, challenges the team to stimulate higher-quality thinking

Team members serving this role:

Coordinator: connects ideas and inputs from others, clarifies how ideas are related to the previous discussion, creates links, helps the team to see where it has been and where it is going

Team members serving this role:

Completer: keeps track of which tasks have and have not been finished, takes responsibility for making sure that all necessary tasks are completed, records unfinished business and reminds the team about these tasks

Team members serving this role:

Encourager: recognizes the contributions of others; positively reinforces members through praise and support; creates a friendly, open team environment; does not reinforce disruptive behaviors

Team members serving this role:

Gatekeeper: is sensitive to the lack of contribution from some team members; keeps the communication flowing by actively seeking input of all members, especially silent members; invites members to express their opinions

Team members serving this role:

Compromiser: recognizes that prolonged disagreement can be destructive to the team; helps the team look for tradeoffs, splitting the difference, or other compromise strategies; looks for strategies to resolve differences in a fair and reasonable way; attempts to appease disagreeing members; works toward a compromise when appropriate

Team members serving this role:

Harmonizer: is sensitive to the team's tensions and pressure (ill feelings); recognizes the need to keep communication channels open; attempts to reduce conflicts by telling jokes, stories, or commenting on the tension at appropriate times; may help members smooth over their differences in the interest of creating a pleasant working environment

Team members serving this role:

Energizer: senses a drop in the group's energy, ensures that the enthusiasm and energy of the team does not fall below acceptable levels, tries to pump the group up when members are frustrated or tired, reminds the team of its mission, praises members for progress

Team members serving this role:

Processor: brings up issues the team needs to confront and work through, feeds back his or her own interpretation of below-the-surface feelings, is an empathetic person who is sensitive to member feelings (positive and negative), encourages members to express their feelings and bring them out in the open

Team members serving this role:

Standard Setter: evaluates the team's processes and relationships by comparing them to the standards set by the team for behaviors or productivity, points out when members do not conform to their roles, offers an evaluation of the group's functioning as a way of raising the standards for the group's process

Team members serving this role:

Source: R. Glaser, *Team Communication Inventory* (King of Prussia, PA: Organization Design and Development, Inc., 1993).

ATTITUDES ABOUT TEAMWORK

Instructions:

Using the scale below, circle one response for each item. Afterwards, discuss any similarities and differences in your ratings with your teammates.

SD	D	N	A	SA
Strongly Disagree	Disagree	Neither	Agree	Strongly Agree

Values Attached to Working Alone

1. I prefer to work with others in a group rather than work alone.   SD   D   N   A   SA

2. I would rather do a job where I can work alone than one where I have to work with others in a group.   SD   D   N   A   SA

3. Working with a group is better than working alone.   SD   D   N   A   SA

Personal Independence & Self-Reliance

4. Only those who depend on themselves get ahead in life.   SD   D   N   A   SA

5. To be superior, a person must stand alone.   SD   D   N   A   SA

6. If you want something done right, you've got to do it yourself.   SD   D   N   A   SA

7. What happens to me is my own doing.   SD   D   N   A   SA

8. In the long run, the only person you can count on is yourself.   SD   D   N   A   SA

Norms About Group vs. Personal Needs

9. People should be made aware that, if they are going to be part of a group, then they sometimes will have to do things they don't want to do.   SD   D   N   A   SA

10. People who belong to a group should realize that they're not always going to get what they want.   SD   D   N   A   SA

11. People in a group should realize that they sometimes are going to have to make sacrifices for the sake of the group as a whole.   SD   D   N   A   SA

12. People in a group should be willing to make sacrifices for the sake of the group's well-being.   SD   D   N   A   SA

Source: J. A. Wagner, "Studies of Individualism-Collectivism: Effects on Cooperation in Groups," *Academy of Management Journal* 38 (1995): 152–172. Copyright © 1995 by ACAD of Mgmt. Reproduced with permission of ACAD of Mgmt in the format Textbook via Copyright Clearance Center.

CONFLICT MANAGEMENT STYLE

Instructions:

Think about your behavior on your team when your team is in conflict. Using the scale below, rate each of the following in the space on the left of each item. Be as honest as possible. Using the scoring key, add up your scores for each of the subscales. These indicate the conflict management approaches you use with your team. Compare the responses for everyone on the team in a team discussion.

When my team experiences some conflict, I . . .

1	2	3	4	5
Almost Never	Rarely	Occasionally	Frequently	Almost Always

1. _____ Try to investigate an issue with my team members to find a solution acceptable to us.
2. _____ Generally try to satisfy the needs of my team members.
3. _____ Attempt to avoid.
4. _____ Try to integrate my ideas with those of my team members to come up with a decision jointly.
5. _____ Try to work with my team members to find solutions to a problem that satisfy our expectations.
6. _____ Avoid open discussions of my differences with my team members.
7. _____ Try to find a middle course to resolve an impasse.
8. _____ Use my influence to get my ideas accepted.
9. _____ Use my authority to make a decision in my favor.
10. _____ Accommodate to the wishes of my teammates.
11. _____ Give in to the wishes of my teammates.
12. _____ Exchange accurate information with my teammates to solve a problem together.
13. _____ Allow concessions to my teammates.
14. _____ Propose a middle ground for breaking deadlocks.
15. _____ Negotiate with my teammates so that a compromise can be reached.
16. _____ Try to stay away from disagreement with my teammates.
17. _____ Avoid an encounter with my teammates.
18. _____ Use my expertise to make a decision in my favor.
19. _____ Go along with the suggestions of my teammates.
20. _____ Use "give and take" so that a compromise can be made.
21. _____ Am generally firm in pursuing my side of an issue.
22. _____ Try to bring all our concerns out in the open so that the issues can be resolved in the best possible way.
23. _____ Collaborate with my teammates to come up with decisions acceptable to us.
24. _____ Try to satisfy the expectations of my teammates.
25. _____ Use my power to win in a competitive situation.
26. _____ Try to keep my disagreement with my teammates to myself in order to avoid hard feelings.
27. _____ Try to avoid unpleasant exchanges with my teammates.
28. _____ Try to work with my teammates for a proper understanding of a problem.

Scoring:

Add up your scores for each of the following subscales, and then divide as noted. You should end up with a score for each subscale ranging from 1 to 5. List the highest score as your primary strategy and the second highest score as your secondary strategy. These are the strategies you are most likely to engage in to address conflict in your team. Compare your results with those of your teammates.

grating	items 1 + 4 + 5 + 12 + 22 + 23 + 28 =	_____ / 7 =	_____
oliging	items 2 + 10 + 11 + 13 + 19 + 24 =	_____ / 6 =	_____
Dominating	items 8 + 9 + 18 + 21 + 25 =	_____ /5 =	_____
Avoiding	items 3 + 6 + 16 + 17 + 26 + 27 =	_____ / 6 =	_____
Compromising	items 7 + 14 + 15 + 20 =	_____ / 4 =	_____

Primary conflict management strategy: _____

Secondary conflict management strategy: _____

Source: The Rahim Organizational Conflict Inventory-II. M. A. Rahim and N. R. Magner, "Confirmatory Factor Analysis of the Styles of Handling Interpersonal Conflict: First-Order Factor Model and Its Invariance Across Groups," *Journal of Applied Psychology* 80 (1995): 122–132. Copyright © 1995 by the American Psychological Association. Adapted with permission.

TEAM LEADER ASSESSMENT

Instructions:

As a team, you may wish to examine the effectiveness of your leader's role in working with your team. After everyone has completed the instrument, compare your responses. Based on your findings, you may want to make some modifications in the leader's role with the team. Using the scale below, circle one response for each item.

SD	D	N	A	SA
Strongly Disagree	Disagree	Neither	Agree	Strongly Agree

Approach

	SD	D	N	A	SA
1. The leader allows the team to make important decisions.	SD	D	N	A	SA
2. The leader allows the team to make work assignments.	SD	D	N	A	SA
3. The leader encourages the team to make peer evaluations.	SD	D	N	A	SA
4. The leader encourages team accountability.	SD	D	N	A	SA
5. The leader does "real work" for the team.	SD	D	N	A	SA

Balance

	SD	D	N	A	SA
6. The leader strives for the right balance between action and patience within the team.	SD	D	N	A	SA
7. The leader promotes constructive conflict and resolution.	SD	D	N	A	SA
8. The leader constantly challenges the team to sharpen its common purpose, goals, and approach.	SD	D	N	A	SA
9. The leader inspires trust in people by acting in concert with the team's purpose.	SD	D	N	A	SA
10. The leader creates opportunities for others.	SD	D	N	A	SA

Purpose and Performance

	SD	D	N	A	SA
11. The leader articulates a team purpose and acts to promote and share responsibility for it.	SD	D	N	A	SA
12. The leader identifies and acts to remove barriers to team performance.	SD	D	N	A	SA
13. The leader tries to remove any obstacles that may cause problems for the team.	SD	D	N	A	SA

Source: Adapted and reprinted by permission of Harvard Business School Press. From *The Wisdom of Teams: Creating the Performance-Performance Organization* by J.R. Katzenbach and D.K. Smith. Boston, MA 1993, pp. 146–147. Copyright © 1993 by McKinsey & Company, Inc., all rights reserved.

PART 2

Getting Started in Business

Chapter 3

Dominique Garval
Reims Management School

Business Strategy
Formulation and Implementation

"All things are ready, if our minds be so."

William Shakespeare, *Henry V*

ORIGINS AND NECESSITY OF BUSINESS STRATEGY

From the Art of War to Business Strategy

As a word and as a concept, *strategy* can be traced back to ancient Greece. Five centuries before Jesus Christ, the Athenians used to elect a council of 10 "strategists" ($\sigma\tau\rho\alpha\tau\eta\gamma o\xi$ from $\sigma\tau\rho\alpha\tau o\xi$ "army" and $\alpha\gamma\eta\iota\upsilon$ "to conduct"), who were in charge of protecting the city through diplomacy and, if needed, of ensuring its defense through the use of armed forces. In many cities of Greece, as well as in other civilizations around the Mediterranean Sea including Byzantium and Egypt, the word "strategy" subsequently became synonymous with leading an army.[1] Although always associated with the conduct of war, the meaning of the word has very much evolved with time, and it is now used in many different ways and contexts such as national policy, diplomacy, military operations, sports, games, and business.

According to Desreumaux,[2] "strategy" was first used in a business context in 1947 by Von Neumann and Morgenstern[3] in their game theory. Since then, the concept has been the subject of much research and debate by academics, management consultants, and practitioners. In 1998, Mintzberg, Ahlstrand, and Lampel[4] listed and described not less than 10 different schools of strategic thought developed from 1965 on (see **Exhibit 3.1**). They concluded that every strategy process has to combine various aspects of the different schools.

From Business Administration to Business Strategy

Why did strategy all of a sudden become the focus of attention in business situations? The answer is fairly obvious. In all situations said to be of a strategic nature,

---

Exhibit 3.1: *Different Schools of Strategy Formation*

Three prescriptive schools
1. Design school: strategy formation as a process of conception
2. Planning school: strategy formation as a formal process
3. Positioning school: strategy formation as an analytical process

Seven descriptive schools
1. Entrepreneurial school: strategy formation as a visionary process
2. Cognitive school: strategy formation as a mental process
3. Learning school: strategy formation as an emergent process
4. Power school: strategy formation as a process of negotiation
5. Cultural school: strategy formation as a collective process
6. Environmental school: strategy formation as a reactive process
7. Configuration school: strategy formation as a process of transformation

Source: For a more complete discussion, see H. Mintzberg, B. Ahlstrand, and J. Lampel, *Strategy Safari—A Guided Tour through the Wilds of Strategic Management* (New York: Free Press, 1998).

BEST-USE CORRELATIONS

Without a strategy, your team is doomed to opportunistic and reactive decision making, with scant chance of succeeding in *Marketplace*. So, where to start? With the guidance provided in Chapter 3.

Three Simple Questions

You must find good, plausible answers to (1) Where are we? (2) Where do we want to go? and (3) How do we get there?

At the beginning of simulation play, your answers may be relatively naive and tentative, but as your experience builds, so too will the sophistication of your responses. By the time your team prepares its business plan in Q5, your understanding of the market and your firm's capabilities will be immense. Your answers should be just as advanced.

Mental Discipline

Teams experience a regular course of strenuous training in strategic planning as the simulation continually drives teams through all steps in the planning process. Teams that apply the objective-strategy-tactic regimen best achieve a crucial advantage—an integrated mental picture of their firm.

Implementation Is Strategy in Motion

Marketplace is a highly tactical exercise. Products must be designed, produced, priced, distributed, promoted, and sold; money must be collected and expended; information must be assembled and distributed. Chapter 3 proposes a model that enhances teams' abilities to translate strategy into specific actions.

The Readiness Is All

In *Marketplace,* the more you think in strategic terms, the better your state of readiness; the better your state of readiness, the better your position to counter threats and to take advantage of arising opportunities.

there is a constant—competition. Politicians and diplomats, generals, athletes, and managers must think in strategic terms simply because they live, think, and act under the competitive pressures exerted by other countries, armies, contenders, or businesses. In order to be successful, they are left with only one option, which is to be better than their adversaries. And this is where the essence of strategy lies: *strategy is all about being better than other players in competitive situations, where simply knowing the tools of the trade to get things done is not sufficient any more.* In environments where competition exists, an approach is required which takes fully into account the competitive dynamics of the situation. This is where the mental discipline of strategy becomes critical. Let's see how strategy has applied to business during the past decades.

Starting in the 1970s, factors such as market evolution, globalization of trade, technological change, management sophistication, and industry deregulation have caused the intensity of business competition to increase dramatically worldwide. Kenichi Ohmae's[5] strategic triangle illustrates the resulting transition from the classical business administration approach to the newer strategic management approach to running a business (see **Exhibit 3.2**).

Thirty to forty years ago, and in situations of lower competition levels, a manager's main concern was to *administer* (i.e., doing *well* in administering the operations of the firm to serve markets). Back then, most business schools were named schools of business administration. Nowadays, and in situations of much higher competitive intensity, a manager's essential responsibility is to *manage strategically* (i.e., doing *better* than competitors in serving markets). As a consequence, most business topics, even in schools of business administration, now revolve around strategy formulation and implementation at various levels of the organization as well as in various management disciplines.

In a business environment, the fact that strategy actually stems from competition is even more striking than in other domains, because we have all witnessed and are still witnessing the above change of paradigm as competition has increased over the last 40 years.

Complexity and Turbulence

Not only is today's business world becoming more competitive, but also it is becoming more complex, more unstable, and therefore more unpredictable. The markets evolve very quickly. So do the competitive dynamics. Moreover, the general environment of the firm also keeps changing at an ever-increasing pace, and its impact on the firm's posture and profitability may in some instances be tremendous. Under this new set of conditions, applying the mental discipline of strategy becomes even more difficult, more time consuming, more intellectually demanding, but also more necessary. These ever-increasing levels of complexity and turbulence lead firms to a permanent quest for better ways to proactively adapt and compete. As an illustration, **Exhibit 3.3** lists some of the strategic concerns shared by a group of executives in the management of their firms.

This chapter is about strategy formulation and implementation. Its primary

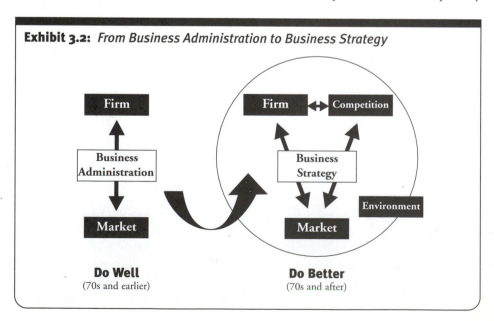

Exhibit 3.2: *From Business Administration to Business Strategy*

Firm → Business Administration → Market

Do Well
(70s and earlier)

Firm ↔ Competition → Business Strategy → Market / Environment

Do Better
(70s and after)

Exhibit 3.3: *Strategic Challenges*

- What bases exist for new competitive advantage?
- How do you position your company to be a permanent industry revolutionary?
- How many products do you buy from companies that did not exist a generation ago?
- There never has been a better time to be an aggressive newcomer.
- Never has life been more dangerous for complacent incumbents.
- Protective barriers are breaking down.
- Competitive positions can be overturned overnight.
- From competition between products or services to competition between business models.
- Strategy life cycles become shorter.
- Companies have to reinvent themselves continually.
- The biggest risk is not inefficiency, but irrelevancy.
- Merger and acquisitions happen because of a shortage of ideas for wealth creation.
- Sustaining success is more and more difficult.
- When successful, do you know what to do next?
- Change is not linear any more.
- If you miss a trend, you may not catch up.
- Strategic metamorphosis: From "build to last" to "build to change."
- From "We try harder" to "We try different."
- Ultimate futility of competing in the old ways.
- You don't find new ideas within your industry.
- Top management is trained to kill innovative ideas because there are no data to evaluate.
- The challenge is not to imitate, but to invent something new.
- Most of success has come from changing the rules of the game.
- Rule makers and rule takers are obsessed by organizational issues.
- A good obsession is the architecture of industry transformation.
- Today's innovator may be tomorrow's straightjacket.
- Most companies are the last bastion of Stalinism.
- Plurality of voices in developing strategy.
- Worry about lenses through which people look at their industry.
- The future is created by heretics, not by prophets.
- Breaking industry orthodoxy.
- 90 percent of useful learning comes from outside the industry.
- We have to reinvent the management process.
- How do you make innovation and wealth creation into a deeply embedded characteristic of the organization?
- Three markets in Silicon Valley: ideas, talent, and capital.
- Change never starts at the top.
- Do you understand how to create activists in your company?
- Employees have brains: Use them and give them a share of say in the future of the corporation.

Source: After G. Hamel, "Creating the Future," 1998 Stanford Executive Briefing.

objective is to propose a model of action to achieve objectives in complex organizations that operate in a competitive and changing environment. At the end of the chapter, a template for strategy formulation will be proposed.

STRATEGY FORMULATION
Concept of Strategy

The concept of strategy has now been a focus of attention in companies, universities, and consulting firms for years, and the definitions of strategy have proliferated without any consensus on a common one. To eliminate this ambiguity, we might turn to a hyperabstraction of the concept, such as the one proposed by General Beaufre.[6] He argues that strategy is a dialectic of the forces that are present, or better, a dialectic of the wills exerting forces. From that standpoint, the essence of strategy lies in the abstract game that emerges from the opposition of wills.

But business schools have not sought to boil all of the perspectives on strategy down to a single definition. On the contrary, business authors seem to have adopted the opposite view, which is to accept a multiplicity of definitions as a necessity to fully comprehend and exploit the richness of the concept. For example, Mintzberg, Ahlstrand, and Lampel[7] argue that strategy requires a number of definitions, five in particular, which they call the five P's:

1. Strategy is a Plan.
2. Strategy is a Pattern.
3. Strategy is a Position.
4. Strategy is a Perspective.
5. Strategy is a Ploy.

Our objective is to propose a definition that allows immediate applicability in a business context. Thus, we will use De Smit's[8] definition, which translates business strategy into a series of goals to be achieved. Taking into consideration the internal and external environments in which an organization operates, strategy is:

1. The development of a clear understanding of the fundamental ends of the organization.
2. The design and implementation of a system of actions and resources to bring about those ends in the shortest possible time at the lowest possible cost.
3. The focusing of the organization on the activities that are essential to the achievement of those ends and the disposal of the activities that are not.
4. The continuous adaptation of both means and ends to account for change in the environment and experience gained from past actions.

Key Ingredients of Strategy

In practice, formulating strategy is similar to charting the course of a ship on an ocean map. It essentially consists of finding a good answer to each of three questions:

1. Where are we?
2. Where do we want to go?
3. How do we get there?

Taking the analogy further, strategy formulation and execution are actually quite like participating in an ocean race. From this simple image, the key ingredients of strategy can easily be identified as shown in **Exhibit 3.4**, where:

1. The final destination of the race corresponds to the setting of objectives.
2. The departure point (in terms of location, ship and equipment preparation, crew's experience and morale, race rules, sea and weather conditions, etc.) is

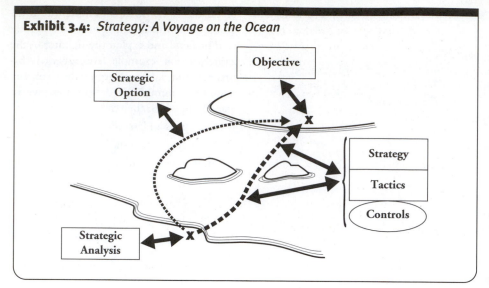

Exhibit 3.4: *Strategy: A Voyage on the Ocean*

defined in terms of the conclusions of a strategic analysis.

3. The actual course charting, sailing, and navigation correspond to strategy formulation, tactics, and controls.

4. Alternative routes are strategic options.

Having these strategic components in mind, we can now focus our attention on how to organize them in a clear and convenient multistep process.

Strategy Process

Someone exercising responsibilities in a competitive environment will invariably declare that strategy is formulated according to a very well-defined format, which in essence does not vary with country, culture, time, or context. This format has been termed Objectives—Strategies—Tactics (OST) and is depicted in **Exhibit 3.5**. P. E. Haggerty,[9] former president of Texas Instruments, institutionalized the OST system at TI, arguing that it actually provides management with a mechanism for identifying, selecting, and pursuing the strategies and tactics that are necessary to attain the objectives sought.

In essence, the OST model is simply the formalization of the key questions to be addressed by a management team in order to implement a thoughtful solution to a problem:

1. Which problem is to be solved? (**O**bjectives)

2. What is the relevant information? (Environmental analysis of the problem) (**S**trategic Analysis)

3. Which of all our available resources do we allocate to this particular problem? (**S**trategic Plan)

4. What are the options? (**S**trategic Plan)

5. Which option should we choose and for which reasons? (**S**trategic Plan)

6. How should we implement the chosen solution? (**T**actical Plans)

7. Implementation of chosen solution including controls. (**T**actical Execution)

Note that, although the OST model seems to imply a linear and sequential approach, that is certainly not the case in reality. A more accurate representation would probably necessitate drawing all kinds of feedback loops. For example, the results of the strategic analysis may lead to the redefinition of the problem to be solved (of the objectives), or lessons drawn at the tactical level may lead to a more accurate strategic analysis or a change of strategy. We will circumvent this difficulty by using two-way arrows in the model. Note that these arrows not only represent logical relationships but also symbolize flows of information.

Another point to be kept in mind is that strategy formulation is a convergent as well as dynamic process. The process is convergent because it may take several iterations circling the various feedback loops of the model before a consistent, integrated, and optimized set of OST is eventually formulated and deemed satisfactory. The process is dynamic in that this OST sequence constantly needs to be adjusted to hit targets, respond to changes in the environment, or take advantage of experience gained.

Objectives, Strategy, and Tactics

It is important to clarify the distinctions among objectives, strategy, and tactics:

1. **Objectives are results to be attained on or before a certain date.** The ultimate objectives of a firm or business entity are defined relative to its stakeholders, and in most instances they will include measures of profit and/or growth and/or cash. These ultimate objectives will then be broken down into chains of coherent subobjectives at different levels and in different functional specialties, all of them contributing to achieving the business's ultimate objectives.

Note that the three objectives of profit, growth, and cash are usually incompatible in the short term. As an illustration, it is obviously impossible for a firm to maximize profits when it is investing for growth. Thus, the formulation of objectives is normally expressed in terms of a realistic trade-off, such as a certain level of growth at a certain level of profit. Long-term, the three types of goals become indeed compatible, and they all work together to create shareholders' value.

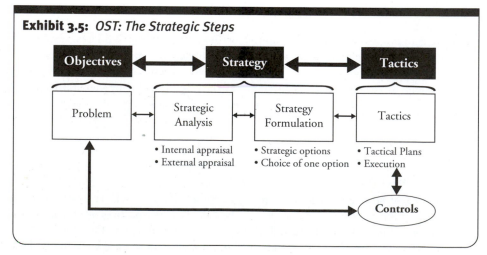

Exhibit 3.5: *OST: The Strategic Steps*

Exhibit 3.6: *Strategy Formulation OST: The Strategic Steps*

- Objective:
  To get from Copenhagen to Helsingborg as soon as possible and as cheaply as possible
- Strategic Analysis:
  Departure point/Prices/Weather conditions/Sea conditions/Traffic conditions/Departure times/Duration of journey . . .
- Strategic Options:
  Bus? Car? Helicopter shuttle? Boat?. . .
- Strategy:
  Take the bus
- Tactics:
  Choose departure time/Prepare luggage and sandwiches/Buy ticket/Board the bus/Choose a seat/Fasten seat belt . . . .

---

2. **A strategy is a set of carefully selected and integrated business priorities (strategic thrusts) to achieve objectives.** For example, a company that has an objective of growth might choose geographic expansion as one of its key strategic thrusts.

Very often, objectives and strategies are not clearly distinguished in people's minds. This is so because the strategies at a particular level are the objectives of the subordinate level. In the preceding example, geographic expansion becomes the objective of the firm's marketing department. It is therefore important to remember that the status (objective or strategy) of a particular business priority is in fact level dependent.

An additional difficulty originates from the fact that, depending upon the context in which it is being used, the meaning of the word *strategy* may include different steps of the strategic process:

Strategy = Strategic thrusts (above definition), but also

Strategy = S = Strategic analysis + Strategic options + Choice of one option + Resulting strategic thrusts

or even

Strategy = O + S + T = Objectives + Strategic analysis + Strategic options + Choice of one option + Resulting strategic thrusts + Tactical plans + Execution + Controls

3. **Tactics are the actual actions and operations that are necessary to execute strategies.** Tactics necessarily flow from the strategy as a set of carefully planned and interconnected actions.

People also get confused between strategies and tactics. To put it bluntly, "strategy" means thinking with a long-term perspective and for large amplitude movements, whereas "tactics" means acting usually with a shorter-term perspective and for smaller amplitude movements. Taking again the preceding example, the resulting strategy for the marketing department would entail the selection of target countries for expansion, and the tactics would include the opening of new offices, the recruitment and training of sales personnel and agents, the translation of brochures and documents into foreign languages, and so forth.

Exhibit 3.6 illustrates these definitions in a day-to-day life example. Objectives, strategy, and tactics are obviously logically interlinked. They flow naturally from each other, and their formulation must obey two principles: *coherence* and *optimization*. A first planning *principle of coherence* must be adhered to:

1. Coherence among objectives-strategy-tactics, also called *integration*.
2. Coherence between the objectives stated, between the strategic thrusts chosen, and between the tactical actions carried out, also called *coordination*.
3. Coherence with the strategic environment (internal and external factors relevant to the problem and its solution), also called *viability*.

A second planning *principle of optimization* must also be kept in mind so that the combination/timing of strategies and the combination/timing of tactics produce the biggest impact toward objectives,

given the limited resources and the time constraints.

The usefulness of applying those two principles is clearly demonstrated by Shapiro[10] at the marketing mix level, for which he recommends that a good fit (which he defines as being consistency, integration, and leverage) exists between all elements of the marketing mix. He also insists on the required mix-market, mix-firm, and mix-competition fits.

Strategy Formulation: Example

This simple generic model is universal and can obviously be applied to any kind of situation. Its application to solving a marketing problem is depicted in **Exhibit 3.7** and further discussed in **Exhibit 3.8**. Observe that all the classical steps of the Strategic Marketing Process clearly fit the OST sequence. An illustration of the OST approach in a real business life example is shown in **Exhibit 3.9**.

The Piper Heidsieck example clearly illustrates the differences that exist between the various OST components:

1. Objectives are clearly defined as *results to be attained over time*.
2. Strategy is a set of *carefully selected and integrated business priorities* to achieve objectives.
3. Tactics are the actual *actions and operations* that are necessary to execute strategies.

Vertical Perspective

Although business organizations differ in the way they are designed, they are generally vertically structured into several organizational layers, such as:

1. Group—Strategic Business Units (SBU)—Operating companies.

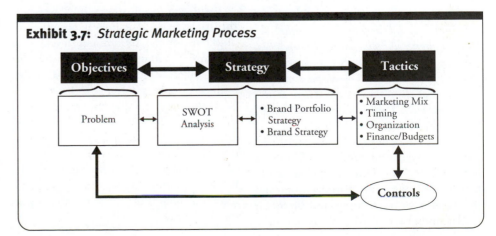

Exhibit 3.7: *Strategic Marketing Process*

Exhibit 3.8: *OST Framework Applied to Marketing Strategy*

Objectives: (assume new product launch):

Which problem is to be solved:　　　　　　　　　　　　　　**(O**bjective)
➜ Increase market share and product profit contribution over time

Strategy:

What is the relevant information?　　　　　　　　　　　　**(S**trategic Analysis)
(Environmental analysis of the problem)
➜ Strategic analysis
Internal analysis (firm):
Strengths and weaknesses
External analysis (market/competitors/environment):
Opportunities and threats

Which of all our available resources do we allocate
to this particular problem?　　　　　　　　　　　　　　　**(S**trategic Plan)
➜ Product portfolio strategy
Allocation of resources across product markets

What are the options?　　　　　　　　　　　　　　　　　　**(S**trategic Plan)
Which option to choose and for which reasons?　　　　　**(S**trategic Plan)
➜ Product strategy
Targeting and positioning

Tactics:

How to implement the solution?　　　　　　　　　　　　　**(T**actrical Plan) &
➜ Marketing mix: Product, price, promotion, place　　　**(T**actical Execution)
➜ Scheduling aspects
➜ Organizational aspects
➜ Financial/budgetary aspects
➜ Controls

2. Firm—Divisions—SBUs.
3. Firm—Geographical Areas—Countries, and so on.

Within the layers people work at different hierarchical levels.

Since strategies have to be formulated and implemented everywhere in the organization, it is obviously critical that all of them work as a coherent assembly and that they all concur to the same ultimate objectives. *One solution to this problem lies in the application of a cascade principle, whereby for a strategy to work at a particular level, a certain number of objectives have to be met at the level below, for which strategies will also have to be developed. Thus, a strategy at a particular lower level depends upon a coherent objectives-strategies-objectives chain from the top down to this particular level.* This model is described by Poirier[11] and depicted in **Exhibit 3.10**.

In order to understand the vertical perspective fully, consider the case of Johnson Screens, a St. Paul, Minnesota–based company specializing in the manufacturing and selling of industrial screens and filters for the chemical industry, the oil well industry,

and the water well industry. Starting in the 1970s, Johnson launched a massive strategic initiative to increase its market presence and revenue through a worldwide geographical expansion strategy. In Europe, it did so from its Western European bridgehead (England and France) into Eastern European countries. **Exhibit 3.11** illustrates the application of the cascade principle from the Minnesota head office down to one of the local Eastern European operations (we will take Poland as an example).

Exhibit 3.11 illustrates how strategic thrusts at a particular level become the objectives of the subordinate level. It is therefore important to remember that the status (objective or strategy) of a particular business priority is in fact level dependent.

At this stage, it is also important to note that strategy formulation is both a top-down and a bottom-up process. It is top down because the strategy at any level dictates the objectives at the level immediately below. It is bottom up because a lower level can (and should) influence the strategy at the level above.

Horizontal Perspective

Within the same organizational level, there are usually several centers of responsibilities, such as SBUs, operating companies, country operations, or individuals. Each has its own specific capabilities and constraints, and they collaborate in search of shared information, coordination, and synergies in the formulation and deployment of their own strategies (see **Exhibit 3.12**). This continuous exchange of information provides the added benefit of significantly contributing to organizational learning. **Exhibit 3.13** provides an illustration of how Egmont, a Danish media house with international operations, goes about taking full advantage of the horizontal perspective opportunities.

OST Network of Strategies

The combination of vertical and horizontal frameworks results in a network of interrelated and congruent strategies, and the complex architecture of strategy throughout an organization can actually be mapped as illustrated in **Exhibit 3.14** (the case of a classical corporate / SBU / product-market structure).

As discussed earlier, strategies will vertically link to each other through a coherent "objectives-strategies-objectives" chain. Parent entities should add value to subordinate units. Subordinate units should both influence and adapt to parent entities. Simultaneously, lateral synergies should be sought between entities belonging to the same horizontal level.

The classic Boston Consulting Group portfolio approach to allocating resources is a typical example of the application of both the vertical and horizontal perspectives.[12] Assuming an SBU made of three product-markets with an overall target return on investment (ROI) of 15 percent, and placing ourselves at the product-market level of Exhibit 3.14, the following can be observed:

1. **Vertically.** The target ROI of each product market (product-market level **O**bjective) is a function of its parent SBU portfolio strategy (SBU level **S**trategy).

2. **Horizontally.** Lateral synergies are critical because product-markets cannot be managed independently. First, they are not independent from a resource standpoint because question marks and possibly stars are funded by cash cows.

Exhibit 3.9: *Piper Heidsiesk—The Success Story of Marilyn Monroe's Favorite Champagne (I)*

Piper Heidsieck is a very well-known "House of Champagne." The company head office and production unit are located in Reims, where all the kings of France were crowned and the capital of the Champagne region, approximately 150 kilometers northeast of Paris. In 1997, the Piper Heidsieck brand had a turnover of 400 million French francs (FF). It was considered to be a well-known but weakening brand, and the following strategy was implemented:

<u>Objective:</u> Increase both sales volume and sales price over time.

<u>Strategy:</u>

1. New <u>Targets</u>: Consumers who drink Champagne at occasions when Champagne consumption is not an obligation/tradition (weddings, anniversaries, year-end celebrations, etc.) but a desire (for pleasure, seduction in any type of interpersonal relationships, etc.), *and* nonconsumers who drink other products (such as vodka and whisky brands having a strong image) that better communicate who they are.

2. New <u>Positioning</u>: Pleasure, emotion, transgression, excitement, elegance vs. tradition.
   Note: The above strategic choices are to allow adequate volume potential as well as the building of a stronger brand image to legitimate price increases (with the added benefit of minimizing frontal competition against other Champagne brands).

<u>Tactics:</u>

1. <u>Product</u>: Quality (Very high and constant with Piper Heidsieck)—Innovation (Introduction of Baby Piper—a small bottle one can drink with a straw; and introduction of Piper "corset bottle" designed by Jean-Paul Gaultier, the French fashion designer)—Red instead of yellowish bottle label color (a Piper Heidsieck proprietary color which symbolizes the contrary of innocence).

2. <u>Price</u>: Progressive increase over time.

3. <u>Communication</u>: Superior quality not mentioned (although unanimously recognized to be present)—Construction of a universe of desire built around the brand—New claim: "Take a walk on the red side!"—Promotion centered around movie stars and movie industry events such as the Cannes festival—Organized visits of the cellars and Piper hospitality complex in Reims (100,000+ visitors per year).

4. <u>Distribution</u>: Distribution partnerships towards night life locations (versus fine restaurants)—Launch of "Piper Espaces"and Piper Clubs in Europe and the United States.
   Note: An absolute coherence of all the marketing mix elements around desire and sensuality was considered to be essential to success.

The results were stunning. Brand turnover went up to 800 million FF in three years with a simultaneous bottle price increase of about 25 percent. Piper Heidsieck is now sold in 140 countries (20 percent in France, 65 percent elsewhere in Europe, and most of the rest in the United States, Canada, and Australia).

Source: Personal interview with Jean Poulallion, marketing director, July 2001.

Exhibit 3.10: *Strategy Formulation: The Vertical Perspective*

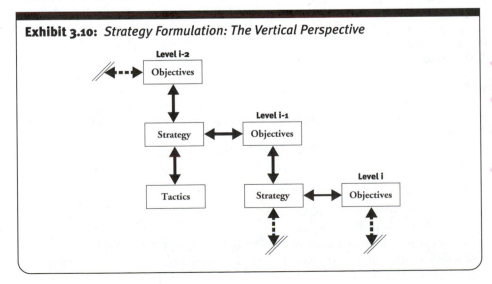

Second, product line effects do occur in the minds of the customers, and eliminating a non-competitive question mark (or a dog product) may produce negative results on the rest of the portfolio.

Exhibits 3.15 and **3.16** summarize these relationships.

STRATEGY IMPLEMENTATION
Tactical Plans

Implementation is the materialization of strategy; implementation makes strategy tangible, audible, and visible to all. But it should be remembered that what anyone can feel, hear, and see is only the tip of the iceberg; a significant part of the whole plan (namely the upstream tasks of setting objectives, performing strategic analysis, formulating strategic options, and selecting one option) remains hidden below the surface. Although these "hidden" elements are kept in the brains of people and saved on the hard disks of computers, they are absolute prerequisites to strategy implementation, so that what is supposed to be a carefully planned course of action does not turn into a sterile agitation of a mostly random or reactive nature.

Implementation is strategy in motion and requires the preparation of detailed tactical plans that, for the firm's employees and especially for those directly involved, should be clear instructions as to the what, where, who, when, how, and why of their actions. Tactical decisions derive directly and logically from the chosen strategy and translate into operations. The core of a tactical plan is the specification of a series of interconnected operations optimally combined and timed for maximum impact.

A complete tactical plan is made of the following ingredients:

1. A list of actions.
2. The scheduling of these actions.
3. The organizational aspects of these actions.
4. The projected financial impact of these actions.
5. A control system.

Tactical Actions

The action items are essentially problem specific. In the case of marketing, these actions would entail the marketing mix

Exhibit 3.11: Johnson Screens—From Saint Paul to Warsaw

	Level i-2	Level i-1	Level i
	Worldwide operations Saint Paul	European operations London	Poland operations London
Objectives	Increase Sales	Geographical expansion	Polish market entry
Strategy	Geographical expansion	Polish market entry . . .	Polish marketing strategy

Exhibit 3.12: Strategy Formulation: The Horizontal Perspective

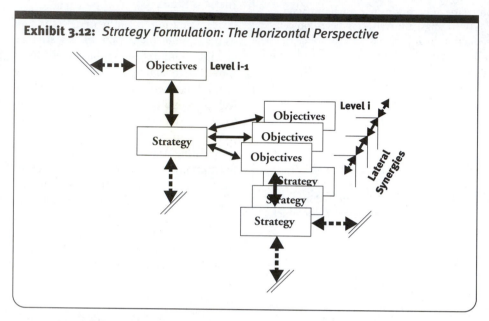

Exhibit 3.13: Egmont—Where Horizontal Collaboration Counts

Egmont is a Danish entertainment media house with a wide and colorful range of offerings, including magazines, comics, animation, video, cinemas, games, and online services. Its 1999 total revenue was 1.1 billion Euros.

Two years ago, Egmont reorganized from five business sectors into 16 SBUs, which have direct responsibility for setting strategies and meeting goals. This new structure was aimed at giving more flexibility to individual businesses. It also increased demands on cooperation.

Below are a few lines selected from the Egmont Website. They describe the underlying philosophy of the new structure and illustrate how the horizontal perspective is put into action for optimum results.

"Every SBU has its own board, that includes members from other business units. They meet regularly, contributing knowledge and skills from their areas and taking the experience and know-how of others with them. Working like this means that business ideas are not allowed to be forgotten or remain untested. . . . In addition to exchanging knowledge, skills, and inspiration, the boards are charged with building and supporting development in the strategic business areas."

Today, Egmont has more than 4,200 employees in 30 countries. It is the leading provider of entertainment in Scandinavia and the largest in printed entertainment for kids and teens in the rest of Europe.

Source: www.egmont.com, accessed April 2001.

decisions. Strategy formulation is a problem-driven process that takes the organization from a set of objectives to a selected course of actions through analysis and imagination. Strategy implementation takes the firm from these actions back to its stated objectives through a series of cause and effect relationships. These two paths

are described in **Exhibit 3.17**. When planning these actions, the strategist must ensure that they all contribute to the overall objectives and that, given limited resources, their combination is optimized so as to produce maximum results. As an illustration, there is no point in increasing the advertising spending if a modest R&D effort aimed at improving product quality would bring more value to the market and more profit to the firm.

Scheduling

The scheduling of actions should result in a detailed timetable that logically sequences operations so as to meet deadlines. It can take the shape of a Gantt chart (see **Exhibit 3.18**), on which activities are plotted as segments against time. Gantt charts are easy to prepare and are often used during staff meetings.

When scheduling execution, the fact that operations may be time linked should not be overlooked. In such instances, some tasks cannot start until a certain number of other tasks are completed, and the schedule should reflect these interdependencies. As shown in Exhibit 3.18, the manufacturing of a modified product (task 6) cannot start until the required engineering work has been completed (task 2) and the production line reorganized (task 3). Should relationships between activities become more complex, more sophisticated planning methods do exist such as Program Evaluation and Review Technique (PERT) or Critical Path Method (CPM).

Organizational Aspects

Organizational aspects must be considered because one cannot dissociate the strategy from the organization and the people in charge of executing it. Adaptive moves such as restructuring, training, recruiting, or cultural change might thus be required.

Peters and Waterman[13] have developed an interesting model to diagnose a firm's capacity to reach objectives, which is known as the McKinsey 7-S framework (see **Exhibit 3.19**). From their study, they conclude that strategy is only one of seven elements for business success:

1. Strategy.
2. Structure.
3. Systems (procedures and systems).
4. Style (management style).
5. Staff (people).

Exhibit 3.14: *The OST Network of Strategies*

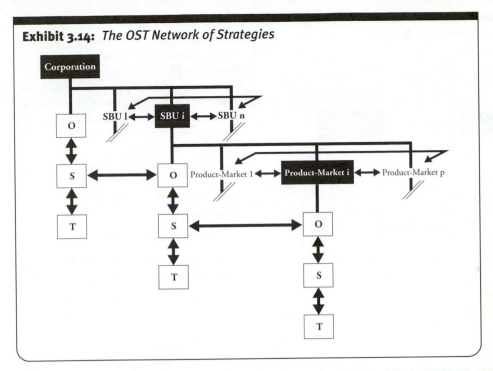

Exhibit 3.15: *From SBU Strategy to Product-Market Objective—Illustration of the Vertical Perspective*

SBU overall Target ROI	15%		
SBU Product-Markets	A	B	C
SBU Resource Allocation Strategy	Cash Cow	Star	Question Mark
Product-Market Target ROI	26%	15%	10%

Exhibit 3.16: *Lateral Synergies—Illustration of the Horizontal Perspective*

Funds Movement			
SBU Product-Markets	A (Cash Cow)	B (Star)	C (Question Mark)
Product-Line Effects			

6. Skills (present and hoped-for corporate strengths).

7. Shared values (culture).

For their part, Thompson and Strickland[14] list eight permanent managerial tasks for successful strategy implementation, seven of them being directly people or organization related:

1. Building an organization with the competencies, capabilities and resource strengths needed for successful strategy execution.

2. Allocating ample resources to strategy-critical activities.

3. Establishing strategy-supportive policies.

4. Instituting best practices and pushing for continuous improvement.

5. Installing information, communication, and operating systems that enable company personnel to better carry out their strategic roles proficiently.

6. Tying rewards and incentives to the achievement of key strategic targets.

7. Shaping the work environment and corporate culture to fit the strategy.

8. Exercising the strategic leadership needed to drive implementation forward.

Just like thinking in strategic terms, the implementation process impacts every part of the organizational structure. Hence, all managers are strategy implementers in their areas of authority and responsibility, and all employees are participants.

Financial Projections

The projected financial impact of these actions is, of course, crucial. Where possible, financial projections should go as far as a proforma income statement, balance sheet, and cash-flow statement. A strategic plan is only as good as its resulting financials.[15] This is the reason it is of the utmost importance to forecast those financials before execution starts, both to validate the plan and to avoid any subsequent difficulty. Should the financial projections prove unsatisfactory, the plan should be reviewed, revised, and its financial consequences recalculated. This convergent process is continued until the projected results are on target (see **Exhibit 3.20**) or until the strategy is judged inapplicable due to unacceptable financial results. In the process, pessimistic and optimistic scenarios are often developed to bracket the real future outcomes with a reasonable level of confidence and to hedge against forecasting errors.

Controls

The control system translates the strategy into tangible objectives and measures to control deployment, pilot activities, detect early any implementation problem, and allow immediate corrective action if needed. In today's turbulent and fast-moving markets, such systems should be anticipative by design, not simply the classical reporting tools providing a productivity and financial synthesis of the past. For maximum efficacy they should also be purposely built for action. The information

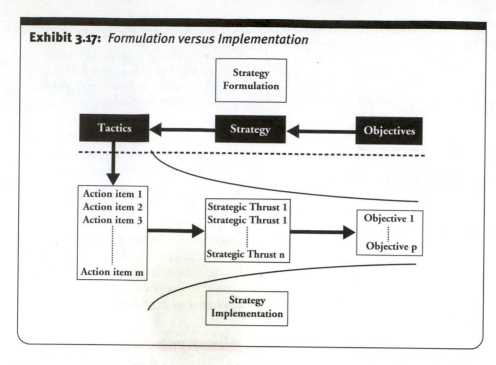

Exhibit 3.17: *Formulation versus Implementation*

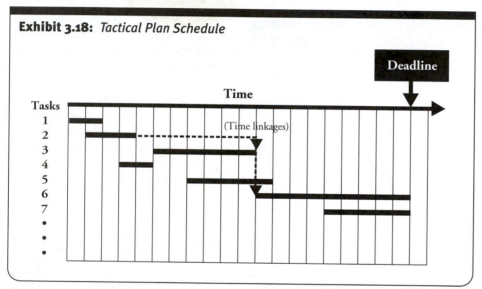

Exhibit 3.18: *Tactical Plan Schedule*

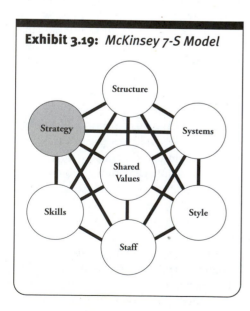

Exhibit 3.19: *McKinsey 7-S Model*

retention rate versus operating income).

These characteristics are summarized on **Exhibit 3.21**.

These new requirements imposed onto traditional control systems have turned them into powerful strategic management systems, which have very much gained the favor and the confidence of management during recent years. The performance scorecard and the balanced scorecard are two strategic management systems very often used. They are the topics of the two following sections.

Managing Strategic Deployment with the Performance Scorecard

The performance scorecard technique is a strategic management system that was born in France between the two world wars. Although developed independently of the OST model, it stems from the exact same logical approach. The performance score-card is used to monitor and manage the deployment of a business strategy. It gained wide acceptance under the name "tableau de bord" (control panel) by analogy to a car's dashboard or an airplane's control panel.

Constructing a performance scorecard is essentially a two-step approach (Loning et al.,[17] Mendoza et al.[18]):

1. The first step focuses on the formulation of a firm's or business entity's strategy. It results in the identification and listing of its **O**bjectives, **S**trategies, and **T**actics and in the assignment of the resulting responsibilities to subordinate units (called *responsibility centers*) using a two-dimensional matrix (see **Exhibit 3.22**). The matrix simply acts as a filter to identify the subordinate units concerned by a particular strategic thrust of the parent entity.

2. Using this matrix, the second step requires the concerned subordinate units to translate the strategic thrusts of the parent unit (hence their own objectives) into their own strategies and tactics. The process cascades down as long as appropriate.

At each level, **O**bjectives, **S**trategic thrusts, and **T**actics are then converted into a few selected indicators to be compared against predefined benchmarks (see **Exhibit 3.23**). A total of approximately 12 indicators per responsibility center is usually considered to be the optimum. For an example of a performance scorecard, see **Exhibit 3.24**.

they give should therefore exhibit the following characteristics:

1. Provided in a manageable amount (carefully selected).

2. Useful (pertinent and important).

3. Understandable (well presented and easy to interpret).

4. Compared to reference values (benchmarks, standards, targets, or history).

5. Immediate (collected and communicated in real time).

6. Financial and nonfinancial.

7. Internally and externally focused (i.e., on firm service processes and resulting client service experiences[16]).

8. Pertaining to both performance drivers and resulting performance (i.e., client

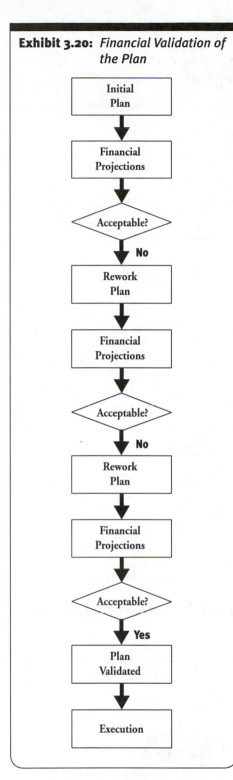

Exhibit 3.21: *Strategic Management Systems*

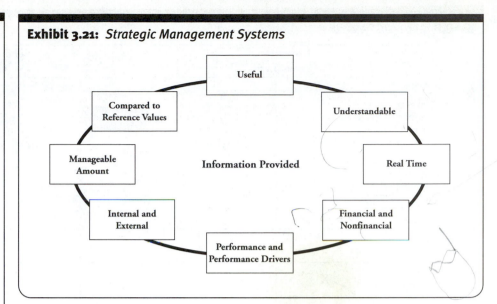

ing and growth). The goal is to answer the following questions:

1. **Financial perspective.** To succeed financially, how should we appear to our shareholders?

2. **Customer perspective.** To achieve our vision, how should we appear to our customers?

3. **Internal business process perspective.** To satisfy our shareholders and customers, at what business processes must we excel?

4. **Learning and growth perspective.** To achieve our vision, how will we sustain our ability to change and improve?

Additional perspectives can be added if specific conditions dictate.

Within each perspective, the strategy is translated into objectives to be met for which performance indicators and their corresponding targets are defined. The approach is depicted in **Exhibit 3.25**.

The balanced scorecard is typically developed at the corporate or SBU level. The underlying assumption is that each subordinate entity throughout the structure will direct its efforts toward achieving the objectives of the organization. This is accomplished by identifying the objectives and measures of the scorecard that the subordinate entity could influence and then building its own linked scorecard.

In their approach, Kaplan and Norton claim to achieve three types of balance between:

1. Financial vs. nonfinancial measures.
2. Internal (internal business process—learning and growth) vs. external (financial—customer) measures.

3. Outcomes measures vs. performance drivers measures.

Exhibit 3.26 shows the typical indicators usually associated with each perspective. A properly designed balanced scorecard should spell out the strategy of the business unit concerned through a chain of cause-and-effect relationships between outcomes and the performance drivers of those outcomes. It should be the translation of the business unit strategy into a set of linked indicators that both define the long-term strategic objectives as well as describe the strategic levers to be acted upon to achieve them. **Exhibit 3.27** gives a sample of a simplified balanced scorecard illustrating this principle.

Strategic Management Systems: From OST to OSTC

The relevance and usefulness of strategic management systems such as the balanced scorecard or the performance scorecard would probably legitimate that a "C" (for control) be added to the OST sequence, which would thus evolve from OST to OSTC. For the sake of simplicity, we will consider that controlling is part of the actual operations (tactics). Thus, we will keep OST as the term to be used to describe the whole strategic process.

At this stage, note that the underlying assumption of strategic management systems is that managers should not confine the revision of their strategic plans to the company's regularly scheduled planning cycle. Strategy is to be modified or adjusted when needed.

Managing Strategic Deployment with the Balanced Scorecard

Like the performance scorecard, the balanced scorecard is another strategic management system, developed in the 1990s by Kaplan and Norton[19] to monitor and manage the deployment of strategy. It highlights an integrated set of measurements directly derived from a business unit strategy using four perspectives (financial, customer, internal business process, learn-

Exhibit 3.22: *OST Matrix*

Strategic Thrusts of Parent Entity = Objectives of Subordinate Units Concerned	Objectives of Parent Entity		Subordinate Entities Concerned			
	Increase Sales	Improve Margins	Management	Marketing & Logistics	Engineering Production	Human Resources
Improve Product Quality	X	X			X	
Generate New Key Accounts	X		X	X		
Decrease Lead Time	X			X	X	
Decrease Prod. Costs		X			X	
Improve Coordination		X	X	X	X	X
Develop Service Culture	X		X			X

Strategy Implementation: Example

Exhibit 3.28 provides a good illustration of swift and efficient strategy implementation. It continues the Piper Heidsieck example described in Exhibit 3.9 and covers the action-listing and action-timing aspects of the tactical plan. It also illustrates four points very well:

1. The differences in essence and nature that exist between tactical and strategic activities.

2. The way tactical plans are first adjusted to reflect knowledge gained.

3. The absolute coherence sought between the stated objectives and the results anticipated or yielded through execution.

4. The vertical and horizontal flow of information during planning and execution.

MANAGEMENT OF STRATEGY
Who Should Think in Strategic Terms?

Strategic thinking is often thought to be the privilege of top management. This is wrong for at least three reasons:

1. We have already seen that competition impacts all functions and all levels of an organization. As discussed in the earlier section "From Business Administration to Business Strategy," it is therefore everybody's responsibility, at any senior-ity level and in any functional specialty, to think and act better than their counterpart from the competition—that is, to think and act as a strategist.

2. Since strategy formulation is both a top-down and a bottom-up process (see the earlier section, "Vertical Perspective), strategic thinking should be a concern at any level of the organization.

3. The vertical perspective leads to the very same conclusion, since the cascade principle can be pursued down from the most senior levels (say a marketing vice president) to the most junior levels (new sales recruit in a particular sales territory).

Considering these two last cases, **Exhibit 3.29**, which assumes an industrial marketing context, illustrates that both the marketing

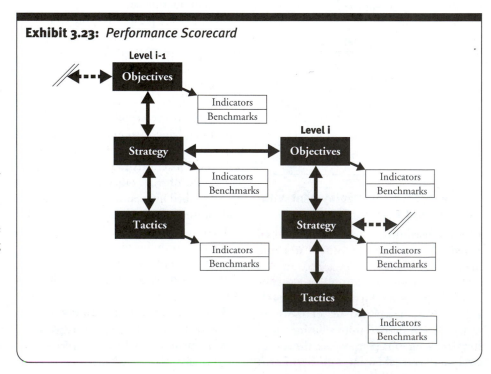

Exhibit 3.23: *Performance Scorecard*

Exhibit 3.24: *Performance Scorecard*

Objectives	Indicators / Benchmarks
Double Volume of Sales Increase Operating Profit by 20%	Revenue / Budget Operating Profit / Budget
Strategic Thrusts	
Geographical Expansion	Number of New Countries Entered / Objectives
Refocus Marketing Efforts	Market Shares in Target Segments / Objective
Rationalize Production	Unit Production Cost / Budget Production Time / Objective
Tactics	
Open New Sales Offices	Number of New Offices Opened / Plan
Introduce Key Account Management Structure	Number of Trained Key Account Managers / Plan
Renegotiate Suppliers Contracts	Number of Renegotiated Contracts / Number of Contracts Procurement Cost / Budget
Improve Changeover Time	Changeover Cost / Target Changeover Time / Target

Exhibit 3.25: *Balanced Scorecard*

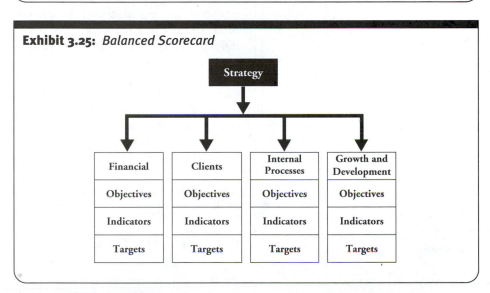

Exhibit 3.26: *Typical Indicators*

Financial	ROI, gross margin, net profit, operating cash flow, share value. . . .
Client	Brand image, brand awareness level, customer retention rate, % of turnover generated by new clients, customer satisfaction. . . .
Internal processes	Time to market, productivity indexes, % of objectives attained, changeover times, % of defects. . . .
Growth and Development	Employees' satisfaction, turnover, productivity, skills, motivation. . . . Information system capabilities. . . .

vice president and the junior salesperson do in fact apply the mental discipline of strategy and follow the OST format. The differences mainly revolve around:

1. **Time scale.** The more senior the manager, the longer his planning horizon.

2. **Scope.** Senior management define key orientations. Junior personnel may be allowed a certain degree of freedom around these key orientations (they also define their own lower-level orientations).

3. **Stakes.** Senior management responsibilities are a matter of life and death for firms or businesses. Junior personnel impact on the success or failure of individual products and projects.

Plans, Planning, and Luck

The best-planned strategies will not survive the test of battle

—General George Patton

Whether the arena is war, sports, games, business, or everyday life, no matter how thorough the preparation and how well conducted the action, things almost never turn out to be what they were expected to be. In other words, plans always prove to be more or less wrong, mainly because the number of parameters to be taken into consideration is very large, these parameters are often unpredictable, and the relationships between them are somewhat unknown. Given this undoubted reality, one could legitimately ask this question: If plans are so often wrong, why should one spend so much time and effort making them? The answer lies in a somewhat provocative statement from the chief commander of the Allied Forces in Europe during World War II:

Plans are nothing—planning is everything

—General Dwight Eisenhower

By exaggerating the opposition between plans (the proposed paths to the end results) and planning (the process to produce these proposed paths), General Eisenhower forcefully conveys his message. What the message really means is obviously more subtle. Plans of course are of critical importance because they communicate the what, who, when, how, where, and why of the action. They also play the role of a baseline from which deviations are measured to take corrective actions when needed. But of at least equal importance is the planning process, because when planning, the strategist does apply a mental discipline that forces him to examine and understand each and every important aspect of a problem. By doing so, he minimizes the risk of overlooking any important parameter of the situation.

The benefits of applying the mental discipline of strategy appear even more far reaching in exploring the relationship between luck and success:

Are you lucky?

—General Napoleon Bonaparte

Coming from one of the leading strategic thinkers in history, this question (which

Exhibit 3.27: *Balanced Scorecard*

Financial Perspective			
Objectives	**Indicator**	**Achieved**	**Targeted**
Grow revenue	% growth		
Add $1.00 per share	Operating profit		
Improve asset utilization	Return on assets		

Customer Perspective			
Objectives	**Indicator**	**Achieved**	**Targeted**
Take lead in target segments	Market shares		
Develop new business	Customer acquisition rate Market share in new segments		
Enhance customer loyalty	Customer retention rate		
Achieve highest satisfaction	Satisfaction ratings by customers of firm and competition		

Internal Business Process Perspective			
Objectives	**Indicator**	**Achieved**	**Targeted**
Achieve fast customer response	Product development time Product production time Product delivery time Percent of orders shipped on-time and complete		
Reduce service response time between departments	Intranet installation (% completed) Service reorganization (% completed)		
Develop supply chain relationship with vendors	Cost reductions due to outsourcing Total procurement cost (% sales) EDI set-up (% completed)		
Reduce Inventory	Work in process inventory level Finished goods inventory level		
Streamline manufacturing process	Lost time due to changeover		
Adopt Total Quality Management (TQM)	Number of errors per 100 orders Customer perceptions of product reliability		

Learning and Growth Perspective			
Objectives	**Indicator**	**Achieved**	**Targeted**
Develop market-oriented culture in organization	Number of personnel trained		
Develop positive organizational climate	Employee satisfaction Employee turnover		
Develop skill base of employees	Number of personnel trained		
Expand product capabilities	Size of research and development investment projects underway		

Napoleon used to ask his colonels when he was about to promote them to the rank of general) has again a somewhat hidden meaning. With this very simple interrogation, Napoleon was in fact testing the ability of his officers to think strategically because he well knew the positive relationship existing between luck and mental readiness. The more one thinks in strategic terms, the better his state of readiness, and therefore the better his position to counter any unexpected threat or to take advantage of any opportunities as they arise. In other words, as Louis Pasteur (the French scientist who invented the vaccine against rabies) said:

Chance favors the prepared mind

Planned and Emergent Strategy

As noted earlier, strategies as planned and strategies as realized are not always identical. Mintzberg[20] explored the subject and proposed the model shown in **Exhibit 3.30**. He observed that realized strategies differ from planned strategies in response to environmental changes, unexpected events, or experience gained. In reality, most strategies exhibit both a planned and an emergent component. If strategies were planned only, there would be no learning; if strategies were emergent only, there would be no control. In other words, strategies have to form and be formulated, and the management of strategy requires agility while maintaining a sense of direction.

How to Assess the Soundness of a Strategy

As formulation and execution progress, assessing the soundness of a strategy is obviously of vital importance to the strategist for the following reasons:

1. **Before implementation:** to maximize the probability of success while minimizing risk.
2. **During implementation:** to make adjustments or modifications if necessary.
3. **After implementation:** to evaluate performance and learn from experience gained.

Before implementation has started, the strategic plan can be judged only on the basis of its format and content. Once implementation has begun, it is then natural to judge the plan on the basis of results, which means that the combination of both strategy and tactics is in fact what is evalu-

Exhibit 3.28: *Piper Heidsieck—The Success Story of Marilyn Monroe's Favorite Champagne (II) from Bottle Design to Product Launch*

Strategy formulation (See Exhibit 3.9)

Strategy implementation

<u>1996</u>

Apr. 15	Packaging brief to agency
May	Agency presents rough n°1 (red label rejected)
May 15	Agency presents rough n°2 (modified red label accepted)
May 31	Presentation to Piper Heidsieck management
Jun.	Tests:
	Measurement of cognitive response via focus groups
	Measurement of affective response via customer sample
Jul. 1–15	Analysis of test results (excellent impact measure, but unsatisfactory acceptance levels)

Note: At this stage, test results are not encouraging and the following is decided:

1. Strategy to be kept

2. Execution to be revised

	New brief to agency
Aug. 1–Sep. 15	Work with advertising agency, packaging agency, and printer–Final label definition
Sep. 30	Delivery of labels to bottling plant
Oct. 15	20,000 bottles ready for field test
Oct. 20–Nov. 15	Field test:
	Measurement of conative response via market testing and forecasting model (excellent sales projections against time and negative elasticity of demand to price)

Note: Field test results are in absolute coherence with stated objectives of simultaneous sales volume and price increases versus time.

<u>1997</u>

Nov. 15–Mar. 31	Final label definition for brut, rose, and vintage bottles
	Preparation of full-scale launch
Apr. 2	First truck out to England

Note: During the above time period, a meeting was scheduled every quarter to constantly liaise with the firm's management as well as with the managers in charge of foreign subsidiaries

Source: Personal interview with Jean Poulallion, marketing director, July 2001.

ated. At this stage, it would be logical to apply some kind of attribution theory to determine which part of success is attributable to either strategy or tactics. As an illustration, one may think of an objective met through a somewhat poor quality strategy followed by an excellent—however long and costly—execution. For the sake of simplicity, we will lump together strategy and tactics and describe techniques aimed at evaluating the results obtained through the combination of both. For the same reason, we will call all these techniques *strategy assessment techniques.*

The critical points in time at which strategy assessment is normally conducted are listed on **Exhibit 3.31**, and the corresponding methods are described here.

Before implementation, there are essentially two acid tests that a manager can run through to validate a formulated strategy: a checklist, and a simple question.

The first acid test is a bullet-point checklist called **OLACS**, where each letter stands for a critical item to be verified:

- **Objectives.** Setting the ultimate objectives to be attained is the very first step of an OST sequence because there is a need for a plan only if there are goals to achieve. Without clearly stated objectives, strategy remains purposeless and becomes pure verbosity as well as a sterile intellectual exercise. Moreover, as seen earlier, objectives and subobjectives must be found everywhere in a strategic plan:

- From upper to lower organizational levels, objectives and strategies derive from each other as a coherent chain (see the earlier section, "Vertical Perspective");

- Within the same organizational level, subobjectives do exist at each and every step of the OST development, and they all contribute to meeting the initial objectives (refer to the earlier section, "Objectives, Strategy, and Tactics").

The Johnson Screens example of Exhibit 3.11 is further developed in **Exhibit 3.32** to illustrate this point.

- **Long term.** The ultimate goal of a strategy is not to propose a quick fix solution. By nature, the purpose of strategy is to produce and implement long-term solutions to problems. A long-term perspective is therefore required, and it must percolate throughout the strategic plan. This question then follows: What is long term? The answer is quite straightforward: Just like the status of a business priority, the meaning of "long term" is level dependent. The president of a company and a junior manager do not face the same time horizons. In the development of their respective strategies, long term might mean five years to the president and only 12 months to the young manager.

- **Allocation of resources.** Managers think and act under constant constraint. They must fulfill their mission with scarce resources, whether those resources are time, cash, skills, or any other input required to achieve objectives. Among all business opportunities and levers of action available to them, they must carefully choose the ones that appear the most promising and selectively invest in them. In other words, because available resources are limited, *strategy is all about allocating resources and results in a series of selective investment decisions.* Proper resource allocation decisions are critical to success, and such decisions must be present at each and every step of the strategic development. Taking again the example of a firm's marketing strategy, this point is illustrated in **Exhibit 3.33**.

- **Competitive advantage.** As discussed in the section "From Business Administration to Business Strategy," *strategy* means attempting to think and to act better than other players in competitive situations. A strategic plan must therefore clearly state the competitive advantage(s) on which to base action. A competitive advantage can be defined as any factor specific to a firm that, when skillfully managed, produces long-term superior

Exhibit 3.29: *Time Scale, Scope, and Stakes Differences in OST Sequences as a Function of Organizational Level (Assume industrial marketing context)*

Strategic Steps		Marketing Vice President	Junior Salesperson
Objectives	Market Presence	Market Share over next 5 Years	Sales Volume over next 12 Months
	Profit Level	Marketing Contribution over next 5 Years	Product Contributions over next 12 Months
Strategy	Allocation of Resources	At Market Level across Product-Markets	At Territory Level across Product-Clients or at Client Level across DMU* Members
	Targeting and Positioning	At Market Level	At Client Level or at DMU Member Level
Tactics	Product	Product Line and Product Strategies	Negotiation of Product Options
	Price	Pricing Strategy	Negotiation of Pricing Rebate
	Communication	Communication Strategy	Face to Face
	Distribution	Distribution Strategy	Direct Selling

*DMU stands for decision-making unit. In industrial marketing, a purchasing decision is usually taken or influenced by several people having different roles, expectations, and relative weights in the decision-making process. As an illustration, a sales engineer selling a high performance pump to be installed on a production line may have to convince persons from engineering, purchasing, production, and management in the client organization.

Exhibit 3.30: *Planned & Emergent Strategy*

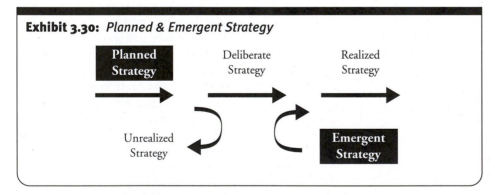

Exhibit 3.31: *Strategy Assessment, Timing, & Techniques*

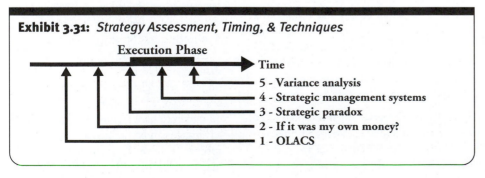

performance as compared to the competition. Competitive advantages have to be carefully managed; they must be identified, created, and maintained through investment because they usually erode with time.

Day and Wensley[21] provide an integrated view of this concept. They explain that competitive advantage:

1. Originates from superior skills and resources in which a company keeps investing.

2. Leads to superior performance which subsequently allows this investment.

This view is represented in **Exhibit 3.34**. See **Exhibit 3.35** for several examples of competitive advantages for selected firms.

• **Simple.** Last but not least, a strategic plan should be as simple as possible, given the market situation, or it will be neither well understood nor properly executed by those in charge. However, one should avoid being simplistic since there are seldom simple solutions to complex problems.

Once the plan has been formulated and verified using the OLACS checklist, the second acid test can be conducted by the strategist before execution starts. It consists of honestly asking oneself this very simple but incisive question: *"Would I invest my own money into this plan?"* Should there be any hesitation in formulating a positive answer, the plan should be reworked and improved until the answer becomes an unambiguous yes.

These two techniques are clearly not guarantees for success. They should merely be considered as conditions necessary—however, not sufficient—for success. Plainly, they are only indications that one is not likely to head straight into the wall.

During implementation, classical strategic management systems such as the performance scorecard or the balanced scorecard should be used for evaluation purposes as well as to initiate corrective steps if needed (see the sections "Managing Strategic Deployment with the Performance Scorecard" and "Managing Strategic Deployment with the Balanced Scorecard").

The beginning of the implementation phase deserves special consideration. Assuming that a firm has a well-planned and well-executed strategy at this point in time, it is very likely that this will severely

Exhibit 3.32: *The Requirement for Objectives Throughout the Plan (Johnson Screens: From Saint Paul to Warsaw)*

	Level i-2	Level i-1	Level i
	Worldwide Operations Saint Paul	**European Operations London**	**Poland Operations London**
(i) **Objectives**	Increase Sales	**Geographical Expansion**	**Polish Market Entry**
Strategy	Geographical Expansion	Polish Market entry . . .	Polish Marketing Strategy leading to a <u>set of coherent objectives and sub-objectives</u> in terms of: • Market presence • Profit level • Cash flow • Investment level • Target segment • Desired positioning • Allocation of resources across marketing mix levers • Timing • Etc. . . .

(ii)

Exhibit 3.33: *Resource Allocation/Selective Investment Decisions in Marketing Strategy*

	Strategic Steps	**Examples of Decisions**
Objectives	Problem to be Solved	Resource Allocation Decisions across Problems in or out of Domain of Acceptable Activities (Consistent with firm's Mission Statement)
Strategy	Strategic Analysis	Selective Investment into Carefully Chosen Competitive Advantages (Consistent with Firm's Competitive Strategy)
	Product Portfolio Strategy	Resource Allocation Decisions across Product-Markets
	Product Strategy	Selective Investment into Target Markets
Tactics	Operations	Resource Allocation Decisions across Operational Levers
	Controls	Selective Investment into Corrective Actions

---

threaten or hurt its competitors and therefore trigger their prompt and forceful retaliation. In most instances, the better the firm's strategy, the stronger the competitive reactions. The nature and the strength of competitive reactions are often a clear indication of the effectiveness of the firm's strategy. This particular phenomenon is called *the strategic paradox* because the more competitive a firm is, the more it attracts competition initially.

After implementation, the final results are compared with the objectives to determine whether the strategy has been successful and draw lessons for the future. Even if the objectives have been met, significant variances between planned and actual may have occurred that could have compensated each other. As an illustration, a satisfactory sales figure may hide a lower than planned market share in a higher than planned market growth. Thus, it is worthwhile to carry out a variance decomposition aimed at explaining which factors have produced which positive or negative variances. If nothing else, the variance analysis gives the manager a set of very pertinent questions to ask others in the organization. For an extensive discussion of variance decomposition, see Hulbert and Toy[22] and Lusch and Benz.[23]

When to Modify a Strategy

Assuming that a formulated plan does not exhibit any evident mistakes in format or content, there are mainly three reasons why this plan would necessitate that modifications be made at any OST level once execution has started (see **Exhibit 3.36**).

Differences between planned and actual performances are obviously the first reason. As noted earlier, constant adjustments have to be made through the proper use of scorecards (see the two earlier "Managing Strategic Deployment" sections). Should the firm constantly not reach its objectives, or should it meet with unexplained success, the plan should be reviewed and probably vastly changed or even abandoned. Such situations are in fact sheer expressions of a strategic failure when managers are driven by their environment and lose control over their firm's results and destiny.

Unexpected changes in the environment are a second reason, Among the classical environmental changes of business life are unforeseen events (such as unpredicted competitive initiatives, strikes, energy crises, wars, sudden technological breakthroughs,

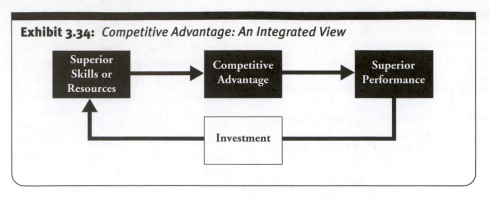

Exhibit 3.34: *Competitive Advantage: An Integrated View*

Exhibit 3.35: *Examples of Competitive Advantages*

Firm	Competitive Advantage(s)
Visa/Mastercard	Efficiency of EDP Operations
American Express	Brand Image/Range of Services Offered
FedEx	Brand Awareness/Service Quality
Motorola	Product Quality
Coca-Cola	Brand Awareness/Proprietary Formula
Audi	Reliability/Design
3M	Capacity for Innovation

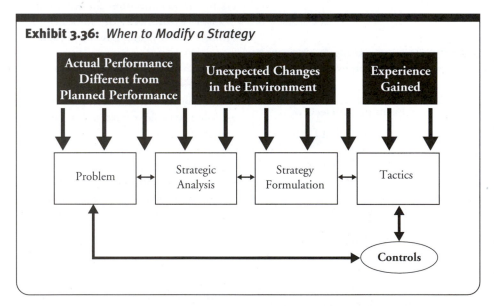

Exhibit 3.36: *When to Modify a Strategy*

leadership change in government) or management changes (such as appointment of a new CEO or acquisition by another firm).

Experience gained is the third reason. Learning from past actions to increase performance is certainly one of the strategist's key missions. Typical examples would be feedback from clients resulting in product improvements and refined marketing approaches, as well as employee suggestions resulting in substantial productivity increases.

How to Modify a Strategy

In order to address the issue of modifying a strategy, it is useful to go back to the basic distinctions existing between objectives, strategy, and tactics, and to consider as an illustration the case of a firm competing on the basis of relative delivered cost (see **Exhibit 3.37**). Let us further assume that this firm does not meet its manufacturing costs objectives. Before effecting any drastic changes to her initial strategy (say from competing on relative delivered cost to

competing on perceived differentiation), a manager confronted with this particular problem will first attempt to improve the situation by acting on the tactical levers she initially chose to work with (i.e., partnering, facility improvement, process improvement, technology acquisition, and training of production personnel). If unsuccessful, she will then move on to explore other operational options at her disposal such as subcontracting the production of selected components or renegotiating suppliers' contracts. It is only after she has investigated and tested all possible tactical solutions that she will reconsider her initial strategy and modify some of its ingredients.

By proceeding so, a manager gives strategy a chance to fully unfold, and she gives herself a chance to at least partially solve her problem in a quicker way.

Pending satisfactory results, adjustments and modifications are pursued along the OST sequence through the strategy level up to the objectives level until the limit case— where the firm's management judges it is in fact tackling the wrong problem and abandons it for a better opportunity. This process is summarized in **Exhibit 3.38**.

Contingency Plans

The business world tends to be more and more unpredictable, and the preparation of a plan requires the making of hypotheses such as market growth rates, or the date at which a new technology becomes available, or the evolution of legal and regulatory obligations in a foreign market, or a probable long-term trend for the cost of raw materials. Making assumptions is obviously unavoidable when planning, and there is in fact absolutely nothing wrong with it, provided that these assumptions are validated as soon as possible. Should they prove to be wrong, it then becomes extremely important not to be caught by surprise. Facing a brand new situation in the absence of a revised plan could have disastrous effects. This is the reason why it is essential to prepare a contingency plan for each and every key assumption made (see **Exhibit 3.39**).

Thus, the strategist should always:

1. Make a thorough review of his plan's underlying assumptions.

2. Evaluate the potential impact of their being wrong on future outcomes.

3. Prepare a contingency plan for those assumptions that he thinks could significantly influence the end result.

Exhibit 3.37: *Strategic Steps*

Objective	Strategy	Tactics
Purpose		
Set Ultimate Objectives	Meet Ultimate Objectives	Meet Contributing Subobjectives
Activity		
Thinking	Thinking	Acting
Time Horizon		
Longer Term	Long Term	Short Term
Magnitude of Effects		
Larger Amplitude	Large Amplitude	Small Amplitude
Example (considering only one of the plan's strategic thrusts)		
Firm wanting to improve its profitability by (among other things) . . .	. . . gaining and maintaining a competitive advantage based on lowering manufacturing costs through (among other things). . .	partnering for economies of scale
		manufacturing facility improvement
		manufacturing process improvement
		acquiring new manufacturing technology
		training of shop floor personnel.

Exhibit 3.38: *How to Modify a Strategy*

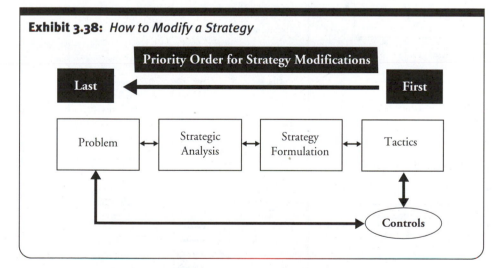

Ideally, he should also consider the case where several assumptions simultaneously turn out to be wrong. By doing so, he reduces his business risk exposure by maintaining his state of readiness at a sufficient level.

Key Strategic Lessons

Following this rather formal study of business strategy, it is probably useful at this stage to provide a series of good lessons drawn from experience by seasoned man-agers, well-known academics, or experienced consultants from all over the world. These lessons should be kept in mind to better understand some aspects of the strategic process, worry less, gain time, and avoid falling into well-known traps.

1. **Strategy formulation is painful.** In addition to being a difficult discipline in itself, strategy requires from those in charge that they successfully deal with many obstacles, including time pressure, lack of information, and conflicting opinions. It also requires the courage of making difficult decisions under uncertainty and of taking one's own personal share of the associated risk.

2. **There is rarely a single solution to a business problem.** There might be no solution, in which case the firm should stop attempting to solve this particular problem in order to avoid wasting more resources. There might be many solutions, in which case the firm should adopt the one that it identifies as its best option.

3. **There is usually no pure analytical solution to a business problem.** As seen earlier, the number of relevant parameters is usually too big, and the exact relationships between them are somewhat unknown. Solutions are often empirical: They derive from cumulative experience, imagination, or trials and errors, and their validation is by nature ex-post.

4. **For these reasons, a decision maker just cannot afford to strictly believe theoretical business models**—but she cannot afford to neglect them either, because their value is tremendous to initiate and structure reflection.

5. **When faced with a business problem, people are sometimes tempted to jump straight to a solution, or, on the contrary, to drown in an endless and inconclusive analysis effort.** Those two situations are classical traps, often termed "extinction by instinct" and "paralysis by analysis." Both lead to reactive decisionmaking and suboptimal performance. Although constantly time pressed, a manager should always give himself the privilege of reflection and also clearly decide when to stop reflection and start action.

6. **An "optimum" long-term strategy is not a succession of "optimum" shorter-term strategies.** If that were the case,

a firm should immediately stop investing to maximize next quarter's profit. In other words, firms must strike the right balance between short-term and long-term objectives. Although hard pressed for immediate performance, managers should never build their firm's present position at the expense of its future position.

7. **Business continues during refurbishing.** A plan calling for a major reorientation or reorganization of the firm should not distract managers and employees from the present day-to-day operations.

8. **In a turnaround situation, long term is short term, and performance is cash.**

CONCLUDING REMARKS

The objectives of this chapter were to propose a model of action for complex organizations operating in a competitive environment and to provide the reader with a template for strategy formulation. To meet these two objectives, an Objectives-Strategy-Tactics model has been presented, and a strategy template deriving from it is given in **Exhibit 3.40**.

Additional objectives have also been met corresponding to the needs and concerns expressed by students in the classroom or by managers in executive seminars:

1. The description of a mental discipline.

2. The shared definition of a common vocabulary.

3. A clearer understanding of the complex architecture of strategies within an organization.

4. A useful help in adopting a strategic spirit and attitude toward business problems.

The answers given to the following questions may also prove to be useful to the practicing manager:

1. How do we build a strategic plan when the company is not organized into strategic business units and functions that lead to the classical corporate, business, and functional strategies as described in many books?

2. How do we develop a strategic plan at my level, where my main challenges are much more selling products or recruiting and retaining talents than developing a vision, formulating a mission statement, or managing a portfolio of businesses?

3. How do we develop and use a scorecard?

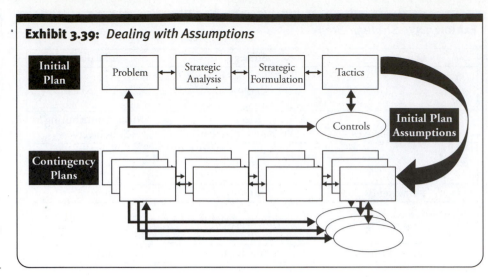

Exhibit 3.39: *Dealing with Assumptions*

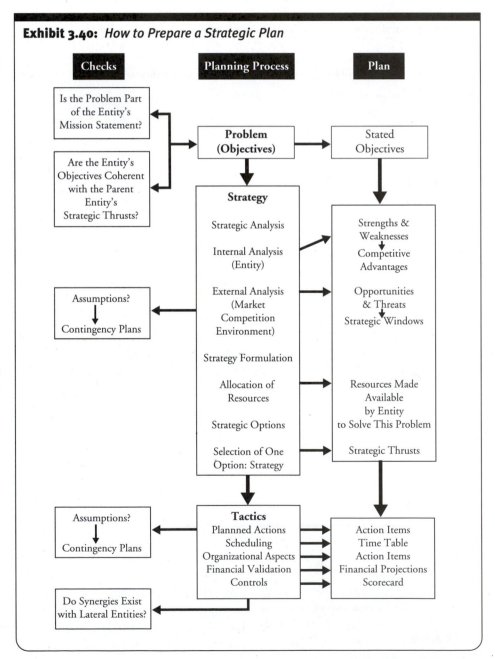

Exhibit 3.40: *How to Prepare a Strategic Plan*

1. Jean Marie Mathey, *Comprendre la Stratégie* (Economica, 1995): 9–10.

2. Alain Desreumaux, *Stratégie* (Dalloz, 1993): 8.

3. John Von Neumann and Oskar Morgenstern, *Theory of Games and Economic Behavior* (Princeton University Press, 1947).

4. Kenichi Ohmae, *The Mind of the Strategist* (Penguin, 1982): 91–98.

5. Henry Mintzberg, Bruce W. Ahlstrand, and Joseph Lampel, *Strategy Safari–A Guided Tour through the Wilds of Strategic Management* (Free Press, 1998).

6. Général André Beaufre, *Introduction à la Stratégie* (Armand Colin, 1965): 16.

7. Mintzberg, *Strategy Safari,* 9–14.

8. Jacob De Smit, Reims Management School, private communication, 2001.

9. Patrick E. Haggerty, "The Corporation and Innovation," *Strategic Management Journal* (April–June 1981): 98–118.

10. Benson P. Shapiro, "Getting Things Done— Rejuvenating the Marketing Mix," *Harvard Business Review* (September–October 1985): 28–34.

11. Lucien Poirier, *Stratégie Théorique II* (Economica, 1987): 62–63.

12. Boston Consulting Group, *Perspectives on Experience,* Boston Consulting Group, Inc., Boston, Mass. (1982).

13. Thomas J. Peters and Robert H. Waterman, Jr., *In Search of Excellence: Lessons from America's Best Run Companies* (Harper Collins, 1982).

14. Arthur A. Thompson and Alonzo J. Strickland, *Strategic Management—Concepts and Cases* (McGraw-Hill, 1998): 270–271.

15. The two key factors in any strategic investment decision are return and risk, and as financial theory suggests, higher-risk businesses should be required to yield higher rates of return. Failure to account for risk leads to faulty decisions, such as accepting inappropriately risky ventures or forgoing profitable opportunities. For a complete discussion see D.A. Aaker and R. Jacobson, "The Role of Risk in Explaining Differences in Profitability," *Academy of Management Journal* (June 1987): 277–296.

16. A *service offering* is considered to be a carefully managed process from the service provider standpoint resulting in an experience from the client standpoint. For a more complete discussion see, C. Lovelock and D. Lapert, *Marketing des Services* (Publi-Union, 1999).

17. Hélène Loning and Yvon Pesqueux, *Controle de Gestion* (Dunod, 1998).

18. Carla Mendoza, Marie-Hélène Delmond, Françoise Giraud, and Hélène Loning, *Tableaux de Bord pour Managers* (Editions Revue Fiduciere, Paris, 1999); and Carla Mendoza and Robert Zrihen, "Les Tableaux de Bord au Cœur des Processus de Changement," *Revue Echanges* 153 (Mars 1999).

19. Robert S. Kaplan and David P. Norton, *The Balanced Scorecard* (Harvard Business School Press, 1996).

20. Henry Mintzberg and J. A. Waters, "Of Strategies, Deliberate and Emergent," *Strategic Management Journal* 6 (1985):257–272.

21. George S. Day and Robin Wensley, "Assessing Advantage: A Framework for Diagnosing Competitive Superiority," *Journal of Marketing* (April 1988):1–20.

22. James Mac Hulbert and N.E. Toy, "A Strategic Framework for Marketing Control," *Journal of Marketing* 41 (April 1977):12–21.

23. Robert S. Lusch and William F. Bentz, "A Marketing-Accounting Framework for Controlling Product Profitability," in *Marketing Effectiveness*, ed. S. Shapiro and V.H. Kirpalani (Allyn and Bacon, Inc., 1984).

Chapter 4

Ernest R. Cadotte
University of Tennessee

Market Opportunity Analysis for New Products

To be successful, any new venture requires good market intelligence. Market opportunity analysis (MOA) is a systematic method for gathering and organizing information about a believed market opportunity.* Properly executed, an MOA will provide information about:

• The macroenvironment and the forces that will shape the market opportunity in the future.

• The market's structure and where your new product is likely to fit in the market.

• The minimum requirements to serve the market as determined by profiles of end users, channel customers, and competitors.

With this information, you will be better able to develop an effective strategy and have a clear understanding of your product's or service's unique contribution to the market. This information also facilitates the forecasting of market potential and demand. The ultimate objective is to reduce the risk to investment that results from insufficient knowledge of the market.

This chapter presents a logical approach to market opportunity analysis. The focus is on new products. The new product may be as rudimentary as an idea or a drawing, or it may have progressed to the bench-model stage. In many cases, it may represent the competency, capability, or know-how of an individual or an organization. Instead of considering inventions that are incremental improvements of an existing brand, we focus on those cases that represent new ways of doing things in markets unfamiliar to the developer/entrepreneur. This focus emphasizes the importance of starting a formal analysis early in the development process. However, the MOA framework can also be used to help revise an existing product or service

Learning Objectives

After reading this chapter, you should understand:

1. The situations in which an MOA is useful.

2. The process by which you can systematically evaluate an MOA.

3. The kind of information to collect, where to collect it, and how to organize it.

4. The critical impact of the macroenvironment on the viability of a market opportunity.

5. The way to position a product.

6. The way the customer, competition, and channel affect not only the viability of the opportunity but also the very nature of the strategy.

7. The need for a unique advantage that pushes the strategy out of the norm and into the limelight such that a sustainable differential advantage can be achieved.

8. The way to use data on macroenvironments, product structure, competition, customers, channels, and unique capabilities to formulate a strategy that is consistent with current market requirements but exceeds customer expectations and competitor offers.

9. A procedure for forecasting potential demand and evaluating the limits of that forecast via sensitivity analysis of key forecast parameters.

Marketplace

http://www.marketplace-simulation.com

BEST-USE CORRELATIONS

Market Opportunity Analysis

The MOA framework presented in this chapter will help your team organize a vast array of bewildering *Marketplace* data. At the outset of the game, it will help you identify potential target segments. Later, as you gain game experience, it will help you evaluate and reassess customer segments, channel options, and competitive threats. Use it to make choices based on information, not intuition.

Profiles

In Q2, your team develops profiles of potential target segments then selects two segments to target from among them. You also formulate an initial strategy, which you then tactically execute in Q3. In Q4 *Marketplace* feeds you a vast array of additional data on customers and competitors. Our advice: look to the MOA framework to make sense of the data and to hone your firm's unique advantages.

Market Requirements

How do you begin to weigh the merits of expanding production capacity against the merits of opening new sales channels? Use this chapter's MOA framework to assess investment risks and possible investment outcomes.

In Q5 your team also must prepare a business plan and compete for venture capital to fund its growth goals.

The spoils of venture capital recruiting belong to the team that shapes the most persuasive argument that its product offerings, prices, promotions and sales channels serve its markets more profitably than its rivals. Use chapter discussions of market requirements to ensure that your pursuit of new capital is adequately rewarded.

---

because it ensures systematic coverage of the subject matter. We recommend regularly revisiting this process in order to update relevant information.

SITUATIONS REQUIRING AN MOA

Three situations benefit from an MOA. In the first, a need or want is identified, but no product or service is identified to satisfy it. In this case, we often find an entrepreneur who is in search of a solution that can be turned into a commercial endeavor. Products invented in response to a recognized need include coffee cup warmers, snow blowers, weed eaters, garage door openers, the Holiday Inn (low-cost lodging for the traveler), and Domino's Pizza (home delivery). Industrial products invented to satisfy a need include sprayers for paint application, jigs for holding parts in place for machining, and conveyor systems for moving materials in the factory. There is much truth to the adage that necessity is the mother of invention.

In the second case, a product exists, but the need or want for that product is not well understood. The product may be an idea, a theory, a prototype, or it may have no more definition than the capability to do something. For example, at the Oak Ridge National Lab (ORNL), we explored the market opportunity of the triple effect absorption chiller. We had no prototype, only a theory for using natural gas to cool commercial buildings. Shortly after the MOA was completed, a prototype was created and used to test the theory. After considerable fieldwork, the prototype evolved into a product now on the market.

A marketless invention may have been created as a by-product of basic research, as a result of solving another problem, or simply as an inspiration of a clever person. There are many examples of marketless inventions, including synthetic rubber, carbon fiber, xerography, Teflon, Velcro, and the adhesive on 3-M Post-it notes. More recently, we see this situation with intermetallic compounds, cloning, and gene splicing. In a sense, the original McDonald brothers created the first fast-food restaurant without knowing much about its true market potential. The McDonald brothers created the first fast-food restaurant—and Steve Jobs built the microcomputer—without proof of a market. We might argue that many garage shop inventions fall into this category.

In reality, there are many more examples of marketless inventions than might be expected. If you consider any research center (universities, national laboratories, or business research facilities), the know-how of the technical staff represents any number of capabilities. The marketless invention might be the capability to work with artificial intelligence, advanced structural ceramics, polycarbons, nonintrusive measurement devices, or even a wind tunnel. The challenge is to find a suitable market need and apply that capability in a commercially profitable manner.

A marketless situation exists when any firm wishes to capitalize on its established know-how in unrelated markets. For example, J. P. Stailey investigated new markets for its fermentation capability at an underutilized ethanol production plant and found that the process could be used to convert waste paper to ethanol. Coors Ceramics of Golden, Colorado, explored new applications beyond internal combustion engines for its advanced structural ceramics capabilities. And some years ago, McDonald's examined the extension of its fast-food hamburger preparation and delivery capability into the breakfast category. In each case, we essentially have a solution searching for a market-worthy need.

The third case requiring an MOA is perhaps the most unusual: No product is identified and no want or need is identified. In this case, we have someone who is looking for a way to profitably invest his or her money, time, talent, or other resources. Venture capitalists are usually in this category, as are many want-to-be entrepreneurs. Occasionally, organizations—such as Roman Adhesive, Inc., the leading manufacturer of wallpaper adhesive—will face this situation. Roman Adhesive recently concluded that there were few opportunities in the mature wallpaper industry. To achieve its growth objectives, the company needed to diversify beyond its core technology of starch-based adhesives to include related products such as wallpaper hanging kits, wallpaper repair kits, and vinyl paper cleaners.

OVERVIEW OF THE MOA PROCESS

The major elements of an MOA are shown in **Exhibit 4.1**. While specific details will vary from case to case, the process itself should always have these basic steps.

1. The analysis begins with an examination of the macroenvironment and the

Exhibit 4.1: *The MOA Approach*

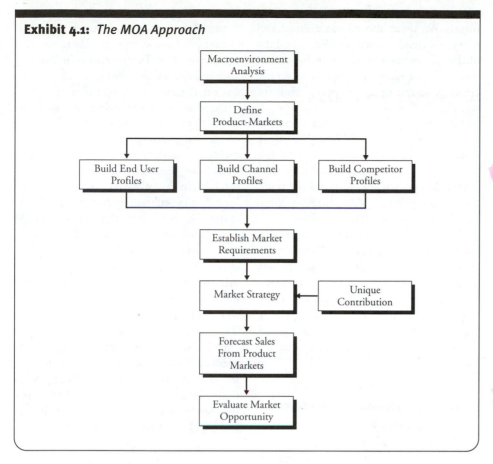

major forces (economic, social, technological, legal, and natural) that might affect the market opportunity. These forces are beyond the control of the players in the market but can greatly expand or shrink the market opportunity, sometimes within a period of years or even months. Some of these forces are broad, affecting many industries (such as an economic downturn, a new U.S. president with different attitudes toward government regulations, or an increase in the number of single-parent households). Others are more specific to a given market (such as the way the availability of e-mail, cellular phones, portable computers, and video conferencing is changing how and where people work).

2. The next step in the analysis is to identify the major markets in which the product might compete and then to segment the markets into a product-market structure. The short-term objective of gathering this information is to understand the organization of the market. The more strategic objective is to determine in which segment(s) and against what products the invention is likely to compete.

3. The third step is to gather a wealth of information on each of the more promising market applications in order to learn as much as possible about the end users, competition, and appropriate channels of distribution. These profiles will lay the groundwork for establishing the minimum requirements for entering the market and constraining and guiding the development of a strategy.

4. The fourth step is to identify the minimum requirements for entering the market (based on what the third step has discovered) and to evaluate the product's own unique contribution to the market. Will the invention, know-how, or approach offer a differential advantage when compared to existing customer needs, competitor offers, and distribution requirements? Can the organization make a unique contribution to the market? How easily can the invention be copied? How fast can the organization innovate to stay ahead of imitators?

5. The fifth step in the MOA process is to develop a strategy, including a tactical approach to the market. The strategy should flow from an understanding of the "normal" way of doing business in

the market and the unique contribution you can make as entrepreneur. As much as 80 percent of the strategy and tactical details will be determined by minimum requirements of the current market. The rest will depend on the creativity and uniqueness of the firm's competitive offer. To be successful, you must establish a strategy that gives the firm an unmistakable differential advantage.

6. The sixth step is to develop a sales forecast for the new venture. The forecast will depend on both the strategy and the market potential; the strategy converts market potential into demand. If the new entry is an incremental improvement on existing brands, then demand will come at the expense of the current competitors as they lose market share. If the innovation brings new capabilities or substantially lower costs to the market, then sales may result from an expansion of the market as new customers enter from the sidelines.

7. The final step in the MOA process is to evaluate the attractiveness of the market opportunity. Any new venture requires considerable time to become established in the market. Thus, you or any entrepreneur can expect heavy up-front investments in product development, production capability, and marketing. Cash flows will be negative throughout the early stages. Does the organization have sufficient resources to stay in the market until the cash flow becomes positive? Is this opportunity consistent with the core competencies and long-term objectives of the firm?

The balance of this chapter will review each of these seven steps of the MOA process in depth.

ANALYZE THE MACROENVIRONMENT

At any given moment, many forces are acting on a market. Some are deliberate attempts by the players in the industry (end users, competitors, distributors, and suppliers) to shape the market. Others are beyond the control of these participants. These other forces are part of the *macroenvironment* and include economic, demographic, social, technological, governmental, and geographical conditions. Macroenvironmental forces can be strong enough to make or break a market for a new technology, almost regardless of the initiatives of those trying to develop it. The macroenvironment may force the market in one direction or another, perhaps causing one segment to expand and another to shrink. Many entrepreneurs have seen their bubbles burst by changes in the macroenvironment; others (a relatively few lucky ones) have been in the right place at the right time. The macroenvironment almost always places constraints on a market opportunity, and the entrepreneur must figure out how to work around and within these constraints.

The objective of a macroenvironmental analysis is to identify the relevant demand forces, determine their relation to the market, and predict how they might change in the future. Consider this example, an analysis (simplified) of the market for school desks. Demand for school desks is a function of the number of school-age children. If we are interested in a short-term forecast (one to five years), then we need only look at the number of preschool children alive today and fast-forward the right number of years to find out how many will be starting school in a given year. For example, we know from the 2000 census data that the number of elementary school-age children was 39,689,000 in 2000 and will decrease to 38,646,000 by 2005. As a result, the demand for school desks should also decrease. (See **Exhibit 4.2**.)

Predicting beyond the five-year period is more complicated. We would need to know the number of women of childbearing age and estimate their likelihood of having children. Again, we can use census data to predict the number of women alive today

who could have children in the foreseeable future. We must also consider social and economic trends to help us understand the likelihood of their wanting to have children. Will the economy continue to shrink, creating fewer career opportunities for women? Will women who have postponed childbearing to develop careers decide to take time off to have children? Will there continue to be less of a stigma for single people to raise children, or will there be a return to the nuclear family and the traditional family roles? Will there be social pressure to have even fewer children?

The school desk example illustrates that there are usually multiple, conflicting forces affecting the potential demand for any product. Which aspects of the macroenvironment will be relevant or dominant is not always clear. The analyst's challenge is to examine the forces affecting the market opportunity and evaluate their probable impact.

Current Macroenvironmental Forces

At the outset of the MOA, you will want to gather a host of information on the macroenvironment and then determine whether the industry is growing, shrinking, or shifting as a result of market forces. For example, demand for robotics equipment in the United States was shaped both by the efforts of the robotics suppliers and by forces largely outside of their control, especially by foreign competition in the markets the robotics industry served. The erosion of competitiveness for many U.S. manufacturers was the direct result of competition

from Asian manufacturers who had lower production costs and a better ability to change production lines quickly to respond to changes in market demand. In industry after industry, U.S. firms came to the realization that the rules of the market had changed and their very existence was threatened. To match the low cost and flexibility of the Asian competitors, U.S. firms individually and collectively concluded it would be necessary to re-engineer their production facilities. As a result, demand for robotics technology has increased dramatically, especially that which could provide low-cost, flexible manufacturing.

In a similar way, the television industry currently bears outside pressures that promise to reshape it in profound ways. Historically, TV has been viewed as a *window* to the world. The emerging vision of TV is that it will be the *portal* to the world. This is not the vision of TV suppliers or network programmers but of outsiders who see an opportunity to expand their businesses by connecting with the household through the TV. These investors see that:

- Nearly every household has a TV.
- It is not hard to connect the TV to a cable, phone line, satellite dish, or cellular system.
- The TV is a dumb terminal, and all the investors need to do is add smarts (usually in the form of a set-top box).
- Consumers are responding to easy-to-use point-and-click PC and Internet functionality, and it is not difficult to build the same features into a TV.
- The thresholds for the necessary hardware, software, and communication technology are within reach.

As a result of this assessment, massive investments are now being made by software suppliers (Microsoft and Sega), microchip manufacturers (Intel and Motorola), file servers (Sun Microsystems and IBM), telecommunications firms (AT&T and the regional Bells), entertainment conglomerates (AOL–Time Warner), and a host of narrow segment service providers (banking, grocery shopping). Within a few years, the consumer will step through this portal to use the TV to:

- Conduct business (banking, home shopping, and telecommuting).
- Interact with family, friends, and interest groups with TV add-ons (phone, video, and Internet connections).
- Be entertained through normal TV programming but also through video on

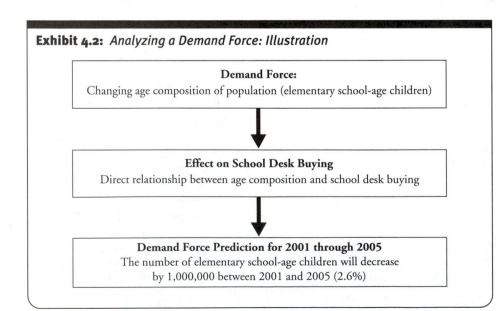

Exhibit 4.2: *Analyzing a Demand Force: Illustration*

Demand Force:
Changing age composition of population (elementary school-age children)

↓

Effect on School Desk Buying
Direct relationship between age composition and school desk buying

↓

Demand Force Prediction for 2001 through 2005
The number of elementary school-age children will decrease by 1,000,000 between 2001 and 2005 (2.6%)

demand and interactive games with remote players.

- Be informed with the addition of narrow segment TV shows, channels, and tailored news summaries beamed by satellite to select audiences and internet news groups.
- Access distance learning and the broadcast of high school and college courses.
- Run the household with the family calendar (now on the wall), messages within family (now on refrigerator), messages from outside (answering machine), and security systems (turning lights on and off, monitoring windows and doors).

In a less exotic market, the vegetable canning industry is responding to new opportunities that outside forces have made available to it. For example, the large influx of immigrants from Mexico prompted the emergence of many Mexican-style restaurants, first as independents and later as chains. As the larger U.S. population became accustomed to Mexican-style food and experimented with different dishes, our palate began to change. We now prepare Mexican-style food at home. As a result, canneries such as Bush Brothers have expanded their product offering to include refried beans, Chili Hots (a chili starter), and bean salsa. Chili Hots also capitalizes on the reduced cooking skills in the household, the limited time available for meal preparation, and the long-standing desire to feel as though you made the meal from scratch. With Chili Hots, all you have to do is add ground beef and tomato sauce to serve chili made "from scratch."

The most striking example of a macroenvironmental force was the terrorist attack of September 11, 2001. The horrific events of that day have caused many people to shun flying, which in turn has caused huge layoffs in the travel industry, including airline companies, convention sites, tourist attractions, and the hotels and restaurants that serve them. Out of fear of future terrorist attacks, many people have avoided crowded places such as shopping malls and movie theaters. These behaviors have also affected consumer purchase rates. And the overall uncertainty of future terrorist attacks and potential layoffs further encouraged consumers to restrict their purchases, further slowing the economy. As consumer spending and confidence waned, retailers and suppliers of consumer goods were adversely affected, causing more layoffs and a general reluctance to expand and invest in the future.

Another widely impacting environmental force was the rapid decline of many "dot.com" firms in 2000 and 2001. This new technology sector had been growing faster than internally generated resources could fund. Large investments had to be made in infrastructure and marketing in order to generate the revenues of the future. When the future revenues did not arrive as soon or in as large an amount as promised, the investment sector lost its patience and stopped additional funding, which caused large numbers of dot.coms to fail. As a result, the venture capital community became wary of further investments in this sector, which in turn affected almost all entrepreneurs with technology ventures.

It is these kinds of industry-shaping macroenvironmental forces that need to be cataloged. How has the industry changed in the last 5 years? What were the driving forces? How is it likely to change in the next 5 to 10 years? What forces are behind this anticipated change?

Conclusion

Understanding the macroenvironment is an important first step in evaluating the market opportunity for a new product or new technology. The macroenvironment can kill the business opportunity, place constraints on it while still leaving room for business, or propel the opportunity forward. Consider the phenomenal success of the all-star hockey player Wayne Gretzky. When asked what he attributes his success to, he says, "Knowing where the puck is going to be." The same is true of a market opportunity. Importantly, knowledge of an invention's macroenvironment can provide valuable signals as to where the opportunity (puck) will be in the market (ice rink).

DEFINE THE PRODUCT MARKET STRUCTURE

Markets differ widely in their structure, from the highly competitive to the vastly underserved. A useful jumping-off point in defining product-market structure is to take an early and broad look at the competition.

Who Is the Competition?

The competition is not just direct competitors but also those who might offer different ways of doing the same thing. Less direct or obvious competitors might turn out to be serious alternatives for the customer to consider. (Detailed profiles will later be drawn of key competitors.)

Anyone who can satisfy the same need is a competitor. The threat of competition emanates not only from suppliers of the same technology but also from alternate technologies for doing the same thing. Take, for example, the Aluminum Company of America (Alcoa), which provides aluminum sheet metal for distributors of soft drinks and beer. The company's immediate competitors are other aluminum companies that provide sheet metal for cans, including Reynolds Aluminum and the Aluminum Company of Canada (Alcan). These are the most obvious but not the only competitors for Alcoa. Alcoa also competes against glass and plastic container suppliers. Plastic container suppliers are probably the greatest threat to Alcoa's soft drink container business.

In the last decade, the aluminum can has lost ground to the plastic container, which offers better production and distribution economies. The aluminum can's share of the business was further eroded by Coca-Cola's introduction of a 16-ounce plastic bottle in the classic hourglass shape in 1994. The contoured plastic bottle is unique, well known, *and* proprietary. It conveys the nostalgia of the original glass bottle and possesses the production and handling advantages of plastic. Coca-Cola has now shifted a large portion of its bottling activities to the contoured plastic bottle.

The Alcoa situation demonstrates that the *threat of competition* emanates not only from suppliers of the same technology but also from alternate technologies for doing the same thing. To restate this proposition, your product or service will compete with alternative product types (for example, family self-service restaurants versus family table-service restaurants—McDonald's vs. Denny's) as well as with similar brands of the same product type (McDonald's versus Wendy's). You must be alert to both kinds of competition. Thus, it is essential to start with a broad look at competition within a generic class of products and then to narrow it down to competition between product types and finally to similar brands of a product type.

The beverage container market also illustrates that an *opportunity* for competition may exist across product markets. Where Alcoa finds threats in plastic, Eastman Chemical finds opportunity. As the number 1 supplier of polyethylene terephthalate (PET) in the country, Eastman

Chemical pushes the advantages of plastic over aluminum to beverage suppliers, distributors, and consumers. Eastman's objective is to take the business away from the aluminum companies; it could not be happier with Coke's discovery of the contoured plastic bottle.

Often, opportunities for competition will come at the expense of established competitors in established product markets. For example, personal computers have captured business from the electric typewriter, the minicomputer, and the mainframe. The PC is also capturing business from the television as more and more children and their parents turn to it for entertainment. PC suppliers such as Apple and Sony hope to replace current TVs with a "smart" version that acts as a user-friendly PC. On the other hand, TV and phone makers see great opportunity in selling Web surfers that use TVs or new screen phones to access the World Wide Web. They expect to take some of the business back from the PC and, more importantly, add new business as more and more consumers become accustomed to e-mail, information searching, and entertainment on the Web.

There are many other examples of one technology attacking other technologies in related product markets. In large information storage and retrieval applications, the DVD is taking business from paper and microfiche and is rapidly taking over the videotape business. Direct digital satellites have allowed the satellite TV business (previously limited to remote locations) to capture home subscribers from local cable TV companies. Soon, cellular systems will compete against both. Personal watercraft that can now pull skiers compete against ski boats. Off-road vehicles with better suspension systems and more comfortable interiors now compete against the family sedan. And raspberry juice and grape juice were added to cranberry juice to move the latter beyond the Thanksgiving and Christmas holiday market. Cranberry juice now competes in the broader juice market against apple and orange juices and to some extent in the broader beverage market against soft drinks.

In summary, the opportunities for competition may come in the form of novel and better ways of doing well-established tasks and activities. The MOA must recognize the product markets and competitors that can be attacked, as well as those that must be defended.

What Is Product Market Structure?

Probably the most important and difficult challenge for an MOA is to define the market structure and determine the requirements of the market. *Market structure* is the arrangement of groups or segments of buyers constituting a total market. Notably, each segment differs from others in the way its buyers respond to a marketing strategy. Customers in different groups have at least somewhat different market requirements. Market requirements are the benefits that buyers expect from products as a condition of buying.

A good starting point for understanding market structure is to study existing product offerings. If a need is present, the overwhelming odds are that some products already satisfy that need. Rarely would a new product create an entirely new market. For the most part, new products provide new ways of meeting existing needs. However, new technologies *are* capable of expanding demand if they relax the constraints on what is possible at a given price.

The relationship between market needs and products is the basis for the concept of product market structure. The similarities and differences in the available product and technology offerings reveal a great deal about the needs being served: The more pervasive a feature is in the available offerings, the more likely it satisfies a widely felt need. Differences in features, functions, or capabilities among regularly purchased products suggest that the market is sensitive to these differences and that they somehow represent a natural segmentation of the market.

The "need" to eat out in restaurants—where most elements of the meal including menu selection, food preparation, serving, and cleanup are provided for the customer—offers an illustration of product market structure. The generic class of products available to satisfy this need is food service (see **Exhibit 4.3**). One type of food service is restaurants, which are in turn divided into subclasses including fast-food, family, and atmosphere restaurants. Each restaurant subclass may be further broken down into specific types of fast-food restaurants such as hamburger, pizza, and chicken. Notice that each restaurant type represents a unique way to meet the underlying consumer need, providing a unique combination of benefits and costs. Thus, customers must choose which benefit and cost combination is best for them.

Each restaurant product-type category may be further broken down into competing brands, with each brand meant to build an edge over competitors. Of course, a brand has the characteristics of one of the

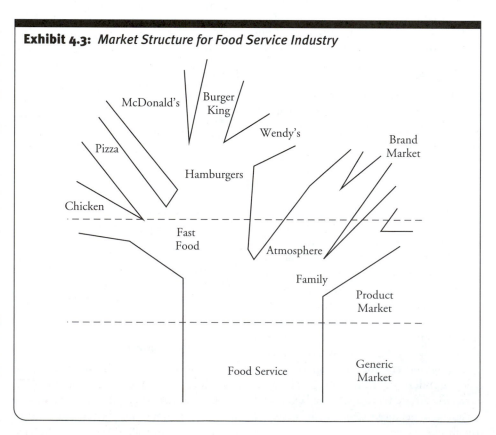

Exhibit 4.3: *Market Structure for Food Service Industry*

McDonald's · Burger King · Wendy's · Hamburgers · Pizza · Chicken · Fast Food · Atmosphere · Family · Brand Market · Product Market · Generic Market · Food Service

product types in the generic class: McDonald's, Burger King, and Wendy's represent similar brands that compete in the hamburger fast-food restaurant product type.

Generic classes, product types, and brands compose a market arena. Each company and its brands are competing for business in this arena, taking on both similar and dissimilar brands of other product types when competing for a share of sales. McDonald's is really competing with other fast-food hamburger restaurants, other fast-food restaurants (e.g., chicken and pizza), and other types of restaurants (e.g., family-style table service, family-style self-service, ethnic, atmosphere). An MOA must develop a picture of this larger arena.

How Are Product Markets Pictured?

The product-market structure represents the interface between the available products and the market's needs. Products (the best current solutions for meeting the needs of customers) and markets (customers with their needs, wants, and values) are essentially opposite sides of the marketing equation. Any product or service that does not fulfill some need will be killed off by the market through lack of demand.

The objective of marketing is to maximize customer satisfaction by providing products and services that satisfy customer needs better than anything else on the market. The challenge is to determine what these needs are and how to make money by fulfilling them. There are two approaches to understanding customer needs.

The first is simply to ask end users about their needs. In the chapter on customer value, Sarah Gardial and Bob Woodruff introduce methods for determining customer value. The techniques of laddering and grand tours are wonderful methods for exploring attributes preferred, consequences desired, and values sought. However, you will discover that end users are imperfect in articulating factors that really motivate their behaviors. End users either do not want to say what is really on their minds, do not know how to say it, or really do not consciously know what motivates them. Another challenge is the diversity of the market; it is impractical to ask all possible customers about all of their needs and wants.

The second approach to understanding customer needs is to observe their behavior in the marketplace. Look at what products they buy, and then infer the attributes, consequences, and values they want. In some respects, it is an easier task to assemble all of the available brands (or their descriptions) and compare and contrast their features and how they meet one need or another. The objective is to look at what attributes exist in products on the market and to speculate on needs being served. The underlying assumption is that the current product offerings reflect a natural segmentation in the market. If customers are buying a given model on a regular basis and not buying others on the market, then there must be something special about the model's ability to satisfy some need or want better than other models.

What Are the Steps in Developing a Product-Market Structure?

The first step in developing a product-market structure is to identify all of the ways in which a need is currently being satisfied. The alternatives are usually competing brands drawn from the same technology, but different technologies able to satisfy the need should also be included. Taken together, all of these options represent the generic market offering.

The second step is to sort the offerings into a treelike structure, where each branch represents a finer segmentation of the products based upon shared features, functions, or capabilities. (See **Exhibit 4.4**.) Offerings that are similar in important ways should be grouped together into product types, and the offerings within one product type should be noticeably different from those within other product types. Look for a hierarchy of important differences.

The limitation of the analysis is that the current market structure does not reveal what else customers want but only that the current brands are the best available for meeting their needs and wants. For example, in the model train industry, the predominant product offerings were 12-gauge and 24-gauge train sets. A focus on only the existing product offerings would not have revealed a dissatisfaction with these offerings. Independently and unknown to each other, many model train enthusiasts wished that model train makers would build a bigger train set that would be easy to assemble, could go around the room or the garden, and had cars that felt more lifesize. Eventually, one company listened to these wishes and created the very popular, although expensive, larger-scale train set (G-gauge, for garden gauge). A study of existing product categories and brands is unlikely to reveal the opportunity to create something that is not on the market.

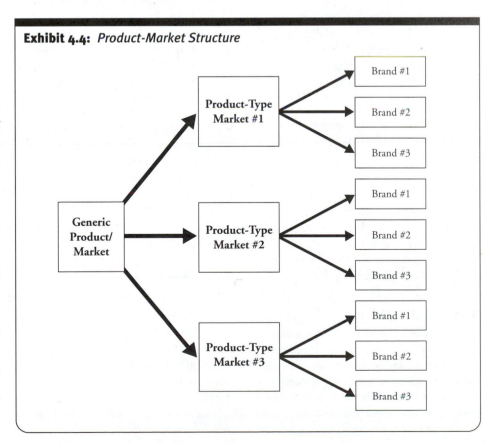

Exhibit 4.4: *Product-Market Structure*

Another major disadvantage of focusing on purchase behavior alone is that you must speculate on the factors motivating purchase and use, which is difficult to do accurately. A combination of the two techniques is best, asking end users what they value and studying the features they are actually buying on a regular basis. If we work both sides of the equation (products and markets), we can maximize our understanding of customer needs and how to fulfill them.

The ultimate goal is to overlay the two types of information: customer values and the product-market structure. Only then will you be able to fill in many of the blanks in your knowledge of the markets you want to serve.[1]

What Are the Benefits of Understanding the Product-Market Structure?

The value of developing the product-market structure is multifold. First, it should help you visualize the natural organization of the market. It will lend order to what might appear to be a chaotic assortment of products and customers.

Second, the product-market structure should help you realize that there are many ways to satisfy a basic need. Customers usually have no intrinsic loyalty to a particular solution. Rather, they will migrate to whichever technology provides the greatest delivery of benefits desired. Thus, your competition may include other technologies or product types. You increase your vulnerability by considering only competitors and technologies basically equivalent to your own.

Finally, the product-market structure should help you realize that the market is not homogeneous. Different solutions evolve in response to different market conditions. If a product market exists, it is because some unique combination of features provides value not achievable by the other product offerings. Thus, the market is composed of any number of segments looking for tailored solutions.

BUILD PROFILES

After you develop a broad understanding of your market, the next step is to gather very specific information about your competitors, end users, and channel partners. This information will help you to determine the minimum requirements for entering the market and to see where you might have

the opportunity to make a unique contribution and gain some differential advantage. This information will enable you to develop your market entry strategy.

As you build the profiles of competitors, end users, and channel partners and focus on building one profile at a time, it is still wise to watch for data points or clues relevant to the others. A good starting point is the competitor profile, both because it follows logically from the product-market analysis and because competitor knowledge, especially of brand offerings and advertising themes, will help you to structure your questions for end users. End user profiles should probably be developed next. Channel profiles can be last; they will build on your knowledge of the competition's distribution tactics and on end user practices and preferences regarding sources or suppliers of the product or service.

Building Competitor Profiles

This section focuses on building competitor profiles. The logical approach is to begin broadly, collecting information about the industry as a whole. With this knowledge as a backdrop, you will be able to narrow the search to a limited number of key competitors. You will want to collect detailed information on the business and marketing practices of these important competitors.

Industry Sales Trends

Discovering industry sales trends is also an important early part of the industry analysis. In fact, the industry sales trends must be studied in conjunction with the macroenvironmental trends and the product market structure. As you will probably discover, the pattern in sales for the industry as a whole and for specific product markets will be linked to the macroenvironmental forces that the industry has encountered for the past decade or more.

The typical questions to ask in an industry sales analysis are:

- What has been the pattern of sales over the last 5 to 10 years?
- What has been the pattern of growth?
- Are some sectors experiencing more growth than others?
- Are some product categories becoming more important while others are losing their appeal?
- Is the total market growing, or are competitors fighting for market share in a mature, stable market?

Firms within Product Markets

The next step is to narrow the focus to the firms competing within one or more selected product types. The purpose of this analysis is twofold:

1. To understand what makes each group of firms unique compared to the rest of the industry.
2. To form a picture of the competitive practices typical of the entire industry and to uncover differences in the strategies typical of different product types.

The task is to gather the kinds of information shown in **Exhibit 4.5**.

A good way to start this analysis and to prepare for the next stage of key competitor profiling is to map the competitors onto the product-market structure prepared earlier. For example, **Exhibit 4.6** shows the market structure for information storage and retrieval that we prepared in an MOA for the write-once-read-many (WORM) optical storage invention from Oak Ridge National Laboratory. In this study, we were particularly interested in the magnetic and optical product markets under electronic information storage and retrieval. We identified all of the major players at that time and mapped them onto the market structure tree. Our research objective was to understand how the different groups competed against each other for a share of the electronic storage market.

In reviewing our findings, we saw that Sony competed in all segments while Hitachi competed in only large-systems markets (both magnetic and optical). Still others such as Maxtor competed in only one product market (small, erasable optical systems). It is apparent that Sony employs a

---

Exhibit 4.5: *Components of an Industry Profile*

What is the industry composition?
- Number of firms
- Industry sales
- Industry structure

What are typical marketing practices?
- Market targets
- Price-feature packages
- Advertising
- Distribution

What changes are anticipated?

What are the industry's strengths and weaknesses?

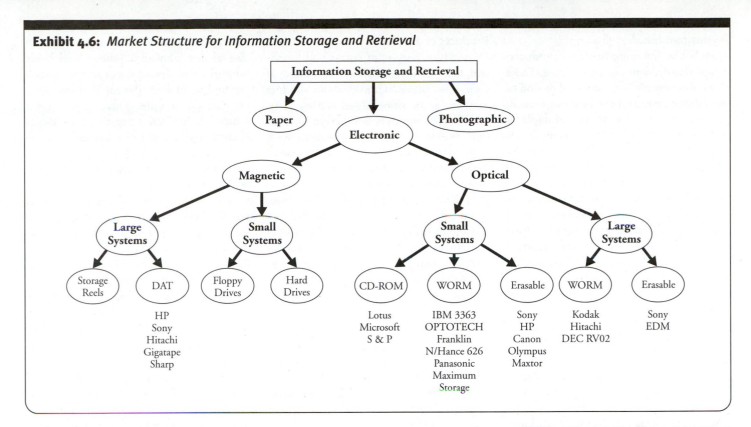

Exhibit 4.6: *Market Structure for Information Storage and Retrieval*

Information Storage and Retrieval
- Paper
- Electronic
  - Magnetic
    - Large Systems
      - Storage Reels
      - DAT — HP, Sony, Hitachi, Gigatape, Sharp
    - Small Systems
      - Floppy Drives
      - Hard Drives
  - Optical
    - Small Systems
      - CD-ROM — Lotus, Microsoft, S & P
      - WORM — IBM 3363, OPTOTECH, Franklin, N/Hance 626, Panasonic, Maximum Storage
      - Erasable — Sony, HP, Canon, Olympus, Maxtor
    - Large Systems
      - WORM — Kodak, Hitachi, DEC RV02
      - Erasable — Sony, EDM
- Photographic

differentiated market strategy while Hitachi and Maxtor employ niche strategies. Each could be a threat but for different reasons.

This analysis should also be applied to the firms competing in the photographic product market, which will be a good source of business for the new electronic mediums. The photographic storage and retrieval market is composed of firms that sell microfiche and microfilm systems. These photographic systems have been used extensively in libraries (for archiving periodicals, books, and corporate financial statements), banks (for archiving canceled checks), and industrial firms (for parts catalogs). A high-capacity WORM storage and retrieval system has important advantages over microfiche and microfilm in access speed, image quality, and storage space. To sell into this product market, it is necessary to understand the marketing practices and performance capabilities of major suppliers of microfiche, microfilm, imaging, and viewing equipment. To be sure, their strategies and tactics would be different from those of Sony, Panasonic, and Hitachi in the electronic product market.

Key Competitors

The last step in the competitor analysis is to assess key competitors. It is wise to profile the companies that will have the greatest impact on the new venture's ability to achieve its objectives in the market. Your objectives are to:

- Discover the capabilities of the products or services offered by key competitors.
- Learn the tactical details of their marketing strategy.
- Learn their intentions for future products and market development (acquisitions).
- Assess their financial and leadership capabilities.
- Discover any unusual situations that might affect their ability to serve the market.
- Document the basic demographic information of each competitor in terms of the location of its corporate headquarters, location of plants or other key assets, ownership, and so on.
- Discover weaknesses in their position in the market and assess their vulnerability to attack by a new competitor.

Select Key Competitors

This section explains which firms to profile, what information to collect, and where to find it. **Exhibit 4.7** provides a summary of the information to collect.

There are several guidelines to follow in selecting key competitors. Obviously, the firms with the largest market share should be studied because they probably set the pace for the industry and the terms of cus-

Exhibit 4.7: *Components of a Key Competitor Profile*

What is the key competitor's financial size and strength?
- Sales
- Profit margins
- Total assets
- Debt
- Equity
- Various financial ratios

What are the key competitor's technical, marketing, and management capabilities?
- Mission and business objectives
- Market share position and trends
- Management capabilities and limitations
- Technical and operating capabilities
- Target market strategies
- Access to key resources

What changes are anticipated?
- Size and strength
- Market targets
- Marketing objectives
- Marketing mix

tomer satisfaction. Do not assume, however, that they are invulnerable. General Motors, IBM, AT&T, and Sears have demonstrated that dominant players leave certain niches open and serve others poorly.

You should know which niches are comparatively unprotected.

Hot new emerging firms (or products) should also be identified and studied. These businesses may give clues to the direction of the industry in the future. Find out what all the excitement is about. For example, a competitor analysis of PC add-on boards identified the hottest CD-ROM company in the industry. Further investigation revealed that the company's CD-ROMs had an access speed four to six times faster than the norm. The excitement was certain to presage a future requirement of at least six times the current norm for this product market. Today, the writeable CD is quickly becoming a standard, and the writeable DVD is likely to be the next hot add-on board.

In the competitor analysis, it is also important to study firms that are down on one knee or on their death beds. Where did they go wrong? Did they cause their own undoing, was someone else smarter and more adept, or did the market change, removing the need for what they provided? For example, why is Kmart having such difficulty in the retail market? Is it because its stores have gotten too old and run down? Are the stores now in poor locations given the normal migration of their target clientele? Have consumer tastes changed since Kmart's heyday? Did Sam Walton outsmart Kmart with larger, better stocked, and better located stores (Wal-Marts and Sam's Wholesale Clubs)?

Finally, if it is your objective to raid the market turf of alternate technologies (such as WORM technology taking on the microfiche and microfilm technologies, or plastic bottle suppliers taking on the aluminum can suppliers), then you need to know as much as possible about the dominant players in these other product markets. How do these firms normally sell their products? What are the benefits they sell and the inconveniences they cause? What are the typical service levels, selling terms, promotional techniques? If there are norms of any kind, they will be reflected in the mind-sets of the buyers you hope to recruit. Your marketing strategy must either adapt to or attempt to change these predispositions.

The industry analysis described earlier helps in identifying the key competitors, enabling you to see the dominant players across product markets and strong niche players in your specific target market.

Discover Capabilities of Competing Products or Services

Detailed knowledge of competing brands will help tremendously in the design of your new brand. Consider the product market for in-office blood testing. This market has historically been served by send-out reference labs with sophisticated, high-volume blood-processing equipment. These labs would pick up blood samples from doctors' offices each evening, transport them overnight to a central location, run the panel of tests specified by the doctor, and either call back the results or send them by courier the next day. In time, large hospitals bought similar equipment and made the same service available to doctors affiliated with the hospital. Later, several companies entered the market with automated equipment that performed a limited number of frequently run blood analysis tests. These were sold directly to doctors' offices, allowing the doctors to perform their own blood analysis quickly and profitably (typically providing an 1,800 percent return in the first year).

Exhibit 4.8 lists the major brands of blood analyzers on the market and their key features. The data in this figure indicate the minimum requirements to enter the market. If a feature is offered on multiple brands, that suggests it is valued by the market. Offering less places a firm outside the norm. In the case of the blood processor, we see in Exhibit 4.8 that whole blood can be processed on three of the six leading brands. The other three brands can handle only serum or plasma. This observation raises the question: Is the market moving in the direction of whole blood processing? Perhaps whole blood processing is faster or more convenient for the medical staff and, therefore, a growing preference among buyers. Will it be a requirement for any new brand to enter the market?

In Exhibit 4.8, we see that the base cost for the equipment ranges from a low of $4,495 to a high of $12,900. Interestingly, the more expensive equipment has the lowest cost per blood test but the longest processing time. This information raises questions about the trade-offs doctors are willing to make for in-office blood testing.

The tables you compile should highlight the unique features of different brands, possibly suggesting the supplier's strategy for product differentiation and market segmentation. From this example, it appears that Kodak targets the high end of the market

while Boehringer Manheim targets the low end, probably small office clinics. We can also see that Johnson & Johnson is the only supplier to use a magnetic card type technology and that Chem-Pro can perform up to 60 tests per minute. These specs suggest Johnson & Johnson is targeting larger clinics likely to have a higher blood-testing volume.

If brand design and feature data are gathered over a period of time, you can see the evolution of the product category and how the market responds to the need for higher perceived performance. In the blood processor example, we found that the market demanded more and more tests be performed in the doctor's office. Brands that offered the greatest variety of blood tests were preferred over faster or less expensive machines. Many doctors seemed to prefer models that offer a standard set of tests (called *panels*) at one time, thus reducing the need to send blood samples to reference labs for the more common panels. At the same time, small offices were happy with a simpler machine that performed standard tests used in monitoring health conditions rather than diagnosing the causes of poor health. Thus, the market was multimodal, and one brand would not meet all of the needs.

Finally, it is instructive to place one's own product or service in the brand/feature table. Do your brand's features fall within or outside the norm? If you are below the norm, is it on a common feature (suggesting a standard), or is it a specialty feature that appeals to selected segments? Does your offer exceed the norm on important features? Do you offer features no one else offers? By comparing your product to competing brands, feature for feature, it is possible to size up your potential in the market and see whether there is a need for additional work to meet or beat the competition.

Learn the Tactical Details of Your Competitors' Marketing Strategies

Just as your product and prices must fall within the acceptable limits of the market, the rest of your market strategy must consider the tactics of your competition. These tactics represent benchmarks against which you can judge your own.

For example, if a key competitor develops strong brand awareness through frequent advertising, ask yourself whether you have the same advertising dollars or whether you will need another mechanism to get your name in front of the customer. If a competitor brings out a new product

Exhibit 4.8: *Feature Comparison/Blood Analyzer Competitors*

	Analyst Dupont	DT-60 Kodak	Vision Abbott	Reflotron Boehringer Manheim	Johnson & Johnson	ATAC 2000 Biochem LabSystems
Size	8.5 × 25 × 13	19 × 14 × 7	11 × 21 × 17	12 × 14 × 8	20 × 18	46 × 19 × 9 basic unit
Weight	42	25	70	12	19	73
Technology	rotor	slide	cartridge	strip	card	rotor
Detection	absorbance	reflectance	absorbance	reflectance	reflectance	absorbance
Volumes	30, 60, 71	10	10	30	30	util. vac. tube
Specimen	s. p	s. p	wb. s. p	wb. s. p	wb. s. p	s. p
Throughput (max.)	66	85	60	25	60	60
Analysis Time (min)	10.5	5.2	8	3	<1	10
Schedule Load	one/10.5	up to 6	up to 10	one/3 min.	one/min.	one/10
Report	display, printer	display, printer	printer	display	printer, display	printer, display
Instrument Cost	$12,900	+$2,900	$14,995	$4,495	$5,500	$10,000
Average Test Cost	$0.46 (panel)	$2.00	$1.60–3.00	$1.90	$2.10	$.069 (panel)

every nine months, how often should you plan on updates? If most of your competitors use a direct sales force, can you get by with independent reps? If your number 1 competitor has an elaborate 2,000 square foot exhibit at the major trade shows, how will you present yourself?

Knowledge of the marketing tactics of your key competitors may also help you identify gaps in their strategy. For example, if a key competitor does not have a strong presence at regional or local trade shows, it may give you an opportunity to meet the customer without strong competitor interference. Or, if the competition does not offer a 24-hour help line, you may be able to differentiate your product or company by featuring one.

Your market analysis may also show that your key competitor has been slow to enter new channels of distribution. Apple and IBM, for instance, discouraged mail-order sales of their products for a long time out of deference to their established retail outlets. This disposition created an opportunity for Dell and Gateway, which did not have strong alliances with the normal channels of distribution. These newcomers observed a price-sensitive segment of the market willing to take a chance on reliability and return policies in order to buy a PC at substantial savings over local retail.

The kind of tactical information you will need to collect for a competitor analysis is outlined in **Exhibit 4.9**. The sources

of information for an industry and competitor analysis are many and varied. The primary source of information will be the target company's own products, brochures, advertisements, and press releases. Product brochures are a very good source for obtaining detailed product specs on competing products. Financial reports reveal new products and markets. Some information is entirely in the public arena, while much of it will have to be tracked down through key informants and skillful questioning.

Third-party opinions and observations may be quite helpful, including those of reporters and editors of the trade press, managers of trade associations, channel partners, and even other competitors. The trade press is an excellent source of information as it chronicles the fame and fortune of key players, the rise and fall of important competitors, and the introduction of new products and new ideas.

In many technical fields and consumer markets, product comparisons are undertaken by industry experts and reported in trade journals and specialty consumer magazines (e.g., *Infoworld, Multimedia Sound, Consumer Reports, Popular Electronics*). These product comparisons and the editorial commentary that accompanies them can offer substantial insight into the norms of the industry and the emerging trends in product offerings.

Salespeople are a great source of information. They know who is doing what and

Exhibit 4.9: *Components of Key Competitor's Marketing Practices*

Key competitor's marketing strategy:
- Market targets
- Marketing objectives
- Marketing mix

Tactics
- Definition of target boundaries
- Product characteristics
- Prices charged and policies
- Distribution network
- Channel service and incentive program
- Advertising copy, media, layout
- Personal selling appeals
- Sales promotion activities
- Publicity stories

how the customers view each supplier. Talk with more than one salesperson to offset the pride in the salesperson's brand and suspicion of others. Above all, have customers walk you through the consumption process and take note of what they like or dislike. When they note anything unusual, be sure to ask, "Why is that important to you?"

Channel partners of key competitors are also a good source of information. Channel partners are well informed regarding key benefits, features, prices, and so on of the products/services they sell. These channel partners might also become your sales channel, so it is useful to find out how business is normally conducted for any firm wishing to sell through the channel.

Finally, if the industry or competitor is large enough, standardized information sources such as Value Line may track the firm and provide detailed data on its actions and apparent strategy.

Do not expect the firm's strategy to be spelled out for you. In many cases, there is no clearly articulated strategy. It may reside only in the minds of a few key executives, or it may be something that evolves as opportunities and challenges present themselves. No matter how formal or informal the plan is, it is not likely to be public information. Thus, you must try to deduce a competitor's strategy from its decisions and public statements.

Building End User Profiles

The process of grouping consumers into relatively homogenous clusters requires that you look carefully at the final, or end, user.

Who Is the Customer?

This question is more complicated than it first appears. In some cases, the customer is a "channel customer" rather than the end user. For example, grocery manufacturers know that they need shelf space at the retail level and warehouse space at the wholesale level before they can have sales. The retail and wholesale customers are the gatekeepers who can make or break the business. As a consequence, grocery manufacturers focus on the trade (wholesalers and retailers), directing their marketing and promotional efforts there.

Are these wholesalers, brokers, manufacturer agents, retailers, and so on the customer? Yes, they are the *channel customers,* but they are not the customer we want to focus on here.

What if the firm sells a component that goes into another product or service? For example, Philips Speaker Systems of Dendermonde, Belgium, provides a complete audio system (speakers and wiring) to automobile manufacturers such as Porsche and Ford of Europe. Intel, perhaps the best known original equipment manufacturer (OEM) supplier, provides the computing brains to Compaq, Micron, Dell, Gateway, and a host of other microcomputer assemblers (recall their clever advertising theme "Intel inside"). Increasingly, companies are

finding it smart to outsource components to firms that specialize in their design and manufacture. The OEM market is becoming quite large, and these buyers are very demanding.

Who is the customer, the final user or this OEM buyer? Obviously, the OEM buyers are extremely important customers. Failure to satisfy their needs will result in the loss of business. However, they are really intermediaries. Someone else will ultimately be using the component (as part of something else). Philips must consider the businessperson who wants to be cocooned in his or her Porsche while traveling to work or the next appointment. What is the sound effect that must be created within the passenger compartment for this customer to feel cocooned? Porsche's ability to sell its cars depends, in part, upon Philips' ability to create this cocooning effect. Philips' ability to retain the Porsche account also depends upon this same ability.

This section focuses not on channel customers but on end users. You must look all the way down the channel to the final user to understand how the product or service is being used and what need is being fulfilled. The end user may be a secretary, an assembly line worker, a salesperson, a retail clerk, a mother, a soccer player, a recreational skier, or a video game player. These are the people we must understand. Only then can we step back and understand who else might be involved in the purchase and consumption process.

Information to Collect

Exhibit 4.10 provides a summary of the information to collect in order to build an end user profile. Essentially, you will want to know:

- What customers are like as real people.
- How they go about deciding what to buy to satisfy the need/want.
- What outside influences (out of the company's control) are affecting buying decisions.

The following sections provide the rationale for collecting this information and offer suggestions on where to collect it.

Who Are the Potential Customers and Why Would They Want to Buy the New Product?

A good starting point to answer these questions is the customer base for competing technologies. Look for products that cur-

---

Exhibit 4.10: *Components of a Customer Profile*

What are customers like as people?
- Needs and wants
- Important use situations
- Activities and interests
- Opinions and attitudes
- Demographic characteristics
- Values

How do people decide to buy?
- Problem recognition
- Search for and use of product information
- Evaluation
- Purchase procedure
- Satisfaction with past purchase

What outside influences are affecting buying?
- Population and social forces
- Legal forces
- Technological forces
- Economic forces
- Natural forces

---

rently fill the market need and suppliers who are selling into this market. Try to find out who buys these products and why. This initial approach to gathering market information will be efficient because there is usually a wealth of information on existing products and markets.

Try to find out how competing technologies are used. What primary need is being satisfied? What motivates customers to buy? You will be looking for parallels between your new product and those on the market. Can you do the same thing, only better?

To learn about secondary needs and wants, look at the features offered by each competitor. Which features are standard across brands, and which are optional? Which features generate the most interest? Keep in mind that every feature is driven by a need. If a feature did not provide value to somebody, it would not be there. Try to find out why some customers prefer certain features but not others.

As you investigate existing brands and technologies, you will probably discover that some are used for one purpose while others are used for another. One of your goals is to discover how different products fit one application better than another. You will find that this information is similar to the product-market structure discussed previously. One of your objectives in gathering this information is to identify the current market segments.

At this stage you can sort out the applications and market segments that have the greatest relevance for your product or technology. This will be a subjective assessment but will help to streamline further research.

Look for Behavior Patterns

Good researchers rely more on end user actions than on any opinion. As the saying goes, "Actions speak louder than words." Researchers are interested in how end users purchase available products, in changes in the buying patterns, and in what seems to be causing the change.

For an MOA for multimedia sound for the PC, we visited computer stores to talk to salespeople and store managers about buying patterns. We also called mail-order houses and spoke with salespeople. We visited trade shows and spoke with exhibitors of related products. We collected historical data on purchase patterns of sound cards, speakers, and software featuring sound. We counted the number of ads featuring sound in computer magazines and the number of magazines targeting the multimedia market. We looked at the trends in the sale of stereo televisions versus mono-sound TVs. We also tracked videoconferencing sales because videoconferencing requires good sound. We looked everywhere the end user had a chance to choose between one product featuring sound and another not featuring sound. The most valuable information showed us how consumers were spending their money on sound. This was the vote that counted.

Get to Know Customers as Real People

The preceding sources essentially provide secondhand information. It is absolutely imperative to get to know the customers as real people. Do not rely on statistics: They provide a hollow impression of the end user. We advise visiting end users in the places where they use the product or service. The customer should explain, and preferably demonstrate, how the product (or a competing one) is used and the factors that influence performance and satisfaction.

In addition to factual information, the analyst should be looking for emotional expressions of frustration or delight toward the product or its use. From our satisfaction research,[2] we know that emotional responses are correlated with exceptional performance

(good and bad). These reactions may provide additional clues to the requirements of the market (high satisfaction) or opportunities (dissatisfaction) with existing products.

Discover Purchase Patterns

As you gather information about end users, try to understand their purchase patterns. What is the typical size of purchase? How frequently is a purchase made? Are there seasonal swings in purchase, use, and consumption?

The purchase pattern will determine your supply and financing requirements. If it is a seasonal product (sailboats, ski equipment, or school supplies), you will have to fill the supply pipeline some months in advance and taper off production and distribution before the season winds down. In contrast, products with a steady consumption pattern (hamburger, laundry detergent, office supplies) require steady flows out of the factory and through the channels of distribution. Other products and services have a combination of steady demand with peaks associated with major events (hair cuts, greeting cards). In each case, the demand pattern will drive the production schedule and distribution pattern. Of course, there are ways to help smooth out demand by offering rebates, seasonal discounts for placing orders early, or price specials to pull up seasonal dips in demand.

Understand the Buying Process

As you spend time with customers, try to learn about their buying process: How do they go about making purchase decisions? How long does it normally take, and who else might be involved? Is the decision process straightforward or complex? Will a purchase have a domino effect on other parts of the person's life? For example, the decision to move to a new home affects shopping patterns, commuting routes, school systems, and friendships. In the case of a nuclear heart imaging technology we investigated, we found that dozens of decisions were tied to the choice of the nuclear isotope. The hospital changing to our technology would require new imaging cameras, retraining for physicians and technicians, new suppliers and buying procedures, and new storage solutions.

You will find almost all purchases fall into one of three categories: straight rebuy, modified rebuy, and new purchase. The preferred supplier will obviously encourage a straight rebuy. Being the new kid on the

block, you want to break this cycle, but it is very difficult to get buyers to change the way they do things. Buyers will be reluctant to review all of the options and make a new decision. Be sure to ask what it would take to break the hold of the preferred supplier.

As you investigate the buying process, try to determine who else is involved. In a classical sense, there are five buying roles: initiator, influencer, decider, buyer, and user. These roles can be performed by one individual (as in the purchase and consumption of a convenience good such as a hamburger or newspaper) or by many (as in the purchase of a high-priced durable good such as office equipment, a car, piece of furniture, or computer for the home).

The *initiator* is the person who first suggests the idea of buying a product or service. *Influencers* are those who shape the outcome of the decision but do not have the authority to make the decision. The *decider* is the person who decides whether to buy, what to buy, how to buy, or where to buy. The *buyer* is the person who makes the actual purchase. The *user* is the person who consumes or uses the product or service. The important point is determining who is involved in the decision process. You may need separate strategies for the initiator, influencer, decider, buyer, and user.[3]

Understand Customer Value

A solid MOA requires more than the descriptive information outlined here; you should also probe into the motivations of your target end user. Conduct in-depth interviews with a small number of end users. Plan on spending an hour and a half with each person. Although the sample is not large, the depth of understanding you will take away will be enormous. The insight will dramatically affect your whole perspective on the market opportunity and your subsequent market strategy. It is well worth the time.

One of the desired end products of this phase of the investigation is a *means-end hierarchy*, which will help you understand end user motivations. You will want to know how the customer relates to the product at three levels: attributes, consequences, and values. In the next chapter, Gardial and Woodruff describe this important process in detail. The following serves as an introduction.

At the lowest level, you will want to know which attributes—often objectively expressed in terms of physical characteristics, features, or components—of the technologies are relevant to the customer. The attributes of a car are the suspension system, interior fabrics, horsepower, and so on. The attributes of a wine cooler are carbonation, label design, amount of alcohol, size of container, and so forth. The attributes of a computer-controlled turning machine are the range of the variable speed motor, the size of the work space for positioning a piece of metal, the mechanisms for positioning and replacing the cutting tool, the programming language for controlling the cutting bit, and so on. The attributes of a Web search engine include the physical appearance of the site (Google's first page has a clean, simple presentation compared to AltaVista's cluttered look), the ability to click through to preselected, popular sites versus the need to type in search words, and the number of cataloged sites in its database. The attributes of a consulting service are the training and experience of the technical specialist, the speed of the response to inquiries, the logic and evidence behind a recommendation or conclusion, and the ability to communicate and persuade in a meeting, among others.

Each attribute or bundle of attributes has a consequence—either desired or avoided—for the user. In the car example, driving ease is a positive consequence of factors such as instrument layout, seat comfort, and shifting smoothness, among others. Feeling hassled with after-sale support is a negative consequence of slow repair service, pressure tactics to repair "discovered" problems, and being treated as an unintelligent person. Importantly, end users tend to care more about the consequences (the finish on a car holds its shine and does not show dings) than the attribute responsible (polymer rather than sheet metal was used on the side panels). Thus, a new product must be measured in terms of the consequences for the user.

The final element in the means-end hierarchy is values. Values are the ultimate ends that the customer wishes to achieve through the use or consumption of a particular product. Products and services are the means by which these ends are pursued (hence the term "means-end" hierarchy).

The means-end hierarchy should reveal the consequences that are driving or limiting product and service use. The hierarchy helps you picture the elasticity of attribute performance relative to its consequences to the user. That is, if a component or feature could do more (faster, easier, or at a lower price), what would the consequence be for the end user? If the consequences are significant and the incremental improvement in attribute performance falls within the domain of the new product, then there may be great opportunity. If the added capability provided by the new product creates little excitement because the consequences are minor, then there is probably little opportunity.

Knowledge of attribute-consequence elasticity aids identification of elements of the new product or service that are worthy of further investment. In some respect, each attribute or feature represents a constraint on consumption—the product is not fast enough, smooth enough, flexible enough, strong enough, and so on. We need to know the factors that limit use and consumption.

Just as important, further development of features that provide the greatest positive consequence to the user may not only draw consumption away from existing products but also increase consumption in the product category. For example, the expansion of CPU capacity on microcomputers not only drew business away from mainframe computers but also resulted in new applications and expanded markets. Cellular telephone technology, rechargeable batteries, color ink-jet printing, and carbon-carbon fibers all represented improvements in technical capabilities that have caused explosive growth in what were once niche markets. This elasticity concept will be further developed in Chapter Six.

Observe How End Users React

Entrepreneurs are usually very secretive about their inventions. They are afraid that someone will steal the idea, commercialize it, and make a great fortune ahead of them. Although there is reason to be cautious, at some point it will be necessary to find out what end users think of your invention, technology, or capability. They must see it, handle it, and experience what it can do for them.

After selecting a target group, show (or at least describe) the new product to them. It is far better to *show* than *describe*, since our imaginations tend to be both limited and uncontrolled. If asked to envision something new, most likely we will do so in terms of what we already know, in terms of existing products. Our imagination may not do your product justice. Just as bad, we may envision something totally different than what you have in mind. In this case, you run the risk of disappointing people if you do not meet their expectations, even unreasonable expectations. If it is not possible to have a working prototype, try a mockup or at least a detailed, three-dimensional artist's rendering.

Why is it so important to let end users touch, feel, and experience a new product or service? There are two kinds of evaluation of a new product: choice evaluation and use evaluation. You must clear both hurdles. (See **Exhibit 4.11**.)

The first evaluation we all make is choice. We ask ourselves whether the new product looks like it will do what we want or need it to do. If we have no experience with the product, we are limited in the criteria we can use to evaluate it. All of this changes once we use a product. At that point, many more factors will enter the evaluation process.

Suppose you were in a new town and looking for a place to eat. How would you go about choosing? You might walk down the main street and peer in the windows, looking at the furnishings, customers, and employees. Does what you see feel right? Is the restaurant clean and appealing? Is a menu posted, with appetizing dishes in the right price range? Essentially, you are on the outside looking in. You must make a choice with limited information.

Ultimately, you choose what appears to be the best restaurant based upon your needs, the options available, and the constraints facing you. Once you are in the restaurant, notice all the new criteria you can use to evaluate it. Are you seated where you want to be? Are the chairs comfortable?

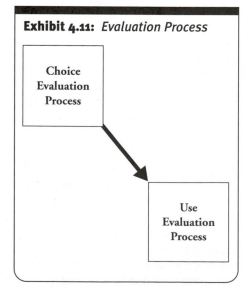

Exhibit 4.11: *Evaluation Process*

Choice Evaluation Process

Use Evaluation Process

Is the waiter friendly, helpful, efficient? Is the food served at the right temperature? Is it tasty? Are the portions the right size? Are the dishes clean? If you go to the restroom, is it clean? What else do you observe along the way? Does it make you feel good or uncomfortable?

The important point of this example is that in consumption there are a thousand things you might notice and evaluate. Any one, and possibly several, could cause you to wish you had made a different choice. None of us can completely judge a product or service without experiencing it.

In new use situations, we are especially attentive to details. Our evaluation is based on three kinds of comparisons. First, we compare what we receive with what we need or want. Second, we compare product performance with what we expected as determined by our initial perceptions of the product (our mental image). Finally, we compare performance with our mental standards of performance based on our experience with the brands in that product category (e.g., fast-food restaurants) or our favorite brand (e.g., McDonald's). In total, our satisfaction depends on how a product performs relative to our needs, our expectations, and the norm for comparable products. Coming full circle, our level of satisfaction affects our perceptions of the product and our willingness to purchase it again or recommend it to others.

Evaluation of a new product is more complex than it might appear. Asking end users to evaluate only the concept of a product will take you part of the way. The more critical evaluation occurs during product use. The number of criteria that must be satisfied in use evaluation is a hundred times greater than in choice evaluation. To find a place in the market, a new product must pass the test of choice and use.

What should you look for when you give a product to a potential customer? Excitement! An eagerness to have it for themselves! A desire to show others how great it is, how their problems have been solved. The response should be instantaneous, emotional, and uncontrolled. You will see it in their eyes and body language. There should be no doubt that they are impressed.

If most customers give you an objective or intellectual response, this is the kiss of death. If they start to discuss the advantages and disadvantages of your product or want

to talk about the utility of this or that feature, you have lost them. Very few of us are forthright enough to say something is a dumb idea or that it will not work, no one needs it, or it is not practical. Instead, we use subtle ways of saying it is not a good idea. We will recommend that you contact this person, or that organization, because they are more likely to benefit from your invention. You can spend a lot of time chasing after these "other" customers.

Another polite way of rejecting the product is to make suggestions on how to improve it. Potential customers will show genuine interest in you and your product and how to make it better. If there is no excitement in their voice, you know you are not even close.

Quantify Your Customer Base

Because the definition of your target market changes as you learn about potential customers, you should gather all of the preceding information before you think about defining relevant target markets. Learning about potential customers, you may discover:

- Stronger motivations for buying than expected.
- Additional use situations or applications.
- Interest by a number of new buying groups.

On the negative side, you may discover just the opposite. More likely, you will refine your definition of why someone would buy the product or service and who these people are likely to be.

As illustrated in **Exhibit 4.12**, the task at this stage is to gather all the information you have collected on use situations, benefits sought, use behavior, mind-set (lifestyle or corporate culture), and descriptive characteristics (demographics or business profile). Use this information to look for natural clusters of end users, with a high degree of commonality within each cluster and important differences between clusters.

Part of this task is to define the boundaries, or differences, between relevant market segments. In some cases, these boundaries will be precise. For example, being 21 years of age is a clear-cut boundary for the consumption of alcohol.

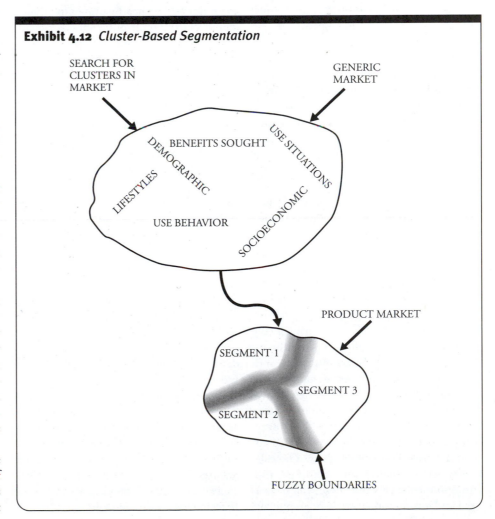

Exhibit 4.12 *Cluster-Based Segmentation*

SEARCH FOR CLUSTERS IN MARKET

GENERIC MARKET

BENEFITS SOUGHT

DEMOGRAPHIC

LIFESTYLES

USE SITUATIONS

SOCIOECONOMIC

USE BEHAVIOR

PRODUCT MARKET

SEGMENT 1

SEGMENT 2

SEGMENT 3

FUZZY BOUNDARIES

Similarly, all banks clearly need a way to store and retrieve images in very large numbers.

Unfortunately, few market boundaries are so clear. As you add criteria to refine the definition of your segments, the boundaries become increasingly fuzzy. For example, suppose you are interested in the product market of health-conscious people. Within this market, you will find some people who express this health consciousness in the way they eat while others will express it by exercising. This boundary between diet and exercise seems clear cut. Taking a closer look at those who prefer to exercise, we find a variety of preferences, including walking, jogging, running, swimming, and biking. Others prefer to play sports such as soccer, golf, tennis, or baseball. Again, the boundaries are fairly precise.

As we attempt to further refine our target market, the boundaries start to become fuzzy. Suppose we want to promote a new product to those who exercise by jogging. Will age or income help to define the segment? We might expect that young people (under 18) will be less inclined to jog and be outside the main segment. As our target group ages, interest in jogging might increase until the age of 40 and then start to decline as older people favor less strenuous activities. In terms of income, we might find that joggers span most income brackets but that those with lower incomes do not jog very often and those with higher incomes tend to take up sports such as golf, tennis, or skiing or buy expensive home exercise equipment.

Notice that age and income do not provide distinct boundaries. There is a tendency to increase or decrease certain physical activities as age or income increases. Market segmentation is characterized by fuzzy boundaries like these. (See Exhibit 4.12.)

The real difficulty in segmentation work is finding the correspondence between motivations and demographic characteristics. Purchase and use are driven by motivations (e.g., I want to stay healthy so that I can enjoy life). Access to markets and media is usually driven by demographics (age, income, location) or other descriptive information (preferred television programs, magazines, or radio stations). The fuzzy boundaries occur when you try to match up motivations with demographics. The difficulty is usually in finding the correspondence between those who have a need and a common set of demographic or descriptive characteristics. As illustrated earlier, health-oriented people can vary greatly by age, occupation, income, or family composition.

Despite this challenge, you will want to try to add demographic dimensions (or industry characteristics, in the case of business products) to your market segmentation descriptions. The data will help you quantify the size and location of your markets.

If you can precisely describe your market segment, you will find that there are considerable data available on almost every characteristic. In the United States, population information is collected by the U.S. Census Bureau and is available through any public library. There are also innumerable service firms that break out the census data into naturally occurring buying groups by geography, age, stage in family life cycle, income, occupation, and so forth. Similar information can also be obtained on industrial, wholesale, retail, and service firms from the U.S. Census Bureau—a complete business census is undertaken every five years—and numerous commercial firms. See the reference librarian at your town's main library or a nearby university library. Embassies and trade offices of other countries are a good place to start gathering information on the populations and industries of other countries.

Conclusion

The objective of this section has been to identify information to collect on the potential end users of your product or service and show how to collect it. It is important to look at the end user, the person who will actually use and benefit from the invention. The end user is always a person, whether a member of an organization or a household.

You will want to learn as much as possible about these end users. Have they demonstrated (as indicated by prior purchase or use) a preference for the capability you have to offer? What is their purchase pattern? When do they buy and how much do they buy? Who is involved in the buying process?

It is important to understand end users as real people rather than as statistics. What attributes or features of current products are most appealing to them? What are the consequences (benefits and costs) of certain features? What are the values or goals that are really driving the purchase of one brand or technology versus another?

When possible, give end users a chance to react to your technology. Look for excitement and be wary of objective or emotionless evaluations.

When all of this work has been done, sort through the information and look for natural clusters of end users who have similar motivations, uses, buying patterns, and descriptive characteristics. As you are able, gather quantifiable information on the number of people, households, or businesses who are likely to fall into these clusters or segments. Ultimately, try to narrow the target group (segment) down to those with the highest probability of buying. These will be the end users who need to be profiled in terms of their numbers, location, alternate sources of supply, and so on.

In the next section, guidelines will be offered on profiling channel customers. Together, the profiles of your competitors, end users, and channel customers will help you to establish minimum requirements to enter the market with your new product or technology.

Building Channel Profiles

The channel of distribution has been the key to success for many entrepreneurial firms. For example, Computer Technology and Imaging (CTI) developed the capability to produce a high-performance Emission Computed Axial Tomography (ECAT) brain scanner at a comparatively low price. CTI's price advantage made it possible for many regional medical centers to purchase scanners whereas previously only research hospitals could afford to buy them. One of the company's major obstacles was the channel: No one knew CTI. CTI also encountered a very long selling cycle because ECAT scanners represented a major capital expenditure. CTI salespeople spent all their time flying around the country in order to make countless presentations to hospital committees. CTI's distribution agreement with Siemens turned these problems around. It gave the customers a name they could trust and CTI a worldwide sales force. CTI was free to focus on improving its production facilities and developing new products, while Siemens focuses on creating sales.

In contrast to CTI, Phyton Technologies found it necessary to distribute a high-tech product (cloned horticultural plants) through low-tech channels. Phyton had perfected the technology to clone Boston ferns and rhododendrons but had no idea how to sell them to end users. It discovered that the channels for horticultural products were many and diverse. Its plants could literally end up in the garden shop of Kmart, in the local nursery, or in the florist's shop down the street. Phyton had to learn how shrubs and household plants were sold throughout the country. What trade shows should representatives attend? Who are the distributors? How far in advance could they book their orders? When do nurseries pay their bills? These and many other questions had to be answered before the business could become viable.

These examples illustrate the value of the channel of distribution. It is usually more practical to sell through established intermediaries than to sell direct. As payment for their services, third parties take a percentage of the final selling price, but the increase in volume will often more than offset the loss in margin.

One important outcome of using distribution partners is that the new venture has an additional customer who must be satisfied. In fact, the channel itself is usually the first customer and thus the gatekeeper to the market. Unless these intermediaries stock, promote, and distribute your goods or services, there will be no meaningful market. What makes it so difficult is that almost everyone has a full warehouse or store and hundreds of suppliers trying to get in. Distributors basically have their pick of products and choose to carry only the best ones. Thus, it is important to know not only the channels that can be used to sell to the end user but also how to motivate the intermediaries to sell your product aggressively.

Direct Selling

While selling through intermediaries is the dominant form of distribution, there is a large number of very successful firms that sell direct to end users: consumers, businesses, educational institutions, and government bodies. For example, in the microcomputer business, Dell has carved out a niche for itself by selling direct to end users, relying on massive advertising to inform and persuade end users, and using a Web address for placing orders. With a one- to five-day delivery promise, it can practically build PCs to order. Thus, Dell is able to avoid substantial inventories in the distribution pipeline and the associated risks of obsolescence. By avoiding the retail channel, Dell's costs and risks are substan-

tially lower, and it can charge more competitive prices, which is the basis for its niche in the market.

Many factors determine the feasibility and attractiveness of direct channels. **Exhibit 4.13** is a summary of the key determinants. Direct selling is often appropriate when the number of customers is small (e.g., automobile manufacturers), they are highly concentrated (furniture manufacturers in North Carolina), or they buy infrequently in large quantities. Direct selling is often required when the goods are custom designed, have a high value, or require special support services. Suppliers will also set up their own selling force when they have a large assortment of goods and are able to pay for inventory storage and distribution as well as order processing. Finally, direct channels are used when suppliers have been unhappy with the performance of the traditional distribution outlets.

In contrast, intermediaries are used most frequently when customers are numerous, widely distributed, and frequent buyers. Intermediaries are usually found when the product has a long shelf life, is small in size and value, and is not customized to individual customer needs. Finally, small suppliers and those with limited financial resources frequently find it advantageous to employ intermediaries to streamline order processing and cash flow. In this respect, it is much easier to do business with a handful of inter-

mediaries who pay regularly versus doing business with hundreds or thousands of end users, many of whom pay irregularly.

Who Is the Channel Customer?

The channel customer is every organization standing between you and the end user of your product. This section describes several kinds of channels. Directly or indirectly, every member of the channel is a customer who must be served and satisfied before your product reaches the final end user.

Why Are There So Many Kinds of Channels?

The channel for canned vegetables is distinctive in that there are multiple paths to the end user. (See **Exhibit 4.14**.) Multiple paths evolve in response to the different needs of customers. For example, consumers want groceries available near their homes, so canned vegetables will be stocked in all grocery and convenience stores in the country, and even in some snack vending machines. A large manufacturer such as Procter & Gamble might have its own sales force calling directly on retail chains, while a smaller manufacturer such as Del Monte might use brokers because its volume does not justify hiring a sales force. The paths a product or service takes to the end user mirror differences in the needs and dispersion of the market segments and depend upon the resources of the supplier.

Exhibit 4.13: *Factors Determining Method of Distribution*

	Using Intermediaries	Selling Direct
Customer characteristics		
number	large	small
dispersion	wide	narrow
purchase pattern	small, frequent	large, infrequent
Product characteristics		
product life (perishable)	long shelf life	short shelf life
size	small	large
design	standard	custom
unit value	low	high
accompanying services	few	many
Manufacturer distribution policy	intensive	exclusive
Supplier characteristics		
size, extent, and share of market	small	large
financial strength, credit	weak	strong
product mix	narrow	wide
past channel experience	good	poor

Source: Philip Kotler, *Principles of Marketing Management.*

Exhibit 4.14: Channel for Canned Vegetables

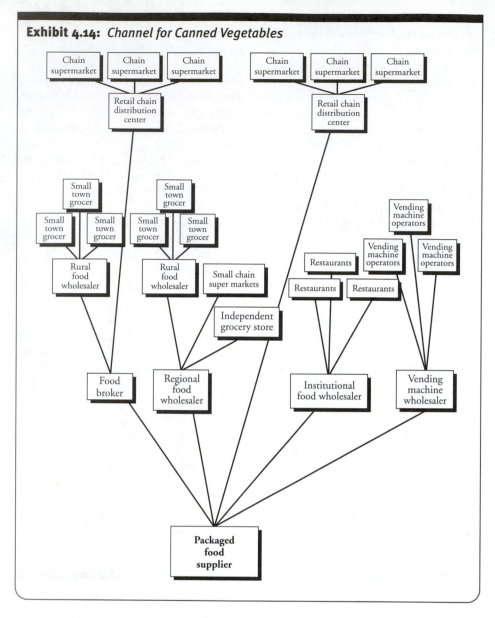

will have a better perspective for developing your own channel strategy and tactics.

Exhibit 4.15 illustrates the kinds of information to collect from end users. This information will help the strategist learn about the buying practices of end users, kinds of support needed from the channel, which intermediaries are effective, and other channel options. The information should provide leads to specific channel firms for later interviews with channel participants. These same contacts may become important for the organization of your own distribution system.

Exhibit 4.16 illustrates the kinds of information to collect on the distribution practices of key competitors. Special attention should be given to firms in the competitor's channel (e.g., brokers, drop shippers, wholesalers, rack jobbers) and what their normal functions are. In all cases, it is important to know the protocol

---

Exhibit 4.15: *How Do End Users Normally Purchase Similar Products?*

Who are their sources of supply (determine major players)?
How do they contact suppliers?
  salesperson makes regular calls
    employee of supplier
    independent rep
  order out of catalog
  track down supplier as needed
How do they learn about new technology?
  salespeople
  trade shows
  professional meetings
  company and product literature
  word of mouth
What are their purchasing procedures?
  information collection
  review process—who needs to sign off
  budgeting requirements and timetable
How do they evaluate suppliers?
  brand performance
  price
  support requirements
    availability
      brand
      supplies
      parts
    training
    maintenance
    trouble shooting
  proven track record

Distribution channels can be quite long and have multiple customers and influencers along the way. For example, American Matrix produced ceramic whiskers (tiny hairlike pieces of ceramic) that, if evenly distributed throughout a plastic part, would greatly increase the strength of the part. American Matrix faced the daunting task of convincing everyone up and down the channel that whisker-reinforced plastics provided superior performance relative to current materials. These customers included the producers of plastic raw materials, of plastic components (original equipment manufacturers), and of finished products, as well as the channel to the end user and the end users themselves (e.g., purchasers of tennis rackets, skis, sailboats, airplanes).

Constructing a channel profile gives you a picture of the channel structure. To construct a profile, identify the many paths that comparable products take from the original supplier to the end user. These channels are the logical alternatives for your organization to take as it distributes its products. Even if novel channels are employed, this picture and related analysis will help the entrepreneur evaluate the comparative features of each.

Gathering Information

The channel equation can be solved by working first the buy side and then the supply side. First, identify end users who are using comparable products and determine how they normally go about finding and buying what they want. Second, follow up on your competitor analysis, profiling their sales and distribution procedures. By understanding both sides of the transaction, you

Exhibit 4.16: *How Is the Product Normally Sold?*

What are the typical sales and distribution procedures of comparable suppliers?

Direct sales force
- number of salespeople
- distribution
  - geographic
  - market segment
- training
- compensation

Network of independent middlemen
- types of firms involved in sale
  - merchant wholesalers
  - brokers and agents
  - distribution specialists
- distribution
  - geographic
  - market segment
- normal operating procedures
  - markups/fees/allowances
  - functions performed (i.e., order taking only versus storage, billing, credit checks, etc.)
  - number and overlap of product lines
  - order process
- typical services and materials which accompany the product
  - training
  - maintenance
  - supplies
  - related equipment
  - other related services
- influence/power of distributors relative to suppliers

Influencers—others important to sale (i.e., system developers such as general contractors, architects, consultants)

What are the mechanics of sale and distribution of the goods?

Describe a typical sale
- what organizations are involved
- what do they do
- when
- how much do they receive for their efforts

Create flow chart
- participants
- activities
- movement of inventory, information, money
- timing

Exhibit 4.17: *Selected Distribution Policy Alternatives*

I. Price Concessions
  A. Discount Structure:
  - trade (functional discounts)
  - quantity discounts
  - cash discounts
  - anticipation allowances
  - free goods
  - prepaid freight
  - new product display and advertising allowances (without performance requirements)
  - seasonal discounts
  - mixed carload privilege
  - drop shipping privilege
  - trade deals
  B. Discount Substitutes:
  - display materials
  - premarked merchandise
  - inventory control programs
  - catalogs and sales promotion literature
  - training programs
  - shelf-stocking programs
  - advertising matrices
  - management consulting services
  - merchandising programs
  - sales "spiffs"
  - technical assistance
  - payment of sales personnel and demonstrator salaries
  - promotional and advertising allowances (with performance requirements)

II. Financial Assistance
  A. Conventional Lending Arrangements:
  - term loans
  - inventory floor plans
  - notes payable financing
  - accounts payable financing
  - installment financing of fixtures and equipment
  - lease and note guarantee programs
  - accounts receivable financing
  B. Extended Dating:
  - E.O.M. dating
  - seasonal dating
  - R.O.G. dating
  - "extra" dating
  - postdating

III. Protective Provisions
  A. Price Protection:
  - premarked merchandise
  - fair trade
  - franchise pricing
  - agency agreements
  B. Inventory Protection:
  - consignment selling
  - memorandum selling
  - liberal returns allowances
  - rebate programs
  - reorder guarantees
  - guaranteed support of sales events
  - maintenance of "spot" stocks and fast delivery
  C. Territorial Protection:
  - selective distribution
  - exclusive distribution

Source: Bert C. McCammon Jr., The University of Oklahoma.

---

for conducting business within particular channels, including the normal terms of trade, special discounts and fees, minimum order quantities, lead time requirements, seasonal purchase patterns, promotional support requirements, and so forth. For example, it is now customary in the grocery trade to buy shelf space for test marketing (this is termed "slotting allowances").

Exhibit 4.17 lists many of the distribution tactics deployed, and often expected, in different channels. Determining which of these tactics are required for the preferred channels will help the strategist decide which channels to enter and how to begin calculating cost.

It is imperative to visit a representative set of the intermediaries identified in the end user interviews and the competitor profiles. The objective is to learn how they function and what would motivate them to carry a new line. Keep in mind that the means-end hierarchy applies to business buyers as well as consumers. The attributes are different (i.e., pricing, packaging, shipping, warehousing, billing), but there are still consequences and values to be considered. The motivation to switch to your product will come only from superior delivery of positive consequences and personal and organizational values.

Finally, the analyst should be watchful for organizations or individuals who do not participate directly in the flow of your product but who influence its flow. System developers such as general contractors, architects, consultants, and engineering design firms fall in this category. When they are unfamiliar with a new material, process, or product, they will be unlikely to build it into their design specifications or recommend it to their clients.

ESTABLISH MARKET REQUIREMENTS

The purpose of developing the customer, competition, and channel profiles is to establish the minimum requirements for entering the market. In many respects, this knowledge will define a large part of the strategy. Perhaps 80 percent or more of the tactical details will be the same as what is customary in the market. Let us summarize important points made earlier.

- First, the anticipated new product must be at least as good as available commercial products. These products are the norms against which the new product will be judged.

- Second, if we are establishing minimum requirements, we need to look not only at standard features but also at trends; if something is not a standard feature now, it may soon be.

In reviewing more than 60 technologies at the Oak Ridge National Laboratory, the NASA Langley Research Center, Philips Consumer Electronics, and numerous entrepreneurial firms, we determined that the number 1 problem in new products is the failure to be as good as the competition on *all* dimensions important to the end user. Generally, these new products and technologies have been engineered to have one or two outstanding capabilities. The problem is that inventors/entrepreneurs do not worry about all the features and benefits of existing brands. In some cases, the task was narrowly defined. In other cases, the entrepreneur was excited about developing only one aspect of the product.

In contrast, a commercial product selling for the same end use has probably had the benefit of years of continuous improvement. There are many forces in the market demanding change in order to increase the value for end users. Suppliers are continually being pushed to improve their products across a broad spectrum of features. If you look at the development path of any product currently on the market, you will find many incremental enhancements that appeal to an assortment of customers and applications. The end result is a more uniform advancement of the technology, perhaps at the expense of exceptional performance in certain areas.

Inventors and customers have different perspectives on new products. When a commercial product is compared to a laboratory prototype, the inventor will focus on the exceptional new feature of the prototype while the end user notices what the prototype lacks. When we conclude that a technology or product is not ready for commercialization, it is usually because it is not as good as the competition on an array of the other features that the end users have come to expect.

Minimum market requirements must be met in other ways as well. For example, end users will expect products of the same type to be sold in much the same way. If comparable products sell for $99, then it will be difficult to sell your product for much more. If trade shows are the normal way to promote a new industrial product, then you need to be there. If other brands are normally sold with a 12-month warranty or with a seasonal discount for early orders, then look at making similar offers.

The normal distribution channel will also constrain choices. For example, a consumer who is looking for a new garage door opener will search out retail stores that normally sell garage door openers. And if a clinic wants the latest nonintrusive digital thermometer, the office manager will turn to products that the distributors normally carry. Except in unusual circumstances, end users expect products to be where they normally are, which can be good for the sellers. The starting point of every strategy is to match the normal way of business. Customer, competitor, and channel profiles can show an entrepreneur the way to approach a market. Many tactical details will emerge from this information-gathering effort—and the profiles will provide benchmarks against which to gauge the market strategy of the new product.

WHAT IS YOUR UNIQUE CONTRIBUTION?

Obviously, it is not enough to meet the minimum requirements; some unique contribution must be added. The technology must be better, faster, or cheaper than current options. For instance, the unique advantage of an optical tool-setting device created at the Oak Ridge National Lab is its ultra-high precision of plus or minus .0001 inches. The unique advantage of the whole blood processor is its ability to do a panel of tests in the doctor's office or at home. The unique advantage of the triple effect absorption chiller is its ability to cool large commercial buildings with a less expensive fuel—gas. The unique advantage of ceramic whiskers is their ability to increase the fracture strength of ceramics and plastics, and so on.

Let us consider this issue of unique contribution from both a theoretical and practical viewpoint. From a theoretical perspective, a new product or service must fall outside of the "zone of indifference." (See **Exhibit 4.18**.)[4]

Think about how we evaluate any product or service we use. Instead of paying attention to the performance of every feature of every product we use, we pay attention only to unusual events. That is, we learn through experience about the normal carbonation of a soft drink, the braking distance on our car, and the color contrast on our television, the cycle time of the punch press, the flow properties of molten metal, and so on. We also learn about normal variation. Not every hamburger, hotel room, rental car, photocopier, cellular phone, robotic arm, or chemical batch will be the same even when it is sold by the same company. We tolerate small differences, probably not even noticing most of them. This is our *zone of indifference.*

As long as our current experience falls within the zone of indifference, we virtually ignore what is happening. Only when performance falls outside the zone do we become conscious that something unusual is occurring.

As marketers, we are especially interested in performance outside the norm because of what happens next. First, unusual performance will usually generate an emotional reaction. If performance is noticeably less than normal, it can lead to annoyance, frustration, and even anger. If it is noticeably better, it can result in pleasant feelings of surprise or delight.

If there is an emotional response, it can, and often does, trigger action on the part of the end user. Frustration may lead to complaints and possibly a search for a better product. Delight is likely to encourage repurchase and favorable testimonials. Understanding this evaluation sequence can help in planning the product offer.

The first step is to be aware of the norms of prospective customers. For some, the

Exhibit 4.18: *Zone of Indifference*

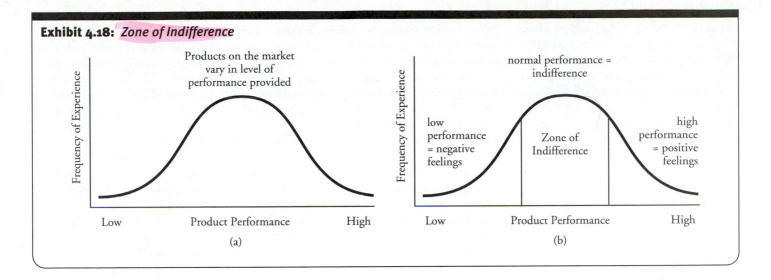

norm is the best brand in the product category (e.g., a Hilton). For others, it is the typical performance of an assortment of brands with which they have experience (e.g., Holiday Inns, Ramada Inns, or Orbis). For a third group, it might be the brand they currently use (for example, if my firm has a special rate with Marriott Hotels, that is where I would stay).

Second, the design of the new product must not result in performance below the norm on any important feature. The awareness and emotional response that comes from "below par" performance will kill sales.

Third, the new product must be above the zone of indifference in some important way. If the new offering is only as good as the norm, it will not even be noticed. It must have something to attract attention and generate excitement—a "gee whiz" response. Without a strong emotional response, nothing will happen. Satisfaction with the current choice creates tremendous inertia; your goal is to motivate customers to change. This motivation comes only from a lopsided performance evaluation.

Fourth, continual innovation will be necessary to keep the product in the forefront of the end user's mind. If your firm does not strive constantly for exceptional performance, good feelings about the brand will slowly decay through repeated use or the introduction of similar brands. In short, your product can become so similar to the norm that the zone of indifference shifts to include your product within its range. As a result, customers become indifferent to the brand.

Finally, you can expect the market to be in perpetual upward motion. If one firm is successful in creating excitement, other competitors must imitate the new capability or lose market share. This imitation will cancel negative comparisons, but it will not create excitement. To gain back market share, smart competitors must do even better. The end result is that the zone of indifference (industry standard) moves steadily upward, and the price of playing in the game keeps going up.

How much of an improvement is sufficient? What does it take to be outside the zone of indifference and to create the excitement necessary to motivate potential customers to buy? We offer a very practical but harsh guideline. Many industrial products require a tenfold increase in the key selling feature before users will give a new technology much attention. There are many reasons for this requirement. First, there is skepticism that the technology will be as successful in practice as it was in the lab. As a rule of thumb, a potential adopter will discount any claims by 50 percent or more. Second, there is an expectation that the technology will be deficient in some unknown and probably unpredictable way. These unwelcome surprises may appear during the initial trial of the new product. Almost certainly, there will be problems with the product in the hands of inexperienced end users. To be sure, hardly anyone will do anything the same way it was done in the lab. Last, customers are unwilling, even averse, to change the way they do things. For example, a major obstacle to the adoption of the new nuclear radioisotope, iridium, for imaging the heart and blood flow was 30 years of experience with technetium. All of the procedures, personnel, and materials for working with technetium

had been streamlined to the point that no one had to think about them. The cost of change and the disruption it would cause would be enormous. A reduction in the half-life of a radioisotope from hours to minutes was not worth all of the trouble to change.

Not all products or services must make such a drastic improvement over the norm to capture the attention of the market. Whatever the threshold, the acid test is that your unique contribution must be sufficiently great to create excitement among a large number of potential customers.

DEVELOP MARKET STRATEGY
Price and Performance

The normal ways of doing business in your industry and the unique advantage of your technology will largely determine your market strategy. Much of the balance of the strategy proceeds from the following interconnected questions:

- Which market segments should be targeted initially?
- Where should the product be positioned on the price-performance continuum?

The answers and the resultant strategies tend to fall at opposite ends of the price-performance continuum. Let us begin by looking at the argument that leads to a high-end strategy.

For many new technologies, it is safe to assume that both the marketing and production costs will be initially high and the cash flow negative. Very few end users and intermediaries will know much about the technology, forcing the entrepreneur to invest heavily in promotional activities to create awareness and provide extra support and incentive to encourage customers to try the product. Also, production costs will be high because of limited manufacturing experience, capacity, and volumes. Cash flow will be negative because the investments required to add capacity, inventory, and sales capability must be made in advance of the revenue they generate. (See **Exhibit 4.19**.)

All of these factors tend to favor a market entry strategy of high price and high performance, with the product targeted at a high-value, price-insensitive market. This strategy was proposed for the ultra-high capacity, write-once-read-many (WORM) optical disk drive. The initial strategy was to target the high end of the market (large banks, the armed services, and NASA) that have very large volume data storage requirements. These players were already solving the problem with cumbersome and expensive systems that switch large diskettes in and out of disk drives in much the same way as a jukebox (which is what they are called). In these applications, the price the market is willing to bear is determined by the real savings the new technology will allow in effort, time, and money. In a sense, the market is insensitive to the price of the technology but is very sensitive to its cost advantage over the existing solution to the problem.

The advantage of charging a high price (regardless of production cost) is that the extra margins will help pay for the high selling costs required to convert doubters into experimenters, as well as the intensive hand-holding required to ensure the customer is satisfied. High prices may also allow investment in manufacturing that will lead to

further cost reductions. As the supplier gains experience, costs come down, and the market becomes familiar with the technology, the entrepreneur can phase in larger and more price-sensitive market segments. This strategy has been used with many new technologies, including aluminum, carbon fibers, integrated circuits, and lasers.

A contrasting strategy is to penetrate the market deeply by offering both performance and cost advantages. The assumptions are that the market is highly price-sensitive, other competitors can quickly enter the market, or there is a first mover advantage in creating brand loyalty. In this case, pricing is based not on current costs but on anticipated costs. The objective is to drive down unit production and marketing costs by selling large volumes of product. This strategy was pioneered by Henry Ford and the Model T, reinvented by Texas Instruments, and emulated in many other industries. In the consumer products arena, there is the pervasive belief that all demand is price-sensitive and that more must be offered for less. The chief limitation of this strategy is that it requires abundant resources to sustain the high negative cash flow requirements of the initial market entry. It also requires confidence that the product will be right the first time.

Promotion

All market strategies must consider how the company will cultivate awareness, interest, trial, and adoption. With few exceptions, the entrepreneur has an uphill battle. From the end user's perspective, there is great risk in switching from something that works to something that may not work.

Keep in mind that the cost of the product may be small relative to the retooling or reengineering of the current solution. For example, a manager of a ceramics processing plant reported that he would have to shut down one of his two lines for three months to convert it to whisker-reinforced ceramics, something he was unwilling to do without a proven market for the material. Because of the high cost of either error or changeover, we often find decision makers willing to tolerate performance limitations rather than try something new. As the saying goes, "Better the devil you know."

What to do? There is extensive research on the diffusion of innovation that offers some guidelines.[5] The major factors influencing adoption are relative advantage, compatibility, complexity, divisibility, and communicability.

- *Relative advantage* is clear, and we have already talked about the need for dramatically improving performance.
- *Compatibility* refers to the degree to which the innovation matches the values and experiences of the end user. In short, it is necessary to understand how things are done currently and mold the innovation into existing operations and lifestyles.
- *Complexity* refers to how difficult it is to understand or use the product. Even if something is sophisticated, it should be packaged so that people can easily use it and appreciate what it can do for them.
- *Divisibility* is the degree to which something can be tried on a limited basis. Look for ways customers can gain experience with low risk or cost. Let them sample the value delivered. Free samples, free trials, lease-buy options, and introductory prices should be considered.
- *Communicability* is the degree to which the results are observable and describable. Once you know what outcomes your target market wants, develop demonstrations and promotions so that the outcomes are obvious to your customer. When the customer uses your product, it should be obvious that the desired benefits are in fact being delivered. Do not assume the customer will recognize them for what they are. Your familiarity with the technology will heighten your sensitivity. Help the customer to see, feel, and understand the positive consequences.

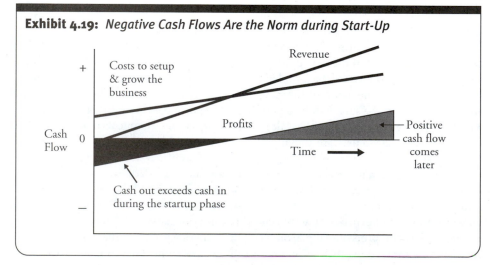

Exhibit 4.19: *Negative Cash Flows Are the Norm during Start-Up*

Distribution

Keep in mind that the channel is your first customer. Unless the wholesalers, retailers, manufacturer's reps, and brokers buy and distribute your product, end users will never see it or be able to buy it. Intermediaries can help or hinder the execution of your marketing strategy. They are independent customers who must be motivated to act in a manner consistent with your overall objectives and strategy.

There are two things that motivate a channel customer: money and making their job easier. For example, when Hanes first introduced its line of L'eggs panty hose, it guaranteed a $1,300 profit for just 2.5 square feet of space, sold the hosiery on consignment, employed route girls to stock the shelves, provided a distinctive display to attract consumers and help them select the right size and color, and spent $10 million on advertising and another $5 million on coupons in order to pull customers into the store. Thus, the retailer was promised lots of profit, no investment, and little work.[6]

When considering the financial incentives, start with the profit equation. A channel customer makes a profit by selling low volumes at high margins or large volumes at low margins. The emphasis is on profit, where profit equals margin times volume.

There are many other financial incentives, including trade (functional) discounts, quantity discounts, cash discounts, prepaid freight, new product displays, advertising allowances (without performance requirements), and seasonal discounts. You might even have to pay a hefty "slotting allowance" in order to gain space in a reseller's warehouse or retail store. For a distributor to drop a proven product in favor of a new untried one, the new one must offer financial returns substantially greater than the norm.

Channel customers will also be responsive if you can make their jobs easier. For example, if you create the demand for your product, they do not have to. Strong advertising, promotion, brand design, and prices will pull customers into the store. If they are required to create the demand, distributors will expect you to provide any number of the following to help: display materials, premarked merchandise, catalogs and sales promotion literature, shelf-stocking programs, merchandising programs, sales "spiffs," payment for demonstrators, and promotional and advertising allowances. (Refer again to Exhibit 4.5.)

Channel customers are also likely to be responsive to management assistance. That is, you must anticipate their needs and problems and provide effective solutions. This support may come in the form of technical assistance, management consulting services, training programs, or inventory control programs. Finally, they may want assurances that their investment will be protected. They might look for price protection, inventory protection (consignment, liberal return allowances, reorder guarantees), and territorial protection. In the end, knowing your channel customers and helping them to accomplish their goals will lead to less conflict, more cooperation, less risk, and a higher probability of a long-term relationship.

FORECAST SALES FROM PRODUCT MARKETS

Forecasting sales is the last information-intensive step in the MOA. The objective is to estimate demand over time given your knowledge of the business environment, product market, customers, and competition, and your market strategy. These numbers will ultimately determine whether or not to pursue the market opportunity and, thus, invest substantial time, money, and effort. The risk of error is great. You do not want to recommend going ahead if the market is insufficient to justify the investment. Nor do you want to drop a project that could develop into a major profit generator. Thus, this step is critical to the entire MOA process and your firm's future.

Begin by establishing realistic expectations. First, forecasting is no more than logical guessing about the future. The logical element derives from market knowledge and a strategy developed from that knowledge; otherwise, it is only guessing. Second, the forecast is at best an order-of-magnitude estimate. For example, will the market be 100 units, 1,000 units, 10,000 units, or 100,000? It is not reasonable to try to predict whether the market is 12,000 or 14,000. All you can say is that it is likely to be more than 10,000 and less than 15,000 units. Last, there is no single best way to forecast. There are many techniques, each with its own strengths and limitations. Use of multiple forecasting techniques may be desirable.

We recommend the inclusion of a rather simple forecasting technique, the customer aggregation model. Specifically,

$$Forecast_t = n_t \times p_t \times q_t$$

where

$Forecast_t$ = the number of units customers (current or potential) are willing to purchase in time period t under stated market conditions

n_t = number of customers in the target market in time period t

p_t = probability of purchase in time period t

q_t = quantity of purchase in time period t

Our reasons for recommending this model are as follows. First, statistical forecasting techniques require historical sales data that, depending on the newness of the technology, may not exist or be insufficient. Second, the assumptions of sales trend techniques may not apply if the technology or market strategy is radically different from current offerings. In one way or another, statistical techniques assume that historical patterns will continue into the future. If you are introducing a new technology, it is your hope to change these patterns. Third, statistical forecasting techniques provide estimates of market demand given historical conditions. Typically, they do not provide estimates of the market potential and unmet demand. It is hoped that the new technology will serve to convert some portion of this unmet demand into new sales. Last, we want to analyze the effect on sales of changes in population, market segment boundaries, or usage (that is, relax or tighten assumptions). Given the uncertainty of the future, it would be wise to conduct sensitivity analysis on our major assumptions about the market.

As you begin, keep in mind that there are three kinds of forecasts—market potential, market demand, and untapped demand—and each kind can be made at three levels. Market potential is an estimate of those who have a need but may or may not be buyers. Market demand is a subset of market potential, reflecting customers who have demonstrated both the ability and willingness to buy under current conditions. Untapped demand is the difference between market potential and market demand. It includes those who have a need but either do not have the ability or do not have the willingness to buy. Any new product or technology should capture part of the current demand (steal market share from existing competitors) as well as generate new business (attract buyers from the sidelines), either by making it easier to buy (lower the cost) or by providing more value for the same price.

Market forecasts can also be made at three levels: generic market, product type, and brand. In the following illustration of the customer aggregation model, we will estimate unit market potential at the product-type level for large-scale, electronic data storage devices. The technology we will use as an example is the write-once-read-many (WORM) technology previously proposed. The forecasts have been adjusted for proprietary reasons but are representative of the process employed.

Developing the forecast requires several steps. First, we review the business and market conditions and project any changes that might affect demand. With these in mind, we estimate n (number of customers in the target market), p (probability of purchase), and q (quantity of purchase). Finally, we multiply these figures to obtain an estimate of potential in the product market.

Note that we are not projecting demand but only potential. These numbers represent our best guess of what demand could be under ideal conditions. Demand will be a function of potential (the more opportunity in the market, the more likely we will be able to sell the product) but will ultimately depend upon the firm's sales and marketing tactics and investments.

To illustrate this point, consider an extreme case in which the new venture does not employ any salespeople or engage in any advertising. How many units are likely to be sold? None. "Build a better mousetrap and the world will beat a path to your door" is all wrong. Do not count on anyone knocking at your door. As you add salespeople, promote your goods in trade shows and appropriate media, and recruit distributors to carry the line, you will begin to convert market potential into market demand.

The important point here is that demand estimates are built from the ground up. How many salespeople will you employ (1, 10, 100, 1,000), and where will they be located? How many units can each salesperson sell? What can be done to increase that number? Will you need new product features, an assortment of model options, lower prices, more advertising, nicer looking brochures, more prominent locations in trade shows, more sales outlets, better logistical support?

Business and Market Conditions

The first step in the forecasting process is to review what was learned from the rest of the MOA. Identify business and market conditions that are likely to affect demand in some significant way. The objective is to determine whether these conditions will positively or negatively affect demand, by how much, and over what time frame. Is the population in the target market increasing or decreasing? Are competitors entering or leaving the market? Are customers demanding more as a result of increased competition and rapid innovation? Are new regulations likely to affect demand? Are we entering a period of economic growth or decline?

With the exception of population changes, it is difficult to quantify the probability, direction, and magnitude of the effect of these conditions on the market. Nonetheless, it is important to keep them in front of you while you try to build a customer aggregation model. At the very least, you should develop "what-if" scenarios around these possibilities and perform sensitivity analysis on the key parameters of the model.

Estimating n: The Number of Customers

To estimate n, you need to

1. Identify the target markets.
2. Define the boundary characteristics of these markets.
3. Find the data on the number within the boundaries.
4. Project changes in the numbers in each target market.

For example, **Exhibit 4.20** identifies three target markets for the WORM optical disk drive and lists the possible applications for each. Through census data, it is possible to see how many organizations fall in each category. However, we know there will be a great diversity at this level of aggregation. If we can further define the boundary of who is in the target market and who is not, it will greatly facilitate data collection and lead to more realistic forecasts. For example, we might ask whether all government agencies are likely to need this type of technology for data storage. Probably not. Small municipalities may not have much need for or the ability to purchase this equipment. Therefore, we might draw the line to include city governments with populations of 1,000,000 or more. We would probably include federal agencies with high data usage such as the IRS, Census Bureau, NASA, and so on.

We want to define these boundaries as tightly as possible. If they correspond to demographic characteristics (age, gender, location, size of company, industry, etc.), our task is comparatively easy. If they correspond to a state of mind (apprehension about one's job), then it is quite difficult. Of necessity, we need to find the correspondence between the state of mind and

---

Exhibit 4.20: *End User Target Markets WORM Optical Disk Drive*

Government	Insurance	Banking
National defense	Actuarial information	Mortgage loans
Census	premium levels	Consumer loans
IRS records	Customer databases	Investment accounts
Stock exchange records	Investment accounts	Trust accounts
Economic databases	Policy service	Credit cards
Legal/case files	Claims processing	Demand deposits
Spying	Agent administration	Certificates of deposit
Crop prediction databases		IRAs
Environmental clean-up		Business loans
FDA drug evaluations		
EEO statistics		
FAA flight safety databases		
Library of Congress files		
NASA R&D		
OMB budget databases		
Selective Service databases		
Social service databases		

demographic or organizational characteristics. For example, those who are concerned about sex appeal are more likely to be young; those who are tired of the same old rat race are more likely to be middle aged; and those who are more venturesome are more likely to work in small start-up companies.

Whenever possible, it is wise to further subdivide those within a target boundary into subcategories. This subdivision will later facilitate estimating the probability of purchase. In all likelihood, there will be variation in the probability of purchase. If you can anticipate which demographic or organizational characteristics will be associated with an increase or decrease in probability, you can then try to obtain information of that kind. For example, we can anticipate that larger banks will probably be more likely to need or be willing to risk the purchase of the WORM optical disk drive system. As shown in **Exhibit 4.21**, we collected data on the number of banks by size of assets.

The last piece of information to collect is the projected change in the target market. Keep in mind that a forecast should extend several years into the future. If you can anticipate that your target market is changing, then you will want to quantify the changes. For example, the banking community has seen a large number of mergers and acquisitions as the laws restricting multicity or multistate banking have been relaxed. As a result, the number of banks had declined steadily for the previous 10 years, with the most striking decline in the number of banks with assets under $100 million. What would be the projection for this consolidation in the

next 10 years? Obviously, consolidation could impact both the number of banks in our target market and their willingness to purchase the WORM technology.

The sources of information on n are many and varied. The Census Bureau is the best single source for population data. They also conduct a census of manufacturing, wholesaling, and retailing every five years. There are many commercial market research firms that can provide estimates for many population subgroups or industries. Trade associations are valuable sources for industry information. Importantly, these same sources often provide additional data on how the population in various segments is changing.

Estimating p: The Probability of Purchase

To estimate the probability of purchase, try to determine the proportion of customers in the target segments currently using a competing product or technology. In the case of the WORM technology, the most direct competitor was the jukebox disk storage and retrieval system. Which banks and how many of them were using or experimenting with these systems? Try contacting the most likely buyers (large banks in major financial markets) to see if they use the technology or know others who have. The trade press might reveal how many units have been sold to the banking community, and given the number of large banks that would be possible customers, we can estimate the likelihood of purchase.

We might also look at indirect competitors (other product markets). For example, the WORM technology could be a substitute for magnetic tape systems in some

applications. Thus, banks with these systems would have a higher probability to purchase WORM technology. On the other hand, banks that use microfiche for data storage and retrieval are less likely to switch systems because microfiche is not compatible with digital data handling.

If there is not a corresponding product on the market, look for a complementary product or one on which your product might be dependent. For example, we might try to estimate the proportion of banks with supercomputers. These data would indicate the level of sophistication of a bank and its willingness to spend money on data processing. You might also look at the adoption rate of other innovations in the industry or market (e.g., automated teller systems or home banking). How quickly and in what numbers have these innovations been adopted?

For example, in an MOA on multimedia sound, we looked at the adoption rate for compact disks among microcomputer buyers. We hoped the adoption rate for multimedia sound would parallel that of the CD. We chose CDs for four main reasons. First, it was the most recent significant technology to be adopted by the industry. Second, both technologies represented added value to the PC, but neither is necessary to the use of the PC. Third, the demand for CDs depends upon the development of the software and applications that use it. The same condition is true for stereo sound. Last, the availability of CD players and software is likely to be a major driver in the demand for stereo sound. Good sound requires large data storage capabilities, and the CD has this capability.

In order to estimate p, we computed the ratio of CD sales to PC sales for the previous eight years. We found that this ratio was very small for the first four years, and only in the last two did it increase markedly. For these reasons, we felt this pattern was likely to repeat itself with stereo sound.

There are other ways to estimate p. For example, the Simmons Study of Media and Markets[7] is an excellent source of data on consumer preferences. Relying on self-report usage, this firm estimates the relative preference for many consumer goods. This information is segmented by gender, age, income, race, and other demographic variables.

Scanner data are available from many retailers, and it can provide sell-through quantities by store. If this information is

Exhibit 4.21: *Sales Potential of WORM Drives*

Size of Banks	Number N	Probability of Purchase P	Quantity Likely to Be Purchased Q	Sales Potential = (units)
<$5 M	221	0.050	1	11
5–10 M	914	0.075	1	69
10–25 M	3,688	0.100	1.5	553
25–50 M	3,684	0.125	1.5	691
50–100 M	2,899	0.150	2.5	1,087
100–500 M	2,236	0.175	2.5	978
500 M–1 B	431	0.200	4	345
>1 B	125	0.200	4	100
Total				**3,834**

combined with the census data on the store's trading area, it is possible to estimate the frequency of purchase by the households in the area for any product category over any time period (i.e., the number of units sold in 12 months divided by the number of people/households in the target market). By comparing sales rates for different stores in different demographic areas, it is possible to estimate differences in the propensity to purchase by different demographic groups.

Regardless of how the estimate for probability of purchase is obtained, it is necessary to adjust the number over time. Other factors to consider are:

- The stage of the product life cycle.
- The increase or decrease in the number of situations in which the new product would be valued.
- The amount and quality of promotional effort being directed at the customers within the target market(s).

If the new product is in the introductory stage of the product life cycle, the fraction of customers willing to buy will be very small, perhaps in the range of 2 to 4 percent. As customers become familiar with the technology and positive word of mouth spreads, more customers will be willing to make a purchase. Also during this early period, suppliers will be gaining market experience that will result in better products, advertising, prices, and distribution. The market will probably respond favorably to these adjustments, and the fraction willing to purchase should increase. For example, in the growth stage, it may rise from 10 to 30 percent over the course of a year.

The difficult part in estimating p several years out is projecting the time in the future when the sales curve will turn upward. The introductory period could be quite long, with comparatively few sales. It may take several years before market conditions turn favorable if they do at all.

A final factor to consider in estimating p is the amount of competition in the market. Although it may appear to be counterproductive, competition may be more of a help than a hindrance to a new technology or product category. If you have no competition, you must sell both the technology idea and your product. The sell cycle is likely to be very long. When you have several competitors selling the same technology and telling the same story, more customers will learn about its value, ulti-mately leading to a higher probability of purchase. Consider how many cars are likely to stop at an exit for food if there is only one restaurant at the exit. What happens when there are a dozen?

Philips Consumer Electronics acknowledged the value of competition when it licensed the CD-ROM technology to its major competitors. It resulted in many more people learning of the technology than would have if Philips had kept the sole responsibility of promotion. The licensing move also served to create the standard for the industry that further enhanced the sales potential for CD-ROM.

Estimating q: The Quantity of Purchase

In estimating q, it is important to consider the normal repurchase cycle. That is, will an end user purchase the product once every few days (milk and bread), once every few weeks (toothpaste and dish soap), once every few months (oil change), once a year (vacation), once every few years (car or personal computer), or once every 10 years (new home)? If the forecast is for a year, you must consider how often the end user is likely to purchase during the year.

In estimating q, also consider how many units will be purchased at one time. For example, a typical consumer might buy things such as a loaf of bread, a six pack of beer, a dozen eggs, a box of five video tapes, or a personal computer one at a time. In contrast, an industrial customer might buy 10, 100, or 1,000 personal computers at a time. The number of units purchased might also be a function of the time of the year; for example, consider the seasonal demand for snow blowers versus wind surfers. The demand for industrial products might also be seasonal, especially those that derive their demand from consumer goods and services. Finally, trial demand is likely to be less than the normal quantity of repurchase. In order to reduce the risk of purchasing a new and unproven product, a buyer might make a small initial purchase to try it out.

The primary source of information on q will be products that satisfy a similar need. In the case of WORM technology, we tried to determine how many hard drive "jukeboxes" were purchased by agencies with large volume data needs. In almost every case, only one had been purchased, and it was frequently on a trial basis. In the case of the blood analyzer, we discovered that medical clinics were likely to buy only one analyzer. It made little difference if there were 2 doctors or 10 doctors working in the clinic. The number of turning machines purchased by a machine shop depended upon the size of the shop and the kind of work done. As a rule, they would buy only one to satisfy the current workload. Once the machine was operational, then the shop would sell the capability to other customers and add another machine only when they had sufficient demand to justify another investment—usually a year or two later.

As you can see, forecasting is largely educated guessing. Everyone wants a formula that can be solved by plugging in the right variables. The formula is not the problem. The problem is coming up with reasonable estimates of the key parameters. Substantial leg work is required. Also, you may not like the process because there is too much guesswork, even if it is educated. Still, there is no way around it.

Multiple Estimates of Sales Potential

Exhibit 4.21 shows the number of banks by size (n), their probability of purchase (p), and the quantity of WORM drives likely to be purchased (q). Multiplying these factors gives us an estimate of sales potential.

The estimate of sales potential is a reasonable guess. Are there other reasonable guesses? Perhaps we should develop a set of numbers for each of the next five years; after all, we could reasonably expect the interest among banks to grow as they get experience with the new technology and it proves itself. Thus, the probability of purchase should increase over time, as might the number of units purchased at one time.

We might also look at creating more pessimistic (decrease p and q) and optimistic (increase p and q) forecasts. We might adjust n if we have reason to believe that the consolidation trend will continue. We develop multiple forecasts in order to assess the operational and cash-flow implications if the market potential is substantially less or greater than expected. The advantage of the customer aggregation model is the ease of modifying key parameters once the model is set up within a spreadsheet.

EVALUATE MARKET OPPORTUNITY

At this point in the MOA process, all the ingredients for an evaluation of market opportunity are available. The challenge is to put them together into an overall picture of market opportunity, including the best segments to target and a tentative marketing strategy to obtain sales from these customers.

There is both a qualitative and quantitative aspect to the evaluation. The description of the market arena is qualitative. This description includes five major components:

1. The structure of the market.
2. The market requirements of the customers.
3. The capabilities and requirements of distributors.
4. The strengths and weaknesses of competition.
5. The important environmental trends expected to cause change in market opportunity.

Each of these factors plays an important role in selecting target markets and planning a marketing strategy for the new venture.

Market structure provides a picture of the market groups or segments that are potential target markets for the company. An entrepreneur needs this input in order to select a targeting strategy. Market requirements must be met by the company's marketing mix (product, price, promotion, distribution, and service). Management must assess the capability of the company to successfully meet the requirements of each market segment. This assessment is an important factor in deciding which segments eventually become targets. Further, the requirements provide important guides as to what to build into each component of the marketing mix.

Channel capabilities and requirements determine how much work the entrepreneur must do in selling to the end user versus how much can be farmed out to distribution specialists. This determination is especially important if the new venture does not have the resources to contact the final customer directly. In addition, existing channels may be able to accommodate the new product readily, with very little increase in selling effort. The entrepreneur must know the distribution options and be able to identify the factors necessary to attract key distributors.

Competitive strengths and weaknesses must also be considered in selecting market targets. No company wants to enter market segments that are saturated with competitors. More often than not, the success of a new venture depends on finding market segments where the company can develop a competitive edge. Further, management will need guidelines on how to compete with key competitors in each target segment. The strengths of competitors must be matched or avoided, and the weaknesses must be scrutinized for possible ways to create differential advantages. Finally, environmental trends are important for determining how stable or long-lasting the opportunity in the market segments will be.

This qualitative information should also facilitate the selection of segments to target and the formulation of a tentative marketing strategy. In fact, the degrees of freedom are usually limited once the market's requirements are well understood. However, you must be clever in the addition of your unique contribution, the element that will give you the differential advantage in your target market. Your offer must be clearly outside the norm, or zone of indifference, if you hope to succeed.

The selection of the target markets and preliminary strategy will, in turn, allow you to proceed with the second aspect of the evaluation of the market opportunity, forecasts of sales potential. The forecasts of sales potential provide estimates of the magnitude of the market opportunity. These estimates, in turn, are crucial for determining financial performance of a new venture. Analyses of profits, return on investment, payback periods, cash flow, and other such performance measures all depend on having reasonable estimates of sales.

A manager will consider many factors before deciding whether to proceed with a new venture. No doubt, a manager will always rely on subjective judgment or "feel" in making the final decision. In fact, an MOA is not intended to be a substitute for experienced judgment. An MOA cannot eliminate all of the risks and uncertainties that accompany new venture decisions, but an MOA can help the businessperson clarify and better understand the dimensions of the risk and uncertainty. An MOA's real contribution is to help decision makers see all facets of the opportunity as well as to understand possible threats. In this way, an MOA ensures that the judgment is an informed one.

*   I would like to acknowledge the substantial contribution of Robert Woodruff in the development of the Market Opportunity Analysis framework and process. He pioneered the MOA approach at the University of Tennessee and shared his many ideas with me as we both taught the subject in many undergraduate and graduate classes. The MOA framework is largely his. I have simply applied it to the analysis of new products, drawing heavily on my own experience.

1. For additional direction on preparing market structure trees, please see Ernest R. Cadotte, *Market Opportunity Analysis for New Technology, New Products and New Markets,* work in progress.

2. Ernest R. Cadotte, Robert W. Woodruff, and Roger Jenkins, "Expectations and Norms in Models of Consumer Satisfaction," *Journal of Marketing Research* (August 1987): 305–314; and Robert W. Woodruff, Ernest R. Cadotte, and Roger L. Jenkins, "Modeling the Consumer Satisfaction Process Using Experience Based Norms," *Journal of Marketing Research* (August 1983).

3. Philip Kotler and Gary Armstrong, *Principles of Marketing,* 9th ed. (Englewood Cliffs, NJ: Prentice Hall, 2001).

4. Cadotte, Woodruff, and Jenkins, "Expectations and Norms"; Woodruff, Cadotte, and Jenkins, "Modeling."

5. The following discussion draws heavily on the work of Everett M. Rogers, *Diffusion of Innovations* (New York: Free Press, 1962). See also his third edition, published in 1983.

6. "Our L'eggs Fit Your Legs," *Business Week,* March 25, 1972.

7. Simmons Study of Media and Markets (New York, Simmons Market Research Bureau, 1998).

Chapter 5

Understanding Customer Value

Sarah F. Gardial
*Associate Professor
of Marketing
University of Tennessee*

Robert B. Woodruff
*Proffitt's, Inc.
Professor of Marketing
University of Tennessee*

Companies that deliver the greatest value to their customers have the highest potential for competitive advantage, success, and longevity. But what is customer value? Value is not inherent in the product, but is something the *customer experiences and perceives* as a result of buying/consuming/disposing of a product or service. (Unless otherwise noted, the term *customers* will be used throughout this chapter to refer to channel and business customers, as well as end users.) There is an old marketing saying: "No one really wants a quarter-inch drill bit—what they want is a quarter-inch hole in their wall."

Looked at this way, it becomes clear that a manager's objective is to create a bundle of attributes that deliver superior consequences and higher goal attainment to a target group of customers. However, in order to do this, you must first determine what it is that your customers value. Once identified, customer value can then become a central focus for the organization, the "north star" around which operations, activities, and systems find their purpose. Customer value provides the organization with a unifying theme that is capable of cutting across functional areas and management levels in order to direct the delivery of value to target customers and thus leads to long-term success for the organization.

WHY STUDY CUSTOMER VALUE?

Putting systems and processes in place to understand and track customer value is expensive and time consuming. Especially in these times of downsizing and creating "leaner" organizations, managers are sometimes reluctant to invest the resources necessary to support first-rate customer

> ## Learning Objectives
>
> After reading this chapter, the reader should be able to:
>
> - Clearly define how customers view the value delivered by a product or service.
> - Use the value hierarchy framework to explore customer needs and desires.
> - Be familiar with the research methods that are most effective for gathering customer value data.
> - Understand how customer value data can be used to guide and support a variety of the firm's strategic decisions.

tracking systems. However, the payoffs of understanding your customer are startling. Consider the following estimates:

- Generating a new customer costs three to five times more than retaining an existing customer.
- "Highly satisfied" customers are six times more likely to repurchase than just "satisfied" customers.
- Studies have shown that even a 5 percent increase in customer retention can raise profitability by 60 percent.[1]

For these reasons, the popularity of quality initiatives and value delivery strategies has grown enormously in recent years. However, customer value has been conceptually linked to company performance for a long time. In the 1950s, Peter Drucker argued that what a customer perceives as value

BEST-USE CORRELATIONS

In *Marketplace,* getting close to the customer is a key element of business success. Chapter 5 aims to provide you with superior skills in understanding customer value and, in the process, position your team to outperform its rivals.

Customers Buy Benefits, Not Components

As you begin to design new products in Q2, you must commit yourself to understanding the mental processes that drive customer decision making. Don't know how to focus? Chapter 5 provides lots of useful advice, with special emphasis on the customer value hierarchy—attributes, consequences, and desired end states.

Means-End Hierarchy

In *Marketplace,* your firm will produce a variety of PC components. But in making their purchasing decisions, are your customers buying ease of use? portability? power? Your challenge is to select the correct computer components (attributes) so that the final product delivers desired benefits. Chapter 5 provides a useful tool—the means-end hierarchy—to help you pinpoint the links between available PC components and the benefits that customers derive from them.

Laddering Is a Good Thing

Laddering is a very useful interviewing technique for exploring attributes preferred, consequences desired, and benefits sought. Because *Marketplace* directly tests your ability to link product attributes (components) to benefits and values, the insights your team gains from experimenting with laddering will dramatically affect your whole perspective on market opportunities and your subsequent market strategy. Teams that take the time to conduct in-depth interviews with PC users generally agree that the exercise is "well worth the time."

plays a decisive role in business performance.[2] More recently, marketing communications have used these terms to tell customers of their organization's commitment to meeting their needs:

> "Yet Escort has always been able to separate itself from the pack by establishing a strong tradition of value" (Ford Motor Company).

> "Performance, compatibility and room for the future—three reasons the i486 DX2 processor is today's best value" (Intel).

Attention to customer value is especially critical in markets that are highly competitive and dynamic. In these cases, managers must track customer value changes over time in order to anticipate and respond to them accordingly. Markets change, and no matter how great the company, it must change, too. Sometimes even the best will overlook the inevitable.

The fall of one of Procter & Gamble's most venerable brands, Crest Toothpaste, is a good illustration of what happens when a company takes its eye off of the customer value ball. Crest had been one of the leading toothpastes on the market since its introduction in 1955. Its value proposition, cavity prevention, was originally both a compelling message and a competitive advantage. However, as consumers' needs moved beyond decay prevention, Crest did not. P&G failed to understand emerging consumer concerns, such as yellowing teeth, sensitive gums, and bad breath. This allowed other competitors to erode Crest's market share by creating and delivering additional value beyond healthy teeth. Between 1987 and 1997, Crest's market share slipped from 39 percent to 25 percent. In 1998, Crest finally lost market leadership to archrival Colgate with its introduction of Total, a toothpaste that fought everything: cavities, tartar, plaque, bad breath, and gingivitis.[3]

Loss of market position usually results from a company's inability to change or improve internal processes for delivering value to customers. The tragedy is that past successes may create an atmosphere of invincibility and complacency. Market position may erode so slowly that management has too little incentive or ability to change strategies or the way decisions are made. New competitors emerge to take advantage of opportunities created by changing customer needs. Sometimes it takes a crisis for a company to begin mak-

ing internal changes in processes needed to compete effectively in evolving markets. Procter & Gamble is now responding, and certainly the game is not over for P&G.

For most organizations the reality is that their customers' perceptions of value change over time; what customers want today may not be what they desire tomorrow. In one study, we found that how customers assess product value can change between when they make a purchase decision and later when they use the product.[4] Longer-run changes are even more likely. These changes in customer value create market opportunity for those suppliers who see them coming. Others may be left behind. The difference lies in how well individual suppliers are able to anticipate changes and respond to them.

WHAT IS CUSTOMER VALUE?

"What is customer value?" "What is it that *our particular customers* value?" "How do I know if we are delivering value to our customers?" These are questions that must be asked and must be asked continually, for the answers are complex, dynamic, and changing all of the time. In addition, it is our premise that most organizations are not able to answer these questions as well as they should.[5]

- First, some managers will honestly admit that they do not understand what their customers value, especially when marketplaces are changing so rapidly that it is difficult to keep up with competition, technology, or mercurial customer attitudes.

- Second, managers may incorrectly assume that they *know* what customers value. This may occur when managers fail to read and interpret the environment correctly. The previous Crest example is a case in point. Or, more arrogantly, managers may believe they know *better* than the customer, who can be "coached" into the correct mindset.

- Third, many managers cannot answer these questions because they never ask the *right* questions.

Defining *value* can also be difficult. Although we all believe we know what "value" means, in fact there is a multitude of different definitions and perspectives. The concept of value has roots in many disciplines, including psychology, social psychology, economics, marketing, and management. Even when we narrow our interest more specifically to consider customer value with a particular product or service, there are multiple meanings. For instance, for many organizations customer value is simply an economic consideration: What did the customer receive for her money? While economic value is certainly part of the puzzle, it is necessary to define value more broadly in order to understand value from the customer perspective.[6]

The following definition of value has been adopted for our purposes:

> *Value* is the customer's perception of the extent to which use of a product allows him or her to accomplish some desired purpose or goal. This evaluation is judged within the context of a particular use situation, and it is the net result of trade-offs between the positive and negative consequences of product use.

This definition requires additional discussion. (See **Exhibit 5.1**.)

Consumption Goals: Value In Use and Possession Value

What kinds of consumption goals are customers trying to fulfill? The specific purposes and/or goals of product use are many and varied. However, these can be generally understood in two broad classifications: value in use and possession value.[7]

"Value in use," as the name suggests, is an outcome, purpose, or objective that is served directly through product consumption.[8] For example, having a cup of coffee wakes the consumer up in the morning, using a computer increases a user's productivity, or purchasing from a particular parts supplier may increase a manufacturer's product reliability. Other examples of value in use might include time efficiency, thirst quenching, dependable transportation, entertainment, easy cleanup, and so on.

The specific type of value in use that the customer requires will vary considerably by the type of product or service. However, less obvious is the notion that, even for a specific product/service, there may be a number of value in use objectives that the product must meet. For example, consumers of the same microwave dinner may have very different purposes in mind (nutrition, low-cost meal, good taste, quick meal preparation, etc.). Understanding value in use, especially as it relates to your target audience(s), is critical for managers.

Second, customers can derive value from simple product possession. This notion of *possession value* acknowledges that products

---

Exhibit 5.1: *Defining Customer Value*

Customer value is the customers' perception of what they want to have happen (i.e., consequences) in a specific use situation, with the help of a product/service offering, in order to accomplish a desired purpose or goal.

Three Important Elements of the Definition

1. Products are the means toward accomplishing customers' purposes. The purposes of product use can be broadly classified as Value In Use (where goals are served by actual product consumption) or Possession Value (where aesthetic or symbolic goals are served through simple ownership).
2. Products create value through the delivery of consequences. Consequences are outcomes which are experienced by the customer, rather than product characteristics.
3. Value judgments are highly influenced by and best determined within the constraints of a particular use situation. These judgments are subject to change across use situation, over time, and due to specific "trigger" situations.

---

can contain important symbolic, self-expressive, and aesthetic qualities that accrue to the customer through mere proximity and association.[9] This type of value is often associated with products that have a very high "pride of ownership" component, such as luxury items, a family heirloom, state-of-the-art technology, or rare art pieces. However, possession value can also apply to relatively inexpensive items, such as a treasured item found at a garage sale or the latest style shoes for the fashion innovator. Consumers may accrue possession value from any item with which they have high involvement or interest, despite its cost. Services also have a parallel "pride of usership" component. Consider the status and prestige that can accrue to the individual who dines at a fine restaurant or the company that retains a world-renowned advertising agency.

Of course, these two product-use goals are not mutually exclusive. Consider the ownership of a corporate jet, which might create both value in use and possession value. This classification is not meant to imply an either/or mentality but to alert the manager to multiple goals that may be associated with the consumption of his product.

Consequences of Product Use

Value judgments are closely associated with the consequences of product/service consumption. It is important to define what we mean by *consequences*. *Consequences* are *outcomes that are experienced by the customer*, as opposed to characteristics of the product itself. Some consequences of product consumption are positive. These are the desired outcomes, benefits, or realizations that the customer enjoys as a result of product/service possession and consumption, and they

can be far reaching in scope. Some positive consequences may be relatively objective in nature, for example, infrequent trips to the service department, minimal time and effort involved in assembly, and a short waiting line. In contrast, some positive consequences are more subjective in nature: stress relief, self-confidence, efficiency, productivity, and so forth. Positive consequences may result from the presence of a single product/service attribute, such as front wheel drive (an attribute) providing "better handling on snow" (a consequence). Likewise, consequences may accrue across a number of product attributes and features. For example, many individual features of a car might combine to determine the consumer's perception of "a comfortable ride," including its suspension, size, upholstery, instrument configuration, and so on.

Price is the most commonly considered negative consequence of product consumption. However, negative consequences go well beyond monetary considerations. Thinking more broadly—for every positive consequence that is associated with the use of a product—there is a corresponding negative consequence that the customer must bear if the benefit is not received. For instance, when the positive consequence "ease of use" is not received, the negative consequence might well be "difficult to operate" or "takes too much of my time (or effort)." Negative consequences may include psychological costs (such as stress), the time and effort associated with purchasing and consuming the product, opportunity costs of not choosing other alternatives (e.g., lost productivity due to choosing an unreliable supplier), and various other sacrifices that might be associated with the product or service.

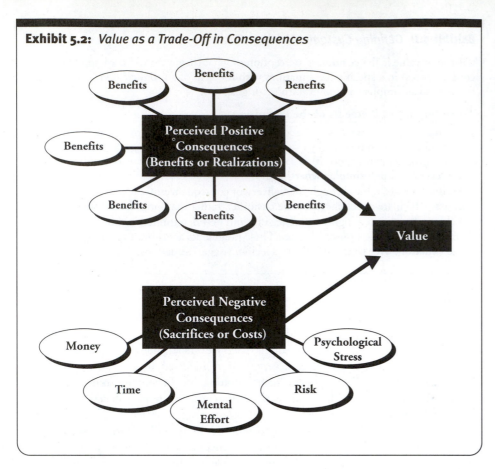

Exhibit 5.2: *Value as a Trade-Off in Consequences*

- Benefits
- Benefits
- Benefits
- Benefits

Perceived Positive Consequences (Benefits or Realizations)

- Benefits
- Benefits
- Benefits

Value

Perceived Negative Consequences (Sacrifices or Costs)

- Money
- Time
- Mental Effort
- Risk
- Psychological Stress

Earlier, we defined *value* as the extent to which a product allows the consumer to accomplish a desired purpose or goal. Positive and negative consequences are the means by which goal achievement is either accomplished or inhibited (see **Exhibit 5.2**).[10] Product/service providers must keep in mind that customers will realize multiple consequences associated with product use, and it would be highly unusual for these consequences to be all positive or all negative, for that matter. For example, a consumer's new car may provide comfort, a feeling of security and luxury, and better handling. However, these positive consequences may be offset by having to cope with frequent repairs, dealing with insensitive service providers at the dealership, or psychological stress over the price. Managers must, therefore, attempt to understand the consequence trade-offs that their customers experience and, thus, the value that is associated with their product.

Understanding consequence trade-offs can, in fact, provide strategic opportunities for businesses that might want to reconsider traditional industry practices. For example, FedEx redefined the package delivery industry by reconsidering the consequence trade-offs that its customers were willing to make. For decades the package delivery service was considered a commodity: The service was basically considered to be moving a package safely from point A to point B. The accepted strategy was to offer this basic service at a low price. However, Federal Express CEO Fred Smith saw the industry differently. Specifically, he believed that knowledge about the cargo's origin, present whereabouts, destination, estimated time of arrival, price, and cost of shipment were as important customer benefits as was safe delivery. And he bet that customers would actually pay a higher price to gain these additional benefits. To accomplish this, he built a state-of-the-art information system alongside the air and vehicle networks, and FedEx has become a success story in the industry.[11]

Importance of Use Situation

It is also important to note that value is the end result of the coming together of a product and a user within a particular use situation (see **Exhibit 5.3**).[12] Adding this situational perspective is important because customers' judgments about product value are based upon the requirements of their use situations. In fact, it is difficult to deter-

mine whether a product "generally" provides value for an individual or organization without asking, "How will the customer be using the product?" or "What does the customer desire in a particular consumption situation?" For example, a consumer may consider purchasing a bottle of wine for many use situations, including a dinner at home with the family, a picnic, entertaining important guests, or as a gift for a friend. The value that a particular bottle of wine has for the consumer may vary considerably depending upon the requirements of the specific use situation for which it is intended.

A good example of this "triangulated" thinking comes from Nissan and is drawn from its development of the Maxima.[13] Positioned as a family sedan (users) maker, Nissan considered the various ways in which the Maxima would be used (situations). One situation considered was "women juggling groceries." Specifically, this situation put additional emphasis on the need for a trunk that is easy to open and close. Therefore, Nissan designed a trunk (product) with a counterbalanced lid so that it would work more easily.

In another example, NEC used field research to study the situations in which persons use notebook (or portable) personal computers. They found that individuals using the computers while on the telephone might need to open the machine with one hand instead of two, or that during a meeting the user might need to show the

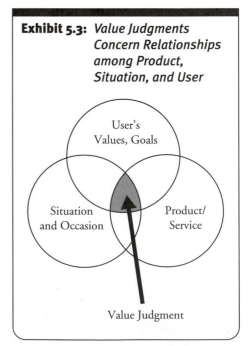

Exhibit 5.3: *Value Judgments Concern Relationships among Product, Situation, and User*

- User's Values, Goals
- Situation and Occasion
- Product/Service
- Value Judgment

computer screen to others in the room and might like the option of a display screen that could be turned to face others. In fact, NEC took its sensitivity for the consumer's various use situation requirements to an extreme. NEC's Versa Notebook Computer allowed every major component (e.g., display screen, disk drives, power supply, and memory) to snap in and out. This design effectively allowed the user to configure the machine for different use situations, such as home, office, or travel.[14]

The influence of use situation on value judgments has important implications. First, it implies that the perceived "value" of a product may, in fact, change over time and across use situations.[15] For instance, while a compact sedan may be entirely adequate (and thus create value) for an individual who is commuting to and from work, its value may diminish when judged within the context of an extended family vacation.

We recently saw an example of situation-driven value when we interviewed Department of Transportation (DOT) employees in two states. We wanted to understand how these "customers" judge the value they receive from suppliers with whom they contract to complete projects, such as building bridges or interstate exchanges. We found that "value" could be defined only by specifying the situational context. When suppliers were trying to negotiate the complex preproject government bidding process, the DOT customers judged supplier value on the basis of dimensions such as "frankness and honesty during negotiations," "minimal documentation errors," "doesn't try a cookie cutter approach to our unique problems," and "ability to understand our needs." In contrast, after a supplier had won the bidding process and was engaged in actually managing the contract and project, other value dimensions emerged as DOT customer concerns, such as "reduces our lead times," "becomes an extension of our staff," "minimal changeover in personnel," and "communicates well."

Second, product or service providers must realize that value is often a moving target, changing with the requirements of the use situation. And, rather than viewing value as static, it might be best to view it as dynamic, as something that is created over time, across a number of use situations during the "life" of the product or service (see **Exhibit 5.4**). Some specific use occasions

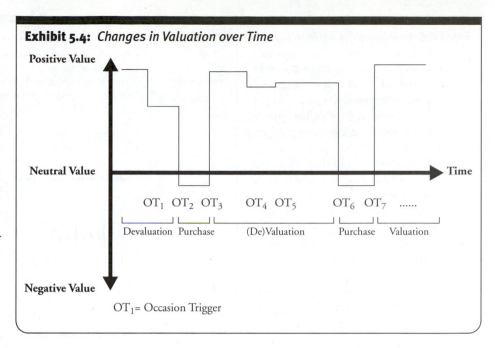

Exhibit 5.4: *Changes in Valuation over Time*

OT_1 = Occasion Trigger

can be identified that provide the "triggers" for changing product requirements and, thus, changing value judgments (these are known as *occasion triggers,* or OTs in Exhibit 5.4). For example, notice in Exhibit 5.4 how value judgments drop significantly at occasion trigger OT_2, or rise dramatically at occasion trigger OT_7. It is clearly important for managers to know where these critical occasion triggers exist for their customers as well as what changing requirements will be used to judge the value of their products in those situations.

For example, most car dealers understand that a critical occasion trigger is the new car buyer's first visit to the service department. At this time, it is likely that a completely different set of value dimensions will be used to judge the responsiveness of the dealership than were used during the product purchase, such as friendliness of the service department employees, promptness in repair, getting it right the first time, adequately explaining what service the car required, or returning a clean car. What are those dimensions? How can dealers track their customers in order to identify exactly when they will reach this occasion trigger? What might be done by the service department to respond to these new requirements?

Many managers have noticed that their customers' requirements change or become more demanding over time.[16] The reasons for this are many; for example, new brands may enter the market with better features, the customer may better understand product requirements after increased product experience, or the characteristics of the use situation itself might change. For any of these reasons, a product/service that once created value may diminish in value over time (i.e., the product "fails," in not responding to changing needs). In addition to noting this tendency with customers we have interviewed, we have encountered managers who are intuitively, or sometimes painfully, aware of how devaluation has occurred in their customer base over time.

Summary

Clearly, perceived product value is a dynamic concept. We have defined *value* as multidimensional (based upon both consumption and possession goals), as resulting from a trade-off (in terms of a variety of positive and negative consequences), and as dynamic (the judgment can vary across different product usage situations). Therefore, it is clear that attempting to understand and measure value will be a challenge. To this end, it would be helpful to have a systematic way to think about customer value. The customer value hierarchy has provided such a framework.

CUSTOMER VALUE HIERARCHY

There was a time when watch manufacturers thought in terms of timepieces. The most important product dimensions included reliability, precision, durability, and cost. However, Swatch watches found a way to redefine the market, primarily by paying attention to the reasons why consumers bought watches.[17] Swatch discovered that consumers in a portion of the market owned not one, but multiple watches to serve as accessories to different types of clothes. The idea of a watch as a fashion item or accessory, rather than a timepiece, took hold and propelled Swatch to the top of a highly competitive product category. Had Swatch paid attention only to the physical properties of the watch, this opportunity would never have been realized. What it did, instead, was to pay attention to the benefits that consumers desired and to understand that the watch itself was only a means to a more important end (fashionable appearance).

Means-End theory suggests a hierarchical representation of how customers view products (see **Exhibit 5.5**).[18] It suggests that how products relate to customers can be represented by three levels: attributes, consequences, and desired end states. As we will see, these levels become increasingly abstract with movement from the lower to higher levels, as well as becoming increasingly relevant to the customer.

Attributes

At the lowest level, the customer defines the product in terms of its attributes. These are physical characteristics (for tangible products), features, component parts, or activities (for services). Attributes are typically what would be mentioned if a customer was asked to describe a product (e.g., "it is a 4-door utility vehicle with 4-wheel drive, leather interior, anti-lock brakes. . . ."). One might also consider these as the "options" that are offered by a particular brand. Attributes tend to be defined fairly objectively, and there may be multiple attributes and bundlings of attributes that make up any particular product or service.

Exhibit 5.6, drawn from our research, is a *value hierarchy* that was constructed from an in-depth interview with a car owner. This hierarchy includes several attributes that the consumer noted in discussing her car. These were attributes associated both with the car itself (location of switches, layout of instruments, size, plushness of the interior, and mpg) or associated with the service surrounding the sale and maintenance of her car (the use of pressure tactics by salespeople, competence of the mechanics, responsiveness of the service department, etc.). Again, because "product" is defined broadly, the customer may consider both tangible product and service attributes.

Exhibit 5.5: *Customer Value Hierarchy*

Desired End States
(Personal and Organizational)
Describes the person or organization

- Their core values
- Guiding principles
- Most fundamental and overriding motivations
- The "ends" which are served by product/service "means"

Consequences
What the product *does* for the user

- Realizations, benefits, desired outcomes
- Sacrifices, costs, undesired outcomes
- More abstract and subjectively defined
- Subgoals which are met through product/service use

Attributes
Describes the product/service

- What the product *is*
- Product features, service activities
- Component parts
- Options
- Tend to be more objectively defined

It should be noted that companies traditionally have defined what they do by way of an attribute focus. Customer satisfaction surveys provide compelling evidence of this because they almost invariably measure satisfaction with product attributes or features (more will be said about this later). Make no mistake, understanding and improving product attributes is important, and, in fact, we will argue later that this is a critical exercise for organizations. However, as will become evident, when an organization's focus *stops* at attribute determination and fails to consider upper levels of the value hierarchy, that is where difficulties (and failures) lie.

Consequences

At the middle level of the hierarchy are the customer's more subjective considerations of the consequences (both positive and negative) that she derives from product use. In interviewing users of a variety of products, we have noted that they frequently speak in terms of consequences when describing their product experiences. For instance, one consumer discussed the effects of inflexible leather soles on a pair of sandals in the following way: "They were kind of stiff. They had the kind of flat-footed effect of a flop, flop, flop because they wouldn't bend." Likewise, a boat owner discussed the location of some of the boat's instrumentation: "You have to be a contortionist to read your autometer. It is usually mounted between the two hatches (in the bilge), and you can't get your body in there." These examples highlight the change in perspective from the attribute level. While attributes describe the *product*, consequences are the results that accrue to the *customer* as a result of product use and possession.

Another way to think about the difference between attributes and consequences is to consider what types of questions one would have to ask in order to elicit each one. At the attribute level, one could simply ask the customer to describe the product or service. At the consequence level, one

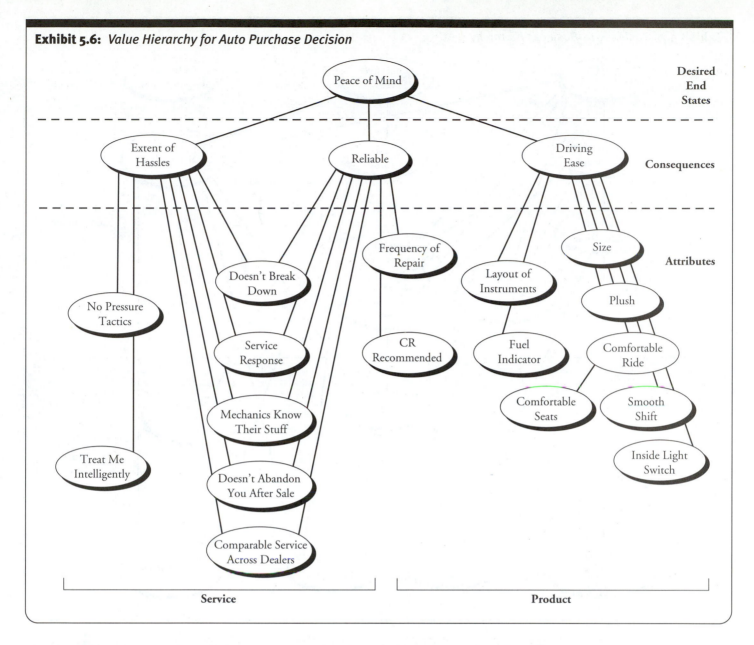

Exhibit 5.6: *Value Hierarchy for Auto Purchase Decision*

Desired End States

Peace of Mind

Consequences

Extent of Hassles — Reliable — Driving Ease

Attributes

No Pressure Tactics
Treat Me Intelligently
Doesn't Break Down
Service Response
Mechanics Know Their Stuff
Doesn't Abandon You After Sale
Comparable Service Across Dealers
Frequency of Repair
CR Recommended
Layout of Instruments
Fuel Indicator
Comfortable Seats
Size
Plush
Comfortable Ride
Smooth Shift
Inside Light Switch

Service

Product

would instead ask questions that are directed at the product user, such as "What happens when you use this product?" or "What does this product do for you?" These are different questions that yield different answers.

A good example of a consequence is found in the process by which Oldsmobile designed the Aurora, its 1994 entry into the luxury car market.[19] As early as 1988, Oldsmobile engineers interviewed owners of European luxury cars such as Mercedes-Benz and BMW to understand the needs of luxury car owners. To be sure, the owners mentioned attributes such as leather seats and wood trim, multivalve engines, and four-wheel disk brakes. However, the characteristics that Olds determined were most critical to defining luxury car experience were consequences: these cars "inspired

confidence and security, gave the vehicles an opulent hush, and isolated drivers from bumps and jolts." Of course, it was left to the Olds engineers to determine which combination of attributes could produce those desired consequences. They decided that the key was a "rock solid body structure," and they began to define what specific combination of materials, design, and assembly (attributes) could produce the desired effects.

As another example, **Exhibit 5.7** depicts a different kind of value hierarchy. It is a representation of how value might be perceived in a business-to-business situation. Again, the distinction between attribute and consequence level is highlighted. Under this scenario, the attributes provided by the supplier might be helpfulness of the staff, on-time delivery, accurate order fill-

ing, EDI services, and so on. However, the consequences to the customer organization might be the extent to which the supplier helps deliver value to the customers, reduce inventory, eliminate downtime, meet the customer's own schedules, and so on. Exhibit 5.7 illustrates how the concepts of a value hierarchy can be adapted not only to service providers but also to business-to-business as well as manufacturer-to-customer relationships.

As stated earlier, consequences of product use can be both positive (benefits, desired outcomes, or realizations) and negative (sacrifices, costs, undesirable outcomes). Consequences tend to be more abstract in nature than attributes and are more subjectively defined by the product user. Although customers might easily agree on a description of a product's attributes,

Exhibit 5.7: *Business-to-Business Hierarchy*

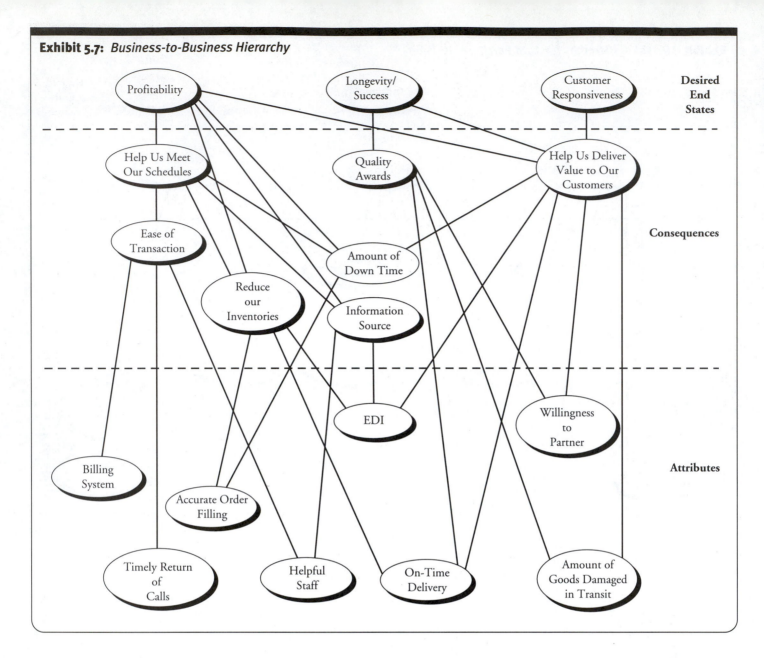

they may have considerable disagreement over its consequences. For instance, two consumers might objectively describe and agree upon the design of a laptop computer (attributes). However, they may disagree completely on whether the design is user friendly (consequences). Another way to think about consequences is that they are the key to understanding why customers prefer certain attributes or attribute combinations over others, that is, based upon their ability to deliver (or avoid) desirable (or undesirable) consequences.

Another characteristic of consequences must be kept in mind; although there may be a one-to-one correspondence between some attributes and some consequences, it is also true that a consequence may be the result of a combination of many attributes.

For example, Ford Motor Company found that many of its consumers complained of scuffed shoes when riding in the back seats of their cars (negative consequence). In responding to this negative consequence, several attribute adjustments were made, including sloping the underside of the seats, widening the space between the seat adjustment tracks, and making the tracks out of smooth plastic rather than metal.[20]

Desired End States

Finally, at the top of the hierarchy are desired end states, which are the most basic or fundamental motivators for the individual, family, or organization. They may be personal or organizational values that are deeply held principles or priorities, as well as goals or purposes that underlie consumption

behavior. In short, these are the ultimate "ends" that the customer wishes to achieve either in life (e.g., peace of mind) or more specifically through the consumption of a particular product (e.g., variety). Products and services are the means by which these ends are pursued (hence, the term *means-end* hierarchy). Again, examples from our interviews illustrate the conscious way in which desired end states shape decisions to buy and use products. One boat owner discussed the purchase as a way of engendering family unity: "We got our boat to hopefully keep our teenagers interested in being with us for a few years longer. It keeps us all together." Likewise, a user of a health and fitness center commented: "[As a result of my exercise] I feel better about everything, I guess, and my outlook on life is better."

Our consumer in Exhibit 5.6 valued peace of mind very highly, both in her life in general and, more specifically, surrounding the use of her automobile. (It should probably be noted that her history was characterized by a string of undependable and repair-ridden "lemons.") By selecting a car that contained a specific configuration of attributes (both product and service) and that provided her with three key consequences (absence of hassles, security, and effortless driving), she attempted to enhance her overall peace of mind.

The types of end states that impact behaviors may be unique to an individual product user as well as shared by organizations, including families, social clubs, religious institutions, or businesses. Examples of end states that are valued by consumers might be self-fulfillment, confidence, entertainment, variety, getting along with others, or ecological responsibility. Organizational end states might include corporate longevity, a sense of unity or community, customer responsiveness, quality, or shareholder wealth.

IMPORTANT CHARACTERISTICS OF THE VALUE HIERARCHY

There are several characteristics of the hierarchy that stand out when one thinks about applying this concept in practice (see **Exhibit 5.8**).

Interrelationship between the Three Levels

As implied earlier, there is definitely an interrelationship among the three levels of the hierarchy. Product attributes are the "means" by which consequences are delivered to the customer. In other words, customers will make inferences about the likelihood that certain attributes or combinations of attributes will lead to benefits or sacrifices. In Exhibit 5.6, for instance, instrument layout, size, and seat comfort are three attributes that the consumer believes contribute to effortless driving.

Another example of the interrelationship between attributes and consequences can be found in the experiences of the Power Tool Division of Stryker.[21] When Stryker employees went into their customers' factories to see where and how their tools were being used, they came across a surprising fact: Half of the product users were women. They noticed that one conse-

quence of their product design was that these customers had difficulty gripping their tools. As a response to this negative consequence or "sacrifice," they had to reconsider the related attributes (design and construction) of their tools. They subsequently redesigned the tools with variable size grips made of rubberized plastic, providing easier gripping for the users. As an unexpected result, they also found that these products sold well among Japanese users, who had smaller hands.

Likewise, customers form perceptions of the extent to which the consequences derived from product use will help them obtain valued end states. For example, cars that provide security and effortless driving help create peace of mind (see Exhibit 5.6).

Level of Abstraction

As mentioned earlier, the level of abstraction increases at higher levels in the pyramid. While attributes tend to be the most objectively and concretely defined, consequences (the benefits and sacrifices of use) tend to be more abstract in nature and desired end states the most abstract. One result of this tendency is that it becomes much more challenging to measure and understand the higher levels of a customer's value hierarchy. Consumers and organizations may not as readily articulate their product desires at the higher levels of the hierarchy, and those attempting to understand and measure the customer perspective will have to dig more deeply to get at consequences and desired end states. This issue will be addressed later in the section, "Measuring Value Hierarchies."

Stability over Time

Another characteristic of the hierarchy has to do with stability over time. There is a tendency for stability to increase at higher levels of the hierarchy. According to psychologists, individuals' core values (or desired end states) are some of the most enduring and stable traits of individuals. While core values might change and evolve over time, generally this process is a very gradual one. The same can be said for organizations.

At the middle level, the consequences that are desired by individuals are probably less stable than valued end states, especially given their tendency to change across situations. Nonetheless, the consequences are much more stable and much less apt to change than are product attributes.

> **Exhibit 5.8:** *Characteristics of Value Hierarchy*
>
> 1. There are three levels of the value hierarchy: attributes, consequences, and desired end states. These three levels are interconnected with each other in the sense that "lower levels" are the means by which "higher level" ends are achieved.
> 2. The level of abstraction tends to increase at higher levels in the hierarchy.
> 3. Stability of the hierarchy tends to increase at higher levels in the hierarchy.
> 4. The value dimensions which appear in the hierarchy are directly influenced by the situation in which the product or service is used.

Finally, at the lowest level, the actual attributes or bundles of attributes that are available in the marketplace are continually changing over time. Product life cycles are decreasing, technological change occurs at an astounding rate, and there is a changing multiplicity of offerings in any given product category. For example, in 1997 alone, some 25,000 new food, health, beauty, and pet products were introduced in the United States, or some 69 launches per day.[22] It is not surprising that in this constantly changing marketplace, customers are continually revising their ideas regarding the desirability of specific product or service attributes.

Importance of Use Situation

Finally, touching back on our previous discussion, we must remember that there is no such thing as "the" value hierarchy for a product or service. Use situation will be a critical determinant of value, and therefore the components of the value hierarchy may change significantly as the use situation is altered. For example, there are many use situations that prompt individuals to visit restaurants (family meals, romantic evenings, and business meetings). Not surprisingly, these restaurant use situations create very different value hierarchies in terms of the attributes, consequences, and desired end states that the consumer is concerned about. For example, based on their understanding about the increasing propensity of consumers to mix eating with business, Starbucks has opened a new restaurant in San Francisco that features high-speed Internet connections with credit

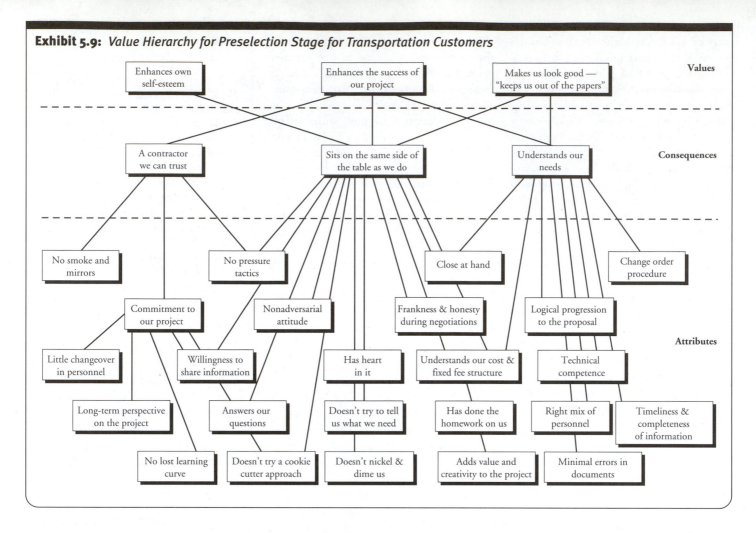

Exhibit 5.9: *Value Hierarchy for Preselection Stage for Transportation Customers*

Values

- Enhances own self-esteem
- Enhances the success of our project
- Makes us look good — "keeps us out of the papers"

Consequences

- A contractor we can trust
- Sits on the same side of the table as we do
- Understands our needs

Attributes

- No smoke and mirrors
- No pressure tactics
- Close at hand
- Change order procedure
- Commitment to our project
- Nonadversarial attitude
- Frankness & honesty during negotiations
- Logical progression to the proposal
- Little changeover in personnel
- Willingness to share information
- Has heart in it
- Understands our cost & fixed fee structure
- Technical competence
- Long-term perspective on the project
- Answers our questions
- Doesn't try to tell us what we need
- Has done the homework on us
- Right mix of personnel
- Timeliness & completeness of information
- No lost learning curve
- Doesn't try a cookie cutter approach
- Doesn't nickel & dime us
- Adds value and creativity to the project
- Minimal errors in documents

---

card swipe-through machines and a conference room equipped with audiovisual equipment.[23] Clearly, these restaurant attributes and their related consequences (convenience, productive meal time, etc.) will be valued in some use situations (e.g., business meals) but not in others.

Likewise, in an earlier example, we discussed how Department of Transportation employees considered different value dimensions when dealing with their suppliers during preselection stages (qualifying and bidding) versus during the contract management stage (project implementation). **Exhibits 5.9 and 5.10** represent how business-to-business value hierarchies can differ by situation.

APPLYING CUSTOMER VALUE HIERARCHIES IN PRACTICE

A legitimate question to ask is why managers should go to the trouble to understand and measure the entire value hierarchy. We believe that there are several compelling reasons (see **Exhibit 5.11**).

Delivering Superior Value

Through the eyes of many product or service providers, their product/service offering *is* a bundle of attributes or features. They produce their product or service by a process that combines component parts, features, or activities. Their research and development (R&D) efforts are frequently aimed at improving their offering by adding, refining, or deleting attributes. They very often differentiate their products from those of competitors by adjusting the attribute options that they offer versus those offered by competitors. In fact, it appears that many companies view customer value in terms of attributes, and therefore their actions tend to be associated with product attribute features.

In contrast, the customer value hierarchy clearly shows that in order to understand value, one must understand the purpose for which a product is intended and used. One must understand what particular set of consequences is (or is not) desired by product users, as well as what use

or possession objectives customers are trying to achieve. Also, one must be familiar with the end states that are deemed desirable by product users. Unless these upper levels of the hierarchy are understood, there is no "north star" to guide managers in the selection and choice of attributes that should be incorporated into the product or service. One study indicated that consequences are more closely related to choice than attributes.[24]

Understanding value hierarchies will also remind the product/service provider that no two customers' (or market segments') value hierarchies will be exactly alike and that these differences provide both challenges and opportunities. For example, Safety Kleen, a commercial waste disposal business, found that its smaller customers required a great deal of face-to-face service tailored to their needs. This requirement was largely due to the customers' lack of understanding of regulatory requirements associated with commercial waste. In contrast, this need was not in the value hierarchies of larger businesses, which tended to have staffs more astute to these

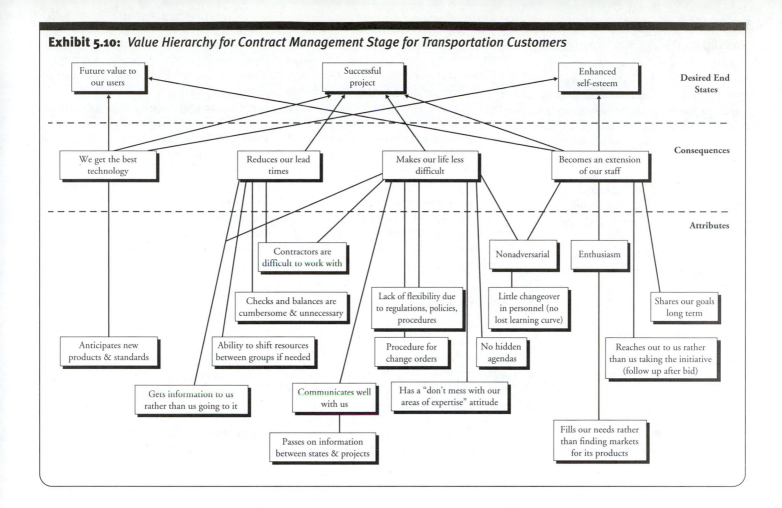

Exhibit 5.10: *Value Hierarchy for Contract Management Stage for Transportation Customers*

issues. Consequently, Safety Kleen was able to offer its larger customers a "stripped-down" service that met their unique needs.[25] Interestingly, this example also implies that it is possible for organizations to build features into their products that do not create customer value and thus are candidates for elimination.

Likewise, if a manufacturer truly understands customers' value hierarchies, it might be able to identify "high-impact" attributes or features that serve multiple consequences for the customer, thus enhancing value. For example, LCD readouts on a car dashboard may provide several benefits for the driver, including being easier to read, providing pride in owning the "most recent technology," and being luxurious. In this way, manufacturers may find that they are undervaluing (and underpricing, in some instances) some of their product or service features by failing to recognize their multiple benefits to the customer.

In sum, without knowledge (or with a misunderstanding) of these upper levels, it will be almost impossible for management to agree upon what the basic product offer-

---

Exhibit 5.11: *Managerial Implications of the Value Hierarchy*

1. Managers must stop defining their product or service offerings strictly in terms of attributes.
2. Managers must understand that value is judged by customers at the upper levels of the hierarchy, specifically in terms of consequence trade-offs.
3. Managers who have a clear understanding of the entire value hierarchy will have better criteria for comparing the merits of alternative products or services.
4. Understanding the linkages between attributes and consequences can help managers to identify "high impact" attributes which provide multiple benefits for the customer.
5. Rather than a "bottom-up" approach, the hierarchy suggests a "top-down" approach to decision making, where one must understand the higher levels before deciding which attributes to include in the product.
6. Managers who concentrate their attention on changing unstable attributes will find themselves chasing a moving target, whereas consequences and desired end states provide a more stable decision making orientation.
7. Upper levels of the hierarchy have an inherent "future" orientation, while the attribute levels tend to focus on historical or current offerings.
8. Upper levels of the hierarchy provide more opportunity for significant and creative changes in the product or service, while an attribute focus tends to result in smaller, incremental changes.

---

ing should be. Or, more likely, management will have insufficient knowledge with which to judge the advantage of one alternative offering against another. It is clear that many business practitioners are increasingly viewing the creation of "value" as a competitive advantage and, more specifically, believe that providing sustainable superior value has a direct impact on profitability.[26]

"Top-Down" Decision Making

The hierarchy suggests a "directional" approach to product or service design. Many organizations that are product driven start at the bottom of the hierarchy, bundling attributes and setting design engineers to work to "build better mouse traps." Later, the organizations go in search of customers or markets that might desire their offerings. The hierarchy suggests a top-down approach. The organization begins with an in-depth understanding of the upper-level consequences and end states that are important to the customer and then works "downward" to try to design a bundle of goods or services to deliver those consequences. In other words, "value" is first determined in the mind of the customer, not in the minds of the R&D department. An organization must understand both value in the customer's mind and the higher means-end levels before it can even attempt to answer the question of how to create and deliver value through any particular bundle of attributes.

More Stable Decision-Making Orientation

It was mentioned earlier that the hierarchy represents increasing stability at higher levels. One obvious implication of this characteristic is that managers who are focused at the attribute level will be chasing a moving target. An attribute focus can introduce a frantic sense of catching up, keeping up, or staying ahead of the competition, often without producing strategic advantage for the product/service provider. A case in point is the technological one-upsmanship that has been practiced in the consumer electronics industry. Manufacturers are finding that their "innovations" are often quickly imitated by competitors, providing only short-term advantage. A marketing manager for a major airline once told me that its new, improved seat design for business class probably had a six-month window before being matched by competitors.

On the other hand, concentrating on the higher levels of the hierarchy, the goals are more stable and are less apt to change. While management will still have enormous opportunities to pursue how they can deliver desired consequences to customers, the objectives can remain more focused for longer periods of time. Think back to the earlier example about the Oldsmobile Auro-

ra. If engineers are focused on creating a sensation of "cocooning" the driver from the road, there may be a multitude of ways to deliver this perception. Rather than a one-shot change, the quest for this consequence could be an evolutionary, continuous improvement process, including changes in multiple product dimensions over time. They might begin with the more obvious attributes, such as the frame structure and suspension, and later move to less obvious attributes that can fine-tune the car's performance, such as the sound the door makes when it closes, the way the seats "hug" the passengers, or the soundproofing of the car from road noises.

Eye on the Future

Consumers are not very good at answering, in the abstract, "What should our product (service) look like in five years?" Ask any manager who has tried. Consumers are not well equipped to project, create, and imagine offerings that they have not experienced.[27] There are probably several reasons for this, but two are most obvious.

First, consumers are very oriented toward "what is." They tend to think in terms of what they already know or have experienced, and this mind-set often limits their ability to see beyond the obvious. (Similar effects have been noted in memory research in the field of psychology. Studies show that you can actually limit an individual's ability to provide a broad range of responses to a question by first suggesting what some of the responses might be.) This tendency to ground responses in "what is" obviously has the limitation of leading to incremental or marginal improvements in existing offerings. However, in many cases product/service providers are looking for more dramatic breakthroughs that literally redefine the industry. It is such breakthroughs that lead to significant improvements in customer value, as well as competitive advantage. Consumers are simply not very good at visualizing such breakthroughs.

The other reason that consumers are not particularly good predictors of the future is simply their limited knowledge. In many instances they lack the (technical, mechanical, chemical, process, systems, resource, etc.) know-how to understand or even imagine what the possibilities are. In fact, in most instances the product/service provider is much more knowledgeable about what *potentially can be*.

So, how should managers understand their customers' future needs? An attribute focus has a greater tendency to focus on what is; as stated earlier, incremental change for existing attributes is a common route for new product development. Think about what would happen if you asked consumers to design the personal computer for the year 2020. By and large they would probably think in terms of size, keyboards, memory, and so on. However, managers can more accurately predict what customers' future needs will be by understanding the consequence level (e.g., the ability to translate ideas into a readable format, the need to integrate databases containing a variety of different information types and formats, accessibility, portability). Once the manager has a keener understanding of these consequences (which are less likely to change in the future than attributes), he can turn an eye toward endless possibilities and alternatives (at the attribute level) for delivering them.[28]

Opportunities for Significant, Creative Breakthroughs

Finally, it is increasingly evident that the objective of delivering consequences yields more opportunity for creativity and for significant, dramatic change than concentrating on improving attributes. It is at this higher level that managers can free up their organization to consider many, sometimes very different options for the customer. It allows them to think beyond their current (attribute) offerings and current systems capabilities. Instead, it challenges them to think more broadly in terms of future directions and opportunities for serving the customer.

For example, an attribute-based survey of car buyers might inquire about their attitude toward side impact beams (an attribute). Consumer response to this query would most likely be positive, and the manufacturer may feel it can "solve" consumers' safety concerns by adding this particular feature to the next generation of cars. However, it may be that what the consumer really wants is to fulfill the consequence of "feeling that my family is secure and safe in our car." By not asking consequence-level questions, the product provider may cut off creative opportunities to enhance customer consequences through a variety of options or features. Additional, creative ways to enhance a feeling of security for car buyers may need to be considered, such as how well the doors and windows seal, the tightness of the steering mechanism, the feel of the suspension system, the construction of the "cage," and so forth. Because consequences provide broader opportunities for creativity than attributes, one R&D employee at a consumer package goods firm told us, "A consequence focus is liberating."

Consider the Starbucks restaurant example noted earlier.[29] Clearly, Starbucks is operating off of a mind-set broader than simply creating a restaurant as "a place to eat." Starbucks understands that persons mixing business with meals often consider restaurants to be "an extension of my office," a consequence for these customers. This consequence provides a much broader, more creative target from which to consider the types of attributes, features, and services that might create value for that target customer group, moving beyond simple food preparation and service to include a broader variety of communications and work-efficiency features.

Another example of this creative thinking may be found in Apple's early development of a laptop computer.[30] The firm's initial efforts, which ultimately failed, concentrated solely on making a smaller and lighter version of its existing desktop machines (an attribute focus). Once the market rejected these, Apple turned to consumers for redirection. By observing consumers using laptops on airlines, in cars, or even in bed (in a variety of *use situations* in which laptops are used), Apple was able to come away with a clearer understanding of the consequences of certain product designs. For instance, a mouse was of little use when the consumer was trying to work on a small airplane tray-table or off of his lap in a taxi. From this, the inclusion of a built-in cursor mechanism was born, a design feature that was innovative at the time and that is now a standard feature on all laptops. We guess that the possibility of a successful redesign might have been less likely had Apple executives gone out and directly asked consumers what kind of attributes they wanted on their laptop, or worse yet, simply sent their design engineers back to the drawing board to try something different.

In short, we believe that substantive, radical, and strategically sustainable advantage is more likely to result when organizations step back from their more narrow focus on attribute improvement and consider the broader issues of conse-

quence and value delivery. In turn, this perspective is likely to provide a more strategically sustainable competitive advantage than simply improving attributes on the margins.

MEASURING VALUE HIERARCHIES

One way to think about measuring customer value is to imagine an onion with many layers. Beginning with the surface, each of these layers must be peeled back, exposing new surfaces beneath until the heart of the onion is reached. Understanding customer value requires such a "peeling-back" process. When first asked to discuss their relationship to product/service offerings, most customers will begin with the most "surface" and objective perspective, that is, attributes. This information is important, and you should pay close attention to customers' perspectives on this level of the value hierarchy. However, you must also encourage customers to explore their relationship with the product at deeper levels (higher in the value hierarchy). You must probe and explore and encourage the customer to discuss important outcomes of product/service use, such as positive and negative consequences. You must dig deeply to allow often deep-seated desired end states to come to the surface. And most importantly, you must let the customer lead the conversation to issues that *the customer* feels are important. It is often impossible to know a priori where such an interview might lead or what new insights might be discovered when the customer dictates the direction of the interview. This "peeling back" process is much more conducive to open-ended, loosely structured questions. It also requires significant amounts of time (beyond the few minutes that one can generally expect respondents to spend on a survey). All of these issues point away from traditional, quantitative survey techniques toward greater use of qualitative methods in the early stages of gathering customer value data.

We have found two different qualitative interview techniques, laddering and grand tours, to be very effective ways to uncover and measure value hierarchies. Each of these will be briefly described next.

Laddering

Laddering is a semistructured interviewing method specifically designed to measure the means-end associations (attributes, conse-

quences, end states) that customers have toward different products or services. This method has been rather widely used in conducting research, and the details of its implementation, analysis, and interpretation are available elsewhere.[31] However, the basic method will be overviewed here.

Beginning at the bottom of the value hierarchy, you must first get the customer to state all of the attributes that he believes are useful to describe/distinguish different brands or products in the category of interest. Several types of questions may be used to elicit attributes. One method is to ask the participant to consider two or three different products (or brands), and then to discuss what the differences are between them. For example, "You said you would consider drinking water or a sports drink while running. In what ways are these two drinks similar? In what ways are they different?" Another method asks the respondent to identify a preferred brand (supplier) and then discuss why it is preferred over other brands. For example, "You stated that you had switched to supplier B after using supplier A for several years. Why do you prefer supplier B?"

In using either of these methods, it is often helpful to place the participant in a particular context, such as purchasing or using the product/service. These contexts often help cue the participant to recall important differences, as opposed to discussing them in the abstract. For example, "Think about being in a dealer's showroom. What do you look for in a car?" or "Think about driving your car on a long trip. What are the things about your car that you like the most?" Although these initial questions may uncover consequences and desired end states in addition to attributes, our experience is that product users typically begin answering at the attribute level, and it is only through more thorough probing that the higher levels in the hierarchy emerge.

Once the participant has listed attributes, you will want him to separate important from relatively unimportant ones. There is generally not enough time to create ladders for all product attributes, and understanding the most important attributes is clearly more strategically meaningful than is pursuing ladders for relatively unimportant attributes. This subgroup of "important attributes" then becomes the basis for the laddering.

Beginning one attribute at a time, you then ask a series of probing questions, such as, "Why is that important to you?" You should continue to ask these questions until the participant has worked his way up the ladder from attributes to consequences to end states. The result should be the construction of a "ladder" for each attribute.

For example, a participant might state that she considered the location of instruments on the dashboard when comparing the cars in her prepurchase consideration set. The following value hierarchy might emerge as a result of laddering.

"I was concerned about the location of the instruments."

"Why was that important to you?"

"Because I don't want to have to search around for them."

"Why don't you want to search?"

"Because it makes me uncomfortable to have to search."

"What do you mean by uncomfortable?"

"It distracts me from paying attention to the road."

"And distractions . . . ?"

"Distractions endanger myself and my family."

"What happens when your family is endangered?"

"They aren't safe."

"Why is family safety important to you?"

"Because I love my family."

This ladder might be represented as in **Exhibit 5.12**. As you can see from this example, the end goal of laddering is not only to get the product user to discuss each level of the value hierarchy but also to make the connections between them explicitly.

As you can tell from the preceding sequence, one of the difficulties in using laddering is how to ask repetitive questions to which the answers often seem obvious. There is also the potential for respondent fatigue. Great care must be used in setting up laddering, as well as with other types of interviews, in a way that assumes naiveté on the part of the interviewer and allows the participant to indulge the interviewer's questions even when they seem too obvious. Customers must be convinced that they are the experts and their opinions are valued. Another potential problem with laddering is that the customers may fairly quickly figure out what kinds of information the interviewer is after, so that the customer can actually be making up ladders. This problem must be overcome with the establishment of rapport that encour-

ages honesty, open communication, and an absence of specific expectations on the part of the interviewer.

As you might guess, the ability to analyze and summarize laddering data across several interviews is often the most difficult aspect of using laddering. Each participant can generate a significant number of ladders, and these must be summarized across multiple participants. However, laddering is clearly one of the most direct and established methods for measuring means-end hierarchies.

Grand Tours

Our research has led us to a different technique for measuring customer value that we call the *grand tour*. This technique helps you understand the value hierarchy more indirectly by exploring in detail how the product or service is experienced by the customer in a particular context.[32]

To begin the grand tour, the interviewer asks the participant to imagine himself in a typical, real-life situation. (Obviously, it would be even better if you can actually, physically "tour" with the customer. However, this is not always possible.) This situation should be one that typifies some point in the consumption context (prepurchase, purchase, use, disposal) and a context in which the customer normally or regularly has product interaction. The interviewer then asks the participant to describe, in as much detail as possible, what is going on in that situation. In essence, the objective is to get the participant to "walk you through" his typical experiences with the product. For example, "Tell us about a typical workout that you have at the fitness center. Beginning with when you pull up in the parking lot, walk me through, step by step. I want you to tell me what you are doing, what is going on around you, what you are thinking about, and what you are feeling. No detail is insignificant."

As the participant works through his grand tour, the interviewer is free to probe for additional details and meaning. Probes should especially be used to add clarification, get deeper meaning, understand what feelings or emotions might be present, get a better understanding of the connections between value hierarchy levels, or get a sense of the importance or intensity associated with particular statements. Examples are "You said that you always like to go to the same locker. How important is that to you?" and "What are you thinking about or feeling at this point in your workout?"

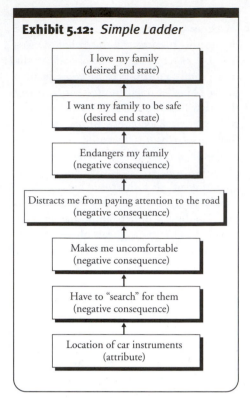

Exhibit 5.12: *Simple Ladder*

- I love my family (desired end state)
- I want my family to be safe (desired end state)
- Endangers my family (negative consequence)
- Distracts me from paying attention to the road (negative consequence)
- Makes me uncomfortable (negative consequence)
- Have to "search" for them (negative consequence)
- Location of car instruments (attribute)

Unlike laddering, the grand tour does not directly pursue value hierarchies. If the connections between levels are not made explicit during the participant's response (and they frequently are not), they may have to be inferred from the context of the participant's response. On the positive side, we have found that, compared to laddering interviews, grand tours tend to yield much more "rich" information about customer value, about the situations and their associated product use requirements, and about customers' evaluative and emotional responses. One research project that involved a direct comparison of the two techniques showed that grand tours produced three times the number of value hierarchy dimensions as did laddering techniques.

This type of interview is less structured than laddering; as a result, it can be somewhat longer to complete. In addition, its lack of structure calls for a great deal of interviewer skill to move the interview along to relevant issues, to probe for value hierarchy linkages and meaning, to pick up on important issues for additional probing, and so on.

Laddering and grand tour are two very different methods for gathering value hierarchy information; their pros and cons are summarized in **Exhibit 5.13**.

It should be obvious that the types of measures that are used to understand cus-

Exhibit 5.13: *Pros and Cons for Laddering and Grand Tour Interviewing Techniques*

Laddering	Grand Tour
Pros	**Cons**
Structured interview which eases moderator's task	Need greater interviewer skill because of the lack of structure and need for probing
Reasonably short time frame (about 45 minutes to 1 hour)	Generally longer to conduct (approximately 1 to 2 hours)
Connections between attributes, consequences, and desired end states are explicitly made	The connections between levels of the hierarchy are rarely explicit and must be inferred from the responses
Cons	**Pros**
Respondent fatigue may lead to omission of some information	Yields tremendous insights on product/service use; can uncover strategic opportunities
Respondents catch on to what you are looking for; can lead to social desirability responses and the "creation" of linkages that don't really exist	Yields significantly more information about all levels of the value hierarchy vs. laddering
Doesn't reveal much about how use situations and other activities may influence product/service value	In-depth understanding of customer's situations and product/service related activities

tomer value are very different from those we typically associate with traditional customer satisfaction measures such as paper and pencil surveys. Traditional customer satisfaction measures most commonly consist of survey items that ask the customer to compare "experienced" product performance against what was "expected." For the most part, these questions focus on the attribute level of the hierarchy. While customer satisfaction measures may be helpful to understand how the customer *feels* about the product, they are not adequate to truly "peel back the onion" in a way that provides a rich understanding of customer value. We believe that customer satisfaction measures are like thermometers that provide a quick read on how the customer is feeling. However, to really get to the root of the customer-product relationship, a full examination is necessary, and the laddering and grand tour techniques are more appropriate measurement techniques.

USING CUSTOMER VALUE DATA FOR A STRATEGIC ADVANTAGE

The University of Tennessee used a customer value orientation to completely redesign its MBA program. For several years MBA programs across the country,

and more specifically their graduates, have been sharply criticized by corporate America and the press. Given that most programs are educating today's business students based on an education model developed in the early 1960s, this is hardly surprising. Like many other schools, Tennessee began to explore what the MBA program of the future would look like (a classic product design problem).

In order to answer this question, the school went to MBA program "customers," that is, MBA students and business managers who hire MBA graduates, to determine what this new product should be. Knowing very little about academia, curriculums, and pedagogy, these "customers" were ill equipped to provide an attribute-level description of a new program. However, they were able to articulate the negative consequences that they experienced as a result of the current offerings (dollars/time spent on retraining, analytical solutions that were devoid of the "people" element, the lack of a cross-functional management perspective, and so on). Likewise, they articulated desired consequences that were not being provided (leadership skills, the ability to work in teams, communication skills, consensus building). It was clear that marginal, attribute-level changes to the existing program (adding one more class)

would be insufficient to achieve these ends. Thus, these consequences became the focus for a radical reconfiguration of the MBA program.

Using "top-down" decision making, a cross-functional faculty team came up with innovative solutions (attributes) to meet customers' consequence requirements. These changes included team teaching by faculty from many functional areas, a focus on the quality movement (an area for frequent postgraduate retraining), a more concerted treatment of the "softer" managerial issues, and a just-in-time (JIT) delivery system that allowed the students to immediately apply their classroom knowledge to a company situation. The new MBA "product" that resulted was one that might never have been envisioned by the providers (educators) without the vision of the customer. The University of Tennessee also continues to monitor its customers to assess the perceived value of its MBA offering, as well as pursue opportunities for continuous improvement.

Understanding customer value can help companies improve their performance because, as mentioned earlier, customer value serves as a common goal, or "north star," around which activities and decisions are oriented. We next briefly summarize some of the many uses for customer value data for strategic decisions.

Identifying and Serving Target Markets

Understanding customer value should rather quickly reveal differences in the needs and requirements of different market segments whose value hierarchies might look very different, for example, business versus leisure travel. This might lead to larger decisions about which markets to target, how to respond differently to different markets, and which markets might provide the best match with the company's capabilities.

Customer value knowledge is also helpful in determining which specific product features or service activities are most important to targeted customers. Identifying the most strategically critical value dimensions should help managers see what attributes might be used to enhance consequences for their targeted customer. Likewise, they might determine that some attributes are not related to important consumer consequences and thus might be targets for elimination.

Customer Relationship Management

Customer relationship management (CRM) is an emerging managerial philosophy.[33] Closely related to the idea of segmentation and targeting, CRM suggests that businesses should try to develop, enhance, and maintain relationships with their "best customers." Frequently, "best" translates into those customers who are going to create the most long-term value (profitability) for the firm. Using transaction-based data and data-mining analyses, companies are able to identify those *specific* customers (as opposed to large groups of segments of customers) who are most profitable for the organization to serve. Typically, the Pareto principle is in effect—some 20 percent of the customer base accounts for some 80 percent of the profit to an organization. Once these customers are identified, their organization can focus on understanding and delivering the value required by those specific customers, often on an individual, customized basis.[34] The key is developing strong brand equity based upon an understanding of key customers' value propositions, to increase the "share of customer" that the company can capture, as well as to retain that customer over time. Clearly, customer value understanding is key to the implementation of a successful CRM strategy.

Developing New Products

Developing new products is a critical process for most organizations. Being able to predict future product/service offerings is important not only for competitive purposes but also because cycle times require organizations to make decisions and put resources in place months or years ahead of actual product delivery. Our previous discussion suggests that new product development should be facilitated by the fact that customers are better able to articulate consequences than to describe and predict future attribute configurations, as well as by the inherent stability that is found in a consequence perspective.

To be sure, understanding higher-order consequences and desired end states will not take managers completely off the hook. To them is left the very important job of translating customer requirements into a configuration of attributes and of doing so in a way that is creative, effective, efficient, appropriate, and hopefully unique relative to competition (as in the earlier MBA

example). However, these decisions are no longer made in the dark. Customer value provides the guide and focus of this translation process.

Pricing Decisions

Pricing is an area that can benefit significantly from a value perspective. Product/service pricing has typically been pursued from a cost perspective. Recently, the emphasis on "value pricing"[35] has led to efforts to cut costs and compete primarily based upon price, as the "low-cost leader." We believe that once managers truly understand the value that is created by their products, they can broaden their perspective from "value pricing" to "pricing as an indicator of value." The latter perspective suggests that pricing should reflect a wider range of consequences to the customer than simply costs. Managers must strategically consider the value that is created by their product and then bring the price of their offering in line with the provided value (not vice versa). Such a perspective may even warrant price increases at times as products and services that provide superior value can command higher prices. For example, Ritz Carlton, a recent Malcolm Baldrige Award winner, has carved out a competitive (premium) niche by competing on service rather than on price in the very competitive hospitality industry.

Promotion

An important consideration for managers is how to communicate product/service value to current and potential customers. One of the primary objectives of promotion should be to help customers understand the value that is created through the consumption of a particular product or service. The product provider may want to place special emphasis on the product attributes or consequences that are critical determinants of customer value. Consequences, in particular, can be highly effective as positioning themes for marketing communications, for example, "When it absolutely, positively has to get there overnight. . . ." An understanding of use situations requirements can also be helpful. Advertisements can connect very effectively with customers by showing the product in use, responding to the important requirements of their particular use situations.

Promotion can also actively and directly influence customers' perceptions of the value that is created by a product or service.

Prior to purchase, it can suggest which value dimensions should be used to assess value. (However, one note of caution should be made here. We must be careful about the potential downside of emphasizing value dimensions on which our product/service cannot deliver.) Promotion will also have an obvious role to play when, as has been suggested, an organization wishes to price its product/service to reflect superior value. In this case, the arguments for reasons a higher price is warranted (which higher-order consequences and end states are delivered by the product) will fall heavily on the promotional tools that are used.

It should also be noted that promotion, in and of itself, can be used to create value, such as the value of advertising to channel customers or the value of interpersonal relationships between a salesperson and customer. For the end user, promotion (both before and after the sale) can enhance the reputation of the product, as well as the product provider. Cognitive dissonance studies, for example, show that consumers may actually read more advertisements for products *after* they have been purchased than before. Clearly some value (e.g., feelings of security, validation of the decision, dissonance reduction) is being provided by the advertisement in a way that may both enhance the subsequent perceived value of the product and influence repeat purchase.

Quality Function Deployment

Another good use of customer value information is associated with quality function deployment (QFD), which will be explored in a later chapter. QFD is being used in many organizations to translate external customer requirements into physical product characteristics (as a part of the product design process). The starting point for this process is an understanding of customer requirements from studies of end users. These may include attributes as well as consequences that the end users perceive as important to them. A team of individuals from different functions can then jointly discuss what product and service specifications are needed to meet these preferences. It is easy to see how customer value data could provide important input for this process.

Logistics and Transportation

In a recent survey of logistics and transportation managers, 9 of 10 responded that customer service had increased in importance in the last 10 years, a majority judging the increase "substantial." In addition, respondents said that customer service is now clearly seen as the most important element of the marketing mix, ahead of price and product features.[36] Like product design, customer service can quickly degenerate into a discussion of which attributes to add, such as EDI, better on-time delivery, and more accurate order filling. However, organizations that are truly customer responsive will look for a variety of creative ways to help customers achieve their higher-order, desired end states, such as reduced inventory, profitability, or being better informed about the industry. The value hierarchy can provide direction for the logistics/transportation function to use its resources to "think out of the box," to increase the customers' experienced positive consequences and decrease their negative ones. It can help move the focus of the logistics function well beyond the simple objective of achieving competitive parity on attributes.

SUMMARY

The objective of this chapter is to promote the need for a customer value orientation as a guide to making strategic business decisions. It is our contention that most companies have difficulty understanding what their customers value. This chapter has tried to show how determining customer value, specifically through a value hierarchy perspective, can provide a rich and meaningful way to understand customers, their needs, and their desires. We believe that for companies to understand value more effectively, they must both reorient their thinking (from a product/attribute to a customer/consequence perspective) and reexamine and possibly revise their current market information–gathering systems.

Clearly, gaining a better understanding of customer value does not solve all of an organization's problems. Even after customer value data have been gathered, there are considerable issues surrounding how that information is disseminated and used by decision makers in the organization, with issues related to both information systems management and organizational psychology. In addition, once customer value information has been disseminated, the very difficult and complex task of translating value requirements into a product or service is necessary. This task goes well beyond the design of the product or service and hinges on the ability of all aspects of the organization to employ people, resources, and processes in a way that results in value delivery.

While customer value determination is only a piece of a clearly larger and complex organizational effort, we believe it is a critical piece, for without a clear and accurate understanding of customer value, it does not matter to what extent other aspects of the organization (its information systems, its communications, its structure and management) are efficient or effective. Systems for delivering value are useless unless pointed in the right direction. While probably not the case, understanding customer value might appropriately have been on the mind of the person who said, "If you don't know where you're going, any road will get you there."

1. Howard E. Butz, Jr., and Leonard D. Goodstein, " Measuring Customer Value: Gaining the Strategic Advantage," *Organizational Dynamics* 24 (Winter 1996): 63–77.

2. Peter Drucker, *The Practice of Management* (New York: Harper and Brothers Publishers, 1954).

3. Katrina Booker, "Can Procter & Gamble Change Its Culture, Protect Its Market Share, and Find the Next Tide?" *Fortune,* April 26, 1999, pp. 146–152.

4. Sarah Fisher Gardial, D. Scott Clemons, Robert B. Woodruff, David W. Schumann, and Mary Jane Burns, "Comparing Consumers' Recall of Prepurchase and Postpurchase Evaluation Experiences," *Journal of Consumer Research* 20 (March 1994): 548–560.

5. Robert B. Woodruff, "Customer Value: The Next Source for Competitive Advantage," *Journal of the Academy of Marketing Science* 25 (Spring 1997): 139–153.

6. Robert B. Woodruff, David W. Schumann, and Sarah Fisher Gardial, "Understanding Value and Satisfaction from the Customer's Point of View," *Survey of Business* (Knoxville, TN: University of Tennessee, Summer/Fall 1993): 33–40.

7. Mary Jane Burns and Robert B. Woodruff, "Value: An Integrative Perspective," *1990 American Psychological Association Proceedings*, ed. Curtis P. Haugtvedt and Deborah E. Rosen (Knoxville, TN: University of Tennessee, 1991): 59–64. See also Mary Jane Burns and Robert B. Woodruff, "Delivering Value to Consumers: Implications for Strategy Development and Implementation," *1992 American Marketing Association Winter Educator's Conference Proceedings* (Chicago, IL: American Marketing Association, 1992): 209–216.

8. Morris B. Holbrook and Kim P. Corfman, "Quality and Value in the Consumption Experience: Phaedrus Rides Again" in *Perceived Quality: How Consumers View Stores and Merchandise*, ed. Jacob Jacoby and Jerry C. Olson (Lexington, MA: D.C. Heath and Company, 1985): 31–57.

9. Morris B. Holbrook, "Aims, Concepts, and Methods for the Representation of Individual Differences in Esthetic Responses to Design Features," *Journal of Consumer Research* 13 (December 1986): 337–347. See also Deborah A. Prentice, "Psychological Correspondence of Possessions, Attitudes and Values," *Journal of Personality and Social Psychology* 53, no. 6 (1987): 993–1003.

10. Robert Jacobson and David A. Aaker, "The Strategic Role of Product Quality," *Journal of Marketing* 51 (October 1987): 31–44.

11. Linda Grant, "Why FedEx Is Flying High," *Fortune,* November 10, 1997, pp. 156–160.

12. Robert B. Woodruff, David W. Schumann, D. Scott Clemons, Mary Jane Burns, and Sarah F. Gardial, "The Meaning of Consumer Satisfaction and Dissatisfaction: A Themes Analysis from the Consumer's Perspective," Working Paper Series, Customer Value and Satisfaction Research Program, University of Tennessee, Knoxville. See also Valerie A. Zeithaml, "Consumer Perceptions of Price, Quality and Value: A Means-End Model and Synthesis of Evidence," *Journal of Marketing* 52 (April 1988): 35–48.

13. Richard Melcher, "A New Era for Auto Quality," *Business Week*, October 22, 1990, pp. 88–95.

14. Gary McWilliams, "A Notebook That Puts Users Ahead of Gimmicks," *Business Week*, September 27, 1993, pp. 92–96.

15. Gardial, Clemons, Woodruff, Schumann, and Burns, "Comparing Consumers' Recall."

16. Daniel J. Flint , Robert B. Woodruff, and Sarah F. Gardial, "Exploring the Customer Desired Value Change Phenomenon in a Business-to-Business Environment," Journal of Marketing, forthcoming August 2002. See also Daniel J. Flint, Robert B. Woodruff, and Sarah Fisher Gardial, "Customer Value Change in Industrial Marketing Relationships: A Call for New Strategies and Research," *Industrial Marketing Management* 26 (March 1997): 163–175.

17. Russell Miller, "A Switch in Time: The Success of Swatch," *Business Week,* July 28, 1985, p. 93.

18. Jonathan Gutman, "A Means-End Chain Model Based on Consumer Categorization Processes," *Journal of Marketing* 46 (Spring 1982): 60–72. See also Jonathan Gutman and Scott D. Alden, "Adolescents' Cognitive Structures of Retail Stores and Fashion Consumption: A Means-End Chain Analysis of Quality," in *Perceived Quality: How Consumers View Stores and Merchandise*, ed. Jacob Jacoby and Jerry C. Olson (Lexington, MA: D.C. Heath and Company, 1985): 99–114; W. Steven Perkins and Thomas J. Reynolds, "The Explanatory Power of Values in Preference Judgments: Validation of the Means-End Perspective," *Advances in Consumer Research* 15, ed. Michael J. Houston (Provo, UT: Association for Consumer Research, 1988): 122–126; Donald E. Vinson, Jerome E. Scott, and Lawrence M. Lamont, "The Role of Personal Values in Marketing and Consumer Behavior," *Journal of Marketing* (April 1977): 44–50.

19. Kathleen Kerwin, "GM's Aurora: Much Is Riding on the Luxury Sedan –And Not Just for Olds," *Business Week,* March 21, 1994, pp. 88–95.

20. Stephen Phillips, Amy Dunkin, James B. Treece, and Keith Hammonds, "King Customer," *Business Week,* March 12, 1990, pp. 88–94.

21. Bruce Nussbaum, "Hot Products: Smart Design in the Common Thread," *Business Week,* June 7, 1993, pp. 54–57.

22. Michelle Wirth Fellman, "Forecast: New Products Storm Subsides," *Marketing News,* March 30, 1998 (Chicago, IL: American Marketing Association): 1.

23. "Behind Starbucks' New Venture: Bean, Beatniks, and Booze," *Fortune,* May 15, 2000, p. 80.

24. Dennis H. Geistfeld, G. B. Sproles, and S. B. Badenhop, "The Concept and Measurement of a Hierarchy of Product Characteristics," in *Advances in Consumer Research* 4, ed. W. D. Perreault, Jr. (Provo, UT: Association for Consumer Research, 1977): 302–307.

25. Kevin T. Higgins, "Business Marketers Make Customer Service Job for All," *Marketing News*, 1989, pp. 1–2.

26. John C. Narver and Stanley F. Slater, "The Effect of Market Orientation on Business Profitability," *Journal of Marketing* 54 (October 1990): 20–35.

27. Amanda Bennett, "Making the Grade with the Customer: Firms Struggle to Gauge How Best to Serve," *The Wall Street Journal*, November 12, 1990, pp. B1, B3. See also Lynn W. McGee and Rosann L. Spiro, "The Marketing Concept in Perspective," *Business Horizons* (May-June 1988): 40–45.

28. Gary Hamel and C.K. Prahalad, "Seeing the Future First," *Fortune,* September 5, 1994, pp. 64–73.

29. "Behind Starbucks' New Venture."

30. Nussbaum, "Hot Products."

31. Thomas J. Reynolds and Jonathan Gutman, "Laddering Theory, Method, Analysis and Interpretation," *Journal of Advertising Research* (February-March 1988): 11–31.

32. James G. Barnes, *Secrets of Customer Relationship Management* (New York: McGraw Hill, 2001): 83.

33. Ibid.

34. Don Peppers and Martha Rogers, *The One to One Future* (New York: Doubleday, 1993).

35. Christopher Power, Walecia Knorad, Alice Cuneo, and James Treece, "Value Marketing," *Business Week,* November 11, 1991, pp. 132–140.

36. "Customer Service: The Great Differentiator," *Traffic Management* (November 1992): 40–44.

Chapter 6

Ernest R. Cadotte
University of Tennessee

Tactical Considerations in Designing Marketing Strategies

The formula for success in business and marketing is very simple: Make a lot of people happy and you can earn a lot of money. Here are the rules:

- Find out what people want (market research).
- Give them what they want (product design).
- Tell them you have what they want (advertising).
- Go to where they work and live and personally explain how you have the solution to their needs (distribution).
- Collect the money for a job well done (price).

Sounds easy, right? Of course, there are a couple of things that get in the way.

First, not all customers are alike. People have different tastes, preferences, and needs. One offer will not work for everyone. As a result, many potential customers will wait until they find the "right" solution for their needs. To paraphrase a famous quote, you can satisfy some of the people all of the time, but never all of the people all of the time. So, demand may not be as great as you would like.

The way around this problem is to discover the differences in needs among your customers (market research), break the customers down into smaller groups with similar needs (segmentation), and then develop a strategy for each group (target marketing).

Another challenge is that everyone wants more for less. Sure, you would like to sell for less, but you have to pay your expenses and earn a profit. One solution to this pricing dilemma is larger sales volumes, which result in lower cost per unit. Lower costs will allow you to lower your prices and/or increase your profits.

How do you create larger sales volumes? Offer a better product at a better price and tell everyone about it (advertising and sales force).

You will always find that someone wants to make money in the same market as you. Competitors will emerge and try to take your sales and profits. How will they do this? Smart competitors will study customers' needs and what you have to offer (benchmark) and then create and sell something better. Usually, they find a group (segment) whose needs are not met and develop a superior strategy targeted at that group.

Customers will almost always gravitate toward the better offer. Your job is never done: You must always check your offer against the customers' evolving needs (satisfaction level) and competitors' offerings (benchmark) to make sure you have the better product, price, promotion, and distribution.

In a nutshell, be the best at creating what customers want, finding the customers, and telling them how good you are at meeting their needs. This should create many sales, drive down your costs, and thus allow you to offer good prices with good profits. Of course, success is not this easy, but this is the essence of marketing.

CHAPTER OVERVIEW

This chapter offers a set of guidelines for making effective tactical decisions as part of an overall marketing strategy. It is assumed that you already have an organizational strategy (see Chapter 3) and a marketing strategy that flows from it (see Chapter 4). In this chapter, we begin with the implementation of the tactical details of the marketing strategy. Once you know what

Marketplace
http://www.marketplace-simulation.com

BEST-USE CORRELATIONS

Chapter 3 advised teams to answer three questions: (1) Where are we? (2) Where do we want to go? and (3) How do we get there? Chapter 6 picks up this storyline by focusing on the execution of marketing strategies.

Strategy Is 1 Percent Inspiration, 99 Percent Perspiration

In Q2 and Q3, teams formulate their initial marketing strategies and go to test market. Although goals often remain fixed and strategy remains fairly stable, new problems, threats, constraints, and opportunities continually present themselves, forcing teams into round after round of tactical adjustment. By the end of Q4, given the range of tactical choices and the discretion teams have in executing them, many teams come to the conclusion: strategy is inspiration, tactical execution is perspiration.

Marketplace Secrets

Knowing how a market is likely to respond to a change in price, the addition of a new feature, a larger advertising program, or more salespeople depends on how well your team is able to discern the market's response functions and then exploit them.

Working on the Margin

How do you use response function to your advantage? By applying marginal analysis to each tactical option under consideration. A fundamental challenge in any business is where to spend the next dollar, euro, or yen. In Marketplace, teams with a well-informed sense of the market's response functions make better tactical decisions.

Change Is the Only Constant

Revaluation and skillful adjustment of earlier decisions is the norm in Marketplace. Keep in mind that the ability to act in ways not predicted by rivals and the timing of actions are factors of immense tactical importance.

you want to accomplish and how you will get there, you must then focus on the implementation of the plan. This requires many tactical decisions that individually and collectively support and follow through on the plan. One of the reasons we focus on these tactical details is that 99 percent of the work is in the execution of the plan. To paraphrase Thomas Edison, strategy is 1 percent inspiration and 99 percent perspiration. The strategy is the inspiration. The tactical execution is the perspiration. Or as Admiral Rickover was fond of saying, "The Devil is in the details."

We also want to take you to the lowest level of strategic planning so that you can build a strategy from the bottom up, as well as from the top down. This kind of knowledge will help you to formulate strategy in the future. You must know your tactical options and the requirements to actually implement them. These represent the building blocks of future strategies.

Another reason to take this perspective is that the deployment of tactics is in a constant state of flux. While goals often remain fixed and strategy fairly stable, skillful adjustment is the rule in execution. New problems, threats, constraints, and even opportunities continually present themselves. The dynamic environment in which strategies are executed once again requires that you fully understand your tactical options.

In this chapter, the marketing fundamentals of market segmentation, target marketing, and the marketing mix are stressed. These pervade the entire discussion. The heart of the chapter deals with the elements of the marketing mix, product, price, promotion, and distribution. Selection of the right marketing tactics depends upon knowing how the market is likely to respond to these tactics. Thus, we need to understand the effect of things such as a change in price, the addition of a new feature, a larger advertising program, or more salespeople. In other words, how much excitement or frustration will result if you choose Option A or Option B?

There are tools for quantifying these response functions.[1] This chapter will take a more intuitive approach.

We are capable of discerning many of the market's response functions. Good salespeople know the "hot" and "cold" buttons of each customer. They know when to back away and when to press forward. The salesperson is responding to experience-based response functions. The same can be

said of experienced ad copywriters or merchandisers. With experience, we begin to understand where we are on the response curve and in which direction we should go in order to create more excitement in the eyes of the customer.

You do not have to wait years to develop an intuitive feel for the market's response. By knowing that these response functions exist and what they might look like, you can be watchful for their presence in the market. Just looking for them will help you find them and use them to your advantage.

There are many response functions that can fit any number of marketing contexts. This chapter suggests various functions. These are not the only ones, but they occur with some regularity and so are a good place to start.

How do you use the response function to your advantage? You use it by applying marginal analysis to each option you are considering. For example, a fundamental challenge in marketing is where to spend the next dollar, euro, or yen. Should it be in new product development, sales force incentive programs, more advertising, or lower prices? Where would we get the highest return for our marketing investment? If we have a sense of the market's response function in each case, we can make an educated guess about the likely impact of option A, B, or C. We would choose the option with the best marginal return.

Let's now turn our attention to a discussion of the fundamentals of marketing. The primary focus will be on product design and pricing since it is easier to discuss the concepts of response function and elasticity in these contexts. To a lesser extent, I will describe how these ideas play out in advertising and distribution. After reading this chapter, you should have a good understanding of how to look for and work with response functions and market elasticity with regard to almost everything you will do in marketing. It is this knowledge that will give you the proper perspective in choosing the tactical options for an effective marketing strategy.

PRODUCT DESIGN

Product design and pricing are the most important factors determining market demand within any marketplace. All of the other variables modify the effect of these two.

Product development and design are rather complex. Each of the following product development issues will be discussed in detail:

- Customers buy benefits, not components.
- The attractiveness of a product is built up by combining a set of components that satisfy the expressed needs of the market.
- More of a feature will not always satisfy a customer—sometimes less is better.
- A feature's benefit can be enhanced or diminished, depending upon which other features are included with it.
- Different segments have different response functions for the same feature.
- When customers cannot achieve all of their goals, they make trade-offs among the desired benefits.
- We can become fixated on improving or adding features and lose sight of the goal of maximizing overall customer satisfaction.
- The differentiating power of a feature will evaporate once all the competition adopt it—the feature then becomes a requirement.
- Response functions can be deduced from our reactions to and choices from what is available.
- Cost considerations, especially production changeover issues, can limit what is offered but need not do so.
- Each segment has a minimum performance requirement you must fulfill as you select features to include in your product or service.
- A firm's product design is compared not only with the absolute requirements of the segment but also with the relative attraction of competing products.

- The appeal of older technology will evolve as new and better features enter the market.
- Multiple product designs can appeal to the same segment, although the costs will differ, and cannibalization is a factor to consider.
- Brand loyalty can be built up over time, although it is safer to assume brand loyalty is always at risk.

An excellent treatment of the product planning process is provided by Kenneth B. Kahn in *Product Planning Essentials* (2001) from Sage Publications, Inc.[2]

Customers Buy Benefits, Not Components

There is an old saying attributed to Revlon: "In the factory, we manufacture cosmetics. At the beauty counter, we sell hope." Whoever said this knew that customers do not buy components (cosmetic ingredients); they buy benefits (hope). These benefits help users to accomplish their ultimate goals and realize certain values or end states. In the personal computer (PC) business, customers buy ease of use, ability to work while traveling on a plane, and ability to work on tiny details in engineering design. These benefits allow them to be more productive, advance in their companies, and thus earn more money and achieve greater security in life.

While customers buy benefits to achieve end states, manufacturers produce components such as disk drives, modems, and monitors. The challenge is to select the correct components in your product designs so that the final product will deliver the desired benefits.

For example, being able to use the computer on the road is an important benefit for the traveling segment of the personal computer market. Which features or components provide this benefit? At the least, the traveler PC should have (1) a flat display to reduce the computer's size and weight, (2) a rugged design so that the computer can be carried around and handle bumps and falls, and (3) an Internet connection in order to send and receive information with customers and the office.

The challenge is to determine how different components contribute to each benefit and then to select those components that yield the greatest value. A good way to start is to apply the means-end hierarchy introduced by Gardial and Woodruff that's in Chapter 5. Let's apply this logic to the design of a portable computer for the traveler PC segment. (See **Exhibit 6.1**.)

First, take the most important benefits desired by each segment and lay them out in a row. Second, place all of the available components (also referred to as the *features* or *attributes*) below them in another row. Third, speculate on which components or services will be necessary to deliver these benefits. Fourth, draw lines linking the benefits with components that are useful or required in satisfying the need. Several components might be necessary to provide the complete benefit, and in a few cases only one component might be necessary to fulfill the need or application. You may wish to add a row of values and end states and extend the lines upward in order to show the linkages with the values being sought through these benefits. You need to build several component-benefit-value

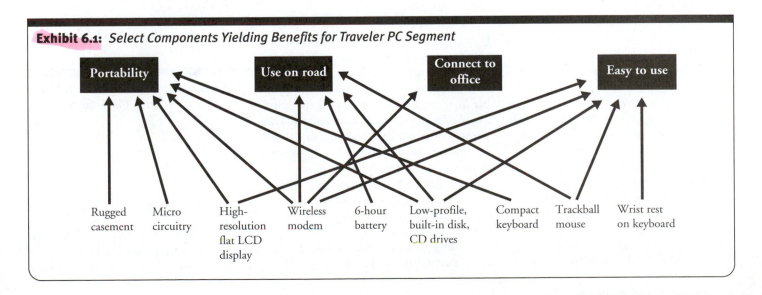

Exhibit 6.1: *Select Components Yielding Benefits for Traveler PC Segment*

ladders for each segment and then try to bring them together into a coherent whole.

A variation on this approach is to start with the components and speculate about resultant benefits. The ultimate goal with either approach is to match up the benefits provided by a component with the benefits sought by a target segment so you will know which features will likely appeal to which segments. While the exercise is not foolproof, it should provide a logical basis for designing products. It is complementary to the quality function deployment (QFD) process presented by Ivan Slimák in Chapter 7.

Even when you use this process carefully, product design is very difficult. The analysis is very complex, and the information from potential customers is imperfect. Buyer opinions are notoriously inaccurate because consumers cannot always know what they will want in the future, especially with an unknown product. Thus, you should approach the product design decision with caution. The best strategy in the early stages of a product's life cycle is to try out a few designs and gauge the market's reaction to these designs. A concept test, prototype trial, and even a test market will provide increasingly better information on customer preferences.

Creating Customer Satisfaction

You create the potential for customer satisfaction by selecting components from the list of available options. Each component in a group of components has a certain want-satisfying capability. Those components that provide more of the desired benefit will yield greater satisfaction with the final design. Thus, a 10-inch, flat LCD screen will obviously provide greater satisfaction for the traveler segment than a 21-inch, high-resolution, desktop monitor. A 12-inch, flat LCD screen will probably cause even greater satisfaction than a 10-inch flat screen.

The task is to build up the satisfaction level, layer by layer. As you choose components, the value of the product design goes up or down, depending on how well each component meets the needs of the target segment.

Consider again the product design for the portable computer. There are many features that affect the customer's ability to use a computer on the road. In addition to the display, ruggedness, and an Internet connection, we also want to consider features such as the type of mouse (touch pad or track ball), size of disk drives and their location (built in or external), size of the keyboard, space on the keyboard to rest one's wrists while typing, physical dimensions, and weight. All of the features can add to or detract from an ability to use a computer on the road. Think of how these same features contribute to ease of use if that is also important.

To practice choosing components that will lead to customer satisfaction, go to a computer supplier Web site to design your own computer. Dell Computers, for example, allows potential buyers to customize computers for their own needs at http://www.dell.com/. You can select the hard drive, monitor, memory, sound card, speakers, CD/DVD player, zip drive, mouse, keyboard, modem, and so on. As you add features, you will discover that your feelings of excitement, anticipation, and even fulfillment will increase. Each selection will add to your anticipated satisfaction. Some components will create much excitement; others will add very little but are perceived as necessary. You may find that certain components cause anxiety and are avoided. Other components are perceived to have no real value and are ignored.

The realization that different components have different want-satisfying capabilities is very important and is the focus of the next two sections.

The Elasticity of the Peanut — More Is Not Always Better

The usual assumption is that more of a feature always adds value for the customer. This is not true. There are many different ways customers could respond to more of a feature. We call these potential reactions *response functions*.

Assume for a moment that you have been asked to design a candy bar for college-age students who like to eat candy bars for a snack. Suppose you must decide how many peanuts to include in the candy bar. Your target customer likes to experience a crunch while eating a candy bar, and the peanut has just the right texture to deliver this benefit. Should the candy bar have no peanuts? A few peanuts? A lot of peanuts? Or a whole bunch? Since you are probably in this segment, let's start with your own preferences. What would you prefer? None, a few, a lot, or a whole bunch?

Assuming you like the crunch of a nut in a candy bar, could we keep adding peanuts and keep increasing your happiness? Or might we reach a point where your excitement about eating the candy bar would go down with the addition of more peanuts?

We could actually draw a curve to reflect your preferences about peanuts in a candy bar. On the *y*-axis, we would show your excitement (happiness, satisfaction, fulfillment). On the *x*-axis, we would show the number of peanuts in the candy bar. We would try to determine how much excitement the candy bar would generate as we added 1, 2, 3, 4, . . .20, . . .30 and more peanuts. We would then plot the excitement level for each amount of peanuts. We call the resulting line or curve a *response function*.

If you are typical of most college students that I have surveyed, your preference curve for peanuts would look like **Exhibit 6.2**. That is, no peanuts would make you unhappy or dissatisfied. A few peanuts would make you the happiest. A lot of peanuts would cause your satisfaction level to turn down, but you might still be somewhat happy. A whole bunch of peanuts would make you unhappy, perhaps as much as no peanuts at all.

I have asked more than a thousand students about their preferences for Milky Way, Snickers, Baby Ruth, and Payday candy bars. Milky Way has no peanuts, Snickers a few peanuts, Baby Ruth about twice as many as Snickers, and Payday has the most (the entire exterior of the bar is coated with whole peanuts). Few students like the Payday. Not many more like Milky Way. Most like Snickers, and many of the remaining students like Baby Ruth, suggesting that a few peanuts is just right. (See Exhibit 6.2.)

You could consider other ingredients— coconut, chocolate, caramel, rice, peanut

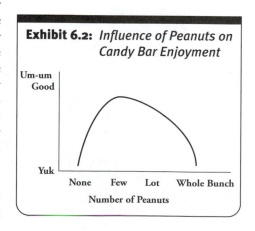

Exhibit 6.2: *Influence of Peanuts on Candy Bar Enjoyment*

butter—in the same way. How much does the excitement increase with increasing amounts of these ingredients?

What do you think the response curve is for coconut? Most students do not like coconut in a candy bar. It causes unhappiness, dissatisfaction. In other words, the response curve is negative. Coconut has a gritty texture when the candy bar is first bit into. It also becomes chewy, but a pasty kind of chewy—again, not appealing. And, of course, it adds its own unique flavor that only a few people like.

The challenge in designing any product is knowing how far to go in adding components. How far should you go in making something smaller, faster, smarter, easier, cheaper?

Potential Market Response Functions

We can extrapolate seven response functions from the candy bar example (shown in **Exhibit 6.3**) that should be considered when designing any new product.

1. **More of a feature is always better.** (See Exhibit 6.3a.) This is the assumption most engineers and product managers make, and, in a large number of cases, it is true. For example, a faster processor on a PC will create increasing excitement and product use among calculation- and data-intensive end users. More miles per gallon, longer battery life, more insulating capability, and more revolutions per minute (RPM) are the kinds of things that are almost always desired.

   But it is wrong to assume that more of a feature is *always* better. Some customers have different response functions when more does not add value and may even detract from it. Thus, adding more function keys to a keyboard might excite one segment, add little value for another, and actually turn another one off.

2. **More of the feature will add value up to a point but then ceases to add anything more.** (See Exhibit 6.3b.) For example, TV manufacturers found that the addition of stereo sound to a TV created much enthusiasm at first. As a result, almost 90 percent of all primary TVs sold today have stereo sound. However, adding further sound capability—adding a broader range of sound reproduction or more powerful speakers—created no further excitement and

few additional sales. The value of better sound reached a plateau, or a point of diminishing returns.

Some customers feel this way about the processing speed of a personal computer. If all one is doing is word processing, financial spreadsheets, and e-mail, there is little need for all the horsepower being built into the state-of-the-art processors by Intel. In fact, this group has been slower in upgrading its computers.

Customers might reach a plateau with the number of channels on cable TV, the size of a PC monitor, the cleanliness of a delivery truck, or the durability of an industrial fabric. It simply does not pay to pursue more of these capabilities.

3. **More of the feature will add value up to a point, and beyond that point more of the feature will detract from enjoyment.** (See Exhibit 6.3c.) For example, romance in a movie can be enjoyable, but too much romance can be overbearing. Attentive waiters and waitresses can be an asset to a restaurant but can quickly become a nuisance to customers if they constantly interrupt the dinner conversation. And the amount of carbonation, syrup, and water in a fountain drink all have tight tolerances; too much or too little is undesirable.

In a market opportunity analysis (MOA) of a metal-turning machine, we discovered that the ability to achieve a smooth surface to one-thousandth of an inch did not excite potential cus-

tomers; rather, it actually turned people off. At the time of our study, machine shop operators were very happy with a precision of one-tenth of an inch. They had few requests for anything more. When offered the potential of one-thousandth precision, they worried that the higher precision would be more difficult to maintain and would probably cost a lot more.

The inventors were dumbfounded by our findings. They assumed that the market was like themselves—more and more precision would always be exciting.

4. **A little of a feature is just right; more only takes away value.** (See Exhibit 6.3d.) Some consumers want very simple calculators. They do not want anything more than the basic four functions: addition, subtraction, division, and multiplication. Each additional function only adds to confusion and frustration. They would never buy a scientific calculator. Ease of use is more important than having a function for every possible calculation.

Some older bicycle riders do not see the value of having more than three gears on a bicycle. Most people do not want to deal with any user manual that is longer than a few pages, even when a big manual would help them get more out of the equipment. And who wants a lot of seasoning in their food when a little bit is just right?

5. **Any amount of the feature is bad.** (See Exhibit 6.3e.) As discussed earlier, some consumers do not like coconut in a candy bar. Other consumers find that

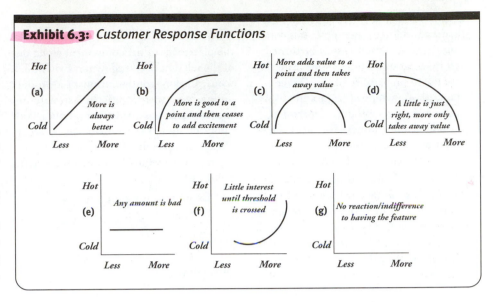

Exhibit 6.3: *Customer Response Functions*

(a) Hot / Cold — Less / More — *More is always better*

(b) Hot / Cold — Less / More — *More is good to a point and then ceases to add excitement*

(c) Hot / Cold — Less / More — *More adds value to a point and then takes away value*

(d) Hot / Cold — Less / More — *A little is just right, more only takes away value*

(e) Hot / Cold — Less / More — *Any amount is bad*

(f) Hot / Cold — Less / More — *Little interest until threshold is crossed*

(g) Hot / Cold — Less / More — *No reaction/indifference to having the feature*

any violence in a movie or TV show is bad and will not watch programs containing it. A consumer may be turned off by sugar or caffeine in soft drinks, the use of prepared foods in a restaurant, plastic-wrapped fruits and vegetables in the produce department, or polyester in clothes. The inclusion of these features can decrease satisfaction and may even create dissatisfaction.

6. **There is little interest until a threshold is crossed.** (See Exhibit 6.3f.) In some cases, more of a feature does not cause the desired positive response until some threshold is crossed. For example, ease of use is a primary benefit of computers and the Internet. Not until the introduction of Windows 95 did computers become easy enough to use that the home market for PCs took off. Similarly, the World Wide Web crossed the threshold of ease of use when Netscape was introduced. In the case of personal computers, they did not become real scientific and engineering tools until the arrival of the Pentium processors.

For some, the cell phone has still not crossed the threshold of reliable, static-free service. Web search engines still do not provide ease of use, considering the thousands of irrelevant sources that are presented with each search. Hydrogen-powered automotive engines, distance learning over the Internet, and in-flight entertainment systems have not crossed the performance threshold for widespread adoption.

7. **The presence of some features in a product can have no effect on consumer excitement.** Notice that in Exhibit 6.3g there is no graph. For example, a graphic artist would not care if there is a spreadsheet or accounting program on her Macintosh computer but would be more concerned about a high-resolution screen and imaging software. Other customers might be indifferent to features added to their purchases, such as a fuel-injection carburetor, a call log on a cell phone, resealable packaging, or quick-release tires on a bicycle.

Interaction Effects

Imagine that we apply some kind of mental arithmetic in evaluating the total attractiveness of any product that we are considering for a particular application or use situation. Every component that might be built into

the product has a want-satisfying score attached to it. These scores probably reflect the placement of the component along one of the relevant curves shown in Exhibit 6.3. Thus, for any configuration of a product design, we can theoretically estimate our excitement in possessing that product based upon the sum of the want-satisfying ability of each component. The equation for scoring a product would be something like the following:

$$\text{Excitement toward product } j = \Sigma_i^n \text{ want-satisfying ability of component } i$$

Where n is the set of components contained in product j.

As the equation suggests, our excitement increases with the inclusion of more and more features that satisfy wants. The inclusion of features that detract from our satisfaction would reduce the total score and excitement.

This simple model misses an important point in the creation of customer excitement: there are interaction effects among the components. In some cases, two or more components work well together, adding value beyond the sum of their individual contributions. In other cases, components may have a negative effect on satisfaction when combined.

For example, the addition of a built-in mouse works better for a portable computer than an external mouse. An external mouse would reduce the value of the whole design while a built-in mouse would multiply the value of the portable design.

We can go deeper with this kind of logic. Among built-in mice, you have the option of a touch pad, a track ball, and an eraserlike joystick built into the keyboard. You also have different keyboard layouts. A dominant design includes a space below the keys for resting your wrists. Another keyboard design has no such space—the keys end at the edge of the encasement. Which of these options will work best with the keyboard in terms of making keystrokes easier, faster, and less error prone? To answer this question, we must consider the combination of the keyboard layout and the pointing device. A keyboard that leaves space for a mouse pad or track ball would be better for a full-function laptop computer, while a smaller keyboard with a joystick would be better for a limited-function, handheld computer.

Let's consider a different example. Suppose you worked for McDonald's, and it

was your job to design the crispy chicken sandwich. What ingredients would you choose? Which ingredients go well together and which should be avoided? The combination of mustard, lettuce, tomato, and chicken is most likely far less appealing than the combination of mayonnaise, lettuce, tomato, and chicken. Mustard probably does not go well with lettuce and tomato, even though many people like mustard in its own right.

Really sophisticated product designers worry about all of the combinations and how their interaction might impact the resulting experience and enjoyment of the product. In McDonald's case, they even worry about the order of the ingredients on the bun because the ingredients have different effects on the palate, depending upon which ingredient encounters the taste buds first, second, or third.

Returning to our mental model, we would need to add an interaction term as follows:

$$\text{Excitement toward product } j = \Sigma_i^n \text{ want-satisfying ability of component } i + \Sigma_{ij}^n \text{ want-satisfying ability of the combination of } ij$$

Conceivably, we should consider all combinations of components i and j. Practically speaking, we need only the most intrusive interactions.

The inclusion of the interaction terms is reflected in the quality function deployment (QFD) model presented by Slimák. QFD is a powerful method for formulating and evaluating different product designs. The mathematics behind the method effectively employ the preceding equation in determining the relative attraction of different product configurations.

Different Segments Have Different Response Functions for the Same Benefit

Returning to our peanut example, Exhibit 6.2 might represent the response function for the typical consumer, but every customer does not feel the same. There is a segment that loves the crunchiness of peanuts. This is the segment that likes Paydays. If we drew the response function for this group, we would conclude that it looks like Exhibit 6.3b, "more is good, but there is a point of diminishing returns."

We know that more mileage per gallon is desired by all of us. But our purchases of sport utility vehicles (SUVs) and other high-performance/comfort cars suggest that mileage is not the most important factor in our choice. Probably Exhibit 6.3b is closer to the truth.

The lesson here is that different segments have different response functions for the same benefit and feature. If you provided only a candy bar, car, PC, photocopier, punch press, or jet plane for the "typical" customer, you would miss out on other segments or niche markets that could be profitably served. You need to pull apart the market into distinct segments, determine the response function for each, and design a different product or service tailored to the segments targeted.

Impact of Competing Benefits and Response Functions

There is another lesson here to learn. That is, we make trade-offs. People who buy SUVs have a stronger preference for what we might call luxurious ruggedness than for mileage economy. To be sure, almost all of us would want greater fuel economy; but when choosing between an SUV with greater luxury and one with more miles to the gallon, it would appear that fuel economy takes a backseat.

As a designer of products or services, you must always ask yourself, "How far do I go in pursuing the various benefits desired by the customer?" To answer this question, you need to understand how the pursuit of one benefit impacts the pursuit of another. Benefits and their response functions cannot be fully considered in isolation from one another.

The classic trade-off is between price (saving money for other things) and almost all other benefits (speed, throughput, ease of use, or reliability in the case of business products, and fun, confidence, or peace of mind in the case of consumer products). In isolation of other considerations, we want it all (as in Exhibit 6.3a). But when price is figured in, our response function may reshape itself to look more like Exhibit 6.3b.

Within our price constraint, we also make other trade-offs. For the same price, would you buy a high resolution color printer that prints at 7 pages per minute, or a medium resolution printer that prints 14 pages per minute? Do you want to look great or to look good and get the work done fast?

This idea of trade-offs is really important. Customers are always faced with constraints. Money and time are the most

serious ones. When people are constrained in their ability to achieve desired benefits, they make trade-offs. Response functions shift between Exhibits 6.3a and 6.3b. You must discover what is good enough and what is insufficient.[3]

You must also realize that the shape of the response function may change over time. The terrorists' attacks of September 11, 2001, have caused us to value security. The value of other benefits has been diminished. Environmental factors (high fuel prices, the political party in power, government regulation, economic conditions, the weather, a shift in religious tolerance, etc.) will cause our response functions to reshape in significant ways.

Competitors can also change the response functions of your customers. Apple computer introduced the iMac with see-through casing. It was like a hidden response function that Apple stumbled upon. Many people liked it, and now there are plenty of imitators. The ultra thin notebook computers are reshaping our response function for portability. In each case, what was sufficient has just jumped up a notch.

How Far to Go in the Pursuit of a Benefit

In any business, you will be destined to refine and improve your products and services. You will make them better in order to attract more customers and/or to keep away the competition.

As inventors or creators of products and services, we can become too enamored with features. We become so focused on doing better with some aspect of our product that we fail to realize that we have already done well enough. This was the mind-set of the metalworking inventors who tried to sell lathes with one-thousandth of an inch precision. Their achievement exceeded what the market wanted. No one was willing to spend the money on this capability.

Consider digital TV. Is the market ready for it? Most surveys suggest consumers are happy with their current color televisions. Few are willing to pay the premium to watch movies on a high-resolution screen, yet the government is mandating the change for the "good of the industry."

Let me give a more personal example. For more than a dozen years, I have been refining the *Marketplace* business simulation. Realism has always been my number 1 goal. I reasoned that the more realistic the exercise, the better the learning experience

for executives and students. I thought my customer's response function looked like Exhibit 6.3a, more is better. What I failed to realize was that more realism also translated into more complexity. As I added complexity, I increasingly made it more difficult for participants to learn, a fact that hit home when I began targeting a new segment, undergraduates in an introduction to marketing course. Added realism in this case caused dissatisfaction, and the curve looked more like Exhibit 6.3c. I realized that "ease of use" was the goal I should be pursuing for segments with less business experience. Much like Windows and Netscape, the easier I made it to learn, the happier my customers became. Thus, ease of use has become my number 1 goal (Exhibit 6.3a), and I provide sufficient realism that the important lessons are learned (Exhibit 6.3b).

Overdoing It

The desire to keep adding functionality to any product is the curse of all product managers. The trap we fall into is that a group of customers has said, "I can see how you can make your product better (for me). Why don't you add such-and-such feature/capability to your product?" We hear this all of the time, and we receive different requests from different customers. We reason that we could make this group or that group happier by adding more of this or more of that. We also reason that the incremental cost of adding a feature is much smaller than the cost of adding an entirely different model to sell. Before long, we have overfeatured our product or service.

This problem of overdoing it is very obvious with my family's recent purchase of a JVG video camera. The camera has so many buttons and functions—date and time stamping, backlighting, low light recording, framing, replay, editing, viewing —that we can barely figure out how to turn it on and record. What ever happened to "point and shoot"? In a different context— blood-testing equipment—but a similar experience, clinics previously bought rather simple machines for quick blood work at the doctor's office. They were so easy to use that any member of the staff could operate them. Now some equipment has so many different blood tests and features that a nurse requires a week's worth of training to learn to operate it.

We fall into the trap of incrementally creating a product that is meant to satisfy many different people. We abandon our segmentation strategy and, by default, adopt a mass-market one. When we do this, we begin to add features that elicit response functions that look like Exhibit 6.3c through 3f: It is too much; I do not like it; or I do not care if it is there. The cumulative effect is that we reduce the satisfaction of buying and using our product.

The lesson is clear: Do not try to create a product that is all things to all people. A segmentation strategy—giving each customer only what he or she wants—will make more customers happy.

Hitting the Wall

In some cases, we find a benefit to pursue that generates much enthusiasm and business. In order to excel on this dimension, we work hard to improve related features over time. As we get better and better, we continue to add customers and revenues. But, at some point, it is not possible to achieve significantly better performance, and we lose our differential advantage—we hit the wall.

To illustrate, the CEO of a tank truck carrier that hauls bulk chemicals found that his firm could attract and retain customers by offering better pickup and delivery than the competition. At the time, the tank truck industry was achieving only 70 percent on-time pickup and delivery. He conducted a quality improvement study and found that by providing cell phones, geographical positioning instruments, and an alarm clock (so drivers would not sleep through the delivery time), he could achieve 80 percent on-time delivery, significantly above the norm. As a result, business, market share, and profits expanded.

The carrier's success was not lost on the competition, which noticed the loss of business and initiated efforts to improve their own pickup and delivery performance. The CEO anticipated these events and was able to raise the bar to 85 percent on-time performance, once again staying outside of the zone of indifference.

Competitive pressures continued to push the zone ever upward. Today, all significant competitors can deliver 97 percent or better on-time service. At this point, on-time service is no longer a differentiating factor in selecting a carrier; it is a requirement. The tank truck carrier hit the wall. The frustration for the CEO is that it has not been easy to find another hugely differentiating factor. Now, the firm must compete on price, where it is difficult to obtain a sustainable competitive advantage.

For anyone who uses a cell phone, it is clear that reliable, static-free reception is the current holy grail. As telephone companies are able to improve on this aspect of performance, customers will migrate to the better system. Eventually, all cell phones will offer reliable, static-free service just as land lines have done. At that point, such service will cease to offer a differential advantage. Every competitor will be required to offer it.

There are many other instances when a capability offered tremendous advantage for a time but ultimately ceased to be a differentiating factor in customer choice (for example, just-in-time delivery, electronic data interchange). Therefore, we must take advantage of the differentiating feature but anticipate that it will be necessary to discover and develop a new capability before the old advantage runs out of steam.

How to Deduce Customer Response Functions

You can deduce the customers' response functions by reviewing the literature in the field, learning directly from customers, studying buying patterns among existing products, and conducting surveys of customer needs and wants.

To understand customer response functions, start by reviewing the industry and popular press. Editorials, articles, and advertisements all can reveal what is causing excitement, indifference, or frustration among different buying groups. Benefits, features, and applications will be evident in many of these sources. The literature review is a foundation for all additional research. It gives you the language of the industry and customers, highlights major response functions, and, suggests what to look for in the rest of the research.

The next step is to get to know customers as real people. Visit them at work, at home, or anywhere they purchase or consume the product or service. Ask them to physically walk you through their use of their current product. Employ Gardial and Woodruff's interviewing techniques. Watch for excitement, frustration, and indifference. Listen to the tone of their voice; watch their body language. We communicate what pleases or displeases us in many ways. Behind these nonverbal cues lie the customer's response functions, which can guide the development of your marketing strategy.

After you get to know your customers, study their behaviors in the market. How customers spend their money is a strong indicator of their motivations. They will not spend money on something they do not want but will spend more money on things that really meet their needs. You can deduce a segment's preferences and response functions by studying purchase patterns of the products on the market. Try to determine whether more or less of a feature is correlated with higher demand and customer satisfaction.

For example, if we wanted to know how important fuel economy is in the purchase of an automobile, we could look at the miles per gallon (mpg) ratings of all cars and trucks sold. We would find that sales do not increase linearly with mpg (Exhibit 6.3a is not true). For some segments, there is almost a downturn in sales with higher mpg, reflecting the pattern in Exhibit 6.3c. This downturn does not necessarily mean that consumers do not value higher mpg; it is just that they are willing to trade it off for other benefits that seem more important, such as a feeling of being pampered or a desire to regain youth.

We can also study purchase patterns and learn about response functions for pages per minute in a printer, revolutions per minute in an electric motor, calories in a soft drink, fat in a restaurant entrée, and so on. Will we find that customers flock to a new product whenever a new capability is introduced? Or do only certain groups of customers respond aggressively, while many others move slowly and only when they would normally replace the product or service? Speed of response and the number who respond are strong indicators of response functions and underlying needs and values.

Customer surveys on the importance of a variety of needs, wants, and applications are also very useful in sorting out the relative priorities of different segments. Surveys are best conducted at the end of the data-gathering trail when literature searches, in-depth interviews, and buying trend analyses lend perspective on what to include in formal surveys of customer preferences. Surveys allow you to systematically add data across a broad spectrum of customers and use situations. You can test your assumptions of the market's response functions on a large scale. Perhaps you can discover whether your insights are applicable to a sufficiently large number of customers so that you can earn a profit with something new.

As you gather data of all kinds, keep in mind that end user preferences may or may not match your expectations or prior assumptions. In fact, what you think makes sense is not important. The objective is to give the end users what they want, not what you think they should want.

Role of Test Marketing

It is very difficult, if not impossible, to optimally design a product the first time. For example, if you told me precisely what you wanted when you ate a candy bar (crunchy, chewy, gooey, long-lasting, and a mouth full of flavor) and what ingredients you liked (chocolate, peanuts, caramel) and did not like (nougat, rice, coconut, almonds), I would still be hard pressed to design the perfect candy bar for you. I would probably go into my commercial kitchen and create five different recipes with varying combinations and amounts of what you wanted. If I then gave you the five samples in a blind taste test, you would probably not give any of the bars a 100 percent rating. Most likely, none would rate more than 70 percent, even with the best information I could ever obtain. Why? It is not until you taste the candy bar that you will actually know what you really like. It all depends on what you experienced when you first held the candy bar, when you took your first bite, and when you rolled it around in your mouth as you chewed the candy.

The lesson here is that customer opinions, preferences, and intentions are notoriously weak in predicting behaviors. To complete your research, you must let your potential customers taste your product and observe how they react to different combinations of features and benefits. Where is there excitement, indifference, or frustration? What would they buy and what would they leave on the shelf? All of this information provides clues to the target segment's response functions.

It is not uncommon for a new venture to upgrade its products almost immediately after launch. This happens because it is virtually impossible to fully anticipate all ways a product can be used (or misused). Thus, product evaluation should be done throughout the product development process, especially during the concept and prototype stages. Prior to launch, it might even be desirable to have a limited test market to ensure that the whole brand concept has been well executed. The objective of all these forms of test marketing will be to learn what you did right and what needs to be improved. Then you can quickly revise your design to better match end user requirements.

The product design decision is unavoidably obtuse. There is no one to tell us what the right configuration is to satisfy a given set of needs. Trial and error, looking for patterns, is the best instructor. Once you recognize the patterns, designs can be greatly improved. Those who are successful at this deductive reasoning and critical thinking will have a real competitive advantage.

Evaluate the Effect of Product Design on Production Costs and Changeover Time

Your product design decisions must rest on more than target market needs. You must also look into the factory to assess how different designs will impact your production operations. One fundamental issue revolves around the incorporation of common or unique components into multiple products.

In an ideal world, your goal as a marketer would be to maximize customer satisfaction by providing every customer with exactly what she needs. Conceivably, there would be as many product designs as there are customers. The better you can meet individual needs, the more likely it is that you will sell large volumes of product, charge better prices, and make tons of money. Let's follow this thinking to its logical conclusion.

Suppose, for example, that your firm produced and sold PC monitors. You would probably sell three different kinds of monitors: large cathode ray tube (CRT) desktop monitors, flat screens for desktop use, and flat screens for portable computers. You might want to produce and offer two dozen or more different monitors to meet different needs. Such a large selection would make many customers happy, certainly happier than if you just offered six or eight.

Let's look at this from the viewpoint of the production manager, who would probably prefer just one monitor so that a long production run would be possible. Adding models would make production more complicated and increase procurement and production costs.

Perhaps the most visible effect of disparate products is on production scheduling; changing a production line over to a different model causes delays in production. To change from a 17-inch, low-resolution monitor to a 21-inch, high-resolution monitor means that the incoming parts (i.e., CRT tubes, casings) must change, which necessitates changes in fittings and fixtures that hold and position the parts. Line changeovers result in lost capacity because nothing can be built while the line is being torn down and rebuilt for the next product.

The problem with lost capacity is that the factory still incurs operating expenses during the changeover time. Workers must be paid, and the factory must have heating, electricity, and so forth. These idle expenses will be charged against the products being produced, adding to their cost. Therefore, plant managers like common components because they reduce changeover downtime, effectively adding production capacity.

Knowledge of the market's response functions can be very helpful in keeping changeovers to a minimum. If more or less capability does not cause much of a change in customer excitement/satisfaction, then the marketer has some freedom to choose a component that would reasonably satisfy multiple customers and reduce changeover time and costs. Have you ever noticed the number of General Motors' automobiles that have the same radio, headlights, electronic locking system, and tires? Within a broad price range, customers are apparently not getting excited or frustrated by the available offering. GM has some flexibility in product design and is using it to reduce changeover costs and increase purchasing economies. At the same time, customers willing to pay for ultra luxury, high-fidelity sound, and a very quiet ride are able to find the product of their choice as well.

Consider this guiding principle. Give each segment the product features that create excitement/satisfaction and incorporate common features where the change, or delta, in excitement is comparatively small. In other words, the uniqueness of each product should be highly correlated with those benefits and components that cause the greatest excitement for a particular segment. If a higher performance component does not cause much additional excitement, then a common component might be the better choice. To the eye of the customer, the product should appear unique and tailored to his needs. Those things that cause the greatest excitement should be included and highly visible. Underneath and not highly visible, the different products may look very much alike with many common components.

Marketing and manufacturing should, of course, work together to manage change-over time and cost. Smart firms discover it is possible, through incremental steps, to continuously reduce the amount of time and money required to change the production line over from one model or product to another. Improvement may result from a change in operating procedure, the layout of the work flow, the machines themselves, or even construction of special equipment to facilitate the change. In some cases, products need to be redesigned to make swapping components fast and easy.

If changeover times can be reduced to minutes or seconds, the production line can effectively run continuously, making changeover a nonissue. Marketing can offer a larger assortment of products and satisfy even more customers. This is called *mass customization*. It is a viable goal for many organizations.

Minimum Performance Requirements

It is fundamental to all marketing that segments are different in what they want and how much they want. I call this their *minimum performance requirements*. For example, in the automotive market, Cadillac and Lexus buyers have very high standards. Features that are optional for mid-class car buyers are minimum requirements for this elite car segment. Saturn and Honda Civic buyers, by contrast, do not expect as much. While they would love to have all the latest gadgets, the gadgets are not necessary to make them happy.

In almost every industry, there is a group of customers that might be called the *Mercedes* segment. These customers have sophisticated needs and want the best of everything. They will generally pay more and are not easy to satisfy. (See **Exhibit 6.4**.) There is often a cost-cutter segment, as well, with fewer, more straightforward needs. Its minimum performance requirements are usually less. Preferences are low price and ease of use.

Of course, there is usually a broad middle segment. I call it the *workhorse* segment. The focus of this group is on functionality, with a touch of class. This segment usually has a broader assortment of needs than the cost-cutter segment but far less than the Mercedes segment. Price is important but is balanced against greater utility and style.

Every market will also have a small niche segment called *innovators*. Innovators take extra risk and pay more to be at the leading

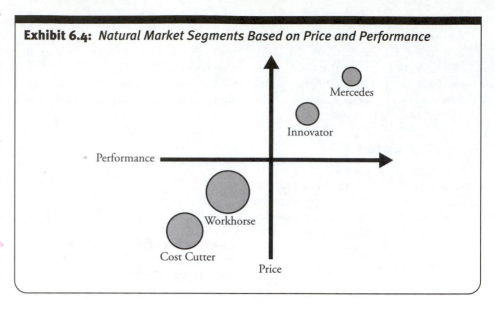

Exhibit 6.4: *Natural Market Segments Based on Price and Performance*

edge of the market. They may also be very knowledgeable customers, which partially explains their willingness to take risk. Their minimum performance requirement probably exceeds that of the workhorse customers but is less than that of the Mercedes customers, who prefer little risk.

Each segment has a minimum performance requirement. Niche segments also have unique requirements. The traveler segment of the personal computer business requires portability. Many of the products in this segment will have features in common with other segments. In fact, within the traveler segment, there are likely to be sub-segments that look like smaller versions of the cost-cutter, workhorse, innovators, and Mercedes segments. Thus, you can have segments within segments, each with its own minimum performance requirement.

Minimum requirements can also vary geographically. Industrial nations have the highest performance requirement; developing economies have slightly lower requirements.

The concept of a minimum performance requirement also helps explain the natural groupings of products within a market. There is what is called an *evoked set*. That is, if you ask people in the Mercedes segment what brands they would consider buying, the set that comes to mind will be remarkably consistent and probably be high performance, high price. You would encounter a different set of brands if you asked the workhorse or cost-cutter segments. If you look at the entire market, you will find clusters of brands; each cluster is similar in a variety of ways but different in important ways from other clusters.

It is obviously quite important to understand how these groupings are formed. What criteria do customers use to sort through the available products and select a smaller set that will satisfy their needs? What is common among the products that compete within this cluster? What is the minimum performance requirement of the segment? What are the differences between this cluster and the other clusters?

Typically, your product will compete within a cluster of products that meet the minimum performance requirements of a segment. Are you well positioned within that segment and cluster of products? Is your product invoked when customers are asked to list competing products?

Relative Performance

Customers compare a product not only to their minimum standards but also to every other product targeted at their segment. Customers gravitate toward the best products in a segment and pull away from lesser products. When a customer can compare products feature for feature, the better products will get a larger share of the market. At a given price point, it is not sufficient to meet the minimum needs in the market, but you must be better than the average competitor.

Evolution of Product Requirements

No market is stagnant. Markets evolve as customers gain experience in a product category. What delighted customers yesterday is commonplace today and insufficient tomorrow. For example, we now expect our cars to have cruise control, power windows,

CD players, stereo sound, remote control door locks, and so on. Not too long ago these were considered elite options. The elite options of today are on-board computers, heads-up displays, global positioning systems, hands-free cell phones, and impact warning systems. In time, they will become the standard options for the mass market.

Each new round of want-satisfying technology can induce the evolution of the market. Once a segment becomes accustomed to today's features, the features enter the "zone of indifference" where the feature no longer adds excitement or causes the customer to think much about it. Being outside the zone of indifference is what it will take to reexcite the customer. Needs do not change, but what it takes to satisfy these needs does.

As new technology and features enter the market, demand will tend to increase because the new features (smaller, easier, faster) are usually better able to meet the needs of one or more market segments. These conditions trigger an evolutionary phase in market requirements. The features that satisfied the cost cutters will slowly drop out of favor. The cost cutters will begin to prefer features that previously satisfied the workhorse segment. The workhorse customers will look for features that satisfied the innovator and Mercedes segments. The Mercedes group will want only the best. The best competitors anticipate the evolutionary nature of the market, expecting to migrate their products from higher to lower segments over time.

As the technology becomes more commonplace and less of a differential advantage, a sharp competitor might shift its previous high-performance products and features to lower segments. As these products are repositioned for the mass markets, primarily by lowering price but also by the novelty of the new features in these lower segments, demand goes up and production costs go down.

Eventually, new technologies migrate down to the lowest segments, where competition is based more on price than other aspects of marketing. In a sense, the firm can trade on the equity built up for the product through prior advertising, promotions, and sales efforts. Although prices are low, production economies are well established, and marketing expenses per unit will be lower than those for newer products. Thus, these products have the potential to become a source of cash for the firm; they are called *cash cows*.

Consider the normal evolution of technology through the market, and build this condition into your strategy to manage a portfolio of products over time and segments.

Multiple Products in a Segment

You will always be challenged by the decision of how many features to give a segment. In many cases, additional or better features create more customer satisfaction and cause the cost of the product to go up, sometimes disproportionately. Thus, you are faced with the trade-off between offering higher performance or offering lower prices.

There are several strategic options to consider. Your customers would like you to offer both high performance and low price. This option is difficult to execute successfully; it requires large production volumes to be profitable, which is possible only if your firm has other products that are driving down overall production costs through their high volumes.

Another option is to compete on price and offer less performance. Price is a powerful motivator and can attract large numbers of customers, often from the more price-sensitive segments. If demand is high enough, then production volumes will be large and production costs low. It is possible to be very profitable with a high-volume/low-price strategy.

A third strategy is to compete on performance. Offer the best in the class and charge higher prices, operating more on high profit margin and less on sales volume. This strategy works best with the best product in the segment because the best product tends to draw customers away from lesser products.

A fourth strategy is to offer an assortment of products to a segment, perhaps a good, better, and best product. This strategy recognizes that there are subsegments that can be simultaneously targeted within a segment. The more price-sensitive customers within a segment might be willing to accept less performance to pay a lower price. The quality-oriented customers might be willing to pay a higher price for all the desired functionality. Each new product will cannibalize any existing products, but this form of microsegmentation should cause the total demand for all products to be higher, helping the firm maximize market share and profits.

There is a tendency to offer a limited assortment of products within a segment.

Often there are practical reasons for this, such as insufficient production capacity or high changeover costs. But the most often cited reason is the fear of cannibalizing a well-performing product.

There are important lessons to learn here. One is that not all customers are the same, even within a segment. There are microsegments that can be profitably served. Another lesson to learn is that cannibalization is not all bad. It may even be preferable when it improves the total demand.

The best example of favorable cannibalization is Diet Coke. It definitely stole part of the market from regular Coke, but the total demand was much improved. Decaffeinated Coke and Diet Decaffeinated Coke had similar effects. Each new formulation of Coke better served a microsegment within the cola market. The result was that total demand for Coke improved. Other examples exist, including different sizes for Baby Ruth candy bars, different kinds of Holiday Inns (i.e., Holiday Inn Express), and different configurations for a Saturn (two-door versus four-door or sedan versus station wagon).

Again, the lesson here is that you need to manage a portfolio of products. These products will serve not only different segments but also different price and performance points within a segment.

Brand Loyalty

Many people buy only Nestlé chocolates, IBM mainframe computers, General Motors cars, Toshiba computers, Dover elevators, or Rockwell aviation components. This phenomenon is called *brand loyalty* or *brand equity*. It offers a great strategic advantage for any firm.

The goal is to build a loyal set of followers who have a strong preference for your particular product or company by providing superior service and performance over repeated purchases and use. Customer loyalty is earned over time, not in a single event or purchase.

The advantages of brand loyalty are obvious. It is a barrier to comparable products and services. Only a vastly superior product or service is likely to cause a loyal customer to switch to a competitor. Brand-loyal customers are attractive because the cost to retain a customer is usually far less than the cost to attract a new customer. A large base of loyal customers allows the firm to project demand more reliably, leading to lower operating and production costs. Because customer loyalty is built up over time, it might erode just as slowly, giving the firm a cushion against sudden shocks to the market.

However, one must not be too complacent with brand-loyal customers. The cynical view is that brand loyalty is strictly a function of consistent superior performance. A much better offer from a competitor will draw away even loyal customers. Xerox, AT&T, Kodak, and even Motorola have all been strong brand names, but the luster has faded or disappeared in light of superior performance by competitors.

If you are entering a new market, you need to consider the loyalty that established players have built up. The new entrant will succeed only by being better in some important way (better product designs, better advertising, better prices).

Brand loyalty allows firms to turn older products or models into cash cows and milk them until they are dry. The reason they can be milked is that prior investments in advertising, sales, and promotions have created a residual preference among customers that takes time to decay. Thus, the firm can shave marketing costs and trade on built-up equity.

Again, one must be very careful about trusting too much in brand equity. One frozen food producer thought it could trade on its well-known brand name during an economic downturn and cut marketing expenses. For the first couple of months, the strategy seemed to work—sales declined but not in a worrisome way. After six months, the downward drift picked up speed and could not be easily stopped. In fact, it took several months to reverse the decline and years to recover the firm's former position in the market. In the end, it cost the firm much more to reverse what it had started than if it had continued to invest in its product identity.

A conservative, even cynical, posture in relation to brand loyalty is probably safest: Think of brand loyalty as strictly a function of consistent superior performance. Every day you must once again demonstrate that you are the best on the market.

PRICING

In the marketplace, price is a very important driver of demand. Pricing is probably just as important as product design in either stimulating or curtailing demand. There are several factors to consider in setting price:

- What the market will bear.
- What the market can afford and natural price points.
- Competitive behavior and prices.
- Price image and market positioning.
- Impact of a differential advantage on price elasticity.
- Cost considerations.
- Price substitutes and promotions.
- Profit goals.

What the Market Will Bear

Pricing is a very important part of a firm's marketing strategy. As any economist will tell you, price increases stifle demand, while price decreases stimulate demand. Most markets are very elastic or responsive to price changes, but not all markets are equally price sensitive. Price elasticity differs by segment. For example, a $1,000 price increase for a Lexus automobile will have less effect on demand than a $1,000 price increase for a Saturn or a Honda Civic. In part, price elasticity is determined by what a customer is willing or able to pay. Thus, if a customer is thinking about buying a $35,000 car, the $1,000 price increase is not as much a shock as it is for the customer looking to buy a $15,000 car. The Lexus car buyer might not react as strongly until the price increase exceeds $2,000 or $3,000.

Price elasticity must be fundamental to the strategist's way of thinking. Every price and every price change are affected by the price elasticity or sensitivity of the target market. Knowledge of price elasticity can yield strategic advantages. Failure to consider price elasticity can lead to disaster. **Exhibit 6.5** illustrates how a change in price might affect a change in demand. If the target segment is inelastic, then demand will drop slowly as prices go up (notice the gently sloping line at the top of the graph). If prices drop, demand will go up slowly. In short, price is not a big factor in a customer's decision to make a purchase. On the other hand, if the segment is highly elastic, then a small increase in price will cause demand to drop quickly (notice the steeply dropping line at the bottom of the graph). Conversely, a small decrease in price should cause a huge increase in demand.

There are many different response functions in the market. You might expect the

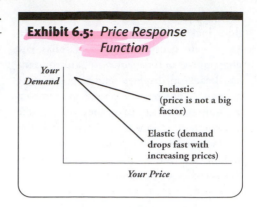

Exhibit 6.5: *Price Response Function*

cost-cutter segment to be very price sensitive, the workhorse segment to be moderately price sensitive, and the Mercedes and innovator segments to be the least price sensitive. Niche segments also tend to be less price sensitive since the products targeted at them generally offer unique benefits that are difficult to obtain elsewhere. What is important is to realize that price elasticity varies by segment, so you must determine the elasticity of your target segment.

It is also important to realize that response functions take many different shapes. Consider, for example, **Exhibit 6.6**. In this case, small price changes have little effect on demand. But as the changes increase, so does the effect on demand. Thus, the market is relatively inelastic for small price changes and highly elastic for large price changes. (In other words, the change in demand increases out of proportion to the change in price.) This assumption might be better to make than the assumption that elasticity is constant or the same across all possible price increases.

All of this suggests that it is important to test the market in order to better understand the price elasticity of your target segments. This knowledge will help you to decide whether to use penetration pricing

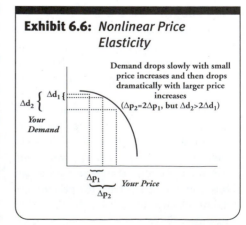

Exhibit 6.6: *Nonlinear Price Elasticity*

Demand drops slowly with small price increases and then drops dramatically with larger price increases ($\Delta p_2 = 2\Delta p_1$, but $\Delta d_2 > 2\Delta d_1$)

(deep price cuts), market prices, or skim-the-cream pricing (premium prices). Here are a few other considerations. Do not assume that any segment is price inelastic. While inelastic segments do exist (i.e., luxury items), they are rare. Price competition will have its greatest impact in the lower price/performance segments. Higher-performance segments and niche segments will be less sensitive to price increases or decreases. Also consider that it is easier to lower prices than to raise them. A price increase will almost always discourage buying, while a price drop will almost always encourage more customers to buy.

Price increases do not always cause demand to decline, and price decreases do not always cause demand to increase because there are special conditions that can result in counterintuitive changes in demand. For example, a drop in price might signal a new model is coming out and encourage customers to wait for something better. Or it might signal that times are rough for the supplier and it is desperate to move inventory. Maybe the supplier will not be around to support its products in the future.

A price increase might signal shortages in supply: Future availability will be reduced and additional price increases may be forthcoming, or a price increase might signal a fundamental change in quality and/or prestige.

Threshold Price

In addition to overall price elasticity, each segment will have a threshold price at which it is willing to enter the market. This threshold is probably a reflection of at least two factors: the typical price for a product of a certain quality and the customers' ability to pay.

The typical price for a product of a given quality is defined by the collective actions of buyers and sellers. For example, a cheap bottle of wine might cost $5, a good bottle $12, and a very good bottle $30 or more. Vineyards create wines to match these price points, and customers choose among the wines at a given price point.

The customers' ability to pay is probably the most important factor in determining the price at which they will enter the market. For example, at the outset of the cell phone industry, service fees and phone costs exceeded the threshold price for most consumers. People in real estate, construction,

sales, and other time-sensitive and value-sensitive professions were the only ones who could justify the expense. However, as prices dropped, different segments one by one entered the market. Currently, a large portion of the middle class can afford to use cell phones, but prices have not dropped far enough for the lowest economic segments to use cell phones in large numbers.

Within the PC industry, there are also different price points. The cost-cutter segment has the lowest threshold price, and the Mercedes segment has the highest. The threshold price can also vary by geographic region. For example, the price customers are willing and able to pay in China or Brazil is substantially lower than what customers are willing to pay in developed countries such as the United States, Canada, and Germany.

Your product design decision must include consideration of the price the market is willing to pay. There is always a price/performance trade-off. Higher performance features will generally cost more than lower performance features. Will the target market pay for the additional capability?

Your MOA should help you to determine how sensitive your target market is to price vis-à-vis performance. Consider establishing a price point for each segment and then designing products within that constraint. If the projected selling price is higher than you think the market will bear, you should consider scaling back the product design to fit the price. Alternatively, you might pursue ways to reduce the cost of highly valued components so that you can offer higher levels of performance within the price limits of the segment.

Keep in mind that as the price of a product rises above the threshold of a segment, demand will decline. The greater the difference between this price point and the asking price of a product, the greater the drop in demand. In this respect, all segments are price elastic.

The opposite is also true. As industry prices come down, total market demand generally goes up because more customers can afford to buy and more segments enter the market. The rate at which customers enter the market as prices drop will vary by market segment. One might expect that as the selling price drops toward each segment's threshold price, the number of customers will increase exponentially. Once the threshold is passed, then growth will be driven much less by the segment's ability to

buy than by other factors in the marketing mix, competitive environment, or economic situation. Competitive prices, in particular, will increase in importance. In other words, if you can afford either competitor A's goods or B's goods and both have approximately the same value, you will shift to the lower price.

We will discuss relative pricing in the next section and return to it again in a later discussion of marketing strategy over the life cycle of the product. We can expect that over the life cycle of the product, the threshold price for a segment will evolve. For automobiles, the threshold prices keep inching up. For electronics, threshold price keeps inching down.

The movement in the threshold price depends upon economic conditions (purchasing power), the underlying costs to produce, and our minimum requirements to be satisfied. For goods such as automobiles and houses, we keep wanting more, putting upward pressure on the price we are willing to pay. For electronic goods, we have come to expect that prices will keep falling and that what we can buy next year will be better than what we can buy this year.

Be aware that you could price below what the market will bear. But if a lower price does not draw large numbers of customers, then why give away money? The market's response function might be such that there is a range around the segment's price point where the market is relatively price insensitive. Small differences might not be noticed or might be less important than other considerations such as reliability, credit terms, availability, and so on.

Competitive Prices

Another consideration in setting prices is the action of your competitors. If all other things are equal, customers will tend to shift toward the lowest-priced product. The magnitude of this product switching depends on the sensitivity of the segment to pricing issues and the size of the price difference.

Exhibit 6.7 illustrates the impact of competitor prices. On the *y*-axis is your demand, and on the *x*-axis is your competitor's price. As the price of a competitor's product increases, your demand will increase. What is more worrisome is that the opposite is also true. As your competition lowers prices, your demand will shrink, all other things being equal.

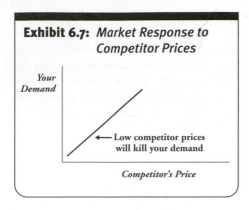

Exhibit 6.7: *Market Response to Competitor Prices*

Your Demand

← Low competitor prices will kill your demand

Competitor's Price

Another way to understand this issue is to look at the elasticity of the difference in prices between you and a competitor. Let's recast Exhibit 6.6, labeling the x-axis as the difference between your price and that of the competition. (See **Exhibit 6.8**.) In this curve, small differences in price will have little effect on demand (low elasticity). This is probably a reasonable assumption because you are likely to have built up some product loyalty, and/or the cost of switching products is greater than the small premium that you charge.

However, as the magnitude of the price difference increases, so does its impact on demand: The elasticity increases. Again, this is a reasonable assumption. It is difficult for buyers to remain loyal if they have to pay a significant premium for your product. As the premium increases, you would expect loyalty to evaporate at an ever-increasing rate. If there are switching costs that retard a change in products, then at some point the price premium will overtake these costs, and it will be more economical to switch products.

This point is not lost on your competition. If they can offer a similar product at a noticeably lower price, they will have a good chance of stealing customers from you. Price is a powerful motivator to buy or

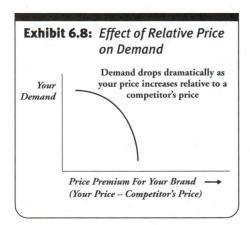

Exhibit 6.8: *Effect of Relative Price on Demand*

Your Demand

Demand drops dramatically as your price increases relative to a competitor's price

Price Premium For Your Brand →
(Your Price − Competitor's Price)

switch products, and a price change is an easy tactic to implement. Thus, your competition will always scrutinize a price cut as a tactic to gain new customers at your expense. The more competitors you have, the higher the likelihood that someone will be cutting prices soon.

Finally, this price sensitivity extends to your firm's own product line. Lower-priced models will attract attention from higher-priced models. Even if no other supplier is in a market segment, your products will compete with each other for market share.

Nature of Competition

Let's consider the number of competitors further. If you were the only supplier in the market, a monopoly, it would not be difficult to keep prices firm. In fact, this is the problem with monopolies; they tend to charge high prices in a market that has no choice but to buy from them.

In a market with just a few competitors, an oligopoly, it does not take long for firms to realize they are tied together when it comes to pricing. Suppose there are three comparable firms in an industry and one firm drops its price. If the other two firms do not drop prices, then the first firm will gain sales at the expense of the other two. Switching costs and a certain amount of product loyalty will slow the migration, but the longer the price differential is in effect or the greater it is, the higher the rate of exodus to the lower-priced firm. Thus, when one firm drops prices, you can expect the others to imitate the change or suffer lost sales.

In an oligopoly, there is also what is called *price leadership*. Price leadership can drive prices down or up, depending on circumstances. For example, United Airlines might announce or signal that it is raising fares on all international flights by 5 percent. It is hoping that other carriers will follow suit. If British Airways makes a similar announcement, there is a chance that the whole industry will follow and that everyone will be at a new parity but with a little more flowing to the bottom line. Unfortunately, it takes only one spoiler to ruin the strategy. If Northwest Airlines decides to keep prices firm, it will have a significant competitive advantage, and before long all air carriers will be back at the old prices. Prices tend to be more stable in oligopolies because competitors realize that price decreases will be quickly copied and price increases tend not to be followed.

As the number of comparable products increases, so does price competition. When there is very little difference between products and many sources of supply, a product becomes a commodity. Under these circumstances, the market moves quickly to the lowest cost provider. This is pure competition. Most businesspeople do not like to compete in this kind of market: Profit margins are razor thin or nonexistent because there is constant pressure to lower prices.

To illustrate, suppose Firm A is able to lower costs and pass the savings on to customers; it will have a competitive advantage and gain new customers. But few of its competitors can afford to give up a significant share of their customer base, so there is strong pressure for competitors to cut profit margins in the short term to match the lower price, hoping they will be able to find similar cost savings and soon be back to their normal profit margins. Unfortunately, by the time they achieve these cost savings, the market may have moved on to another round of price cuts, and profit margins become permanently shaved.

Price competition becomes destructive when a firm cuts prices below its costs. Although this may seem unwise, the firm is clearly better off to price below costs in order to keep the business alive. It might need the production volume in order to keep overall costs down. In the short term this can be wise, but sometimes the short term stretches into the long term and the firm is strangled by the market.

Price Image and Market Positioning

Competing on price is a very powerful way to attract business. In fact, segments are often defined by their price sensitivity. A cost-cutter segment is very price sensitive, and a Mercedes segment is much less so. Suppliers respond to this sensitivity by creating different offerings that are consistent with the price requirements of the segments. Thus, we have clusters of products arrayed by price and performance. (See Exhibit 6.4.)

Every firm has a price-performance image. Marriott Hotels, Sony Consumer Electronics, Trane Heating and Air Conditioning, and the Harvard Business School all have a high-price/high-performance image. Budget Inn, Panasonic, Carrier HAC, and the University of Phoenix offer scaled-down versions but at very attractive prices. The firm's price-performance image is garnered from its assortment of products, its prices, and the image it created through advertising and sales efforts.

The important point is to decide which segment you want to compete and what price-performance image you wish to create. Do not let the market form its own image of your competitive position. Be proactive: Define the position and image you want to hold, and then organize your marketing activities to place your firm squarely within that segment of the market.

Creation of Little Monopolies to Avoid Price Competition

As much as possible, marketers prefer not to compete on price. Although price is a powerful marketing tactic, a price cut is comparatively easy to copy, so price advantages are often short lived. Price cuts also come at the expense of bottom-line profits. When profits suffer, so does the stock price, and so do the bonuses of the executives.

Marketers prefer to compete on everything but price. If they can create the impression that their offering of products and services is better than the competition, they will create a small monopoly for their goods. In other words, if they can create a differential advantage, they can shift the demand curve so that it is flatter or less elastic. (See **Exhibit 6.9**.) This, in turn, will allow them to price above the market and realize a measure of monopoly profits.

One of the reasons to pursue niche segments is that they are easier to monopolize than are larger mass markets. Every market is filled with unique segments. The more finely you divide the market, the more likely you will find groups of customers that are not quite happy with the current offerings.

Exhibit 6.9: *Differential Advantage Can Reduce Price Elasticity*

If you can uniquely serve one of these segments, its attraction to your firm will be enhanced. If the customers think they cannot find what they want elsewhere, they will be more willing to pay a premium for what you have to offer.

Thus, smart businesspeople will go to great lengths to find and serve unfulfilled segments. Through a combination of product design, service, communication (advertising, public relations, sales presentations), and even price, they try to create an image that they are uniquely tuned to serving the needs of the segment.

Another reason to pursue this image is that it is more difficult for the competition to combat. When price is easily imitated, to replicate all that goes into an image is much more difficult. Thus, a differential advantage based on superior performance is more sustainable than one built on price.

As we move up the price-performance chart, we find more uniqueness and less price sensitivity. But even within a segment (a given price point), you can consciously try to build a differential advantage, reducing the market's sensitivity to price differences between your products and those of your competition.

Cost Considerations

The price ceiling for a product or service is probably defined by what the market will bear. The price sensitivity of a market indicates the relative advantage of a price-skimming strategy—charging high prices because the market is less price elastic—or of a price penetration strategy—charging low prices because the market is highly elastic. The competition imposes further constraints. A noticeably higher price will probably cause a loss in demand, and a noticeably lower price will probably cause the competition to lower prices to match a price advantage. Of course, a strong differential advantage from product design, image, or distribution will provide some latitude to charge premium prices.

One other factor to consider in setting prices is the cost to produce, deliver, and service your products. Over the long term, your prices must pay for all expenses associated with the product, contribute to all other expenses to run the company, and, most importantly, provide a fair profit to the owners.

The most direct costs are those associated with producing a product. These include

everything that goes into production, including raw materials, already assembled components purchased elsewhere, the labor to create parts and assemble the product, and the cost to change over a production line from one model to the next. These costs are easy to associate with a particular model or product and are assigned directly to the cost of goods sold.

Sometimes these costs are called *variable costs* or *direct costs* because they vary directly with which model is being produced and with its production volume. In general, as the production volume goes up, the variable costs go down. Variable costs, or per unit production costs, usually go down as a result of the firm's ability to acquire parts, raw materials, and supplies at increasingly better prices. Production costs also go down as the firm gains experience and learns how to be efficient in the handling and assembly of materials.

There are also indirect production costs, such as heating and cleaning the facilities, maintenance on the equipment, and so on. These costs generally benefit all products equally and are usually assigned to each model's cost of goods in proportion to its production volume.

The cost of goods is a very important number. It is often compared to the selling price to determine the gross margin.

$$\text{Gross margin} = \text{Selling price} - \text{Cost of goods sold}$$

At the very least, the firm wants a positive gross margin, so the selling price must pay for all costs to produce the good. The gross margin must also pay for all other expenses of the firm and provide profit for the owners.

In addition to production costs, the price you charge must reflect your company's overhead expenses, often referred to as *general sales and administration* (GSA). Overhead includes marketing, advertising, sales, warehousing and shipping, interest on loans, R&D, engineering, depreciation, leases, training, and administrative costs, to name a few. Many GSA expenses tend to support all products equally. These expenses can be allocated to each product in proportion to its sales or production volume. However, some GSA expenses should not be allocated to a product simply based upon the number of units sold or produced.

Suppose you spent $300,000 in total advertising. Should this cost be charged to the overhead of the firm as a selling expense? If so, then every unit sold would effectively carry the same advertising burden. But what if we know that $200,000 was spent on Product A and $100,000 was spent on Product B? Would it not make more sense to charge Product A with the larger advertising burden?

We can similarly charge each product with its relevant demand-creating costs (point-of-purchase displays, sales force incentive, rebates). There might even be other specific costs to manufacture (larger parts inventories, more storage space, special equipment), distribute (special warehousing, handling, and transportation), and service a product. When all of the revenues and costs are properly allocated, we can discover which products are making the greatest contribution to the profitability of the firm.

We can similarly evaluate the sales territories or regions in which the firm sells. It is not difficult to allocate revenue or cost of goods sold to a geographic area, but we can also assign costs associated with the regional rebates, sales force salaries, office leases, and advertising costs. Again, our objective is to learn the relative profitability of each region so that we can allocate our resources effectively.

The technique of allocating expenses and revenues to their correct activity is *activity-based costing* (ABC). (James Reeve devotes much of an entire chapter to ABC.) ABC is a powerful tool for evaluating the financial contribution of each product, sales territory, or marketing activity.

In the past, many marketing and distribution expenses were not assigned to specific products or sales territories. Thus, there was no direct accountability. For whatever reason, one product might be given more advertising, promotional, or sales support than another. Or one channel or advertising medium might simply be more expensive for the same level of activity. If all of the marketing and distribution expenses were lumped together, how would you know whether the expenditures for a particular product were financially justifiable? The objective in applying ABC is to track down all costs associated with the creation of a sale and assign them to the product or market that generated the sale. Thus, you will know the real profit contribution of the activity, a figure that is more useful than just the gross margin of the product.

The ABC analysis will clarify the profit or loss contribution of every product and sales territory, but it will not tell you what to do. Should you eliminate all products that do not make a positive contribution? Not necessarily. You may elect to retain a product if it helps you to accomplish other objectives, such as having a full product line or achieving economies in purchasing components for all products. It will take time to build business for a new product, which may not become profitable for several quarters. Regardless of the reason, if you are losing money, you should know it. And, if you are making more money on some products than others, perhaps you should reallocate some resources to take further advantage of these gains.

Price Substitutes and Promotions

There is a variety of price discounts, price substitutes, and financing options you can offer to the distribution channel or end users. **Exhibit 6.10** lists many that target the distribution channel. All of the tactics in Exhibit 6.10 deal directly or indirectly with the price sensitivity of the market. It is clear that the market favors lower prices and responds well to any support that lowers the costs of handling and selling a supplier's goods. The tactics outlined in Exhibit 6.10 indirectly but effectively lower the total costs of buying from a particular supplier. Thus, they are responding to the price elasticity of the market.

Exhibit 6.10: *Selected Distribution Policy Alternatives*

I. Price Concessions
  A. Discount Structure:
    trade (functional discounts)
    quantity discounts
    cash discounts
    anticipation allowances
    free goods
    prepaid freight
    new product display and advertising allowances (without performance requirements)
    seasonal discounts
    mixed carload privilege
    drop shipping privilege
    trade deals
  B. Discount Substitutes:
    display materials
    premarked merchandise
    inventory control programs
    catalogs and sales promotion literature
    training programs
    shelf-stocking programs
    advertising matrices
    management consulting services
    merchandising programs
    sales "spiffs"
    technical assistance
    payment of sales personnel and demonstrator salaries
    promotional and advertising allowances (with performance requirements)

II. Financial Assistance
  A. Conventional Lending Arrangements:
    term loans
    inventory floor plans
    notes payable financing
    accounts payable financing
    installment financing of fixtures and equipment
    lease and note guarantee programs
    accounts receivable financing
  B. Extended Dating:
    E.O.M. dating
    seasonal dating
    R.O.G. dating
    "extra" dating
    postdating

III. Protective Provisions
  A. Price Protection:
    premarked merchandise
    fair trade
    franchise pricing
    agency agreements
  B. Inventory Protection:
    consignment selling
    memorandum selling
    liberal returns allowances
    rebate programs
    reorder guarantees
    guaranteed support of sales events
    maintenance of "spot" stocks and fast delivery
  C. Territorial Protection:
    selective distribution
    exclusive distribution

Source: Bert C. McCammon Jr., The University of Oklahoma.

There are many reasons a supplier might wish to use these tactics rather than a simple, straightforward price cut. These tactics can be used as bargaining chips to encourage or reward certain channel partner behaviors. For example, a seller might want a buyer to take on a new product, buy in larger quantities, place an order early, expand distribution to other outlets, and so on. The supplier might, therefore, give an extra case per pallet load, extend the time to pay for the goods, increase the discount for early payment, or provide some advertising money. Thus, the supplier negotiates price-like concessions to obtain important support in marketing, distribution, or sales from its channel customer to influence what happens in the sale of its products.

The tactics listed in Exhibit 6.10 also add to the overall image of the firm while taking the focus off price, since maintaining a differential advantage on price alone is difficult. The differential advantage is more sustainable if the supplier is perceived as helping the buyer achieve its goals in many different ways. It is not easy to translate the price substitutes and financing options in Exhibit 6.10 into a net selling price. The complexity and indirectness of these price-like tactics make it difficult to determine how the total, delivered price is affected. Thus, the buyer is left with a less specific image that the supplier is helping the customer to lower costs and otherwise achieve its goals. As this image of being a "good provider" increases, so does the supplier's competitive, or differential, advantage. This in turn gives the supplier a little more flexibility in setting price.

The supplier might like the tactics in Exhibit 6.10 because the cost to implement them is less than the perceived value to the customer. You might offer a channel partner an extra case for every new pallet load purchased. The buyer would probably think of the extra case at its wholesale price, but the cost to you is the production cost, perhaps 50 percent less. You might instead offer advertising money to a retailer to include your products in advertising. This is called *co-op advertising*. Clearly, this benefits the retailer, but it also benefits you. Your products will appear more often and in many more venues than if you had to design the ads and schedule and pay for the media yourself. Your image also benefits from its association with a reputable retailer.

As you can see, there are many reasons to use these tactics in your marketing strat-

egy. They appeal to the price sensitivity of the market and allow you to gain some influence over the marketing and sale of your goods in the channel.

These same tactics might also be employed in building relationships with end users that are businesses. Although these tactics will not influence resale of your goods, they will influence the manner in which your goods are purchased and consumed.

Finally, there are many price promotions aimed at consumers. Many companies offer rebates, coupons, or price specials. Price promotions are a short-term stimulant to market demand. They create excitement and encourage customers to buy *now*. They appeal to all segments, especially to highly price-elastic ones.

Suppliers strategically use price promotions to reduce inventory of overstocked products, to attract attention to a new product, or to attack an established competitor. One advantage of using a rebate or coupon with the introduction of a new product is that it reduces the risk of trial for the consumer and offers a temporary price incentive.

Another advantage of rebates and coupons is that the supplier gets the benefit of being perceived as a low-price provider without actually having to lower its revenue by the full amount of the price incentive. Price incentives will motivate many consumers to buy, but perhaps only 50 percent will actually cash in a rebate or coupon.

There are at least four disadvantages to the use of price promotions. First, many customers probably would have bought the product without the promotion. Your price promotion just allows them to save some money. For these customers, you lose money on everything they bought. Second, some customers will stock up on the goods that they probably would have bought at a later time, and demand may decline as your customers work off the inventory they have built up. Thus, you may be borrowing sales from the future. Third, it is difficult to maintain the excitement of a price promotion; as soon as it ends, interest returns to normal. Also, while price prompts customers to act now to get the deal, price promotions do not sustain an image of being a good provider. Finally, if the promotion is discontinued, it can disproportionately dampen demand; to the customer, it is a price increase.

Low-Price Provider

You need to be very careful about trying to dominate the market by price leadership. Suppliers usually assume that a very low price will lead to huge demand that, in turn, will drive down per unit production and supply costs. The demand will come from either a shift in market share from competitors or an increase in new customers.

This strategy can work if you have a structural advantage in the cost to produce and deliver the product. In other words, your labor, production methods, equipment and facilities, raw materials, and/or supply chain must be significantly less expensive than that of your competition. If it is cheaper for you to produce and deliver goods, your cost advantage will allow you to maintain prices your competition cannot. You drive them from the market because they cannot afford to stay in it.

Without a structural advantage, the price leadership strategy may lead to bankruptcy because you can expect that your competitors will cut their margins rather than lose business. They will probably even be willing to price below costs if they believe business is threatened. If they can sustain their losses longer than you, you might be the one driven from the market. Without a structural advantage, the only other way this strategy will work is for there to be another organization or person with deep pockets to cover your losses until demand improves or competitors leave the market.

ADVERTISING

Your overall marketing strategy should include an integrated marketing communication (IMC) strategy. That is, all forms of communication with your target audience should be designed to have a common message and support each other. In this section, our attention will primarily be on one element of the IMC strategy, advertising. However, the basic principles apply to other forms of communication such as promotions (coupons), media events (NASCAR races), public relations, and so forth.[4]

The role of advertising is to create awareness, interest, desire, and, ultimately, a purchase from your firm. Advertising usually involves presenting information in a persuasive way so that potential customers buy your products. In its simplest form, good advertising requires that you determine the message you want to convey, create an effective presentation of this message (print, video, or sound), select the appropriate media to reach the maximum number of people in your target audience, and run the advertisement an appropriate number of times in that media to maximize the number of potential customers exposed and the frequency of exposure.

Advertising campaigns usually target individual segments. The message, copy, and media are all selected to impact the target segment and may not be seen by or relevant to other segments. Thus, advertising tends to be a highly focused endeavor. Overall, your ability to draw customers from a target segment is dependent upon the quality and the quantity of your advertising relative to that of your competitors and the quality of your offer.

This section addresses creating an ad, weighting elements in it, evaluating its effectiveness, selecting appropriate media, and analyzing the effect of exposure frequency and budgets.

The advertising decision is actually much more complex and sophisticated than presented here. Considerable creativity and effort are required to deliver effective advertising. Our focus is limited to a few key response functions that are likely to be at play in the market. This section offers a sampling of the functions that underlie the market's response to a delivered message. The goal is to sensitize you to look for response functions and employ this knowledge to create more effective advertising.

Relative Priority of Advertising

Even before you start planning your advertising campaign, you must think through the trade-offs inherent to your marketing strategy. Would it be better to spend the next $100,000 on advertising, or would you realize a higher payoff by spending it on further product development, lower prices, more sales outlets, more salespeople, or more incentives to resellers? Or would you realize a higher payoff by investing in additional plant capacity, quality improvements in production, or even the money market?

The size of your advertising budget relative to other expenditures implies a set of priorities and assumptions. For example, if you spend $2,000,000 on salespeople and $100,000 on advertising, you apparently have concluded that the marginal return on salespeople is much higher than the marginal return on advertising. Or if you spend

$300,000 on promotions and other incentives for wholesalers and retailers and only $100,000 on advertising, this implies that you consider a *push strategy*—getting resellers to stock and sell your product—to be much more effective than a *pull strategy*—getting customers to come looking for your goods.

To make effective marketing decisions, you must know your investment options, estimate their payoffs, and consciously establish your strategic priorities. You will find that these priorities will change as your firm and the industry pass through the introductory stage of the product life cycle to the growth stage and on into maturity.

Advertising Strategy

The advertising strategy needs to be agreed upon at the outset of an advertising campaign. The first step in designing a strategy is to decide on the goal. For example, is your goal:

- To inform customers about a new product, price, outlet, service, or event?
- To persuade customers that you are familiar with their needs and can satisfy them?
- To stimulate awareness of a need that was not well recognized?
- To reposition your image so that it is more consistent with customer preferences or competitive positions?
- To further heighten product recognition and memorability?
- To encourage trial of a new product?
- To increase foot traffic at a retail outlet?

There are many other goals beyond these, but whatever the goal, it must be clearly articulated since everything else flows from this decision.

With the goal in mind, decisions must be made regarding the budget, time/length, and target audience. Next, the media are selected, usually two to three different forms to increase exposure. The message is then created and tailored to the advertising strategy and its constraints and goals. The message should also be tested within the context of the medium and audience. When everything is in place, the ad campaign is launched according to the schedule. During and after the ad campaign, the target audience is sampled for awareness and retention of the message. Finally, an attempt is made to evaluate whether the campaign had the desired effect, such as an increase in foot traffic in a retail store or a change in attitude toward

the brand. We will now turn our attention to issues of the budget, media outlets, frequency, and message.

Advertising Budgets

One of the most important decisions you must make in media planning is how much to invest in advertising. There are four common methods for setting advertising budgets:

1. All you can afford.
2. Percentage of sales.
3. Competitive parity (the same amount as your strongest competitors).
4. Objective and task.

Theoretically, the objective and task method is the most attractive because it requires that you spell out your objectives, assumptions, and the expected payoff of the amount of money invested. Practically speaking, the first three methods help to establish benchmarks for comparison between products and competitors and should be part of the decision.

The fundamental reason that the first three methods are not optimal is that they fail to consider the marginal return of the investment. Perhaps you think you can afford only $100,000 today based on past experience and projected cash flows. But ask yourself what would happen to your projected revenues if you doubled your advertising budget to $200,000. Would revenue not increase? Would it increase enough to pay for the extra $100,000 in advertising? To say that a certain amount is all you can afford implies that the marginal return for the next dollar is effectively zero. What you can really afford depends on what the extra money would generate in new revenues.

The same is true for the percentage of sales method. The percentage you spend on advertising should probably fluctuate. During the introductory phase of the product life cycle, heavy advertising is probably warranted. As a percentage of sales, it is probably very high. In contrast, the percentage might decline during the mature phase because awareness is already strong and sales volumes high.

Competitive parity is a serious consideration in setting advertising budgets. The market responds not only to the total pull of the advertising campaign on a segment but also to its relative pull. As illustrated in **Exhibit 6.11**, the more a competitor advertises, the less your likely demand. Thus, the

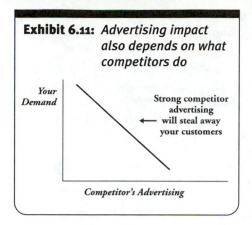

Exhibit 6.11: Advertising impact also depends on what competitors do

Your Demand

Strong competitor advertising will steal away your customers ←

Competitor's Advertising

firms with the better advertising campaigns will attract more customers than those with weaker advertising programs. Clearly, if you do not keep up with your competitors, they will steadily take your customers away, all other things being equal. Just consider the huge advertising battles being fought by Coke and Pepsi or Kellogg and General Mills. Similar battles are being fought over sales of microprocessors, cell phones, credit cards, and so forth.

While it is very important to constantly monitor the amount and type of advertising your competitors are engaged in, it is not financially wise to simply spend as much as they do. Perhaps they are not spending their money as wisely as they should. Perhaps rebates, coupons, tie-ins, sporting event sponsorship, and so on would be more effective on the margin. There are also many kinds of trade incentives and sales force incentives that could be employed and that might provide a better marginal return. For example, Bush Beans has concluded that good shelf location in retail grocery stores is more important in generating sales than advertising to the consumer. As a result, its advertising expenditures are much less than its investment in incentives to wholesalers and retailers. Bush relies much more on a push strategy—getting resellers to carry the product—and much less on a pull strategy—getting customers to look for and ask for the product.

The objective and task method is a good way to establish an advertising budget. This approach takes your objective as the foremost consideration. Is the objective to get potential customers to try the product for the first time? If so, then perhaps a combination of heavy advertising and couponing would be best. Is the objective to get wider distribution among the wholesale trade? Then perhaps trade shows and channel incentives might be best. Is the objective to excel in product recognition? Then a wide variety of media and promotional options may be necessary in order to appear pervasive in the market. Is the objective to sell the most profitable product in your portfolio? Then perhaps sales force incentives may work best. The goal is to build the budget up from the ground based upon what you want and need to accomplish.

You can also apply the principles of activity-based costing. Each product, segment, and sales territory should be evaluated in terms of the full revenues and costs associated with it. Once you know the profitability of each product, segment, and sales territory, then consider spending proportionately more on the most profitable.

There are many considerations in setting a budget and allocating money to promote a product or service. At the very least, you must consider what the competition is doing. Beyond this consideration, you have to ask yourself what you want to accomplish. As you try to answer this question, look at which products and markets provide or could provide the greatest return to the company. Consider all of your promotional options, and then choose those options that give the best marginal return for money invested.

Selecting Media Outlets

Advertisers use multiple outlets to ensure that their ad campaign is seen. A very important element in planning your advertising campaign is deciding where and how often to run your advertisements, often called the media mix. In general, the more often you expose your potential customers to your message, the more likely it is that they will learn about you and your products and be persuaded to buy. Of course, there are many factors to consider in making this decision.

One goal is to select media outlets that your target segments will likely see and that are consistent with the message you want to convey. If you are focusing on the health-conscious consumer, you would focus on media outlets that cater specifically to this group, such as *Health Today*, *Cooking Light*, or *Runner's World*. Some outlets target a segment directly.

On the other hand, many health-conscious consumers do not read these magazines at all. Thus, you must find magazines where being healthy is conveyed less directly. For example, many young women like to look good, and so fashion-oriented magazines might also be good outlets. Even among these magazines, should you choose *Glamour*, *Vogue*, or *In-Style*, or would *Cosmopolitan* be a better outlet to convey your message to your target audience?

To help you choose media outlets, you must find out to which magazines, TV shows, radio programs, and so on your target segment is exposed. Some outlets will be directly linked to the benefits sought by the segment, but many others will be tangentially linked or not linked at all. Suppose health-conscious people also have more education and income. Perhaps many are over 30 and do not read fashion magazines any more. Would general news magazines such as *Time* or *Newsweek* be good outlets? If potential customers are also mothers, perhaps *Ladies' Home Journal* would be viable. The goal is to pick outlets that have the highest probability of conveying your message to your target audience.

Your media selection decision should also consider advertising waste. You would like to choose outlets that give you a direct avenue to the target segment, which is often difficult because of the diversity of customers in the market. Although *Info Week* might be read by computer-savvy customers, many do not read it. So, you must select outlets that are viewed by a more diverse group of people, many of whom are not in your target group. To the extent that you place advertisements in media that cover more than your target group, you have advertising waste. Essentially, the message falls on deaf ears.

To evaluate your advertising investment, it is important to compute the cost per exposed target segment customer. For instance, if an ad in *Cosmopolitan*'s international edition costs $500,000, you figure the cost per person exposed to the message, which is certainly not based on the total readership of *Cosmopolitan* (say 10,000,000 people), or 5 cents per exposure. Use instead the number of readers that fit your target segment, which might be only 10 percent of the total readership. Thus, the real cost would be 50 cents per potential exposure.

In today's advertising world, it is possible to tightly focus advertising by geography and demographics. *Time* magazine has regional editions, allowing you to target the Northeast United States or the Province of Ontario. *Time* also has editions that are targeted by demographics such as age, education, or income. To the extent that your target segments have clear demographic correlates with audiences of these media, you can increase your advertising precision and limit waste.

As you move away from tightly focused media, you will have many other options to consider. At the far end of this continuum, you would find local newspapers, news shows, radio stations, billboards, and so forth. Although they are highly focused geographically, local media reach a broad demographic base otherwise. Local media are very good for drawing attention to local companies and the products and services they offer, but they can fail to target specific benefit-oriented segments.

Your media placement decision must take into account the number of customers that have access to your products, along with the cost and effectiveness of the media. An advantage of local media is that you can place your ads only in markets where the product is available. There would be less waste than with national or regional media that provide exposure in markets not served. As your customer base becomes larger and more dispersed, larger-scale national media become more financially attractive.

You must compare the lower cost and lower precision of dispersed advertising with the higher cost and higher precision of tightly focused advertising. The former is a mass-marketing approach; the latter is a differentiated marketing strategy. You must evaluate the number of potential customers that could be exposed to your message versus the cost to deliver that message. A billboard might be very inexpensive, but the exposure is low. In contrast, an ad during the Super Bowl or the World Cup soccer finals might be very expensive, but the exposure to your target segment could be very high.

Frequency of Advertising

After selecting the right media for a particular market segment, you must decide how many times the ad will run. For example, *Time*, a weekly magazine, might be the preferred news magazine for a given segment. Do you run the ad once a month or once a week? Can we say anything about how often a message is presented and its effectiveness?

We might imagine that the response function for exposure to a message looks like the S-shaped curve in Exhibit 6.11.

That is, low exposure might have little effect on the awareness, interest, or desire to purchase because it just does not cross the threshold of memorability. As the frequency of exposure increases, so does its effect on the target population. On the other hand, it is possible to overexpose and run the message too often. If the same ad is run over and over, people may discount the message, become exasperated by its repetition, or simply tune it out altogether. Advertisers sidestep boring their audience by varying the content of ads. An ad might run every week in *Time*, but with the content changed periodically so the delivery is fresh.

Another tactic is to distribute advertising across multiple outlets in the same category. For example, you might advertise in both *Time* and *Newsweek*. While some of the people who read *Time* will also read *Newsweek*, each magazine is likely to have its own set of unique readers who are in your target market.

Keep in mind as well that your target customers are exposed to many different media outlets. They may read news, financial, and sports magazines. They might also watch TV news networks or drama shows late at night. They might watch wrestling or NASCAR racing. As you expand your budget, consider more than the highest-rated outlet. Exposure in multiple contexts will increase the probability of the message getting through the clutter of the media and the customer's natural defenses against advertising.

Exhibit 6.12 suggests that varying the message and the outlet is wise. That is, before you reach the point of negative returns for having saturated the outlet with your message, you might try multiple messages and media in order to keep your message fresh. Each new message and outlet will have its own response function such as Exhibit 6.12. The goal is to work at the inflection point on each curve (just before diminishing returns set in) in order to maximize your advertising impact.

As a general rule, the more often you advertise, the more likely you will move a potential customer through the awareness, interest, decision, and selection sequence. However, this rule has three limitations:

1. Additional insertions in the same media with the same message will eventually result in diminishing returns.

2. The ads must be on target to be effective.

3. Your advertising will be judged against the quality and quantity of advertising of your competition; if your competi-

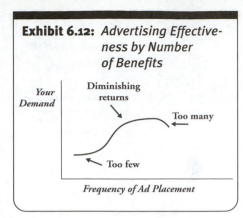

Exhibit 6.12: Advertising Effectiveness by Number of Benefits

tion does a better overall job than you do, it will capture a larger share of the market.

Advertising Message

The formulation of the advertising message is critical to the campaign. It flows from the goal of the campaign, the media selected, and the mix of other messages and media employed at the same time. We will focus on the creation of a single ad, a print ad for a magazine. The principles presented here apply to multiple messages and media.

As we discuss the process of ad design, we will concern ourselves with only three key dimensions:

• What to say in the ad.
• How much to say in the ad.
• The priority of the content.

For illustration purposes, let's assume you have been assigned to create a print advertisement for a national magazine, and you have hired an ad agency to help you. The advertising agent assigned to you is skilled in the mechanics of copy preparation and media placement. She also has access to the creative talents of copywriters, graphic designers, photographers, models, and so forth. While the ad agency will know more about how to deliver a message, we would assume that you know more about what message to deliver. You must provide the agency with the content of the advertisements and decide on the message or theme to convey. To assist the advertising agency, you must select and prioritize the messages in your ad. The ad agency will take your guidelines and create an attractive advertisement that conveys the intended message.

If you are unsure about how advertisements are designed, try studying ads in almost any print media such as *Time*, *USA Today*, or the *Financial Times*. Ads have a multifaceted message: Several major and minor points are addressed in the ad. These points highlight needs of the consumer or benefits of the product or company.

You can almost rank order the different points made in the ad by the size of type and their placement on the page (i.e., large bold letters at the top versus small letters in the lower right). There is probably some key benefit that gets top billing. There is likely to be some image that portrays customers in a use situation. The picture probably also illustrates the benefit or value the customer would like to achieve. The ad probably includes a product or company name and logo. All of these factors combine to create a message to a targeted audience.

Customers Buy Benefits, Not Features, So Promote Benefits

It is easy to get excited about new features, especially if you have worked hard to create them. You have probably seen ads for the processing speed of a new Intel microprocessor, the added horsepower in a Mercedes engine, the additional inches between the seats on an American Airlines airplane, or the placement of additional drop boxes for Federal Express package pickup. These are all features, not benefits. Customers buy the benefits of these features.

Let's recast these features into benefits. More processing speed can help users (1) be more productive because they can do the same work in a shorter time or (2) do more interesting work because they can tackle bigger problems that have been unsolvable in the past. More legroom on an airplane might allow a customer to (1) arrive more rested or less stressed or (2) carry an additional item on the plane and thus avoid checking baggage and the long wait for baggage claim at the end of the trip. Additional shipping locations might mean the customer can (1) work a little longer on a project to fine-tune it, (2) be less likely to miss shipping an important package that could affect the life of the company or his career, or (3) arrive home a little early and spend more time with his kids.

Your ads must stress the value to the customer of any new gadget, service, or promotion. If you choose to emphasize features, make sure you also communicate the benefits those features provide.

Prioritizing Benefits in an Ad

Not all ad messages have equal appeal or importance to every target segment. The

benefit "slim rugged design to make the PC easy to travel with" might attract the traveler segment but not the Mercedes and work-horse segments. The benefit "high resolution monitor to facilitate detailed work on images" might appeal to the Mercedes and innovator segments but not other segments.

Among those benefits that appeal to a given segment, some benefits will have a stronger draw than others. The traveler segment would be drawn to "slim rugged design for easy travel," "easy to use to reduce stress," and "fast Internet connection to save time and be more productive." But which one would have the most appeal? And so forth? The goal for the advertiser is to infer the relative importance of each benefit to a target segment. Those that have the greatest importance should be given the highest priority in the ad design.

To help visualize the effect of ordering benefits, let's use font size to indicate the relative importance of the benefits within the ad. Consider the benefits in an ad for a personal computer in **Exhibit 6.13**. This example illustrates that the last few benefits in the list will probably not be read or remembered with any clarity.

How Much to Say in an Ad

One of the challenges of designing ads is knowing when to stop to avoid crowding everything into one ad. For example, in computer-related advertisements, you will frequently find seven, eight, or nine benefits or features in a single ad. To be safe, the designer probably included anything that might remotely appeal to the segment. But more is not always better. (See **Exhibit 6.14**.) Who will read an ad filled with so much detail? With so many benefits, the ad can easily exceed the point of readability

and persuasion. Ads filled with clutter are less effective. It is your job to decide which benefits to include in what order. The best ads might have little text and a focused message. It might be better to design multiple ads with multiple messages rather than put everything into one.

Scoring an Ad

Ad agencies try to evaluate the effectiveness of their ads before placing them in the media to determine potential problems and optimize the ad's design before a substantial amount of money is spent in media placement. Often, agencies will present an ad to a group of potential customers to obtain feedback on the message and method of delivery. The agency might show customers a number of ads and ask them to tell about

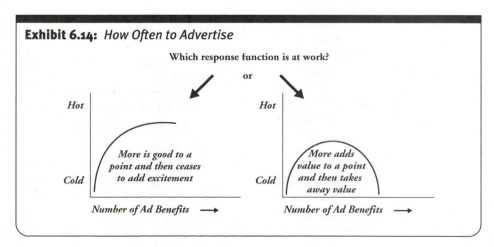

Exhibit 6.14: *How Often to Advertise*

Which response function is at work?

or

Hot

Cold

More is good to a point and then ceases to add excitement

Number of Ad Benefits →

Hot

Cold

More adds value to a point and then takes away value

Number of Ad Benefits →

their impression of the product being promoted and which ads they like best.

How do customers make decisions about which ad they like best? We might imagine that the customers consider the importance of benefits featured in an ad and how strongly each benefit is communicated. Let's assume all possible benefits can be scored from 0 (benefit is not important) to 10 (benefit is very important). Let's also assume that the strength of the communication can vary from 0 (not communicated) to 1.0 (strongly conveyed).

We know the importance of the benefit is different for different customers, so we have to guess at the importance based upon our market research. In contrast, the strength of the communication depends largely on the ad agency and the priorities set by the sponsor. More or less, we have control over this part of the outcome.

With these conditions in mind, the model for scoring the effectiveness of an ad might look such as this:

Ad effectiveness $j =$

$\sum_i^n$ benefit i importance $\times$ communication strength i

Where n is the set of benefits contained in ad j

Let's apply this model to the ad illustrated in Exhibit 6.13. Recall that the size of type indicates how strongly the benefit is communicated in the ad. The larger the font, the stronger the communication. Assuming that the ad agency gives the most important benefits the highest priority, the order probably also indicates the importance of the benefit. See **Exhibit 6.15** for the way the ad agency evaluated the sample ad data.

The strategy in this ad is to draw the reader in by featuring low price and then get her to realize the product also offers ease of use and comfort. These first three benefits are assumed to be the most important. If the reader commits to reading the rest of the ad, she discovers the computer is also fast and has software applications that meet the customer's needs (also illustrated by the picture placed in the ad). Finally, readers will want to know the name of the product so they can look for it when buying a computer the next time.

You could vary which benefits are placed in the ad and their order. Obviously, you would want to include important benefits and give the highest priority to the most important of the important benefits, but it is not so easy to get an ad right. Let's

assume that the customer perceives the elements in the ad in Exhibit 6.13 as is shown in **Exhibit 6.16**.

In this case, the value of the ad is perceived to be much lower than anticipated by the creators. The ad is rated lower because customers perceived the importance of benefits and the strength of communication to be lower than the designers planned.

This example illustrates how critical it is to understand the value of different benefits to the customer. If the designer knew the true importance of each benefit, the priority and communication strength could have been substantially changed to create a more effective ad. "Ease of use—reduce stress" would have been given top billing, and perhaps "fast—save time" would not have been mentioned at all.

This second reading of the ad also illustrates the value in understanding how strongly a benefit or theme is actually received by the potential customer. If the designer knew how poorly certain benefits were communicated, the design would have been adjusted to improve the strength of communication in these areas. If the ad designer had better knowledge of what is important to customers and greater control over the strength of the message, the ad might be designed as shown in **Exhibit 6.17**.

You might argue to increase the strength of communication for all benefits. You might even suggest that every point should be communicated at the highest strength. But imagine the effect of the ad if everything in it was shouting at you. You probably would not pay attention to anything. An ad is like a painting that draws your eye first to one point and then to

---

Exhibit 6.15: *How the Ad Was Envisioned by the Agency*

Benefit	Importance to Customer	Strength of Communication
Low price—save money	9	0.9
Easy to use—reduce stress	8	0.8
Designed for comfort—more productive	8	0.7
Fast—save time	7	0.6
Office software—do necessary work	7	0.5
Picture office workers—productive, less stress	6	0.4
Name of product—product loyalty	5	0.3

Thus, we can score the above ad as follows:

Ad Effectiveness

$= 9 \times 0.9 + 8 \times 0.8 + 8 \times 0.7 + 7 \times 0.6 + 7 \times 0.5 + 6 \times 0.4 + 5 \times 0.3$
$= 8.1 + 6.4 + 5.6 + 4.2 + 3.5 + 2.4 + 1.5$
$= 31.7$

Exhibit 6.16: *How the Customer Reads the Ad*

Benefit	Importance to Customer	Strength of Communication
Low price—save money	8	0.9
Easy to use—reduce stress	9	0.8
Designed for comfort—more productive	6	0.7
Fast—save time	3	0.5
Office software—do necessary work	5	0.4
Picture office workers—productive, less stress	6	0.2
Name of product—product loyalty	7	0.1

So the score this time would be:

Ad Effectiveness

$= 8 \times 0.9 + 9 \times 0.8 + 6 \times 0.7 + 3 \times 0.5 + 5 \times 0.4 + 6 \times 0.2 + 7 \times 0.1$
$= 7.2 + 7.2 + 4.2 + 1.5 + 2.0 + 1.2 + 0.7$
$= 24.0$

Exhibit 6.17: *Redesigning the Ad*

Benefit	Importance to Customer	Strength of Communication
Easy to use—reduce stress	9	0.9
Low price—save money	8	0.8
Name of product—product loyalty	7	0.7
Designed for comfort—more productive	6	0.7
Picture office workers—productive, less stress	6	0.6
Office software—do necessary work	5	0.5
Fast—save time	3	0.4

This ad design would be scored as follows:

Ad Effectiveness

$= 9 \times 0.9 + 8 \times 0.8 + 7 \times 0.7 + 6 \times 0.7 + 6 \times 0.6 + 5 \times 0.5 + 3 \times 0.4$

$= 8.1 + 6.4 + 4.9 + 4.2 + 3.6 + 2.5 + 1.2$

$= 30.9$

Exhibit 6.18: *Advertising Impact Also Depends on What Competitors Do*

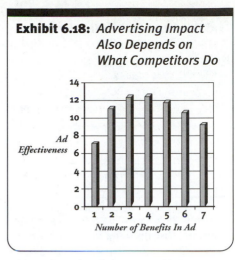

other parts. A good artist controls how you look at the painting in order to achieve the desired effect. The same can be said for an ad; the designer wants to take you into the message along a certain path in order to create a convincing argument.

So how does the number of benefits play into ad creation? Let's assume that each additional benefit detracts just a little from the overall impact of the message. As we add benefits, we add to the weight of the message but also to its clutter, which diminishes the effectiveness of the message. If we wanted to express the negative effect of ad clutter on the total score of an ad, we could take the earlier formula and add an exponent that reduces effectiveness for each additional benefit:

Ad effectiveness $j =$

$(\Sigma_{i}^{n}$ benefit i importance $\times$ communication strength $i)^{\text{clutter elasticity}}$

Where n is the set of benefits contained in ad j.

clutter elasticity $= 1.0 -$ number of benefits $\times 0.05$

(educated guess)

If we score our ad redesign taking clutter into account, we get:

Ad effectiveness $= 30.9^{0.65} = 9.3$

As the score suggests, the effect of clutter greatly reduces the effectiveness of the ad.

You might wonder what the optimal number of benefits is given the knowledge of benefit importance, strength of communication, and clutter elasticity. With the preceding formula, it is possible to plot the impact of each added benefit to the total score. In **Exhibit 6.18**, we have plotted the scores for the ad redesign assuming differ-ent numbers of benefits in the ad. The first bar indicates how the ad would be scored if only the first benefit was included in the ad. Bar two shows the score if only the first two benefits were included in the ad, and so forth. We can see that maximum effectiveness occurs when only the top four benefits are included in the ad. After that, the weight of including another benefit is counterbalanced by the addition of more clutter in the message. Thus a shorter, more focused ad would be more persuasive.

We might imagine that the effect of ad clutter will vary by segment. Probably the most adventuresome segment—innovators—would be happy to read detailed ads in order to learn as much as possible about a product. On the other hand, cost-cutter and workhorse segments might be discouraged from reading past the first point if there is too much information in an ad. Thus, we would adjust the clutter exponent to reflect the tolerance or appeal of additional information in an ad.

The effect of an ad will also vary by medium. Print media allow the greatest detail or number of benefits. In contrast, you would be more limited with 30-second TV commercials; 30-second radio spots would be even more limiting. With these media, you need to keep the message very focused. As we move to nonprint and outlets of shorter duration, we would need to increase the ad clutter coefficient to reflect the limitations inherent in the medium for communicating much information.

Knowing how an ad might be interpreted by a customer can be very helpful. Obviously, it is best to include the most important benefits. The temptation to keep adding benefits hoping to hit on some "hot" button in the consumer's mind should be tempered by the realization that more could be less.

If you can learn to think along these lines, you should be able to multiply the effect of your advertising expenditures. Even modest improvements in ad design can greatly extend your advertising expenditure. Suppose an ad could be rated from 0 to 100 in terms of its persuasive effectiveness. A 60 rating would be like getting 60 percent of the effectiveness of the ad or getting 60 cents on the advertising dollar. By improving an ad's rating from 60 to 90, your advertising effectiveness jumps by 50 percent ([90−60]/60). This is like getting 90 cents on the dollar. If you design more effective messages, you may not need to advertise as frequently to have the same effect, so you can save advertising money for other promotional activities that provide a greater marginal return.

DISTRIBUTION AND SALES MANAGEMENT

The final major element of your marketing strategy is distribution, the way you get your goods to your final customer. If good products, good prices, and good advertising create demand, then good distribution creates sales. Thus, the best advertising promoting the best products at the best prices will result in nothing if customers do not have the opportunity to buy. Your market strategy should consider the intensity of distribution and the management of salespeople.[5]

Sales Channel

It is said that the three most important factors in retailing are location, location, and location. You could say that the three most

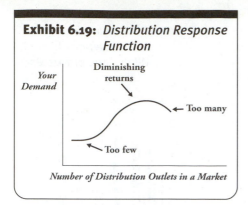

Exhibit 6.19: *Distribution Response Function*

Your Demand

Diminishing returns ↘

← Too many

↗ Too few

Number of Distribution Outlets in a Market

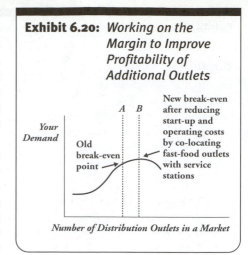

Exhibit 6.20: *Working on the Margin to Improve Profitability of Additional Outlets*

Your Demand

A B

Old break-even point

New break-even after reducing start-up and operating costs by co-locating fast-food outlets with service stations

Number of Distribution Outlets in a Market

important factors in creating sales are distribution, distribution, and distribution. There is no question that demand is directly driven by the number and quality of distribution outlets. The more contact points you have with your customers, the more opportunity they will have to buy. If there are no distribution outlets, there will be very little demand (in most cases). If one sales outlet will create a certain level of demand, two outlets should create even more, but does this logic hold indefinitely? If you keep adding distribution outlets, will demand increase with each additional outlet?

Most marketing theorists believe that the market response follows an S-shaped curve. (See **Exhibit 6.19**.) That is, when there are very few distribution points, additional outlets will cause demand to increase disproportionately. The function reflects a belief that there must be a certain number of sales outlets in a market in order to reach a critical mass and that there is synergy in having more than a few.

As the number increases, total demand is expected to continue to increase, but at a lower rate. It becomes increasingly more difficult for the additional channel partners to find new customers and persuade them to buy.

At some point, total demand will peak and then begin to decline with additional sales outlets. Demand begins to decline when there are so many distribution points in a market that they begin to get in each other's way and even compete for the same customers. Given this response function, what is the right number of channel outlets? The answer again lies in the marginal cost/marginal revenue line of thinking.

The usual strategy in selecting channel partners is to begin with those that promise the greatest opportunity for sales and profits. In any industry, it is easy to spot the largest distributor, broker, wholesaler, retailer, and so on. Who could do business

in groceries without selling to Kroger or Safeway in the United States, Loblaws-Superstore in Canada, or Carrefour in Europe? For consumer electronic goods, you would want to sell through Circuit City, Best Buy, or Wal-Mart. For machine shops, you would have to consider selling through Ingersoll International or Drake Atwood Tool and Supply Inc.

The primary outlets are easy targets. As you move to secondary and tertiary channels, the decision becomes more complex. One of the large consumer electronics firms applied activity-based costing to prune its channel outlets. The big buyers were easily identified as worthy channel outlets. A very large part of the supplier's volume was sold through just a few resellers. In contrast, the mom and pop neighborhood appliance store accounted for the largest number of channel customers but the smallest share of revenues and profits. When all the costs and revenues were properly accounted for, this part of the market was just not economical. As a result, management refocused the firm's selling efforts from the small neighborhood outlets to its top retail accounts. The intermediate-size appliance stores were also financially attractive.

Where we find many suppliers reducing the number of channel partners in order to provide better support and supply chain management (see J. Thomas Mentzer's chapter), others are continuing to expand their distribution options. The classic example is the beverage industry. You can buy a soft drink in any supermarket, convenience store, discount store, and restaurant in the developed world. You can also buy soft drinks in almost every school and office building in the United States and Canada. If you want something to drink, Pepsi and Coca Cola do not want you to have to walk very far to find their beverages. In fact, the people at Coke's headquarters speak of "share of belly" instead of share of market. They consider every other beverage, including water, to be their competitor; if they can place a beverage within easy reach, they are betting you will choose a flavored beverage over water most of the time. In case they are wrong, they will even sell you bottled water.

We also see firms such as McDonald's, Kentucky Fried Chicken, and Subway expanding distribution in areas where the economics did not previously justify an outlet. Over the decades they have continued to reduce the distance between

fast-food outlets so that we all can easily buy their products. Every time they add a new store to a market, it makes it easier for people in the area to buy, and they do buy as a result of this convenience. Yet they also take away some business from nearby outlets, cannibalizing some of their existing business.

What is most interesting is that these fast-food restaurants have found a way to reduce the marginal cost so that marginal revenue does not have to be so great to justify a new outlet. They are co-locating with service stations and convenience stores so they can substantially reduce their fixed and variable costs because they share many expenses, including the cost of the building, land, utilities, parking, and so forth, and each one serves as a magnet for the other.

Let's think about this strategy in terms of our response functions. In **Exhibit 6.20**, we have the S-shaped response curve for new sales outlets in a market. The dotted line A represents the previous break-even point for new sales outlets. By finding ways to reduce the start-up and operating costs via co-location, these businesses are able to shift the break-even point upward to line B. This is a powerful lesson. When the marginal cost of the next distribution outlet exceeds the marginal revenue, it is probably time to look for ways to reduce the costs, just as these restaurant chains did.

Shifting the Demand Curve

The S-shaped demand curve is assumed to be static for any given set of market conditions and marketing tactics; if all other things are equal, demand will follow the S-shaped curve described.

However, all other things do not need to be static. As noted in the last section, you

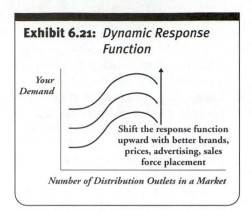

Exhibit 6.21: Dynamic Response Function

Your Demand

Shift the response function upward with better brands, prices, advertising, sales force placement

Number of Distribution Outlets in a Market

can work on the cost side of the equation in order to make marginal distribution options profitable. You can also work on the demand side so that the marginal revenue improves as well. You can shift the S-shaped demand curve upward by designing better products, offering a wider assortment, managing salespeople more effectively, selling at lower prices, and presenting better advertising. (See **Exhibit 6.21.**)

The touchtone phone, the cordless phone, and now the cell phone were successful in shifting the demand curve upward for the telecommunications industry. In the PC industry, Microsoft's Windows 95 caused the demand curve to shift upward. The jumbo jet shifted the demand curve upward for the airline industry. There is hope that the new digital television will shift the demand curve upward in the television sector, just as color and stereo sound did earlier. The greater reliability and more comfortable designs of the Japanese and European car makers shifted their demand curves upward in the United States.

The assortment of products offered for sale also has a direct impact on the demand in a geographic market. The addition of a breakfast menu shifted the demand curve upward for fast-food restaurants. McDonald's, in particular, is constantly exploring new menu options to attract more and a greater variety of customers. Every time it successfully adds a new item, it shifts the demand curve upward. As a result, the trading area that can sustain a profitable outlet shrinks, and the company can add more distribution points, creating even more demand.

Most buyers like variety in products and prices. Their needs are varied, and when one model might not meet their needs, another could. Thus, providing customers a portfolio of products can help shift the demand curve upward. The best example is Dell Computers. Customers can essentially design their own product on the Web. Giving customers exactly what they want has made Dell one of the best technology firms on the market.

In the trade, having a complete assortment of products to meet a variety of customer needs is called *category dominance*. Toshiba dominates the laptop market, Siemens dominates the medical equipment market, Mattel dominates the toy market, and *Marketplace* dominates the business simulation market.

Like the number of distribution outlets, the market's response to product selection is believed to follow an S-shaped curve. That is, when a supplier offers only one or two products for sale, additional products will cause demand to increase disproportionately. It is assumed that customers would prefer to do business with a supplier that has an assortment of products, not a limited offering. As the number of products offered increases, total demand will continue to increase but at a slower rate. At some point, total demand will peak and then actually begin to decline with additional products. Demand begins to decline when there are so many products on the market that they begin to compete with each other and cannibalize each other's demand. In practical terms, too large a selection will burden the customers as they try to sort out the differences in benefits from one design to the next.

There is a genuine reluctance to have many products on the market. Part of the hesitation is the difficulty in managing multiple products and real capacity constraint issues. Economies of scale and changeover issues can also pose a serious obstacle to profitability. Still, the market is more responsive to a wider selection of products than a narrower one. The challenge then is to reduce the costs associated with multiple products and to make it easier for customers to sort through the options so that they find (or build) the product that meets their particular needs. For customers, it is not the assortment that attracts but the ability to easily satisfy their needs.

The upward shifting of the demand curve can occur as a result of many small marketing decisions that add up to substantial change. Take, for example, sales force management. Salespeople are needed whether the firm sells directly to the end user or indirectly through a channel of distribution. Procter & Gamble (P&G) sells its products through a vast network of wholesalers and retailers, hardly ever coming into direct contact with an end customer. P&G employs a small army of salespeople to call on its channel customers of all sorts, located everywhere. There is hardly a supermarket, convenience store, or drug store in the developed world that does not sell P&G products. Somehow, all of these channels must be actively recruited, maintained, and expanded.

Market demand is directly impacted by the presence of salespeople. If there are no salespeople, there will be very little demand (in most cases), but having many salespeople is probably not productive either. Again, the S-shaped curve is probably at work, and marginal analysis is required to determine the optimum number. It makes sense to keep adding salespeople until the marginal cost equals the marginal profit.

Even the reallocation of salespeople may cause the demand curve to shift upward. If your salespeople are assigned to different segments, geographic markets, or distribution channels, you can analyze the marginal return of the last salesperson in each target market. Activity-based costing applied to markets or customer groups would provide similar valuable information. If one customer group is outperforming others, it suggests that additional salespeople should be assigned. These salespeople could be new hires or reallocated from markets that are not performing as well.

There are many other ways to help shift the demand curve upward via your sales force, including better training, sales tools, and incentives. Professional training programs can help salespeople develop teamwork, interpersonal, presentation, negotiation, or proposal-writing skills. Demonstration kits ensure a professional presentation of your products and services that is standardized across salespeople, regions, and products.

Salespeople are strongly motivated by financial incentives. You can channel their energies toward a specific group of customers or a specific set of products by offering commissions, bonuses, and contests. If a product is especially profitable, the salespeople can be challenged to spend even more time selling that product.

Exhibit 6.22 illustrates the relative impact and duration of various types of programs designed to help shift the demand curve up via your sales staff. The professional training and sales tools such as demonstration kits are modest demand stimulators but have a relatively long payback period. In contrast, bonuses and contests provide a

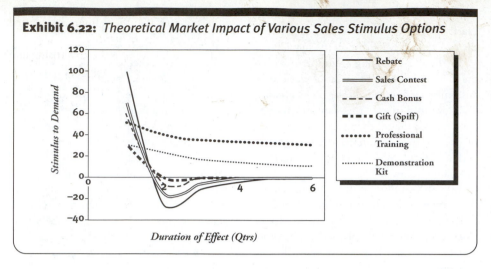

Exhibit 6.22: *Theoretical Market Impact of Various Sales Stimulus Options*

Legend:
- Rebate
- Sales Contest
- Cash Bonus
- Gift (Spiff)
- Professional Training
- Demonstration Kit

Y-axis: *Stimulus to Demand* (−40 to 120)
X-axis: *Duration of Effect (Qtrs)*

---

short-term spike in demand, often borrowing sales from the future.

As previously argued, most markets are price sensitive. In case after case, we have seen the demand curve shift upward dramatically as the overall market price dropped. Henry Ford demonstrated this with the automobile, and we have seen it with calculators, cell phones, computers, blood-testing equipment, CAT scanning equipment, and computer-aided design equipment, to name just a few. Essentially, falling prices put a desired good within the financial reach of more and more customers.

Being the low-cost provider within a segment is also one way to shift the demand curve upward. Another option is to provide a portfolio of products at different price points. Thus, the price-sensitive customer within a segment will be just as likely to find the desired product as the performance-driven customer. And, of course, there are many other pricelike incentives that stimulate potential customers to buy.

Perhaps the most pervasive approach to shifting the demand curve upward is advertising. Recognizing that it takes time to develop truly new and better products and that price is not what most suppliers like to compete on, advertising is an attractive option to expand the market base by exposing more potential customers to the want-satisfying characteristics of a product or service.

The logic is compelling. If there are potential customers who do not know about you, are not convinced that you can meet their needs, do not know where to buy your products, or simply have forgotten how good you are, then you can move the demand curve upward by providing informative and persuasive information.

The goal is to change the way people think and, thus, their propensity to buy (assuming you do have the right product at the right price).

The important point of this discussion is that there are many options to improve the balance in the marginal revenue/marginal cost comparison. Improvements on either side of the equation can result in expanded opportunities for distribution and, thus, sales.

MARKETING OVER THE LIFE CYCLE OF A PRODUCT

Where a product is in its life cycle can greatly influence the relative efficacy of marketing tactics and thus its place in the marketing strategy. Philip Kotler has prepared an excellent summary of product life cycle characteristics, objectives, and strategies. **Exhibit 6.23**, an adaptation of Kotler's model, indicates which marketing tactics tend to have stronger response functions at each stage of market development.

In the early stages of a market, the emphasis is on creating the right product (which can require multiple redesigns), generating awareness of the new solution, and encouraging customers to try it. Product design, advertising, and promotion dominate relative to product assortment, prices, and distribution. Price can be less important if consumers think a new product can satisfy some unmet or poorly met need.

In the growth phase, the goal is to maximize sales volumes via more intensive distribution, large-scale advertising campaigns, and a broader assortment of products with multiple price points. Marketers are much more aware of the market's response functions in this phase, and they employ many tactics to stimulate growth.

In the maturity phase, competitive pressures play a greater role in shaping demand and marketing tactics. Demand is no longer rising, and so there is greater competition for available demand. The market is relatively knowledgeable and can readily compare products and prices. To better serve the market, build market share, and fight competitive pressures, suppliers engage in microsegmentation, yielding a wider assortment of products and prices. Advertising shifts from building awareness to highlighting the relative advantages of one product over another or maintaining product recog-

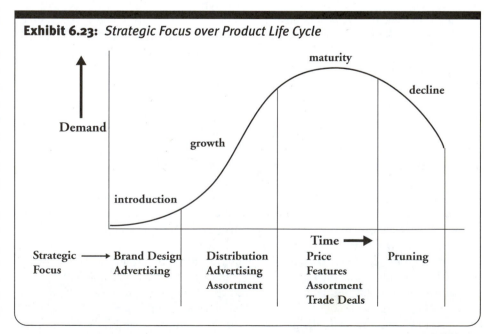

Exhibit 6.23: *Strategic Focus over Product Life Cycle*

Demand vs. Time curve showing: introduction, growth, maturity, decline

| Strategic Focus → | Brand Design Advertising | Distribution Advertising Assortment | Price Features Assortment Trade Deals | Pruning |

nition. Trade promotions become more important as suppliers fight for shelf space. Further expansion of distribution is limited because the marginal revenue of additional outlets becomes fairly thin.

During the decline phase, the goal is to trade on the built-up equity of the product. The product line is streamlined to only the most profitable models, advertising is scaled back, and distribution is reduced to the most profitable, or willing, outlets. Prices tend to weaken in an effort to stimulate demand, but profits can still be good because expenses are reduced.

CONCLUSION

A marketing strategy is a plan of action, a series of interconnected tactics purposely organized to be executed in a particular order over time in order to achieve specific goals. Formulating and executing an effective marketing strategy requires a keen understanding of the market's many response functions and how to exploit them to your advantage.

Many of the tactics discussed in this chapter were at play in the introduction of Hanes' L'eggs pantyhose in the early 1970s, which serves as an example of great marketing strategy. *Business Week* wrote a brief review of the strategy at the time (reprinted in **Exhibit 6.24**). Let us see what we can infer about the Hanes strategy and how its marketing executives were successful in applying the market response functions to the selection and deployment of their tactics to achieve their market objectives.

The strategic planning process for L'eggs began with a careful analysis of the market. The executives made several important discoveries. First, women primarily wanted to "look good." They also wanted convenience. As more and more women entered the work force during the late 1960s and early 1970s, their time became limited. Women did not, therefore, have much time for shopping for good hosiery at department stores. Hanes also discovered that women were willing to buy health and beauty aides from supermarkets, drugstores, and other convenience stores, yet pantyhose were not selling well in these same stores. The problem was that the quality did not meet the customers' requirements, failing to satisfy the primary value desired—looking good. Even at deep discounts, they did not sell.

Hanes had a potential solution to the pantyhose problem. A new method had been developed to make pantyhose that allowed the material to expand and contract around the natural contours of a woman without changing its look (the apparent density of the fabric). Hanes could now create pantyhose that consistently provided the value, "good looks." What is more, one size would fit many different women. (Hence the slogan, "One size fits all.")

At issue was how to market the new pantyhose through supermarkets, drugstores, and convenience stores in order to deliver on the other desired benefit—saving time. The objective was to profitably market the new pantyhose through new channels of distribution. Here is what the company did.

First, Hanes decided to create a distinctive brand name. Another low-profile brand would be lost in the crowd. Hanes had to overcome the bad experiences and impressions of pantyhose sold through these channels. Fortunately, the lack of brand recognition in these stores created a great opportunity for it to do this.

The name "L'eggs" was a clever play on words and attracted attention. It also led to a clever package, the white plastic egg. The egg was distinctive, attention getting, and easily recognized. It reinforced the brand name, reminded women about pantyhose, and had after-sale utility as storage and as a plaything for children (which helped to continuously remind mothers about L'eggs).

Hanes was a premium brand, and so L'eggs came with a premium price. The price reinforced the premium image.

Strong brand identity was developed with a $10 million introductory advertising campaign, spending more than double the rest of the industry. Hanes bought its way into the consumer's mind. It also came up with a clever advertising theme, "Our L'eggs fit your legs," and portrayed attractive women in roles and social situations consistent with the consumer's self-image. Everywhere, Hanes appealed to and reinforced the "look-good" value. And the advertising appeared everywhere women were likely to look—women's magazines, popular TV shows, the news.

Couponing was also very effective in encouraging women to try the brand. Many people love a bargain, and a time deadline on the coupon encourages early action. A 30 cent coupon also reduced the effective price of the brand so that it was more in line with the better brands sold through these outlets. It reduced the consumer's risk of trial. It allowed Hanes to keep the sticker price high with the implicit understanding that the coupon represented a temporary price reduction.

The combination of the advertising and couponing was a "pull" approach to marketing. The objective was to create a large volume of demand so as to pull the brand through the channel. If customers are asking for the brand, the retailer would be hard pressed to ignore the potential revenue.

Hanes also employed a push strategy, pushing the brand through the channel with various incentives. First, the pantyhose were sold on consignment. As a result, the retailer had no money tied up in inventory. Also, Hanes hired "route girls" to stock the shelves. Therefore, the retailer did not have to spend money on employees to order and stock the hosiery.

Hanes also guaranteed a $1,300 profit for just 2.5 square feet of space. Very few brands could generate this level of income, and so the competition for space was easily won. Finally, Hanes provided a very distinctive point of purchase display, the L'eggs Boutique, to help sell the merchandise. Its design reinforced the egg package and provided shelf space for hundreds of pairs of pantyhose in several colors. The push strategy complemented the pull strategy. Hanes created demand for millions of pairs of pantyhose and then had millions of pairs in the pipeline and stores.

To convince the retailer that the demand would be there, Hanes had to show that it was serious about creating demand. To this end, it armed its sales staff with a demonstration kit that dramatically documented large investments in the media. The retail buyers could see when the advertisements would hit *Good Housekeeping* or *Mademoiselle* or appear on "The Mary Tyler Moore Show" or the morning news. The buyers would also learn when the women in their territory would be blanketed with coupons and start showing up at the stores looking to redeem the coupons. All of these tactics encouraged the retailers to stock up in advance. As a consequence, the consumers found the merchandise in the stores when the ads and coupons stimulated them to go looking for L'eggs pantyhose.

These clever tactics led to many positive outcomes. The L'eggs boutique used only 2.5 square feet of retail space, but it was the best 2.5 square feet of space in the store—the end of an aisle. (An end-of-aisle display can result in a fivefold increase in sales compared to an aisle location.) This favorable location, in turn, helped Hanes achieve the sales and profit objectives for the store.

Exhibit 6.24: *Our L'eggs Fit Your Legs*

At 8:00 a.m. every Monday through Friday, 29-year old Joanne Miller climbs into a white Chevrolet van and drives around the Pocono Mountains countryside of upstate Pennsylvania delivering 5-inch high white plastic eggs to local supermarkets and drugstores. Dressed in a red, white, and blue hot pants uniform, and wearing tinted glasses and knee-high boots, Mrs. Miller is hardly ever taken for the local Easter Bunny. Store people know her instead as "route girl" for a national pantyhose manufacturer—"L'eggs," a new division of the $176 million Hanes corp. of Winston-Salem, N.C., which has kept the highly competitive splintered hosiery industry on the run for the last 24 months.

Joanne Miller and 450 other "route girls" around the country are part of the strong brand image that "L'eggs" has built up in the two years it has been in operation. The elongated white plastic displays which Joanne sets up to hold the supermarket egg packages also promote the image. "L'eggs'" heavy start-up investment and highly sophisticated distribution and control system was a substantial drain on Hanes's earnings for the first 18 months, but it has recently turned a profit. With $35 million in sales for 1971, "L'eggs" has climbed into first place as the largest selling brand of hosiery in supermarkets and drugstores scattered throughout the country.

An extremely secretive business, the $1.84 billion hosiery industry is filled with hundreds of small, medium, and large-sized companies selling some 600 different brands of stockings and pantyhose. Burlington Industries, Kayser-Roth, and Hanes—the top three manufacturers—all have well-known brand names, but extensive private labeling by department stores, discount operations, and more recently, supermarket and drugstore retailers, has swollen the number of hosiery brands in the marketplace and reduced their individual visibility.

NEW MARKET

The pantyhose boom in supermarkets started in early 1969 with the introduction of the Lady Brevoni brand by a leading manufacturer in West Germany. The pantyhose gave stores a margin of 40 percent on a low retail price of 79 cents and was shipped in ready-to-display cartons. "With that promotion, pantyhose became a commodity, not just a fashion item," a competitor notes. Says Ken Peskin, advertising manager of Supermarkets General Corp.: "Pantyhose has become a very big item for supermarkets. It's hardly a little rack in the corner anymore."

About the same time, Hanes Corp. hired 33-year old David E. Harrold, a former marketing man at General Foods Corp., to research how it could sell a newly designed one-size line of pantyhose to the lucrative supermarket and drugstore outlets. Up until this time, Hanes had been selling hosiery to department store outlets only. Hanes paid $400,000 for market research—a high price in the normally conservative hosiery industry. Harrold concluded that women were not particularly impressed by strong price promotion of hosiery in supermarkets and drugstores. And many were disgusted by the lack of uniform quality control for many private labels. "For a while, I always bought medium-tall in the same brand for 79 cents a pair," says Pat Sasha, a New Jersey social worker. "One week they sagged and bagged, the next week I could hardly sit down they were so tight."

Harrold also found that while hosiery and health and beauty aid products were introduced into supermarket outlets at approximately the same time—10 to 12 years ago—supermarkets got only 12 percent of hosiery sales in 1968, while sales of the top 20 health and beauty aid products in the same outlets had grown to 50 percent. With this background, Hanes decided it would gamble on a program geared to building brand loyalty and with ads emphasizing quality rather than price. The new "L'eggs" hosiery, at $1.39 a pair, costs at least 30 cents more than most pantyhose sold in supermarkets and drugstores.

In fact, private labeling has kept other pantyhose prices on a continuous downhill spiral in the last few years. For example, A & P has had price promotions offering private label brands at 39 cents a pair, Waldbaum's at three for $1, and Pathmark at 49 cents a pair.

The route girls helped advertise the brand by demonstrating it. More important, they ensured that the inventory was fresh so that customers would not be disappointed because the selection was depleted or the display was disorganized or dusty. Hanes knew the stock people in the store would be too busy to provide the level of care that it considered necessary.

Another advantage of the route girls was that they entered unit sales into a computerized inventory control system. This system provided the factory with nearly instant information on which colors were selling well and which were not. The information allowed the factory to adjust production in line with demand and keep the levels of unwanted inventory low and the shelves filled with the right selection.

Intensive distribution contributed to the success of route girls. Hanes wanted its pantyhose in virtually every supermarket, drugstore, or convenience store in a market. These stores are so intensely distributed in cities that most of them are only minutes apart. As a result, the route girls spent little unproductive time traveling from store to store and most of their time taking care of merchandise or working with the retailer. There was little wasted time.

The "one-size-fits-all" approach also made the route girl job easier. Consider, for example, a pantyhose assortment of four sizes and six colors. This would result in 24 SKUs (4 × 6). With only one size, there are only 6 SKUs. Think of the savings in store inventory, restocking time, and the size of the delivery vehicles needed to transport the inventory.

"One size fits all" had other advantages. It reduced the number of options that the consumer had to sort through as well as the possibility for error when she picked out her pantyhose. There were also substantial savings in the factory due to fewer changeovers and lower inventory levels.

Hanes' pricing strategy also worked to its advantage. The tactic of consignment selling provided more than a low price to the retailer. It gave Hanes control over the retail price so that it could not be discounted. When a store buys a good, it can set whatever price it chooses. It can discount goods even though that cheapens the brand name and could result in reduced market penetration.

Price control also helped Hanes maintain its intensive distribution goal. Some retailers would love to undercut smaller stores in order to attract more customers. As the smaller retailers lost customers, they would lose their incentive to carry the brand. As the number of resellers declined, the convenience of buying Hanes hosiery would decline, thus diminishing an important benefit to the consumer.

Finally, the premium price did more than reinforce the brand image and add profit to the bottom line; it paid for everything. Hanes spent $15,000,000 on advertising and coupons. It hired route girls and leased delivery trucks. It owned 100 percent of the inventory, and it was in virtually every supermarket, drugstore, and convenience store in the market. It bought a display for every store and promised $1,300 in profits to every store. None of this would have been possible without high margins. High margins generated high revenues that paid for high levels of product

Hanes, however, will not budge on the price it charges for "L'eggs." Says Walter Pilcher, product brand manager for "L'eggs," In Detroit—most discount-oriented city in the country—we have to police the retailers in order to maintain a fair-trade position. I have been called arrogant and stupid because we took our display out of one supermarket where the owner insisted on underpricing "L'eggs."

Says Harrold, who is now a Hanes Corporate vice-president: "We decided that to be successful, any new brand would have to establish a clear-cut identity—something on a par with Maxwell House Coffee or Tetley Tea."

"L'eggs'" subsequent hefty $10 million introductory advertising budget—double the amount spent by the total hosiery industry—neatly tied in its distinctive egg-shaped point-of-purchase display with newspaper and television ads using the slogan, "Our 'L'eggs' fit your legs." The company spent an additional $5 million on national consumer promotion, using introductory direct mail coupons worth 25 cents or 35 cents off on each "L'eggs" purchase. "We used classic consumer marketing techniques to build this brand image," says Robert Odear, who recently took Harrold's place as marketing manager for "L'eggs." "Our advertising," he adds, "took into consideration the fact that consumer brand awareness of hosiery was virtually nonexistent in supermarkets and drugstores, and that brand permanency had to be reinforced to the consumer and to the trade as well."

CONSIGNMENT

"L'eggs'" toughest job, though, was to convince the supermarket and drugstore chain retailers. "We had to trade off a past reputation with department stores into the supermarkets," says Harrold. "All we asked for was two and a half square feet of their store—that was less than everyone else." The key word, however, that sold retailers was "consignment." Typically, retailers buy inventory, but "L'eggs" is completely paid for by the manufacturer. The retailer makes no financial investment at all. Each store averages about $1,300 a year profit from a single "L'eggs" display, and he has no service costs since route girls do all the restocking and cleaning.

To overcome the out-of-stock and service problems that hurt other hosiery manufacturers, "L'eggs" opted for direct store delivery and hired an Atlanta-based management consulting firm, Executive Control Systems, to develop an information-gathering and control system. The ECS system that "L'eggs" now uses integrates all activities—from manufacturing to placement of the product in the store. When the first product assortment is provided on consignment, resupply is based on individual display units. The computerized control system coordinates manufacturing, warehouse distribution, retail inventory balance, sales and market analysis, billings and accounts. "With this system, we can optimize the route girl's workload and schedule her from week to week." says Joseph Neeley, director of administration for "L'eggs." Now selling in 75 percent of the major urban markets across the country, "L'eggs" expects to go completely national this year although executives admit that New York City, with its heavy auto and pedestrian traffic, presents distribution difficulties. "The thought of route girls parking and unloading on Manhattan streets causes my stomach to turn," says Odear.

Meanwhile, back on the road, Joanne Miller is busy fighting the Pocono's rainy, slippery roads, high winds ("It blows my 'L'eggs' away"), and the cookie men, milkmen, and meat men all trying to see store managers. But no matter what, she is always an enthusiastic salesgirl. "A few weeks ago it was down to about 5 degrees," says Joanne. "A woman stopped and asked me while I was unloading, 'What's so great about "L'eggs"?' Why, just look at the way they fit," answered Joanne, and obligingly rolled up her woolen slacks to display a baggy pair of gray long johns. "We both just stood there and roared," said Joanne. "It wasn't exactly a hard sell, but she bought a pair anyway."

---

quality, distribution, and promotion, which were needed to create the high demand Hanes was promising and needed—a truly self-reinforcing strategy.

Clearly, there was much more to the Hanes strategy than might meet the eye. Hanes recognized that it had two customers, the consumer and the channel. It developed a marketing strategy for each customer. Both strategies were well coordinated.

It is also clear that Hanes had multiple objectives. In addition to delivering a high-quality product that provided "good looks" and convenience, it set out to win the channel of distribution over to its way of thinking and marketing. It also had the less obvious objective of reducing its risks in dealing with the channel. Hanes sought to control shelf location, pricing, and inventory. This goal helped it to accomplish its other marketing goals.

Obviously, the current strategy for marketing L'eggs pantyhose is substantially different than the initial one. Competitors have entered the market, emulated the Hanes strategy, and improved upon it. The market has changed. Consumer needs have evolved, and retailers have become smarter in merchandising pantyhose and dealing with suppliers

We can look at the Hanes strategy in terms of its awareness and application of the market's many response functions. Hanes could see that the consumer market was elastic with regard to looking good, elastic with regard to time, and potentially inelastic with regard to price. If the company could help customers improve their looks and save time, the market would allow a premium price.

The promotion campaign employed many venues and messages, although only one major theme, "looking good." "Looking good" was the hot button that caught the consumer's attention. The messages were uncluttered in this respect.

Frequent advertising created tremendous awareness across the targeted segments, but the diversity of media and messages avoided saturation in any single outlet, and, thus, the downslope on the advertising effectiveness curve.

By creating a strong brand identity, Hanes was able to create a little monopoly for its L'eggs brand and thus price above the market. However, this was not true initially. Placement in convenience-oriented stores caused L'eggs to be placed in the evoked set of other brands sold through this channel. Hanes reduced the initial unfavorable price comparison by providing a temporary price reduction through couponing. Thus, the firm was able to play on the historical price sensitivity of the channel.

Hanes also found the response functions of the distribution channel. It provided zero cost, high profit, and little effort to the trade. Hanes came in strong on these tactics in order to counterbalance the historical negative image that hosiery had in the channel.

In conclusion, L'eggs is a great example of a well-thought-out and executed strategy. It demonstrates a clear understanding of the market's many response functions and how to exploit them. Moreover, the strategy was well coordinated over time, self-reinforcing, and clearly designed to achieve specific market objectives.

1   Hanssens, Parsons, and Schultz's textbook, *Market Response Models: Econometric and Time Series Analysis* (2001).

2. See also Robert J. Dolan, *Managing the New Product Development Process: Cases and Notes* (Reading, MA: Addison-Wesley, 1993).

3. Ibid. Conjoint analysis is an excellent tool for understanding trade-offs. Dolan presents a managerial discussion of conjoint analysis.

4. For a more in-depth discussion of these communication options and issues, consult Richard J. Semenik, *Promotion and Integrated Marketing Communication* (Cincinnati, OH: South-Western College Publishing, 2002).

5. For a comprehensive discussion of distribution channels, please see Anne Coughlan, Erin Anderson, Louis W. Stern, and Adel El-Ansary, *Marketing Channels,* 6th ed. (Upper Saddle River, NJ: Prentice Hall, 2001).

Chapter 7

Quality Function Deployment

Ivan Slimák
*Volkswagen Transmission
(Shanghai) Co.*

"Break down barriers between departments. People in research, design, sales, and production must work as a team to foresee problems of production and in use that may be encountered with the product or service."

Dr. W. E. Deming[1]

QUALITY FUNCTION DEPLOYMENT IN THE PAST AND TODAY

We will strive to achieve total customer satisfaction, ensuring that every encounter every customer has with Infiniti is positive. We will evaluate everything we do from our individual customer's point of view. We will build relationships which endure and thereby ensure customer loyalty.

—Infiniti Credo[2]

As early as the 1970s, Japanese companies began using an intricate system of matrices, charts, and tables in order to:

• Speed up design activities, both for products and for processes.

• Identify and prevent problems at early stages.[3]

• Coordinate quality-related activities on a companywide basis.[4]

This approach was called *hin shitsu ki no ten kai*. As with many Japanese phrases, an exact translation into English is impossible. Nevertheless, it has been translated as "quality function deployment," or QFD.

We can begin to understand QFD by comparing typical Japanese and American approaches to engineering changes for a new product, as shown in **Exhibit 7.1**. The classical approach,[5] which is typical in U.S. manufacturing, requires progressively more changes as the start of production approaches, and the changes continue during the first months or even a whole year into production while "the bugs are worked out." In contrast, the QFD approach used by Japanese manufacturers stimulates more changes in the early phases of product development, and then the number of changes decreases as the start of production approaches. By the time the product is ready to be launched, all required changes have been implemented.

Learning Objectives

This chapter explains the philosophy and basic ideas behind quality function deployment (QFD). By systematically addressing the following questions, we learn to apply QFD in a business environment:

• How can we be faster than the competition?

• How can we better satisfy customers?

• How can the company save money?

This approach benefits both the customer and the company.

Simply defined, QFD is a tool for the introduction and future improvement of new products (or services). The American Supplier Institute defines QFD as "a system for translating consumer requirements into appropriate company requirements at each stage, from research and product development to engineering and manufacturing/sales and distribution."[6]

Dr. W. E. Deming, late Massachusetts Institute of Technology professor, proposed a similar system in his 1950s lectures to top Japanese managers, which helped bring about dramatic improvements in Japanese industry. Deming's first principle for management is to "create constancy of purpose towards improvement of product and service, with the aim of becoming competitive, to stay in business, and to provide jobs."[7] The "old" approach used by many companies can be characterized as isolated silos, or chimneys, representing the separate

BEST-USE CORRELATIONS

Product design is a colossally important tactical decision. Many marketing, manufacturing, and distribution decisions flow from it. The right design decisions can lead to tremendous market share and profits. The wrong ones can prove very costly indeed. In *Marketplace*, decisions often involve tradeoffs.

Chapter 7 introduces you to an excellent tool for managing tradeoffs and matching features to benefits: *quality function deployment (QFD)*.

You Can Take the Short, Long Way or the Long, Short Way

In Q2, teams start the brand design process. Each team looks at customer needs, applications, and price points and tries to reason out what constitutes a winning brand. As Chapter 7 points out, quick approaches to brand design represent the long and expensive way to product success, ensuring an unsatisfactory market response and frequent revisions. If your team elects to put the QFD approach into practice, it will require more time to reach agreements on brand design, but over the life of the product, QFD will reduce error, revisions, and the expense of not getting things right from the start.

QFD Is How You Should Be Thinking

The beauty of QFD is that it forces teams to approach design possibilities systematically as you consider how the combinations of components can multiply or diminish the satisfying effect on the customer.

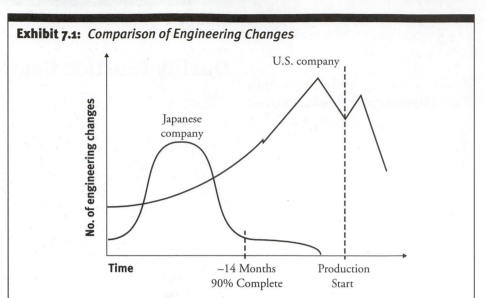

Exhibit 7.1: *Comparison of Engineering Changes*

Source: Adapted from *Quality Function Deployment: Implementation Manual for Three-Day Workshop,* American Supplier Institute. Reprinted with Permission of ASA.

departments or functions within a company. In the old approach, barriers exist between company departments, and each department is held responsible only for partial solutions. As markets become increasingly fragmented, this method of running a business becomes ineffective. As customers demand more and more individualized products, a manufacturer who wishes to be a global player must respond by being able to produce an increasing number of product options. General Motors, in effect, will have to become "Specific Motors."

The QFD process addresses issues not only of quality but also of engineering, manufacturing, and marketing. QFD helps to implement cross-functional product development by establishing simultaneous engineering teams (SETs). These teams represent a dramatically different approach to how departments can work together. In the traditional model (isolated silos), each department would strive for a local optimum, which would usually be in conflict with the goals of other departments or with those of the organization as a whole. For example, a sales department would benefit from a wide product range, while manufacturing would benefit from fewer products. SETs look for an optimum for the whole company, focused on the customer (see **Exhibit 7.2**).

In the early 1990s, U.S. auto manufacturers began to use SETs. When Ford Motor Company used SETs in introducing 4.6-liter engines at the Romeo Plant, the result was a reduction in the number of management levels from seven to four. This reduction improved not only communica-

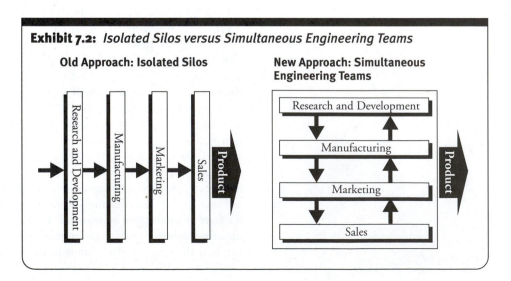

Exhibit 7.2: *Isolated Silos versus Simultaneous Engineering Teams*

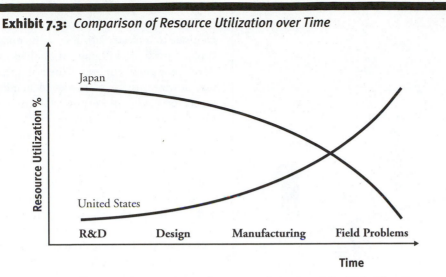

Exhibit 7.3: *Comparison of Resource Utilization over Time*

Source: Adapted from *Quality Function Deployment: Implementation Manual for Three-Day Workshop,* American Supplier Institute. Reprinted with Permission of ASA.

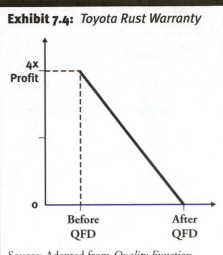

Exhibit 7.4: *Toyota Rust Warranty*

Source: Adapted from *Quality Function Deployment: Implementation Manual for Three-Day Workshop,* American Supplier Institute. Reprinted with Permission of ASA.

tion and decision making but also the overall cost effectiveness of the operation by increasing the proportion of value-added (car-building) personnel. Chrysler Corporation used the SET approach when developing the Vision and the Viper, reducing design changes by 30 percent. Moreover, development was accomplished with approximately 55 percent of the planned staff. For the new concept of simultaneous engineering, the company built the Chrysler Technology Center. Up to 7,000 employees work on new products, testing them in weather conditions ranging from Arctic freeze to desert dust and heat. Chrysler plans to reduce the development time of new models by one to three years.[8]

QFD devotes more resources to the early stages of product development, which significantly reduces the later resource requirements for manufacturing and field problem solving (such as customer complaints and warranty costs). The difference in use of resources over time between the U.S. and Japan is illustrated in **Exhibit 7.3**. Historically, the approach in U.S. manufacturing has just been to be the first to market with the product, but the consequences of neglecting the early stages of development are increased costs later in the form of high warranty costs, rebuilding manufacturing lines to handle additional product changes, recall actions, and even legal fees because of safety problems discovered in cars.[9] **Exhibit 7.4** illustrates how QFD helped Toyota eliminate warranty costs due to rust by preventing cars from rusting during the warranty period.

In today's competitive environment, market share is influenced by the ability to fulfill the criteria of quality, cost, and timeliness. The bottom line of these activities is productivity and profitability. According to a common notion, the problem with dissatisfied customers is that they complain. Actually, voiced complaints should be preferred to those kept silent because the voiced complaints provide the company with valuable feedback on how to improve. It is much worse to have dissatisfied customers who do not complain but who will just switch to the competition. This can happen without warning and can be the cause of a quick death for the company. Volkswagen Corporation is aware of this and explains in its training materials for manufacturing staff: "Quality is when the customer returns rather than the car."

We often hear another common notion, that the bigger wins over the smaller. In business, however, it is more often true that the quicker wins over the slower. A story told at a senior management conference of the Volkswagen Group illustrates this point. Mr. Lopez, a member of the board, warmed up the audience with the following story, which describes his philosophy of doing business:

> Each day the giraffe wakes up in the bush country. She knows that she must run faster than the lion in order to not be eaten. Each day the lion wakes up in the bush country. He knows that he must run faster than the giraffe in order to eat. Each day the lions and the giraffes wake up in the bush country. There is no difference, whether you are giraffe or lion.

The fact is that you must run faster and faster.

Mr. Lopez, a purchasing wizard and zealot of cost cutting and lean production, saved General Motors $7 billion with his improvement programs.[10]

One of the ways that Mr. Lopez was able to realize such huge savings was to begin product improvement at the early stage of product design. At this stage, the payoffs on the investments will be roughly 10 times more than investments made at the next stage, process design, and 100 times more effective than when production begins (see **Exhibit 7.5**). As the old maxim says, "A stitch in time saves nine." Such dramatic differences decide the winners and losers. For these reasons, quality assurance is moving from the manufacturing area to the product design area.

HOW CAN QFD HELP?

QFD can help to create the "constancy of purpose" that Dr. Deming describes in his first point for managers, to prioritize what to do and to find cost-effective ways to do it.[11] The QFD methodology moves from the often fuzzily defined wants of the customers to the more clearly defined production routines in four phases:

- Phase 1: Product planning
- Phase 2: Parts (materials) planning
- Phase 3: Process planning
- Phase 4: Production planning

Sometimes when the customer requires something very simple, the company comes up with complicated and poor solutions.

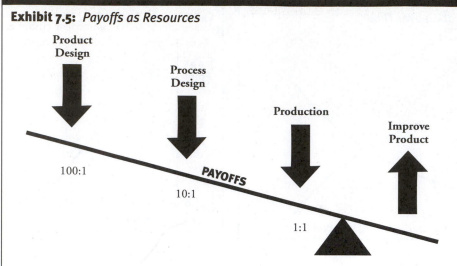

Exhibit 7.5: *Payoffs as Resources*

Product Design

Process Design

Production

Improve Product

100:1

10:1

PAYOFFS

1:1

Source: Adapted from *Quality Function Deployment: Implementation Manual for Three-Day Workshop,* American Supplier Institute. Reprinted with permission of ASA.

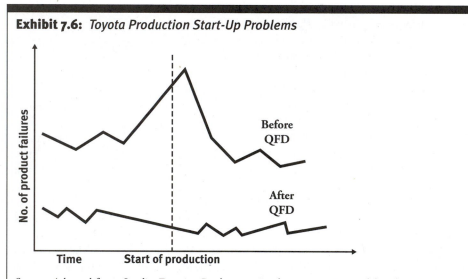

Exhibit 7.6: *Toyota Production Start-Up Problems*

No. of product failures

Before QFD

After QFD

Time

Start of production

Source: Adapted from *Quality Function Deployment: Implementation Manual for Three-Day Workshop,* American Supplier Institute. Reprinted with permission of ASA.

This problem is usually due to the conflicting goals of the isolated silos mentioned earlier. In such cases, results are unsatisfactory for both the customer and the company.[12] As a tool, QFD helps us to both translate customer requirements into product features and plan product research and development to enable effective future improvements. The main benefits of QFD are:

- **Fewer and earlier changes.** The changes are made in the planning stages and are thus less expensive. This is a vital move from being *reactive* to being *proactive*.
- **Time savings in development.** These can be up to 50 percent.
- **Fewer start-up problems.** The problems are solved upstream in the process (see

Exhibit 7.6). For example, Toyota reduced its start-up costs by 39 percent within seven years (see **Exhibit 7.7**).

- **Fewer field problems and reduced warranty claims.**
- **Improved documentation of the whole approach.** This results in a good base for future improvement, training of new employees, and quick know-how transfer within different locations of large companies.[13]

An example of engine development by Japanese companies in the 1980s illustrates how low-cost product changes can dramatically increase customer satisfaction.[14] In the 1970s, the Japanese were successful marketing small cars with small engines in the

United States, partly because of increased fuel prices. Assuming that oil prices would continue to increase, Japanese car manufacturers invested billions of dollars in developing small engines. When oil prices fell, however, the U.S. market demanded bigger cars with more powerful engines. One way to meet these demands would have been major design changes, such as adding more cylinders to the small four-cylinder engine. A major change such as this would have required extensive resources and time, both in development and in redesigning and retooling the manufacturing process.

Instead, the Japanese decided to increase the power of the basic four-cylinder engine by developing a few relatively simple features, which could be added to it. They replaced carburetors with fuel injectors, doubled the valves per cylinder from two to four, and added superchargers and turbochargers to get more power from the same basic engine. Customers were delighted with the small engines because they thought they had a "high-tech" car. Ironically, these new features had been available to manufacturers for a long time (four valves per cylinder since the 1920s and superchargers since the 1930s), but manufacturers had viewed them as being too expensive or complex for mass production. Introducing these features gave Toyota a four-year advantage over GM and changed Toyota's image from "low tech" to "high tech."[15]

This example shows a quick reaction to changed customer requirements. The customer requirements (or *whats*) changed when fuel consumption became less critical and customers wanted more powerful engines. The manufacturer's reaction was to add new features (or *hows*) to the engines to address those changed needs. The result was increased customer satisfaction and sales success for the new models.

FOUR BASIC PHASES OF QFD

You don't need a weatherman to know which way the wind blows.

—Bob Dylan, *Subterranean Homesick Blues*

QFD is a continuous process that helps to define the measurable objectives from product concept to production control. The philosophy presented in this chapter describes only the main ideas behind the first phase, product planning. The other QFD phases are more detailed but are still based on the same philosophy of refining the *whats*

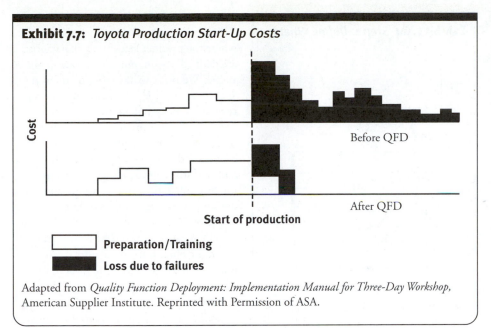

Exhibit 7.7: *Toyota Production Start-Up Costs*

Cost

Before QFD

After QFD

Start of production

☐ **Preparation/Training**

■ **Loss due to failures**

Adapted from *Quality Function Deployment: Implementation Manual for Three-Day Workshop*, American Supplier Institute. Reprinted with Permission of ASA.

Exhibit 7.8: Hows *Become* Whats *in Following Phases*

Phase 1	Product planning	**WHAT**	**HOW**		
Phase 2	Part planning		**WHAT**	**HOW**	
Phase 3	Process planning			**WHAT**	**HOW**
Phase 4	Production planning				**WHAT**	**HOW**

and *hows*. Although this chapter necessarily focuses on the tools of the QFD process, QFD itself is more than just charts. It is a philosophy that lies behind the processes of customer orientation (both external and internal) in the company. The charts are the tools to facilitate those processes.

In the following section, you will see and learn the steps for applying QFD charts to the first phase of product planning (see **Exhibit 7.8**). These steps can be applied similarly in the next phases. Generally, the *hows* from one phase will become the *whats* in the next phase, and, as always, measurable *hows* must be defined.

A detailed explanation of how to use QFD to define both customer requirements and design requirements follows. We will first discuss the basic QFD method and later introduce some extensions to the basic method. The basic QFD method can help you to organize your product design activities from the early stages of product design, including the features or characteristics that address customer desires.

The basic QFD chart consists of three elements: *what, how,* and *relationships*. The basic approach follows these steps:

1. Define *what*.
2. Define *how*.
3. Define *relationships* between *what* and *how*.
4. Analyze whether the *whats* are covered by *hows*.

Timing is everything. It can be deadly to repair your roof when a hurricane is tearing down your home. QFD can help a company anticipate the need for repairs before the storm strikes. Earlier we described QFD as an intricate system of matrices. Sometimes when people encounter the method for the first time, they regard it as overly complicated and are reluctant to try it. However, the ideas behind the method are relatively simple and easy to use.

Step 1. Define *What*

Your first step is to develop a list of customer requirements, or the *whats* of the equation. The *whats* are also called *the voice of the customer*. Customer requirements can be divided into three categories:

1. **Basic requirements.** These are expected by the customer in any case although the customer often does not even express

them. Not fulfilling any of the basic requirements leads to immediate customer dissatisfaction, loss of sales to a competitor's product, or customer complaints. In marketing they are called *dissatisfiers* because they lead to dissatisfaction when they are missing. For example, customers have come to expect that a new car will be equipped with safety belts and mirrors, although this has not always been true.[16]

2. **Performance requirements.** They can be expressed by numbers and specifications but are also often verbalized by the customer (i.e., expressed in words). Examples of this verbalization are low fuel consumption and good acceleration for cars or large hard disk capacity and high processor frequency for personal computers. These requirements are considered critical in marketing. (However, we will later see that what it takes to create a satisfactory feature may lead to dissatisfaction with another feature.)

3. **Excitement requirements.** These are those characteristics not expected by the customer but that can significantly contribute to customer satisfaction. In marketing they are labeled as *satisfiers*. The Chrysler Corporation made a big splash when Lee Iacocca announced that airbags would be included on all of its models without any price increase.

The link between the fulfillment of these three categories of requirements and the customer response is as follows:

- **Basic requirements.** If fulfilled, there is no response; if not fulfilled, the product is rejected.

- **Performance requirements.** If fulfilled, positive response occurs; if not fulfilled, negative response occurs.

- **Excitement requirements.** If fulfilled, there is very positive response; if not fulfilled, there is no response.

The divisions among basic, performance, and excitement requirements are not static. What might have caused excitement a few years ago will tend to become a basic requirement, such as color televisions or catalytic converters. In some cases, a feature might even become required by law, for example automobile safety belts.

Often the first customer expressions of *what* are too vague. Understanding customer needs requires a thorough questioning of customers to find out what lies behind the vague expressions. As an example, consider an industrial computer designed to

Exhibit 7.9: Customer Requirements for Industrial Computer

WHAT

Easy to use	Easy to wire
	Use standard wire sizes
	Easy to set up module
	Easy to program controller

communicate with different instruments and machines. A vague expression of a customer need might be that it needs to be "easy to use."[17] After asking the customer what he means by "easy to use," we might learn a variety of things. For example, it could mean that the computer is easy to connect to other instruments and machines, that the location of its input/output connectors on the case is convenient, or that it uses standard cables to connect to other equipment. The computer might include an "easy set-up module" to prepare the computer to work. It might also include a standard keyboard, be flexible for using a variety of applications, or not require the operator to remember complex commands. As illustrated in **Exhibit 7.9**, the *what* part of a QFD matrix can have several layers/columns. **Exhibit 7.10** shows a list of customer requirements for a computer.

We will build on the computer example throughout this chapter to illustrate how the steps of the QFD methodology tie in with the QFD chart. Exhibits 7.10, 7.13, and 7.15 show the first three basic steps.

Tom Peters said "Niche or be niched."[18] The following shows how customers' gener-

Exhibit 7.10: Step 1. Define Whats

Customer Requirements (*whats*)

Working speed
Low price
Easy to operate
Communications
Data storage
External size

al definition of a "small car" can change and become more specific over time.[19]

Past. The small car.

Today and future.

The small luxury commuter car.

The small personal leisure car.

The small fun young woman's car.

The small comfortable retirement car.

The small family supersafe car.

The small supereconomical "eco" car.

New niches out of existing needs.

Customers' requirements for an "image statement" when they choose a luxury car could include such varied factors as those in **Exhibit 7.11**.

Step 2. Define *How*

The second step in the basic QFD method is to translate the *whats* into *hows* (i.e., how

can we satisfy customer requirements?). This is the step of designing the product where the product features or characteristics are defined. Again, our initial *hows* might be vague. We must work to define them more and more precisely. For example, one feature of a personal computer—shown in **Exhibit 7.12**—might be the pointing device, which is a vague description for the tool needed to locate positions on the screen and perform commands such as fetching or moving objects. One common pointing device is a mouse, which could be cordless or have a cord and have a wheel for scrolling, an optical sensor for tracking, or left/right click buttons. Another group of pointing devices includes light pens (which can point directly at the screen). The *hows*, in **Exhibit 7.13**, need to be defined in such a way that they can be expressed in terms of measurable characteristics, such as the determining resolution of the pointing device or meeting certified specifications (for example, that the device complies with the limits established by FCC rules for a Class B computing device).

Step 3. Define *Relationships* between *What* and *How*

Some of the *whats* may influence several *hows,* and vice versa. The third step in the basic QFD method defines the relationships between the *whats* and the *hows*. The pieces of the QFD chart shown in **Exhibit 7.14** combine the *whats* of Exhibit 7.10 with the *hows* of Exhibit 7.13.

The relationships between the *whats* and the *hows* represent the ways in which the *hows* satisfy the *whats*. For example "easy to operate" (a *what*—or feature—for a personal computer) is satisfied by Microsoft

Exhibit 7.11: Customers' Requirements for "Image Statement"

Good value for money
Overall reputation
Reliable
Dealers have high service standards
Advanced technology
Conservative style
Responsive acceleration
Fun to drive
Sporty style
Elegant style
Smooth ride
Comfortable interior

Well-engineered
Good resale
Safe in case of accidents
Car I would like to own
Handles well
Prestigious
Durable
Attractive styling
Distinctive style
Classic style
Roomy interior
Adequate numbers of dealers
Economical to operate

J. D. Power and Associates, *The Lexus and Infiniti Experience: Redefining Competition in the Luxury Car Market* (August 1991): 79.

Exhibit 7.12: Design Characteristics for a Pointing Device

Mouse					Light Pen*	Touch Pad
Cordless	With cord	Wheel for scrolling	Optical sensor tracking	Left and right click buttons	With cord	Cordless

*special monitor is required

Exhibit 7.13: *Step 2: Define* Hows

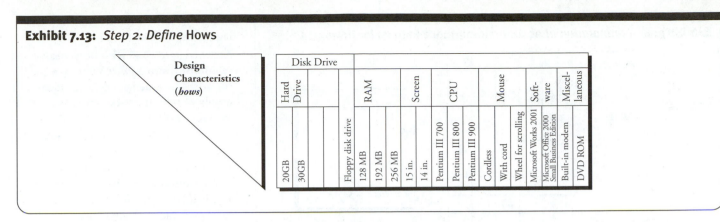

Exhibit 7.14: *Cross-Relationships between* Whats *and* Hows

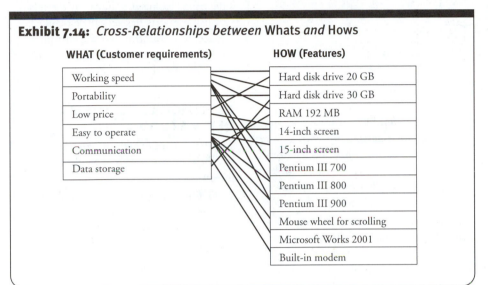

Works 2001. The mouse, as a pointing device, helps the customer to select, mark, copy, or move an object and quickly execute selected commands. Verbalizing the descriptions of relationships between *whats* and *hows* helps in assigning weights of importance to those relationships and helps identify the features of a product that are important to advertise.

The next task is to assign weights of strong, medium, or weak to the relationships between *whats* and *hows*. Usually the relationships are weighted on a scale of 1 to 9 (strong = 9, medium = 3, and weak = 1), but another system could also be used, for example, a scale of 1 to 3 (strong = 3, medium = 2, and weak = 1). Symbols we use to note the weights in **Exhibits 7.15**, **7.16**, and

Exhibit 7.15: *Step 3. Define Relationships between* What *and* How

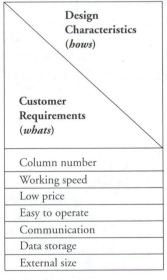

Design Characteristics (*hows*) / Customer Requirements (*whats*)	Disk Drive: 20GB	30GB		Floppy disk drive		RAM: 128 MB	192 MB	256 MB	Screen: 15 in.	14 in.	CPU: Pentium III 700	Pentium III 800	Pentium III 900	Mouse: Cordless	With cord	Wheel for scrolling	Microsoft Works 2001	Microsoft Office 2000 Small Business Edition	Built-in modem	DVD ROM
Column number	1	2	3	4	5	6	7	8	9	10	11	12	13	14	15	16	17	18	19	20
Working speed			○	○		○	●	●			△	○	●							
Low price	△								○											
Easy to operate										○		●	●	△	○	●	●			
Communication																			●	
Data storage		●		●																
External size																			○	○

Relationships

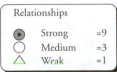

● Strong = 9
○ Medium = 3
△ Weak = 1

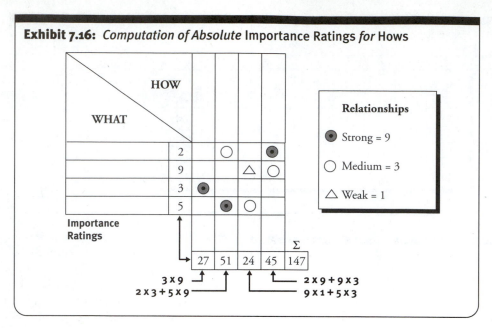

Exhibit 7.16: *Computation of Absolute* Importance Ratings *for* Hows

Relationships
- Strong = 9 (●)
- Medium = 3 (○)
- Weak = 1 (△)

Importance Ratings: 2, 9, 3, 5

Σ row: 27 | 51 | 24 | 45 | 147

3 × 9 →
2 × 3 + 5 × 9 →
← 2 × 9 + 9 × 3
← 9 × 1 + 5 × 3

---

company money without any disadvantage to the customer.

- **Are there any *hows* with only weak relationships to *whats*?** Why have you considered this design characteristic if it only weakly addresses a customer requirement?

- **Does it seem that everything is related to everything else?** This question can be answered in part by prioritizing the *whats*. Consider that there are some characteristics that are "nice to have" (optional) and only some that can be described as "need to have." If the relationship matrix has very little blank space, it is doubtful that the customer needs or design requirements were understood or clearly specified.

7.17 are: strong = ● , medium = ○, and weak = △.

Step 4. Analyze whether the *Whats* Are Covered by *Hows*

In the fourth step of the basic QFD approach, we take the first look at how our design satisfies customer requirements.[20] Now we can clearly see what contributes to customer satisfaction and what does not, as well as which customer requirements are not yet covered in the design. The questions to ask at this stage are:

- **Does each *what* have at least one medium or strong relationship with a *how*?** If there are *whats* that have no relationship or only weak relationships with *hows*, design another *how* to cover that particular customer need.

- **Are there any *hows* without any relationships to *whats*?** If the answer to this is yes, then it seems that this design characteristic does not satisfy any of the stated customer requirements, and you should question why the feature is included. Eliminating the feature might save the

EXTENSIONS TO THE BASIC QFD METHOD

The basic QFD method can be extended by these five steps to provide additional information:

1. Define *importance ratings* for *whats* and *hows*.
2. Define *how much* for *hows*.
3. Define *improvement direction* of *hows*.
4. Define *correlations* between *hows*.
5. Perform *competitive assessments* for *whats* and *hows*.

Step 5. Define *Importance Ratings* for *Whats* and *Hows*

Because our goal is to satisfy all customer needs, it is helpful to know as much as possible about expressed needs.[21] Customer requirements can be quantified by the help of weights or *importance ratings* for the *whats*. The data for allocating weights to each *what* can be obtained from customer research surveys, where the preferences among needs are expressed in percentages or some other numeric value. Within the QFD framework, the weights for *whats* are usually quantified on a relative scale from 1 to 9, with 9 having the highest importance and 1 the lowest. When relevant data are difficult to obtain directly from the customer, the QFD team can collect data from experts or use their own judgment to assess the *importance ratings* for *whats*. This effort is beneficial in situations where trade-offs in product design are needed because customer wants are in conflict. For example, two important attributes for the computer are the processor speed and the price.

Exhibit 7.17: *Step 5. Define* Importance Ratings *for* Whats *and* Hows

Customer Requirements (whats)	Customer importance	Hard Drive 20GB	Hard Drive 30GB	Floppy disk drive	RAM 128 MB	RAM 192 MB	RAM 256 MB	Screen 15 in.	Screen 14 in.	CPU Pentium III 700	CPU Pentium III 800	CPU Pentium III 900	Mouse Cordless	Mouse With cord	Wheel for scrolling	Software Microsoft Works 2001	Software Microsoft Office 2000 Small Business Edition	Built-in modem	DVD ROM
Column number		1	2	3	4/5	6	7	8	9	10	11	12	13	14	15	16	17	18	19/20
Working speed	5		○	○	○	○	○	●	●			△	○	●					
Low price	3	△								○									
Easy to operate	6									○			●	●	△	○	●	●	
Communication	4																		●
Data storage	5	●		●															
External size	7																	○	○
How important		3	45	42	87	15	15	45	81	9	9	5	69	99	6	18	54	54	24	57	93

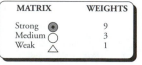

MATRIX	WEIGHTS
Strong ●	9
Medium ○	3
Weak △	1

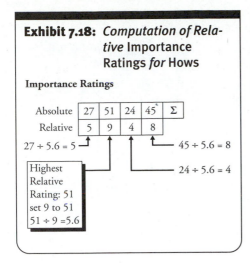

Exhibit 7.18: *Computation of Relative Importance Ratings for Hows*

Importance Ratings

Absolute	27	51	24	45	Σ
Relative	5	9	4	8	

$27 \div 5.6 = 5$

$45 \div 5.6 = 8$

$24 \div 5.6 = 4$

Highest Relative Rating: 51
set 9 to 51
$51 \div 9 = 5.6$

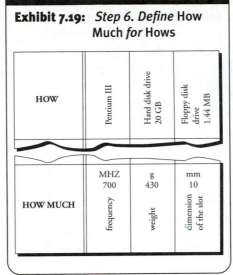

Exhibit 7.19: *Step 6. Define How Much for Hows*

HOW	Pentium III	Hard disk drive 20 GB	Floppy disk drive 1.44 MB
HOW MUCH	MHZ 700 frequency	g 430 weight	mm 10 dimension of the slot

Exhibit 7.20: *Step 7. Define Improvement Direction of Hows*

Improvement direction	↑	↓	○
HOW	Pentium III	Hard disk drive 20 GB	Floppy disk drive 1.44 MB
HOW MUCH	MHZ 700 frequency	g 430 weight	mm 10 dimension of the slot

Increased processor speed adds to the price of the unit (negative) but is desirable for ease of use (positive).

Absolute *importance ratings* for *hows* are then computed and recorded along the bottom of the QFD chart on the line labeled "*How* important" (as in Exhibit 7.17). To compute the absolute *importance ratings* for a *how:*

- Convert the symbols for each *how* to numeric values (i.e., strong = 3, medium = 2, and weak = 1).
- Multiply each numeric value by the value given as relative customer importance for the corresponding *what.*
- Add the products for each relationship in the column of *hows.*

The term *relative* means that the importance ratings for *whats* are expressed on a scale from 1 to 9, and the term *absolute* means that the importance ratings for *hows* are not scaled. (See Exhibits 7.16 and 7.17.)

It is customary with the QFD framework to convert the absolute importance ratings for *hows* to a rating scale of 1 to 9. This simplified scale will be helpful when it becomes necessary to set priorities among design characteristics for trade-offs in design. A simple scaling procedure for obtaining relative importance ratings for *hows* follows. (See also **Exhibit 7.18.**)

- Allocate to the highest absolute importance rating the value 9, that is, the highest relative importance rating (in this example, assign 9 to 51).
- Divide the highest absolute importance rating by 9 to come up with the scaling number ($51 \div 9 = 5.6$).
- Divide the other absolute importance ratings by the scaling number and round the

result. This is the relative importance rating for a given *how* (e.g., $27 \div 5.6 \approx 5$).

Step 6. Define *How Much* for *Hows*

How much better is our design than the designs of our competitors? This is the question engineers and marketing people in the company ask. The answer will require a quantification of the *hows* (design parameters). When the design parameter can be expressed by a number, we know *how much.* If we are not able to quantify many of the *hows,* this might be an indication that the corresponding design specifications are too superficial. For example, the customer requirement (*what*) expressed as the "need for fast data processing" can be satisfied by Pentium III (*how*). This *how* can then be expressed by the frequency of the processor (i.e., 700 MHz, or 800 MHz, or 900 MHz).

Often when the *hows* are specified in more detail, additional refinements may still be needed. For example, to satisfy the *what* "data storage," we might begin with a general design characteristic (a *how*) such as "hard drive." To quantify to *how much,* we might specify 20 GB hard drive. But we can also consider a more specific *how,* such as 20 GB hard drive, and then we might further quantify to *how much* by adding the weight of the drive or its read/write speed to the specification of *how much.*

The medieval scholar Pascal is known for saying, "What cannot be measured does not exist." A design that cannot be expressed in numbers is too vague. The design engineers can provide the QFD team with knowledge about *how much* (see **Exhibit 7.19**).

Step 7. Define the *Improvement Direction* of *Hows*

Another extension of the basic QFD chart concerns the connection between the *hows* and the *how muchs. Improvement direction* is a line describing the direction in which a design parameter contributes to customer requirements. There are three basic *improvement directions* (as illustrated in **Exhibit 7.20**) of design characteristics:

- ↑ = Maximize (the bigger the better). Examples: Hard disk size, RAM memory size, trunk volume.
- ↓ = Minimize (the smaller the better). Examples: Power consumption, engine noise, wind noise.
- ○ = Target value and tolerance around it. Example: Dimensions of floppy disk drive, location of steering wheel.

Step 8. Define *Correlations* between *Hows*

The *correlation* matrix identifies potential conflicts and synergies among the *hows.* Some design parameters may support other parameters. For example, in personal computer design, the mouse (*how*) can contribute positively to Microsoft Works 2001 (*how*), making the computer "easy to operate" (*what*) (see **Exhibit 7.21**). On the other hand, some design parameters may have negative correlations where conflicts can arise. For example, 128 MB of RAM (*how*) can contribute negatively to Microsoft Works 2001 (*how*) because the 128 MB of RAM is not sufficient to run

Works quickly (see **Exhibit 7.22**). In this case, the *what* will not be satisfied.

In such cases, trade-offs are considered. Sometimes it is necessary to sacrifice one solution in favor of another or to do some more research to find a new breakthrough solution; in this case, for example, to develop a method of producing cheaper memory chips. Remember, however, that the winner when trade-offs are required should always be the customer.[22]

Step 9. Perform *Competitive Assessments* for *Whats* and *Hows*

Let us begin our look at conflict in the *competitive assessments* for *whats* and *hows* with a story from the auto industry.[23] The story also depicts two different approaches: the new customer-oriented approach of Company A and the outmoded traditional engineering approach of Company B. In this case, the *what* (a customer requirement for an automobile) was expressed as "experience the feeling of the car's acceleration." In an independent competitive assessment made by a market research company, the fulfillment of this characteristic was rated by the customer as "good" for Company A's product and "bad" for Company B's (see the right side of the QFD chart in **Exhibit 7.23**). The engineers of Company B started their own competitive assessments of design characteristics related to the acceleration of the car. This engineering assessment was made by means of car tests, but the results were confusing. For all design characteristics related to the car's acceleration, the design of Company B was clearly *better* than that of Company A (see the bottom side of the QFD chart in **Exhibit 7.24**). Was the problem in customers who were not educated or intelligent enough to appreciate the meaning of superior engineering?

It turned out that the Company A engineers had been aware that their engine was not as good as Company B's. Rather than pouring money into engine changes, they decided to alter the car seats. When accelerating, the upper body was pushed back into the seat slightly more in the Company A car, giving it more of a feeling of acceleration. The customer requirement of "a feeling of acceleration" was accomplished despite a less powerful and cheaper engine.

Exhibit 7.24 illustrates this story in the QFD charts of the two companies. Com-

pany A better satisfies the customer requirements (the competitive assessment of *what* is 5 for A and 3 for B). However, the two QFD charts differ in other ways. Company

A realized that satisfying the *what* of "a feeling of acceleration" was a function not only of the engine but also of the seat. Moreover, in the roof of the chart for Company A,

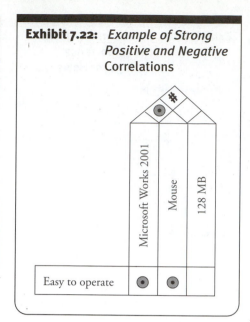

Exhibit 7.21: *Example of Strong Positive Correlations*

Exhibit 7.22: *Example of Strong Positive and Negative Correlations*

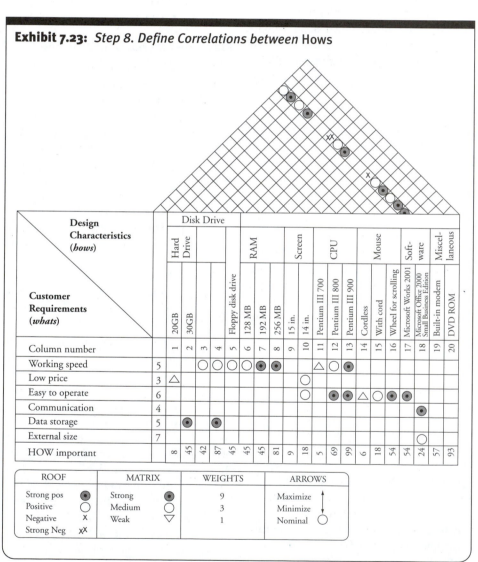

Exhibit 7.23: *Step 8. Define Correlations between* Hows

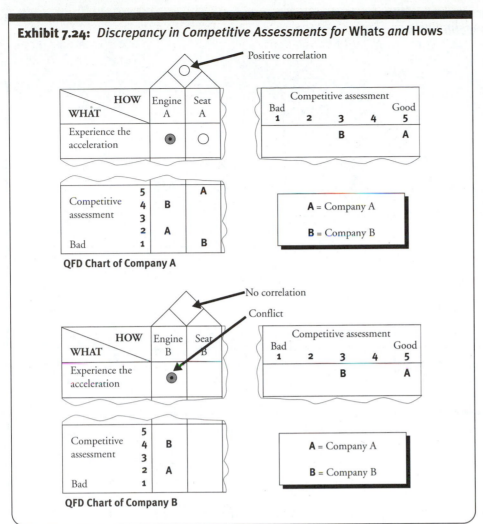

Exhibit 7.24: *Discrepancy in Competitive Assessments for* Whats *and* Hows

QFD Chart of Company A

QFD Chart of Company B

A = Company A

B = Company B

zines, newspapers, and various consumer reports, and they are respected worldwide.

The *competitive assessments* for *hows,* which might also be called *engineering assessments,* compare specific engineering solutions. Companies often buy competing products and test them against their own products under various conditions. The products are scrutinized to the smallest detail. Automobile manufacturers perform "tear-down" analyses, where competitors' cars are disassembled so that the new features and solutions can be illustrated to the engineers. Even the senior executives regularly test-drive competitors' new models and fly around the world from the Arctic to the desert to test their own models. This level of testing requires substantial resources, but valuable data can be obtained about important quality-relevant parameters such as fuel consumption, acceleration, results of crash tests, durability of plastics, and engine noise.[25]

A discrepancy between *what* and *how* in a relationship ("bad" for *what* but "good" for *how*) can be an indication of some failure in our reasoning or internal quality standards. Other problems you might encounter during the QFD process follow; the sign is in bold type followed by the related problem.

Blank rows: Customer requirements are not met.

Blank columns: Unnecessary design features or incomplete customer requirements.

Rows or columns with only weak relationships: Unclear contribution of design features to customer satisfaction.

Unmeasurable *how much:* Vague definition of design characteristic.[26]

More than 50 percent have relationships: Hard to prioritize the design characteristics.

Negative correlations: Trade-offs are needed.

Conflict in competitive assessments: Customer does not appreciate what company regards as superb feature.

BUSINESS OBJECTIVES DEPLOYMENT

The philosophy behind QFD can be used for other purposes in addition to product planning. Remember that each process in the company has its customer (internal or external); thus, the needs (*whats*) can be defined

there is a positive correlation between the engine and the seat, which indicates that the engineers were aware that seat design could contribute to the experience of acceleration. In fact, it was the engineering of Company A making the seat a greater factor in the feeling of car acceleration that was more important for customer satisfaction than the data about the car's acceleration testing.

This story suggests two things to remember:

• Blaming the customer for not understanding your solutions is not useful.

• Do not rely solely on computation when using QFD. Instead of assigning only engineering solutions to customer needs, try to gather the customer opinion on the engineering solution and to understand what is behind apparent "conflicts" within the QFD process. A better understanding of such a "conflict" can show you, as in the preceding case, that you have wrongly assumed that your expensive or complicated engineering solution will satisfy the

customer. In this case, the customer wanted to *feel* the acceleration, not necessarily to have a more powerful engine.

The *competitive assessments* are done for both *whats* and *hows* where the developed product/service is compared to the competition. Much specific data are needed for the comparison.

The *competitive assessments* for *whats* might also be called *customer assessment* since they depict customer opinion. Various customer surveys offer comparative data on how well competing products and services satisfy customers' needs (*whats*). One of the well-known and acknowledged companies in the field of customer satisfaction research is J. D. Power and Associates.[24] This company performs various customer satisfaction surveys over the life of the car, beginning when the car is sold and delivered to the customer and ending five years after the purchase, by which time the everyday problems of the car have become well known to the customer. The results of these annual surveys are published in car maga-

Exhibit 7.25: *Blank QFD Chart with Competitive Assessment*

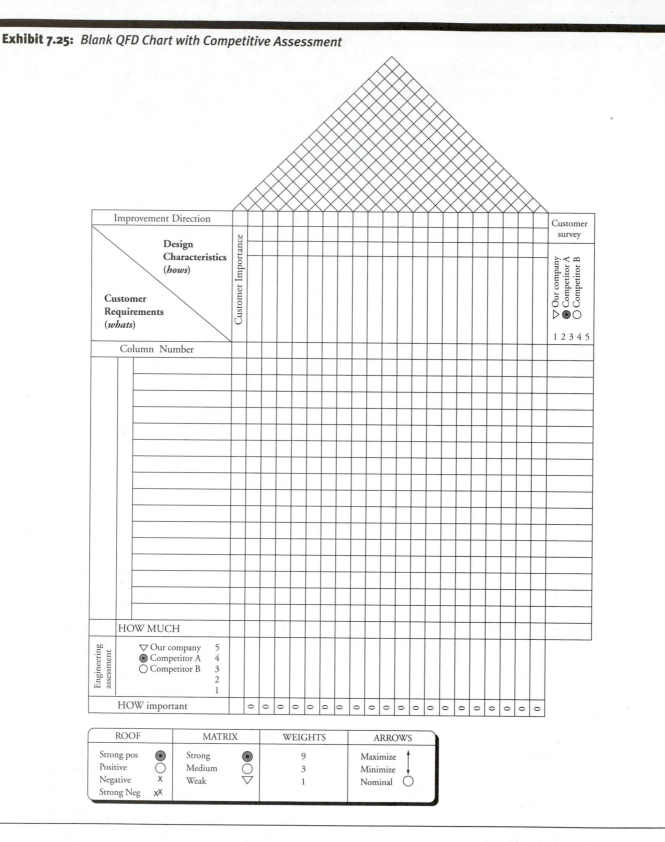

and QFD can begin (see **Exhibits 7.25, 7.26**, and **7.27**). Some examples of *what* definitions for business objectives follow:

- Make money.
- Increase market share.
- Become a high-tech company.
- Become a world-known company.

- Satisfy customers.
- Acquire other companies.
- Become a lean manufacturer.
- Provide a nice place to work.

One application is the deployment of the company mission. You can start with global business objectives and then define business

strategies to suit the measurable goals that are set. Later, the other QFD phases can be used in ways similar to the process for product planning so that the measurable goals can be deployed from the corporate level, through divisions, to individual departments, and finally to each work station. Thus, QFD can be a tool for cascading the

Exhibit 7.26: Blank QFD Chart

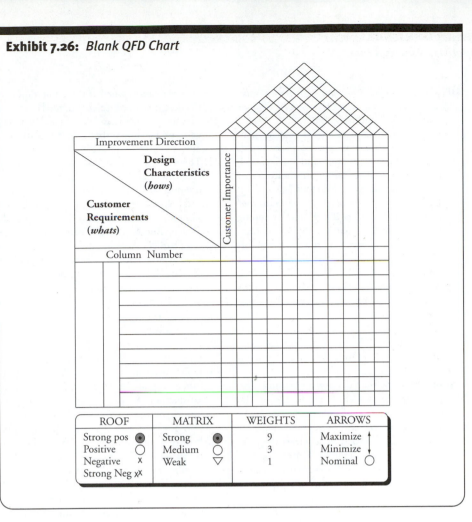

Exhibit 7.27: QFD Chart for Business Objectives Deployment

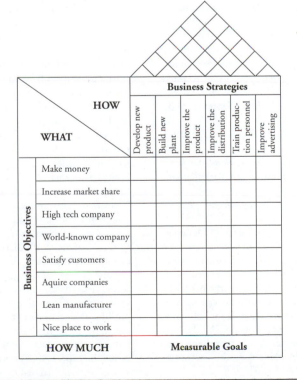

goals throughout the corporation, and for each level of the hierarchy, one phase can be used. It can be surprising to discover that some business objectives have no strategies to support them, that some strategies are in conflict with company objectives, or that management is unaware of the measurable goals that can contribute to business objectives. How can reasonable action be taken if the *whats* are not met by *hows*, and if the *how muchs* are not specified?

CHAPTER SUMMARY

This chapter has illustrated some of the benefits of using QFD, which can help you to

- Avoid having to find and fix problems in production. Instead, you can find and prevent problems in the design stage.
- Differentiate between "need to have" and "nice to have."
- Find and solve problems instead of hiding problems.
- Avoid having to work out bugs in the months after the product launch.
- Be an advocate of the customer.

The basic QFD method has four steps:

1. Define *what*.
2. Define *how*.
3. Define *relationships* between *what* and *how*.
4. Analyze whether the *whats* are covered by *hows*.

The method can be extended with the addition of five steps:

1. Define *importance ratings* for *whats* and *hows*.
2. Define *how much* for *hows*.
3. Define *improvement direction* of *hows*.
4. Define *correlations* between *hows*.
5. Perform *competitive assessments* for *whats* and *hows*.

Implementing QFD might at first be something like managing a home movie project with a new video camera. The camera has many sophisticated features, but an exciting movie will not film itself. It requires planning, experience, and resources. So it is with the QFD method. It requires time and teamwork. Remember that QFD is not like a "paint-by-numbers" job. Rather, it is a philosophy that lies behind the processes of customer orientation (both external and internal) in the company. The QFD charts are the tools to facilitate those processes.

1. Quoted from W. E. Deming, *Out of the Crisis* (Boston, MA: Massachusetts Institute of Technology, 1989). The 14 Principles were the basis of Dr. Deming's lectures on quality to Japanese top managers in the 1950s. Adopting Dr. Deming's philosophy was the beginning of dramatic changes in Japanese industry. As a postwar aide to Japan, Deming helped revitalize Japanese industry by implementing quality improvement methods such as statistical process control, PDCA cycle, Pareto analysis, and so on. In 1983 Dr. Deming was elected to the National Academy of Engineering. Each year the best Japanese companies are awarded the Deming Prize for their achievement in quality.

2. Immediately after it was introduced in the United States in 1991, the Infiniti (a luxury Nissan model) did superbly well in customer satisfaction compared to other non-Japanese luxury models, according to J. D. Power and Associates, *The Lexus and Infiniti Experience: Redefining Competition in the Luxury Car Market* (August 1991): 33.

3. According to J. D. Power and Associates, *1991 Early Buyer New Car Initial Quality Study,* in 1991 the Toyota Lexus models achieved the best-ever score of 47 problems per 100 cars, as compared to the overall industry average of 141. The best non-Japanese model, Mercedes-Benz, received a score of 99 problems.

4. J. D. Power and Associates, *The Lexus and Infiniti Experience,* p. 29. In the 1980s, Toyota started to develop its new luxury car for the segment that had been dominated by traditional U.S. and European manufacturers. Toyota's 1,400 engineers, 2,300 technicians, and 220 support workers were divided into 24 teams, which identified and improved specific engineering elements of the luxury models from the world's renowned companies.

5. More and more U.S. and European companies are implementing the QFD approach (see the example of Chrysler in the text).

6. The American Supplier Institute (ASI) was founded by the Ford Motor Company to improve its supplier industry. ASI has helped to introduce quality improvement methods such as statistical process control, quality function deployment, the Taguchi methods, and many others throughout the world.

7. Deming, *Out of the Crisis.*

8. Quality Concepts 1992 Conference and Exposition, October 1992, Chrysler Technology Center (Auburn Hills, Michigan).

9. Ralph Nader, *Unsafe at Any Speed* (New York: Grossmann, 1965). An example from the 1960s, Nader started a nationwide campaign against GM because of the safety hazards of the Corvair. This book caused serious image problems for GM.

10. Maryann Keller, *Collision: GM, Toyota, Volkswagen and the Race to Own the 21st Century* (New York: Doubleday, 1993).

11. Dr. Deming's first point for management states: "Create constancy of purpose towards improvement of product and service, with the aim to become competitive and to stay in business, and to provide jobs."

12. J. D. Power and Associates, *The Lexus and Infiniti Experience,* p. 29. When developing the Lexus for U.S. markets, the Toyota team even lived in an expensive suburb of California to observe how the customers used their cars.

13. Adapted from American Supplier Institute's *Quality Function Deployment Workshop Manual,* 1989.

14. Adapted from J. P. Womack, D. T. Jones, and D. Roos, *The Machine That Changed the World* (New York: Harper Perennial, 1991): 131–132.

15. In 1994, GM started a new advertising campaign in the Czech Republic. After the change from a centrally planned economy to a market-oriented economy, international car manufacturers started to penetrate the market in the Czech Republic. For a couple of weeks, billboards displayed questions painted in white type against blue rectangles. The questions asked "Do you know who invented . . ." the automatic transmission, safety belts, air conditioning, or airbags. Usually customers would not know the answer. The answer came when new billboards bearing the GM logo and the words "American General Motors" were added. GM wanted to build an image of a high-tech car company. This illustrates that even being the first is not a guarantee that customers will know the products or automatically buy them.

16. John Grant, *Your New Consumer: Sociocultural Trends Affecting the Car Market* (Ashridge: Ashridge Management College, 1993) (lecture delivered September 3, 1993).

17. This example is from Siemens Industrial Automation, Johnson City, TN.

18. T. Peters, *Thriving on Chaos: Handbook for a Management Revolution* (New York: Knopf, 1987).

19. Grant, *Consumer: Socio-cultural Trends Affecting the Car Market.*

20. Some software, such as The QFD Designer II from Qualisoft Corporation, offers features that highlight the blank rows and columns in the relationships matrix and compute the percentages when the matrix is full. Remember that the software can analyze the relationships matrix from a formal point of view, but the person or team who designs the product must decide whether the design requirements already satisfy the customer requirements or whether more fine-tuning of the design characteristics is needed.

21. Beware, according to Murphy's Law, that if you build a system that even a fool can use, only a fool will ever use it.

22. There was a popular joke in former Eastern Bloc countries about research activities. A man came to the National Bureau of Inventions and Patents and said to the patent official who accepted the patent claims, "I have invented a Shaving Robot. It would increase the efficiency of barber's shops around the whole Eastern Bloc by 300 percent." The official replied, "A Shaving Robot must be extremely difficult to perfect since each customer has a different face." To this the inventor proudly replied, "Oh no, it works perfectly. The faces are only different before the first shave."

23. Heard at Siemens Industrial Automation, Johnson City, TN, June 1992.

24. J. D. Power and Associates have also published several special reports on customer satisfaction. In the car industry, the best known of these reports is *The Lexus and Infiniti Experience* cited earlier. It looks at the history and successes of the Japanese car manufacturers Toyota and Nissan in the U.S. marketplace. When the Japanese announced these products, their competitors, especially the European luxury car producers, expressed doubts that companies without a heritage and experience in luxury cars could be serious competitors. However, the companies have scored the highest-ever scores of 170 on the Customer Satisfaction Index in 1991, coming in well ahead of Mercedes.

25. There was a popular joke in former Eastern Bloc countries that illustrates an unexpected analysis of the product: A woman who had worked for 30 years in the Soviet Union State Sewing Machine Company was invited to the director's office and thanked for her work and contribution. The boss asked what she would like to get in appreciation for her work. "I would like a sewing machine," answered the woman. The director was surprised. "After 30 years in the company, you must have had enough opportunities to take home leftover parts and assemble a machine for yourself," he said. The woman answered, "I've tried many times, but it always turns out to be a tommy gun or machine gun, never a sewing machine."

26. In the *Marketplace* simulation, this problem cannot be addressed in product design because the set of design characteristics is predefined. Instead, the task is to select from among predefined characteristics for each product the team designs. The players do not have the ability to redefine the characteristics, and thus some characteristics cannot be expressed in a measurable way.

Chapter 8

James M. Reeve
Deloitte & Touche
Professor of Accounting
University of Tennessee

Financial Reporting
A User's Perspective

As we go through life, it is important to manage our own personal financial affairs. We must be careful to spend within our limits, use our credit cards wisely, pay our taxes, and save enough to meet future needs. Accomplishing these objectives often requires us to monitor our finances. For many of us, monitoring them may be as simple as recording checks and deposits in our checkbooks. Recording transactions in a checkbook is an example of accounting. *Accounting* is defined as an information system that provides reports to various individuals or groups about economic activities of an individual, family, organization, or other entity.

Not only must individuals manage their financial affairs; so must businesses. Accounting is used by corporations to provide information about business events. You may think of accounting as the "language of business" because it is the means by which most business information is communicated.

Assume you inherited $10,000 and wished to invest this money in the stock market (the common stock of public companies). Which stocks would you select? How would you know which stocks were good potential investments, and which ones were not? One way would be to use the information provided in corporate financial statements to assess the financial performance of your prospective investments. The financial statements compose a set of reports identifying the financial position, results of operations, and cash flows for an organization. The financial statements provide information about the:

1. **Financial position**—by reporting the wealth of a business at a point in time.
2. **Results of operations**—by reporting how well the company performed during the most recent period of time.
3. **Cash flows**—by reporting the sources and uses of cash for operating, investing, and financing activities during a period of time.

In this chapter, we will develop a basic understanding of the three major financial statements: the balance sheet, the income statement, and the statement of cash flows. Before we describe the statements themselves, the next section will discuss the financial reporting environment.

FINANCIAL REPORTING ENVIRONMENT
Regulatory Environment

The financial statements of publicly traded companies are required to be submitted and filed annually with the Securities Exchange Commission (SEC), a governmental agency that was established by Congress in the early 1930s to regulate the stock markets and the financial statement disclosures of companies that list their stock on the public stock exchanges. The financial statements are required disclosures in order to serve the needs of external decision makers, such as stock investors, creditors, financial analysts, employees, vendors, and customers. For example, if you were considering a job offer from a public company, you might wish to evaluate its financial statements before accepting the job. After all, you may not wish to be hired by a company that has a weak financial position.

By law, the SEC is responsible for regulating the actual content of the financial statements. However, the SEC has traditionally allowed an independent body of accounting experts to perform this function. The independent body that develops the standards or "rules" for financial reporting is the Financial Accounting Standards

BEST-USE CORRELATIONS

This chapter reviews how to track, and thus manage, your business performance. The focus is on measuring wealth, measuring the change in wealth, and measuring the change in cash.

Financial Statements

In *Marketplace,* after receiving your quarterly results, first check your cash flow statement (did you have enough cash?), then your income statement (how much did you lose or earn?), and then your balance sheet (are you solvent?). In Q5, venture capitalists will evaluate your actual performance through Q4 and your pro forma projections through Q8.

You can see how every choice made affects cash flow, income statements, and balance sheets. As teams make decisions, financial statements are updated so that you can immediately see their impact on accounts and firm profitability.

Cash Is King, or Is It Profit?

Starting in Q5, firms may borrow money and have lots of cash. But remember, investments in R&D and new sales offices are current period expenses. They register on income statements as losses. The losses reduce your retained earnings on the balance sheet, causing owners' equity to shrink. At this point, the auditors step in and limit current period expenses. Thus, profit and the need to add to owners' equity take on significant importance after Q5.

The Loan Shark Is Waiting

If you experience a cash shortfall in *Marketplace,* the bank will call in a loan shark to pay your bills. To avoid the loan shark, project your cash flows every quarter by using *Marketplace*'s easy-to-use pro forma tools. See what could happen if sales fall short of expectations; consider a drop in revenue by 30 to 50%.

Board (FASB). These rules are the guidelines used by accountants in reporting various business events to external users. The FASB does not determine the reporting rules for federal corporate income taxes. These rules are determined by Congress and enforced by the Internal Revenue Service. Thus, corporate tax reporting and financial reporting are two completely different areas. We will not discuss corporate tax reporting in this chapter. The term used for the financial reporting standards is *generally accepted accounting principles* (GAAP). All public companies must report their financial performance according to GAAP.

The annual disclosure required by the SEC is termed a *10-K report.* The 10-K includes information about the company's performance for the year, including the financial statements. The SEC maintains electronic versions of the 10-K report in a database, Electronic Data Gathering Analysis and Retrieval (EDGAR) system. Using the Internet, you can download without charge any public company's 10-K report from EDGAR via a number of Internet services. We recommend the free Edgarscan service provided by Pricewaterhouse-Coopers at www.edgarscan.pwcglobal.com/servlets/edgarscan/.

Generally Accepted Accounting Principles

What could be controversial about reporting business events? Is it not obvious how an event should be recorded? Sometimes this is true, but often there is a great deal of controversy on how business events should be recorded. To take a simple example, how should Walt Disney Corporation account for the trademark value of Mickey Mouse®? Would you agree that Mickey Mouse is a valuable asset of the Disney Corporation? Would it also surprise you that you would not find this asset on Disney's financial statements? The reason is that the rules established by the accounting standard setters allow a company to record trademark assets at cost, not at market value. The cost to establish Mickey Mouse as a trademark was incurred decades ago as mere legal fees. These costs are insignificant. Thus, while Mickey Mouse is a significant economic asset of Disney, he does not show up on its financial statements because of the nature of GAAP.

Taking a more contemporary example, are the stock options awarded to employees a form of compensation expense to be reported on the income statement, and if so, what is the compensation expense to be reported? Under many circumstances no compensation expense is recorded. However, when they should be reported the amount of expense is determined by a set of rules established by the FASB. The actual rules are established by the FASB in *Statements of Financial Accounting Standards* (SFAS), which are issued periodically to address new reporting rules and requirements.

Exhibit 8.1 illustrates the role of GAAP in financial reporting. The "real world" consists of thousands of business events required to conduct business. This underlying economic reality must be measured in order for external users of financial statements to be able to evaluate business performance. The "lens" used to measure these economic events is provided by generally accepted accounting principles. In other words, we see the underlying events of an organization through the lens of accounting measurement. The results of the measurement process are the financial statements. Thus, what we see is strongly influenced by the measurement system itself (the lens, if you will). If the lens is

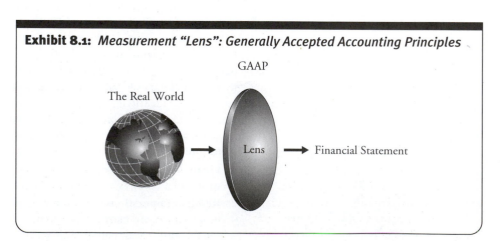

Exhibit 8.1: *Measurement "Lens": Generally Accepted Accounting Principles*

distorted, then so will be the likely interpretation of the real world.

As a (future) manager, you must keep this important point in mind: What you see in financial statements reflects the underlying transactions of a business *and* how they are measured. To illustrate, one of the requirements of GAAP is to record all long-term assets at original purchase cost less accumulated depreciation from the purchase date. How well do you think this rule measures the value of the hotel properties of Marriott International? All the hotel properties of Marriott have a market value that likely exceeds their original cost less accumulated depreciation. Thus, the hotel assets measured under GAAP likely understate their "true" market values.

FINANCIAL STATEMENTS

The financial statements and their relationship to the objectives of financial accounting can be summarized here with the objective in bold followed by the appropriate statement:

Measuring wealth—balance sheet.

Measuring change in wealth—income statement.

Measuring change in cash—statement of cash flows.

Each of the major financial statements can be defined as follows:

• **Balance sheet.** A list of the assets, liabilities, and stockholders' equity as of a specific date, usually at the close of the last day of a month or a year.

• **Income statement.** A summary of the revenue and the expenses for a specific period of time, such as a month or a year.

• **Statement of cash flows.** A summary of the cash receipts and cash payments from operating, investing, and financing transactions for a specific period of time, such as a month or a year.

All financial statements should be identified by the name of the business, the title of the statement, and the date or period of time. The data presented in the balance sheet are for a specific date. The data presented in the income statement and the statement of cash flows are for a period of time.

Financial statements are used to evaluate the current financial condition of a business and to predict its future operating results and cash flows. For example, bank loan officers use an entity's financial statements in deciding whether to grant it a loan. Once

granted, the entity's financial statements will also be used to monitor the business. Other people using financial statements are management, financial analysts, investors, customers, suppliers, and employees. The next sections of this chapter describe the financial statements.

Measuring Wealth: The Balance Sheet

If you were asked "What is your wealth?" how would you respond? The first thing to notice is that you can answer the question only by referring to a specific point in time, as in "What is your wealth *right now*?" The components of wealth are assets and liabilities. *Assets* represent items that confer future economic benefits to the owner. Examples of assets to an individual are cash, investments, car, and house. *Liabilities* are items that obligate the owner to provide future economic benefits to someone else. Examples of liabilities to an individual are student loans, credit card balances, auto note, and house mortgage. The wealth of an entity can be measured as follows:

$$\text{Assets} - \text{Liabilities} = \text{Net wealth}$$

As with an individual, the financial condition of a business at a point in time is a snapshot of its wealth. Thus, businesses also have assets and liabilities. In addition, a business has claims by owners. The owners have invested in the business and have a right to a portion in the financial success of the business. We term the claim of the owners *stockholders' equity*.

The wealth of a business is measured at a point in time using the balance sheet. As we shall see, the balance sheet is the starting place for all of the financial statements. This is so because the balance sheet measures wealth, and it is wealth and what happens to wealth that drive our financial interest.

The balance sheet measures the assets, liabilities, and net worth of a business at a point in time using the following equation:

$$\text{Assets} = \text{Liabilities} + \text{Stockholders' equity}$$

Unlike you or me, a business enterprise has assets and liabilities for a business purpose. Thus, it should not be surprising to observe assets and liabilities on the balance sheet of a business that may at first appear unfamiliar. Examples of assets of a business enterprise are cash, accounts receivable, inventory, and property, plant, equipment. Examples of liabilities of a business enterprise are accounts payable as well as short-term and long-term notes payable.

We shall discuss each of these categories separately, referring to the example balance sheet of Martinez Company in **Exhibit 8.2**.

Assets

The balance sheet assets of a business enterprise are the items that meet the following four conditions:

1. Will result in future benefits (cash inflows).

2. Are estimable in money terms.

3. Are the result of a past transaction.

4. Are owned by the enterprise.

First, all assets must be able to generate future cash flows. This is a core definition of an asset. Second, only assets that can be measured are placed on the balance sheet. There must be some reference point for measurement. Thus, for example, a business's good reputation would not be an accounting asset because it is not estimable. Third, assets and liabilities arise if one side or the other to a transaction performs its side of the agreement. This is termed a *partially executed agreement,* which is how a *past transaction* is defined. For example, if I agree to paint your house and you agree to pay me, this is just a mutual promise. In such a case, there are no accounting assets or liabilities because there is no partial execution. On the other hand, if I paint your house before you pay me, then there is partial execution. I have performed my side of the agreement, and I have an asset—termed an *account receivable.* Lastly, the asset must be owned and under control of the enterprise to be included as an asset on the balance sheet.

Assets can be separated into current assets and fixed assets. *Current assets* are those that will be converted into cash within the next year or operating cycle of the business, whichever is longer. *Fixed assets* represent benefits that will accrue to the business over a longer-term time horizon.

Cash and Marketable Securities

The typical current assets of a business enterprise are *cash and marketable securities, accounts receivable,* and *inventory.* The cash and marketable securities of a business enterprise would be determined much like they would be for an individual. They represent the sum total of all cash accounts, checking accounts, and current investments used by the enterprise for operating needs. Management will invest excess cash balances into marketable securities, such as

Assets

Current Assets

Cash and Marketable Securities	$120,000	
Accounts Receivable (net of allowance for doubtful accounts)	340,000	
Inventory (valued at LIFO)	570,000	
Total Current Assets		$1,030,000
Non-Current Investments		430,000
Property, Plant, and Equipment (net of $800,000 accumulated depreciation)		3,000,000
Total Assets		**$4,460,000**

Liabilities and Stockholders' Equity

Current Liabilities

Accounts Payable	$360,000	
Short-term Notes Payable	120,000	
Total Current Liabilities		$480,000
Notes Payable		1,500,000
Total Liabilities		**$1,980,000**
Stockholders' Equity:		
Preferred Stock		200,000
Common Stock (no par), 50,000 shares issued and outstanding		1,400,000
Less: Treasury Stock 5,000 shares		(160,000)
Retained Earnings		1,040,000
Total Stockholders' Equity		**2,480,000**
Total Liabilities and Stockholders' Equity		**$4,460,000**

stocks and bonds of other companies, or money market funds, in order to capture investment returns. Management must plan cash requirements for future growth, operating seasonalities, investment, and other operating needs.

Accounts Receivable

The *accounts receivable* represent the amount owed to the firm for sales already made to customers. This needs some explanation. Unlike individuals, firms do not conduct transactions with other businesses on a cash basis. The reason is fairly straightforward. When you or I purchase something, we can take out a checkbook and pay for it right then. It is our money; we can do with it what we wish. Companies cannot do this because all employees that wish to purchase something for the firm cannot be given a checkbook! It is not their money; it is the firm's money. Thus, firms separate the decision to purchase something from the paying for it. This is termed *internal control by separation of duties.*

Exhibit 8.3 illustrates the transaction sequence. On February 6 Selling Company ships product to Customer Company with

an invoice. A sale has occurred because the product has been shipped, yet cash has not yet been received from Customer Company. Thus, Selling Company has an account receivable from Customer Company representing the total sales price of the shipped goods. Customer Company processes the invoice and remits a check to Selling Company on February 26. At this time the accounts receivable held by Selling Company is eliminated because cash is received from Customer Company. The time separation between the shipment of the goods (sale) and the collection of the cash gives rise to accounting accruals. An *accrual* is merely an account that connects an economic event that occurs at one point in time to its cash flow at another point in time. Thus, accounts receivable represent an accrual account that links the sale with the eventual cash receipt.

The accounts receivable balance at a point in time will be disclosed on the balance sheet, net of the allowance for doubtful accounts. The *allowance for doubtful accounts* represents the estimated amount of the accounts receivable that is expected to be uncollected. Reducing the

accounts receivable by the allowance for doubtful accounts values the accounts receivable at the estimated amount of cash that the company actually believes will be realized in the future. The allowance is determined from historical experience.

The accounts receivable balance should be carefully managed. If the accounts receivable become too large relative to the underlying sales, this might indicate overly liberal credit terms. The size of the accounts receivable can be measured by the average collection period. This ratio is calculated as follows:

$$\text{Average collection period} =$$
$$365 \text{ days} \div \left(\frac{\text{Sales}}{\text{Average accounts receivable}} \right)$$

Average accounts receivable is the sum of the beginning and ending balance divided by 2. The smaller the accounts receivable balance relative to the sales, the shorter the collection period, and vice versa. The collection period should be compared across time for the same firm or across industry competitors at a particular point in time. To illustrate, Best Buy Co. has an average collection period of only five days. Best Buy has a small accounts receivable balance relative to its sales because most of its sales are done on a cash or credit card basis. Thus, the company does not provide credit to customers (the credit card company pays Best Buy immediately for credit card sales). In contrast, General Electric Co. has an average collection period of 25 days. This is so because General Electric does not sell items to its customers on a cash basis but instead provides credit to customers. GE is collecting its accounts within 25 days, on average, which would be viewed as acceptable.

The collection period helps management maintain the accounts receivable balances consistent with its credit policies. If the collection period is growing, this can indicate a problem with collections, which can result in possible future write-downs. Collection periods stretching beyond 60 days would be considered too long for many industries.

Inventory

A very important current asset of manufacturing and merchandising enterprises is inventory. *Inventory* for a retailer or wholesaler represents purchased goods for resale. For example, the merchandise inventory of Toys 'R' Us would include board games sitting on the shelf for sale. The retailer

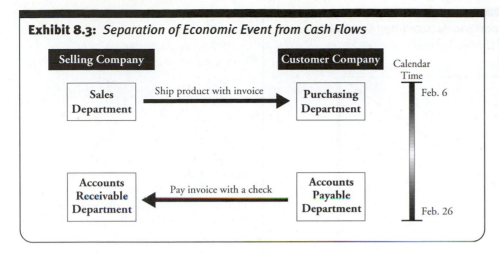

Exhibit 8.3: *Separation of Economic Event from Cash Flows*

purchases goods from suppliers. These goods are added to the inventory balances. When customers purchase the inventory, it leaves the firm and is recorded as cost of goods sold. The *cost of goods sold* is an income statement item representing the cost of sold items matched against the sales revenue. Whatever product is left at the end of the period is the inventory shown on the balance sheet of the firm.

A manufacturer is different than a retailer or wholesaler. A manufacturer does not purchase goods for resale but instead makes goods for sale. In making goods for sale, a manufacturer uses three inventory categories: materials, work in process, and finished goods. These inventory categories are defined as follows:

- **Materials inventory.** These are the costs of materials that have not yet entered the manufacturing process. For example, purchased steel for an automobile manufacturer would be included in materials inventory.

- **Work in process inventory.** These are the manufacturing costs associated with products that have not completed production. The cost of the incomplete cars in the factory would be work in process inventory for an automobile manufacturer.

- **Finished goods inventory.** These are the accumulated manufacturing costs associated with the completed products that have not been sold. For example, the total manufactured cost of completed cars that have not been shipped to dealers would be used to value the finished goods inventory of an automobile manufacturer.

Many manufacturers are using *just-in-time principles* in order to improve their manufacturing operations. One of the results of these efforts is to dramatically reduce the amount of raw material, work in process,

and finished goods inventories required for production.

How much inventory is enough? The inventory efficiency is measured by the *inventory turnover ratio* calculated as

$$\text{Inventory turnover} = \frac{\text{Cost of goods sold}}{\text{Average inventory}}$$

The average inventory is the sum of the beginning and ending inventory balance divided by 2. The higher the inventory turnover number, the more quickly inventory is being turned into sales (which is favorable). The inventory turnover ratio can be compared for a single company over time to identify inventory turnover trends or with other companies in an industry to compare a company with competitors. Different industries will have very different inventory turnover ratios. For example, McDonald's will have a much higher inventory turnover (40 turns) than will Zale's Jewelers (1.53 turns) because food products are more perishable than diamonds.

Noncurrent Investments

Noncurrent assets are those that are held and provide benefits longer than a year. The most common noncurrent assets are noncurrent investments and property, plant, and equipment. Noncurrent investments include sinking funds and minority investments in subsidiary companies. A *sinking fund* is an investment used to repay borrowed funds. Often sinking funds require periodic contributions until the fund is large enough to retire debt. Investments are made in subsidiary companies for the purpose of developing business relationships. For example, Ford Motor Company has a minority investment in Mazda Motors of Japan. This investment provides Ford an opportunity to participate in and learn about the Japanese automobile market.

Property, Plant, and Equipment (Fixed Assets)

The *property, plant, and equipment* (PPE) include all of the physical assets required to deliver products and services. The property (or land) is valued on the balance sheet at original acquisition cost. The balance sheet value is not adjusted for changes in market value unless the market value has been permanently impaired. The plant and equipment are valued at original acquisition cost less accumulated depreciation. The accumulated depreciation measures the amount of the original acquisition cost that has been depreciated since the asset was acquired. Depreciation expense is the amount of acquisition cost allocated to a particular period. The most common method of depreciation is the straight-line method, which is determined as

$$\text{Annual depreciation expense} = \frac{\text{Acquisition cost} - \text{Residual value}}{\text{Useful life in Years}}$$

Exhibit 8. 4 illustrates accumulated depreciation and depreciation expense. Depreciation does not attempt to measure the decline in property and equipment value. Depreciation only matches the service benefits of plant and equipment to accounting periods that benefit from those assets. The property, plant, and equipment are shown on the balance sheet at net book value. *Net book value* (or *net fixed assets*) is the difference between acquisition cost and accumulated depreciation at a point in time.

The efficiency of property, plant, and equipment can be evaluated by measuring the sales earned per dollar of fixed assets (property, plant, and equipment). This is termed the *fixed asset turnover ratio* and is calculated as

$$\text{Fixed asset turnover} = \frac{\text{Sales}}{\text{Fixed assets}}$$

The higher this ratio, the more efficient are the fixed assets of the business. In a sense, this measure provides insight as to how well a company uses its fixed capacity. For example, a hotel experiencing only 60 percent occupancy (i.e., 60 percent of the room nights are occupied by guests) will have a poorer fixed asset turnover than a similar hotel with 85 percent occupancy.

Liabilities

The liabilities of a business enterprise are the items that meet the following four conditions:

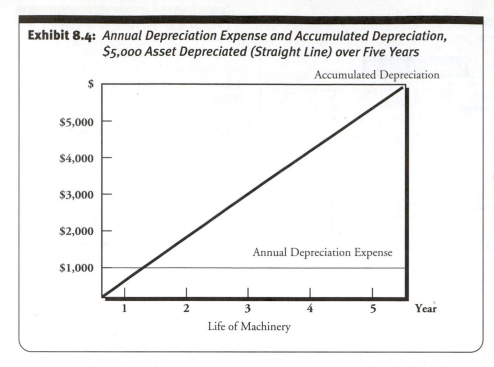

Exhibit 8.4: *Annual Depreciation Expense and Accumulated Depreciation, $5,000 Asset Depreciated (Straight Line) over Five Years*

ties, called a *current ratio,* for several retailers:

Wal-Mart,	0.92
Kmart,	2.00
JCPenney,	1.71
Sears,	1.82
Toys 'R' Us,	1.24
Amazon.com,	1.40

As you can see, there is wide variation in the current ratio across the various retailers. A closer examination of the financial statements helps the reader interpret the ratios. For example, Wal-Mart had an unusually large debt installment payment due within the next year, which increased current liabilities and brought its current ratio below 1.0.

Long-Term Liabilities

Organizations may acquire funds through long-term borrowings, such as mortgages, bonds, and bank notes. These instruments require the company to repay a fixed amount of principal at some date in the future. In addition, the company is obligated to pay a contracted return on the debt. This contracted return, termed *interest expense,* is accrued and paid over the time period that the debt is outstanding. Generally, the outstanding debt is paid back in installments, much like a home mortgage or auto note. The notes to the financial statements will provide detailed information about the amount, terms, and interest rates of outstanding debt. From a financial management perspective, the firm should refund high interest cost debt as market interest rates fall. Management uses the money from long-term debt to make investments that will provide a return that exceeds the interest expense. When the investment return exceeds the cost of the debt, this is termed *positive financial leverage.*

A company must be careful not to be overly indebted. As with individuals, too much debt can cause interest and principal payments to become too burdensome. One measure of debt load is the ratio of total liabilities to total assets. The following are some companies and the ratio of total liabilities to total assets for each:

Adolph Coors,	43%
Sprint Corp,	66%
Procter & Gamble,	64%
American Airlines,	72%
eBay,	12%

As you can see, it is not uncommon for the total debt to exceed 50 percent of total assets.

1. Will result in future sacrifices (cash outflows).
2. Are estimable in money terms.
3. Are results of a past transaction.
4. Are owned by the enterprise.

The liabilities of a business enterprise are defined much like the assets except that liabilities represent future cash outflows. The liabilities of a business enterprise are used to finance operations much like an auto loan is used to finance the purchase of an automobile. Companies use liabilities to provide money to acquire assets, such as inventory and property, plant, and equipment. Liabilities, like assets, are divided into current and noncurrent categories.

Current liabilities are obligations that are expected to be paid within the next year or operating cycle, whichever is longer. The most common current liabilities are *accounts payable, accrued expenses,* and *short-term notes payable.*

Current Liabilities

Accounts payable are generated from purchases made on credit. To illustrate, a credit card balance is an accounts payable for an individual. As discussed in the accounts receivable section, when businesses conduct transactions with each other, it is usually on a credit basis. When a company sells on credit, an account receivable is established by the selling company for the purchase price, while a complementary account payable is established on the purchasing company's books for the purchase price.

The balance of the accounts payable represents the total amount owed to suppliers at a point in time. Cash is remitted to satisfy accounts payable within the time terms of the supplier (generally within a month).

Accrued expenses payable are amounts of cash owed various suppliers for services received but not yet paid. An example would be utilities expense for power consumed but not yet paid. At the end of the month, when financial statements are prepared, the monthly power bill may not yet have been paid, yet a month's worth of power has been consumed. The accrued utilities payable will be satisfied when the company receives and pays the power bill during the beginning of the next month. Other accrued expenses payable are related to wages, advertising, rentals, interest, and contract billings.

Noncurrent notes payable are the amounts of cash owed to a bank for a short-term loan. Often banks provide companies short-term loans to meet the cash needs within the operating cycle. For example, a toy manufacturer may need a short-term loan to manufacture toys for the Christmas season. After the season when the revenues are collected, the bank loan can be paid.

A rule of thumb for many companies is that the current assets should at least be maintained at 150 percent of the level of the current liabilities. This ensures that there are sufficient funds on hand to meet current obligations when they come due. To illustrate, the following shows the ratio of current assets divided by current liabili-

In some capital-intensive industries, such as airlines, the ratio can be much higher.

Stockholders' Equity

The *stockholders' equity* section of the balance sheet measures the owners' claims on the assets of the firm. The common elements of this section are *common stock, preferred stock, treasury stock,* and *retained earnings.*

Common Stock

The common stock of the firm represents the stockholders' original investment in the firm. For Martinez Company, common stockholders have invested $1,400,000 into the firm. This investment could have been an original investment to start the firm or several investments over a period of time. The average price paid by investors was $28 per share ($1,400,000 ÷ 50,000 common shares). It should be pointed out that the common stock amount shown on the balance sheet is not the market value of the firm as determined by the stock price on a stock exchange. The market value of the firm is not reflected on the balance sheet.

Preferred Stock

Companies will often issue a class of stock that has a preference right over the common shareholders. This type of stock is termed a *preferred stock.* Preference rights include preference to dividends. This means that the preferred stockholders will receive a dividend before the common stockholders. However, this dividend is usually stated as a fixed percent of original selling price, or par value, of the stock. Thus, for example, 9 percent preferred stock that has a $100 par value will pay a dividend of $9 per share.

Treasury Stock

Treasury stock represents common stock that has been repurchased by the firm. The firm cannot be considered an owner in itself; thus, it is inappropriate to disclose the treasury stock as an asset. Instead, the treasury stock is more like common stock that has been temporarily retired from the stock market. For Martinez, the treasury stock was repurchased at an average price of $32 per share ($160,000 ÷ 5,000 shares). The treasury stock is disclosed as a reduction in stockholders' equity. The treasury stock may be reissued to the market at a later date or granted to senior executives as part of the executive stock option plans.

Retained Earnings

Retained earnings are the earnings of the firm that have been reinvested since the firm's inception. The income of a profitable firm can be either reinvested into the business or paid out as a dividend to the stockholders. The earnings that have been reinvested into the assets of the firm are added to the retained earnings to reflect the amount of capital retained by the firm. Likewise, if the company experiences losses, the retained earnings will go down by the amount of the loss. Thus, the balance sheet stays in balance because the increase in net assets from earnings retained by the business is "balanced" by the Retained Earnings account.

It is not unusual for the retained earnings balance for a young company to be negative because there have only been losses. As the company matures and is able to earn profits, the retained earnings will begin to become positive.

See **Exhibit 8.5** for the calculation of the end-of-period retained earnings balance for Martinez Company.

The retained earnings are in the stockholders' equity section of the balance sheet because it represents the owners' increase in the book value of the firm after dividends. The retained earnings should not be considered as a "pool of cash" or a "rainy day fund." Retained earnings are no such thing. The retained earnings have already been reinvested in the firm and represent the increase in the net assets of the firm since its inception.

Measuring Changes in Wealth: The Income Statement

The *income statement* measures the change in wealth for the organization over an accounting period. The two major components of the income statement are revenues and expenses. *Revenues* represent increases in wealth from providing goods and services. The corresponding increase in wealth is shown on the balance sheet as increases in assets (e.g., cash or accounts receivable) or reductions of liabilities. *Expenses* represent reductions in wealth from using goods and services provided by others. The corresponding decrease in wealth is shown on the balance sheet as reductions in assets (e.g., cash) or increases in liabilities (e.g., accounts payable).

The excess of the revenue over the expenses incurred in earning the revenue is called *net income* or *net profit.* If the expens-

Exhibit 8.5: *Martinez Company Retained Earnings Balance*

Retained earnings, beginning of period	$ 840,000
Net income for the period	200,000
Less: dividends for the period	0
Retained earnings, end of period	$1,040,000

es of the business exceed the revenue, the excess is a *net loss.* For this reason the income statement is sometimes referred to as a *profit and loss statement,* or P&L. It is impractical to determine the exact amount of expense for each revenue transaction. Therefore, the net income or the net loss is reported for a period of time, such as a month or a year, rather than for each revenue transaction.

The net income (or net loss) is determined using a matching process involving two steps. First, revenue is recorded during the period. Second, expenses used in generating the revenue are matched against the revenue to determine the net income or the net loss. Generally, the revenue for providing a service is recorded after the service has been provided to the customer. The expenses incurred in generating revenue during a period are then recorded and are thus matched against the revenue.

The net income is an important indicator of a firm's financial performance for a period of time. Often the net income is expressed as a percentage of total assets or stockholders' equity in order to aid comparisons across firms. For example, the net income as a percent of total assets and stockholders' equity is shown in **Exhibit 8.6** for Wal-Mart and Kmart.

Exhibit 8.6: *Net Income Information for Wal-Mart and Kmart*

	Wal-Mart	Kmart
Net income as a percent of total assets	8%	2.7%
Net income as a percent of stockholders' equity	20%	6.4%

Exhibit 8.7: Martinez Company Income Statement for the Year Ended 200X

Sales	$6,200,000
Cost of Goods Sold	3,600,000
Gross Profit	$2,600,000
Sales, General, and Administrative Expenses	2,000,000
Operating Profit	$ 600,000
Other Income and Expenses	(250,000)
Income before Taxes	$ 350,000
Income Taxes	150,000
Net Income	$ 200,000
Earnings per share ($200,000/50,000 shares)	$4.00

Exhibit 8.8: Inventory Relationships for a Manufacturer

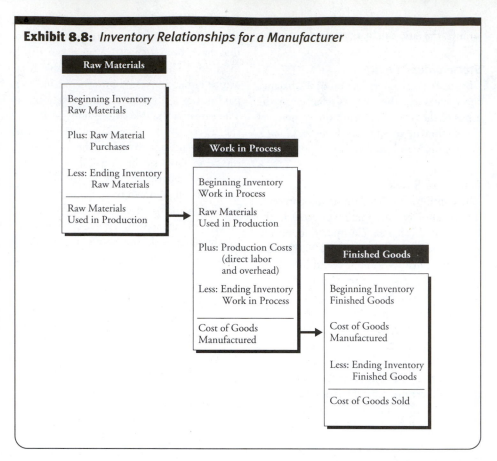

As you can see, Wal-Mart's financial performance was much better than Kmart's. Wal-Mart stockholders are receiving a rate of return nearly 20 percent on their investment, while Kmart stockholders are receiving only a little more than 6 percent return on their investment.

The income statement for Martinez for the year ended 200X is shown in **Exhibit 8.7**. Unlike the balance sheet, which shows the financial position of a firm at a point in time, the income statement shows the results of operations for a period of time, such as for a quarter or for a year. Martinez Company earned $200,000 in net income during the period, which is the change in net assets for the period.

Revenues (Sales)

Revenues are earned by a firm for providing goods and services to customers. Often the terms *revenues* and *sales* are used interchangeably. For example, if a firm sold $3,000 worth of goods to a customer, the revenues would increase by $3,000 as would the cash (or accounts receivable) on the balance sheet. The amount of revenue is determined by multiplying the quantity of goods and services sold by the price charged the customer. The revenue is accumulated in the revenue account until the end of the accounting period. At the end of the accounting period, all of the income statement accounts, including the revenue account, are "zeroed out" in order to begin a new period.

Cost of Goods Sold

The *cost of goods sold* for a manufacturer is the accumulated cost to make a product for sale. These costs include the direct materials, direct labor, and factory overhead. *Direct materials* are the materials used to make a product. For example, electrical components would be direct materials for a personal computer. *Direct labor* refers to the employee costs associated with fabricating and assembling products. For example, the assembly wages would be direct labor for a personal computer. *Factory overhead,* sometimes termed *burden,* represents all remaining costs incurred in production that are not direct materials or labor. Examples of factory overhead include power, plant manager salaries, maintenance, and factory depreciation. The direct labor, direct materials, and factory overhead are frequently termed *product costs* since they are costs directly associated with producing the product.

Exhibit 8.8 illustrates the inventory relationships in a manufacturer. A manufacturer must purchase the raw materials for production. The beginning raw material inventory plus current period purchases, less the ending inventory, yield the raw material placed into production. The raw materials placed in production are added with other production inputs, direct labor and factory

overhead, in order to build product. The inventory of partially completed product is termed *work in process inventory.* The cost of goods manufactured during a period is the sum of all production and material cost inputs, plus the beginning work in process inventory, less the ending work in process inventory. The cost of goods manufactured is added to the finished goods inventory. The cost of goods sold during the period is the beginning finished goods inventory, plus the cost of goods manufactured, less the ending finished goods inventory, to yield the cost of goods sold.

The difference between the revenues and the cost of goods sold is termed the *gross margin* (or *gross profit*). The *gross margin ratio,* which is gross margin divided by sales, can be used to compare companies in an industry. Companies with a high gross margin ratio compared to the industry either control their costs or price their products better than the competition.

Sales, General, and Administrative Expenses

The *sales, general, and administrative expenses* (SG&A expenses) are the costs of nonmanufacturing services purchased by a firm. Examples of SG&A costs include advertising, research and development

Exhibit 8.9: *Dell Computer and Apple Computer Operating Profit Information*

	Dell Computer	Apple Computer
	(All numbers in thousands, except the ratios)	
Consolidated net sales	$31,888,000	$7,983,000
Cost of sales	$25,445,000	$5,817,000
Gross margin	$6,443,000	$2,166,000
SG&A expenses	$3,780,000	$1,644,000
Operating profit	**$2,663,000**	**$ 522,000**
Gross margin ratio	20.2%	27.1%
Operating profit ratio	8.3%	6.5%

(R&D), shipping, office depreciation, office salaries, sales office, and sales force expenses. SG&A expenses are frequently termed *period costs* since they are incurred in and benefit a particular accounting period. Some SG&A expenses, such as R&D, may actually benefit more than one period; however, accounting practices require that they are expensed in the period incurred rather than deferred and matched with future periods benefited.

The difference between the gross margin and the SG&A expenses is termed the *operating profit*. Analysts will often evaluate a company's performance using the *operating profit ratio,* which is the operating profit divided by the sales. To illustrate, consider the gross margin and operating profit ratios of Dell Computer and Apple Computer companies for a recent year (see **Exhibit 8.9**).

The gross margin ratio of Apple Computer is 27.1 percent, while that of Dell Computer is only 20.2 percent. Note, however, that the operating profit ratio for Dell Computer is actually higher than Apple's ratio. Dell Computer has smaller selling and R&D expenses; thus, it is able to operate profitably on smaller gross profit margins. Apple Computer, on the other hand, invests much more in selling and R&D; thus, it must sell its computers at higher gross profit margins in order to remain profitable. Even so, Apple is not able to sell its computers at a price high enough to generate operating profit as a percent of sales equal to that of Dell.

Other Income and Expenses

The other income and expenses include gains and losses from the disposition of assets and interest income and expenses. Some companies may also include income and expenses that are incidental to the principal line of business. For example, licensing income, fines, and litigation gains or losses may be disclosed below the operating profit line as other income and expenses. Gains and losses for disposing of assets are determined by comparing the proceeds upon sale with the book value of the assets. The *book value* is the original cost of the asset less accumulated depreciation. Thus, if an asset that originally cost $10,000 with $4,000 of accumulated depreciation was sold for $8,000, a $2,000 ($8,000 – $6,000) gain would be recognized as "other income."

Income Taxes

The federal tax code requires most corporations to pay income taxes on their earnings. The tax is calculated using tax methods, which frequently differ from financial reporting approaches. The statutory rate can reach as high as 45 percent of earnings. A company that has a loss may elect to carry the loss forward to years in which positive earnings occur. In this way, the loss can offset earnings in future periods and reduce the amount of taxes owed in those years. The net effect is to provide a tax benefit from years with losses to years in which there are positive earnings.

Measuring Changes in Liquidity: The Statement of Cash Flows

The last major financial statement is the statement of cash flows. The *statement of cash flows* explains the change in a firm's balance sheet cash balance from the beginning of the period to the end of the period. Thus, the statement of cash flows shows how a firm acquires and uses cash during an operating year. So, like the income statement, the statement of cash flows provides disclosure for a period of time rather than at a point in time. The statement of cash flows is divided into three sections: operating activities, investing activities, and financing activities. An example of the cash flow from operations for Martinez Company is shown in **Exhibit 8.10**.

Operating Activities

The cash flow from operating activities represents the amount of cash generated from providing goods and services to customers. This amount is determined by subtracting cash disbursed for operating activities from cash received from operations. The major sources of cash from operations are, of course, sales. Notice that the $6,200,000 sales amount shown on the income statement is also the amount received in cash shown on the statement of cash flows. Although these two numbers are equal in this example, this will often not be the case for most companies. This is so because sales are recorded on the income statement when goods are shipped. However, cash is collected at a later point in time. Recording sales in this way, termed *accrual accounting*, causes a timing difference between sales recognition (on the income statement) and cash collection (on the statement of cash flows).

Cash is disbursed for operations to support items related to production, selling, administrative, and taxes during the period. Each of these items corresponds to operating expenses on the income statement. The cash disbursed for production is related to cost of goods sold. The cost of goods sold means the costs matched against sales. However, the cash associated with producing the products may have occurred in prior periods. Thus, the cash outflow for production will often not be equal to the cost of goods sold in any one period. If inventories are building up, the cash outflow for production will exceed cost of goods sold. If the inventories are being depleted, the cash outflow for production will be less than the cost of goods sold.

The cash disbursed for advertising, sales expenses, and R&D is related to the sales, general, and administrative expenses. Notice that the total of these amounts, $2,000,000, is equal to the total sales, general, and administrative expenses in the income statement. The cash disbursed for interest is related to other income and expenses, and the cash disbursed for taxes is related to the tax expense. Again, the cash disbursement numbers may not necessarily be identical to the corresponding income statement expense numbers due to accrual accounting. Additionally, depreciation expense is a noncash expense on the income statement and should not be included on the statement of cash flows. For this reason the cash flow from operations is frequently greater that the net income for most firms.

Exhibit 8.10: Martinez Company Statement of Cash Flows for Year Ended 200X

Cash Balance, Beginning of period		$130,000
Operating Activities		
Receipts from operating activities:		
Sales	$6,200,000	
Interest and other income	50,000	
Total cash receipts from operating activities		$6,250,000
Disbursements for operating activities		
Production	3,300,000	
Advertising	700,000	
Sales expenses	900,000	
Research and development	400,000	
Interest	300,000	
Taxes	150,000	
Total disbursements for operating activities		5,750,000
Cash flow from operations		500,000
Investing Activities		
Purchase of plant capacity	(270,000)	
Sale of subsidiary investment	120,000	
Cash flow from investing activities		(150,000)
Financing Activities		
Issue note payable to bank	600,000	
Retire note payable to bank	(900,000)	
Sell stock to owners	100,000	
Purchase treasury shares	(160,000)	
Cash flow from financing activities		(360,000)
Change in cash flow		(10,000)
Cash Balance, End of period		$120,000

Investing Activities

The investing activities of a firm originate from the changes in noncurrent assets that occur over the period. Increases in noncurrent assets are a use (disbursement) of cash, while decreases are a source (receipt) of cash. For Martinez in Exhibit 8.10 there were two noncurrent asset transactions. Martinez used cash to increase plant capacity, which increases the noncurrent asset, plant and equipment. Martinez received cash through the sale of a long-term investment in a subsidiary. The cash received from this sale is shown as a positive cash flow from investing activities. On Martinez's balance sheet, the subsidiary investment would be reduced to the present balance of $430,000.

Financing Activities

The financing activities of a firm originate from changes in long-term liabilities and stockholders' equity over the period. Increases in long-term liabilities or stockholders' equity are a source of cash. Issuing bonds or stock results in cash inflows to the firm. Decreases in long-term liabilities or stockholders' equity are a use of cash because the firm must use cash to retire debt or repurchase stock, as treasury stock, from the market. Martinez had a number of financing transactions.

Martinez had both a receipt and disbursement in cash from long-term notes payable transactions with the bank. In Exhibit 8.10, Martinez retired $900,000 of notes payable, which required a use of $900,000 cash, and issued new notes for $600,000, which provided cash of $600,000. Why would Martinez retire a note only to turn around and reissue another note to the bank? One likely reason would be to refinance a loan at a lower interest rate.

In addition, Martinez engaged in some transactions with its stockholders. Martinez received $100,000 in cash from issuing new stock to owners and used $160,000 in cash to repurchase common stock for the treasury.

SUMMARY

In this chapter, we have introduced the basic financial reporting environment and financial statements used by public companies. **Exhibit 8.11** provides a summary of the financial statement relationships. To review, the balance sheet measures the wealth (net assets) of an enterprise at a point in time. The income statement explains how wealth changed over a period of time between two balance sheet dates. Thus, the income statement measures the operating performance of a firm for a period of time. The statement of cash flows provides information about the sources and uses of cash over a period of time. The statement of cash flows provides a complete explanation for the change in the cash balance between two balance sheet dates. Thus, all three statements are said to articulate: All three statements are linked together.

Managers often need to read financial information from financial statements. As you play *Marketplace,* you should be able to learn how financial statements reflect the business events of organizations.

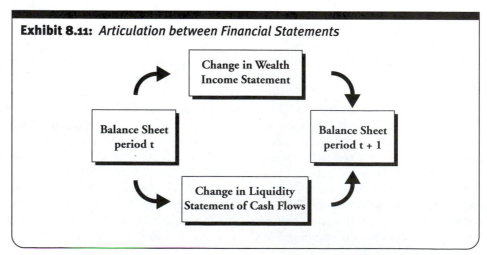

Exhibit 8.11: Articulation between Financial Statements

PART 3

Expanding the Business

Chapter 9

Ernest R. Cadotte
University of Tennessee

Obtaining Venture Capital by Writing and Presenting a Business Plan

Any company, new or growing, needs capital in order to embark on a business venture. The funding needed to back a venture and the inspiration driving the venture typically come from different sources. The entrepreneurs who lead startups and established businesses into new ventures are typically people who have long had "ideas that require substantial capital to implement but [lack] the funds to finance these projects themselves."[1] To solve this problem, entrepreneurs increasingly turn to venture capital funds—instead of bank loans or other sources of debt funding—as a source of capital. "Over the past two decades, there has been a tremendous boom in the venture capital industry. The pool of U.S. venture capital funds has grown from less than $1 billion in 1976 (Charles River Associates 1976) to over $60 billion in 1999. . . . The supply of venture capital is also likely to continue growing."[2]

A partnership with a *venture capitalist*—a term used to refer to anyone investing in a new business venture—promises more than funding. A venture capital firm also contributes to a venture by "identifying and evaluating business opportunities, including management, entry, or growth strategies; negotiating and closing the investment; tracking and coaching the company; providing technical and management assistance; and attracting additional capital, directors, management, suppliers, and other key stakeholders, and resources."[3] Clearly, there are many benefits to a venture capital arrangement.

How does an entrepreneur go about obtaining venture capital? Convincing an investor to believe in an entrepreneur and his management team (as well as in the idea, operating philosophies, and projections of his team) involves three steps. First,

Learning Objectives

After reading this chapter, you should be able to:

- Understand the value of partnering with a venture capitalist.
- Describe the roles of the entrepreneur and the venture capitalist.
- Understand the motivations of both entrepreneurs and venture capitalists.
- Explain the types of commitment an entrepreneur must be willing to make.
- Appreciate the importance of an experienced and balanced management team and a well-thought-out plan.
- Describe the purpose and contents of each section of a business plan.
- List the entrepreneur's goals in presenting a business plan to potential investors.
- Explain the process of negotiating a deal and list challenging questions that an entrepreneur may encounter during negotiations.

the entrepreneur must define his own goals and understand the expectations of the venture capitalist. Next, the entrepreneur and management team will write a business plan, which is the vehicle for convincing the venture capitalist that partnering with

BEST-USE CORRELATIONS

Venture capital is a frequent source of new funding for entrepreneurial firms. In *Marketplace* Q5, teams prepare and sell a business plan to venture capitalists with the goal of obtaining new investment. What do venture capitalists want? If you cannot answer this question, Chapter 9 will steer you in the right direction.

What Goes into a Business Plan?
A business plan is a sales tool that conveys the excitement and promise of a business enterprise to potential investors. It should include (1) an assessment of market opportunity, (2) a review of team performance to date, (3) a statement of overall business strategy, (4) tactical plans with substantiation for how functional operations will together achieve an overall strategy, and (5) historical financial statements and pro forma projections for the future.

What's the Payback?
Investors look for business opportunities with earning power. In *Marketplace,* when you make your business plan presentation, make the venture capital community sit up and take notice. Use this chapter's introduction to valuation and Chapter 10's comprehensive discussion of the concept, to convince them that your firm will make money.

The Devil Is in the Details
In *Marketplace,* teams need to prepare more than one business plan: a rather detailed plan, along the lines outlined in Chapter 9, and an abridged version to give to potential investors. The detailed plan will carry you through far-ranging and precise discussions. The short plan is simply a starting point for the venture capital discussions.

the entrepreneur is a good choice. Finally, the team presents the plan to potential investors and negotiates a deal.

ENTREPRENEUR'S GOALS

Because entrepreneurs and investors are all human, they have an infinite variety of goals. One of the challenges of entrepreneurship is finding a match amid this variety. Before an entrepreneur can invite like-minded potential investors to become involved in his venture, however, he must first be able to articulate his needs clearly. An entrepreneur "needs to be clear about what he or she wants from an investor and then set forth on a course of action that will give him or her the highest probability of achieving that objective."[4] In *Attracting Equity Investors*, Dean Shepherd and Evan Douglas advise entrepreneurs to start out by asking, "What do you want from an investor?"[5]

An entrepreneur must begin his search for funding by honestly, even harshly, evaluating not only his idea, but also himself and his management team. "The risks in entrepreneurship are you, your team, and any fundamental flaws in your venture idea. You must make a reasonable first evaluation of these risks. You should then be able to put together a business plan and avoid many of the early errors . . . that so often cripple new ventures."[6]

Similarly, entrepreneurs should be selective about the investors with whom they choose to partner. This partnership "can be a very significant factor in determining the success of a business development."[7] An early list of potential investors can be narrowed by matching the appetites of investors "for the stage, industry, technology, and capital requirements proposed"[8] with the type of business venture the entrepreneur proposes.

VENTURE CAPITALIST'S EXPECTATIONS

The entrepreneur and management team will not be the only ones to benefit if the venture is a success. Investors will enjoy the rewards of the venture as well. The venture capital industry is based on the premise of supplying "capital and other resources to entrepreneurs in businesses with high growth potential in hopes of achieving a high rate of return on invested funds."[9] In this way, the "relationship between the entrepreneurial team and the investor should be considered a strategic alliance."[10]

A venture capitalist will be willing to become involved in a venture only from which she can see that she will benefit. Experienced and critical, venture capitalists are practiced at predicting the likelihood of venture success. Potential investors look for "ventures that:
- fit within the domain of their knowledge and experience.
- offer a new product or service of superior value.
- serve a long-felt need.
- will grow by rolling out new products, new markets, or both.
- are very likely to be a success."[11]

Investors also expect the entrepreneur to be committed, the management team to be experienced and balanced, and the plans for the venture to be well thought out.

ENTREPRENEUR COMMITMENT
Effectively operating a new venture is all-consuming. Knowing this, a venture capitalist will expect an entrepreneur to commit all of his resources—especially time, energy, and money—to the venture.
- Entrepreneurs talk about "a time commitment. . . not recognized by the 8-, 10-, 12-hour employee or seasoned executive who has just worked hard. . . . [Entrepreneurs know] 15-16-hour days, seven-days commitment, no vacations. . . . The average person does not understand that what it really takes is time."[12]
- An undying personal commitment is also evidenced by an entrepreneur's enthusiasm and competitive spirit. These sentiments must be genuine because venture capitalists are on their guard for dishonesty.
- An entrepreneur must be willing to invest her own money—all of it. Refusal to give up any financial resource will leave a venture capitalist unconvinced of total commitment.

In her article "How to Seduce a Venture Capitalist," Sarah Gracie advises entrepreneurs preparing to approach a venture capitalist that "you need to convince them that you, and only you, are the person to drive the project forward."[13]

Management Team Experience and Balance

An entrepreneur rarely manages a venture by himself. Instead, he assembles a management team by inviting a number of other managers—each with specific skills—to join him in operating the venture. While many factors contribute to the success of a business, venture capitalists tend to focus on the management team as the key success factor. One expert goes so far as to assert that "without the right team, none of the other parts really matters."[14] Venture capitalists would rather "look at a grade-A manager with a grade-B business idea than a grade-B manager with a grade-A idea."[15] The entrepreneur and others who round out the management team should have sufficient, complementary skills and experience to manage effectively, seize opportunities, solve problems, and make profits. Venture capitalists criticize those who blindly attempt to run a business without entrepreneurial skills, technical training, or sophistication in marketing, financial management, production, administration, and research and development.

Few individuals, if any, have all the skills necessary to single-handedly build a business. "A solo entrepreneur would need to simultaneously manage marketing and sales, finance and accounting, research and development, engineering and production, and human resource management, not to mention various other leadership and motivational skills he or she must possess to keep the new business headed toward success."[16] An entrepreneur, therefore, is well advised to construct a management team of people who are strong in her areas of weakness.

Once a management team is assembled, its members must learn to work together as a team. A cohesive management team exudes professionalism and projects an air of success, which fosters confidence on the part of investors. A management team that does not work well together is conspicuous and will not attract investors.

Well-Thought-Out Plan

If an entrepreneur has given serious thought to his own goals and to the expectations an investor will have of him and his management team, then he is already moving toward having a well-thought-out plan. The process of writing a business plan—described in detail later—often helps a management team solidify the goals of the venture and discover critical issues and potential risks that need to be evaluated. According to William Bygrave, "the discipline of the process [of writing a business plan] forces you to articulate your vision and how and when you expect to achieve it."[17]

Investors "prefer ventures with plausible, carefully thought-out plans to address well-defined markets. A solid plan reassures them about the competence of the entrepreneur and provides an objective yardstick for measuring progress and testing initial assumptions."[18]

Venture capitalists may also expect a management team to have a back-up strategy to use in case the original plan fails. The management team needs to be able to prove it is able to think things through in the event of a setback in the proposed strategy.

BUSINESS PLAN

More than anything else, a "business plan is *a selling document* that conveys the excitement and promise of [a] business to any potential backers or stakeholders."[19] The business plan is the most valuable tool an entrepreneur has to convince a venture capitalist to fund his venture. Therefore, "entrepreneurs must learn how to write a plan that stands out from the rest" and need to deal with the fact that "about 90% of business plans sent to venture capital investors are thrown away."[20]

By considering what he wants from potential investors and what he has to offer them, an entrepreneur has already begun to build a business plan. To get the plan on paper, an entrepreneur might "list at least five major benefits that [his] business would receive out of a strategic alliance with this particular investor. Then list five benefits this investor would receive out of a strategic alliance with [his] business."[21]

The business plan must speak for the entrepreneur because this document is the first exposure investors will have to the venture. "If the business plan fails to gain investor excitement, the entrepreneur is unlikely to receive the opportunity to make a presentation or answer any questions."[22]

Most experts agree that "for a venture seeking to raise venture capital or other equity in today's highly competitive environment, a quality business plan is a must."[23] Investors will be motivated to read a business plan that is concise—brief and to the point—and clear throughout. A successful plan will seize every opportunity to show what is special about the venture.

The following is a description of each section of a business plan. The lists of questions to be answered in each section offer a guide to writing such a plan. **Exhibit 9.1** contains an outline for the business plan with suggestions for the number of pages for each section.

Exhibit 9.1: *Outline for Business Plan*

	Recommended Number of Pages
Executive Summary	1 to 2
Description of Business and Industry	2
Your Company	
Industry	
Historical Performance Chart	
Market Opportunity Analysis (MOA)	4
Industry or Market Profile	
Customers	
Competition	
Channel	
Marketing Plan and Sales Tactics	6
Target Markets	
Product Line	
Pricing	
Promotion	
Distribution	
Market Rollout Campaign	
Manufacturing Plan	4
Capacity Investments	
Production Plan	
Continuous Improvements	
Production Costs	
Changeover Time and Costs	
Quality and Product Reliability	
Human Resource Plan	2
Personnel Requirements	
Compensation Packages	
Financial Plan and Financial Request	2
Funding Needs	
Funding Options	
Capital Structure	
Return on Investment to Investors	
Exit Strategies	
Tactical and Financial Planning Documents	
Tactical Time Chart	1
Summary Cash Flow Document	1
Appendices	
A. Place customer profiles here (one per page)	
B. Place competitor profiles here (one per page)	
C. Place market and brand forecasts here	
D. Place historical balance sheet, income statement, and cash flow statement here	
E. Place pro forma balance sheet, income statement, and cash flow statement here	

Executive Summary

The purpose of the executive summary is to condense the main points of the business plan into one or two pages that can be read quickly to determine the value of reading the rest of the plan. Since "investors rarely read past the first two pages,"[24] a disproportionate amount of the work of a business plan falls to the summary. The executive summary is the "first substantive contact the investor will have with [the] business. It must build interest and excitement. If it fails to encourage investors to keep reading, then they may stop reading and not express any interest in [the] business."[25]

Although the executive summary is the first part of the plan that potential investors will read, compiling the summary should actually be the last step in business plan preparation. The executive summary should briefly state the following:

- What is the makeup of the management team?
- How will the team achieve success?
- What is the company's product/service? What are the distinguishing features of the product/service?
- What is the estimated market for the product/service?
- How attractive is the market?
- What are the key projected financial data?
- How much money is the company seeking?
- What form is being requested, debt or equity?
- For what will the money be used?

The executive summary should cover the basics of the proposal rather than delving into specifics. Inciting potential investors to reject your plan "can be as simple as failing to say how much you want to raise and what you will do with the money," says Vivian McCarron, research and development partner with PricewaterhouseCoopers.[26]

Description of Business and Industry

The business and industry section serves to orient a venture capitalist to the entrepreneur's industry and to familiarize her with the entrepreneur's business. Here also is an opportunity for an entrepreneur to show an investor what makes this business special.

Business Overview

The business overview should include a description of the "product/service, possible customers, and regions of operation,"[27] as well as the company's objectives. If the proposed venture is being undertaken by a company already doing business, it is necessary to review the history of the company, including the evolution of its products/services, financial performance, early setbacks and operating losses, and the role each officer has played in bringing the company to where it is today. Entrepreneurs might include a timeline illustrating the milestones in the life of the company. All of this information allows the investor to read this section "to obtain a brief overview of who and what the company is 'about,' that is, he or she needs to develop a 'feel' for the company and to establish whether it fits within the category of businesses the investor wants to pursue."[28]

Industry Overview

The business plan must describe the industry and offer information about the current status and prospects for it. Investors will read this section to determine that entrepreneurs "are entering an industry that is large and/or growing, and one that's structurally attractive."[29] The industry trends should be addressed as well as any major economical, technological, legal, or social threats. The industry overview might "describe the principal participants and how they are performing, growth in sales and profits, and also any published forecasts for the current year, companies that have recently entered or left these markets and why."[30]

Market Opportunity Analysis

The business plan should include market, customer, key competitor and channel profiles, which together convince investors that there is a market for the proposed product or service and that anticipated sales in the targeted areas can be met in the face of competition. This section of the plan is called a *market opportunity analysis* (MOA). The MOA (which is explained in more detail in Chapter 4) is the portion of the business plan designed to provide a "clear identification of the existing and future market needs as well as the niche that will allow a new or smaller growing business to exist and successfully expand."[31]

Conducting the type of market research needed to write an MOA is complex and involved, but producing an MOA is preferable to making the venture capitalist do the analysis himself. The MOA allows entrepreneurs "to argue that the opportunity is real, not a mirage, and that they have at their disposal the resources and skill necessary to force the window [of opportunity] open, grasp the opportunity, and capitalize on it sooner and better than can anyone else."[32]

Market Profile

Analysis of customers and the industry as a whole is crucial. A market profile would begin along the following lines:

- What is the total dollar volume for the market?
- What is the overall unit demand for the product/service?
- Why do customers buy this product (what benefits do they seek)?
- How is the market structured? Identify market segments.
- Who are the major suppliers, and what are their sizes?
- What is the level of product knowledge in the industry?
- What does the future look like?
- What is the growth rate?
- Are there seasonal fluctuations?
- What industry trends address new technical developments and new/changing customer needs?
- How do your company and its products fit into the industry?
- How has your product penetrated the industry?

Customer Profile

Because the venture will ultimately rely on its customers, it is vital to know who the customers will be. The entrepreneur must constantly remind herself of her dependence on customer satisfaction and loyalty.

It is a mistake when entrepreneurs take the "Field of Dreams" approach to customers: "build it, and they will come. That strategy works in the movies but is not very sensible in the real world."[33] Potential investors recognize that "entrepreneurs tend to overestimate the size of their market."[34] If potential investors doubt the entrepreneur's honesty "about your market size and growth estimates, they may lose interest in the rest of your proposal."[35] The customer profile should, therefore, be realistic in answering these questions:

- Who are the major purchasers (business and/or demographic characteristics)?
- Why do they buy the product (benefits sought—convenience, time, and/or money savings)?

- For what do they use it?
- When do they buy the product?
- Where are the major purchasers?
- Does the product fit in with users' priorities?
- Do different groups of customers (segments) exist?
- What are the differences between segments? What are the similarities among segments?
- How big are the different segments?
- Are some segments more price sensitive than others?
- Is price or performance more important?
- Is the sale complex and long or relatively simple and straightforward?
- Is the product a large-cost item or a small-budget item?
- Are the customers brand loyal?
- How often do they buy?
- How do the customers decide what to buy (cautious, thrifty, impulsive, status seeking)?

A customer profile may also include lists of actual or potential customers. Additionally, if there are customers who have stopped purchasing the product, the business plan should explain why this has happened.

Key Competitor Profile

Entrepreneurs should keep two points in mind above all else when considering the competition. First, they should never assume that the competition is not a threat. Second, entrepreneurs need to ensure that their analysis and assessment of competition is comprehensive and realistic. A careful entrepreneur will gather far more information on the competition than he intends to include in the business plan. It is advisable, in fact, to devote an entire three-ring binder to each competitor.

Based on this wealth of information, an entrepreneur can then write a key competitor profile for each of the companies that will be primary competitors, assessing their strengths and weaknesses. These profiles are also the place for entrepreneurs to compare their products/services with those of competitors on the basis of design, price, performance, service, warranties, and other important features. This portion of the business plan might also address how customers rank the product compared with the competition's products.

"Professional investors are very wary of proposals in which competition is treated lightly"[36] or in a less than objective fashion. Entrepreneurs must be candid, honest, and complete in their evaluations of competition. A market profile for each key competitor should answer the following questions:

- What is the company's current sales volume and market share (in units and dollars)?
- Has the sales volume or market share fluctuated over time?
- What are the competitor's objectives and strategies regarding sales (in units and dollars) and market share?
- What is the company's apparent strategy in developing the market (target markets, products, price, promotion, channel)?
- Why is the competitor selling and why are customers buying?
- What are the competition's strengths and weaknesses regarding marketing, operations, management, finances, product, price, promotion, channel, and manufacturing?
- How would you characterize the company's competitive style (aggressive, conservative, careful, hard working)?
- Given recent events, what competitive actions is the company likely to take in the foreseeable future (12 to 24 months)?
- Given your planned future activities, what competitive actions is the competitor likely to take in response?

Channel Profile

The channel of distribution has been the key to success for many entrepreneurial firms. It is usually more practical to sell through established intermediaries than to sell direct. Although the intermediaries take a share of the final sales dollar, the increase in volume will often more than offset the loss in margin.

Constructing a channel profile gives you a picture of the many paths that comparable products take from the original supplier to the end user. These channels are the logical alternatives for your organization to consider as it attempts to distribute its products. Even if novel channels are employed, this picture and related analysis will help the entrepreneur evaluate the comparative features of each.

A channel profile should answer the following questions:

- How do end users normally seek out and purchase similar products?

- How is the product normally sold?
- What tasks and duties do intermediaries perform and how are they compensated?
- What are the responsibilities of the supplier to make a distribution channel effective?
- What is required to motivate an intermediary to carry and promote a new product?

Marketing Plan and Sales Tactics

According to J. A. Timmons in *New Venture Creation: Entrepreneurship in the 21st Century,* "The marketing plan describes how the sales projections will be attained. The marketing plan needs to detail the overall marketing strategy that will exploit the opportunity and your competitive advantages."[37] Simply put, the marketing plan should make clear "what is to be done, how it will be done, and who will do it."[38]

Target Markets

After getting to know the customers, the company will have to decide what type of targeting options it would like to pursue (mass or segmentation) and use the following questions to develop segment profiles:

- What segments will be targeted?
- What are the needs and demographics of each segment?
- How is each segment different from the rest of the market?
- Why were these segments selected for market development?
- Will some segments and/or geographic markets be overlooked at the outset and then targeted at a later date?
- What will be the order of market development and why?
- Will marketing efforts try to overlap segments?

Product Line

Any potential investor wants to know exactly what the venture will sell. This section of the plan should describe in detail the product to be offered and the needs it will satisfy. In *How to Raise Venture Capital,* Stanley Pratt advises entrepreneurs to "emphasize any distinctive features of your product/ service by highlighting the differences between what competitors currently have on the market and what you have or will offer. State candidly each feature's advantage or disadvantage."[39] Questions that should be considered for this section include:

- What is the product?

- What needs will it satisfy?
- At which market segment(s) is it aimed?
- In what way is the product unique/distinctive?
- How is the product different from what competitors have?
- Are there any patents, trade secrets, or other proprietary features?
- Does this product enjoy a favored or entrenched position in the market?
- Is there a natural extension of the product or potential to develop related products/services?

Research and Development

The goal of research and development (R&D) is to identify sustainable competitive advantages such as product quality, brand prestige, product reliability, service, distribution, and/or low cost. Investors "will be looking for reassurances that the technology works; that it will be continually improved upon; and whether or not there is potential for creating new products, generating new markets that will drive the new venture's growth, or both."[40] The following questions should be considered regarding efforts to develop new products:

- Will new technology help differentiate your products?
- What are you doing to increase your technology?
- Is research being directed at matching product designs with benefits sought by targeted markets?
- Will research generate new products or improve old products?
- How much will the research cost?
- How long will it take?
- How will the introduction of this research affect the market?
- Is a specific time frame desirable for the introduction?
- How much has been spent in the past on R&D?
- How much of this has resulted in sales?

Pricing

In a growing market, having the strategy of selling "quality products at reasonable prices" is not the route to take. After convincing investors that an idea is viable, entrepreneurs should not tell them that the product will be priced below the competition. If the product is as good as the business plan says it is, investors may take it

as a sign of poor salesmanship to adopt this pricing strategy.

The price should be discussed, including pricing objectives, policies, and gross profits. The following questions should be considered:

- What is the pricing strategy?
- How is price determined (costs, return on investment, competition, market sensitivity)?
- What are your profit margins by brand?
- How much of the price is designed to cover advertising costs and other marketing expenses?
- How do your prices compare to the competition's prices?
- Is the market sensitive to any differences?
- If the price is high, is it because you can get away with it?
- If the price is low, is it because the competition forced the price down?

Pricing decisions should include three main components: customer requirements, competitive requirements, and cost considerations. Some customers are less sensitive to price than others. Customers who are performance oriented will probably accept a higher price than those who are price sensitive (the latter will probably accept lower performance). Competition serves to set an upper bound on what can be charged for comparable products. Finally, prices must cover costs, including fixed costs, variable costs, profits, and growth. A venture must price for growth. The business plan should show each price broken down into these cost considerations. Activity-based costing (ABC) will be helpful here.

The price established for a product must be right to penetrate the market, maintain market share, and produce profits. This pricing section must "explain how the price you set will enable you to: secure/increase acceptance of your offering, and desirably increase your market share in the face of competition, and produce profits."[41]

The business plan should also include a list of proposed prices and how they compare to competitors' prices for similar brands. If prices are below the competition, the plan is strengthened by an explanation of how the venture will remain profitable and grow with this strategy.

Promotion

It makes no sense to build a better mousetrap if you do not tell anyone about it. Too many

new ventures spend all of their money in product development and production, with almost nothing set aside for advertising and promotion. One electronics firm spent $1,000,000 developing a product and budgeted only $10,000 to advertise it. The company folded for lack of market awareness.

A new venture must advertise while being cautious with the advertising budget. Advertising is very expensive, and to judge its effectiveness is difficult. This expense can be best managed by establishing advertising objectives, evaluating the attractiveness of alternate media relative to the probable use by target markets, and developing a media plan that maximizes market impact per dollar expended. A media plan should be laid out for 12 to 24 months, showing the media, frequency, and cost of each activity. The plan should also include a summary of each advertisement or brochure (or actual ad) and explain how the ad addresses the needs and wants of particular segments. In constructing such a plan, the entrepreneur needs to be sure to consider the following questions in review of the advertising issue:

- How important is advertising to the success of your products?
- Will national or local advertising be used?
- What types of media will you use?
- What will be the message? What benefits will be stressed?
- How much will advertising cost?
- What percentage of sales will advertising represent?
- How do your advertising expenditures compare to those of your competitors?
- How do you measure advertising effectiveness?
- What promotions are you utilizing (displays, conventions, trade shows)?
- What are your service policies for the product?

Distribution

The business plan needs to show how the venture will establish suitable outlets for products and move products to the market. A well-written marketing plan will take into consideration the organizations and individuals—referred to as *intermediaries*—who link producers with end users. Each of these intermediaries "performs particular activities in connecting end-users with desired goods and services."[42] These distribution activities include "procurement, storage, packaging, financing, transportation, and counseling."[43] Bypassing this distribution network in order to lower costs causes entrepreneurs to miss out on the efficiency of distribution systems. Intermediaries can make distribution much more effective by dividing up large quantities for individual end users, offering a wide variety of products in one location, and assuming some of the risk of doing business by purchasing the products they sell from the venture. In writing this part of the business plan, the entrepreneur should determine if it will be more beneficial to distribute products directly, with no intermediaries, or indirectly, with one or more intermediaries.

The plan should consider the following questions:

- What geographic market do you want to enter?
- What are the sizes of the segments in those areas?
- Will distribution be direct or indirect? If indirect, which intermediaries will be involved and when and how much will they be paid?
- What mode of transportation (trucks, airplanes, railroads, waterways) will be most suitable?
- How many salespeople will you assign to each sales channel? Each segment?
- How do you determine sales force size and effectiveness?
- When and where will you open new sales channels?

Market Rollout Campaign

The market rollout campaign combines this list of marketing decisions to become a full-scale strategy, including a time chart that details key decisions for market expansion. An outsider looking at this time chart should be able to assess the underlying marketing objectives and deduce the actions necessary to accomplish them. This chart should match the timeline in the cash-flow analysis. Astute businesspeople are quick to deduce the "real" business plan from the cash flow analysis; the size and timing of expenditures clearly indicate what is planned for the venture.

Manufacturing Plan

This section of the business plan needs to describe how the product will be produced. The manufacturing plan "needs to include such factors as plant location, the type of facilities needed, space requirements, capi-

tal equipment requirements, and labor force (both full- and part-time) requirements."[44] Investors "want to know how the manufacturing of the product or delivery of the service will be performed; what, if any, competitive advantages are derived from manufacturing and operations; and an assessment of associated risks and resulting risk reduction strategies to eliminate, or at least reduce, those risks."[45]

The manufacturing section of the business plan should include a production forecast (in conjunction with the market rollout campaign) including costs at various levels of operation. This plan, which will aid in cash-flow management, should follow the sales forecast. Since production is a venture's greatest expense, this production plan should be very detailed as to how many products will be produced in each time period over the next two years and answer the following:

- How are production levels determined and justified?
- Is production scheduled at the most efficient use of capacity?
- How are inventory levels controlled?
- What is the total cost of carrying inventory?
- Are any supply problems anticipated?
- What is the policy on safety stock?
- When are plant additions/expansions planned?
- What actions are planned to improve plant efficiencies and product quality?

Financial Plan

The financial plan is paramount to a good overall business plan because money ranks so high in the venture capitalist's affairs. Dean Shepherd and Evan Douglas say of the financial plan that "This is where the investor is thinking 'what do they want and what's in it for me?'"[46] The purpose of the financial plan is "to indicate the venture's potential and to present a timetable for financial viability."[47]

If the management team has precisely thought out decisions and strategies up to this point, the financial figures will fall into place and be well justified. The supporting documents, covering a two-year period, should be realistic and all embracing. The financial statements, to include historical data and forecasts, should contain a balance sheet, income statement, cash-flow statement, and key ratio analyses, as well as product-line profitability analyses.

Financial statements included in the plan should be as carefully planned as if an accountant had prepared them. The venture capitalist will scrutinize these statements and projections, and more than likely, "cut these sales and earnings projections in half, and assume that these reduced figures are more realistic."[48] Some will even take a more pessimistic approach and double all expenses, depending on how well justified the plan's projections are (or are not).

The time commitment an entrepreneur puts into studying and understanding the new venture's financial performance is crucial for entering into negotiations with venture capitalists.

- How good is your company at what you do?
- What is the return on investment?
- What is the net profit margin?
- What is the asset turnover?
- What trends have evolved?
- How is your company leveraged?
- What is your debt-to-equity ratio?
- How is the company affected by taxes?
- Has the company made any efforts to shelter some of its income?
- What are your cash-flow requirements for the next two years?

An entrepreneur should be able to defend sales and earnings projections. The investor, meanwhile, wants to know what he gets out of the deal. Venture capitalists are concerned with how much money the venture wants but are driven by how much money they will make in the future and how reasonable are the expectations of making that money.

The financial section should conclude with a statement of cash-flow requirements for the next two years. These analyses should be directly tied into the business plan and the market rollout campaign. The cash-flow statement should clearly indicate projected revenues, expenses, and investments. It is unlikely that a growth-oriented company will be able to generate sufficient cash flow from internal operations to achieve objectives. Therefore, the plan should address cash shortfalls as well as sources of cash, including profits, debt, and equity. The bottom line to the investors is how much money the venture will require from them to achieve market and financial objectives and how much they can expect as a return on their investment.

PRESENTING THE BUSINESS PLAN, VALUING THE BUSINESS, AND NEGOTIATING A DEAL

Presenting the Business Plan

A business plan alone "will not raise money for a company, but it should lead to a meeting between the investors and the company's management team."[49] This meeting is the entrepreneur's opportunity to convince potential investors to become involved in the venture.

The goals of the entrepreneur's presentation are to "get the investor excited about your product or service concept," "convince the investor that the management team adds value," "communicate the financial viability of the new venture," and "pitch the deal and begin the negotiation process."[50] The entrepreneur's presentation should, of course, "emphasize the strengths in [the] proposal. Obvious weak points should be addressed, to illustrate that you recognize them."[51] At the end of the presentation, investors should "have a clear and concise understanding of [the] business, what is unique about it and how [the management team] will achieve . . . projections."[52]

Gladstone lists five suggestions for making your presentation and dealing with venture capitalists:

1. Do not avoid answering questions and do not give vague answers.
2. Do not hide significant problems.
3. Do not bring your lawyer to the presentation and negotiations.
4. Do not press for an immediate decision.
5. Do not be rigid in pricing.

Valuing the Business

If all goes well during the presentation, prospective investors may take a step toward negotiating a deal by initiating a discussion of the value of the business and funding structure. The entrepreneur should be prepared to discuss how much the company is worth and how much of it he is willing to give up.

In order for the entrepreneur to be prepared for negotiations, he should value his business before this first meeting with potential investors. Having done his own valuation, an entrepreneur should then strive to remain flexible, for the valuation of a company will ultimately be determined "through both quantitative analysis and the personal judgment and bias of the venture

capital investor."[53] Venture capitalists prefer to take a leading role in structuring a deal.

Should the proposed structure involve common stock, preferred stock, convertible debt, or a combination of these? Is it possible to form an R&D partnership, or can the company go public? Even though these options should be considered prior to meeting with prospective investors, the funding request section, in addition to a funding proposal, should simply state that the entrepreneur is willing to negotiate a deal.

Following is an illustration of how these factors impact the valuation of an imaginary company, Company X, which needs $300 in capital for a venture. Two approaches to funding structure are considered: *Traditional Pricing* and *Fundamental Pricing*. Assume that Company X projects the following numbers for the first four years of business:

Year	1	2	3	4
Sales	$2,800	$4,300	$6,300	$9,200
Net Earnings:				
Before Tax	420	890	1,300	1,900
After Tax	210	445	650	950

Traditional Pricing Approach

To estimate the value of the company according to Pratt and Morris (57), the entrepreneur "should:

- Consider the business risk associated with the business to determine the rate of return that will be expected by the venture capitalist.
- Estimate the price/earnings ratio based on comparable publicly held companies.
- Estimate the earnings of the firm at some appropriate target time in the future (i.e., four years out).
- Estimate the market value of the venture by multiplying the earnings estimate times the P/E ratio.
- Divide the estimate of the total dollar return the venture capitalist wants by the projected market value of the company. These calculations will yield the percentage of ownership the venture capitalist will need, as of the future date, to realize the desired return."[54]

Applying this logic to Company X, assumes that:

1. The basic profit criterion is five times invested funds in four years, or 50 percent compounded return on investment ($1.5^4 = 5.06$)
2. A price-earnings ratio of 15 in Year 4
3. No explicit adjustment is made for risk[55]

The steps used in calculating the straight equity position given to investors would be as follows:

1. Total value in year 4 is $950 \times 15 = \$14,250$
2. Investor's desired value is (300×5) + $300 = \$1,800$
3. Percentage of equity required is $1,800/$14,250 = 12.63\%$

Probably a more accurate valuation of the company would include discounting the future value back to the present. These steps are:

1. Total value in year 4 is $950 \times 15 = \$14,250$
2. Present value is $14,250/[(1.5)^4] = \$2,814.82$
3. Percentage of equity required is $300/$2,814.82 = 10.658\%$

Fundamental Pricing Approach.

In a Fundamental Pricing Approach, in which the company issues $300 in 7 percent convertible debentures, the "basic premise is that a venture investor ought to receive 20 percent or more on all invested funds."[56] The pre-tax earnings on $300, if invested in a financial market at various compounded rates over the four years, would be as follows:

Rate	1	2	3	4	Total
20%	60	72	86	104	322
30%	90	117	152	198	557
40%	120	168	235	329	852

To determine the equity percentage required under the different returns, simply divide the total earnings (less interest received from the debentures) by the four-year cumulative pre-tax projected profits of $4,510 ($420+$890+$1,300+$1,900). The following equity percentages can be expected:

20% return ($322−$84)/$4,510=5.277%
30% return ($557−$84)/$4,510=10.488%
40% return ($852−$84)/$4,510=17.029%

Thus under this approach the investor holds debt from the new venture, receives annual interest payments, and also acquires some ownership. When planning to propose some type of debt financing, the entrepreneur, referring to the cash flow analysis, should also include a payback schedule depicting the time period over which the investor will be paid back.

It has been suggested that "if the venture capitalist structures an instrument that calls for its payment, he is merely taking back his own money."[57] On the other hand, a venture capitalist may agree to purchase preferred stock with an annual dividend of 6 to 8 percent. This way he will receive annual payments. This agreement may have a deferred put option and a common stock conversion feature. If the company does not fare well, the investors can require liquidation. If the company is successful, the investor can become a common owner.

These two approaches, although simple in nature and based on the valuation of future earnings, give the entrepreneur a way to begin valuing her company.

Venture capitalists may require certain objectives to be met over the term of the investment and/or place restrictive covenants on the company. An objective could involve increasing ROI by 5 percent each year, while a covenant could restrict the D/E ratio to 50 percent.

Remember, the venture capitalist will be valuing the venture based on the entrepreneur's commitment, upside potential, downside risk, additional funds, and the exit vehicle. The above valuation for Company X is based on future earnings. The future earnings and the current investment suggest the investor would get 17.029 percent equity and a 40 percent return over 4 years.

Percent of Investment Approach

The investor may take a different perspective in evaluating her rightful share of the company. Suppose the current equity is $50 and the investor is asked to put up $300 for a total of $350. Her share of the investment would be 85.7 percent (300/(300+50)). Thus she might argue for 85.7 percent of the company.

Of course, this line of thinking fails to recognize the contribution of the idea or the tremendous time and effort (sweat equity) that the entrepreneur has and will invest. If the investor is only to get 10 to 17 percent but put up 85 percent of the money, then the entrepreneur must make a convincing case to justify the lower ownership.

These equity percentages—10 to 17 percent from the entrepreneur's viewpoint and 85 percent from the investor's—provide a range within which to begin negotiations.

Negotiating a Deal

It may be hard to determine when the venture capital presentation ends and financial negotiations begin. The investors will have many questions about the opportunity, plan, financial projections, team, and pro-

posed deal. The questions and answers clearly affect the interest level and negotiating position of each party.

The negotiation process actually takes much longer than one might expect. Rather than being resolved after one or two meetings, the negotiation process can stretch over the course of several months. A protracted negotiation can work to the entrepreneur's advantage. Investors will spend this time getting to know the entrepreneur and the rest of the management team. The more comfortable investors feel with the management team, the more risk they are often willing to absorb. This sets the stage for the final negotiations and making the deal.

Ultimately, "the entrepreneur either must convince the investor of the validity of the assumptions underlying the business valuation, seek an alternative source of equity capital and start the information and persuasion process all over again, or reach a graceful compromise that assures that the funds are actually forthcoming."[58] Shepherd and Douglas describe one method of making a "graceful compromise":

> In the business plan, the subsequent presentation to the investor, or both, the entrepreneur normally will "ask" for a specific level of funding and "offer" a specific share in the company. This offer should be regarded as an opening claim, because the investor certainly will treat it as such. Thus the entrepreneur should consider making an offer that is based on a set of assumptions that he or she expects will be not quite acceptable to the investor. . . . This may allow the entrepreneur to gracefully give ground and be "argued up" to an equity offer that he or she feels is appropriate.[59]

During negotiations, potential investors will certainly test an entrepreneur's resolve, such as by asking negative questions (attempting to determine the risk level of the new venture). The entrepreneur will need a positive and upbeat outlook in order to overcome this negotiating hurdle. Gladstone offers the following list of challenging questions an entrepreneur may encounter:

- What makes you think you can start a new company?
- What problems do you expect to encounter in starting a new company?
- How are you going to solve all the problems of a new company?
- If you do not have enough money to break even, what will you do for the next round of financing?

- What will you do if positive cash flow is not achieved?
- How many of your key managers are skilled in this industry?
- What could go wrong with the business plan?
- What is going on in the market that could destroy this company?
- What strategy might the competition use in the marketplace?[60]

During the negotiation stage an entrepreneur can avoid other pitfalls by keeping in mind "the reasons cited by investors for rejecting investment proposals. . . . The most common reasons are:

- Lack of confidence in management
- Unsatisfactory risk/reward ratios
- Absence of a well-defined business plan
- The investor's unfamiliarity with products, processes, or markets."[61]

CONCLUSION

Obtaining venture capital is a difficult task, with "no more than 2 to 4 percent of the ventures contacting venture capital firms receiv[ing] financing from them."[62] Entrepreneurs can greatly increase their chances of acquiring venture funding by having a clear sense of their own goals and investors' expectations, a great deal of personal commitment, a balanced management team, and a solid approach to writing a business plan and presenting that plan to potential investors.

To help achieve this end, a business plan must be not only thorough and honest but also clear and concise in order to gain investor attention. Further, "a plan must demonstrate mastery of the entire entrepreneurial process, from identification of opportunity to harvest. It is not a way to separate unsuspecting investors from their money by hiding the fatal flaw."[63]

Partnering with a venture capitalist enables entrepreneurs to acquire more than capital; a great deal of expertise and guidance is part of the bargain. Together a venture capitalist and an entrepreneur "can achieve common purposes if the partners complement and support each other's capabilities, respect and understand each other's different perspectives, and develop sensitivity to each other's actions and reactions."[64]

1. Dean A. Shepherd and Evan J. Douglas, *Attracting Equity Investors: Positioning, Preparing, and Presenting the Business Plan* (Thousand Oaks, CA: Sage Publications, Inc., 1999): 5.
2. Paul A. Gompers and Josh Lerner, *The Venture Capital Cycle* (Cambridge, MA: The MIT Press, 1999): 127.
3. William D. Bygrave and Jeffry A. Timmons, *Venture Capital at the Crossroads* (Boston, MA: Harvard Business School Press, 1992): 13.
4. Shepherd and Douglas, *Attracting*, 71.
5. Ibid.
6. Stanley E. Pratt and Jane K. Morris, *Pratt's Guide to Venture Capital Sources* (Wellesley Hills, MA: Venture Economics, Inc., 1987): 13.
7. Ibid., 19.
8. J. A. Timmons, *New Venture Creation: Entrepreneurship in the 21st Century*, 4th ed. (Burr Ridge, IL: Irwin, 1994): 490.
9. "Note on the Venture Capital Industry (1981)," HBS Case 285-096 (Harvard Business School, 1982): 1.
10. Shepherd and Douglas, *Attracting*, 14.
11. Ibid., 41.
12. Jeff Bailey, "Shaking the Tree," *The Wall Street Journal* (May 20, 1985): 20.
13. Sarah Gracie, "How to Seduce a Venture Capitalist," *Management Today* (April 1998): 110.
14. William A. Sahlman, "How to Write a Great Business Plan," *Harvard Business Review* (July–August 1997): 101.
15. Stanley E. Pratt, *How to Raise Venture Capital* (New York: Capital Publishing Corporation, 1982): 15.
16. Shepherd and Douglas, *Attracting*, 58.
17. Bygrave and Timmons, *Venture Capital*, 191.
18. Amar Bhide, "Bootstrap Finance: The Art of Start-Ups," *Harvard Business Review* (November 1992): 112.
19. William D. Bygrave, *The Portable MBA in Entrepreneurship* (New York, NY: John Wiley & Sons, Inc., 1997): 122.
20. Kath Walters, "Get Planning," *Business Review Weekly* (November 17, 2000): 1.
21. Shepherd and Douglas, *Attracting*, 71.
22. Ibid., 80.
23. Timmons, *New Venture Creation*, 376.
24. Walters, "Get Planning," 1.
25. Shepherd and Douglas, *Attracting*, 85.
26. Walters, "Get Planning," 1.
27. Pratt, *How to Raise*, 99.
28. Shepherd and Douglas, *Attracting*, 89.
29. Sahlman, "How to Write," 102.
30. Pratt, *How to Raise*, 101.
31. Pratt and Morris, *Guide*, 19.
32. Shepherd and Douglas, *Attracting*, 91.
33. Sahlman, "How to Write," 102.
34. Pratt, *How to Raise*, 102.
35. Ibid.
36. Ibid.
37. Timmons, *New Venture Creation*, 430.
38. Pratt, *How to Raise*, 104.
39. Ibid., 100.
40. Shepherd and Douglas, *Attracting*, 104.
41. Pratt, *How to Raise*, 104.
42. Bygrave and Timmons, *Venture Capital*, 98.
43. Ibid., 99.
44. Timmons, *New Venture Creation*, 433.
45. Shepherd and Douglas, *Attracting*, 105.
46. Ibid., 108.
47. Timmons, *New Venture Creation*, 437.
48. David J. Gladstone, *Venture Capital Handbook* (Reston, VA: Reston Publishing Company, 1983): 67.
49. Walters, "Get Planning," 3.
50. Shepherd and Douglas, *Attracting*, 120.
51. Pratt and Morris, *Pratt's Guide*, 44.
52. Ibid., 45.
53. Ibid., 151.
54. Ibid., 57.
55. Ibid., 151.
56. Ibid., 151.
57. Ibid., 134.
58. Shepherd and Douglas, *Attracting*, 136.
59. Ibid., 148.
60. Gladstone, *Venture*, 67.
61. Bygrave and Timmons, *Venture Capitalism*, 208.
62. Timmons, *New Venture Creation*, 487.
63. Sahlman, "How to Write," 108.
64. Pratt and Morris, *Pratt's Guide*, 19.

Chapter 10

James W. Wansley
University of Tennessee

Management and Valuation of Financial Assets

MEASURING FINANCIAL PERFORMANCE

Basic financial analysis involves the use of various financial statements. Each financial statement has a specific purpose. First, the balance sheet summarizes the assets, liabilities, and owners' equity of a business at a moment in time, usually at the end of the fiscal or calendar year or at the end of a quarter. Next, the income statement summarizes the revenues and expenses of the firm over a particular period of time, again usually at the end of a year or quarter. While the balance sheet can be thought of as a snapshot of the firm's financial position at a moment in time, the income statement illustrates a summary of the firm's profitability over time. From these two statements (plus sometimes some additional information), certain other statements can be produced, such as a statement of retained earnings, a sources and uses of funds statement, and a statement of cash flows. Examples of a balance sheet, an income statement, and a statement of cash flows for the hypothetical TennCorp. Company are shown in **Exhibits 10.1** through **10.3**.

Ratio Analysis

One common use of financial statements is ratio analysis. This process is simply the determination of various measures (called *financial ratios*) of the firm's health or viability. Financial ratios are often used because they provide a better *relative* measure of the firm's health than the use of the raw numbers on their own. For example, knowing that a firm generated $2 million in gross profits is not as revealing as knowing that the firm earned the $2 million on $10 million in sales. This tells us something

about the firm's ability to generate a reasonable rate of return on sales and allows us to make comparisons across firms. Ratio analysis is used within the firm to answer such important questions as:

- Do we have enough cash?
- Are inventories adequate to support the projected level of sales?
- Can we pay our debts when they come due?
- Is the firm worthy of a line of credit or a bank loan?
- Does the firm have too heavy an investment in accounts receivable, and does this condition reflect a lax collection policy?
- Is our firm earning an adequate return?
- How do we know what is adequate?

We often use ratio analysis within the firm for control and comparison purposes, but analysts also use ratio analysis to monitor the firm's health or progress in comparison to firms in the same or other industries.

Internal Uses of Ratio Analysis

Firms customarily use ratio analysis to judge, or benchmark, themselves against both their own past performance and that of their competition. Analysts within the firm can compare the current state of the firm's profitability or liquidity with past levels and expected future levels. Almost all companies have financial goals or targets, and commonly these targets are expressed in financial ratio terms. For example, one division of a firm may have an objective of increasing sales by 10 percent and earning profits of 15 percent on sales (a 15 percent net profit margin).

When financial ratios are arrayed over a period of years, we can study apparent trends and the composition of change in

BEST-USE CORRELATIONS

In many respects, the management of a firm is the management of its financial resources. Chapter 10 instructs teams to use financial ratios to assess the health and vitality of *Marketplace* enterprises. Ratio analysis represents one of the more important management tools available to simulation players. In *Marketplace,* either learn how to use them or sink.

Skillful Adjustment
As Q5 begins, teams should start using the tools of financial management to skillfully adjust their strategies. If you don't know what the numbers mean, Chapter 10 can help.

Competitive Benchmarking
In *Marketplace*, teams are given a host of financial ratios with which to evaluate strengths and weaknesses and to use to benchmark themselves against their competitors. If you think you are doing as well as you can in some area, it may be sobering to find a rival firm doing better.

How to Make Tough Choices?
You could use intuition to make tough decisions or you can rely on the tools of capital budgeting offered in Chapter 10. Your choice.

Impress the Venture Capitalists
Look smart. Devote a portion of your business plan to presenting key financial ratios in graph form over time.

How to value the firm?
What will be the value of an investment in your firm 1, 3, and 5 years from now? Chapter 10 details how to value companies just like yours.

Exhibit 10.1: TennCorp. Consolidated Balance Sheet at December 31, 20X2 and 20X3

Assets	20X3	20X2
Current Assets		
Cash	$4,061.	$2,382.
Marketable securities	5,272.	8,004.
Accounts receivable	8,960.	8,350.
Inventories	47,041.	36,769.
Prepaid expenses	512.	759.
Total Current Assets	$65,846.	$56,264.
Property, plant and equipment	40,607.	26,507.
Less accumulated depreciation	11,528.	7,530.
Net plant and equipment	29,079.	18,977.
Other assets	373.	668.
Total Assets	$95,298.	$75,909.
Liabilities and Stockholders' Equity		
Accounts payable	$14,294.	$7,591.
Notes payable	5,614.	6,012.
Current maturities of long-term debt	1,884.	1,516.
Accrued liabilities	5,669.	5,313.
Total Current Liabilities	$27,461.	$20,432.
Deferred income taxes	$843	$635
Long-term debt	21,059.	16,975.
Total liabilities	$49,363.	$38,042.
Stockholders' Equity		
Common stock, par value $1, authorized 10,000 shares: issues 4,803 shares	$4,803.	$4,594.
Additional paid-in capital	957.	910.
Retained earnings	40,175.	32,363.
Total Liabilities and Stockholders' Equity	95,298.	75,909.

Exhibit 10.2: TennCorp. Consolidated Statement of Earnings for the years 20X2 and 20X3

Statement of Consolidated Earnings	20X3	20X2
Net sales	$215,600	$153,000
Cost of goods sold	129,364	91,879
Gross profit	$86,236	$61,121
Selling and admin. expenses	$32,664	$26,382
Advertising	14,258	10,792
Lease payments	13,058	7,111
Depreciation and amort.	3,998	2,984
Repairs and maintenance	3,015	2,046
Operating profit	$19,243	$11,806
Other income (expense)		
Interest income	$422	$838
Interest expense	$(2,585)	$(2,277)
Earnings before income taxes	17,080	10,367
Income taxes	7,686	4,457
Net income	$9,394	$5,910
Earnings per common share	$1.96	$1.29

Exhibit 10.3: *TennCorp. Consolidated Statement of Cash Flows for the years 20X2 and 20X3*

Cash flow from operating activities	20X3	20X2
Net income	$9,394	$5,910
Noncash expenses and revenues included in income		
Depreciation and amort.	3,998	2,984
Deferred income taxes	208	136
Cash provided (used for) current assets and liabilities		
Accounts receivable	(610)	(3,339)
Inventories	(10,272)	(7,006)
Prepaid expenses	247	295
Accounts payable	6,703	(1,051)
Accrued liabilities	356	(1,696)
Net cash provided (used) by operating activities	$10,024	$(3,676)

the firm's financial picture. For example, if our profitability has been declining over the past three years, a trend emerges from this internal analysis that focuses our attention on the potential causes of our declining profitability.

Not only is ratio analysis useful in judging how our performance has improved or declined over time, but also it is useful in judging how we are doing relative to our competition. For example, **Exhibit 10.4** shows that TennCorp's return on assets (ROA) was 9.9 percent in 20X3. Was that a good or a poor performance? There is no way of knowing unless we know how the firm did in prior years or how TennCorp's competitors are doing. For example, the 9.9 percent ROA looks very different depending on whether our major competitor had an ROA of 20 percent or 2 percent.

External Uses of Ratio Analysis

A number of individuals make use of a firm's financial ratios besides the individuals in the firm: financial and investments analysts, bank loan officers, portfolio managers, regulators, and the investing public are often interested in a firm's financial ratios. Several investments firms such as *ValueLine* publish software that lets potential investors screen firms on their financial ratios. For example, one such screen might list those firms with high liquidity, low leverage, and high profitability using various financial ratios.

Important users of financial ratios are those firms such as Standard and Poor's, Dun and Bradstreet, and Moody's Investors Services that publish credit ratings for publicly

held firms. These credit ratings range from AAA for high-quality companies to a C or D rating for firms of low or questionable credit quality. Analysts at these credit rating firms use financial ratios as their primary source of information in developing these ratings. *The ratings are critically important to the firm because they determine to a large extent the firm's cost of borrowing funds.* **Exhibit 10.5** shows the rating categories used by two of the most commonly followed rating services, Moody's Investment Services and Standard and Poor's. A rating of Baa from Moody's, or BBB from Standard and Poor's, is considered investment grade; rating grades below these are considered speculative. Recently, the term "junk bonds" has become popular. Junk bonds simply refer to bonds with a Moody's rating grade of Ba or less, or a Standard and Poor's rating of BB or less.

While the various rating agencies do not publicly disclose how they arrive at a rating, it is common knowledge that the rating results from (1) an objective evaluation of the firm's past, current, and projected financial condition, where the financial condition is based primarily on various financial ratios, and (2) a subjective evaluation of the firm's management.

Five Classes of Financial Ratios

While there are a number of different ways to categorize financial ratios, one common classification is the following:

- **Liquidity** measures the firm's ability to meet its maturing short-term obligations as they come due.
- **Leverage** measures the extent to which the firm has been financed by debt.

- **Coverage** relates the financial charges of a firm to its ability to service these charges.
- **Activity** measures how effectively the firm is using its assets.
- **Profitability** measures management's overall effectiveness as shown by the returns generated on sales and investments.

Exhibit 10.4 identifies the five different categories of financial ratios, defines the ratios, and calculates these ratios for the TennCorp. Company for 20X3. One warning about using ratios is always useful to remember: The ratios for different companies may not be strictly comparable if the firms follow different accounting procedures. For example, if one firm uses LIFO (last in, first out) accounting for its inventory, then any financial ratio that uses inventory would not be directly comparable to that for one using FIFO (first-in, first-out) accounting. In addition, the use of generally accepted accounting principles (GAAP) allows the firm some ability to "manage" its earnings. Analysts are usually skeptical of firms that change their procedures for accounting for inventory.

Decomposition Analysis

One frequent use of ratio analysis that seeks to determine root causes of financial performance is referred to as "decomposition analysis" or the "DuPont system" of ratio analysis. This approach recognizes that a firm's performance is multidimensional and is related to its profit margin on sales, use of financial leverage, and level of activity. Thus, a firm's return on equity can be composed into three component parts:

$$ROE = \text{Net income}/\text{Equity} = (\text{Net income}/\text{Sales}) \times (\text{Sales}/\text{Total assets}) \times (\text{Total assets}/\text{Equity})$$

where,

net income/sales is a measure of the firm's level of profitability,

sales/total assets measures the level of firm activity, and

total assets/equity measures the firm's use of leverage.

Using this approach, we can determine the components of ROE and isolate any particular problem area. If our firm's ROE falls below our target level, decomposition analysis can help determine the root cause.

Exhibit 10.4: *Financial Ratios of TennCorp. 20X3*

Ratio Category/Name of Ratio	Definition of Ratio	Ratio Calculation
Liquidity ratios		
Measure the firm's ability to meet its maturing short-term obligations as they come due.		
Current ratio	Current assets/Current liabilities	65.846/27.461 = 2.4 x
Quick or acid test ratio	(Current assets − inventory)/Current liabilities	(65,846 − 47,041)/ 27,461 = 0.68 x
Cash-flow liquidity ratio	(Cash + Marketable securities + Cash flow from operations)/Current liabilities	(4,061 + 5,272 + 10,024)/ 27,461 = 0.70 x
Activities ratios		
Measure how effectively the firm is using its assets.		
Average collection period	Accounts receivable/Average daily sales	8,960/(215,600/360) = 15 days
Accounts receivable turnover	Net sales/Accounts receivable	215,600/8,960 = 24.06 x
Inventory turnover	Cost of goods sold/Inventories	129,364/47,041 = 2.75 x
Fixed asset turnover	Net sales/Net plant and equipment	215,600/29,079 = 7.41 x
Total asset turnover	Net sales/Total assets	215,600/95,298 = 2.26 x
Leverage ratios		
Measure the extent to which the firm has been financed by debt.		
Debt ratio	Total liabilities/Total assets	49,363/95,298 = 51.8 %
Long-term debt to total capitalization	(Long-term debt/Long-term debt + Stockholders' equity)	21,059/(21,059 + 45,935) = 31.4 %
Debt to equity ratio	Total liabilities/Stockholders' equity	49,363/45,935 = 107.5 %
Coverage ratios		
Measure relationship between financial charges of a firm to its ability to service these charges.		
Times interest earned	Operating profit/Interest expense	19,242/2.585 = 7.4 x
Fixed charge coverage	(Operating profit + Lease payments)/ (Interest expense + Lease payments)	(19,243 + 13,058)/(2,585 + 13,058) = 2.1 x
Profitability ratios		
Measure management's overall effectiveness as shown by the returns generated on sales and investments.		
Gross profit margin	Gross profit/Net sales	86,236/215,600 = 40.0 %
Operating profit margin	Operating profit/Net sales	19,243/215,600 = 8.9 %
Net profit margin	Net earnings/Net sales	9,343/215,600 = 4.4 %
Return on assets	Net earnings/Total assets	9,343/95,298 = 9.9 %
Return on equity	Net earnings/Stockholders' equity	9,343/45,935 = 20.5 %

Exhibit 10.5: *Ratings by Investment Agencies**

Moody's Investors Services		Standard and Poor's	
Aaa	Best quality	AAA	Highest grade
Aa	High quality	AA	High grade
A	Upper medium grade	A	Higher medium grade
Baa	Medium grade	BBB	Medium grade
Ba	Possess speculative elements	BB	Speculative
B	Generally lack characteristics of desirable investment	B	Very speculative
		CCC-CC	Outright speculation
Caa	Poor standing; may be in default	C	Reserved for income bonds on which no interest is being paid
Ca	Highly speculative; often in default		
C	Lowest grade	DDD-D	In default, with rating indicating relative salvage value

* The top four grades, through Baa, are considered "investment grade." Grades beginning with Ba are considered "noninvestment" grade or speculative grade. Bonds with these lower ratings are sometimes referred to as "junk bonds."

Did we fail to generate sufficient sales? Were our sales less profitable than we expected? Or do we need to use additional debt financing to leverage or magnify our return on assets? These are the types of questions that decomposition analysis might help answer.

Because different industries have different financial structures, we should expect ROE components to be different for firms across different industries. For example, firms in heavy manufacturing industries or in the utility industry necessarily have large fixed cost commitments to plant and equipment, while software or biotechnology firms can produce products without such large fixed investments. **Exhibit 10.6** displays the 2001 ROE decomposition for selected companies and shows how different components of profitability contribute to a firm's ROE. Notice, for example, the way that both Merck and Wal-Mart arrive at a final ROE of approximately 21 percent. Merck has a very high profit margin, but low turnover. Wal-Mart's profit margin on each unit sold is a modest 3.46 percent but its total asset turnover (sales/total assets) is five times that of Merck. Compare also the leverage used by Microsoft and USX. Virtually all of Microsoft's assets are financed with equity since its total assets are only 1.17 times its equity. On the other hand, USX makes liberal use of debt financing. USX's equity multiplier of 4.496 implies that for every dollar of equity on its balance sheet, it has $3.49 of debt.

Common Size Statements

Since firms that we might like to compare ourselves to may be substantially larger or smaller, one common practice among those who use financial ratios is to put the balance sheet and income statement items on a comparable basis. When this is done, these statements are called *common size statements*. They express balance sheet items as percentages of total assets and income statement items as percentages of net sales. These percentages can be directly compared to industry norms or to those for competitors. **Exhibit 10.7** illustrates a common size balance sheet, and **Exhibit 10.8** illustrates a common size income statement for the TennCorp. company. We can see in Exhibit 10.7 that inventories represent 49 percent of assets. If the average company in our industry invests only 30 percent of its assets

Exhibit 10.6: *2001 ROE Decomposition for Selected Companies*

Company	Net Profit Margin: Net income/Sales	Total Asset Turnover: Sales/ Total assets	Equity Multiplier: Total assets/ Equity	Return on Equity: ROE
Coca-Cola	15.59 %	1.130 x	2.622 x	46.19 %
Exxon	4.82	1.30	2.418	15.15
Merck	20.60	0.527	1.989	21.60
Microsoft	25.40	.986	1.174	29.40
USX	−1.43	1.040	4.496	−6.69
Wal-Mart	3.46	2.547	2.459	21.67

Exhibit 10.7: *TennCorp. Common Size Balance Sheet at December 31, 20X3*

Assets	20X3
Current Assets	
Cash	4.3 %
Marketable securities	5.5
Accounts receivable	9.4
Inventories	49.4
Prepaid expenses	0.5
Total Current Assets	69.1 %
Property, plant, and equipment	42.6
Less accumulated depreciation	12.1
Net plant and equipment	30.5
Other assets	0.4
Total assets	100.0 %
Liabilities and Stockholders' Equity	
Accounts payable	15.0 %
Notes payable	5.9
Current maturities of long-term debt	2.0
Accrued liabilities	5.9
Total Current Liabilities	28.8 %
Deferred income taxes	0.9
Long-term debt	22.1
Total liabilities	51.8
Stockholders' equity	
Common stock, par value $1, authorized 10,000 shares; issues 4,803 shares	5.0%
Additional paid-in capital	1.0
Retained earnings	42.2
Total Liabilities and Stockholders' Equity	100.0 %

in inventories, then it would be reasonable to question whether or not our firm has too much invested in inventories. With this in mind, other questions related to our inventories arise. Will we have to sell at reduced prices to reduce inventories? Do these excessive inventory levels indicate we are buying the wrong type of goods to sell? A dairy company, for example, with perishable inventories, would be more concerned about excessive inventories than a retailer of nuts and bolts.

Index Statements

Another common use of financial statements is the creation of index statements. These are balance sheets and income statements in which the various items such as current assets are indexed to their level in some prior year, the year of the index.

Exhibit 10.8: TennCorp. Common Size Income Statement for the year 20X3

Statement of Consolidated Earnings	20X3
Net sales	100.0 %
Cost of goods sold	60.0
Gross profit	40.0
Selling and admin. expenses	15.2
Advertising	6.6
Lease payments	6.1
Depreciation and amort.	1.9
Repairs and maintenance	1.4
Operating profit	8.9
Other income (expense)	
Interest income	0.2
Interest expense	1.2
Earnings before income taxes	7.9
Income taxes	3.6
Net income	4.4

Exhibit 10.9: TennCorp. Index Balance Sheet for December 31, 20X3. The year of the index is 20X2

Assets	20X3	20X2
Current Assets		
Cash	170.5 %	100.0 %
Marketable securities	65.9	100.0
Accounts receivable	107.3	100.0
Inventories	127.9	100.0
Prepaid expenses	67.5	100.0
Total Current Assets	117.0 %	100.0 %
Property, plant and equipment	153.2	100.0
Less accumulated depreciation	153.1	100.0
Net plant and equipment	153.2	100.0
Other assets	55.8	100.0
Total assets	125.5 %	100.0 %
Liabilities and Stockholders' Equity		
Accounts payable	188.3 %	100.0 %
Notes payable	93.4	100.0
Current maturities of long-term debt	124.3	100.0
Accrued liabilities	106.7	100.0
Total Current Liabilities	134.4 %	100.0 %
Deferred income taxes	132.7	100.0
Long-term debt	124.1	100.0
Total liabilities	129.8	100.0
Stockholders' equity		
Common stock, par value $1, authorized 10,000 shares; issues 4,803,000 shares	104.5 %	100.0 %
Additional paid-in capital	105.2	100.0
Retained earnings	124.1	100.0
Total Liabilities and Stockholders' Equity	125.5 %	100.0 %

Exhibits 10.9 and 10.10 display index statements for TennCorp. In **Exhibit 10.9**, for example, notice that the 20X3 level of cash is 170 percent of its 20X2 level. Is all that cash necessary? Analysts know that dollars invested in cash increase the firm's liquidity but reduce the firm's profitability.

Index statements give us another perspective on the various accounts that comprise the balance sheet and income statement. As another example, notice in Exhibit 10.9 that TennCorp's accounts payable increased by 88 percent, while **Exhibit 10.10** shows that sales increased only 40 percent. Is accounts payable becoming a problem area for the firm?

CAPITAL BUDGETING

Long-term investment decisions are difficult but crucial to the success or survival of a firm. For most firms, the majority of their assets are invested long term, and furthermore, the most profitable investments are long term. Many firms reveal their basic strategic plans based on the type of capital investments they are willing to make. *Capital budgeting* is the process of planning for purchases of assets whose returns are expected to continue beyond one year. A *capital expenditure* is a cash outlay that is expected to generate a flow of future cash benefits lasting longer than one year. Several different types of cash outlays may be considered as capital expenditures and evaluated using the framework of capital budgeting models, including the following:

- Purchase of new equipment, real estate, or a building in order to expand an existing product or service line or enter a new line of business.

- The replacement of an existing piece of equipment, such as an automated assembly line.

- Expenditures for advertising or research and development.

- Investments in employee training and education.

- The refunding of an old bond issue with a new issue having lower interest rates.

- Lease versus buy analysis.

- Merger and acquisition evaluation.

A variety of methods exists to help us with capital budgeting decisions. Like most techniques, capital budgeting procedures depend critically on the estimates of costs and revenues that go into the decision. The very long-term nature of projects associated with capital budgeting means that the cash flows may be difficult to forecast accurately. For example, if we are considering investment in a new product line, we probably have imperfect information on the demand for the product, and we may not even be sure of the pricing of the product. Additionally, it is always difficult to forecast what our competition will do in response to a strategic investment on our part. In spite of these and other problems associated with capital budgeting, all firms make capital investment decisions, and the capital budgeting decision rules are designed to assist the firm in selecting the most appropriate projects for selection.

Exhibit 10.10: *TennCorp. Index Statement of Earnings for the year 20X3. Year of index is 20X2*

Statement of Consolidated Earnings	20X3	20X2
Net sales	140.9 %	100.0 %
Cost of goods sold	140.8	100.0
Gross profit	146.0	100.0
Selling and admin. expenses	123.8	100.0
Advertising	132.1	100.0
Lease payments	183.6	100.0
Depreciation and amort.	134.0	100.0
Repairs and maintenance	147.4	100.0
Operating profit	163.0	100.0
Other income (expense)		
Interest income	50.4	100.0
Interest expense	113.5	100.0
Earnings before income taxes	164.8	100.0
Income taxes	172.4	100.0
Net income	159.0	100.0
Earnings per common share	151.9	100.0

Basic Steps in the Capital Budgeting Process

Many firms have adopted the following four-step procedure for a complete capital budgeting process.

- Selection of proposals.
- Estimation of incremental cash flows.
- Evaluation of alternatives and project selection.
- Project postaudit and review.

Generating Capital Budgeting Proposals

New ideas for capital budgeting come from a variety of sources both from within and outside the firm. Some firms have special staff with the responsibility for identifying and evaluating capital expenditures. In fact, however, anyone within the firm can develop a capital budgeting proposal. For example, a plant manager may suggest that the plant needs expansion or modification. Capital budgeting proposals may fall into one of the following three categories: (1) projects generated by growth opportunities; (2) projects generated by cost-reduction opportunities; and (3) projects generated to meet legal requirements and health and safety standards.

Estimating Incremental Cash Flows

The capital budgeting process involves the estimation of the *incremental after-tax cash flows* associated with an expenditure. For a typical project, this entails an initial cash outlay followed by several years of cash inflows. In practice, some projects (such as construction of a nuclear electricity generating plant) involve cash outlays for a number of years before the project comes on-line and can generate some profit. In addition, there are some projects, usually referred to as *non-normal or nonconventional* projects, with cash-flow patterns with more than one sign change—that is, a cash outlay followed by a cash inflow followed by another cash outlay. These projects can cause additional analytical problems.

Several key points should be remembered when estimating cash flows for a capital budgeting project. First, cash flows should be measured on an incremental basis. All changes in the firm's revenue, cost, and tax stream associated with the project should be considered. Cash flows that would not be changed by the investment should be ignored. Second, cash flow estimation should be made on an after-tax basis. Because the initial outlays required to fund the investment are made with after-tax dollars, the returns from the project should also be considered on an after-tax basis. Third, all of the indirect effects of a project should be included in the cash-flow calculations. For example, if a proposed plant expansion requires that working capital be increased for the firm as a whole, perhaps as larger cash balances or more inventory, then the increase in working capital should be added to the initial investment.[1] Fourth, sunk costs should not be considered when evaluating a project. Since sunk costs are an outlay that have already been made and cannot be recovered, they should not be considered in the decision to accept or reject a project. Fifth, and finally, the value of resources used in a project should be measured in terms of their *opportunity costs*. Opportunity costs of resources (assets) are the cash flows that those resources could generate if not used in the project under consideration. Suppose the cost of a piece of land is $1 million, but a recent appraisal indicates it could be sold for $5 million. If a firm builds on this land and thus cannot sell it, the appropriate opportunity cost of the land is $5 million, not the original cost of $1 million. All projects should be evaluated relative to the alternative opportunity of selling the land for $5 million.

Evaluating Alternatives

Once the costs and incremental after-tax cash flows have been estimated, several analytical approaches exist to consider the acceptability of various projects. These approaches include:

- **Net present value (NPV).** The dollar difference in the present value of the stream of net incremental cash flows from a project minus the project's net investment.

- **Internal rate of return (IRR).** The discount rate that equates the present value of the net cash flows from a project with the present value of the project's cost or net investment. It is also the discount rate that causes the NPV to equal zero.

- **Profitability index (PI), also sometimes called the *benefit-cost ratio*.** The ratio of the present value of future cash flows over the life of the project divided by the project's net investment.

- **Payback period.** The amount of time required for the cumulative cash inflows from a project to equal the initial cash outlay.

These four capital budgeting methods are summarized in **Exhibit 10.11**, including their acceptance decision rule and their respective strengths and weaknesses. **Exhibit 10.12** shows the formulas used to

Exhibit 10.11: *Summary of Capital Budgeting Methods*

Model	Acceptance Criterion	Strengths	Weaknesses
Net present value	Accept if project has a positive or zero NPV, evaluated at the firm's cost of capital.	Considers the timing and magnitude of cash flows; provides an objective, return-based criterion for decision making; and most conceptually correct method.	Some find it difficult to work with dollar return value, instead of percentage returns.
Internal rate of return	Accept if IRR equals or exceeds the firm's cost of capital.	Same benefits as NPV. Easy to interpret the meaning of IRR.	Multiple rates of return possible; sometimes gives decision that conflicts with NPV.
Profitability index	Accept project if PI is greater than or equal to 1.0.	Same benefits as NPV. Useful to guide decisions in capital rationing problems.	Sometimes gives decision that conflicts with NPV.
Payback (PB)	PB should not be used in deciding whether to accept or reject an investment project.	Easy and inexpensive to use; provides a crude measure of project risk; provides a measure of project liquidity.	No objective decision criterion. Fails to consider the timing of cash flows and fails to consider cash flows beyond the payback period.

Exhibit 10.12: *Capital Budgeting Decision Rules*

Net present value

$$NPV = NCF_1/(1 + k)_1 + NCF_2/(1 + k)_2 + \ldots + NCF_n/(1 + k)_n - NINV$$

Internal rate of return

$$IRR = NCF_1/(1 + r)^1 + NCF_2/(1 + r)^2 + \ldots + NCF_n/(1 + r)^n - NINV = 0$$

Profitability Index

$$\left(\sum_{t=1}^{n} NCF_t/(1 + k)^t \right)/NINV$$

Payback period

$$PB = NINV/\text{Annual net cash inflows}$$

where

INV = the project's net investment:
k = the project's appropriate discount rate;
r = the project's internal rate of return; and
NCF = the project's incremental after-tax net cash flows

calculate the NPV of a project. Four different methods are shown here since some firms use each of these methods. Most firms, however, use several approaches in making capital budgeting decisions, and the NPV (net present value) and IRR (internal rate of return) decision rules are most commonly used. Fortunately, most commonly used spreadsheets such as Excel and Lotus have built-in functions that facilitate the actual calculations. One caveat should always be kept in mind when using these spreadsheet models to implement capital budgeting procedures. Be sure the spreadsheet calculates the decision rule the way you believe it is being calculated. For example, in some calculations Lotus and Excel are somewhat different when they

find the present value of a stream of cash flows.

If only one rule is used, it should be net present value. That is, firms should rank projects based on their net present value and select first those projects that have the highest NPV. The reason for this is simple—*the NPV of a project measures the increase in a firm's wealth associated with accepting a project.*

At this point, perhaps an example will be helpful in illustrating how the various capital budgeting rules work. **Exhibit 10.13** shows the cash flows and decision results from four independent projects when the firm's marginal cost of capital is 10 percent. Independent projects simply are those whose acceptance or rejection in no way affects the

decision on another project. In Exhibit 10.13, project A might be an investment in a production process while project B might be a decision on whether to buy new and unrelated hardware. If we decide to invest in the production process (project A), it does not affect in any way whether we still want to buy the hardware (project B).

Exhibit 10.13 shows that project B seems best if we make our decisions using NPV or PI, while project C seems best if we use IRR or payback period to decide. What is a company to do? Remember, as I mentioned earlier, in case of doubt or conflict, rely on NPV. That is, choose project A even though its rate of return is lower than that for project C. It adds more value to the firm than either of the other two projects being considered.

Here is the appropriate place to point out some good and bad news. The bad news you can see for yourself in Exhibit 10.13: Different evaluation techniques such as NPV and IRR will rank projects differently. In Exhibit 10.13, project B has the highest NPV while project C has the highest IRR.[2] This creates some confusion. The good news is that while project ranking may differ, the basic decision of whether to accept or reject a project will not differ across the three techniques of NPV, IRR, and PI. That is, if a project has a positive NPV, it will also have an IRR greater than its cost of capital, and if the IRR is greater than the cost of capital, it follows that the NPV will also be positive.

Exhibit 10.13: Four Independent Projects. Cost of Capital = 10%

Year Cash Flows	Project A	Project B	Project C	PV Factor at 10 %
0	−1000	−1,000	−1,000	1.000
1	0	100	200	0.909
2	0	200	300	0.826
3	300	300	500	0.751
4	700	400	500	0.683
5	1,300	1,250	600	0.621

Decision Criteria Results

Project	NPV[1]	IRR[2]	PI[3]	Payback[4]
Project A	$510.70	20.9 %	1.51	4 years
Project B	530.75	22.8	1.53	4 years
Project C	519.20	25.4	1.52	3 years

[1]The NPV of project A ($510.70) is the solution to the following equation:

$$NPV_A = \$510.70 = -\$1000 + \$0/(1.10)^1 + \$0/(1.10)^2 + \$300/(1.10)^3 + \$700/(1.10)^4 + \$1300/(1.10)^5$$

[2]The IRR of project A (20.9 %) is the solution to the following equation:

$$IRR_A = 20.9 \% = -\$1000 + \$0/(1 + r)^1 + \$0/(1 + r)^2 + \$300/(1 + r)^3 + \$700/(1 + r)^4 + \$1300/(1 + r)^5$$

where r is the internal rate of return. Notice that this equation has more than one unknown, so it cannot be solved directly. It must be solved by iteration. All spreadsheet packages, such as Excel and Lotus, have IRR functions that will solve this equation for an IRR.

[3]The profitability index (PI) is defined as the present value of the cash flows divided by the initial investment. For project A, the PI is $1510.70/$1000 = 1.51.

[4]The payback is the number of years or parts of a year required to recover the initial investment. For project A, the payback is 4 years since the initial cost of $1000 is recovered only after the receipt of the $700 cash flow in year 4.

Incorporating Risk into the Capital Budgeting Decision

Explicitly incorporating risk is an important part of any capital budgeting decision. When the NPV approach is used, the appropriate discount rate is the firm's marginal cost of capital, and when the IRR method is used, we have suggested that a project should be accepted when the project's IRR equals or exceeds the firm's marginal cost of capital. While this is a correct approach, it assumes that all projects under consideration are similar in risk to the existing firm as a whole and that acceptance of the project would not alter the firm's business-risk attributes. Of course, this is not always the case. Firms often consider projects that have varying degrees of risk, and managers should incorporate these different risk levels into the capital budgeting decision. *In fact, failure to recognize explicitly significant risk differences among projects biases the project selection toward risky projects.* The firm is taking on more

Many firms recognize two different approaches for adjusting the discount rate to recognize differences among projects under consideration: the total project risk approach and the portfolio or beta risk approach.

Total Project Risk Approach

This approach measures the chance that the project may not perform up to expectations. It often is measured by either the standard deviation or the coefficient of variation of the project's expected cash flows. For example, consider two projects with equivalent after-tax cash flow but whose standard deviation of cash flows differs. The project with the larger standard deviation of cash flows would have more risk and should justify a larger discount rate. Thus, we as managers would not be indifferent between these two projects, even though there are no cash flow differences between them.

Many firms use the best-case/worst-case scenario to evaluate risk levels. Although this approach has the benefit of allowing us to quantify the risk of the cash flows, it does not tell us by how much to adjust the discount rate to properly penalize the cash flows of the riskier project. **Exhibit 10.14** displays the data a firm might collect in an attempt to use the total risk approach to determine an appropriate discount rate. In this exhibit, the firm is considering three projects: an automated production line, a new cooling system, and a totally new product line. To make life easy, I have assumed the total costs and

Exhibit 10.14: Total Project Risk Determination

Project Description	Project Cost	Annual increase in sales or decrease in costs (000s)			Range (000s)	Standard Deviation (000s)	Coefficient of Variation
		Average	Best Case	Worst Case			
Automated production line	$1 million	$200	$300	$100	$200	$40	0.20
New cooling coils	1 million	200	220	180	40	10	0.05
New product line	1 million	250	400	50	350	100	0.40

expected annual increase in sales or decrease in costs to be the same for all projects. Does this mean the firm would consider these three projects to be equivalent? It appears not, since the new product line is the riskiest project given the range of possible outcomes and its large standard deviation and coefficient of variation of cash flows. New cooling coils are the least risky project and should be evaluated using the lowest of the three discount rates. The simple rule of thumb is that riskier projects should have higher discount rates when determining their NPVs and less risky projects should have lower discount rates. While this part seems easy, again it is not clear from the total risk approach how much discount rates should be adjusted upward or downward to properly reflect risk. This is a disadvantage of this approach.

Beta Risk Approach

This approach is conceptually sounder than the total risk approach and focuses on the contribution to firm risk associated with accepting a given project. It measures the interaction between the cash flows of the project and the existing firm. Beta risk is taken from the capital asset pricing model, which states that the appropriate risk level of a given project equals the risk-free rate plus some risk premium multiplied by the project's beta level. Beta, in turn, is measured as the covariance between the project's and the existing firm's cash flows divided by the variance of the market returns.

$$K_j = RFR + [E(R_m) - RFR] \times \beta_j$$

Thus, K_j is the appropriate discount rate for the project, RFR is the risk-free rate of return, $E(R_m)$ is the expected return on a market portfolio, and β_j is the project's beta. As an example, suppose a given firm has a beta of 1.2 and is financed exclusively with internally generated equity. The market risk premium $[E(R_m) - RFR]$ is 7 percent. When considering projects of average risk—that is, projects whose cash flows are highly correlated with the firm's existing cash flows and have a beta similar to the firm's beta (β) of 1.2—the firm should use the computed 13.4 percent cost of equity. When the project is substantially riskier, say the project's beta is 1.8, the appropriate cost of equity discount rate rises to 17.6 percent.

Exhibit 10.15: *Life Cycle of a Typical Firm and Logical Financing Alternatives*

Stage of Firm's Life	Description of Stage	Financing Alternatives
Start-up stage	First year of company's life; no track record of sales or proven products.	Owner's equity Venture capital
Development	Product developed and initial sales generated; company not at break-even level of sales.	Owner's equity Trade credit Bank lines of credit Venture capital
Expansion	Company is marketing product with some success; company near or above breakeven; cash needs are great.	Trade credit Bank lines of credit Venture capital Public sales of equity
Growth	Company is generating profits, but cash needs are great.	Trade credit Bank lines of credit Venture capital Public sale of equity Public sale of debt

Average project: 13.4% = 5% + (7%) × 1.2
Risky project: 17.6% = 5% + (7%) × 1.8

While this approach is certainly elegant, it is frequently difficult to arrive at reasonable estimates of $E(R_m)$ and especially the project's beta. What is important to remember, however, is that project risk should be incorporated into the decision process. For a more detailed discussion of how to calculate a firm's beta or a project beta, see Appendix 2 in this chapter.

Sources and Costs of Capital

Most new businesses are financed exclusively by their owner's equity. The reason for this is simple. A new business with no proven track record is simply too risky for most banks or other creditors. As the firm grows, its need for capital to finance that growth increases. Eventually, the owners exhaust the capital they are willing or able to invest in their business, and they have to seek alternative sources of funding for their business. These sources of funding can take a variety of shapes and forms. They can be various forms of credit extended by a bank or other lending institution; they can be venture capital supplied by an outside individual or venture capital firm; or they can be outside equity injected into the firm through a public offering of the firm's stock.

The most important source of funding for most companies is monies that the company generates internally through the retention of profits. These funds are called "retained earnings" on the balance sheet and represent the cumulative retention of past and current after-tax profits that have been plowed back into the company's assets to increase the company's profit potential or to grow the company.

While retained earnings are an important source of funds for most companies, new companies (or companies in their initial years of start-up) have no retained earnings, or the retained earnings may be negative if the firm has suffered losses in its early years, a not uncommon occurrence.

External Sources of Funding

Thus, while internally generated sources of funding are important for many companies, external sources of funding get the company started. **Exhibit 10.15** lists various stages of the firm's life from start-up through the growth phase and indicates likely sources of external funding at each stage. For example, in the earliest start-up phase, when the company has no track record, the most likely source of financing is the owner's own funds (owner's equity), although many entrepreneurs will seek out venture capital financing at this point also. As the firm grows through the research and development stage, and through the stage at which it is actually selling products and generating revenues, and perhaps even profits, the number of alternative sources of funding grows also.

Venture Capital

In the early years of a company's life, it is unlikely that the firm can sell equity to the public in a public offering because of the firm's size or its lack of a track record. Most firms at this point are just too risky for there to be much interest in public ownership. Therefore, if the owners need additional capital, they may turn to venture capitalists or to a venture capital fund. Venture capitalists are individuals who loan money to or make equity investments in smaller, start-up firms. Venture capital funds also exist. These are investment companies that invest shareholders' money in new, very risky, but potentially very profitable business ventures. Although venture capitalists may loan money, like a bank, for a fixed rate, usually they prefer to make equity investments in start-up companies. That is, they invest money and receive partial ownership in the firm. Because the typical investment of venture capital in start-up companies is extremely risky, venture capitalists generally impose high requirements on their investments. It is not unusual for venture capitalists to require returns as high as 50 percent and paybacks as short as two years. A study by Bruno and Tyebjee,[3] which surveyed 193 entrepreneurs, found that the overall equity yielded by their firms to venture capitalists averaged 45.1 percent. The average equity amounts obtained by investors in financing rounds one, two, and three were 31.5, 19.7, and 10.2 percent. By the second round of financing, the average firm had given up 51.2 percent, or a controlling equity position, to the outside venture capitalists or venture capital firm. Frequently, the negotiations between the firm's owners and capital suppliers, in this case venture capitalists, revolve around how much investment is needed by the firm and how much equity or ownership the owners are willing to trade for the investment.

Bank Debt

As an alternative to selling a substantial ownership position to venture capitalists, many start-up companies will turn to bank debt as a source of short-term capital. Bank debt is not a good source of long-term capi-
tal for a variety of reasons. First, banks generally do not lend for more than two to three years, and most start-up companies need the investment in more permanent types of assets, such as plant and equipment. Since the entrepreneurs do not plan to liquidate their plant and equipment at the end of two to three years, they may likely not have sufficient funds to repay the loan. Thus, most bank debt is used as a source of shorter-term funds.

Examples of bank debt used by start-up companies would be revolving credit agreements and bank lines of credit. A revolving credit agreement is a binding agreement that commits a bank to make loans to a company up to a predetermined credit limit. To obtain this type of commitment from a bank, a company usually pays a commitment fee based on the unused portion of the pledged funds. A line of credit is an agreement that permits a firm to borrow funds up to a predetermined limit at any time during the life of the agreement. Under both arrangements, banks usually require the company to maintain agreed upon financial standards. For example, to protect their position, a bank may create a provision in the line of credit agreement that would not allow the company to add additional debt. Alternatively, a common provision is one that requires the company to maintain a certain level of liquidity, such as maintain a current ratio at some predetermined level. Many industry analysts consider a current ratio of 2.0 to be an acceptable level of liquidity, although this varies widely.

External Equity: Selling Stock to the Public

Frequently entrepreneurs have as their ultimate objective taking their company public through the public sale of their stock. Apple Computer and Microsoft are relatively recent examples of start-up companies that have made their original owners and investors millionaires, and in the case of Microsoft and Bill Gates, a billionaire. Selling stock to the public usually involves one of two forms: (1) private placement or (2) public sale. A private placement is much the same as venture capital. A public sale is much the more complicated because it involves meeting the legal requirements of state and federal laws, including the Securities Act of 1933 and the Securities and Exchange Act of 1934.

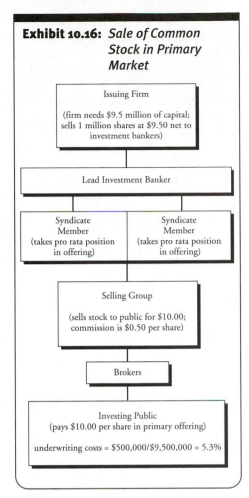

Exhibit 10.16: *Sale of Common Stock in Primary Market*

Issuing Firm
(firm needs $9.5 million of capital; sells 1 million shares at $9.50 net to investment bankers)

Lead Investment Banker

Syndicate Member (takes pro rata position in offering)

Syndicate Member (takes pro rata position in offering)

Selling Group
(sells stock to public for $10.00; commission is $0.50 per share)

Brokers

Investing Public
(pays $10.00 per share in primary offering)

underwriting costs = $500,000/$9,500,000 = 5.3%

The mechanics of a public offering are shown in **Exhibit 10.16**. Technically, the issuing firm sells stock to a syndicate made from a number of investment banking firms, which in turn sells the stock to the public. Generally, the investment banking firms have contracted to sell the stock for a fixed commission, which is the difference between what the investment banking firm pays for the stock and the price at which they agree to sell the stock to the public. Since the underwriters generally assume the risk of an unsuccessful sale of stock, issuing costs are greatest for those securities types for which the investment bankers bear the greatest risk, namely equity. **Exhibit 10.17** illustrates the relative costs to the firm of selling different types of securities. The riskier the security type, the larger the underwriting costs. Thus, secured debt usually involves the lowest underwriting costs, and these costs range from 0.50 to 1.50 percent, while the costs of selling equity average around 6 percent but can be as large as 15 percent for a small start-up company.

Determining the Cost of Capital

The firm's cost of capital is an important element in managing the firm's financial resources. Only when managers understand their cost of capital can they make appropriate long-term investment decisions. Generally, the rule when making such decisions is to invest only in projects whose returns exceed the company's cost of capital. There are three steps necessary to compute a firm's cost of capital: (1) determine the after-tax component costs of capital; (2) using market values, determine the weights that the particular capital source has in the firm's current capital structure; and (3) calculate a weighted average cost of capital. For example, assume that a firm has only debt and equity in its capital structure. In this case, the firm's weighted average cost of capital (WACC) would be determined as follows:

$$WACC = [MVD/(MVD+MVE)] \times K_d +$$
$$[MVE/(MVD+MVE)] \times K_e$$

If the firm also had preferred stock, then the WACC equation would be adjusted as follows:

$$WACC = MVD / (MVD + MVE + MVP) \times K_d +$$
$$MVE / (MVD + MVE + MVP) \times K_e +$$
$$MVP / (MVD + MVE + MVP) \times K_p$$

where MV, MVD, MVE, and MVP represent market value, market value of debt, market value of equity, and market value of preferred stock, and K_d, K_e, and K_p represent the firm's cost of debt capital, equity capital, and preferred stock.

Perhaps an example will be helpful. In **Exhibit 10.18**, consider a firm with a total market value of $100 million, where this value is divided among debt, preferred stock, and equity. If the component costs of capital are as shown in Exhibit 10.18, and if debt, preferred stock, and equity represent 20, 10, and 70 percent, then the firm's weighted average cost of capital is 13.27 percent.

Occasionally, managers may want to tie the rate of return from a project to the specific costs of financing that project, say with debt financing. The manager may think that it is acceptable to undertake a project with a 10 percent rate of return if the firm is able to finance the project with a par debt issue having an 8 percent coupon rate. This is a mistake. Since the firm cannot sell an unlimited amount of debt, it soon will be forced to use equity to finance projects and will find that it is forced to reject projects with returns greater than 10 percent but lower than the firm's cost of equity financing. Even if debt financing were unlimited, investors would soon become uncomfortable with the firm's debt level and begin demanding higher rates of return on succeeding projects.

Cost of Debt

The appropriate component cost of debt is an after-tax cost. Because the corporate tax code allows interest expense as a deduction when calculating the corporate tax liability, interest expense reduces the firm's tax liability. Consider two firms that are alike in all respects, except one uses $100,000 of 8 percent coupon debt while the other firm has no debt. This example is shown in **Exhibit 10.19**. Notice that while Firm A (the firm with debt financing) incurs interest expense of $8,000, it pays $2,400 fewer in taxes. Thus this firm's after-tax cost of $100,000 in debt is the interest expense of $8,000 minus the tax savings of $2,400, for a total cost of $5,600, or 5.6 percent.[4]

Cost of Preferred Stock

Most preferred stock is perpetual and does not mature. If the preferred is selling at par or if the company can issue preferred stock at par, then the cost of preferred stock is simply the coupon rate on the preferred. Since preferred dividends are paid with after-tax dollars, there is no adjustment to calculate

---

Exhibit 10.17: *Expected Issuance Costs (%): By Security Type*

Security Type	Average Costs	Range of Costs
Senior debt	1.00%	0.50–1.50%
Junior debt	1.25	0.75–1.75
Preferred stock	3.00	2.00–5.00
Common stock	6.00	5.00–15.00

Exhibit 10.18: *Calculation of a Firm's Cost of Capital*

Security Type	Number Outstanding	Market Value per Share of Stock or per Bond	Market Value of Security Type	After-Tax Cost of Capital
Senior debt (8%, 20 years)	17,857	$1120	$20M	8%(1 − .30) = 5.6%
Preferred stock (9.5%)	100,000	100	10M	9.5
Common stock	2,000,000	35	70M	16

Exhibit 10.19: *Determination of a Firm's After-tax Cost of Debt*

	Firm A (with debt)	Firm B (no debt)
EBIT	$50,000	$50,000
− Interest	8,000	—
= EBT	42,000	50,000
− Taxes (30%)	12,600	15,000
= EAT	$12,600	$15,000

After-tax cost is $5,600, not $8,000; so $K_d = 5.6\%$, not 8%. For the general case,
$$K_d = (\text{before tax cost})/(1 - t)$$

the after-tax cost of preferred stock. The preferred dividend is already after tax. If the preferred stock is not selling at par, then the cost of preferred stock equals the preferred dividend divided by the market price of the preferred stock. As an example, if the company's 8.25 percent preferred stock is selling at $82.50, the cost of preferred stock is 10 percent ($8.25/$82.50).

Cost of Equity Capital

The cost of equity capital is the most difficult component of capital to estimate, principally because its cost is frequently not explicit (like paying interest expense on debt) or may be unknown. The major implicit cost of equity capital is the growth rate or the change in the company's stock price that investors are demanding or anticipating. Even the explicit cost of equity capital, dividends, is difficult to estimate because firms change their dividends from quarter to quarter or year to year.

There are at least three methods used frequently to determine a firm's cost of equity capital. The first is the dividend growth approach. Under this approach, the firm's cost of equity capital (K_e) is based on the expected dividend yield and the firm's expected growth rate in earnings, $K_e = D_i/P_0 + G$, where D_i is the expected upcoming annual dividend, P_0 is the current market price of the firm's stock, and G is the expected growth rate in earnings. While this approach seems easy, it is appropriate only for those firms whose dividends and earnings have been and are expected to continue to grow at a relatively constant rate for the foreseeable future. Of course, this approach is not feasible for those firms that do not pay dividends.

The second approach to calculate the firm's cost of equity capital is the bond yield approach. It estimates K_e as the yield to maturity on the firm's bonds plus a risk premium to reflect the additional risk associated with equity. Estimating the risk premium is the difficult part and is frequently done on an *ad hoc* basis. Analysts usually estimate the risk premium to be between 3 and 7 percent.

The third approach to estimating the cost of equity capital is usually referred to as the capital asset pricing model. In this approach, K_e is estimated by starting with the risk-free rate and adding components for a market risk premium and an estimate for the level of the riskiness of the company.

$$K_e = RFR + [E(R_m - RFR)] \times \beta_j$$

This approach hinges on the determination of a firm's beta (β_j), which is its co-movement with the market. Firms with βs > 1.0 are more volatile than the average stock and hence require more return. Firms with βs < 1.0 are less volatile than the average stock and hence require less return. If the expected return on the market is 14 percent and the risk-free rate (T-bill or bond) rate is 6 percent, a stock with a beta of 2.0 would have a required rate of 6 + (14 − 6) × 2.0 = 22 percent. Most stocks have betas that are between 0.20 and 3.00. A few rare stocks actually have negative betas, indicating that these companies are expected to do well when the market is suffering negative returns and do poorly when the market experiences high returns.

CONCEPTS OF VALUATION

A plethora of methods exist that afford the valuation of real and financial assets. Some are as outlandish as random guessing to estimate value, and some are more scientific in nature, such as the use of continuous time techniques to value future cash flows. In this section we focus on the more scientific and less subjective methods of firm valuation.

Before we delve into the mechanics of valuation, take a moment and ponder why firm valuation is important. Ask yourself: Why is it important for the investors to be able to correctly value the firms that they invest in? A pretty straightforward answer exists: Without valuation techniques that yield normatively desirable valuation estimates, investors would be left in the dark and the efficiency of the financial markets would crumble. Investors who cannot correctly value firms may be less likely to invest in them or may require a premium for the added risk that they are accepting by investing in firms of unknown value. This entire process would lead to financial market instability or collapse. Thus the valuation of firms is an important aspect of healthy financial markets and is paramount for healthy economies.

A thorough understanding of the concept of value should be founded before we progress further. There are many ways to classify value, and thus many different values that could naively be maximized. The most basic concept of value that could be analyzed is the liquidation value of a firm. This value corresponds to the value at which the firm's assets could be sold on a piecemeal basis. More precisely, liquidation value is the value of the firm's raw assets without consideration of their worth in the context of the organization. For example, think of the street value of a smelter, then compare that to the value of a smelter to a steel manufacturer within the context of its entire business operation. It is obvious that the smelter is more valuable to the steel manufacturer than to the person on the street. When we examine the value of a healthy business we should always evaluate its value in a framework that considers the value of the firm as a going concern. This value corresponds to the value the shares would hold if all pertinent information about the firm's value were reflected in the price of the security. This value does not always equal the market value of the firm's equity, often because of market imperfections. When finance professionals refer to the maximization of firm value they are referring to the maximization of the present value of all of the future cash flows of the firm, which corresponds to a maximization of shareholder wealth.

Firms in their infancy often find capital acquisition a difficult process, and in many cases reach a point where internally produced financing can no longer supply funding for the growth prospects of the firm. At this point the firm must decide which method of financing is best given the market conditions and also given the opportunity set of available choices to the firm. Firms at this stage in their life cycle often enlist the help of an investment banker. The investment banker undertakes the process of valuing the firm and often uses their established network of securities dealers to sell the equity of the issuing firm to market place. When the investment banking firm underwrites the shares of the firm on a *best efforts* basis the investment banker agrees to undertake their best effort to issue the securities. The do not agree to purchase the securities from the firm and they do not accept the risk associated with the shares not selling. The investment banking firm could have committed to selling the shares for the firm. The *firm commitment* method of underwriting involves the investment banker buying the shares from the firm at a certain price and selling them to the public. The investment-banking firm bears the risk of market down turn and of non-placement.

Equity Valuation

Similar to the methodologies employed in calculating net present value, firms can be valued using discounting techniques.

$$V = \frac{D_1}{(1 + K_e)^1} + \frac{D_2}{(1 + K_e)^2} + \frac{D_3}{(1 + K_e)^3} \cdots \frac{D_\infty}{(1 + K_e)^\infty}$$

$$= \sum_{t=1}^{\infty} \frac{D_t}{(1 + K_e)^t}$$

Where D_1 is the dividend in period 1, and K_e is the discount rate used to discount the dividends of the firm, it is also known as the *required rate of return*.

Myron Gordon developed the model presented below to value firms, and this model assumes that the growth rate will stay constant forever. Granted this is not the most realistic assumption, but this model is quite tractable and allows for the extension of multiple growth rates along different periods of time.

$$V = \frac{D_0(1 + g)}{(1 + K_e)^1} + \frac{D_0(1 + g)^2}{(1 + K_e)^2} + \frac{D_0(1 + g)^3}{(1 + K_e)^3} \cdots \frac{D_0(1 + g)^\infty}{(1 + K_e)^\infty}$$

$$V = \frac{D_1}{(K_e - g)}$$

One major limitation of the constant growth model is the relationship between K_e and g in the denominator. If g is greater than K_e then the value of the stock, as indicated by the model, is negative. This suggests that the current equity holders should pay others to take the stock off their hands! No matter how enticing this may seem, this result is not reasonable. The lowest value a share of stock can attain is zero.

Let's examine the result more closely through an example: Assume that TennCorp has a current dividend of $1.00 and this dividend is expected to grow at 10 percent forever, and the current required rate of return, or K_e, is 12 percent. The value of the share could be easily calculated using the discount model as outlined above. We proceed as follows:

$$V = \frac{D_1}{(K_e - g)}$$

$$\$55 = \frac{\$1.00(1 + .10)}{(.12 - .10)}$$

We should emphasize that the current dividend was not used to calculate this value. We used D_1, the dividend next period to estimate the value of TennCorp. If we assume that the dividend is growing at 10 percent a year forever then the dividend next period would be $1.10. Using this result we obtain a value of $55 for one share of TennCorp's stock.

Now let's assume that TennCorp has a current dividend of $1.00 and this dividend is expected to grow at 13 percent forever, and the current required rate of return, or K_e, is 12 percent. The value of the share could be easily calculated using the discount model as outlined above. The numerical result:

$$V = \frac{\$1.00(1 + .10)}{(.12 - .14)}$$

$$-\$55 = \frac{\$1.10}{(-.02)}$$

First, let's ask ourselves if this result seems realistic. If we used this value we should expect the current holder of the equity to pay us $55 to take it from them. Not a bad deal, at least for some shares.

Also, let us note the sensitivity of changes in the entire value calculation to changes in the denominator. Slight changes in the discount rate or in the growth rate can have dramatic effects on the firm's value. With the difficulty involved in estimating the true growth rate and discount rate of the firm, valuation may become very subjective if hard and fast scientific rules are not used in the measurement of these variables. Therefore, efforts should be made to estimate these variables with the greatest possible accuracy under the assumption that the costs of estimation do not become prohibitively large.

Before we move on let's examine two changes in the denominator of the constant growth equation. First, let's change the growth rate from the original problem above. Assume it changes to 8 percent:

$$V = \frac{D_1}{(K_e - g)}$$

$$\$27.50 = \frac{\$1.00(1 + .10)}{(.12 - .08)}$$

Now, change the required rate of return from the original problem above. Assume it changes to 15 percent:

$$V = \frac{D_1}{(K_e - g)}$$

$$\$22.00 = \frac{\$1.00(1 + .10)}{(.15 - .10)}$$

Notice the sensitivity of the value of the share to changes in values in the denominator. Keep in mind that the original price calculation was $55 a share!

No Growth Case

Let's evaluate the value of TennCorp assuming that its dividend is expected to stay constant forever, that is, a no growth rate. Modify the original formula as follows:

$$V = \frac{D_1}{(K_e - g)}$$

$$V = \frac{D_0(1 + 0)}{(K_e - 0)}$$

$$V = \frac{D_1}{K_e} = \frac{D_0}{K_e}$$

Now let's assume that TennCorp has a current dividend of $1.00 and this dividend is expected to stay constant forever, and the current required rate of return, or K_e, is 10 percent. The value of the share could be easily calculated using the discount model as outlined above. The numerical result:

$$V = \frac{D_0}{K_e} = \frac{D_1}{K_e} = \frac{\$1.00}{.10} = \$10$$

Keep in mind that this value is only valid if we assume that the firm's dividends will never grow and that they are maintained at their current level.

Multiple Growth Rates

As seen here, the general form could be manipulated to accommodate different growth rates through time.

$$V = \sum_{t=1}^{n} \frac{D_0(1 + g_1)^t}{(1 + K_e)^t} + \sum_{n+1}^{\infty} \frac{D_n(1 + g_2)^{t-n}}{(1 + K_e)^t}$$

It can reasonably be assumed that most stocks will not grow at a constant rate forever, and thus this extension of the constant growth model is appropriate in many circumstances.

First, let's assume that TennCorp has a current dividend of $1.00 and this dividend is expected to grow at 20 percent for three years, and then at 5 percent forever after, and the current required rate of return, or K_e, is 11 percent. The value of the share could be easily calculated using the discount model as outlined above. The numerical result:

Step One: Find the present value of the dividends from t_1 to t_3

Time Period	Dividend	Present Value Calculation	Present Value of Dividend
0	1.00	—	—
1	1.20	$\dfrac{1.00(1 + .20)^1}{1.11}$	1.08
2	1.44	$\dfrac{1.00(1 + .20)^2}{(1.11)^2}$	1.17
3	1.73	$\dfrac{1.00(1 + .20)^3}{(1.11)^3}$	1.27

Step Two: Find the present value of the stock in period 4 using the constant growth method outlined before:

$$V_3 = \frac{D_4}{(K_e - g)} = \frac{(1.00(1 + .20)^3) \times (1.05)}{(.11 - .05)} = \frac{1.81}{.06} = \$30.24$$

Now discount this amount back to the present:

$$V_0 = \frac{\$30.24}{(1 + .11)^3} = \$19.92$$

Step Three: Sum the present values of all dividends and the value of the stock in period 4.

$$V = \sum_{t=1}^{n} \frac{D_0(1 + g_1)^t}{(1 + K_e)^t} + \sum_{n+1}^{\infty} \frac{D_n(1 + g_2)^{t-n}}{(1 + K_e)^t}$$

or

$$V = \frac{1.00(1 + .20)^1}{(1 + .11)} + \frac{1.00(1 + .20)^2}{(1 + .11)^2} + \frac{1.00(1 + .20)^3}{(1 + .11)^3} + \frac{\dfrac{(1.00(1 + .20)^3) \times (1.05)}{(.11 - .05)}}{(1 + .11)^3}$$

$$V = \$23.44$$

Now let's assume that TennCorp has a current dividend of $1.00 and this dividend is expected to grow at 20 percent for three years, and then at 15 percent for 2 years, and then 5 percent forever after, and the current required rate of return, or K_e, is 11 percent. The value of the share could be easily calculated using the discount model as outlined above. The numerical result:

Step One: Find the present value of the dividends from t_1 to t_3

Time Period	Dividend	Present Value Calculation	Present Value of Dividend
0	1.00	—	—
1	1.20	$\dfrac{1.00(1 + .20)^1}{1.11}$	1.08
2	1.44	$\dfrac{1.00(1 + .20)^2}{(1.11)^2}$	1.17
3	1.73	$\dfrac{1.00(1 + .20)^3}{(1.11)^3}$	1.27
4	1.99	$\dfrac{1.73(1 + .15)^1}{(1.11)^4}$	1.31
5	2.29	$\dfrac{1.73(1 + .15)^2}{(1.11)^5}$	1.36

Step Two: Find the present value of the stock in period 5 using the constant growth method outlined before:

$$V_5 = \frac{D_6}{(K_e - g)} = \frac{((2.29 \times (1 + .05)))}{(.11 - .05)} = \frac{2.40}{.06} = \$40.00$$

Now discount this amount:

$$V = \frac{\$40.00}{(1 + .11)^5} = \$23.74$$

Step Three: Sum the present values of all dividends and the value of the stock in period 6.

$$V = 1.08 + 1.17 + 1.27 + 1.31 + 1.36 + \$23.74$$

$$V = \$28.57$$

Valuation Using Multipliers

Let's examine valuation from a different perspective. First, think of the earnings available to shareholders. There are two components to this amount. There is one component that will be retained in the firm and another that will be paid to shareholders as a dividend. The ratio of the amount the firm retains to the total earnings is called the *plowback ratio*, or retention rate. Let us denote this percentage as R_t, and, for this analysis, let's assume that this percentage is constant through time. If this were the case, we would observe:

$$(1 - R_t) = \frac{D_1}{E}$$

or

$$(1 - R_t)E_1 = D_1$$

We could incorporate the constant growth model to solve for V. This would result in:

$$V = \frac{(1 - R_t)E_1}{(K_e - g)}$$

Assume that TennCorp has current earnings of $2.50 per share. These earnings are expected to grow at 17 percent forever, and the current required rate of return is 20 percent. Let's assume that the firm retains 50 percent of their earnings every year. The value of the one share could be easily calculated using the discount model as outlined above. The numerical result:

$$V = \frac{(1 - R_t)E_1}{(K_e - g)}$$

$$V = \frac{(1 - .50)(2.50(1 + .17))}{(.20 - .17)}$$

$$V = \$48.75$$

We can also manipulate the formula to solve for an earnings multiplier.

$$EM = \frac{(1 - R_t)}{(K_e - g)}$$

Assume that TennCorp has current earnings of $2.50 per share. These earnings are expected to grow at 17 percent forever, and the current required rate of return, or K_e, is 20 percent. Let's assume that the firm retains 50 percent of their earnings every year. The value of the one share could be easily calculated using the discount model as outlined above. The numerical result:

$$EM = \frac{(1 - .50)}{(.20 - .17)}$$

$$EM = 16.67$$

Thus: $V = 16.667 \times \$2.50(1 + .17) = \$48.75$

As can be seen this approach yields the same value as the calculation above.

Free Cash Flows Approach

What about firms that do not have current dividends or are seeking an estimation of their value? The firm would have to estimate its free cash flows to equity. The calculation is outlined below:

FCFE = Net Income
      + Depreciation
      − Capital Spending
      − ΔWorking Capital
      − Principal Repayments
      + New Debt Issues

FCFF = FCFE		EBIT $(1 - T)$
+ Interest Expense $(1 - t)$		+ Depreciation
+ Principal Repayments	or	− Capital Spending
− New Debt Issues		− Δ Working Capital
+ Preferred Dividends		

Similar to the valuation of dividends:

$$V_0 = \sum_{i=1}^{n} \frac{\text{FCFE}_1}{(K_e - g)}$$

$$V_0 = \frac{\text{FCFE}_1}{(K_e - g)}$$

or

$$V_0 = \frac{\text{FCFF}_1}{(\text{WACC} - g)}$$

Thus, using the techniques outlines before, one is able to value the firm given a correct estimate of free cash flows.

Comparable Company Approach

The comparable company approach is a valuation technique that uses information about other firms to gauge value for a firm that seeks a valuation estimate. The first step in the process consists of finding other firms that are very similar to the firm that seeks valuation. The second step entails collecting past financial data on the similar firms. Collection and evaluation of earnings, sales, cash flows, book value, and other financial data would all be made. Then the firm could use these estimates to estimate multipliers for its value. Assume that TennCorp wants to go public, and there are two very similar firms that are currently publicly traded. FloridaCorp and AlabamaCorp are of similar size and are almost identical to TennCorp, and their financial data follows:

Measure	TennCorp	FloridaCorp	AlabamaCorp
EPS	$1.50	$2.00	$3.00
CFPS	$2.00	$3.40	$5.00
BVPS	$14.00	$20.00	$25.00
Price	?	$60	$60
P/E	?	30×	20×
P/CF	?	17.65×	12×
P/BV	?	3×	2.4×

We could use the multipliers from the similar firms to gauge estimates for TennCorp's price. By using the values from FloridaCorp and AlabamaCorp financial statements TennCorp could estimate its own price using the multipliers given in the table above. The table below demonstrates how TennCorp would undertake the process.

Valuation Estimates

Indicator	High	Low	Average
P/E	$45	$30	$37.5
P/CFP	$35.30	$24	$29.65
P/BVPS	$42	$33.60	$37.80

Grand Average: $34.98

Thus TennCorp would estimate its value at approximately $35 a share, given the information from the similar firms.

Estimating Components

Now that the valuation models have been derived let's examine how the components of the models are obtained. One difficult component to estimate is the growth rate of the firm's dividends for use in the dividend discount model. It should be noted that for short run equity analysis, growth rates of earnings and dividends must be estimated separately because they are not necessarily positively correlated, even though that is normally the case.

Assuming that earnings were growing at some constant rate and the payout ratio stays constant over this same period, we would expect, as is the result, that the dividend growth rate equals the earnings growth rate over the same time period. However, if the retention rate decreases, the growth rate of dividends would have decreased, and if the retention rate increases then the dividend growth rate would have increased over time. A number of factors could lead to payout ratios increasing or decreasing over time. Thus it is paramount that we estimate the dividend growth rate and not naively estimate the earnings growth rate and assume that the dividend growth rate is identical if we are investing in the short run. For most firms these two ratios will be highly correlated if growth rates are positive, because firms tend to pay higher dividends the higher the earnings, but this is not the case for negative growth rates. If firms are experiencing negative earnings growth they tend to avoid dividend reductions and the growth rate in dividends becomes less correlated with the growth rate in earnings. It should be noted that over the long run the growth rate of earnings is highly correlated with the growth rate of dividends. This is a logical conclusion given the fact that there must exist a bound on how long the divergence in these two ratios can continue. We can estimate the growth rate in earnings by use of the following formula:

$$g = (\text{Retention Rate}) \times (\text{Return on Equity})$$

$$g = (R_r) \times (\text{ROE})$$

As can be seen, the growth rates of the earnings are a function of the retention rate of earnings and the return on equity. This growth rate estimate implicitly assumes that the only funding that the firm uses is being generated internally. This is intuitively appealing because we can decompose the two separate factors that affect growth. If a firm retains more of its earnings there will be more capital to invest in projects, ceteris paribus, than if a portion of the earnings are paid to investors as dividends. Thus it's logical to conclude that higher retention rates would lead to higher growth rates.

As seen before, ROE can be further decomposed as:

$$\text{ROE} = \text{Profit Margin} \times \text{Total Asset Turnover} \times \text{Financial Leverage}$$

$$\text{ROE} = \frac{\text{Net Income}}{\text{Sales}} \times \frac{\text{Sales}}{\text{Total Assets}} \times \frac{\text{Total Assets}}{\text{Common Equity}}$$

$$\text{ROE} = \frac{\text{Net Income}}{\cancel{\text{Sales}}} \times \frac{\cancel{\text{Sales}}}{\cancel{\text{Total Assets}}} \times \frac{\cancel{\text{Total Assets}}}{\text{Common Equity}}$$

$$\text{ROE} = \frac{\text{Net Income}}{\text{Common Equity}}$$

where the individual components of return on equity are outlined in the section of financial ratios. We can derive directly from this equation a relationship between the growth rate of earnings and any of these three components of ROE. If net income, total asset turnover, or financial leverage increase, the growth rate in earnings should also increase, and vice versa.

Let's examine this closer through an example: Look at the balance sheet and income statement of TennCorp for 20X3. You can easily locate the financial values and solve for ROE as outlined below. Assume that TennCorp's historic retention rate is 50 percent.

$$\text{ROE} = \frac{\text{Net Income}}{\text{Sales}} \times \frac{\text{Sales}}{\text{Total Assets}} \times \frac{\text{Total Assets}}{\text{Common Equity}}$$

$$\text{ROE} = \frac{9{,}394}{215{,}600} \times \frac{215{,}600}{95{,}298} \times \frac{95{,}298}{45{,}935}$$

$$\text{ROE} = \frac{9{,}394}{45{,}935}$$

$$\text{ROE} = 20.45\%$$

To solve for the growth rate:

$$g = (R_r) \times (\text{ROE})$$

$$g = (.50) \times (.2045)$$

$$g = 10.225\%$$

Assuming the retention rate was 30 percent we would have:

$$g = (R_r) \times (\text{ROE})$$

$$g = (.30) \times (.2045)$$

$$g = 6.135\%$$

Examine what effect this difference in retention rates can have on the value of TennCorp stock. Using the original example and the two derived growth rates it can be seen that dramatic differences in value can result in differences in growth rates.

$$V = \frac{D_1}{(K_e - g)} \qquad\qquad V = \frac{D_1}{(K_e - g)}$$

$$\$22.00 = \frac{\$1.00(1 + .10)}{(.15 - .10)} \qquad \$12.22 = \frac{\$1.00(1 + .10)}{(.15 - .06)}$$

K_e, the required rate of return on the firm's equity, can be estimated by use of the CAPM. As outlined in the previous section, K_e can be directly estimated by the CAPM if we have access to the firm's beta and expected return. Recall the formula as:

$$K_e = RFR + [E(R_m - RFR)] \times \beta_j$$

where K_e is the investors required rate of return, RFR is the risk free rate, R_m is the expected market return, and β is the beta of the stock. But how can beta be estimated if the security is not publicly traded? To estimate a beta for a firm that is not publicly traded an approach similar to the comparable company approach could be used. An industry average beta could be used as a proxy of the firm.

Through an example we can examine this process closer. Assume that the average firm in the industry that is most similar to TennCorp has a beta of 1.5 and the market is expected to return 12 percent and the risk free rate has been estimated at 3 percent. Using the CAPM we can calculate K_e as follows:

$$K_e = .03 + (.12 - .03)1.5$$
$$K_e = 16.5\%$$

1. *Working capital* is defined as total current assets minus total current liabilities. When the scope of a manufacturing facility increases, the facility usually requires greater cash balances, greater inventories or receivables to run the facility. These increases should be incorporated into the capital budgeting decision.

2. The reason for potential differences in ranking has to do with the different assumptions used by NPV and IRR regarding the reinvestment of intermediate cash flows. NPV assumes that cash flows are reinvested at the firm's cost of capital, while IRR assumes the cash flows are reinvested at the IRR.

3. Albert V. Bruno and Tyzoon T. Tyebjee, "The Entrepreneur's Search for Capital," *Journal of Business Venturing* 1 (1985): 61–74.

4. This example assumes the firm has sold or can sell this debt at par. In general, the before-tax cost of debt should be the yield to maturity on the company's debt. If the company sells the debt at par, then the coupon rate and the yield to maturity will be the same.

1. SOURCES OF COMPOSITE FINANCIAL DATA

Industry Norms and Key Business Ratios. Dun & Bradstreet Credit Services, Dun's Analytical Services, One Diamond Hill Road, Murray Hill, New Jersey, 07974-0027. Tel: 800/223-0141. Annual data cover 800 specific lines of business, classified by 2- and 4-digit Standard Industrial Classification (SIC) code numbers. Balance sheet and income statement figures are given for each industry group. Three figures are listed for each financial ratio: the median, and the upper and lower quartile.

Annual Statement Studies. Robert Morris Associates, One Liberty Place, Philadelphia, PA. 19103. Tel: 215/851-9100. One of the most well-known sources of financial ratios. Contains broad product breakdowns for manufacturing, wholesaling, and retailing plus a selection of services and construction. Three figures are listed for each financial ratio: the median, and the upper and lower quartile.

2. CALCULATING BETA FOR A FIRM OR A PROJECT

Beta is a measure of sensitivity. It indicates how much the value of a firm or a project will change given a change in the market. The formula to compute beta is:

$$\text{Beta} = \frac{\text{Cov}_{i,m}}{\text{Var}_m}$$

where $\text{Cov}_{i,m}$ is the covariance of the returns of company i with a portfolio of market-based securities, and Var_m is the variance of the returns on the market-based securities. An alternative way to calculate beta is to regress the market returns on the company returns using a spreadsheet package such as Excel or Lotus. The slope of the regression line will be equivalent to the beta as calculated above. A number of investment advisory companies such as ValueLine or Standard and Poor's compute and publish betas for companies.

Betas for projects are more difficult to estimate. Some analysts find a comparable company, calculate its beta, and make adjustments for comparability. Other analysts use quarterly earnings instead of returns and calculate beta as indicated above. Even with the best of data, estimates of beta are subject to measurement error, and management should use this approach with caution.

Chapter 11

Harry J. Bruce
CEO
Illinois Central Railroad

Corporate Governance
How the Board of Directors Holds a Corporation's Management Accountable to Its Shareholders

"Quis custodiet ipsos custodes?" (Who will guard the guardians themselves?)
Juvenal, *Satires* 2.6, *c.* 116 A.D.

INTRODUCTION TO CORPORATE GOVERNANCE
Issues of Management, Power, and Accountability

- Who owns today's business corporations? What does it mean to be the owner of a share—or of a million shares—of a corporation's stock?
- Who really runs today's corporations? Management? The board of directors? The shareholders? The large institutional investors? How does personal ownership of shares influence management decisions?
- To whom are corporations accountable in their conduct and performance? The board of directors? The shareholders? The law? The employees? The customers? Government?
- What institutions, agencies, or individuals have a right to demand a particular level of performance from corporations? How can corporations be held accountable to those who exercise such rights? How do those making demands on corporations bring about the responses they seek?
- How much should the chief executive officer and top managers of corporations be paid? Should excellent managers be paid more than mediocre ones? Who decides what constitutes excellent performance by a CEO? What kind of compensation package is most likely to stimulate effective performance?

The proper term for the subject of all these questions is "corporate governance"—the distribution of power and accountability within the modern business corporation. In particular, corporate governance is concerned with the enormous power exercised by the management of the modern corporation. The purpose of this chapter is to describe key issues in corporate governance—issues of management, power, and accountability—by looking at the history of American corporations; the relationship among shareholders, top management, and the board of directors; the board's fiduciary duties and legal powers; and the way the board actually does its job (both outside and inside the boardroom). The better one understands such key issues in corporate governance, the better chance one has to control them (or not fall victim to them).

The modern corporation has the power to change the lives of millions of people for good or for bad. The largest Fortune 500 companies have revenues that exceed the annual budgets of many national governments: Mitsubishi is bigger than Indonesia; Ford is bigger than Turkey; Wal-Mart's resources exceed the gross domestic product of Poland.[1] The dollars these companies pay to their employees and their suppliers, along with the taxes they pay to various governments, produce enormous economic impact. So do the products and services corporations bring to the world marketplace. So does the growth in shareholder wealth that occurs when a corporation is successful. For these reasons, the top executives of modern business corporations are among the most powerful people ever to appear on the stage of history.

Such power can be dangerous unless those who wield it are part of a wider system that holds them accountable. Just ask any Enron employee who was forced to stay vested in the company's stock just as the firm was suddenly to go bankrupt. New York corporate lawyers Arthur Fleischer, Jr., Geoffrey C. Hazard, Jr., and Miriam Z. Klipper state the problem this way:

BEST-USE CORRELATIONS

In *Marketplace,* your firm's board of directors begins to take on a leading role in Q5. To prepare you for this new dimension in simulation play, Chapter 11 provides an in-depth review of corporate governance practices and obligations.

Who Will Be on Your Team's Board?

In Q5, teams sell part of their companies to venture capitalists in return for an infusion of investment funds.

A board can be very helpful to a young company. Directors can provide experience and connections that the executive team does not have. Does your team lack financial, marketing, or technical expertise? Does it need connections to banks, other investors, key suppliers, or important customers? Think strategically. Who should join your board?

Who Decides Who Sits on Your Board?

In *Marketplace,* you will know your investors very well and they will insist, rather forcefully, on knowing you equally as well. As the condition of their investment, they will want representation on your board, probably a majority position. Chapter 11 will prepare you to deal with the demands of outsiders who want a voice in management decisions.

You Can Be Replaced

The most important decision a board makes involves the selection and retention of the chief executive officer. In *Marketplace,* Q5 and beyond, a board may exercise its power to remove a team's CEO (and, potentially, other top managers) if it concludes that management is floundering.

To be secure, power has to be legitimate, and for power to be legitimate, whether public or private, it has to be accountable. The modern business corporation is accountable according to its constitutional law, just as the government is accountable according to constitutional law. The constitutional law of the business corporation is called the law of corporate governance, which defines the accountability of directors to shareholders and of officers to directors. Corporate-governance law is important law because ultimately it affects every shareholder and the entire economy.[2]

Senior corporate managers ("officers," as Fleischer, Hazard, and Klipper call them) thus must be held accountable. But to whom? And for what? How is corporate governance supposed to work? How well *does* it work? To understand that, we need to understand how corporations originated, how they developed over time, and how finding a balance between accountability and initiative within corporate governance has evolved into a persisting contemporary dilemma.

Historical Evolution of Boards and Corporations

The corporate form of business organization is relatively new. Until about the mid-18th century, when the Industrial Revolution in England brought about the first mass production of goods in mechanized factories, virtually all private business was conducted by sole proprietors, families, or partnerships. Small workshops and cottage industries, selling hand-crafted products direct to a small and mostly local consumer market, had little need for the large amounts of capital and division of labor coordinated by a professional management that corporations provide.

"Perpetual Existence"

Although private *business* corporations did not exist until the mid-1800s, other types of corporations had been around for centuries: City governments, universities, monastic religious orders, charitable organizations, hospitals, and even the Roman Catholic Church were organized according to a corporate model. Incorporation enabled them to enjoy what lawyers term "perpetual existence." Today's business corporations also enjoy this potential for "perpetual existence"; they are legal entities distinct from either their members or their leaders.

Another similarity between today's business corporations and earlier institutions built on the corporate model is that they can hold property in their own name—another way the corporation perpetuates itself. This property belongs to the corporation, not to its members or its officers. The officers control the use of the property, but only so long as they hold office. The power really belongs to the corporation, which delegates it to the officer.

The origin of the word "corporation" helps make this clear. It comes from the Latin word *corpus,* meaning "body." A corporation is a group of people organized in such a way that they can act as if they were literally one body. Because corporations enjoy many of the same legal rights and privileges as a living individual, lawyers often call a corporation "a person on paper."

Joint-Stock Companies and "Limited Liability"

The first demands for the application of this corporate model to profit-making business came with the great voyages of exploration and the establishment of overseas colonies in the 15th and 16th centuries. These ventures required more capital than any single individual or a few partners could raise, and they threatened to overtax government treasuries as well. So the sovereigns of the exploring nations, chiefly Great Britain and the Netherlands, issued royal charters authorizing the creation of "joint stock companies" to pool the resources of dozens, perhaps even hundreds, of individuals willing to risk some of their capital for the chance of long-term gain.

To attract as much capital as possible, the charters establishing these early corporations promised investors not only a share of the profits but also "limited liability": If the corporation ran up debts that exceeded its earnings, the investors would not be personally liable for making good the losses. An investor might lose all of his original stake, but he could not be dunned for more. The creditors, not the investors, would bear any residual risk. To this day, British corporations still carry the name "Limited" to indicate that their shareholders enjoy the protection of this "limited liability."

Mergers and Boards of Directors

In addition to large amounts of capital, a colonizing expedition required a more complex organization than the typical

The December 2, 2001, collapse of Enron Corporation, the largest corporate bankruptcy in history, seemingly took the business world by surprise. Investment analysts, business-school professors, economists and high-profile business journalists pronounced themselves shocked and puzzled that billions of dollars in shareholder value could implode almost overnight. Less than two months earlier investors were valuing Enron at $28 billion, and a few months before that three McKinsey & Company consultants, Ed Michaels, Helen Handfield-Jones and Beth Axelrod, praised the Houston-based energy trading giant in lavish terms: "Few companies will be able to achieve the excitement extravaganza that Enron has in its remarkable business transformation," they wrote, "but many could apply some of the principles."[1] *Fortune* magazine voted Enron "The most innovative company of the year" for 2000.

How were so many "experts" able to fool themselves for so long about Enron? Possibly because they failed to take a searching look at the company's governance structure and its board of directors. Had anyone with a basic understanding of corporate governance taken the trouble to examine Enron's board in the months preceding the scandal, he or she quickly would have picked up danger signals of the type described in this chapter. Let's look at the more benign danger signals first.

Board size? In the year prior to the collapse, the Enron board had 15 members, including Chairman/CEO Kenneth Lay. The author considers this about twice the number required for an effective board. Once the number of directors goes beyond seven or eight, communication becomes difficult and the board tends to break down into an "inner" group of relatively active members and a less-involved "outer" group of "go-along" types.

Board composition? Enron's directors included some names with strong corporate-management credentials, such as Norman Blake, Jr., Chairman, President and CEO of Comdisco and former CEO and secretary general of the U.S. Olympic Committee; and Herbert Winokur Jr., Chairman and CEO of Capricorn Holdings and former senior executive vice president of Penn Central Corp.

But it also included Charles Lemaistre, M.D., president emeritus of the M.D. Anderson Cancer Center at the University of Texas, as well as John Mendelsohn, M.D., the Anderson Center's current president. Placing a medical doctor from a high-profile research and teaching hospital on a corporate board may lend the board some prestige, but it's not clear whether such a move brings any serious breadth of experience or policy judgment to a corporation dealing in highly complex and abstract financial instruments such as Enron's futures contracts. Putting two M.D.s from the same institution on the board only compounds the error.

Board activism and participation? Enron director Ronnie Chan, CEO of Hong Kong-based real estate firm Hang Lung Group, missed 75 percent of the Enron board's meetings. William Patterson, director of the AFL-CIO's office of investment, noted that Chan also sits on the board of Motorola, Inc., and Standard Chartered plc. "Chan is a classic example of a director who sits on too many boards," Patterson said.[2]

But the attendance records and professional qualifications of the Enron board members were small change compared to the compromising relationships into which roughly half of the directors allowed themselves to be drawn by the company's management. Technically, all of the board members except Chairman Lay were "outside directors," supposedly independent because they did not serve as part of the company's management. But six of them had effectively renounced their independence and become management insiders by accepting company favors.[3]

- Director William Powers Jr., dean of the University of Texas School of Law, sat on the Enron board at the same time that Enron management donated $250,000 to his law school and $3 million to the university at large. In addition, Enron's law firm, Vinson & Elkins, endowed a chair at the law school.

- Director Robert Belfer, CEO of Belfer Management, established a company called Belco Oil & Gas Corp., which became one of Enron's customers. It was all out in the open. Since 1996 Enron's proxy statements have included the disclaimer that "Belco Oil & Gas Corp. has entered into natural gas and crude oil commodity swap agreements and option agreements with Enron Capital & Trade Resources Corp." In 2000, Enron earned $33 million in connection with the Belco agreements.

- Director Herbert Winokur, Jr., who joined the Enron board in 1985, is affiliated with the National Tank Co., a vendor of oil-industry supplies which in 2000 received $370,294 in orders from Enron. This information was disclosed in Enron's most recent proxy.

- Director Lord John Wakeham, a former minister of energy in the British cabinet, received $70,000 in consulting fees from Enron while sitting on the board.

- Wendy Gramm, wife of U.S. Senator Phil Gramm (R-Tex.), received a seat on the Enron board in 1993, only a few weeks after the federal agency she headed, the Commodity Futures Trading Commission, ended restrictions on the types of energy trades in which Enron management planned to engage (she left the CFTC before joining Enron).

- Former Enron Director John Urquehart received consulting fees from the company while he sat on the board. In 2000 he received $493,000 in such fees on top of his $50,000 annual director's fee and an additional $10,000 received for sitting on a committee.

Amazingly, all of these relationships were disclosed in Enron's proxy statements and thus available for securities analysts and portfolio managers to evaluate. Virtually all of these investment professionals either chose to ignore the danger signals or simply failed to recognize that board members' cozy relationships with management were likely to compromise their capacity for evaluating management's performance objectively on behalf of the shareholders.

Not revealed in any proxy statement, but perhaps more damaging to Enron's corporate governance, was a statement made in 1989 by board member Robert Jaedicke, dean of the Graduate School of Business at Stanford University, an accountant and head of the Enron board's audit committee. According to *Vanity Fair* writer-at-large Marie Brenner, Jaedicke visited with Enron's internal-audit staff in March 1989 and was asked, "How do you view your role as an independent director?"

"I'm here to support management," Brenner says he replied. "I'm here to support Ken Lay." Brenner concluded: "The two auditors took this remark as an indication of where Jaedicke's loyalties lay."[4]

Jaedicke's remark is astonishing—and discouraging. If the dean of the number-one-ranked U.S. business school[5] can misconstrue the duty of a corporate director by 180 degrees—viewing himself as responsible not to the shareholders but to the chief executive officer—then shareholder capitalism may be in bigger trouble than anyone has imagined. The dean's remark suggests that tomorrow's business leaders are emerging from one of the world's most prestigious institutions of higher learning unaware of their true legal and ethical responsibilities, unprepared to distinguish between the interests of the shareholders and the interests of management, and unable to act correctly when a conflict between the two arises. Indeed, they may not even be able to discern the very existence of such a conflict.

The ultimate impact of the Enron collapse on the corporate system and economic growth remains to be seen. Already, one great American auditing firm, Arthur Andersen & Company, appears headed for extinction in the wake of its alleged collaboration with Enron management in a scheme to mask losses and confect bogus profits. While the Enron collapse is unlikely to lead directly to the demise of other firms, the public cynicism it generated may be acting like a low-level pollutant, repelling potential investors from committing their wealth to the care of corporate managers and retarding the global economic growth on which the welfare of billions depends. That consequence may best be summarized in a remark made to the author by Dr. Tony Maingot, director of Caribbean Research–Yale University:[6]

"Without trust in leaders of institutions, both private and public, there is growth in cynicism. Without trust there is no growth."

[1] "Why honesty is the best policy," *The Economist*, March 9, 2002, p. 9 ("Back to Basics" supplementary insert).

[2] Ron Orol, "Critics: Time to overhaul corporate boards," The Deal.com, Feb. 6, 2002

[3] Robert Manor, Stephen J. Hedges and Melita Maria Garza, "Critics: Enron probe pretty soft on board," *Chicago Tribune*, Feb. 5, 2002, Sec. 3, p. 4.

[4] Marie Brenner, "The Enron Wars, *Vanity Fair*, April 2002, p. 206.

[5] *The Best Graduate Schools for 2003*, special publication by *U.S. News & World Report*, 2002.

[6] Tony Maingot, Ph.D., personal interview, Rio de Janeiro, April 2002.

proprietorship or family enterprise of the period. Many individuals with different skills were needed, plus a cadre of especially skilled and motivated people to coordinate and direct their work—managers. To make the colonizing ventures successful, these managers had to be given broad power and authority over the company's employees, property, and funds.

The shareholders in the new joint stock companies gave their managers this power but under a condition: The managers had to be accountable to the shareholders for what they did with the wealth and power entrusted to them. Because the managers were going overseas and could not be observed or supervised directly by the people putting up the capital, a mechanism of accountability was needed. This *board of directors* consisted of men not involved in the day-to-day management of the enterprise. Their responsibility was to periodically examine and evaluate the managers' performance, report their findings back to the shareholders, and replace the managers if their performance was deemed inadequate. The first two private corporations that colonized America for the British, the Virginia Company of London and the Virginia Company of Plymouth, both had boards of directors specified in the royal charters that established them. In fact, they each had *two* boards—a local council in the New World and a "supervisory board" in England.

Monopolies

The first joint stock companies chartered by the British and Dutch crowns (as well as the earliest American corporations) were basically monopolies, chartered by government to private entrepreneurs to accomplish some acknowledged public purpose, public work, or internal improvement that government could not finance by itself: construction and operation of canals, ports and harbors, toll bridges, turnpikes, plank roads, and other public infrastructure; colonial settlements; and overseas trading corporations that shipped spices back to England and Holland. Each corporation was awarded a royal monopoly to engage in a particular activity or to dominate a particular geographic area. Government let private investors keep the profits in return for assuming financial risk and undertaking management of the venture. At this stage of development, corporations were actually an extension of the power of the Crown.

The American Corporation: Less Public Purpose, More Private Profit

After the Revolutionary War, Americans continued to use the British model of corporate organization but with two important differences. The first American innovation was that the charter authorizing private individuals to form a corporation came not from the king but from the legislature of each state. American corporations also differed from the British model in that they gradually shed their original public character and migrated into what we today call the *private sector.*

It took several generations of evolution in public consciousness before investors, lawyers, and the public could accept the idea of placing a powerful wealth-multiplying mechanism such as the corporation in the hands of businesspeople solely interested in making a private profit while competing with others for the same business. Even after Adam Smith's *Wealth of Nations* was published in 1776, there was a lag of several decades before the public at large accepted Smith's notion that private profit brought public benefits. As J.M. Juran and J. Keith Louden write:

> There were fears (amply justified) that the charter rights would be abused. There were apprehensions about breathing life into immortal creatures. There was downright disgust about the idea of limited liability, which was widely regarded as welshing on one's honorable debts. The opponents of corporations saw trouble ahead if the way were opened to a new breed of immortal monsters, each unlimited to growth, yet limited as to liability.[3]

Adam Smith's belief in the public benefits of private profit and competition got a much better reception in the new American republic than in its country of origin, Great Britain. In this country, many advocates of independence envisioned a healthy private corporate sector as a strong counterweight to the kind of powerful centralized government the colonies had just rejected. One of these advocates was the new nation's first treasury secretary, Alexander Hamilton. In November 1791, Hamilton obtained a charter from the New Jersey legislature authorizing him to form a corporation known as the Society for Establishing Useful Manufactures (SUM), which was to produce a series of products ranging from sailcloth to women's shoes.[4] Hamilton's SUM was different from today's corporations in three respects:

1. Hamilton had to appeal directly to the legislature for a special act granting SUM a corporate charter. Chartering a corporation today is a routine administrative procedure that any entrepreneur may undertake simply by filing a special form and paying a registration fee. This change was made to eliminate the once-common practice of bribing legislators to obtain a charter. Today, each state has a General Corporation Law setting forth the rules for incorporation of any type of business. This "one-size-fits-all" set of guidelines makes further legislation superfluous and enables virtually anyone to establish a corporation.

2. Corporate charters no longer specify that a corporation confine itself to a certain type of business, to a specific territory, or to the production of certain products, such as making shoes, milling flour, or running a railroad between Point A and Point B. Today, a corporation may engage in any lawful activity, and a charter obtained in one state authorizes the company to engage in business in any of the others.

3. Finally, corporate charters no longer grant monopolies. Corporate businesses are expected to compete in free markets.

Differences between Corporations and Other Businesses

All businesses need management. Why do corporations require not just management, but governance? Governance is required primarily because a corporation differs very substantially from the other two common formats for organizing a business—the sole proprietorship and the partnership. In proprietorships and partnerships, the same people who own the business also manage it. They are financially responsible only to themselves, and if they manage poorly, they usually lose. But in a business organized as a corporation, ownership and management are divorced. All the owners do is invest their money in the business; professional managers run the business for them. If the managers fail, they do not automatically lose wealth, but the investors do. In fact, corporate managers can do a poor job for extended periods of time—years, even decades—and still keep their well-paid jobs while shareholders watch the value of their investment drop.

Because the interests of managers can conflict with those of shareholders, the law requires that corporations have a governance structure to make sure the activities of the managers are carried out for the benefit of the owners. If this is not done, there is a danger managers will exceed their legal authority and begin operating the corporation for their own benefit rather than for the shareholders. For example, they may decide to increase their salaries even though profits are not growing, or they may award some of the corporation's business to outside firms they control. Or they may engage in ill-advised acquisitions or mergers that increase managerial power and salaries without necessarily raising shareholder value or long-term corporate viability.

The Upside of Corporations:
Fast, Strong Growth

Separating ownership and management according to the corporate model increases the practical benefits to a business, particularly a business requiring large amounts of capital. Having a multitude of owners each contributing a small amount of money enables a business to raise far more capital than it could attract from a few individual owner/managers using their own funds. Keeping the management function separate from the ownership function also leaves the professional managers with more freedom to take risks and to act aggressively than if they were funded solely with their own money or with borrowed funds that must be paid back with specified interest on a definite schedule.

The combination of strong capitalization and professional management can have a powerful liberating effect on managerial effort—and on results. If corporations are powerful, it is because the corporate system of separating management from investment unleashes the maximum potential of each component.

Downside of Corporations:
Disenfranchised Owners and
Unaccountable Managers

But the economic advantages of the corporate form of business organization come at a price: The owners of a business corporation are radically disenfranchised, while the managers are supplied with vast discretionary power. Although separation of ownership and management raises economic performance, it also leaves every corporation with a problem of accountability: When managerial power is concentrated

in the hands of a small number of skilled professionals while ownership is dispersed among a vast number of uninvolved, non-managing owners, what assurance is there that the powerful managers will use their power for the benefit of the powerless shareholders?

History and Mechanisms of
Shareholder Disenfranchisement

The potential for shareholder disenfranchisement is always present in any corporate business. But it apparently was not a major problem until the post-Civil War era, when the development of the telegraph and the ticker tape enabled investors all over the United States to trade shares on the New York Stock Exchange. Prior to that time, most corporations were small, local businesses with a few dozen—or perhaps a hundred—large shareholders, all living in or near the city where the corporation was headquartered. If these shareholders became concerned about the conduct of the business, they could communicate directly with the board of directors. Most held their shares for long periods—even for life. Dumping their stock was not the option it is today; lack of a nationwide stock-trading system made it hard for sellers to find buyers. For these early shareholders, communicating their dissatisfaction to the company (exercising their "voice") was a comparatively strong option, while choosing to sell their stock (choosing "exit") was a comparatively weak one.

Students of business history say many of these early corporations actually behaved more like large partnerships than like today's true corporations. William T. Allen, Chancellor of the Delaware Court of Chancery, says that up until about the mid-19th century, corporate shareholders had "a sense, but only a weak sense, of a distinctive artificial corporate entity."[5] Another source views the corporations of that period as "little more than limited partnerships, every member exercising through his vote an immediate control over the interests of the whole body."[6]

All this changed in the huge outburst of post-Civil War business expansion that knitted the United States together into a single, nationwide, industrial economy. Legally, corporate shareholders were still entitled to accountability from management. Practically, however, the increasing numbers and geographic dispersion of

shareholders, along with the ease of liquidity made possible by a national stock market, isolated shareholders from management and made accountability difficult to enforce.

Today, three factors keep shareholders, the owners of a corporation, from enjoying the powers of proprietors and partners who own other kinds of businesses. Together, these factors add up to what students of organizational behavior call the "collective-action problem" (i.e., the inherent difficulty of organizing large numbers of dissimilar people into an effective operational group).

The first factor in the shareholders' collective-action problem is *sheer numbers*. A typical large corporation will have hundreds of thousands of shareholders. Some will be individuals holding a few hundred to several thousand shares each, while others will be institutional investors: mutual funds or pension funds holding millions of shares on behalf of hundreds of thousands of individual plan members who are the beneficial, though not legal, owners of the shares. Some of the shareholders will even be other corporations. Most of these shareholders will be unknown to one another, since only the management of their company holds a complete list of all its investors. Unable to communicate with one another, the shareholders cannot act as a group to defend their interests.

The second factor in shareholder disenfranchisement is *geography*. While the top management of a corporation normally is found all in one place—corporate headquarters—shareholders are spread across the nation and the world. This geographic dispersion makes it even more difficult to organize a multitude of shareholders into an effective group. Even with today's most advanced telecommunications technologies, loose ownership cannot easily obtain information controlled by a tightly coordinated management.

The third factor is *liquidity*, the ease with which corporate shares can be bought and sold on a modern stock exchange. Because today people can trade stock almost as easily as they can hold it, a shareholder who is dissatisfied with the financial performance of his stock is more likely to sell it and reinvest the proceeds in another stock than to exhaust himself in a futile attempt to reach out to management and get it to do a better job. When traders dump a stock that has not met their expectations, they call it "walking the Wall Street walk." The disgruntled investor "votes with his feet" by walking away from the under-performing corporation rather than trying to stimulate it to do better. If the investor were for some reason unable to sell the stock, he would be more strongly motivated to communicate with the board of directors and seek some sort of managerial reform, to exercise "voice." Today, for all but the largest investors, "voice" is impossible to achieve. Because the shareholder is voiceless, it is easier just to "exit."

BOARD OF DIRECTORS

Total Accountability to Disenfranchised Shareholders; Limited Authority over Powerful Managers

In one respect, Alexander Hamilton's SUM corporation of two centuries ago was strikingly similar to today's Fortune 500 companies: Its prospectus said, "The affairs of the company [are] to be under the management of thirteen directors." The current General Corporation Law of the State of Delaware, where more than 50 percent of the nation's publicly traded corporations are incorporated, reads, "The business and affairs of every corporation organized under this chapter shall be managed by or under the direction of a board of directors."[7] The incorporation laws of the other 49 states employ almost identical language.

Note the expression "managed by or under the direction of." Managing is a full-time job. A board of directors, which normally meets no more than five to eight times a year, cannot actually manage a corporation. The courts have held, however, that the expression "under the direction of" gives the board the right to *delegate* its management authority to professional managers. This means *managers are legally accountable to the board for their actions* because it is from the board that they receive their authority and powers. It also means *the board in turn is accountable to the shareholders for the performance of the managers* because it is from the shareholders that the corporation receives its capital. The courts have found that it is really the board's own managerial authority that the managers are exercising. This authority, in turn, comes from the shareholders, whose equity provides the managers with the financial means to carry out their work. Thus, in the corporate system, it is ultimately the shareholder investment that legitimizes management power.

(Mythical) Model of Corporate Governance

Corporate governance involves three elements: the shareholders, who own the corporation but have no voice; the managers, who operate the company and have virtually total voice; and the board of directors, who supervise the managers on behalf of the shareholders and supply at least a token of the voice the shareholders have relinquished.

The central element is the board, ideally a strong, independent-minded panel of experienced businesspeople who meet periodically to evaluate management's performance, appraise management's proposals for the forward movement of the enterprise, approve recommended gain-sharing (dividends) from time to time, and determine whether management is doing an adequate job of multiplying the shareholders' wealth in compliance with the law. Should the directors determine that management's performance has been inadequate, they may exercise one of their most important powers by discharging the chief executive officer and retaining a new one.

The board is supposed to serve as the voice for the voiceless shareholders, representing them and making sure management acts in their interest. Under the law of corporate governance, shareholders relinquish the right to manage their property, but they do not relinquish their right to retain effective management. Proper management of the shareholders' property is the manager's obligation, and the board of directors is there to make sure that management carries out its side of the bargain.

More Realistic Model

Unfortunately, the model described above contains more myth than reality. The way boards of directors work is very different from what the public imagines. It is even different from what most business managers imagine. Neither the shareholders nor the board is at the top of a chain of command. For reasons already discussed, the shareholders are largely powerless. And except in a few areas (such as discharging the chief executive officer and retaining a new one), the board, too, is largely powerless.

The way a corporation really works is that virtually all power to initiate action is vested in management. All of the company's goals, plans, and strategies for growth are developed at the management level. So are all of the programs, including the bud-

get, that enable the managers to implement those plans and realize their goals. The board can at best only periodically monitor and review the way those plans and strategies are being implemented and determine whether the goals are being reached.

Wakeup Call to U.S. Boards: The Global Economy

In order to work, management's accountability to shareholders must have a mechanism: corporate governance centered in a strong and relatively independent board of directors. But by the early 1970s, it began to be apparent that is not the model which America's growing new industrial economy got.

The first signs that something might be amiss with corporate governance in the United States came in the 1970s, when several large corporations were caught breaking the law. Lockheed Aircraft Corp. admitted paying bribes to Japanese government officials to obtain contracts in that country; Gulf Oil was found guilty of making illegal political contributions;[8] and ITT used corporate funds to support CIA activities against Chile when that nation's new Marxist government threatened to nationalize the company's telecommunications properties.[9] A few media critics chastised the boards of these companies for ignoring management's excesses, but the business community saw little reason to question the governance mechanism. Profits had not suffered, so why get upset?[10]

Attention focused on boards again in the late 1970s when civil-rights advocates noted that virtually every boardroom was totally male and totally white. To mollify the critics, many companies named a token female, black, Hispanic, or labor-union official to their boards, a cosmetic change that fooled no one and left the existing corporate-governance format intact. The new directors accepted their places in the system without challenging its fundamental assumptions about governance.

Starting in 1981, however, corporate governance at last began to come under real scrutiny and real demands for change. This time the challenge to corporate America was not legal or racial but economic: For the first time, U.S. corporations were facing serious competition, and some of them were losing the battle. Throughout the 1980s and into the early 1990s, millions of investors learned for the first time that holding a blue chip stock no longer meant safe, steady growth and uninterrupted dividends. Household names such as Weirton Steel, Pan American World Airways, Chrysler Corporation, International Harvester—even venerable public utilities such as Chicago's Commonwealth Edison—found themselves struggling with unforeseen challenges. As the decade of the 80s progressed, some of those household names did the unthinkable: They disappeared through liquidation. Pan Am and Eastern no longer are around. Neither are some of the steelmakers. Gone, too, is a whole laundry list of less-than-truckload motor carriers whose managers proved unable to adjust to free-market competition after Congress deregulated their industry in 1981. Spector, Dohrn, Red Ball, Time-DC, Campbell Express, Wilson, PIE, and a host of smaller truck lines simply went out of business.

By the mid-80s, even companies once considered untouchable—companies such as IBM and General Motors—were in deep, deep trouble, watching helplessly as their market share dribbled away to upstarts at home and abroad. Yet their boards appeared to be sleepwalking, leaving the same CEO and management team in place for years. As these businesses unraveled, critics began to ask, "Why doesn't the board do something?"

Today's corporate managers and directors operate in a changed environment and therefore experience their roles differently. Management performance is being judged by world competitive standards. Most large American business corporations directly confront, in their own backyards, competition from businesses in every other part of the world—businesses that are run by relentless competitors who have their own sources of manpower, innovation, and capital and often the overt or covert support of their governments.

Even business competition within the United States has become far more dynamic as a result of greater technical innovation and product change, to mention only two factors. Hence, every business is much more vulnerable than in the past to the adverse consequences of ineffective management. An investor can no longer invest in a "good sound company" and simply relax. That good sound company might turn out to be a Republic Steel or Swift & Company. Neither can management assume that they "have it made" when they have "made it." "We

have to earn our wings every day," as Frank Borman, then CEO of Eastern Airlines, said before he lost his.[11]

In this new and more dangerous competitive environment, the board of directors takes on fresh importance. Under the laws of corporate governance, only the board has the authority to replace the chief executive officer when management appears to be losing the battle for corporate viability and growth. If the board fails to act in time, shareholder choices quickly dwindle. A proxy fight staged by a disgruntled investor may lead to ousting of the incumbent board and its management, but only a large shareholder with deep pockets can afford such a campaign. Stanford Law School Professor and former Securities and Exchange Commissioner Joseph Grundfest notes that "the costs of a 1992 proxy contest at Jefferson-Pilot Corp. [a North Carolina-based insurance and broadcasting conglomerate] exceeded $5 million."[12] Or a takeover company may offer the shareholders a premium for their shares, but this is likely to happen only if the acquirer perceives the target company to have considerable value left. Takeover artists look for underperforming companies, not dying companies.

In any case, proxy fights and takeovers only beg the question of how the target company came to be a chronic underperformer in the first place. Here the finger points back at the board. The absolute minimum duty incumbent upon a board of directors is that of safeguarding the shareholders' capital, taking care to see that their investment is not diminished. Beyond that, the board's duty is to see that management multiplies that capital to the greatest extent practicable. If growth fails to occur or losses begin to accumulate, the board is the shareholder's first and to a large extent only line of defense. The board's most important duty is to evaluate management's performance and to act promptly and appropriately if it finds that performance inadequate.

At this point the question becomes: Does the board have what it takes to hire the right CEO, track his performance, and replace him if he fails to protect and multiply the shareholders' assets?

Myth of the All-Powerful Board

When Lee Iacocca was brought in to rescue the technically bankrupt Chrysler Motor Corporation in 1980, he knew the compa-

ny's sleepy management had been ignoring innovation and giving away market share to vigorous Japanese competitors for more than a decade. What he could not understand was why Chrysler's board had never seriously questioned what management was doing.

I often wondered: where was the board while all this was going on? . . . When I became chairman, I moved in on the board members very gradually. I wasn't crazy enough to point my finger at a group that had just hired me and tell them: "It's all your fault." But once or twice I did ask the board, as politely as I could: "How did management ever get their plans past such a distinguished group of businessmen? Didn't you guys get any information?"[13]

Iacocca's question was rhetorical. As a veteran of the Ford Motor Company under its quixotic chairman Henry Ford II, Iacocca knew perfectly well that few boards of directors actually perform all of the oversight functions assigned to them by the law and entrusted to them by the shareholders.

And he probably knew why: Although directors are legally obligated to defend the interests of the shareholders, most boards are mere appendages of management. The failure of the public to grasp this reality has led to the growth of a whole board-of-directors mythology that differs radically from the facts. The following myth/fact inventory suggests why boards usually rubber-stamp management when they are supposed to question and challenge it.

Corporate Governance Myth-Fact Inventory

• **Myth No. 1: The board of directors is the supreme power in the corporation.** The board appoints the chief executive officer. The CEO and senior management answer to the board and can be replaced if management performance does not meet the board's standards. *Fact:* Most U.S. boards are *de facto* subordinate to management, not superior to it. The directors are selected by the head of the management team—the CEO—and owe their prestigious positions and their many privileges to him. As for the chairperson of the board, in more than 75 percent of U.S. corporations the CEO and the chairperson are the same person, and the CEO persona prevails. In effect, management runs the board, not vice versa.

• **Myth No. 2: Shareholders own the company.** *Fact:* Ownership of shares in a business corporation does not bring with it the same rights and privileges as ownership of other types of property. Legally, the holder of corporate shares is considered an investor rather than a proprietor. He has no access to what he "owns" and no say in how it is used or managed. All he has is a right to a share of the profits and a right to an accounting by management of the company's performance.

- **Myth No. 3: The board manages the company.** *Fact:* The board cannot manage the company. The board meets only five to eight times a year for approximately four hours per session and maintains no ongoing communication with the many specialized departments and functions essential to a modern corporation. It delegates the management function to professional managers who work full-time in their specialized areas. Only these managers have the expertise to plan, organize, coordinate, and control the day-to-day functions of the enterprise.

- **Myth No. 4:** *The board represents the shareholders and makes sure management acts in their interest.* **Fact:** See Myth No. 1. Boards do a better job of representing management—or representing themselves—than representing shareholders.

- **Myth No. 5: The board takes the long view, grasps the big picture that management misses due to its need to focus on the details.** *Fact:* The board is in the dark because management controls all essential information about the firm. The head of the management team, the CEO/chairperson sets the agenda for board meetings. The chairperson thus controls the amount and kinds of information the directors receive.

- **Myth No. 6: While quiescent in normal times, the board becomes active during periods of trouble. It probes, investigates, interrogates management, gets to the bottom of the problem.** *Fact:* See Myth No. 1. Directors are reluctant to challenge the CEO because in most cases he was the one who gave them their directorships. A collegial, "old-boy" culture discourages confrontation in the boardroom while encouraging an ethos of "to get along, go along." Even when they suspect problems are developing, directors are slow to react until pressure from major shareholders, lenders, the news media, or a tender offer forces a response.

- **Myth No. 7: If shareholders feel certain directors are delinquent in holding management accountable for corporate performance, they can vote such directors out of office at the annual meeting.** *Fact:* The annual election of corporate directors in the United States closely resembles the "elections" of delegates to the Central Committee of the Communist Party of North Korea.[14] There is only one slate of candidates, and it is picked by management. Shareholders can either vote for the entire slate or abstain. Most corporate bylaws offer shareholders little more than the chance to ratify measures on which management already has decided. Contesting a board election usually involves a proxy contest likely to cost an insurgent shareholder at least $500,000—much of it for legal fees, the rest for advertising and direct mail appeals to other shareholders. As a forum in which management can be challenged, much less changed, the annual meeting is almost useless.

"The notion that shareholder meetings are hollow rituals is hardly new," writes Joseph Grundfest, citing Adolph A. Berle's remark in 1957 that the annual meeting is "a kind of ancient, meaningless ritual like some of the ceremonies that go on with the mace in the House of Lords."[15]

Origins of the Board Myth

How did the myths of corporate governance come to be so widely believed? Governance guru Nell Minow says it happened because management wanted it that way. "Managements perpetuate those myths to lull the shareholders," Minow says. "Shareholders feel more secure if they believe a wise board of directors is watching and correcting management."[16]

Managements do not need an expensive or carefully orchestrated propaganda campaign to get the corporate-governance myths into circulation. All that is required is a typical corporate public relations department with a professional grasp of press-release language. For example: "The Board of Directors of XYZ Corporation today declared a dividend of 12 cents per share of common stock to shareholders of record as of May 15," reads the opening line of a typical release. Reading this kind of language, even veteran investors cannot help visualizing a dozen silver-haired wise men of industry grouped around a mahogany table to address the solemn issue

of how much of the company's current earnings should be distributed to the shareholders. The reality is that the CEO and the chief financial officer decided how large the dividend should be, and the directors routinely ratified their decision.

Another release might read, "The Board of Directors of Intercontinental-Universal Incorporated today elected Daniel C. Smith as Chairman and Chief Executive Officer, effective October 1. Mr. Smith will succeed Thomas M. Jones, who is retiring." Like the release announcing the dividend, the disclosure that the board "elected" a new CEO conceals a baser reality: The CEO picked his own successor, and the board accepted that choice. In the real world, most boards accept with only token dissent almost everything management proposes. Most board resolutions, in fact, are adopted unanimously.

Boards vote with management because board members are appointed by management and paid by management; they owe their perks and privileges to management. Under the law, boards work for the shareholders; they are not employees of the corporation and hence not subordinate to its management. In the boardroom, however, corporate directors find themselves enmeshed in a powerful web of other obligations and relationships that can be very difficult to evade.

Methods and Motives for Keeping Boards Loyal to Management Rather Than to Shareholders

Between the fees, the perks, and the prestige—all controlled by the powerful chairperson/CEO—it is not surprising that boards frequently fail to perform the governance duties that the shareholders and the law expect of them. If the CEO is of the "imperial" variety, unscrupulous dispensing of perks can draw the board deeper and deeper into the orbit of management, detaching the board further and further from the interests and perspective of the shareholders—and even the customers.

For example, during the mid-1980s, when General Motors management stood virtually helpless as Japanese competitors ate deeply into GM's historic market dominance, the corporation's directors were totally in the dark about the widening quality gap between GM's cars and those of its popular Japanese competitors. GM cars had become legendary for falling apart after 10,000 miles or rusting out after one bad winter. Yet GM's directors remained ignorant of the company's quality problems. Why? Because GM's Chairman/CEO Roger B. Smith made sure that each director got a brand-new GM car for personal use every 90 days. The cars were replaced before any director had a chance to experience personally the infuriating manufacturing errors that were turning GM from a legend into a laughingstock.[17]

Dilemma of Corporate Governance: Initiative vs. Accountability

The extraordinary amount of power and freedom that senior executives are given to use other people's money in pursuit of economic growth is one of the important keys to the great economic productivity of the corporate form of business organization. If this managerial initiative were to be seriously curtailed, the corporation's potential for multiplying shareholder value could be crippled. Thus, any restriction on management power must be applied with extreme care and discretion, and by law that discretion belongs to the board of directors. The board must keep the managers law abiding and loyal to the stockholders, but it must do so without exerting a chilling effect on managerial initiative or effort.

How much freedom should corporate managers be allowed? Total power is not advisable. "Power corrupts, and absolute power corrupts absolutely," wrote British historian Lord Acton (1834–1902). But governance that involves too much monitoring, too many restrictions and guidelines and rules can err in the other direction, stifling the creativity and extra effort that build high performance. A business corporation is a wealth-generating machine. Its only reason for existence is to create customers and produce profits. Fettered, frustrated managers working in a military-style chain-of-command structure cannot generate the profits investors seek when they put their capital at risk.

Corporate governance, then, is not just a problem or a task. It is a dynamic dilemma, a perpetual effort to maintain a balance between excessive freedom and excessive monitoring. An effective board of directors is continually trying to balance the management's need for initiative and freedom against the shareholders' entitlement to an accounting of management's performance.

Unfortunately, many boards find that balancing act too demanding. Instead of mediating between the management's need

for power and the shareholders' entitlement to accountability, they identify with and embrace management. And with good reason: Management has more to offer.

How CEOs Can Seduce Their Boards

Serving on a corporate board of directors is rewarding in many respects. At the typical Fortune 500 company, such positions offer $25,000–$50,000 per year for between five and eight four-hour meetings (banks are an exception; by law their boards must meet monthly). About two-thirds of the total represents a retainer, or flat annual rate, while the balance represents fees of $1,500 to $2,000 for each meeting the director attends. A director who serves on a board committee receives additional compensation for each committee meeting attended.

The sums cited may seem small compared to the seven- or eight-figure salary-plus-bonus packages of top CEOs, but directors work part-time while CEOs work full-time and then some. In addition, retainers and meeting fees may be only the tip of a much bigger financial iceberg for some directors. These are directors of corporations in which the CEO bonds with the board by routing his corporation's business to firms owned or managed by his directors. That might mean lucrative contracts for a director's consulting company, legal business for a director's law firm, loan business or deposits for a director's bank, corporate contracts for a director's insurance company, or charitable donations from the corporation to a director's *alma mater* or favorite charity. In a 1993 article in *New York* magazine, reporter Christopher Byron explained how James Robinson, the embattled chairman of American Express Corporation, kept board members loyal to him even after the company suffered a decade-long string of business reverses. Among his directors were former Secretary of State Henry Kissinger and former President Gerald Ford. Each received Amex consulting contracts. In 1991 alone Kissinger's foreign-affairs consulting firm received $500,000; Ford received $100,000.[18]

Because a board seat brings both income and prestige, most directors are careful not to engage in behavior that might endanger their eligibility for continuing board membership. That basically means getting along well with the chairperson/CEO and the other directors, which means not being too independent and not leading a fight to

upend the CEO's plans and programs. The old rule prevails: To get along, go along.

In companies ruled by an imperial chairperson/CEO, a dissenting director is unlikely to be renominated at the end of her term. In effect, she is fired. Once she is let go, the intercorporate grapevine may label the dissident as "not a team player." She could be dropped quietly from consideration for membership on other boards.

Disenfranchised Owners, Powerful Managers

The combination of disenfranchised shareholders and boards of directors too beholden to management opens the door to many kinds of abuse. Such abuse of managerial power and authority is not just a potential but a reality. In recent years the media have carried a growing number of stories detailing managerial conduct that was in conflict with the interests of the shareholders. Some typical examples:

- Managers award themselves salary increases and bonuses even though the company is failing to earn profits.
- Managers (or directors) use corporate (i.e., shareholder-owned) assets for their personal leisure or that of their families and friends.
- Managers (or directors) use corporate bank accounts to grant themselves low-interest loans, interest-free loans, or loans so open-ended that they need never be repaid.
- Managers award corporate business to a company in which they or a family member holds a financial interest (so-called "sweetheart deals"), often bypassing other vendors offering better products or services at lower prices.
- Managers act on inside information to trade profitably in their company's stock before outsiders have had a chance to learn the state of the company's performance (insider trading).
- Managers acquire other companies and engage in "empire-building" in order to raise their power, status, and salaries, even though the acquisitions mesh poorly with the core corporation and contribute little or nothing to long-term growth or financial viability.
- Managers break the law, subjecting the corporation to large fines or legal settlements that are paid not out of the managers' personal wealth but out of shareholder equity.

Arguably the most common form of managerial abuse is plain old mediocre performance: The managers run the company just well enough to generate good salaries for themselves but not well enough to build value for the shareholders. During the 1980s, takeover specialists made it their business to identify such underachieving corporations, and they found hundreds of them. Many of these companies were successfully acquired when takeover companies convinced shareholders that the value of their stock would never grow as long as the company was being run by its incumbent management. To take control of the company, the raiders offered the shareholders a premium over the market price for their stock. In many cases, the shareholders willingly sold out, and the takeover firm then installed a new board and executive team.

Abuse of power by managers is dangerous because it can erode the long-term economic viability on which shareholder value depends. Shareholders invest their capital in a corporation for one reason: to multiply their wealth. When corporate assets or corporate power and authority are converted to serve the private interests of managers, shareholder wealth is diminished and investor confidence is eroded. So is the company's fundamental economic strength—its ability to develop good products that will generate profits and jobs.

What makes managerial abuse really problematic, however, is that it is hard for shareholders to identify it and document it, much less stop it. Thus, to a large extent, corporate shareholders are without power. They need a governance system to keep managers accountable because without such a system there is almost nothing they can do to affect the performance of the company in which their money is invested. Without strong and responsible governance, a corporation is a faceless, self-governing, nonaccountable—and extremely powerful—entity that cannot be controlled through the historic mechanisms of reward and punishment that society uses to control its individual members.

This potential for nonaccountability is why the French call a corporation a *société anonyme* and the Spanish call it a *sociedad anónima*, an "anonymous society." It is also why the British Lord Chancellor Edward, Baron Thurlow (1731–1806) complained: "Did you ever expect a corporation to have a conscience, when it has no soul to be damned and no body to be kicked?"[19]

CORPORATE GOVERNANCE AND THE LAW

The Board's Fiduciary Duties and Legal Powers

What Good Boards Are Supposed to Do

Robert Kirk Mueller, former chairman of Arthur D. Little, Inc., and author of seven books on boards of directors, writes that "governance is understood as the continuous exercise of authority and decision over, and the performance of, political functions of policymaking and resource allocation. That's fancy language for overseeing and monitoring a company's conduct, i.e., bugging the management to get with it."[20]

In recent years, corporate-governance analysts have begun focusing more sharply on just what governance is and why it is essential to strong corporate performance.

> The single major challenge addressed by corporate governance is how to grant managers enormous discretionary power over the conduct of the business while holding them accountable for the use of that power. Shareholders cannot possibly oversee the managers they hire. . . . In theory, at least, the law imposes on the board a strict and absolute fiduciary duty to ensure that a company is run in the long-term interests of the owners, the shareholders.[21]

If the duty of a board is so clear, why do so many boards fail to do their duty? A clue can be found in the somewhat evasive qualifying phrase, "In theory, at least." Under the law of corporations, which is virtually identical in every state and relies on a British precedent more than 250 years old, corporate directors are held to be "fiduciaries" of the stockholders. A fiduciary—from the Latin *fides*, faith, *fidere*, to trust, and *fiducia*, a thing held in trust—means someone who can be trusted to be faithful to another's interest, to care for another's property as if it were his own. The law expects corporate directors to exercise what it calls *fiduciary responsibility* toward the shareholders' property. In theory, the law would appear to hold corporate directors to a very high standard of behavior.

In fact, the law goes even further, breaking the general concept of fiduciary responsibility down into two specific duties, the *duty of loyalty* and the *duty of care*. The duty of loyalty means that in all official conduct, a director is to act solely on behalf of the shareholders, never on behalf of another party or herself. She may

not place herself in a conflict of interest—a situation in which she uses her corporate powers to serve her own interest at the expense of the interests of the shareholders. (Managers are under the same obligation when they exercise their corporate powers and use the corporate resources the shareholders have placed at their disposal.) Monks and Minow elaborate:

> *Duty of loyalty* means that a director must demonstrate unyielding loyalty to the company's shareholders. Thus, if a director sat on the boards of two companies with conflicting interests (both trying to buy a third business, for example), he would be forced to resign from one board because clearly he could not demonstrate loyalty to the shareholders of both companies at the same time.[22]

The basic principle of loyalty is not complicated. Stealing from the company is disloyalty in its extreme form. Yet even mild forms of disloyalty can have very destructive effects, because disloyalty necessarily diminishes profits to shareholders and almost inevitably demoralizes the organization. This happened at Chrysler in the 1950s, when top management stole from the company by setting up sweetheart contracts with supplier companies that they controlled. Receiving unjustified compensation is stealing from the company. But what level of compensation is unjustified?[23]

The other duty, the duty of *care*, means directors must be *careful* when exercising judgment and making decisions. They must take *care* by giving appropriate consideration to the issues they are called upon to decide. They must pay attention to what they are doing by asking appropriate questions so that they do not act out of ignorance or negligence. They must display what the courts have called "reasonable diligence" before coming to a conclusion. They must consider all the alternatives before coming to a decision.

Business-Judgment Rule: Escape Hatch for Directors

Fiduciary responsibility, with its charge that directors must treat shareholder interests with loyalty and care, would seem to be an ironclad guarantee that directors will always act in the best interests of owners. If they do not, they can end up on the wrong end of a shareholder lawsuit.

But that threat exists more in theory than in reality. In reality the number of successful lawsuits against corporate directors is relatively small because the courts have evolved another rule that to a great extent cancels out much of the doctrine of fiduciary responsibility. It is called the "business-judgment rule," and it means that the courts will not try to second-guess a director's business decisions unless there is evidence that the director benefited personally at the expense of the corporation or engaged in extreme neglect of his responsibility.

The business-judgment rule evolved because the courts recognized that when corporate directors make a business decision they must act in real time, without knowing all of the facts that might become known later during a court trial.

> The business-judgment rule protects a director who acts in good faith, who is adequately informed, and who has no personal interest in the transaction. In such circumstances a director is not liable for consequences of his decision unless the decision lacks any rational basis. The rule is known as a "safe harbor," providing a director broad discretion to act without fear of second-guessing.[24]

Directors are allowed this wide latitude because it is nearly always impossible, and hence unfair, for a court to substitute its after-the-fact judgment for what business decisionmakers had to decide under pressure.

> Two strikingly different realities can operate when a business transaction is being put together: the reality perceived by businesspeople and the reality perceived by lawyers. The businesspeople are living in real time, plagued by uncertainties that often must be resolved immediately. They must decide one way or another, on the basis of reasoning they have not time to expound. . . . The business person's focus is the bottom line—*what* to do, not *why* it is being done.[25]

Because of the business-judgment rule, the courts will not find against a director or officer simply because shareholders experienced a negative outcome. Businessmen and businesswomen are allowed to fumble, to make errors of judgment, to make bad guesses. They are allowed to be human and fallible as long as they are not demonstrably negligent, careless, or fraudulent.

> All [that] even the strictest fiduciary standard asks is that decisions be undertaken with care, good faith, disinterestedness, and without abuse of discretion. As one court has said, "The entrepreneur's function is to encounter risks and to confront uncertainty, and a reasoned decision at the time may seem a wild hunch viewed

years later against a background of perfect knowledge."[26]

In essence, the business-judgment rule provides that if any rational purpose exists for the directors' or officers' decisions, they are not liable for errors in judgment, even when the decisions turn out to be wrong.[27]

Despite the apparently strong language of the fiduciary standard, the business-judgment rule allows directors' loyalty to the shareholders to be diluted by loyalty to management. And, as we shall see, there are other factors that enhance this tendency, including boardroom culture, the CEO's ego, the directors' egos, the power of the CEO to seduce the board with retainers, fees, and glamorous privileges—and the makeup of the board itself.

Makeup of Today's Boards: Trends and Issues

The following findings on the composition and conduct of contemporary boards represent a digest of several studies conducted during the 1990s, along with analysis and comment from the author and some 30 current and retired CEOs.

Board Size

Boards are getting smaller. In a 1993 study, the consulting firm SpencerStuart found that half of the corporate boards it surveyed had 13 or fewer directors. The same firm's 1988 survey had shown half the firms to have 15 or fewer directors.[28] Proponents of strong and responsible corporate governance tend to prefer a smaller board. A smaller board has more potential to restrain an imperial CEO because it can act more quickly and decisively than a large one. Large boards take more time to share information and arrive at a consensus. They are more easily subjected to an imperial CEO's divide-and-conquer strategy. If the board members are not only numerous but geographically scattered as well, vital time may be lost in convening them to handle an emergency.

The idea that "small is beautiful" when it comes to boards is receiving an increasing amount of official sanction. A survey of 653 CEOs conducted in 1992 by the National Association of Corporate Directors found an overwhelming majority in favor of "small, proactive, informed and truly independent boards."[29] Corporate-governance specialist John E. Balkcom, of the Chicago management-consulting firm Sibson &

Company, says even large corporations now seem to be moving toward a standard board size of fewer than 10 directors.[30]

Insiders vs. Outsiders

A very definite trend is under way toward fewer inside directors and more outside directors. The 1993 SpencerStuart study of the boards of the 100 largest U.S. corporations showed the median ratio of outsiders to insiders—directors unaffiliated with the company vs. directors employed by the company—at 3:1. More than a quarter of the companies surveyed had an outside/inside ratio of 5:1 or better. In the five years leading up to the 1993 survey there was a net loss of 91 inside directorships and a net gain of two outside directorships, suggesting that elimination of inside directors may be fueling the board-shrinkage trend. Only seven of the boards in the survey had a majority of inside directors, while 14 had only one insider, the CEO. SpencerStuart says the drop in inside directorships has been going on steadily for at least a decade. In 1980 only 20 out of 100 boards had an outside/inside ratio of 3:1 or better. By 1990, 51 boards had reached that level.[31]

Also on the decrease is the class known as "affiliated outsiders" (i.e., directors not employed by the corporation but receiving some sort of benefit from it that could place a director in a conflict of interest). In 1980, for example, 32 percent of the boards included a director who also served as the company's outside legal counsel. By 1990, however, this figure had dropped to 21 percent.

SpencerStuart concluded in its 1991 *Index*: "Since 1980 . . . the combined total number of inside directors for all the SSBI companies has fallen from 584 to 410. That's a decline of 30%."[32]

Corporate-governance advocates welcome the trend toward outside directors because outsiders are viewed as more likely to act independently in the event that management's performance falls and the CEO needs to be replaced. Outsiders are perceived as less obligated to the CEO than corporate managers who owe their jobs directly to a CEO appointment and serve on the management team.

Nevertheless, the encouraging trend toward outsiders needs to be tinctured with a dose of realism. Although outside directors technically are not employees of the corporation and are putatively "elected" by the shareholders, they are really appointed by the CEO and naturally feel an obligation, making them something like "brevet" insiders even if not formal members of the organization. Juran and Louden acknowledged that outsiders can be insiders when they wrote in 1966:

> When we examine why in the world a nonemployee is called an insider, it turns out that for important investors the word "inside" is used in a sense totally different from employment. The word is used in the sense of being in the inner circle, having an inside track, being part of the inner power structure (like political "in's" versus "out's"). Some writers have used the term "proprietary director" for such cases.
>
> The Securities and Exchange Commission (SEC), in particular, makes use of the term "corporate insiders" to describe officers, directors, and "controlling stockholders." In the dialect of the SEC, the word "inside" includes a strong connotation of possessing "inside information," thereby having the potentiality to take advantage of those who are not "in a special relationship with a company and privy to its internal affairs."[33]

Perhaps more important, however, outside directors' objectivity remains under intense CEO pressure because most outsiders share a secret bond with the CEO: They are CEOs too.

Board of Directors or CEOs' Club?

What kinds of people do CEOs like to have on their boards? One answer has remained consistent over the decades: other CEOs.

Data collected by SpencerStuart and published quarterly in the "Directors Roster" section of *Directors & Boards* magazine show that CEOs remain the most popular category from which to recruit new directors. In the Spring 1995 issue, for example, the "Directors Roster" reported 297 new U.S. corporate board appointments for the preceding quarter. Of those, 32.2 percent came from the "Chairman/CEO" category, making this group the largest bloc in the roster.

Not surprisingly, the second-largest bloc, 21 percent of the total, came from "Senior Officers" of business corporations (i.e., those most likely to become CEOs in the future). Together, these two corporate-officer categories made up the overwhelming majority of the new directorships—53 percent.

There are good reasons to have current or former CEOs on—or even dominating—a corporate board. Successful, seasoned business executives are more likely than any other category of director to have the experience, judgment, and organizational skills necessary for monitoring management's performance. They understand what the CEO is trying to accomplish, and they understand the difficulties he is likely to encounter in accomplishing it.

But this very familiarity with the CEO mentality can make a CEO director overly sympathetic to a CEO who is doing poorly and needs to be replaced. Along with the retainer, meeting fees, and perquisites the CEO has bestowed on him, an emotional bond with the CEO can interfere with the objectivity required for effective representation of stockholder interests.

Seniors Dominate

Despite many misconceptions about directors and their work, one popular myth turns out to be true: Most corporate directors are mature, if not actually elderly. A demographic analysis of SpencerStuart's 1994 study showed that of 1,003 outside directors representing 100 major corporations, only one percent were under 45 and only six percent were under 50.

"By contrast, 30% of the 1,003 directors were 66 years old or older and an astounding 58% were 61 or older," the report noted. This situation is unlikely to change, since CEOs normally cannot spare their young and busy subordinates for work on another company's board. Juran and Louden found that only 17 percent of CEOs they interviewed encouraged younger subordinates to sit on the boards of other companies. The remainder either actively or tacitly discouraged such board membership.

The "Boardaholic"

The 1992 Korn/Ferry survey revealed that 65 percent of the directors they surveyed served as outside directors on the boards of more than two companies. Over 20 percent of those surveyed served on four or more boards, with the most active respondent serving on 11 boards.[34]

In 1993 the *Washington Post* reported that former Reagan Administration Defense Secretary Frank Carlucci, at that time a full-time consultant, was serving on 20 corporate boards as well as 12 boards of nonprofit organizations. Reporter Kathleen Day told *Post* readers that in 1992 Carlucci had a board meeting every business day of the year and even attended one meeting by telephone conference call from his physician's office.[35]

Juran and Louden, writing in 1966, referred to these virtually full-time board members as "professional directors"[36] and seemed to feel they had much to offer, especially if they were retired CEOs. In the opinion of this author and his CEO colleagues, however, anyone expecting to do an effective job as director of more than four or possibly five corporations in the severely challenging business environment of the twenty-first century is kidding himself. A person taking on more than four or five directorships should probably be called a "boardaholic" rather than a "professional director." The job is simply too taxing to be performed repeatedly and effectively.

A 1995 study by *Business Week* of 120 underperforming corporations targeted by either the California Public Employees Retirement System or the Council of Institutional Investors documented statistically what many observers had long suspected intuitively: There is a numerical correlation between poor corporate performance and the presence of "boardaholics" among the directors. "Boardaholic" No. 1, Lilyan Affinito, turned up on the boards of Kmart Corp., Tambrands, Chrysler, Jostens, Lillian Vernon, and Caterpillar, three of which had been cited two years or more in a row for underperformance. The magazine said Ms. Affinito was collecting an aggregate $300,000 per year in meeting fees and retainers for her service on the six boards. Confirming what the Washington *Post* had suggested in 1993, *Business Week* named Frank Carlucci "boardaholic" No. 2 for sitting on the boards of troubled companies such as Westinghouse, General Dynamics, Northern Telecom, and Upjohn, two of which had been cited by investor watchdog groups as troubled for more than two years running. "To a remarkable degree," the magazine wrote, "the country's most troubled companies share an overlapping cast of directors."[37]

Ideal Board: Small Is Beautiful; "Outsiders" Are "In"

Over the years the 30 active and retired CEOs contributing to this text have headed a wide variety of corporations large and small. Industries represented include footwear, pharmaceuticals, defense technologies, consumer electronics, banking, transportation, adhesives, insurance, investment funds, refractory brick, and office supplies, to name just a few. Company size ranged from $30 million to more than $10 billion in annual revenues. Some of the CEOs devoted their entire professional careers to one firm; others climbed the corporate ladder by moving from firm to firm and even from industry to industry.

Despite the wide disparities in their business backgrounds, however, all of these CEOs agreed that the governance of today's corporations would improve substantially if four fundamental changes were to occur in the composition of corporate boards: Boards must be (1) smaller, (2) more independent of management, (3) more professionally competent, and (4) more frequently renewed through mandatory retirement of older directors.

What disturbed the CEO panel was that most boards today are too large, have too many inside directors, are too closely interlocked with the boards of other companies, and are "too old" (i.e., they keep the same directors for so long that the entire board's median age is in the geriatric end of the spectrum). While boards are often large in size, too many of them are thin in competence due to an excess of elderly directors, celebrities, boardaholics, or other directors lacking in professional competence relevant to the corporation's needs.

On December 8, 1995, the new board model that emerged from the deliberations of this CEO panel was aired before 60 members of the International Academy of Management when they held their annual meeting at the Harvard Business School.[38] The mixed audience of business executives and professors of management greeted the proposals almost with a sense of relief. On January 29, 1996, Chicago *Tribune* reporter David Young printed the proposals in his "Biz Tips" column in the Monday business section.[39] The proposals for the ideal board are few and simple, starting with the principle of "Small is Beautiful":

- The board should consist of no more than seven directors, including the chairperson.
- All directors except the chairperson should be outsiders (i.e., neither current nor former employees of the company or its affiliates).
- No director should be a personal friend or relative of the chairperson/CEO, but all should be known to him by business reputation.

- No director should sit on the board of another director's corporation or non-profit institution.
- The company at which a director is employed in management must not accept business from a company he serves as a director.
- Each director should have a core competence in a specialty important to the corporation she directs, be it law, engineering, computer science, marketing, finance, logistics, or R&D.
- Directors should serve under some sort of term limits, such as mandatory retirement at age 70 or after two successive three-year terms.

What Today's Boards Cannot and Must Not Do

Let's assume that a certain corporation has a board that exemplifies all the ideals agreed upon by the most serious students of governance reform. What exactly can this ideal board do to advance the interests of the shareholders it represents? Actually, very little. So little, in fact, that before discussing the relatively few things a board can and must do, it is more important to understand the many things a board cannot do:

- **A board is not a "super-management."** It does not second-guess management by critiquing management's plans, suggesting alternatives, or reserving unto itself certain big decisions deemed too challenging for management's capabilities.
- **A board is not a representative body like a legislature.** It is not expected to represent or balance the interests of a variety of contending constituencies, such as the company's employees, customers, vendors, or lenders, nor does the board represent any outside critics impacted by the company's operations, such as environmentalists, the government, or consumer activists. No director is elected to serve as the representative of a specific constituency. All directors serve at large, and all serve only one constituency, the shareholders. Nor is any director elected by any specific group of shareholders, such as pension-fund members, mutual-fund members, or individual investors. Each director is obligated to all of the common shareholders as a single body. (*Note:* This provision does not apply in certain European countries, some of which mandate that boards include a representative from organized labor, the

corporation's major banks, its largest vendors, or, in some cases, the national government itself.)

- **The board does not normally exercise initiative or leadership (i.e., it does not "go first").** Management makes the first move. The board can do no more than review the results of management's initiatives.
- **The board is not a court of last resort or a corporate ombudsman.** The board is not a place to which whistleblowers or disgruntled employees and customers can run with reports of trouble that management has ignored or overlooked. Troubleshooting is both a management prerogative and a management responsibility. If management is not spotting and treating problems effectively, a properly functioning board will become aware of such dereliction during the normal course of reviewing performance. If it finds such dereliction and is convinced that the current management is unlikely to restore effective performance, the board's appropriate response is to replace the CEO.

Violating the One-Chain-of-Command Principle

Boards historically have been restricted from engaging in managerial activities out of respect for a fundamental reality of organizational behavior: There can be only one chain of command. Accountability works only when lines of authority are clear and unambiguous, and when each subordinate reports to one superior. If a board were to intrude into managerial prerogatives, top managers would become confused about whether to take orders from a director, from all of the directors acting collectively as the board, or from the CEO. The CEO would bristle—rightly—at this dilution of his authority. Organizational effectiveness would erode. No corporate management wants or expects to answer a question from a director outside the formal structure of a board meeting, and no serious or experienced director wants to become involved in management by doing an end run around the CEO. If a director feels he or she is not getting adequate answers from management within the classic board-meeting structure of formal reports followed by Q&A, the proper course is to resign. Becoming a one-man or one-woman fact-finding committee is tantamount to establishing a second chain of command.

Clear lines of reporting between top management and the board are sometimes compromised in another way—when a CEO retires but remains on the board. This can leave the former CEO's subordinates confused as to whether their ex-boss really has relinquished his powers and authority or whether he actually plans to continue exercising them informally by managing from his seat on the board. The strain can be particularly hard on the new CEO. Just when he needs to take firm command of the organization, he finds himself glancing back over his shoulder to find out whether his predecessor is quietly second-guessing his decisions.

Howard D. Sherman, author of the Institutional Shareholders Services 1991 report, felt that retention of former CEOs on corporate boards has the potential to weaken the board's effectiveness as a monitor and check on management.

> They could dominate the board agenda and decisions. . . . [M]any, if not all, inside directors may owe their jobs to the retiring CEO, and would be reluctant to contradict his views out of a sense of loyalty and/or fear: CEOs often continue to exercise enormous power even after their retirement. The same combination of fear and loyalty can appear to the non-executive [outside] directors recruited by the retiring CEO.[40]

Although the retired CEO possesses considerable experience that may be useful to a successor, most corporate-governance authorities today recommend that if the new management or the board feel in need of her advice, she should dispense it from a position as outside consultant—paid or unpaid—rather than from a seat on the board. Walter Wriston, the former CEO of Citicorp, came to a similar conclusion:

> One reason for mandatory retirement is to assure the corporation of fresh leadership to meet changing conditions. If the new leadership wants to consult the old, no corporate structure is necessary; if consultation is not desired no corporate arrangement will assure it. On the other hand, if the new CEO wants to get moving with his or her agenda, a board seat occupied by the retired CEO may be seen as an impediment to getting on with the job, particularly if new management feels that radical measures are called for.[41]

Finally, a third kind of violation of the one-chain-of-command principle makes it difficult if not impossible for boards to discharge their accountability to shareholders if they are also saddled with a legislative-type duty to represent a variety of constituencies or stakeholders, such as employees, communities where the company has plants or offices, or demographic minorities. The board's effectiveness is crippled by the need to report to so many different superiors. Dilution of responsibility can be just as corrosive as dilution of authority. If you are accountable to everyone, you are accountable to no one.

What Today's Boards Can and Must Do

Although boards cannot and must not manage, the law nevertheless insists that they govern. It gives them very few powers to do so, but these powers carry considerable authority and can prove to be very strong when applied at the critical time and in the appropriate sequence:

- The board has the sole authority to elect the corporation's chief executive officer.
- The board has the sole authority to review the performance of the CEO and determine if it has been satisfactory (shareholder value has grown at an acceptable rate). It has the sole authority to set the CEO's salary and bonus in such a way as to reward him for performance.
- The board has the sole authority to determine whether managerial performance has been in compliance with the law.
- If the board deems that the performance of the CEO and his management team has not been successful, through either failure to grow the shareholders' investment or failure to comply with the law, it has both a fiduciary obligation to the shareholders and the sole legal authority to discharge the CEO and replace him.

These four functions are the core of the board's legally mandated mission. If we look at them closely, however, we realize they really add up to one function: Make sure the chief executive officer is working for the shareholders. This is virtually the definition of corporate governance.

Boards also have exclusive authority over another critical corporate function, but one that tends to occur only at random intervals: change of ownership. Only the board can authorize the sale or merger of the company, the issuance of additional shares of stock or new classes of stock, the buying back of stock, the splitting of stock, or the conversion of one form of stock into another.

Even here, however, the board does not normally *initiate* the action. A proposal to merge, acquire, be acquired, or divest, or to issue, buy back, split, or convert stock typically will come from—or through—the CEO. The board will merely ratify his proposal. The decision to declare a dividend bears the same stamp: Management proposes; the board disposes.

So too when management asks the board to approve certain large expenditures and to review and approve major programs for the future growth of the company. In many corporations the bylaws mandate that the board approve all corporate expenditures above a stated sum. On paper, at least, such a bylaw would appear to give the board ultimate control of much of the CEO's spending and investing authority.

But here, too, the reality is otherwise, for it is the CEO who initiates the budget request, while the board merely ratifies it. Should a director question the size of the proposed expenditure, the CEO almost invariably will prevail because the CEO's information on the company's day-to-day operations is vastly superior to that of even the best-informed director. When Harvard Business School Professor Myles L. Mace compiled his 1971 monograph, *Directors: Myth and Reality* (reprinted in 1986, from which this citation is taken), one of the CEOs he interviewed told him:

> In the seventeen years I've been with this company, and my previous associations, I haven't been turned down by the board yet, that I can consciously remember. If I was, it was on some inconsequential thing, nothing important. The board is not in a particularly good position to say no to management. They don't know the industry. My operations people do. And if they come in and say we ought to expand a particular plant from 2000 tons to 5000 tons a month, how can any outside director say no? Nine hundred and ninety-nine times out of a thousand, the board goes along with management, and our batting average on making the right decisions is not that good.[42]

The real source of the board's power, therefore—the one critical area where it can act on its own initiative and at its own discretion—is its exclusive authority to hire, reward, penalize, and, if necessary, fire the chief executive officer, the one individual whose performance as a leader is the single biggest key to corporate success or failure. The relationship between the board and the CEO is the central theme of the ongoing drama of corporate governance and the reason that governance came under such intense critical scrutiny during the late 1980s and early 1990s. This is the period when many proud U.S. companies went into a prolonged performance slump that should have led to decisive intervention by the board, ending in the selection of a new CEO.

Why did so few boards actually take this step while they still had time to do so? While the answer is not entirely clear, there is at least some evidence that many directors do not actually understand the nature of governance. As the 1991 Institutional Shareholders Services study and the 1994 Boardroom Consultants studies indicated, something like 30 percent of the nation's corporate boards apparently do not fully grasp the difference between governance and management—and prove it by permitting the retiring CEO to remain on the board. Meanwhile, anecdotal evidence collected by the author from active and retired chairmen/CEOs suggests that many corporate directors are unclear about what their governance duties actually are and how they are to be carried out. "Granted that a board can't manage," these directors seem to be saying, "but if it can't manage, what exactly *does* it do?" What is the governance process, and how is it supposed to interact with the management process?

Governance in Essence: Oversee. Review. Monitor.

If we examine governance literature, including more than two centuries of court decisions in Britain and North America, three verbs recur in descriptions of the corporate board's activities: "oversee," "review," and "monitor." This choice of verbs reflects an enduring sense on the part of scholars, jurists, and practical businesspeople alike that it is not the responsibility of the board to take the *initiative*. The first move belongs with management; the board waits for management to act and then reviews management's performance.

The board's reviewing, monitoring, and oversight of management are largely confined to two distinct periods in the governance process. The first period of board activity comes when management *proposes* a business initiative and the board reviews the proposal prior to approving it; the second period of board activity takes place after management has *implemented* an initiative and a sufficient time has passed for the results—especially financial results—to be evaluated.

Reviewing Management's Plans

A major opportunity for the board to review management's plans and proposals comes once a year when management presents its annual budget to the board for approval. In essence, approval of a budget means approval of the activities which the budget is designed to support. Thus, the board's decision to accept and authorize the budget effectively tells management it has the board's authority to proceed with implementation of the corporate plan.

Typically, the board will approve management's plan and budget unanimously. If anything less than unanimous approval is forthcoming, the meaning is unmistakable: The chief executive officer does not have the full confidence of the board, and the unhappy director either will resign soon or will not be asked to serve again when the term expires.

If, however, a larger number of directors begin to withhold approval of management's plan or budget, it is the CEO who is likely to resign or be replaced.

What is not likely, however, is that the board will become involved in changing or fixing the plan. The board does not engage in planning—even strategic planning—because planning is a management responsibility.

Approval of a plan and budget means the board has authorized management to use a number of valuable resources belonging to the shareholders, including the corporation's capital, credit, facilities, and employee skills.

In approving management's plan and budget, however, the board has tacitly granted management another valuable resource—time. Only over time will corporate management be able to grow the shareholders' investment sufficiently to earn an acceptable profit. How much time? Since no two industries are alike, no two corporations are alike, no two corporate managements are alike, and no two business situations are alike, it is up to the board, with its combination of varied business experience, to determine whether a CEO's program is progressing at the proper rate and showing acceptable financial results within a reasonable amount of time.

This decision is when the distinction between corporate governance and corporate management becomes critical. Once the board has authorized management to proceed with a program, it stands back and leaves management alone, delegating to management a vast amount of discretionary authority to organize personnel, spend money, acquire equipment and supplies, perform operations, enter into contracts with other businesses, and commit the company in dozens of other areas too detailed to be observed by the board. Management must be allowed to get on with its work and must be granted a so-called "decent interval" in which to carry out at least a portion of the tasks it has set for itself before undergoing review by the board. In the words of Robert K. Mueller, the appropriate behavior for the board during this period is "Nose In, Fingers Out (NIFO)," meaning the board keeps its "nose" in the business by evaluating the management reports presented at board meetings, but it keeps its hands off the actual tasks required to manage the business. The board watches, but it does not touch anything. Mueller's advice to boards is, "Concentrate on overseeing and monitoring management's performance, and then get out of the way."[43]

In addition to its annual approval of the budget and the strategic plan underlying it, the board may be called upon at other times during the year to review and approve certain types of management proposals. Under most corporate bylaws, the board must approve any management initiative that affects the capitalization of the company, such as the decision to declare a dividend, to split the stock, to issue additional shares or create a new class of stock, to make a major capital investment, to sell a subsidiary or spin it off as a dividend to the shareholders, to acquire another company, or to offer a stock option to employees, officers, or directors. In addition, the board must review and approve changes in employee benefits and health coverage.

Reviewing Management's Performance and Results

The board's second period of entry into the corporate governance process comes *after* management's programs have been under way for a sufficient time to have produced measurable results. At its regularly scheduled meetings, the board reviews the quarterly financial statements prepared by the chief financial officer. On the basis of these reports, as well as additional information supplied by other corporate officers, the board tries to determine whether the company's results are meeting—or are likely to meet—the shareholders' expectations for investment growth.

If we examine the behavior of boards with regard to management, we find that boards are reactive rather than proactive. This quality is the reason that board meetings are infrequent and usually last no more than half a day. *Boards actually do not have much to do. Governance is by definition a minimalist activity.* The board listens to management's accounts of its plans and its performance, but it does not tell management what to do. Although a board may suggest ways for management to improve its performance, it is not obligated to do so. It is obligated only to review management plans and performance so that it can assure the shareholders it is holding management to the highest practicable and legal level of performance.

We have already learned who makes up the typical board and how the directors get appointed to their jobs. Now let's examine how they do their work of monitoring the CEO's performance and rewarding or penalizing it appropriately. The theater in which this work occurs is the regular board meeting.

INSIDE AND OUTSIDE THE BOARDROOM

How Informal Director Dialogues and Formal Board Meetings Add Up to Good Governance

Informal Governance: Outside the Boardroom

Some of the most important work that directors perform on behalf of the shareholders takes place outside the boardroom as well as outside of the formal governance structure.

What exactly makes up this important work that never appears in the minutes of board meetings? Nothing more or less than advice and counsel to the CEO on critical matters of management. True, boards do not manage, but these advice-and-counsel activities are not conducted by the board acting collectively or formally but by individual directors acting informally, usually outside the boardroom.

Juran and Louden noted this informal background activity when they identified two separate components of directors' work. The board's legally mandated fiduciary duty to oversee management on behalf of the shareholders they defined as the *trustee-*

ship role; the nonbinding, informal component they identified as the *advisory* role. The latter, they pointed out, is strictly optional and off the record.[44] Advising and counseling the CEO thus has no legal standing and is not understood to be part of a director's fiduciary obligations.

If we look closely, we see that the two roles—advising the CEO informally while monitoring the CEO's performance formally—interact in ways that can very strongly affect the outcome of the governance process. We also see that the interaction can have both positive and negative aspects. Ideally, a proper advice-and-counsel relationship between a CEO and the board can help the CEO do a better job. This happens when the CEO is a fundamentally secure individual who can recognize the need for advice and can use it effectively without becoming overly dependent on it. She knows her job, but she also knows her limitations, and she has a reliable panel of advisors to whom she can turn when she senses that her own abilities need to be supplemented by others.

The negative side of advising and counseling surfaces when a CEO becomes overly dependent on board input. Harvard Business School Professor Jay W. Lorsch said the directors he interviewed split 50/50 on this question, with half of his subjects expressing apprehension that "the CEO's reliance on outside contact could be interpreted as a sign of inexperience."

The advisory role of the board can develop another negative aspect: If the board members become too vested in advising the CEO, if his decisions become their decisions, they risk losing some of the critical distance essential to an objective review of the CEO's performance, the core of the board's legally binding fiduciary duty to the shareholders. Being solicited by the CEO for input can be flattering to a director's ego; if used to excess, however, it can draw the directors and the CEO into a relationship so chummy that the directors will instinctively avert their eyes from any evidence that the CEO's leadership may be faltering. To put it another way, by contributing too many of their own views to the CEO's decisionmaking, the directors effectively sneak back into management through the back door, which effectively robs them of the ability to perform their governance role.

Fortunately, this tendency to cross the line into management can be offset if, in addition to their informal relationship with the CEO, the outside directors also enjoy good relationships with one another. By discussing company affairs from time to time—informally, off the record, in groups of two or three—without the CEO present, the outside directors are more likely to form a cohesive unit capable of acting as a counterbalance to any excesses or neglect on the part of management. Informal though they be, these off-site, informal discussions are essential to good governance because they help cement the outside directors into a proshareholder body capable of ousting the CEO if his performance falters. Only in these informal contacts can directors establish the kind of relationship that will make it possible for them to ask one another: "Is the CEO doing an effective job, and if not, how do we go about replacing him?" Before we look at the critical issue of evaluating the CEO's performance and deciding to replace the CEO—the issue which is the acid test for any board—let us first examine the structure of the normal board meeting.

Preparing for the Regular Board Meeting

Most corporate boards hold between five and eight regular board meetings per year. This figure does vary, however. Professor Graef S. Crystal of the Haas School of Business at the University of California at Berkeley found that in 1990 the board of grocery wholesaler Wetterau held only four meetings, while the board of Chemical Bank met 17 times (in most states, corporate charters issued to banks mandate monthly board meetings).[45] Regardless of the number of regular meetings, however, additional meetings can be held at the discretion of the chairperson to handle extraordinary business, and multiple meetings are a must when the board is faced with the decision to accept or reject a tender offer.

Emergency meetings to respond to a takeover attempt, however, are clearly atypical. Most regular board meetings start at 9 A.M. and last less than a day. Many conclude with lunch. Governance critics down through the years have remarked that the format of the typical regular board meeting is so routine as to be a stale ritual. To a large extent these comments remain true. The dates of meetings usually are set a year in advance, and in many corporations the regular meeting times are specified in the bylaws (e.g., the fourth Tuesday of each month except in July, August, and December). Although an effective chairperson/CEO will do her best to keep the meeting interesting, a certain irreducible minimum of meeting time must nevertheless be spent on legally mandated procedure, such as approving the minutes of the previous meeting, hearing committee reports and approving committee resolutions, and reviewing financial reports.

Before the regular board meeting convenes, however, two other formalities—distribution of the advance briefing package and committee meetings—normally precede it.

Advance Briefing Package

A week or more before the regularly scheduled board meeting, each outside director receives by mail or courier a briefing package containing informational materials on matters to be discussed at the upcoming meeting. This package usually will contain a copy of the agenda as prepared by the chairperson/CEO. This agenda will contain the schedule of business matters to be brought before the board (i.e., matters requiring a vote), but in most corporations today it will also list certain non-business items, such as informational presentations by members of management, which do not require a board response. For example, if the CEO has scheduled the vice president of international marketing to tell the board about the company's plans to launch a special line of products in Eastern Europe, the board will receive notice of his presentation in its advance briefing package even though such a presentation is not part of the formal *Robert's Rules of Order* agenda to be voted on and recorded in the minutes.

The advance briefing package is a practical tool at a number of levels. First, it expedites the handling of business at the meeting. "The board meeting can then be used more as a discussion and decision-making forum rather than as a slow-paced information bureau," write Juran and Louden. "A meeting devoted to discussion and decision-making is a far more rewarding experience than one devoted to digging out information."[46]

Juran and Louden point out that the advance briefing package also acts as an important social lubricant. "The decorum of board operation, no less than the need for effective conduct of board business, requires that there be no surprises," they note. "Matters of *importance* [emphasis in original]

should not be brought up for decision without adequate notice and preparation."[47]

Perhaps most important, the briefing package can protect directors against the possibility of a shareholder lawsuit charging negligence. Since at least 1642, when the House of Lords—at that time the British equivalent of today's U.S. Supreme Court—ruled in a case called *Charitable Corporation v. Sutton,* the law has held that under their duty of care directors can be held liable if they fail to inform themselves adequately about the issues facing the company. This obligation got a resounding reaffirmation 343 years later when the Delaware Supreme Court issued its 1985 ruling against the directors of Chicago-based Trans Union Corporation in the now legendary case known as *Smith v. Van Gorkom.* The court found that the Trans Union directors had been "grossly negligent" in approving a 1980 merger between Trans Union and the Marmon Corporation because they acted without having seen the merger agreement itself, which had been negotiated privately between Trans Union Chairman Jerome Van Gorkom and Marmon Chairman Jay Pritzker.

As Fleischer et al. point out, the court did not attempt to second-guess whether the $55-per-share price that Pritzker agreed to pay for Trans Union was adequate.[48] The court was interested only in whether the directors had acted on sound information as to how the two CEOs had arrived at a price. The court concluded the directors had never obtained such information.

The 1985 *Smith v. Van Gorkom* decision had a profound effect on board meetings. Advance briefing packages for even the most routine board meetings became larger and more detailed—to the point where many directors began to complain about the additional hours of preparation required for effective performance at meetings. The greater size and complexity of post-1985 briefing packages is a major reason that so many governance specialists now warn "boardaholics" to limit their intake to three or four directorships at most. Reading and understanding a briefing package may require a day or more of study and perhaps some phone calls to clarify obscure technical or legal points. These activities can seriously cut into the time a director has set aside for his own business or retirement activities.

The *Van Gorkom* ruling had an even stronger impact on special board meetings

called in response to merger offers. To make sure directors are adequately informed about whether to accept or reject an offer, board chairpersons now invite the company's investment bankers to attend emergency board meetings and advise the directors as to whether a buyout or merger proposal represents real value for the shareholders. Outside legal counsel is present as well to brief the board on both its obligations and its options in the face of an offer for the company's shares. Although few directors can absorb the mass of intricate financial and legal detail laid down by the consultants appearing at these sessions, management nevertheless pays top dollar for such guest lecturers because their presence in the boardroom serves as a kind of insurance policy against shareholder lawsuits later. By showing that the board availed itself of the best legal and financial advice, the directors and management can take shelter under the business-judgment rule, which protects them from a potential shareholder lawsuit as long as they can demonstrate that they deliberated appropriately and took all reasonable measures to inform themselves prior to acting.

Committee Meetings

Before the members of a corporate board convene at their regularly scheduled 9 A.M. meeting, they often participate in a series of smaller committee meetings usually lasting an hour. Virtually all boards are divided into standing committees, of two to five directors each, to handle specialized duties. During their meeting these committee members will approve a report that their committee chairperson later will deliver to the full board meeting.

Reviewing the Audit

The most important of the committees is the audit committee. Its duty is to oversee and review the work of both the corporate accounting department and its outside auditing consultants to determine whether their picture of the corporation's financial performance is accurate. Because corporate governance is primarily concerned with holding management accountable for preservation and enhancement of the shareholders' capital investment, the work of the audit committee is absolutely fundamental to the board's performance; it is the shareholders' only way of learning whether their investment is earning an adequate return. The audit committee also is important from a legal standpoint. If management has been engaged in any kind of financial misconduct, this committee should be the first component in the governance system to become aware of it. The audit committee is the last stop before the board accepts management's account of the company's financial condition and discloses that account to the shareholders and the public. Invariably, the full board will accept the audit committee's findings. Whatever the audit committee determines thus will become the company's official report of its condition to the shareholders, the SEC, the IRS, and the investment community.

The audit committee makes this determination in a more or less ritualized fashion. An hour before the start of the full board meeting, the audit committee meets with the company's outside auditors. Usually this meeting also will include the company's chief financial officer, the controller, and perhaps others from the company's financial staff. The members of the audit committee review the quarterly or monthly financial report that management plans to present to the board and discuss it with the lead outside auditor.

At this point the chairperson of the audit committee asks the outside auditor, "Do you have anything to tell us?" Usually the answer is no. If the auditors had detected any discrepancies in the financial report, they would have mentioned them earlier. The audit committee adjourns, and its members then join the rest of the directors in the full board meeting, which will almost certainly feature a report by the chief financial officer.

Setting Executive Pay

While the audit committee is meeting, so are the other committees, the most common of which are the compensation committee (sometimes known as the compensation and organization committee) and the nominating committee.

The compensation committee has the responsibility to advise the board on the salaries to be paid, as well as any bonuses or stock options to be awarded, to the CEO and other senior executives. The board has the sole legal authority to set the CEO's compensation (and that of all top management). Hence, any decision by the board to increase the CEO's salary, bonus, or perks is an implicit endorsement of current leadership. The work of the compensation committee therefore is critical to good gov-

ernance. Giving the CEO more money is the board's way of saying, "We think you're doing a good job of running this company and we want you to keep doing it." Since hiring, evaluating, rewarding, and replacing the CEO are really the only formal tools the board has for safeguarding the shareholders' investment, bestowing or withholding rewards is one of the few ways a board has of "grading the CEO's exam."

During the 1980s, when many large U.S. firms began to lose market share and profitability in the face of intensified competition, corporate-governance critics homed in on executive-compensation practices as a major culprit. In company after company, the board was routinely authorizing an annual salary increase and even a bonus for the CEO despite falling market share, dwindling return on investment, and a stagnant or even falling stock price. This practice is indefensible.

Recruiting Directors

Most companies also have a nominating committee to identify and evaluate candidates for current or soon-to-be vacant positions on the board. At its best such a committee can act as an informal, internal head-hunting firm, listing three or four "possibles" for each vacant seat and letting the board make its choice. It may even make its own determination and submit the candidate's name for ratification by the full board.

As Lorsch points out, however, it is in the nature of the selection process that the nominating committee normally will not enjoy the same level of autonomy as the audit or compensation committees because director selection historically has been a prerogative of the CEO. In Lorsch's 1988 survey, "55% of the directors reported that the CEO was the major source of new ideas for new candidates, while only one-third considered the nominating committee the most important source." Moreover, Lorsch notes, "42% of the directors reported that the CEO's candidates rarely were rejected by the nominating committee."

Although nominating committees are becoming more common, with 84 percent of directors interviewed saying their boards had such a committee, Lorsch concludes that, "Nevertheless, in many companies, these committees still have limited influence compared to that of the CEO." He even reports that many CEOs still are heard using the expression "my board," or "my directors."[49]

Regular Board Meetings

Regular board meetings (as opposed to emergency board meetings called to deal with a crisis) are a paradox: They're all alike, yet each one is different.

Regular meetings are all alike because to be legitimate they must follow the routine laid down in *Robert's Rules of Order*. Each session begins with a formal call to order by the chairperson, approval of the minutes of the previous meeting (usually without a reading), and a succession of business items requiring a vote by the board. A vote to adjourn brings the meeting to an end.

What makes each board meeting different is the precise nature of the business to be voted on. These items might include approval of a proposal for the company to increase its indebtedness; declaration of a cash or stock dividend; a decision to split the stock or convert one class of stock into another; a decision to proceed with a major investment in new plant or technology; or approval of some major change in the company's holdings, such as acquisition of another company or divestiture or spin-off of a major division or subsidiary. There could be a vote to approve the appointment of a new director or to accept the resignation of an incumbent one. Based on the recommendation of the compensation committee, the board might vote to approve a salary increase, a bonus, or a stock option for the CEO and his senior executives.

Almost invariably, the formal business handled by a board at one of its regular meetings will amount to a ratification of actions already decided upon by the CEO and the top managers. This does not necessarily mean that the CEO owns the board, or is acting in an imperial fashion, or that the directors are nothing but "ink pads for the chairperson's rubber stamp." It simply reflects the reality discussed earlier: Proper corporate functioning requires management to take the initiative in all matters and the board to stick to the job of reviewing management performance. Unless the directors have become seriously apprehensive about the way the company is being managed, they are not likely to confront the CEO during a regular board meeting with initiatives of their own. They may subject the CEO to some serious but civil questioning about plans and programs before they vote, but when the Q&A period comes to an end, a unanimous ratification of management's proposals is the norm.

Not everything that happens at a typical regular board meeting comes under the formal heading of "business" (i.e., matters requiring a vote). Much of what happens is simply informational. After formally calling the meeting to order, the chairperson normally will make some opening remarks. This is not called for by *Robert's Rules of Order* or the bylaws; it is simply a courtesy to help the directors reorient themselves to a company with which they have had little contact since the previous meeting.

After the minutes of the previous meeting are read and approved, another informational presentation—the chairperson's report or management report—is delivered. The chairperson, who in most U.S. companies is also the CEO, will update the directors on the progress of the company's programs, alert them to any unforeseen problems that have arisen, and discuss management's plans and expectations for the future—the next quarter, perhaps the next year. At many corporations, one meeting each year is set aside for briefing the board on the company's three-year strategic plan. Like most reports delivered at today's board meetings, the management report is likely to be accompanied by slides, particularly when graphs and charts are required to clarify complex numerical material. Lorsch says:

> Directors consider the "Report of the CEO" the most important event of a normal meeting. It's also the most time-consuming, with the CEO informing the directors about what is going on at the company and describing his plans for the future. This report often includes assessments of the firm's financial performance, results of various divisions, changes in management, and an update of events since the previous meeting.
>
> Specific management proposals are next in importance and are given ample discussion time. Top managers, who report to the CEO, generally present the proposals, then it's the directors' turn to ask questions and offer suggestions.[50]

Depending on the chairperson's agenda, an additional management report might be made by operations, marketing, strategic planning, engineering, legal, or almost any other management department headed by a senior vice president, or by the president of a subsidiary. Normally, time will permit only one such report in any given meeting. Each committee chairperson will make a report, and a report from the general counsel is virtually obligatory if the company is involved in any major litigation.

One presentation that is never skipped, however, is the financial report, usually delivered by the chief financial officer. This is the basic information that enables the directors to learn how well the company has performed its core mission of increasing shareholder value. Some chairpersons/CEOs see the financial report as so fundamental that they treat it as a *de facto* CEO's report, with the CEO simply delegating the reporting function to the CFO. There is nothing wrong with this. Since a corporation is basically a machine for generating wealth, financial performance and corporate performance are essentially the same thing.

> Reviewing past financial results is the third most important and time-consuming activity, giving directors an opportunity to scrutinize the company's overall performance, as well as its various businesses. This report generally includes budget forecasts, which enable directors to consider probable future financial results. On many boards, the presentation, distinct from the CEO's report, is given by the chief financial officer and the controller and contains more financial detail than the CEO's overview.[51]

A characteristic typical of the CFO's report is that if the company is doing well, the report will be short, while if the company is doing poorly, the report will be longer due to management's greater need to "explain" poor results (i.e., attribute them to factors outside of management's control). This is the part of the board meeting where directors must be particularly alert for signs of trouble, as well as for signs that management might be concealing something unpleasant.

Following the informational reports, the CEO may introduce a report on something management is planning or asking authorization to do, such as investing money in a large new capital project. The presentation typically will include slides showing what the new facility or equipment will look like, and some of the slides will use graphics and tables to display the CFO's projection of the anticipated payback from the investment. The presentation will be followed by a Q&A during which one or more directors will ask how the payback schedule was determined. This is where it pays to have a director or two with a core competency in finance and engineering. As a rule, the board will authorize the expenditure unanimously after discussion.

When the CEO Has to Go: How the Board Arrives at a Consensus

The development of a board consensus that the CEO's performance is faltering is not the kind of formal, *Robert's Rules of Order* business likely to be placed on the agenda for discussion and a vote at a regular board meeting. The CEO, who in 80 percent of U.S. corporations is also board chairperson, sets the meeting agenda. He is not likely to arrange for his own execution.

Nor is it likely that a director who has lost confidence in the CEO will bring up such concerns under "New Business." To do so without some sort of preliminary discussion with the other directors would violate the unspoken "no-surprises" rule of boardroom etiquette and would sabotage the collegial atmosphere essential to the conduct of effective board meetings.

For these reasons, much of the work the board performs in evaluating the CEO is virtually forced into the informal arena of casual private conversations outside the boardroom. First one outside director, then another, begins to worry about the company's performance under the incumbent CEO. Concerned Director A invites Potentially Concerned Director B to a friendly game of golf or a business lunch and, at first guardedly, then with greater concern and candor, begins to air his doubts about the CEO's performance. If Director B agrees with Director A's suspicion that there is a problem, and if both view the problem with roughly the same sense of urgency, each of the directors will arrange to reach out to one or more other outside directors they believe might share their concerns. Again, the process remains informal and off-the-record, with the consensus gradually building in a series of private one-on-one conversations.

At this point events can diverge in either of two directions: If the concerned directors meet resistance from directors who continue to believe the CEO's performance is adequate, and if the pro-CEO faction appears larger and more determined than the anti-CEO faction, the latter will most likely drop—or at least relax—their campaign. Often the ringleader will quietly resign, her effectiveness as a director having been chilled by her aborted attempt at an anti-CEO initiative.

In the other alternative, the anti-CEO faction succeeds in convincing a majority of the outside directors that the CEO has been underperforming, that improvement is not likely, and that protection and enhancement of the shareholders' investment requires that the CEO be ousted by the board and replaced by someone with greater potential.

Even at this dramatic juncture, however, nothing occurs in a formal board meeting. The fateful decision is made entirely in the informal arena as one outside director after another falls in with the insurgents calling for the CEO's ouster. Is the process somewhat conspiratorial? Yes, but not necessarily sinister, especially if the directors see themselves as the law sees them: duty-bound to protect billions of dollars worth of endangered shareholder equity that the disenfranchised owners of the company cannot protect by their own efforts.

How is the actual termination performed? Softly. One of the outside directors will be designated to invite the CEO to a quiet, private meeting at an off-site location. After a few moments of chit-chat, the director selected to deliver the bad news will say something like, "You know, several members of the board have become concerned about the direction the company's been taking lately. We've come to the conclusion that maybe it would be a good thing for all concerned if you were to step aside—maybe take early retirement so we can bring in somebody with some fresh ideas." Usually the CEO will "get it." He will submit a letter of resignation, which the board will accept unanimously, often in a conference-call phone meeting. If the CEO goes into denial, however, the bearer of bad tidings usually can bring him back to reality by explaining that the outside directors already have been polled and that the CEO has lost the support of the majority of the board.

The corporate news release announcing the resignation will be kind. It will say something very much like this:

> The board of directors of Intercontinental-Universal Incorporated announced today that it has accepted the resignation of Chairman and Chief Executive Officer J.T. Smith, effective Sept. 1.
>
> In a statement to the board, Ms. Smith, who has held the post for three years, said, "I have contemplated this change for some time because of the need to spend more time with my family. I feel I have essentially completed the work I set out to do and can now safely entrust the next phase of the company's growth to fresh, new leadership."

Even if the business pages reprint the news release without further coverage or comment, few veteran readers will be fooled by the careful language. They will understand that the board—possibly under pressure from unhappy investors—gave up on the CEO and asked her to step down.

The little charade has its uses. A messy boardroom battle has been avoided. The departing CEO is portrayed as leaving at her own initiative, with most of her dignity intact. The board is portrayed merely as having rubber-stamped her decision. The hunt for a successor—probably under way informally for several weeks—can now be conducted openly. Corporate life goes on.

Tough Job of Reviewing CEO Performance

What is important in such situations, however, is not so much the *mechanism* the directors use to remove the CEO as the *process* by which they arrive at a consensus that he has failed and that they must summon the collective will to remove him. Deciding to discharge the CEO is the single most difficult and sensitive job a director ever will face.

Some of the most useful thinking on the problem of CEO evaluation and removal by the board came during the late 1960s, when Harvard Business School Professor Myles L. Mace was collecting material for his 200-page 1971 monograph titled *Directors: Myth and Reality*. Using data from hundreds of interviews, Mace found that at least some boards removed their CEOs for underperformance during the largely prosperous 1960s, but many others that needed to do so were reluctant to face their responsibilities. Mace's valuable—and still very applicable—conclusion is reproduced here in full (please note that Mace's 40-year-old language uses "president" instead of today's "chief executive officer").

> It was found that boards of directors of most companies do not do an effective job in evaluating, appraising, and measuring the company president until the financial and other results are so dismal that some remedial action is forced upon the board. Any board has a difficult job in measuring the performance of a president. Criteria are rarely defined for his evaluation. The president's instinct is to attribute poor results to factors over which he has no control. The inclination of friendly directors is to go along with these apparently plausible explanations. Control of the data made available to the board which provides a basis for evaluation of the president is in the president's

own hands, and board members rarely have sufficient interest and time to really understand the critical elements in the operations of the company. Only when the company's results deteriorate almost to a fatal point does the board step in and face the unpleasant task of asking the president to resign.[52]

The 30 CEOs and directors who contributed to this section on corporate governance agree thoroughly with Mace on this point. Everyone who has served on a corporate board knows that the most difficult part of the job is not the actual removal of an underperforming CEO, which is only the final act in the boardroom drama, but the painful preliminary process of facing the CEO's performance problem and admitting it will be ended only with his resignation and replacement.

Six Painful Obstacles to Facing CEO Underperformance

There are six reasons that this process takes so long, involves so much agony, and is so frequently avoided:

- Personal loyalty of directors to the CEO.
- Disinclination to believe bad news.
- Disinclination to undertake something unfamiliar and possibly dangerous.
- Difficulty detecting gradual deterioration in conditions.
- Difficulty getting accurate information about the business.
- Unwillingness to disrupt boardroom cordiality and fellowship.
- All of the reasons support one another, creating a fierce wall of resistance to taking action.

Personal Loyalty to the CEO

Directors feel loyal to their CEO, and with good reason. They usually owe their prestigious positions to her. She probably reached out to them personally and invited them to join "her" board. Most of the directors are current or former CEOs themselves. They know what the CEO is going through and sympathize with her situation.

Nor is it simply a matter of the CEO having reached out and brought the directors onto "her" board. The reverse may be just as true: The directors may have sought out the new CEO and unanimously elected her to head the company. If she turns out to be "wrong" for the company, that means the directors must have been "wrong" to name her its chief executive.

While directors owe a legal duty of loyalty to the shareholders rather than to the CEO, the problem is that the shareholders are largely an abstraction, while the CEO is a living, breathing human being with whom the directors have shared values, duties, and responsibilities. Little wonder, then, that the tug of loyalty to one familiar CEO is stronger than the gravitational field exerted by hundreds of thousands of faceless, distant owners.

Disinclination to Believe Bad News

None of us likes to hear bad news, especially when the news carries strong implications that we must respond with some kind of disagreeable action. Psychologists tell us that it is virtually instinctive for people receiving bad news to react initially by exclaiming, "Oh, no!"—as if the utterance could somehow command the facts to reverse themselves.

Denial is a natural human reaction, and business executives, including corporate directors, are human. They do not like dealing with bad news any better than the rest of us. This natural tendency only enhances the difficulty of dealing with poor CEO performance.

Disinclination to Undertake Something Unfamiliar and Possibly Dangerous

Calling for the resignation of a CEO is a venture into unknown territory for most boards. It is done so seldom that no one ever acquires a skill in it—or a taste for it. Hence, even the most experienced board feels a little shaky approaching this particular moment of truth. There is no self-help manual on how and when to remove a CEO; each CEO is different, and so is each company's situation. There is no telephone hot line or late-night radio call-in show to dispense advice. A bungled attempt to oust the CEO can embarrass the board and damage the personal reputations of the directors, possibly barring them from service on other boards in the future. With so little outside support to rely on and so much at stake, prudence and caution can easily slide into timidity.

Difficulty Detecting Gradual Deterioration in Conditions

Although boards tend to respond well to a sudden crisis, such as the unexpected death of the CEO, they are notoriously slow to take action as the result of a gradual slip or a nearly imperceptible drift in corporate performance, especially when it is unclear whether the reasons are external (negative industrywide trends) or internal (poor leadership from the CEO). Detecting the change is particularly difficult if the gradual deterioration follows a prolonged period of strong performance. In this situation, directors may be so lulled into taking performance for granted that they lose the capacity to detect a deviation. When evidence of deterioration does surface, it becomes easy to rationalize each successive event as insignificant and unique rather than as part of a developing pattern. If the CEO is glib in explaining away underperformance, or if the company is well known and prestigious, as IBM and General Motors were during their prolonged slippage through the 1980s, the directors may dwell in a dream world for years without facing the fact that even a legendary flagship of industry can drift off course and become stranded on a shoal.

Difficulty Getting Accurate Information about the Business

In business as in life, decisions are supposed to be based on information, not guesswork. But for a corporate board, sound information on corporate performance is not as easy to come by as many people might think.

- The CEO controls the information the board gets, and he releases and discusses it only intermittently—at the regular board meetings.
- Outside directors are by definition veterans of other businesses and industries, not the one they monitor as board members.
- Indices of corporate dysfunction do not always mean the same thing from one industry to another or one business to another.
- It is hard to know how much time to allow management to come to grips with a situation.

Unwillingness to Disrupt Boardroom Cordiality and Fellowship

The mystique of the corporate boardroom exerts a powerful effect on the directors who conduct their meetings there. The usual setting created by the decorators is one of tasteful, understated elegance—not glitter, but a great deal of wood paneling, leather cushions, and earth-toned fabrics set off by just enough brass or steel trim to create some contrast. More often than not, English sporting prints or lithographs of scenes from classical antiquity decorate the walls. The atmosphere straddles the border between businesslike and clublike, between prudent sobriety and cordial comfort:

> Like nearly everything else at PepsiCo, Inc., the room's stately power and elegance made you stand a little straighter. A large abstract painting by Jackson Pollock's widow, Lee Krasner, dominated the far wall. Custom-designed carpeting in earth-toned colors cushioned the floor. The bronze-plated ceiling, perhaps more appropriate for a church, reflected burnished mahogany-paneled walls. High-backed beige leather chairs, so imposing they could have carried corporate titles of their own, surrounded the boardroom table.[53]

The boardroom, in other words, is an excellent place in which to deliberate, ponder, and vote, but a poor place in which to have a confrontation. In the tacit understandings which make up corporate etiquette, arguing, disputing, disagreeing, and confronting are associated with management, not governance. The directors, most of whom have had their share of arguing and confrontation as members of management, expect the boardroom to be something of a refuge above the fray. Hence the disagreeable duty of firing the CEO is brought up in a less sensitive setting off-site. It simply does not fit in the boardroom.

Nevertheless, the mystique of the boardroom continues to exert its comforting effect even when the directors are not physically present there, making it difficult for them to contemplate—even in the safety of their own homes—the disagreeable job of firing the person who brought them together in those comfortable and dignified surroundings. Whatever the CEO's failings, and whatever their effects, the hours spent in the boardroom are valued ones to most directors. Even when discussing difficult matters, most boards maintain a cordiality and collegiality rarely experienced by people who have not faced great challenges and dangerous moments together. To consider discharging the leader of the boardroom tends to violate that spirit and to rupture valued bonds of good fellowship and mutual self-esteem.

CONCLUSION

Boards That Faced the Heat and Replaced the CEO

The failure of corporate boards to replace underperforming CEOs became a major topic in the business news media during the late 1980s and early 1990s. When the rate of growth of a corporation's stock persistently lags the Standard & Poor's 500 index, or when the share price actually sinks over a prolonged period while the same top management remains in place, the media run extensive investigative pieces and exposés that conclude with the inevitable question, "Why isn't the board doing something?" In the cases of General Motors and IBM, not just news stories but entire books were written and published before the respective boards finally removed the CEO. Billions of dollars in shareholder value eroded as directors vacillated.

Nevertheless, the prominence of such episodes should not be allowed to obscure the more positive side of the story: Almost every day, virtually unnoticed, other corporate boards do their duty and replace the chief executive officer without a prolonged bout of boardroom denial or endless months of negative media coverage. Here are three typical examples: Dial Corporation, 1996; Centennial Technologies, Inc., 1997; and Abbott Laboratories, 1989–1990.

Case 1: Dial Corporation, 1996

On Monday, July 15, 1996, the board of directors of The Dial Corporation held a special meeting in Chicago. Late the next day Dial's corporate headquarters in Phoenix issued a news release under the headline: "John W. Teets, Chairman and CEO of The Dial Corp., says he plans to retire early next year."[54] Members of the Phoenix business community were stunned. Teets, 62, had been serving as chairman/CEO of Dial for 15 years and had been a Sunbelt star well before that. His contract at Dial was not due to expire until Jan. 1, 1999. Now he had announced he would leave two years early. Did he jump, or was he pushed?

A week later the story—or at least a good deal of it—emerged in the *Arizona Republic*. Although Teets had led Dial through more than two decades of growth since forming the company in the 1970s out of the old intercity bus and meatpacking conglomerate known as Greyhound Corp., Dial's more recent financial results had begun to slip as the company placed excessive emphasis on short-term cost cutting. "Sales and profits fell sharply last year after years of consecutive, double-digit increases, demanded by bottom-line baron

Teets," the newspaper reported. "Much of the trouble was blamed on a standard inventory-reduction program, but the problems went much deeper, employees and industry analysts say. Years of short-term focus hurt Dial's key brands, and the company was losing market share in such key brands as Dial soap," they say.[55]

An executive who had left the company the year before told *Republic* reporters Dawn Gilbertson and Charles Kelly that Teets's intense focus on short-term cost cutting had come at the expense of long-range market development and brand management. Once the most serious excess costs had been identified and trimmed, the company appeared to have no more tricks in its kit with which to build market share and brand loyalty. "There was almost more of a focus on how to please management than how to please the consumer," the ex-manager said.[56] Disgruntled consumer-product marketing professionals began to flee, with some departments experiencing turnover as high as 50%. An employee newsletter in the fall of 1995 admitted that "costs associated with employee turnover and relocations have cut into profits, and we're having problems with inventories, customer-service levels, brand equity and lower-than-expected sales of some of our core brands."[57]

As if the numbers alone were not bad enough, one of the disgruntled former employees had circulated an anonymous letter implicating Teets in more than poor management. The letter said that Dial's former VP-Human Resources Joan Potter Ingalls, 46, who had taken early retirement in the summer of 1996 amid rumors of scandal, had had a sexual relationship with Teets and had received a multimillion-dollar settlement paid by the company. The letter-writer also complained that Dial's financial reverses, which included closure of six factories and severing of 700 workers, had not led Teets to crimp his luxurious lifestyle. The company still was paying $10–$12 million per year to keep two Gulfstream IV corporate jets, still held partial ownership in professional sports teams and resort properties, and still kept corporate apartments in Manhattan and other locations that Teets and his wife had used for personal rather than business purposes.

Allegations of scandal alone rarely torpedo a corporate chieftain, nor do charges of lavish lifestyles—as long as the shareholders are making money. But after beating the

market for the previous five years, Dial's shareholder value had stalled, stealing the luster from Teets's style. "When things are going good, no one cares about those things," an anonymous Dial executive told the *Republic*. "But when austerity came, people started asking, 'Why do we own the Phoenix Suns? Why do we need to own the building? Why do we need two jets?'"[58]

The unidentified executive was not the only one who asked those questions. So did Wall Street money manager Michael Price, whose Heine Securities held nearly 10 percent of Dial's stock in its Mutual Series family of mutual funds. In the June 24, 1996, edition of *Barron's*, Price charged that a plan by Teets to spin off part of Dial would saddle the shareholders with excessive debt. He even said the name of the new entity, Viad, was "Greek for screwing the shareholders."[59] When business resumed after the 1996 Fourth of July weekend, Price asked the Securities and Exchange Commission to delay the spinoff and urged Dial to unload its airplanes, corporate apartments, and office building.

Both in his public pronouncements and behind the scenes, Price also urged Dial's board to act. The results were not long in coming. Only a week elapsed between Price's SEC filing and the special Dial board meeting in Chicago that brought an end to Teets's reign. "Something happened," an anonymous "observer" told the *Republic*. "Did those guys (Price and company) say, 'We're going to continue the pressure on this end?' Did the board itself finally say, 'Enough is enough?' Did John finally say, 'I fought this thing too long?' I don't know. It was probably some combination of all of the above."[60]

Best of all, it did not take long. Dial's shareholders, unlike those at GM and Kmart, did not have to wait years for board action. The board moved less than a year after viewing the first poor financial results and less than a week after the first public complaints by a major shareholder. In the corporate world, that is speed.

Case 2: Centennial Technologies Inc., 1997

The February 12, 1997, edition of *The Wall Street Journal* carried a news story by reporter Jon G. Auerbach detailing the unexpected firing of a CEO:

> Centennial Technologies Inc. fired its chairman and chief executive officer, removed its chief financial officer, and

announced it had launched an inquiry into the accuracy of its most recently reported earnings and prior financial statements.

The surprise news from the maker of computer memory cards—a company recently touted by widely read investment newsletters—comes after days of swirling rumors about the 1996 stock-market high-flier, whose share price has dropped about 70% since the start of this year.[61]

A steep and sudden drop in the price of a company's stock is the biggest danger investors face. Such reverses seldom are recouped; the sheer size of the sell-off means investors have suddenly realized that their earlier perception of value in the corporation was misplaced. Such misperceptions can represent an honest mistake, particularly in the high-tech industry, where scientists and engineers sometimes generate breakthroughs faster than businesspersons can figure out how to commercialize them and yesterday's hot new technology turns out to be today's has-been. But sometimes the mistake is not an honest one. Sometimes investor expectations rise because a corporate management has misstated—perhaps deliberately—the company's near-term potential. Something like this apparently happened at Centennial, because the *Journal* did not extend Centennial's departed CEO its customary courtesy of saying he had "resigned," and neither had the board. According to Auerbach:

> Centennial said it fired Emanuel Pinez, its 58-year-old chairman and chief executive, and relieved its chief financial officer, James M. Murphy, 45, of his duties. . . . Centennial said the board had met and agreed early yesterday to remove Mr. Pinez after an internal investigation revealed "certain preliminary information" that led it to question the company's reported earnings for the fiscal second quarter ended Dec. 31. [Treasurer and Corporate Counsel Donald Peck] said Centennial had contacted the Securities and Exchange Commission and was actively working to get a "full understanding of what happened."[62]

Under the laws of corporate governance, corporations must comply with the law, and the board of directors is responsible for reviewing management's conduct and determining whether it has been lawful. If the board finds that management has broken the law, its powers are the same as when it finds management has broken its obligation to the shareholders: The board replaces the chief executive officer.

Among the laws that corporations must obey are SEC rules that prohibit corporations from issuing misleading claims about their future profit growth in order to hype the price of their stock. Auerbach's article noted that on the same day Mr. Pinez was fired, a shareholder lawsuit in Massachusetts alleged that "Centennial and certain of its officers made false statements that caused the stock to be artificially inflated."[63]

The *Wall Street Journal* article said further that several investor newsletters had been told that Centennial was anticipating a $10 million order from AT&T Corp. for its Nomad telecommunications gear and a $60 million license fee for a satellite-linked truck communications system. The same assurances had been made to at least one individual investor, according to the *Journal*, while a portfolio manager for a California-based investment fund said he had acquired Centennial stock in May 1996 after the company told him it expected that a contract with AT&T would bring about $100 million in added revenue in 1997 and 1998. AT&T said it had no contract with Centennial and declined to say whether it was negotiating with the company.

A graph appearing with the *Journal* article showed that Centennial's stock price more than quadrupled during calendar 1996, beginning the year at around $10 and peaking at $58.25 in early January. Then, in a little over a month, it plunged nearly all the way back to its starting point, finishing at $16.50 the day the board fired Mr. Pinez and notified the SEC of its actions. Trading in the company's shares was halted.

Considering that only a month passed between the first retreat in Centennial's share price and the firing of the CEO, the board's action would seem to have been extraordinarily swift. For those who held the stock, however, the board's pace was tortoiselike. Centennial's board was faced with a much bigger problem than a gradual slump in earnings. What it really faced was the sudden discovery that the company had experienced almost no earnings at all.

Case 3: Abbott Laboratories, 1989–1990

Most corporations that replace a chief executive officer do so because financial performance has lagged. Profitability is flat or dropping, causing investors to "walk the Wall Street walk" by dumping the compa-

ny's stock. Facing their fiduciary duty, the directors seek new leadership for the company. But sometimes a board of directors replaces a CEO while growth is impressive and the company's affairs appear—to outsiders at least—to be going forward in a normal fashion. This is what happened in December 1989 when the directors of one of the world's largest and most successful manufacturers of pharmaceuticals, Abbott Laboratories, of North Chicago, Illinois, removed chairman/CEO Robert Schoellhorn from his position as chief executive officer and elected Chief Financial Officer Duane L. Burnham to replace him on January 1, 1990. Schoellhorn, who was 61 and not scheduled to retire until he reached 65, retained his post as chairman. But on March 9 the other shoe dropped. The board took Schoellhorn's chairmanship position away and awarded it as well to Burnham. Schoellhorn had been CEO of Abbott since 1979 and chairman since 1981, a period during which, according to the *Chicago Tribune*, "the company has exhibited a consistently dazzling financial performance."[64] Why, then, did the board remove him?

Under the rules of corporate governance, directors are accountable to shareholders not simply for current performance but also for the long-term viability of the corporation as a wealth-generating mechanism. Although many shareholders invest for the short term, making their money in quick trades, the vast majority, including those whose shares are held by pension funds, expect to stay invested for consistent growth over the long term. Directors are expected to look after the interests of these investors by making sure the company is managed for steady long-term growth.

Media accounts at the time of Schoellhorn's ouster suggest that Abbott's directors, while acknowledging Schoellhorn's past performance, were nervous that his leadership skills may have been faltering to a degree that endangered the company's future. They were particularly concerned about Schoellhorn's attitude toward succession. As you learned in Chapter 1, a distinguishing mark of true leaders is an ongoing concern with identifying and developing future leaders. During his most recent years in office, however, Schoellhorn appeared to be doing just the opposite. Three times in a row, a second-in-command had left the company after a series of disagreements with the CEO. Two of these departed stars went on to join biotechnology companies that competed with Abbott. The Abbott board rightly wondered whether Schoellhorn, rather than seeking and welcoming fresh talent, was systematically driving it out of the company and into the more congenial arms of competitors. *Wall Street Journal* reporter James P. Miller acknowledged that Schoellhorn had delivered outstanding profits to the company's shareholders. "Mr. Schoellhorn, however, developed a reputation as an authoritarian manager who could not bear the appearance of a possible contender for the job," he wrote.[65]

In March 1990, Schoellhorn sued the outside directors who made up the succession committee on the Abbott board, charging they had violated the by-laws in stripping him of his job. The lawsuit may have been an ill-advised move, however, because when Abbott's lawyers went to court in April to try to have the suit dismissed, they introduced additional material that might have stayed confidential had Schoellhorn chosen to leave quietly. Wrote Miller:

> Earlier in the week, Abbott alleged for the first time that Mr. Schoellhorn violated his fiduciary obligations and repeatedly defrauded the company during his lengthy tenure. . . .
>
> Last week, Abbott said in court documents it had discovered, through an investigation which began a month ago, that "during much of the past decade Schoellhorn has repeatedly misappropriated Abbott corporate assets for his personal use" and committed fraudulent acts.
>
> The documents contain, among other things, allegations that Mr. Schoellhorn had on a number of occasions used the company's corporate aircraft for "purely personal purposes" and then ordered subordinates to make "false entries" to conceal the wrongdoing. It also claims he "submitted false expense reports" and was reimbursed by the company.[66]

One of the "other things" mentioned in the document was a charge that a gift presented to Abbott by a Japanese company and intended for the company had been appropriated by Schoellhorn as his personal property and was on display in his home.

Perhaps more interesting than the charges against Schoellhorn was his response. According to *Wall Street Journal* reporter Jeff Bailey, Schoellhorn tried to shift the blame for his actions to his successor, Duane Burnham, claiming that as the company's chief financial officer during the period named in the documents, Burnham should have made sure the company's assets were not misused. "It was Mr. Burnham's job to question and rectify anything he thought was improper regarding use of company aircraft or other assets by company executives," Schoellhorn said.[67] Here too it is useful to refer to Chapter 1, where Louis Lundberg reminds us that a real leader takes responsibility not only for his own actions but also for those of his subordinates. Lundberg's remarks suggest the Abbott board made the right decision.

In the fall of 1990 the court ruled that the Abbott board had acted legally in removing Schoellhorn as chairman and CEO. However, it also ordered the board to award Schoellhorn $5.5 million in stock to which he was entitled by virtue of the company's financial results under his leadership. The company's profits in the six years following Schoellhorn's ouster also suggest the board had made the right decision. No one is indispensable. Despite the loss of its star CEO, Abbott continued to be a star investment as it brought out a series of successful new drugs to treat acute and chronic illnesses: $100 invested in Abbott stock at the start of 1991 would have been worth about $170 at the close of 1996. Robert Schoellhorn had left Abbott a $6.2 billion company. Six years later under Duane Burnham it was an $11 billion company. Earnings per share in the last year of Schoellhorn's leadership were 96 cents. Under his successor they reached $2.41. Abbott, moreover, had managed to achieve those results while remaining independent. Its competitors in the pharmaceutical industry had been able to survive only by merging into giant global companies. The Abbott board's decision to replace Schoellhorn with Burnham may have come just in the nick of time.

This chapter has examined a number of key issues involved in the topic of corporate governance and the distribution of power and accountability within the modern corporation. The modern-day disenfranchisement of shareholders, coupled with the enormous power of today's CEOs, places the responsibility for enforcing managers' accountability to shareholders squarely on the board of directors. Yet contrary to popular myth, the boardroom is not the seat of great power, which actually belongs to management. The directors, as we have seen, are without power most of the time. The one occasion when they are supremely powerful is when they choose to replace the chief executive officer. If they do not enter upon their directorships prepared to take that step, they do not belong on a corporate board in the first place.

1. R.C. Longworth, "Corporate Giants Dwarf Many Nations," *Chicago Tribune*, October 11, 1996, pp. 1, 28.

2. Arthur Fleischer, Jr., Geoffrey C. Hazard, Jr., and Miriam Z. Klipper, *Board Games: The Changing Shape of Corporate Power* (Boston, MA: Little, Brown & Co., 1988): 3.

3. J.M. Juran and J. Keith Louden, *The Corporate Director* (New York: American Management Association, 1966): 337.

4. Robert A.G. Monks and Nell Minow, *Corporate Governance* (Cambridge, MA: Blackwell Business, 1995): 180.

5. William T. Allen, address to the Samuel and Ronnie Heyman Centre of Corporate Governance, Benjamin N. Cardozo School of Law, Yeshiva University, April 13, 1992.

6. Joseph K. Angell and Samuel Ames, *A Treatise on the Law of Private Corporations,* 6th ed. (Boston: Little, Brown and Co., 1858).

7. Delaware General Corporation Law Annotated Franchise Tax Law Uniform Limited Partnership Act, amended as of February 2, 1988.

8. Fleischer et al., *Board Games,* 11.

9. Robert Sobel, *ITT: The Management of Opportunity* (New York: Truman Talley Books, 1982): 302–335.

10. Fleischer et al., *Board Games,* 12.

11. Ibid., 5.

12. Joseph A. Grundfest, "Just Vote No: A Minimalist Strategy for Dealing with Barbarians inside the Gates," *Stanford Law Review* (April 1993): 952 *n.*

13. Lee Iacocca, with William Novak, *Iacocca* (New York: Bantam Books, 1984): 155.

14. Edward J. Epstein, "Who Owns the Corporation?" A Twentieth Century Fund Paper (New York: Priority Press, 1986): 13.

15. Grundfest, "Just Vote No," 866.

16. Telephone conversation, September 22, 1995.

17. Doron P. Levin, "Groping Giant: In a High-Tech Drive, GM Falls Below Rivals in Auto Profit Margins," *The Wall Street Journal,* July 1986, p. A1.

18. Christopher Byron, "House of Cards," *New York*, February 15, 1993.

19. The American Bar Association on Corporate Laws, "Other Constituency Statutes: Potential for Confusion," *The Business Lawyer* (August 4, 1990): 26.

20. Robert Kirk Mueller, *Behind the Boardroom Door* (New York: Crown Publishers, Inc., 1984): 76.

21. Monks and Minow, *Governance,* 179–180.

22. Ibid., 182.

23. Ibid., 64–65.

24. Fleischer et al., *Board Games,* 33.

25. Ibid., 34.

26. *Joy v. North.*, 692 F.2d 880, 886 (1982).

27. Monks and Minow, *Governance,* 86.

28. SpencerStuart Board Index, 1993.

29. National Association of Corporate Directors, *NACD 1992 Corporate Governance Survey* (Washington, DC: NACD, 1992): 1.

30. John E. Balkcom, "The New Board: Redrawing the Lines," *Directors & Boards* (Spring 1994): 27.

31. Monks and Minow, *Governance,* 181.

32. Ibid., 203–204.

33. Juran and Louden, *Corporate Director,* 169.

34. Korn/Ferry International, *Board of Directors Twentieth Annual Study,* 1993, 5.

35. Kathleen Day, "Frank Carlucci and the Corporate Whirl," *The Washington Post,* February 7, 1993, p. H1.

36. Juran and Louden, *Corporate Director,* 333.

37. *Business Week*, November 13, 1995, 78.

38. Harry J. Bruce, "A Corporate Director Looks at Governance Reform," International Academy of Management, Panels on Corporate Governance (Harvard Business School, Boston, December 8, 1995).

39. David Young, "Boring Board: A Call for Fresh Blood," *Chicago Tribune*, January 1996, Business section, 3.

40. Howard D. Sherman, "Catch 22: The Retired CEO as Company Director," Institutional Shareholder Services, July 15, 1991.

41. Monks and Minow, *Governance,* 192.

42. Myles L. Mace, *Directors: Myth and Reality,* Harvard Classics ed. (Boston, MA: Harvard Business School Press, 1986): 46–47.

43. Robert K. Mueller, "Oxenstierna's Law: The Issues of Corporate Governance," International Academy of Management, Panel on Corporate Governance (Boston, MA: Harvard Business School, December 8, 1995): 5.

44. Juran and Louden, *Corporate Director,* 113–114.

45. Graef S. Crystal, "Do Directors Earn Their Keep?" *Fortune*, May 6, 1991, 78. Chemical Bank spokesman John Steffens said the five additional meetings held by that bank's board in 1990 may have been associated with plans for Chemical's merger with Manufacturers Hanover Bank, consummated the following year (telephone interview, June 26, 1996).

46. Juran and Louden, *Corporate Director,* 259.

47. Ibid., 273.

48. Fleischer et al., *Board Games,* 30–31.

49. Jay W. Lorsch, with Elizabeth MacIver, *Pawns or Potentates: the Reality of America's Corporate Boards* (Boston, MA: Harvard Business School Press, 1989): 20.

50. Ibid., 61–62.

51. Ibid., 62.

52. Mace, *Directors,* 41.

53. John Sculley, with John A. Byrne, *Odyssey* (New York: Harper & Row, 1987): 1.

54. Dawn Gilbertson and Charles Kelly, "Dial CEO's departure puzzling," *Arizona Republic,* July 21, 1996, p. A15.

55. Ibid., A15.

56. Ibid., A15.

57. Ibid., A15.

58. Ibid., A15.

59. Ibid., A15.

60. Ibid., A15.

61. Jon G. Auerbach, "Centennial Technologies Fires Chairman," *The Wall Street Journal*, February 12, 1997, p. A4.

62. Ibid., A4.

63. Ibid., A4.

64. Steven Morris, "Fired, Schoellhorn Sues Abbott," *Chicago Tribune,* March 10, 1990, Business section, 1.

65. James P. Miller, "Abbott Ousts Schoellhorn as Chairman, Drawing Lawsuit by Embattled Official," *The Wall Street Journal,* March 12, 1990, B6.

66. James P. Miller, "Abbott Labs Derides Lawsuit by Former Chairman, Seeks Dismissal," *The Wall Street Journal,* April 9, 1990, p. B2.

67. Jeff Bailey, "Ousted Chairman of Abbott Accuses Company in Filing," *The Wall Street Journal,* June 6, 1990, p. A6.

PART 4

Skillful Adjustment and Continuous Improvement

Chapter 12

Joyce E. A. Russell
University of Maryland

Jacquelyn DeMatteo Jacobs
University of Tennessee

Managing the Team to Excellence

"People are very naive about how easy it is to create a high-performance team."
Ed Lawler, Management consultant and professor, University of Southern California[1]

As noted in Chapter 2, the use of teams has been increasing in organizations. In fact, by 1998, 91 percent of Fortune 1000 firms reported that they were using employee work groups, and 79 percent stated that they used self-managing work teams.[2] More and more companies have attributed performance improvements (e.g., productivity gains, defect reductions, reduced turnaround time, improved service quality) to the use of teams.[3]

Teams vary in terms of how successful they are and whether they are in industry, academics, voluntary agencies or other nonbusiness organizations. Some teams are trying to resolve serious problems in an effort to improve to an acceptable level of performance. Other teams already have a satisfactory level of performance yet want to become higher-performing teams. In this chapter, we will focus on managing a team to excellence. Specifically, we will highlight the characteristics of high-performance teams and outline common challenges facing teams. We will also offer tips and strategies for enabling teams to improve their performance to the level of success to which they aspire.

CHARACTERISTICS OF HIGH-PERFORMANCE TEAMS

Highly effective teams are composed of groups of committed individuals who trust each other; have a clear sense of purpose about their work; are effective communicators within and outside the team; make sure everyone in the team is involved in decisions affecting the group; and follow a process that helps them plan, make decisions, and ensure the quality of their work.[4]

Think about various teams you have worked on. What do you believe are the characteristics of effective teams? What are

Learning Objectives

After reading this chapter, you should:

- Understand the characteristics and attributes of effective teams.
- Be aware of the common difficulties and challenges facing teams.
- Be knowledgeable about strategies for improving team effectiveness.

the attributes of ineffective teams? It is a good idea to have team members share their ideas on the "best possible team" and their views regarding the "worst possible team." This is especially helpful when a new team forms so that members can compare notes on their previous experiences and start to develop some guidelines. Appendix 12.A contains an exercise your team can use. Make sure each person writes down his or her individual ideas and shares these with the team to arrive at a consensus regarding your team's views of the most important attributes a successful team possesses. Most team members find that they have many similar ideas regarding what makes a successful team. Talk about some strategies your team can engage in to make sure you become an outstanding team.

Some of the more commonly mentioned attributes for an effective team are described in the following sections.[5] Your team may have mentioned many of these characteristics in your discussion of the instrument in Appendix 12.A.

BEST-USE CORRELATIONS

There are many management tools to help you appraise your situation and skillfully adjust your strategy and tactics. Before you apply such tools, statistical process control, or activity-based costing, make sure your most important asset is performing well: the team. Q6 is a good time to identify the strengths and weaknesses of your team. The assessment tools in Chapter 12 will help you do just that.

Become a *Performing* Team

Candid appraisal is a necessary prerequisite to high performance; so do as advised, avoid groupthink and address, in a forthright manner, social loafing.

Even Leaders Need Feedback

Without constructive feedback, no one on the team knows how to improve. In *Marketplace* as in the real world, teams trying to reach the highest possible level of performance won't get there without an awareness of the factors that enhance and hinder team success.

Change the Organization

Think about changing positions within the team in Q6 or Q7. Let someone else lead. Switch the marketing person with the accountant and move the accountant to manufacturing. Use your *Marketplace* opportunity to gain experience in multiple functions and responsibilities.

High-performing teams have attributes such as these:

- Members with adequate knowledge, skills, and motivation to complete the tasks.
- Purpose or shared goals and vision.
- Commitment by members.
- Cooperation by members.
- High trust and credibility.
- Cohesiveness, or a feeling of being close or bonded.
- Communication among members.
- Involvement by all members and participatory leadership; coordinated, shared work roles.
- Peer feedback and discussions of ways to continuously improve.
- Plans for handling changing deadlines.
- Problem-solving strategies.

Member Knowledge, Skills, and Motivation

For teams to perform successfully, they must have members who have the needed skills, knowledge, and motivation to perform the tasks. A variety of abilities is needed for an effective team, including technical skills, interpersonal skills, decision-making skills, and problem-solving skills.[6] Not every person must have the highest level of each skill set, but the team as a whole should make sure to have all the skills covered. In addition, even if the team has all the necessary skills, if the members are not motivated to perform, they will not be successful. Thus, some level of motivation is needed for the team to be effective. It is also important to keep the members together for some period of time so that they can jell. Stable membership enables the team members to learn about one another and figure out how to work together.

Purpose or Shared Goals

Highly successful teams are those in which team members share a common purpose or goal that everyone is aware of. Members understand how the team fits into the overall business of the organization and what functions they serve. Team members know their roles, feel a sense of ownership, and can see how they make a difference or have an impact on the team. Since members are aligned in the purpose, they can keep focused on meeting their goals and on the task at hand. They can also make sure that everyone

---

is applying her individual talents and creativity to accomplishing the team's goals and purpose. As noted in Chapter 2, when a team is first formed, it is important for the team to determine what its goals are. At the initial meetings, it will be important for members to voice their views and reach consensus on their purpose, otherwise they may experience conflict. For example, some members of a team may decide that being the absolute best in the entire market (or class) is their goal. Other members on the team may decide that being acceptable (in the middle of the pack) is their goal. Unless the team reaches consensus on its primary goals, team members will be likely to work at cross purposes, causing resentment and conflict.

Team goals should meet several criteria, represented by the acronym MAPS.[7] The goals should be:

- **M**easurable
- **A**ttainable
- **P**erformance related
- **S**pecific

Measurable goals are stated in such a way that it is easy to document whether or not the goal is achieved. The statement should indicate how much must be accomplished, to what standard, and by when. For example, the team may say, "We will have the first 10 pages of the report written and proofed once by next Monday." The team should also make sure its goals are *attainable*. Goals that are set too low may not be motivating. Goals that are set too high may be frustrating and demotivating to team members. Goals should be attainable yet challenging for team members. If the team had set the goal of having the entire 30-page report done by next Monday, many of the members may have decided that the goal was too difficult, and given up. If, on the other hand, they set the goal to have the first three pages done by next Monday, then that goal might have been seen as too easy and the members would not push themselves. Goals should also be *performance related*. Members should see the goal as a legitimate thing that their team should be working on. Goals should reflect at least two main purposes: to accomplish higher-quality work and to advance the quality of the team members' lives. Finally, goals should be *specific*. Considerable research indicates that the more specific the goal, the more likely it is that it will motivate people to work toward it. For example, if the team's goal is simply to "do their best," their performance will probably not be as high as if they had set a specific, challenging goal.

Commitment

Successful teams have members who are highly committed or devoted to the team. This means that team members see themselves as belonging to a group rather than as individuals who operate autonomously. They are dedicated to group goals above and beyond their own personal goals. It is important to measure perceptions of the degree to which members feel that everyone on the team is fully committed to the team. If several members feel that one person is not committed to the team (e.g., puts his own needs ahead of the team's), then this can cause conflict on the team. One tool that can be used to measure team members' commitment may be found in Appendix 12.B. After completing the instrument, members should discuss their views on the level of commitment of everyone to the team.

Cooperation

Effective teams are those that foster cooperation among members. Cooperation involves integrated efforts by members to achieve a common goal or objective. In other words, individual team members are working together, rather than competing against one another. For example, if the team has to conduct an oral presentation, the team goal might be to present a top-notch "team" presentation. A cooperative team would have members giving each other constructive feedback on each person's part of the presentation in order to improve the entire presentation. On the other hand, a team with members who are competitive against one another might have members trying to make their own individual parts look better than other members' parts. Individuals might even make comments in the actual oral presentation, such as "I did the financial analysis," to take credit for certain parts of the team presentation. While the individual may believe she will stand out to the audience, generally such self-serving behavior is viewed negatively. To the audience, it often indicates that the individual is not a team player and that the team is not well integrated (i.e., that the team does not seem like a team).

Research indicates that a team should integrate cooperation and competition among its members. In other words, cooperation and a healthy amount of competition (where members encourage each other to work at a high level) are important for a team's success. For example, sports teams are more successful if they have teammates who work together and at the same time push each other to reach higher levels of performance.[8] Some coaches treat practices like real games and record each player's performance after each session. They openly encourage players to benchmark against one another and to try to outperform each other.[9] In fact, in a study of 32 male and female college basketball teams, it was found that teams with the best win-loss records had coaches who promoted a strong spirit of cooperation and a high level of *healthy* competition among their players.[10] The competition should be healthy such that members encourage each other and do not undermine each other.[11]

In addition to fostering cooperation within a team, it is also a good idea to encourage cooperation among teams. Teams that cooperate with other teams may find that all of the teams actually perform at a higher level. For example, suppose teams in one organization all collect market research and share that information with each other. This would enable all of the teams to act on the pooled information instead of having each team waste time researching the same things that others have already explored. Also, the teams may try to illustrate exemplary performance since they know other teams are relying on their work.

Trust

Trust among teammates can be described by the faith and confidence they have in each other and the level of reliability the teammates perceive exists. Trust has also been defined as the extent to which one is willing to ascribe good intentions to and have confidence in the words and actions of other people.[12] Team members trust each other to honor commitments, maintain confidences, support each other, and behave in a consistent and predictably acceptable manner.[13]

Successful teams have members who trust one another. Members know that they can count on each person to do his work on time and at the right level. One common complaint heard among poor teams is that they just cannot count on certain members to do what they say they will; they cannot be trusted to follow through or to pitch in when extra help is needed. Another problem occurs when certain team members make negative or disparaging comments about other members, especially behind their backs. This can cause the team to break up into subgroups. Eventually, if this type of divisive behavior is not addressed, the team is likely to break up. Free riding in teams can also destroy trust among members.

Trust among teammates is one of the most important characteristics of effective teams, especially teams that need to work together over a long period of time. Trust, however, is not easy to acquire. Trust cannot be given to a team; instead, it must be earned by members. In order to assess your team's current level of trust in one another, members should complete the instrument in Appendix 12.C. Some tips for improving trust follow:

- Improve the team's communication such that everyone knows what is going on (policies, decisions, etc.).
- The team should support one another by providing help, advice, coaching, and assistance to each other's ideas.
- Team members should respect one another and listen to each other.
- Members should feel that any feedback or peer performance evaluations are fair, objective, and impartial.
- Team members should be consistent and predictable in their daily affairs and keep their promises regarding what they say they will do.
- Members can enhance their credibility by demonstrating good business sense, technical ability or competence, and professionalism.[14]

Cohesiveness

Teams that feel a sense of team purpose that goes beyond their own individual motives are said to be *cohesive*.[15] They have a bond or good feelings about the team and stick together and are reluctant to leave the group. Cohesion is a sense of solidarity or camaraderie that the members experience by being part of the group. You have probably seen a team where the members sit close together, focus more attention on each other, and seem to get along really well. This would be a cohesive team. Over the years, the nationally ranked University of Tennessee Lady Vols basketball teams have always been very cohesive under the leadership of Coach Pat Head Summitt. In fact, on one team (over four seasons), they had nicknamed three of their players the "Meeks" due to the similarity of their names and the fact that as starters they were responsible for many of the team's points and rebounds. Fans carried signs "The Meek shall inherit the earth" in support of the team.

Team members may experience *socioemotional cohesiveness*, whereby they feel a sense of togetherness based on an emotional bonding with the team. For example, team members might enjoy each other's company and engage in social activities together (lunches, dinners, parties, sporting events, etc.). *Instrumental* cohesiveness refers to team members feeling bound together because they believe the team can accomplish important goals that they cannot achieve individually.

In general, groups that are more cohesive have greater member satisfaction, are more productive, have greater conformity to team norms, and communicate more positively and frequently than low-cohesive groups.[16] Both types of cohesiveness are important to teams, but be warned that too much cohesiveness can be detrimental to team effectiveness if it leads to an emphasis on social activities over task activities, or vice versa.

A number of suggestions are offered here for improving group cohesiveness. These are steps that a leader can take with the team or that the members can take by exerting peer pressure. Sometimes individual team members may play the role of helping the team to bond. On one of the most successful MBA teams at The University of Tennessee, a team member was nicknamed *Elmer* because he was the "glue" that kept the team together. Using a calm yet directive style, he helped the team develop goals as well as confront any problems in an open format. His leadership inspired the team and motivated members to achieve more than they personally thought they could.

Most cohesive teams have one or more members who play the roles of encourager, harmonizer, or energizer (see Chapter 2 for a discussion of these roles). If these individuals leave, the team can lose its level of cohesiveness unless someone else steps into those roles. When a faculty team at a large university unexpectedly lost a highly respected member, it became obvious within a few days that the team had lost its "bond." The team splintered with intrateam fighting and backstabbing, and it took a year of concerted effort for the team to regain some of its cohesiveness.

To enhance your team's *socioemotional cohesiveness*, several steps can be taken:[17]

- Keep the group relatively small (3–8 members).
- Strive for a favorable public image to enhance the status and prestige of belonging to the team.
- Help the team build identity by having them interact more frequently.
- Place the team in close physical proximity.
- Encourage interaction and cooperation.
- Emphasize members' common characteristics and interests and similarities.
- Point out environmental threats to rally the group.
- Spend time socializing together (e.g., lunch, sporting events, concerts).

To increase your group's *instrumental cohesiveness,* you may want to:

- Regularly update and clarify the group's goals.
- Give each group member a vital "piece of the action" (i.e., important tasks).
- Channel each group member's special talents toward the common goal.
- Recognize and equitably reinforce every member's contributions.
- Frequently remind group members that they need each other to do the job and that every member is important to the group's success.
- Challenge the team and use rewards to recognize successes.

Communication

Communication—the style and extent of interactions among and between team members and outsiders—includes written and oral communication as well as listening. Effective listening may be one of the most important characteristics of an effective team. Members of successful teams feel that their views are valued by the rest of the group. They feel free to share opinions and suggestions because they know their teammates will be receptive to their ideas.

Communication includes both verbal and nonverbal expressions. Nonverbal communication is especially important, and members should use appropriate nonverbal gestures (e.g., head nodding, open stance, eye contact) when listening to one another. In effective teams, members look at each other when they are speaking, they avoid interrupting one another, and they show

attention by leaning forward toward the speaker. These behaviors convey that the listener is really interested in what the speaker has to say. As a result, the speaker feels encouraged to offer her input.

Communication also refers to the way the team members handle conflict, decision making, and day-to-day interactions. Effective teams have a climate of open, honest communication. They share positive thoughts as well as problems with the team. Generally, they use a collaborative approach when addressing conflict rather than avoidance, forcing, or accommodating. (Refer to Chapter 2 for a discussion of conflict styles in teams.)

Some tips for improving a team's communication include:

- Ask all team members for their ideas, particularly the more introverted or quieter members.
- Use appropriate nonverbal gestures when listening to a team member (e.g., eye contact, head nodding, open stance).
- Try to resolve any difficulties with a team member on a one-to-one basis before going to any other team members.
- Address conflicts promptly; do not allow them to fester.
- Give team members who are less skillful in communication opportunities to practice and improve their skills. Provide them with feedback or encourage them to get additional assistance (e.g., with speech classes such as *Toastmasters* or *Dale Carnegie*).
- Make sure that all team members have opportunities to participate.
- If a team member is consistently interrupting others, making disparaging comments, displaying inappropriate nonverbal cues (e.g., reading while another person is speaking, rolling his eyes), it is important that someone in the group provide the team member with specific feedback as soon as possible. Have the leader of the group or the person who is closest to the individual provide the feedback that his behaviors are inappropriate.

Involvement and Participatory Leadership

In successful teams, members feel a sense of partnership with each other. They share responsibility for the performance of the work unit. Contributions by members are respected and solicited. A consensus is reached before committing the team to action. Team members are interdependent, and everyone feels involved in the decisions made by the team.

Different leadership styles are needed for the stages of group development. Early in the group's work, a leadership style which is active, aggressive, directive, structured, and task oriented has favorable results. However, if this style continues, it seems to have a negative impact on the team's cohesiveness and quality of work. Instead, in the later stages of group development, leadership behavior that is supportive, democratic, decentralized, and participatory seems to enhance the team's productivity, satisfaction, and creativity.[18]

To improve team members' sense of involvement, the team should:

- Make sure everyone on the team feels that her opinion is valued. Even if there are one or two people who seem to be the leaders of the team, everyone should still feel that her opinions are important to the team.

- Reinforce members for making contributions to team meetings and projects.

- Involve all team members in major decisions about team goals or projects.

- Make sure all team members know about important team meetings. Take everyone's schedule into account when setting meeting times.

- Do not allow any team members to discount another team member's views. While team members may not agree with everyone, they still should show respect and listen to each other.

Peer Feedback

There is nothing greater in the world than when somebody on the team does something good, and everybody gathers around to pat him/her on the back.

—Billy Martin, former manager, New York Yankees[19]

Feedback among group members is critical for the team's success. Although individuals vary in the amount of feedback they desire for tasks, you can be assured that all teammates want some feedback. Some of the common complaints that team members have concerning feedback are that:

- They do not get enough feedback.

- It is not specific enough.

- It is not given in a timely fashion.

- It is primarily of a negative nature.

Successful teams provide members with constructive feedback on their performance, including a good balance of both positive and negative feedback. Often, team members are reluctant to provide each other with feedback that might be interpreted as negative or critical since they do not want to hurt each other's feelings. It is, however, essential to give each other constructive feedback; otherwise members will not know what needs improvement or what they are already doing well. Remember that it is important to be forthcoming with positive feedback or praise. This can serve to motivate as well as inform members about behaviors or work they are doing which is exceptional.

Appendix 12.D contains an instrument that can be used to assess the degree to which you feel you are receiving positive and constructive feedback from your teammates. Note whether team members believe they receive more positive or negative feedback from their peers. If they perceive that they receive too much negative feedback, the group should try to determine why this may be the case.

There are a number of tips for using feedback effectively in your team:[20]

- Do not assume that your teammates will accept your feedback. Check for clarity. It may be misperceived or rejected.

- Feedback is better accepted if it is given in a climate of trust and if members perceive the feedback giver as having expertise (for example, you are more likely to believe feedback from a teammate on a financial spreadsheet assignment if you know that he is an expert in finance).

- Remember, negative feedback is often misperceived or rejected. Be prepared to back up your comments with specific examples (e.g., "Alanna, last week you missed meetings scheduled on Tuesday and Thursday" rather than "You always miss the meetings.").

- In most cases, teammates do not give each other enough feedback, and people desire more, especially positive, feedback.

- Tailor your feedback to the specific person (e.g., "Sean, your introduction to the paper has many good points, but it needs to be proofed.").

- High performers desire feedback that enhances their feelings of competence and personal control (e.g., "Parks, you really got the presentation off to a good start with your enthusiasm; how do you

think we should structure the next presentation?").

- Allow the person who is receiving the feedback to become actively involved in the feedback process. Recipients perceive the feedback to be more accurate if they have actively participated in the feedback session rather than passively received it (e.g., "Aaron, how do you feel about your role on the team?").[21]

- Avoid destructive criticism because it tends to cause conflict and resentment and reduce motivation (e.g., "Maria, you never do anything right; you're a loser.").[22]

- Feedback should not be used to punish, embarrass, or belittle.

- Individuals need to see the feedback as relevant to their work or role on the team (e.g., "Tim, it's important that you come to meetings on time so that you can hear about your assignment.").

- Timing of feedback is important. Make sure it is right after the occurrence. Feedback that is provided too late may not do any good.

- Show the recipient how it is within her power to do something about the feedback. If recipient thinks it is outside her control, she will not change.

- Be careful not to make the feedback too complex or too difficult to understand.

Process Orientation

High-performance teams have established a process or means to reach their goals. The process includes using problem-solving tools, planning techniques, regular meetings, meeting agendas and minutes, and accepted ways of dealing with problems. With these procedures, meetings are more efficient and the team is able to accomplish more work and of higher quality.

Handling Changing Deadlines

Effective teams must be aligned in their expectations about shifting deadlines. In other words, the team members must be comfortable about change. This is important because deadlines are often uncertain or changing. Teammates need to be able to handle shifting deadlines appropriately to manage transitions successfully. Otherwise, they may experience stress, wasted time, overtime work, and conflicts. The team must clarify tasks, goals, and deadlines as well. They need to communicate and agree upon the relative importance of various deadlines. This will improve their own task efficiency.

As noted in Chapter 2, team members who have varying styles (using the Myers-Briggs Type Indicator) may have differing levels of comfort regarding changing deadlines. For example, judging types (J's) have a greater need for structure and closure and may feel more stress with changing deadlines. Perceiving types (P's) tend to be more flexible and spontaneous, feeling less constrained by time. Thus, P's may need to assist J's in maintaining flexibility and openness to new timelines. J's will still need to help ensure that the team reaches closure on its tasks. Both need to make sure that they talk through their own views about shifting deadlines so that the team can identify its strengths (e.g., the team may discover that Duane is the only P in the group, and he may be instrumental to help the team cope with the stress of changing deadlines).

Problem-Solving Strategies

To be effective, a team needs to use a systematic approach to solving problems. The model described in **Exhibit 12.1** outlines four steps a team can use in problem solving.[23] Within each step, the team first expands its thinking and then at the end of each step, it narrows or focuses its thinking. Generally, the team should reach consensus, although it is not necessary for every decision. Consensus decisions have the benefit of getting everyone to buy into the decision, and that may contribute to a higher level of commitment. The drawback is that it often takes longer for the group to arrive at a consensus decision. When a quicker decision is needed, it may make more sense for the team to vote (using majority rule) or to have one person make the decision.

Another example of the key components of effective teams is illustrated in **Exhibit 12.2**. Notice that many of the characteristics that have just been described are presented in this figure.

COMMON CHALLENGES FACING THE TEAM

It's not that teams don't work. It's that there are lots of obstacles.

—Eileen Anderson, author of *The New American Workplace*

Exhibit 12.1: *The 4-A Problem-Solving Model*

Awareness
Expand your thinking to consider all the possible problems by:
>> Using brainstorming
>> Charting or listing all ideas
>> Not criticizing or discussing ideas at this time
Narrow your focus to the one problem you will work on now by:
>> Using criteria to review each problem
>> Writing a one-sentence problem statement

Analysis
Expand your thinking to all the possible causes by:
>> Gathering data
>> Using brainstorming
Narrow your focus to the one to three core causes of the problem by:
>> Using criteria to review each possible cause
>> Picking the significant few causes
>> Highlighting the chief cause

Alternatives
Expand thinking to all the solutions to the chief cause by:
>> Providing individual quiet time to write down ideas
>> Encouraging creative thinking
>> Using round-robin brainstorming
>> Pooling ideas and "hitchhiking" on each other's ideas
Narrow the focus to the best strategy available by:
>> Using criteria (e.g., effectiveness, cost) to screen solutions
>> Seeking consensus decision making rather than majority rule
>> Ensuring the strategy addresses the chief causes

Actions
Expand thinking to all the possible implementation actions by:
>> Specifying what might need to happen in concrete terms
>> Ensuring the strategy is real, not just philosophical
Narrow the focus to who is to do what with whom and by when by:
>> Clarifying individual responsibilities
>> Charting an implementation time line
>> Stating indicators that will verify the problem is solved

Teams are the Ferraris of work design. They are high performance, but require high maintenance and expertise.

—Ed Lawler, Management consultant and professor, University of Southern California[24]

Groups or teams experience a number of common problems or challenges. These include blind conformity, group pressure (Asch effect), groupthink, social loafing, reliance on others, the Abilene paradox, lack of performance appraisals, accountability issues, and conflict due to diverse perspectives in groups.[25] Members in successful teams are aware of these potential issues and address them before they become larger problems. Some of these challenges are briefly described here.

Blind Conformity

Generally, it is important that team members conform to the group's norms, policies, rules, and regulations. Sometimes, however, members may blindly conform to rules and procedures that are out of touch with the changing times. This may stifle the creativity of the team. For example, one member may state "this is how we have always done the financial analysis," even though new techniques are available that would make the team more efficient. To avoid this problem, team members could assign a member to be a devil's advocate to question the group on its practices. Different team members could assume this role at different times so that one person is not always seen as the critic.

Group Pressure (the Asch Effect)

Over 40 years ago, a social psychologist, Solomon Asch, discovered that individual members of groups would often agree with the views of the majority (when those are voiced aloud) despite the fact that the majority is clearly wrong. The "Asch effect" refers to perceived group pressure that causes individuals to go along with the group's view even if the individuals know it is wrong.[26] This may be a problem especially in new groups or groups of strangers where members are trying hard to be polite, accepted, and liked. To go against the group is a difficult thing to do yet necessary if the group is to be innovative in the ideas it generates. Members should be aware that they might have the tendency to succumb to peer pressure. If creativity and original thinking is desired by the group, the team may need to take secret ballots on issues. In this way, everyone's individual opinion can be shared with the group without being influenced by the majority view.

Groupthink

Groupthink has been defined as a type of thinking members engage in when they are highly cohesive and are striving for unanimity.[27] They fail to realistically appraise alternative courses of action. They may neglect reexamining various alternatives or discount experts' opinions. They may also avoid setting up contingency plans since they have a tendency to believe they are right and could not possibly fail. The problem for teams is that by engaging in groupthink, they may commit more errors than they normally would. Groupthink occurs in highly cohesive, tightly knit, very homogeneous groups. Some of the symptoms of groupthink are:[28]

- **Illusion of invulnerability.** An illusion that breeds excessive optimism and risk taking based on the team's past success (e.g., "No one can come close to beating us in the market; we can't possibly fail.").

- **Inherent morality.** Members believe that they are moral individuals who are not likely to make wrong decisions, so they ignore ethical implications (e.g., "Of course we are doing the right thing; we would never knowingly make a bad decision.").

- **Rationalization.** Members protect pet assumptions and rationalize away threats (e.g., "The reason we should always do it this way. . . .").

- **Shared stereotyped views of the opposition**. The group stereotypes its opposition, which enables it to underestimate the opposition's strengths (e.g., "They are accountants; what do they know about marketing?").

- **Self-censorship.** The team stifles critical debate (e.g., a team member decides not to bring up a criticism in order to be accepted by group members or because he thinks maybe he is wrong if everyone else has a different view).

- **Illusion of unanimity.** Silence is interpreted to mean consensus (e.g., a few members of the group speak and the others make no comments, so the leader assumes that everyone agrees).

- **Direct peer pressure.** Loyalty of dissenters is questioned (e.g., "Elizabeth, I can't believe you would bring up that criticism.").

- **Mind guards.** Self-appointed protectors emerge to "protect" the team from adverse information (e.g., Patrick tells Kelly, "Don't listen to Erin and Tony; they are clueless about this project.").

To be sure that a highly cohesive group does not fall victim to groupthink and is able to make sound decisions, several suggestions are offered:[29]

- **Critical evaluator.** In each meeting, at least one member of the team should be assigned the role of critical evaluator of the team's decision. She must actively voice objections and doubts.

- **Devil's advocate.** One person should be given the role of devil's advocate to uncover various possible negative factors. He should make sure that members provide their underlying rationale for their opinions. It is critical, however, that the team is receptive to the devil's advocate and does not ostracize the person playing this role.

- **Subgroups.** Have the team use subcommittees to derive independent proposals.

- **Adopt different perspectives.** Have team members play the role of different constituents (e.g., government, citizens, competitors, higher-level managers).[30]

- **Outside experts.** Use outsiders to bring in fresh, new ideas and to critique the group's decisions.

- **Get buy-in from organizational authorities.** Make sure that the team has to report its decisions to leaders in the organization. This will hold the team more accountable.

- **Second-chance meetings.** Once a consensus has been reached, everyone should be encouraged to rethink her position to check for flaws. Hold a second meeting in the next several days to have the group revisit the idea.

Social Loafing

Social loafing, or the "free-rider" effect, refers to the tendency for individual members' efforts to decline as the group size increases. Thus, as the team increases in size, the individual members feel they do not have to do as much work, so they do not. Some individuals see the opportunity for a "free ride" and rely on others to do their share.[31] Social loafing has been demonstrated in many cultures including India, Japan, Taiwan, among others.[32] There are a number of reasons given for social loafing and the decline in an individual's effort. These include an individual's holding these perceptions:[33]

- *Perceived inequity* in members' efforts (e.g., "No one else is working very hard, so why should I?").

- An individual does not feel personally accountable because of the *diffusion of responsibility*. When they are in a group, some individuals feel less personally culpable (e.g., "The boss won't know that I did not do anything if the group gets the project done.").

- *Motivational loss* due to the sharing of rewards (e.g., "Why should I work the hardest, since I am not receiving any individual recognition and I will just get the same reward as everyone else in the group?").

- *Sucker effect* (sometimes people do not work harder because they are afraid of being taken advantage of by the rest of the team or being considered a sucker for doing all the work. Thus, they hedge their bets and lower their output to see what others will do).

- *Coordination loss* (e.g., "I can never seem to coordinate my work with Ryan, so forget it.").

Social loafing is very common in teams. It is most likely to occur when the task is seen as unimportant, simple, or uninteresting; when members think their own individual work is not identifiable; and when they expect their co-workers to loaf.[34] It is less likely to occur when the members expect to be evaluated or compensated for individual efforts. To curb social loafing, a number of suggestions are offered:

- The team should set up clear expectations for workload issues and deadlines when they first meet and establish their norms. Developing a written contract that everyone signs is best for making sure everyone is clear on the objectives and standards.

- Design a team peer appraisal system, under which members are all individually evaluated and given feedback on their performance.

- Design the task to be challenging, interesting, and important. People feel more motivated to perform when the task is more involved.

- Individuals should be held accountable for their parts of the team's work. Make their contributions identifiable by sending out e-mails or posting lists on bulletin boards detailing who is responsible for each part. If it is public and others can see who is supposed to do each part, it is less likely that members will loaf.

- Reward members for their performance. Rewards can be in the form of monetary or nonmonetary awards (e.g., appreciation by teammates, symbolic rewards or tokens, public praise, acknowledgement by teammates for good ideas). In fact, often nonfinancial rewards are seen as more meaningful by members than money.

- Have the leader build trust among members, and show that he is willing to work hard.

Reliance on Others

In the United States, individuals are often taught to focus on individual efforts and accomplishments rather than on team efforts. A common belief is "If you want to get something done right, do it yourself." As a result, individuals may feel uncomfortable having to rely on others to work on tasks. Shifting from individual accountability to team accountability makes many people uneasy and may be a difficult transition.[35] When a group first forms, members should discuss their expectations and experiences working in teams. They should also describe the areas of expertise that they bring to the group. This may enable members to feel a little more confident about relying on others to complete parts of the group's project. For example, a team that discovers one of its members has six years of work experience in human resources may feel more confident about allowing that person to take the lead on the compensation project the team is responsible for.

Abilene Paradox

In addition to the challenge of managing conflict, teams might have trouble managing agreement. The "Abilene paradox" refers to an inability in the group to manage its agreement, resulting in frustration by team members. The name comes from the story of a family who decided to take a long car ride to Abilene, Texas, on a hot afternoon, despite the fact that the car did not have air conditioning. No one really wanted to go, but because they did not have an open, candid discussion, they went on the drive and had a miserable time.[36] Suppose that in a team setting each person believes it is *not* necessary to work on the team project on Saturday night. In an effort to find out how the group stands on the issue, one person might say "Well, I guess we should think about working on Saturday night." A second team member might want to be supportive to the first and respond, "Yeah, maybe we should work Saturday night." Within a few moments, the entire group has decided to work Saturday night (or take a trip to Abilene), despite the fact that none of the members privately believed it was necessary or a good idea.

The inability to manage agreement within a group generally follows this cycle:

- Team members are basically in agreement about the importance of a situation or issue facing the group (e.g., the goal of finishing the team's project).

- Team members are basically in agreement about what it would take to meet the goal ("We should not need to work past Friday") but have not discussed it.

- One of the group members suggests the opposite of what she is feeling, leading the group to misperceive the collective reality (e.g., "It looks like we need to work Saturday night.").

- With this invalid interpretation of group consensus, team members make collective decisions that lead them to take actions contrary to what they really want to do and thereby make decisions that are counterproductive to the team's intent and purpose (e.g., they work on Saturday night).

- As a result, members experience frustration, anger, irritation, and dissatisfaction with the group. This often leads to the formation of subgroups and placing blame on each other or on authority figures, as members attempt to identify the culprit (e.g., "It was Mike's fault. He suggested working on Saturday night.").

- This cycle often repeats itself if the group fails to confront their inability to manage agreement (e.g., at the next meeting, Steve says, "We should think about whether we should work on Sunday. . . ."). It is important that members recognize when they are getting ready to "take a trip to Abilene." They need to encourage each other to express their true feelings before the group makes a decision that few or none consider wise. To avoid a trip to Abilene, the following suggestions are offered:[37]

- Use critical evaluators and devils' advocates in the group.
- Take votes by secret or private ballot.
- Minimize status differences. Higher-status members should reassure lower-status members that it is important to have open, candid discussions.
- Frame the task as a decision to be made and provide a forum for airing controversial views.
- Create a climate in which teams can make mistakes and then correct them.

No Appraisals of Team Member Performance

As noted earlier, team members often do not provide each other with enough positive or constructive feedback on their performance. As a result, team members do not know how to improve, and the team as a whole suffers. If the team is interested in reaching a higher level of performance, it is critical that members identify how each person can effectively contribute. One way to ensure that team members provide feedback to one another is to use a performance appraisal instrument to evaluate one another. Peer performance appraisal systems are increasingly being used in organizations today, given the influx of teams in U.S. firms.

Team members can rate each person on the team on important dimensions (e.g., participation, leadership, effort). Each person could then receive ratings from all of his teammates. Team members could use this feedback to see how the group perceives their work and what they can do to reach a higher level of performance. If each person on the team improves her own level of performance, the team's effectiveness should be enhanced.

One instrument that can be used in conducting performance appraisal ratings is found in Appendix 12.E. In using such an instrument, the team may want to have an outsider collect the evaluation forms and prepare a report for each member based on that person's ratings and comments from the other team members. A group may decide to use an outsider if it wants to keep specific ratings and comments anonymous (i.e., Kara would not know the exact ratings that Eduardo or Suzanne gave her since she would only see the aggregated ratings and comments). Some teams may decide that they want each person to hear the comments and ratings from all other members individually. In that case, they would not need to keep the ratings anonymous. Regardless of which system is used, some type of peer appraisal can be instrumental in helping team members know how the group views their work and what they need to do to improve it.

Composition of Groups: Diversity Issues

Whenever groups become more diverse in terms of personality, background, work experience, demographic characteristics (e.g., gender, race, age, ethnic background, physical ability), there is the potential for more divergent perspectives to be voiced. One advantage of having a more heterogeneous team is that it might come up with more innovative ideas. However, as a result of the members' more diverse opinions and previous experiences, heterogeneous teams may also experience more conflict.

One type of diversity in teams that has received increasingly more attention has been mixed-gender groups. In general, research indicates that male and female employees work well together in groups, leading to cooperative and supportive social relations.[38] However, there are a number of issues that can arise in mixed-gender groups. Some of these include perceived power inequities, communication problems, sexual harassment, and tokenism or cliquishness.

With regard to communication patterns, research shows that men interrupt others more frequently and successfully than do women. In mixed-gender groups, men interrupt women more than men interrupt men. Women, on the other hand, interrupt less often, and when they do, they interrupt both men and women equally.[39] As a result of being interrupted more frequently, women may be viewed as having less power because they are less forceful in being heard. They may also become more frustrated and passive in the group if they are having trouble getting their ideas across without being interrupted. This is true for all members who feel their views are being interrupted, regardless of gender, but unfortunately, it seems to occur more often to women. To address this issue, it is important for team leaders and members to enforce a norm of listening to each person's input. This includes showing attentive nonverbal or body language (e.g., looking at the person who is speaking, leaning forward, head nodding). Recently, several excellent source books on male and female communication patterns have been written that should help teams better understand gender issues in communication.[40]

Another issue facing mixed-gender teams is that of sexual harassment. Because men and women in a team work in close proximity to each other and often participate in social activities, it is possible for the boundaries around the relationship to become blurred. It is also possible for harassment to exist. For most teams, teammates share equal authority; thus, harassment might take the form of a hostile environment, rather than explicit threats to a person's job. For example, a man on the team may make suggestive sexual comments or tell sexual jokes to a woman on the team, or vice versa. Perceptions of an "offensive" environment may exist to a greater degree when a team member is in a distinct minority with respect to gender or race. A sole man or woman on a team may experience more difficulty voicing displeasure about offensive behavior because such a person might feel outnumbered on the team.

When an individual does not share a common characteristic or interest with the majority of the group, the group is said to be skewed toward one type of individual.[41] In these situations, there is the danger of tokenism or cliquishness interfering with the cohesiveness and effectiveness of the team. The characteristic could be race, gender, disability, religion, age, political views, or even something as seemingly minor as who the team hopes will win the football game on Saturday. The members of the dominant group may consciously or unconsciously make the minority individual feel either uncomfortable or excluded by the topics discussed. For example, in a team with four men and one woman, the men might habitually rate the physical attractiveness of women or engage in cat-calls as other women pass by. Similarly, a team dominated by women might make a solitary man feel uncomfortable if they spend a lot of time talking about shopping for clothes. Or four team members might converse in a language that is not understood by the other two team members. It is very important that teams be sensitive to these issues. When any teammates feel uncomfortable on the team, or left out of team activities and discussions because they do not fit in, then they cannot perform their team tasks to the best of their ability and the team as a whole will suffer. At its most extreme level, cliquishness or tokenism can be as serious as harassment, and team members should be made aware of the legal and ethical implications of these issues.

There are a number of things you should be sensitive to in a highly skewed group. First, everyone has probably felt left out or different from others at some point in their life. It is important to be aware of the feelings of a person who is different and to include the person in the team's activities. Often such individuals may be ignored, interrupted, or have their views discounted. Be aware that this may happen and make sure that you allow them opportunities to participate. On the other hand, sometimes they will be put in the spotlight and asked to serve as the representative for all of their "type" (e.g., having an older person give the perspective for all older adults). They probably do not want to be singled out in this way. In fact, the individual probably prefers to be an active contributor like everyone else on the team. If you are able to bring the person's views into the group, the team will benefit from the alternative perspective.

Diversity in a team's composition can enable teams to arrive at more creative, innovative ideas and decisions. However, diversity must be managed. If diversity is not managed, conflicts may emerge that make it difficult for the team to become a cohesive, high-performing group.

STRATEGIES FOR BECOMING A HIGH-PERFORMANCE TEAM

A team may have worked together for some time yet may still experience some difficulties due to performance or internal conflicts (e.g., personality clashes). Some teams face changing team composition through the addition of new members or the loss of members. This necessitates that they revisit issues of trust, commitment, and purpose. Other teams may suffer some team trauma or lose their edge due to limited training opportunities.

There are a number of things teams can do to try to reach a higher level of performance and team success. Some of the most important things a team can do include securing needed training for the team, allowing for "practice" time to experiment with new ideas, learning how to run efficient team meetings, focusing on success, and being aware of how to monitor and measure the team's progress and performance. These strategies are discussed next.

Securing Training and Support for the Team

Teams often get launched in a vacuum, with little or no training support, no change in the design of their work, and no new systems to help communication between teams.[42]

When asked which factors have most influenced the success of teams, most practitioners point to training and support. Senior management support is critical for the success of teams. Not only should top managers support the use of teams, but also they must create a climate that encourages experimentation, innovation, employee-management openness, and sharing of information. Sufficient resources of funding, time, and technology are critical to show support for teams in an organization. In addition, when teams are formed, if the firm utilizes unions, then they should be involved in the design of the self-managed teams.[43]

Inadequate training has often been cited as one of the largest hindrances to effective team performance. If they want to reach higher levels of performance, it is important that teams secure the additional training they need. Many team-based organizations devote large amounts of time to training.[44] At Corning, team members spend 15–20 percent of their time in training, or approximately one day per week. At Dana Corporation, employees enrolled in 40 hours of training over an 18 month period.[45] At Chaparral Steel, new team members receive technical skills training for four hours a week in addition to participating in an on-the-job training program.[46]

In general, it is important that team members receive training in some core areas as well as continuous training. While a variety of training areas is necessary for teams, they generally fall into three categories: job skills, team or interactive skills, and quality/action skills.[47] All skills are equally important. For example, a team with excellent technical skills will probably still not be successful if its interpersonal skills are poor (e.g., members cannot manage conflict). Likewise, a team with good interpersonal skills may be incapable of becoming a high-performance team if team members do not serve as quality experts capable of identifying and correcting problems. **Exhibit 12.3** lists the training skills needed in these three core areas.

Job skills include the technical knowledge and skills team members need to perform successfully on the job. Depending on the specific job, they may consist of such skills as conducting market research, performing a sales call, operating a piece of equipment, or preparing a budget. Team or interactive skills include the interpersonal and communication skills that team members need to work effectively together. Some of the interpersonal skills include communicating supportively, managing conflict, giving and receiving performance feedback, running effective meetings, motivating others, coaching, managing time and stress, and handling customer issues.[48] Quality/action skills involve being able to identify problems and make improvements. These are important skills for teams because members are often given responsibility for examining the team's performance and making continuous improvements.

Allowing for Practice Time

In order to be innovative, teams need to experiment with new ways of doing things. Yet they often do not have time to do this since they are always under the gun for performance. Unlike work teams, sports teams alternate games with practices. It is in their practice sessions that they try out new plays and learn new techniques.[49] If work teams could follow a similar strategy and build in more opportunities for "practice" or learning, they might be more successful. Perhaps some team meetings or work time could be devoted to brainstorming new ideas and experimenting with new methods. If members are encouraged to take risks, even if they fail, they might be pushed to reach higher levels of performance and more innovative work. Thus, members need to build in time for learning and allow for risk-taking and "intelligent" failures.[50] For example, the well-known consulting firm McKinsey & Company has consulting teams spend at least one day a week at the home office to share ideas in a more relaxed environment than at the client site.[51]

Running Effective Team Meetings

The two biggest problems in America today are making ends meet and making meetings end.[52]

By conducting only meetings that are necessary, well prepared, and well organized, you set the pattern for business efficiency throughout your organization.[53]

Why can some teams pull together, tackle difficult tasks, and solve problems, while other teams cannot? Even when a group has the necessary skills and is highly motivated, it can be ineffective. Typical sources of ineffectiveness stem from poor use of meeting time and weak group processes.

A number of process flaws can sabotage the effectiveness of a meeting and result in frustration, inefficiency, and a lack of productivity among team members. These are known as "meeting breakers" and include anything or anyone who prevents individuals from accomplishing their goals in meetings. Some meeting breakers are listed in **Exhibit 12.4**.

Communicating effectively and making the most of team meetings is critical for team effectiveness. MGM Grand Airlines has a series of private compartments on its airplanes that accommodate four people, enabling groups to conduct business meetings during the long trip from California to New York.[54] Exhibits 12.5, 12.6, and 12.7 provide some practical tips that can assist teams in holding meetings that are focused, well-organized, efficient, and more productive.[55] These tips refer to things a team can do before the meeting (**Exhibit 12.5**), during the meeting (**Exhibit 12.6**), or in ending the meeting (**Exhibit 12.7**). Knowing how and when to bring a meeting to closure is an important skill. Sometimes a team may be well prepared for the meeting and may conduct an efficient meeting yet have difficulty wrapping the meeting up. A team can also assess how effective it is at meetings using the diagnostic tool illustrated in Appendix 12.F.

Your Role in Ensuring Effective Team Meetings

Each team member has a responsibility to make sure the team meetings are run

---

Exhibit 12.3: *Core Training for Team Members*

Team/Interaction Skills
- Listening (summarizing, checking for understanding)
- Giving and receiving feedback
- One-on-one communication (with team members, customers, suppliers, and leaders)
- Handling conflict (identifying and resolving conflict with team members, other teams, customers, etc.)
- Influencing others (gaining the commitment of others)
- Cross-training and coaching others
- Establishing roles and responsibilities for team members
- Group process skills (including meetings)
- Making presentations
- Leading meetings
- Selecting team members
- Assessing team performance
- Gaining team agreement (using consensus building and group decision making)

Quality/Action Skills
- Clarifying internal and external customer needs and requirements
- Identifying improvement opportunities by analyzing the root causes of problems
- Developing and selecting solutions to problems
- Planning, monitoring, and measuring quality projects
- Standardizing improvements and identifying ongoing opportunities for improvements

Job Skills (as relevant to specific jobs)
- Operating equipment
- Safety practices
- Maintenance basics for machines
- Production processes (developing just-in-time systems and material requirements planning)

Source: R. S. Wellins, W. C. Byham, and J. M. Wilson, *Empowered Teams: Creating Self-Directed Work Groups That Improve Quality, Productivity, and Participation* (San Francisco: Jossey-Bass, 1996):169–170.

Exhibit 12.4: *Problems with Team Meetings*

1. Purpose of meeting unclear—meetings scheduled routinely, even when there might be nothing to discuss; meetings for the sake of meeting.
2. Lack of an agenda—even when there are good reasons for a meeting, they are not outlined in an agenda format which results in unfocused, rambling discussions.
3. Agenda is too full—nothing gets accomplished, members discuss so many issues that they cannot reach closure on any particular issues.
4. Agenda does not specify time limits—team members do not complete the agenda because discussion on early agenda items is unfocused and rambles on.
5. Secret or hidden agendas—individual members have plans to accomplish priorities of their own during the meeting which are not on the team's agenda.
6. Lack of preparation by team members—the group cannot make progress until it has seen certain reports or assignments; members will not be prepared to make reports if they are unaware of the meeting agenda.
7. Meetings do not start on time—some members are habitually late, members socialize too much and have difficulty getting down to business.
8. Meetings do not have a clear ending point—discussion wanders, issues are not resolved.
9. Attendance problems—people who miss meetings do not find out what happened, and then come to subsequent meetings unprepared.
10. Lack of accountability—confusion over who is responsible for accomplishing tasks; minutes recording the agreements made in prior meetings are not available.
11. Inappropriate interpersonal behaviors and communication—a team member engages in counterproductive behaviors (interrupts or ignores others, does not listen, monopolizes discussions, discounts others' views, ridicules or overly criticizes ideas generated during brainstorming sessions, pulls rank or status).
12. Inability to deal with conflict during the meeting—members smooth over issues, avoid conflict, accommodate too quickly, or lose control without resolving the conflict.

Exhibit 12.5: Tips for Running Effective Meetings: Before a Team Meeting

1. Decide whether or not it is important to meet

Sometimes meetings are held out of habit when the team may be more productive working individually or communicating through other formats, such as memos, voice mail, or e-mail. Before calling a meeting, it is important to evaluate whether there is a real need for a meeting.

Do meet if . . .

- you need to present information to the team quickly (and a meeting is more efficient than writing it)
- input from others is important
- you need to be sure that the message is understood by all team members
- a group decision is necessary
- you need to gain commitment (buy-in) from fellow team members
- you want to motivate or energize the team about an idea

Don't meet if . . .

- you have nothing important to discuss
- participation from others is not critical
- you have already decided on a course of action
- there is a need for a quick decision
- there is not enough time for adequate preparation

2. Establish objectives for the meeting

Make sure objectives are achievable and specific. Share the agenda and meeting objectives with teammates before the meeting.

3. Prepare and circulate an agenda

Use active verbs in your agenda. Briefly summarize each issue to be discussed. Establish a purpose for each item (e.g., for discussion only; to collect feedback; decision necessary).

Start with the most important items first.

4. Choose a meeting place that reflects the purpose of the meeting

If the purpose is to help members get to know one another and have fun, then a social place such as a restaurant, bowling alley, or picnic area may be appropriate. If the purpose is to outline a new marketing strategy, then a conference room with paper, tables, and flip charts may be more appropriate.

Sources: Modified from K. Fisher, S. Rayner, and W. Belgard, *Tips for Teams: A Ready Reference for Solving Team Problems* (New York: McGraw-Hill, 1995); G. E. Huszczo, *Tools for Team Excellence: Getting Your Team Into High Gear and Keeping It There* (Palo Alto, CA: Danes-Black 1996); and D. A. Whetten, and K. S. Cameron, *Developing Management Skills,* 5th ed. (New York: HarperCollins, 2002).

---

effectively. To be sure that you are fulfilling your responsibility, the following tips are given:[56]

- **Prepare for each meeting.** Complete the projects you were required to do and prepare any questions you have for the others.

- **Be on time.** Being late delays the meeting and hurts morale of the team since it often shows you do not value the other members' time.

- **Ask for clarification on points that are unclear or ambiguous.** Do not be afraid to ask questions since often others will have the same questions.

- **When giving information, be concise, clear, and to the point.** Do not confuse everyone by providing too many details or too much information.

- **Listen.** Maintain eye contact with those who are speaking and show interest in their comments through your nonverbal behaviors (e.g., by leaning forward, looking interested).

- **Show support for other teammates.** Build on their comments and ideas ("Julia has a great point, and I would like to also add that we might. . . .")

- **Make sure everyone participates in discussions.** If you have quieter members or teammates with different language skills (e.g., on an English-speaking team, several members have English as a second language), you might try to encourage

their participation by asking for their input.

- **Be open and candid about the issues.** Avoid bringing "hidden agendas" into team meetings.

Improving the Virtual Team

Today, many teams are not working in one room together or even in one building. Some are located in multiple sites across different countries or even continents. They may be working in offices or telecommuting. Advances in technology have enabled teams to connect through computer networks, e-mail, chat rooms, phone conferencing, faxes, satellite transmissions, and Web sites. There are some reported benefits with virtual teams, such as being able to send messages to the whole team at once, easier time reaching consensus on strategy and making decisions, fewer interpersonal conflicts, and more efficient time spent in teleconferences or conference calls.[57] There are, however, difficulties reported as well, such as problems with technology, loss of social interactions, and the impersonal nature of the communications. Virtual teams should be matched to the task at hand because they may not be appropriate in all situations.[58] One of the biggest challenges faced by virtual teams is that the members may have trouble becoming cohesive and building a social bond. To improve the effectiveness of virtual teams, a few suggestions are offered:[59]

- Initially bring the team members together for a face-to-face meeting to build communication and trust. Generally, it is easier for members to work together in virtual space if they have at least met face-to-face once.

- The team can hold one meeting or several meetings face-to-face to build rapport.

- Use videoconferences for important meetings so members can have closer contact.

- Have members send some e-mails about their backgrounds and lives to build a stronger relationship with their teammates.

Focus on Success

It is critical for the team to experience some early successes since generally members will view themselves more positively. After an initial success, members often aspire to more and expect more of themselves than

Exhibit 12.6: *Tips for Running Effective Meetings: During a Team Meeting*

1. **Identify and clarify the roles of a facilitator**

   Generally, this person makes sure the team follows the agenda, solicits ideas from all team members—especially quieter members, ensures that someone charts the team's comments, summarizes or clarifies perceptions of the group's conversations, and helps the team reach closure on important issues.

2. **Assign roles to a timekeeper and a scribe or recorder**

   Select a person to watch the time and to inform members when they have spent too much time on various agenda items. This is critical if the team is to discuss all agenda items. Assign another person the role of a scribe or a person who is responsible for taking notes at that meeting. Some teams have the person type up notes and send them out to everyone on the team before the next team meeting. Make sure to rotate who serves in each role at every meeting.

3. **Begin the meeting by reviewing the agenda and the objectives**

   Clearly state the issues to be addressed and problems to be solved. This is important since it reminds everyone about the purpose for the meeting. If anyone disagrees with the agenda items or has additional iems for the agenda, these should be briefly discussed at this time.

4. **Encourage participation and solicit input from others**

   - Ask for a show of hands on an issue
   - Use open-ended questions, not "yes/no" questions
   - Utilize a round-robin format in which each member takes turns sharing opinions
   - Use alternative methods to solicit ideas of group members (e.g., present your questions/issue in writing, give all members a copy, ask them to jot down their reaction to your question, collect the responses and read them to the group for reactions)
   - Assign team members turns playing the "devil's advocate"

5. **Summarize often**

   The team can assign someone the responsibility of briefly summarizing the team's decision on each issue after it has been closed.

6. **Use process checks**

   Periodically, have someone check to make sure that the process being followed is an effective one (i.e., there are few interruptions, members are taking turns voicing their opinions).

7. **Stick to the agenda**

   Keep a list of other topics to discuss, don't digress or get sidetracked, and try to keep the discussion focused on one issue at a time.

8. **Control interpersonal and communication problems**

   Deal with dominating members and interrupters. Encourage and reinforce active listening. Allow team members to finish discussing/describing their ideas before commenting. Avoid engaging in one-on-one battles during team meetings. Be open minded and flexible to diverse views. Maintain a relaxed and comfortable atmosphere.

Sources: Modified from K. Fisher, S. Rayner, and W. Belgard, *Tips for Teams: A Ready Reference for Solving Team Problems* (New York: McGraw-Hill, 1995); G. E. Huszczo, *Tools for Team Excellence: Getting Your Team Into High Gear and Keeping It There* (Palo Alto, CA: Danes-Black 1996); and D. A. Whetten, and K. S. Cameron, *Developing Management Skills,* 5th ed. (New York: HarperCollins, 2002).

teams that start out with failures.[60] To ensure that the team starts off on a positive note, members could break up the project into smaller tasks with shorter deadlines so that the team can get some quick successes under its belt. In addition, as the team continues to work on projects, members can remind each other of the successes they have had. If the team finds itself in a downward spiral, members need to reframe the bleak outlook into a positive opportunity or challenge. They need to encourage each other and remind each other of successes they have had in the past. It is critical to maintain a positive outlook and continue focusing on success.

Monitoring and Measuring a Team's Progress and Performance

Highly successful teams are those that periodically assess how well the team is doing in terms of important group processes (e.g., leadership, communication, conflict, decision-making). Even sports teams use a half-time break to review what they have done and what changes they need to make.[61] Similarly, work teams should review their processes and progress at periodic times. Most members are open to conducting a midpoint review of the team, and this allows them to make needed changes and corrections. It is important to have debriefing meetings after receiving team feedback, especially if the team does well. Many teams will feel that they do not need to do a team review if they succeeded on a project, yet this is critical. In some situations, they may have been successful, but the members hated working together. This must be addressed if the team is to survive over a longer time. Whether the team did poorly or successfully, members should provide both positive feedback and constructive suggestions to each other. One factor that distinguishes great teams from poor teams is how they use the feedback they receive. Great teams understand the importance of feedback and learn more quickly from their mistakes so that they do not keep repeating the same mistake over and over again.[62]

Generally, the effectiveness of teams can be measured by using two primary criteria: performance and viability. *Performance* refers to the acceptability of the output to customers (within or outside the organization) who receive the team's products, services, information, decisions, or performance. For student teams, performance may be assessed by how well members are judged or graded on oral case competitions, written papers, decisions made in simulations, and so forth. Others evaluate the quality of a team's work in terms of its acceptability and overall performance.

Another equally important criterion for measuring team effectiveness is team *viability*. This refers to the degree of satisfaction team members have with the team and their continued willingness to contribute to it. That is, are the team members better or worse off for having contributed to the team?[63] Most of us are familiar with teams that excelled on their group projects, yet if you asked them if they wanted to keep working together, they were quick to emphatically state, "No way!" In this regard, a team that does well on projects without being able to resolve major sources of

Exhibit 12.7: *Tips for Running Effective Meetings: Ending the Team Meeting*

1. **Decide in advance how the team will reach its verdicts.**

   If the group decides to use consensus or voting, make sure that the particular procedure chosen has been followed.

2. **Before closing, summarize all key points raised and/or decisions made.**

3. **Establish accountability for actionable items.**

   Inform each member what, if any, his or her assignments are and what he or she needs to bring to the next meeting.

4. **Make sure action items are unambiguous and that deadlines are realistic.**

   Discuss with teammates whether or not the deadlines can be met.

5. **Hold a question and answer session at the end of each meeting.**

   Use this brief session as an opportunity to ensure that all team members are clear on the decisions made and course of action to follow.

6. **Reinforce each other.**

   Thank each other for participating. Provide support to teammates for being willing to share their views, especially those serving as devil's advocates or evaluators.

7. **Do a final review.**

   In the last five to ten minutes, have someone wrap up the meeting by reviewing the meeting (i.e., whether the norms were followed, whether the key objectives were met). Rotate who serves as reviewer at each meeting.

8. **Consider circulating minutes before the next meeting.**

   After the minutes have been prepared, circulate them prior to the next meeting.

Sources: Modified from K. Fisher, S. Rayner, and W. Belgard, *Tips for Teams: A Ready Reference for Solving Team Problems* (New York: McGraw-Hill, 1995); G. E. Huszczo, *Tools for Team Excellence: Getting Your Team Into High Gear and Keeping It There* (Palo Alto, CA: Danes-Black 1996); and D. A. Whetten, and K. S. Cameron, *Developing Management Skills,* 5th ed. (New York. HarperCollins, 2002).

conflict (i.e., never wants to work together again) is not an effective team.[64]

One instrument that can be used to measure your team's progress is included in Appendix 12.G. Essentially; the team must try to assess the factors that are responsible for its success and the factors that might be hindering its performance. In addition, team members need to examine their processes (communication, interpersonal relationships, trust, cooperation, motivation, fun). Another instrument, based on the seven key components of effective teams as shown in Exhibit 12.2, is contained in Appendix 12.H. Regardless of which tool is used, a team should periodically assess how its members view its progress and performance. Only with specific and timely feedback can the team make continual improvements and reach a higher level of performance.

SUMMARY

With the increasing use of teams in organizations, more strategies and ideas are being offered for how to improve the performance of teams. This chapter reviewed some of these strategies by focusing on the characteristics of highly effective teams and the common challenges facing most teams. In addition, some tips for enhancing a team's performance were offered. These tips are valuable for a team that is trying to reach an acceptable level of performance as well as a team that is trying to reach the highest possible level of performance.

When team members are willing and able to work to reach the next higher level of performance, they will be successful in managing their team to excellence. They should recognize, however, that the job is never done. Outstanding teams know that the team's processes and performance must be periodically reviewed in order to make continual improvements and to strive for excellence. Experts recommend that there are two key issues that impact teams for the future. These are (1) the team's ability to learn and become skilled in new and changing technologies and (2) its competence in transferring those technologies to others who need to know. In addition, given the rapid speed of change, the team must be willing to quickly learn and make needed changes.

1. B. Dumaine, "The Trouble with Teams." *Fortune* 13, 5 (1994): 86–90. See also J. Gordon, "Work Teams: How Far Have They Come?" *Training* 29 (1992): 59–65; and B. Dumaine, "Who Needs a Boss?" *Fortune*, May 7, 1990, pp. 52–55, 58, 60.

2. E. E. Lawler, *Strategies for High Performance Organizations* (San Francisco: Jossey-Bass, 1998). See also E. E. Lawler, S. A. Mohrman, and G. E. Ledford, *Creating High Performance Organizations: Practices and Results of Employee Involvement and Total Quality in Fortune 1000 Companies* (San Francisco: Jossey-Bass, 1995).

3. S. G. Cohen and D. E. Bailey, "What Makes Teams Work: Group Effectiveness Research from the Shop Floor to the Executive Suite," *Journal of Management* 23 (1997): 239–290. See also R. A. Guzzo and M. W. Dickson, "Teams in Organizations: Recent Research in Performance and Effectiveness," *Annual Review of Psychology* 47 (1996): 307–338; and Lawler et al., *Creating High Performance*.

4. R. S. Wellins, W. C. Byham, and J. M. Wilson, *Empowered Teams: Creating Self-Directed Work Groups That Improve Quality, Productivity, and Participation* (San Francisco: Jossey-Bass, 1996): 188.

5. D. A. Whetten and K. S. Cameron, *Developing Management Skills*, 5th ed. (Upper Saddle River, NJ: Prentice Hall, 2002). See also L. Thompson, *Making the Team: A Guide for Managers* (Upper Saddle River, NJ: Prentice Hall, 2000); S. Bucholz and T. Roth, *Creating the High-Performance Team* (New York: John Wiley & Sons, 1987): xi; M. A. Campion, G. J. Medsker, and A. C. Higgs, "Relations between Work Group Characteristics and Effectiveness: Implications for Designing Effective Work Groups," *Personnel Psychology* 46 (1993): 823–850; P. S. Goodman, R. Devadas, and T. L. G. Hughson, "Groups and Productivity: Analyzing the Effectiveness of Self-Managing Teams," in *Productivity in Organizations*, ed. J. P. Campbell and R. J. Campbell and Associates (San Francisco, CA: Jossey Bass, 1990): 295–327; J. R. Hackman, ed., *Groups That Work and Those That Don't: Creating Conditions for Effective Teamwork* (San Francisco: Jossey-Bass, 1989); E. E. Lawler, *High-Involvement Management: Participative Strategies for Improving Organizational Performance* (San Francisco, Jossey-Bass, 1986); R. Kreitner and A. Kinicki, *Organizational Behavior*, 3rd ed. (Chicago: Irwin, 1995); and Wellins et al., *Empowered Teams*.

6. Thompson, *Making the Team*.

7. G. E. Huszczo, *Tools for Team Excellence: Getting Your Team into High Gear and Keeping It There* (Palo Alto, CA: Davies-Black Publishing, 1996): 77. See also E. A. Locke and G. P. Latham, *A Theory of Goal Setting and Task Performance* (Englewood Cliffs. NJ: Prentice-Hall, 1990).

8. N. Katz, "Sports Teams as a Model for Workplace Teams: Lessons and Liabilities," *Academy of Management Executive* 15, no. 3 (2001): 56–67.

9. K. Labich, "Elite Teams." *Fortune*, February 19, 1996, pp. 90–99. See also W. Witherspoon, "Champions of Chapel Hill: Anson Dorrance Nurtures Dynasty of Women's Soccer at North Carolina," *Los Angeles Times*, November 18, 1994, p. C1.

10. N. Katz, "Drawing the Best from Both Cooperation and Competition: A Study of College Athletic Teams," Paper presented at the Academy of Management annual meeting, Chicago, 1999.

11. Katz, "Sports Teams."

12. J. Cook and T. D. Wall, "New Work Attitude Measures of Trust, Organizational Commitment, and Personal Need Non-fulfillment," *Journal of Occupational Psychology* 53 (1980): 39–52.

13. Wellins et al., *Empowered Teams*.

14. F. Bartolome, "Nobody Trusts the Boss Completely Now What?" *Harvard Business Review* (March-April 1989): 135–142. See also J. B. Rotter, "Interpersonal Trust, Trustworthiness, and Gullibility," *American Psychologist* 35, no. 1 (1980): 1–7; and Kreitner and Kinicki, *Organizational Behavior*.

15. W. F. Owen, "Metaphor Analysis of Cohesiveness in Small Discussion Groups." *Small Group Behavior* 16 (1985): 415–424.

16. Thompson, *Making the Team*. See also Owen, "Metaphor Analysis"; J. Keyton and J. Springston, "Redefining Cohesiveness in Groups," *Small Group Research* 21, 2 (1990): 234–254; and Kreitner and Kinicki, *Organizational Behavior*

17. D. A. Prentice, D. T. Miller, and J. R. Lightdale, "Asymmetries in Attachments to Groups and to Their Members: Distinguishing between Common-identity and Common-bond Groups," *Personality and Social Psychology Bulletin* 20 (1994): 484–493. See also Kreitner and Kinicki, *Organizational Behavior*; and P. E. Mudrack, "Group Cohesiveness and Productivity: A Closer Look," *Human Relations* (September 1989): 771–785.

18. D. K. Carew, E. Parisi-Carew, and K. H. Blanchard, "Group Development and Situational Leadership: A Model for Managing Groups," *Training and Development Journal* 40, no. 6 (1986): 46–50. See also G. R. Bushe and A. L. Johnson, "Contextual and Internal Variables Affecting Task Group Outcomes in Organizations," *Group & Organization Studies* 14, no. 4 (1989): 462–482.

19. D. Martin, *Teamthink: Using the Sports Connection to Develop, Motivate, and Manage a Winning Business Team* (New York: Penguin Books, 1993).

20. C. Bell and R. Zemke, "On-target Feedback," *Training* 29, no. 6 (1992): 36–38, 44. See also D. R. Ilgen, C. D. Fisher, and M. S. Taylor, "Consequences of Individual Feedback on Behavior in Organizations," *Journal of Applied Psychology* 64 (4) (1979): 349–371.

21. M. DeGregorio and C. D. Fisher, "Providing Performance Feedback: Reactions to Alternate Methods," *Journal of Management* 14, no. 4 (1988): 605–616. See also D. Davies and B. C. Kuypers, "Group Development and Interpersonal Feedback," *Group & Organizational Studies* 10, no. 2 (1985): 184–208.

22. R. A. Baron, "Countering the Effects of Destructive Criticism: The Relative Efficacy of Four Interventions," *Journal of Applied Psychology* 75, 3 (1990): 235–245. See also M. L. Smith, "Give Feedback, not Criticism," *Supervisory Management* 38, no. 2 (1993): 4.

23. Huszczo, *Tools for Team Excellence*. See also R. Y. Hirokawa, "Why Informed Groups Make Faulty Decisions: An Investigation of Possible Interaction-Based Explanations," *Small Group Behavior* 18 (1987): 3–29.

24. Dumaine, "The Trouble with Teams."

25. Kreitner and Kinicki, *Organizational Behavior*.

26. S. E. Asch, *Social psychology* (Englewood Cliffs, NJ: Prentice-Hall, 1952). See also Kreitner and Kinicki, *Organizational Behavior*; and T. Amir, "The Asch Conformity Effect: A Study in Kuwait," *Social Behavior and Personality* 2 (1984): 187–190.

27. I. L. Janis, *Groupthink*, 2nd ed. (Boston, MA: Houghton Mifflin, 1982).

28. C. C. Manz, C. P. Neck, J. Mancuso, and K. P. Manz, *For Team Members Only: Making Your Workplace Team Productive and Hassle-Free* (New York: AMACOM, 1997). See also G. L. Stewart, C. C. Manz, and H. P. Sims, Jr., *Team Work and Group Dynamics* (New York: John Wiley, 1999).

29. Janis, *Groupthink*. See also Thompson, *Making the Team*; R. J. Aldag and S. R. Fuller, "Beyond Fiasco: A Reappraisal of the Groupthink Phenomenon and a New Model of Group Decision Processes," *Psychological Bulletin* 113, no. 3 (1993): 533–552; R. R. Sims, "Linking Groupthink to Unethical Behavior in Organizations," *Journal of Business Ethics* 11, no. 9 (1992): 651–662; M. R. Callaway and J. K. Esser, "Groupthink: Effects of Cohesiveness and Problem-Solving procedures on Group Decision Making," *Social Behavior and Personality* 2 (1984): 157–164; and Whetten

and Cameron, *Developing Management Skills*.

30. M. E. Turner and A. R. Pratkanis, "A Social Identity Maintenance Model of Groupthink," *Organizational Behavior and Human Decision Processes* 73, 2–3 (1998): 210-235.

31. J. A. Shepperd, "Productivity loss in Performance Groups: A motivation analysis," *Psychological Bulletin* 1 (1993): 67–81. See also R. E. Kidwell, Jr. and N. Bennett, "Employee Propensity to Withhold Effort: A Conceptual Model to Intersect Three Avenues of Research," *Academy of Management Review* 18, 3 (1993): 429–456; S. J. Karau and K. D. Williams, "Social Loafing: Meta-Analytic Review and Theoretical Integration," *Journal of Personality and Social Psychology* 65, 4 (1993): 681–706.

32. Thompson, *Making the Team*.

33. Kreitner and Kinicki, *Organizational Behavior*.

34. J. M. Jackson and S. G. Harkins, "Equity in Effort: An Explanation of the Social Loafing Effect," *Journal of Personality and Social Psychology* 49, 5 (1985): 1199–1206.

35. J. R. Katzenbach and D. K. Smith, *The Wisdom of Teams: Creating the High-Performance Organization* (Boston, MA: Harvard Business School Press, 1993).

36. J. B. Harvey, *The Abilene Paradox*, videocassette and book available through Pfeiffer & Company (San Francisco, 1996).

37. Thompson, *Making the Team*.

38. S. J. South, C. M. Bonjean, W. T. Markham, and J. Corder, "Female Labor Participation and Other Organizational Experiences of Male Workers," *The Sociological Quarterly* 24, no. 3 (1983): 367–380.

39. L. Smith-Lovin and C. Brody, "Interruptions in Group Discussions: The Effects of Gender and Group Composition," *American Sociological Review* 54, no. 3 (1989): 424–435.

40. D. Tannen, *Talking from 9 to 5* (New York: William Morrow & Company, 1994). See also D. Tannen, *You Just Don't Understand: Women and Men in Conversation* (New York: Ballantine Books, 1990); and D. Tannen, *That's Not What I Meant!* (New York: Ballantine Books, 1986).

41. R. Kanter, *Men and Women of the Corporation* (New York: Basic Books, 1977).

42. Dumaine, "The Trouble with Teams."

43. R. Hersowitz, "Self Management and the Kaizen Team—Empowerment versus Tasking," in *Kaizen Strategies for Improving Team Performance,* ed. M. Colenso (London: Prentice Hall, 2000): 87–106. See also P. E. Brauchle and D. W. Wright, "Training Work Teams," *Training and Development* (March 1993): 65–68.

44. R. S. Wellins, J. M. Wilson, A. J. Katz, P. Laughlin, and C. R. Day, *Self-Directed Teams: A Study of Current Practice*, Survey Report (Pittsburgh, PA: Development Dimensions International, Association for Quality and Participation, and Industry Week, 1990).

45. J. H. Sheridan, "America's Best Plants," *Industry Week*, 239, 20 (1990): 27–64.

46. Wellins et al., *Empowered Teams*.

47. Ibid.

48. G. M. Parker, "Cross–Functional Collaboration," *Training and Development Journal* 48, 10 (1994): 49–53.

49. Katz, "Sports Teams."

50. S. Sitkin, "Learning through Failure: The Strategy of Small Losses," in B. Staw and L. L. Cummings, eds., *Research in Organizational Behavior* 14 (Greenwich, CT: JAI Press, 1992): 231–266.

51. A. Edmondson, "Psychological Safety and Learning Behavior in Work Teams," *Administrative Science Quarterly* 44 (1999): 350–383.

52. D. Booher, "Holding Your Own Meetings, but Working as a Team," *Training and Development* 48, 8 (1994): 54–59. See also Whetten and Cameron, *Developing Management Skills*.

53. Martin, *Teamthink*.

54. Ibid.

55. Booher, "Holding Your Own Meetings." See also K. Fisher, S. Rayner, and W. Belgard, *Tips for Teams: A Ready Reference for Solving Common Team Problems* (New York: McGraw-Hill, 1995); and Huszczo, *Tools for Team Excellence*.

56. Whetten and Cameron, *Developing Management Skills,* 552.

57. K. Kizer, "Building a Virtual Team," *Training* (March 1999): 34.

58. K. A. Graetz, E. S. Boyle, C. E. Kimble, P. Thompson, and J. L. Garloch, "Information Sharing in Face-to-Face Teleconferencing, and Electronic Chat Groups," *Small Group Research* (December 1998): 714–743.

59. D. L. Duarte and N. Tennant, *Mastering Virtual Teams* (San Francisco: Jossey-Bass, 1999). See also Thompson, *Making the Team*.

60. Katz, "Sports Teams.

61. Ibid.

62. A. M. Barratt, "Future Teams and Implications," in *Kaizen Strategies for Improving Team Performance,* ed. M. Colenso (London: Prentice Hall, 2000): 199–213.

63. E. Sundstrom, K. P. DeMeuse, and D. Futrell, "Work Teams," *American Psychologist* 45 2, (1990): 120–133.

64. Kreitner and Kinicki, *Organizational Behavior*.

EXERCISE ON TEAM CHARACTERISTICS AND EXPERIENCES

Instructions: Have each team member complete the questions listed below.
As a group, discuss your responses.

1. List some of your recent experiences working on teams (e.g., sports teams, community projects, work teams, school teams):

2. Were any of these teams successful or effective teams? If so, describe why you believe they were effective:

3. Are there any other characteristics that you think successful teams possess?

4. Were any of your teams unsuccessful or ineffective? If so, describe why you believe they were ineffective:

5. In general, what do you think are the attributes of ineffective or unsuccessful teams?

6. What could the team do to make sure it becomes a successful, high-performing team? Describe some strategies. Which are most important?

MEASURE OF TEAM MEMBER COMMITMENT

Instructions: Using the scale below, circle one response for each item. Each team member should individually complete the form. Afterwards, discuss any similarities and differences in your individual ratings for the items.

Almost Never	Rarely	Sometimes	Frequently	Almost Always
AN	R	S	F	AA

To what degree do your team members . . .

Stay late, come to work early, or take work home to make sure a job gets done	AN	R	S	F	AA
Attend regularly scheduled meetings	AN	R	S	F	AA
Complete work assignments set by the team	AN	R	S	F	AA
Try to improve the quality of the team's work	AN	R	S	F	AA
Talk about concerns with the quality of the team's work	AN	R	S	F	AA
Speak favorably about the team to others	AN	R	S	F	AA
Help each other when necessary	AN	R	S	F	AA
Go outside the team for help/resources when necessary	AN	R	S	F	AA
Live up to their responsibilities	AN	R	S	F	AA
Get to meetings on time	AN	R	S	F	AA
Spend their free time (e.g., lunch, breaks, after-work hours) with other team members	AN	R	S	F	AA
Work to fulfill the team responsibilities assigned to them	AN	R	S	F	AA
Try to find solutions when there are problems with the team's level of performance	AN	R	S	F	AA
Remain positive when things don't go well for the team	AN	R	S	F	AA
Talk enthusiastically about working together to meet the team's goals	AN	R	S	F	AA
Try hard not to let the team down	AN	R	S	F	AA
Take on extra work to ensure that the team meets or exceeds its goals	AN	R	S	F	AA
Want the team to be successful	AN	R	S	F	AA
Are satisfied with the roles they have in the team	AN	R	S	F	AA
Work to maintain a high level of team spirit and morale	AN	R	S	F	AA
Take feedback about the team's performance seriously	AN	R	S	F	AA
Think of themselves more as members of the team, than as individuals	AN	R	S	F	AA

Source: Modified from: R. S. Wellins, W. C. Byham, and J. M. Wilson, *Empowered Teams: Creating Self-Directed Work Groups That Improve Quality, Productivity, and Participation* (San Francisco: Jossey-Bass, 1991): 221–222.

TRUST IN TEAMMATES SCALE

Instructions: Think about your team, and rate each of the following items using the scale below. Write in one response (1 to 5) for each item in the blank on the left. Add up your scores to get a total score for all 15 items. Compare the responses for everyone on the team. This will help you to understand each other's perceptions of the level of trust in the team.

Strongly Disagree	Disagree	Neither	Agree	Strongly Agree
1	2	3	4	5

_____ If I got into difficulties at work, I know my teammates would try and help me out.

_____ I can trust the people on my team to lend me a hand if I need it.

_____ Most of my teammates can be relied upon to do as they say they will do.

_____ I feel quite confident that my team will always try to treat me fairly.

_____ I have full confidence in the skills of my teammates.

_____ I can rely on my teammates not to make my job more difficult by careless work.

_____ My teammates can be trusted to make sensible decisions for the team's future.

_____ I can expect my teammates to play fair.

_____ I can confide in my teammates and know they have the desire to listen.

_____ I can expect my teammates to tell me the truth.

_____ My teammates would never intentionally misrepresent my point of view to other people.

_____ I can confide in my teammates and know that they will not discuss my views with other people.

_____ If my teammates promised to do me favors, they would carry out those promises.

_____ My teammates are sincere in their attempts to meet my points of view.

_____ I could lend my teammates valuables, (money, books, computer, etc.), and count on getting them back to me as soon as possible.

_____ TOTAL SCORE (Add up responses to all 15 items. Total should be between 15 and 75.)
   67 - 75   High level of trust in the team
   52 - 67   Moderate level of trust in the team
   37 - 51   Minimal level of trust in the team
   15 - 36   Low or very low level of trust in the team

Sources: J. Cook and T. D. Wall, "New Work Attitude Measures of Trust, Organizational Commitment, and Personal Need Non-fulfillment," *Journal of Occupational Psychology* 53 (1980): 39-52.; C. Johnson-George and W. C. Swap, "Measurement of Specific Interpersonal Trust: Construction and Validation of a Scale to Assess Trust in a Specific Other," *Journal of Personality and Social Psychology* 43, no. (1982), 1306–1317.

TEAM FEEDBACK EXPERIENCES

Instructions: Indicate how frequently you have experienced each of the following in your team. Use the scale to write in one response (1 to 5) for each item in the blank on the left. Score your responses below.

Almost Never	Rarely	Occasionally	Frequently	Almost Always
1	2	3	4	5

How often have you experienced your teammates . . .

1. _____ coming to you for advice

2. _____ expressing approval for your work

3. _____ telling you they like to work with you

4. _____ telling you that you are doing a good job

5. _____ commenting favorably on something you have done

6. _____ giving you a compliment

7. _____ asking for mentoring from you because they admire your work

8. _____ telling others about the good work you are doing

9. _____ telling you that you are *not* doing your job

10. _____ speaking poorly about your work

11. _____ trying to avoid working with you

12. _____ talking about your poor performance

13. _____ complaining that you are *not* doing your fair share

14. _____ complaining about your work to others

15. _____ complaining to you about minor aspects of your work

16. _____ keeping you out of things

17. _____ *not* seeking your opinion or advice

18. _____ commenting unfavorably on something you have done

19. _____ insulting or ridiculing your work

20. _____ trying to give you hints on how to do your job

Scoring:

Positive Feedback from teammates: _____

Add up your responses to items 1 to 8. You should have a score ranging from 8 to 40. A score of 32 or higher indicates that you believe that your teammates provide you with positive feedback.

Negative feedback from teammates: _____

Add up your responses to items 9 to 20. You should have a score ranging from 12 to 60. A score of 48 or higher indicates that you believe that your teammates provide you with negative feedback.

Compare your positive and negative feedback scores. Share your findings with your teammates.

Source: D. M. Herold and C. K. Parsons, "Assessing the Feedback Environment in Work Organizations: Development of the Job Feedback Survey," *Journal of Applied Psychology* (May 1985): 290–305. Copyright © 1985 by the American Psychological Association. Adapted with permission.

TEAM MEMBER PERFORMANCE APPRAISAL FORM

Instructions: Have each person on the team complete one performance appraisal form for every person on the team. Have one person, preferably an outsider, compile the ratings and comments for each member of the team so that each person receives his/her own report to indicate how the team as a whole viewed his/her performance.

SECTION A: PERFORMANCE RATINGS

Name of teammate being rated: _____

Not at all Effective	Marginally Effective	Effective	Very Effective	Extremely Effective
1	2	3	4	5

Attendance, Effort, and Participation

Actively and enthusiastically participates in team activities	1	2	3	4	5
Completes and brings assignments to meetings	1	2	3	4	5
Attends team meetings and work sessions	1	2	3	4	5
Consistently attends team meetings on time; does not leave early	1	2	3	4	5

Communication and Listening

Disseminates relevant information about decisions, plans, and activities to teammates	1	2	3	4	5
Talks clearly and concisely using appropriate voice tone, inflection, grammar, and vocabulary	1	2	3	4	5
Effectively uses nonverbal behaviors and gestures	1	2	3	4	5
Listens carefully to others and considers their ideas	1	2	3	4	5

Leading Task Accomplishment

Plans and adheres to a schedule for team activities	1	2	3	4	5
Defines problems and suggests procedures for solving problems	1	2	3	4	5
Makes an active attempt to keep the team focused on the task	1	2	3	4	5

Teamwork

Reconciles disagreements among team members	1	2	3	4	5
Encourages participation from other team members	1	2	3	4	5
Assists others as needed to accomplish team goals	1	2	3	4	5
Coordinates work with teammates	1	2	3	4	5
Brings a positive attitude to team activities	1	2	3	4	5

Interpersonal Sensitivity

Effectively interacts with others in meetings	1	2	3	4	5
Acknowledges valid points made by other team members	1	2	3	4	5
Deals effectively with others regardless of their personal characteristics or style	1	2	3	4	5

Intellectual Contribution

Generates new, creative, or imaginative ideas or solutions	1	2	3	4	5
Correctly identifies the basic issues and problems with team projects	1	2	3	4	5
Demonstrates competence in concepts related to team assignments	1	2	3	4	5
Provides a logical framework for the content of team projects	1	2	3	4	5

Judgment/Decision Making

Provides reasoning behind decisions and suggestions	1	2	3	4	5
Considers and offers alternative courses of action	1	2	3	4	5
Articulates the consequences of proposed actions before reaching a conclusion	1	2	3	4	5

Flexibility and Managing Change

Adapts or modifies behavior when pressured by time, people, or situations	1	2	3	4	5
Maintains constructive behavior despite changing or stressful environments	1	2	3	4	5
Helps the team to respond to changes in assignments	1	2	3	4	5

SECTION B: OPEN-ENDED COMMENTS

Name of teammate being rated: _____

1. Describe the individual's strengths or greatest contributions on this team:

2. Describe the individual's developmental needs or areas for improvement on this team:

TEAM MEETING QUESTIONNAIRE

Instructions: Rate the strengths and weaknesses of your team's meetings using the following scale. For each item, circle the one rating that is most accurate. After everyone on your team has completed the survey, compare your ratings with each other in a group discussion.

Almost Never	Rarely	Sometimes	Frequently		Almost Always
AN	R	S	F		AA

To what degree . . .

Is the purpose of team meetings clarified in advanced	AN	R	S	F	AA
Is an agenda provided in advance for team meetings	AN	R	S	F	AA
Is an agenda followed during team meetings	AN	R	S	F	AA
Is it clear who is or is not expected to attend	AN	R	S	F	AA
Do the members attend meetings regularly	AN	R	S	F	AA
Do team members attend meetings on time	AN	R	S	F	AA
Are meetings interrupted	AN	R	S	F	AA
Do members come to meetings prepared	AN	R	S	F	AA
Do members participate actively enough	AN	R	S	F	AA
Do members understand their roles and responsibilities	AN	R	S	F	AA
Is the time scheduled for the meeting conducive to its purpose	AN	R	S	F	AA
Do members listen to each other	AN	R	S	F	AA
Does the leader/facilitator fulfill his/her role	AN	R	S	F	AA
Do members reflect on the process of the meeting	AN	R	S	F	AA
Do members seem to be acting on hidden agendas	AN	R	S	F	AA
Does the group overdepend on the leader/facilitator	AN	R	S	F	AA
Is the amount of material covered at each meeting appropriate	AN	R	S	F	AA
Are minutes of the meeting put into writing	AN	R	S	F	AA
Do the minutes accurately summarize the meeting	AN	R	S	F	AA
Are the meeting minutes distributed appropriately	AN	R	S	F	AA
Is there follow-through after meetings	AN	R	S	F	AA
Are ground rules and norms clear and adhered to	AN	R	S	F	AA
Is the effectiveness of the meetings evaluated	AN	R	S	F	AA

Source: Modified from G. E. Huszczo, *Teams for Excellence: Getting Your Team into High Gear and Keeping It There* (Palo Alto, CA: Davies-Black Publishing): 129.

TEAM PROGRESS REPORT

Instructions: Using the scale below, circle one response for each item. Each team member should evaluate the team. Afterwards, discuss any similarities and differences in your individual ratings for the items.

Strongly Disagree SD	Disagree D	Neither N		Agree A		Strongly Agree SA

Clarity of Purpose

My team's goal is clear when we begin a project	SD	D	N	A	SA
Each member of my team has a clear idea of the team's goal	SD	D	N	A	SA
Going into a project, our team develops a specific strategy for approaching the project	SD	D	N	A	SA

Satisfaction with Social Relations and Morale

I am satisfied with the respect I receive from my teammates	SD	D	N	A	SA
I am satisfied with the friendliness among my teammates	SD	D	N	A	SA
I feel I am really part of my team	SD	D	N	A	SA
Overall, I enjoy working on my team	SD	D	N	A	SA

Perceived Efficiency of Teammates

My teammates could be more efficient in the way they handle the team workload	SD	D	N	A	SA
My teammates are efficient in doing their team work	SD	D	N	A	SA
Our team meetings are run in an effective manner	SD	D	N	A	SA
The way in which we run our team meetings needs improvement	SD	D	N	A	SA

Peer Competition vs. Collaboration

Most of my teammates try to outperform each other rather than help each other	SD	D	N	A	SA
In our team, members are too competitive with one another	SD	D	N	A	SA
Members on our team need to be more collaborative with one another	SD	D	N	A	SA
Members on our team push each other to perform at higher levels	SD	D	N	A	SA
We have a healthy amount of competition on our team	SD	D	N	A	SA

Participation in Meetings

At team meetings, teammates ask me for my ideas	SD	D	N	A	SA
At meetings, teammates pay attention to what I have to say	SD	D	N	A	SA
I feel comfortable expressing my opinions at team meetings	SD	D	N	A	SA

Working Together

In our team, we seek information from each other to complete our projects	SD	D	N	A	SA
We pass along tasks to each other if we think our teammates can better complete them	SD	D	N	A	SA
We share resources and provide advice to each other	SD	D	N	A	SA
We share insights on projects	SD	D	N	A	SA
We discuss problems and share strategies	SD	D	N	A	SA

Team Viability

I would continue to work with my teammates if the opportunity arose	SD	D	N	A	SA
I want to keep working with my teammates	SD	D	N	A	SA

Satisfaction with Team Performance

I am satisfied with my team's overall performance	SD	D	N	A	SA
I am satisfied with the quality of my team's output	SD	D	N	A	SA
I am satisfied with the amount of effort put forth by members of my team	SD	D	N	A	SA

Source: Items modified from scales in J. D. Cook, S. J. Hepworth, T. D. Wall, and P. B. Warr, *The Experience of Work* (London, Academic Press, 1981).

TEAM DIAGNOSTIC QUESTIONNAIRE

Instructions: Each team member should complete the following questionnaire. The team leader or an outsider should take all of the completed surveys and determine an average for each section. See Exhibit 12.2 for a listing of the dimensions. The team should review their results and discuss their strengths and plans for improvements.

Not at all	Slightly	Somewhat	Considerably	Extremely
1	2	3	4	5

1a. The goals of our team are appropriate and clearly stated	1	2	3	4	5
1b. The members of our team are committed to the accomplishment of our shared team goals	1	2	3	4	5
1c. Our team accomplishes its goals	1	2	3	4	5
2a. Our team collectively contains the full range of talents we need to be an effective unit	1	2	3	4	5
2b. The talents of our team are fully utilized	1	2	3	4	5
3a. The role of leadership is competently fulfilled by one or more people on this team	1	2	3	4	5
3b. Each member of our team clearly understands the role he/she is to play for us to be effective	1	2	3	4	5
3c. Each member of our team clearly fulfills the role he/she is expected to play	1	2	3	4	5
4a. Our team uses effective and efficient procedures to work together to complete our tasks	1	2	3	4	5
4b. Our team uses effective and efficient procedures to identify and resolve problems as they occur	1	2	3	4	5
4c. Our team holds effective and efficient meetings	1	2	3	4	5
4d. Our team uses effective and efficient procedures to ensure that information is shared and received	1	2	3	4	5
4e. Our team uses effective and efficient planning procedures	1	2	3	4	5
4f. Our team effectively monitors its progress	1	2	3	4	5
5a. Our team members deal with conflict in a constructive manner	1	2	3	4	5
5b. Our team members provide enough support to each other to encourage high levels of performance	1	2	3	4	5
5c. Team members provide enough positive challenge to each other to encourage high levels of performance	1	2	3	4	5
5d. Team members get along with each other quite well	1	2	3	4	5
6a. Team members provide each other with enough recognition for our working together as a team	1	2	3	4	5
6b. Our team receives enough recognition from outside sources	1	2	3	4	5
7a. Our team recognizes and actively pursues opportunities available in its external environment	1	2	3	4	5
7b. Our team recognizes and actively addresses the threats it is facing in its external environment	1	2	3	4	5
7c. Our team has good constructive relationships with other teams that we interact with	1	2	3	4	5

8a. Overall, on a 0 to 100 percent scale, how effective would you rate your team? _____ %

8b. Overall, on a 0 to 100 percent scale, how satisfied are you to be a member of this team? _____ %

Source: Modified from G. E. Huszczo, *Teams for Excellence: Getting Your Team into High Gear and Keeping It There* (Palo Alto, CA: Davies-Black Publishing): 43–45.

Chapter 13

Quality Improvement

Ivan Slimák
*Volkswagen Transmission
(Shanghai) Co.*

HISTORY OF QUALITY IMPROVEMENT

To begin the chapter, we trace the evolution of approaches toward quality improvement, showing how the roles of inspection and prevention have changed with the progress of civilization. The first part starts with the dawn of civilization, and the second part is focused on trends in the 20th century. There are some good approaches that have been used from the very beginning, but unfortunately some bad habits are also still commonplace after centuries of experience. Fortunately, history is here to learn from.

Dawn of Quality Improvement

People have always appreciated quality in the goods that make their lives easier or give them pleasure. The earliest quality testing was done by seeing, smelling, tasting, or touching. In prehistoric times, the test for quality was the everyday use of the product. Day after day, the producer, as his own customer, tested the quality of his own products. When the products failed, he experienced immediate hardship, for example, confronting dangerous animals with poor weapons. Early people's lives depended on the quality of their bows and arrows.

Producers and their families formed the first examples of customer-producer relationships. When producers built their family shelter poorly, they slept in wet and cold places, and their children were more prone to illnesses. When homemade garments were not warm enough, hunters could not track wild animals in the woods and thus provide enough food for their families. Day after day, survival of the fittest provided the essential test and incentive for improved quality.

> ### Learning Objectives
>
> The aim of this chapter is to help you understand the basic principles of modern quality improvement needed for running a business in today's market environment. After reading this chapter, students should be able to:
>
> - Define *product improvement* and *process improvement*.
> - Distinguish early attempts at quality improvement from later, more successful methods.
> - Explain the relationship between inspection costs and warranty costs.
> - Define *variation* and describe one way to reduce variation.
> - Describe the role that metrology plays in quality improvement.
> - Explain the value of the normal distribution in statistical quality control.
> - Describe the difference between inspecting for quality and quality improvement.

Customers over the centuries have tried to ensure their claims for product quality. We will look at two examples: Hammurabi's Code from almost 4,000 years ago, and an edict of Tsar Peter the First of Russia from less than 300 years ago.

Codex Hammurabi

Hammurabi's Code, a fragment of Babylonian Law introduced by King Hammurabi

BEST-USE CORRELATIONS

As the old saying goes, "It is hard to remember that your objective was to drain the swamp when you are up to your neck in alligators." You have seen your share of alligators as you started up your company in Q1 and Q2, test-marketed your products and marketing strategy in Q3, significantly revised your business strategy in Q4, and recruited venture capital in Q5. But, have you been paying attention to the quality alligator?

Just How Important Is Quality Improvement?

Ask the auto industry. Or the textile, photocopier, or industrial machine industries. This chapter carefully lays out the process of continuously improving the quality of your manufacturing operations. Learn what enhances and what limits quality.

The Quality Alligator Is About to Bite You

Have the demands of *Marketplace* caused you to lose sight of the quality and reliability of your brands? It is easy to get distracted.

In the second year of *Marketplace*, quality-oriented teams will start to produce more reliable computers. How much share will your team lose if it doesn't do the same or more?

The Payoff

Improving quality requires careful study and extended investments. If a team has the foresight to start this process early, it can achieve a significant differential advantage. Costs will go down and demand will go up.

of Babylonia (1792–1750 B.C.), contains some interesting ideas related to quality. To paraphrase part of the code:

> When a builder builds a house for a man and it is finished, the owner is to pay him two shekels for each sar (1 shekel = 360 grains of wheat = 9.1 grams of silver; 1 sar = 14.88 sq. m.). If a builder builds a house and the construction is not solid, causing it to collapse and kill the homeowner, the builder shall be killed. When the collapse causes the death of the owner's son, the son of the builder shall be killed. When the slave of the owner is killed by this, then the builder shall give one slave of the same value. If possessions are damaged, the builder shall replace everything that was damaged. Because the house was not solidly built, he shall rebuild it at his own expense. If the walls fail because of poor construction, the builder shall rebuild at his own expense.

Edict of Tsar Peter the First, January 11, 1723

The Tsar punished offenders, but he also looked to inspection before final assembly of the product to ensure adequate quality. To paraphrase from the edict:

> I order the flogging of Kamil Belaglasow, owner of the factory in Tula, and that he be sent to work in the monastery, because the scoundrel allowed the sale of unusable muskets to the government. I also order the flogging of the chief inspector, Frol Fux, and that he be expelled to Asow,[1] because he put the test and quality sign on the defective muskets. It is further ordered that St. Petersburg's Armament Bureau will be moved to Tula and that the Bureau will check the quality of the muskets around the clock. The chief supervisor and his staff will constantly monitor the inspectors and the standards for testing and giving the sign of quality. They are personally obliged to shoot the muskets to test their quality. Once a month the chief supervisor of the armament bureau will shoot two muskets until they fail. When the muskets fail in battle because of poor manufacturing, the sinners from the armament bureau will be flogged severely on their naked bodies. The factory owner will get 25 lashes with the whip as well as a fine of 1 tschevonec. The chief inspector will be lashed until he is unconscious. The chief officers of the armament bureau will be degraded to the rank of sergeant. The chief of the armament bureau will be degraded to the position of clerk. The staff of the bureau will not get his Sunday glass of vodka. The new

owner of the Tula factory is ordered to build a house, which will not be poorer than his own, for the chief supervisor of the armament bureau. Should it be, I order that the factory owner be shot.

The two approaches in Hammurabi's Code and Tsar Peter's edict do not differ much. In both cases, customers assert their rights by law and punishment. But Tsar Peter also emphasized a way to ensure quality inspection.

With the specialization of manufacturing activities brought about by Taylorism or "scientific management," the separation between the people who produced the product and those who inspected it was created. Moreover, with increasing quality requirements and complicated manufacturing processes, the number of inspectors increased. But more inspection does not necessarily mean better quality. This concept is expressed in the saying "quality cannot be *inspected in.*" This is illustrated also by the story of a manager who tries to explain to his boss that even after adding a fourth inspector to the line to inspect the third inspector, who inspects the second, and so on, quality is still not improving.

The situation today is slightly better than under Hammurabi or Tsar Peter, at least for producers. The punishment for producers has been replaced by warranty costs (e.g., for a rusty car), and customers can now sue manufacturers if a product has caused them losses, damages, or injuries. Manufacturers are being more cautious now. Everyone has heard of the kinds of major product recalls issued by automobile manufacturers, asking thousands of customers to come in to a service department to have a serious potential problem—such as a faulty air bag—repaired in order to prevent a worse problem in the future.

MODERN QUALITY IMPROVEMENT

When you want to help a hungry man for one day, give him a fish; when you want to help him for a lifetime, teach him how to fish.

—Japanese saying

Modern quality improvement began in the United States in the 1920s when W. A. Shewhart started to use statistical methods for quality improvement. These methods were suitable for mass manufacturing, which was flourishing in the United States. At this time in history, industry could sell all the product it produced; customers demanded more and more. When demand exceeds supply, the emphasis on quality is not so critical. Unlike in the more distant past, producers were no longer their own customers, nor did they meet their customers face to face in the marketplace. The people who influenced quality—workers on the manufacturing lines—were distant from customers and were not paid to understand customer needs. They were rewarded for volume and speed. Economies of scale were more important.

Some companies, such as Bell Laboratories and General Electric, started using statistical quality improvement methods for military contracts during World War II. This helped to stimulate the widespread use of statistics. The introduction of statistical quality control at General Electric helped to reduce the number of inspectors from 5,000 to 2,000.

Even such examples did not lead to statistical methods being used throughout industry in the United States. Quality improvement is not sustainable without pressure for improvement from competitors. After World War II, U.S. industry was dominant in the world market, with customers buying whatever was produced. There was not much stimulus for quality improvement. In a market driven by production, quality is left behind. In such a market, the response to quality problems tends to be limited to a "find and fix" philosophy—detecting the problem, fixing it, but not wasting resources on an analysis of causes, improvement, or prevention.

The introduction of modern quality improvement was still to come; it would happen not in the United States, but in Japan, a country severely damaged by war. Japan was a country with almost no industrial experience whose products were thought to be synonymous with poor quality.

After World War II, the United States sent several experts to Japan to help rebuild industry that was outdated or had been destroyed by the war. Among those experts, Dr. W. E. Deming and Dr. J. M. Juran are remembered as missionary saints by Japanese quality professionals. Deming introduced a philosophy of quality improvement, *statistical quality control,* aimed at reducing variation in processes, thus leading to improved product quality.

The Deming prize was established in 1951 to recognize the contributions of Deming to the development of quality improvement techniques in Japan. Awarded to outstanding individuals and

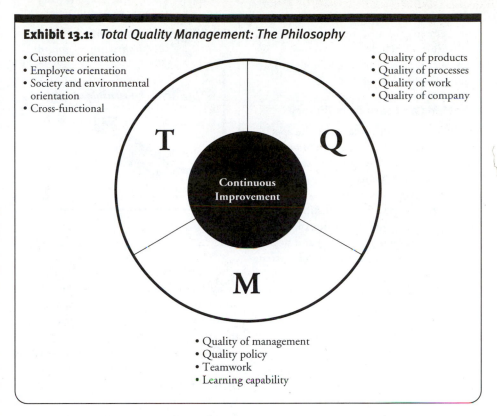

Exhibit 13.1: *Total Quality Management: The Philosophy*

- Customer orientation
- Employee orientation
- Society and environmental orientation
- Cross-functional

- Quality of products
- Quality of processes
- Quality of work
- Quality of company

T Q M

Continuous Improvement

- Quality of management
- Quality policy
- Teamwork
- Learning capability

companies in the field of quality improvement, the prize is highly valued in Japan and throughout the world. Divisions of Japanese companies such as Nissan, Toyota, Kawasaki, Fuji, Mitsubishi, NEC, and Komatsu have received this prize. In 1989 the Florida Power & Light Company earned it, proving that non-Japanese companies can achieve the kind of quality improvement culture that is described in Japan as *company wide quality control* (CWQC) or *total quality control* (TQC).

The Deming prize does not focus on product quality but looks instead at the conditions and activities that are required for quality improvement to occur, such as company policy, organization, and management; education; collection, dissemination, and use of information for analysis; and standardization, quality improvement, and planning for the future. Today such a philosophy of quality improvement at all levels of the company is called *total quality management* (TQM). TQM is a structured approach for satisfying internal and external customers as well as suppliers. TQM integrates the business environment's continuous improvement and breakthroughs with cycles of development and maintenance while changing organizational culture.

The other prophet of quality, Juran, was awarded the Order of the Sacred Treasure by Emperor Hirohito for his contributions to

quality improvement in Japan. In 1951 Dr. Juran published the first edition of his *Quality Control Handbook,* which is now the most recognized reference of quality improvement methods by quality professionals worldwide.[2]

Total Quality Management

TQM focuses on eliminating waste by minimizing manufacturing variance and reducing variance in nonmanufacturing processes such as purchasing and distribution. "Total" means all of the processes, employees, and phases, from design through customer follow-up (see **Exhibit 13.1**). While the most visible components of TQM philosophy are the customer and the employees, the culture of the company is also an integral part. There is an interrelatedness among processes, and improvements should be viewed as an improvement for the whole company. For example, savings on material purchases, which might be seen as an improvement by the purchasing department, might cause problems for other departments if the materials required additional effort or cost before they could be used in the process.

How close the company is to total quality management is not solely determined by the quality of their products but is also judged by criteria such as the commitment of managers to quality and their ability to foster teamwork and learning in their employees and themselves. Thus, the quality policy of an institution includes this statement: "We value our employees and we want to provide them a nice place to work. . . ."

What We Can Learn from History

Quality means conformance to the specifications determined for a given product. These are defined by engineers and used by manufacturing. Quality also means satisfying customer needs and surprising customers with pleasing results in their use of the product. Quality requires knowing what the customers really need and how to reduce variation to deliver a consistent product to them.

The first thing we learn from history is that the best test for product quality is in its everyday use by the customer. When it is time to purchase a new car, customers will consider the reliability and repair history of their current vehicle. If they have had many problems, they will consider switching brands to a manufacturer with better customer satisfaction ratings.

The customer chooses particular products and services based on personal experience, needs, and requirements. Because the customer can generally choose from among several competitors, the competitors themselves provide the biggest drive for quality improvement. To improve quality, the producer has to listen to the customer and watch the competition.

In order not to be punished by the customer, or by the law, producers should consider appropriate use of inspection tools (for example, inspecting safety parts such as brakes). But there are methods besides inspection for improving quality. Modern quality improvement can be characterized by its transition from screening out the bad product from among the good (inspection) to preventing bad product at its source (improving the manufacturing processes by reducing the variation that impairs product quality). The customers want stable quality, to be sure that what they are buying does not vary from the claimed specifications. Reducing process variation is at the core of this solution (see **Exhibit 13.2**).

QUALITY IMPROVEMENT METHODS AND TOOLS
Crankshaft Story

Before introducing quality improvement tools and methods, we will consider a spe-

Exhibit 13.2: *Trend in Modern Quality Improvement*

cific example concerning the crankshaft in an automobile engine. Though the example contains some simplified explanations of processes, it can help us understand the underlying methods.

One of the functions of a crankshaft is to transfer energy (produced in the pistons by the expansion of the ignited gas) to the wheels, which move the car. This shaft revolves thousands of times a minute. If this part does not rotate, the engine cannot move the car.

A couple of unique parameters influence such important features as gas consumption or engine noise. The shaft has to fit into the bearing hole so that the bearing can smooth the rotary movement of the shaft and produce less noise and friction. Therefore, one of the shaft's parameters is its cylindrical diameter. This parameter was set by engineers so that the cylinder would fit into the hole of the bearing. The connection of shaft and bearing is vital for the function of the crankshaft (i.e., for the transmission of energy from the pistons to the wheels). This connection must withstand billions of revolutions at very high temperature during years of vehicle use.

In addition to the diameter of the shaft, which is expressed by a number (for example, 35 mm), the engineer also specifies tolerances for the vital parameters. Tolerance denotes the range (for example, 0.1 mm) or the acceptable interval of the parameter for its proper functioning. Tolerances are specified for everything from the precise mechanical parts in machinery to the contents of packaged food. In the food industry, the nominal weight of a product might be set at 400 grams, with a tolerance of plus or minus 20 grams. In this case, the weight of a particular package would be acceptable from 380 to 420 grams. The tol-

erance range in our crankshaft example would be a lower tolerance limit (LTL) of 34.95 mm and upper tolerance limit (UTL) of 35.05 mm.

When the diameters of the shaft and the bearing hole vary from the designed value (35 mm), it can cost extra money to assemble the shaft and the bearing, or it can cause less efficient function (excessive noise and friction) of the shaft during its operational life. For any parameter, the lower the variation from its designed value, the better. The tolerance represents an acceptable interval for proper function of the given parameter.

On a single crankshaft, there are dozens of parameters with tolerances. These should fit together with parameters and tolerances of other parts—such as bearings and gear wheels—and will influence the proper functioning of the engine, including its gas consumption, noise, durability, reliability, acceleration, and so on. Just this one parameter, the diameter of the shaft, is influenced by several manufacturing processes, including turning of the shaft, heat treatment, and grinding. Each of these processes contributes to variation of the parameters. Thus, we need to improve each of the processes that produce the parameter in order to improve the features that the parameter influences. Variation in a process can be influenced by excessive vibration of the machine. Different operators may use different methods of adjusting the machine, resulting in variation of machine parameters. Using the wrong grinding tool or a poorly designed manufacturing process might cause too much material to be ground off in one operation. This in turn may cause variation in the shaft's diameter. Environmental influences such as temperature changes can also cause variation in the grinding process.

The variation means that when producing 2,000 crankshafts per day, the diameters of all 2,000 of them will not be exactly 35 mm but will vary around this value. For example, if the minimum value for 2,000 parts is 34.97 mm and the maximum value is 35.03 mm, we can see that the variation of the full day's production was within the tolerance with no defective parts (recall that LTL = 34.95 and UTL = 35.05). When the minimum value from those 2,000 crankshafts is 34.91 mm and the maximum value is 35.12 mm, we can see that the diameter of some of the crankshafts is outside the tolerance limits, and therefore there will be some defective units.

Generally, defective units can be divided into two categories: rework and scrap. In the case of a crankshaft, the diameter can be reworked when the actual diameter of the crankshaft is outside the *upper* tolerance limits (greater than 35.05 mm). There is too much material, and it can be removed. When we speak of tolerances or of too much material in mechanical engineering or in electronics, we are describing a dimension comparable to a hair's width. But reworking a crankshaft means extra handling: extra time for adjusting the grinding machine, extra machining time, and extra operator time.

When the actual diameter of the crankshaft is outside the *lower* tolerance limits (less than 34.95 mm), the diameter of the crankshaft cannot be reworked. There is no practical way to add material back to the cylinder, so the whole part must be scrapped. It cannot be used in the assembly of an engine, and a new good part has to be produced to take its place. Scrap means the loss not only of the material needed for the production of the part but also of all other resources used in its production such as machine time, operator time, inspection time, logistics, and overhead. (In some cases the loss of scrap can be at least partially offset by recycling the material.)

Internal defects cause extra quality costs and are a loss for the company. This loss of production is lost capacity. Without the defects, this capacity would have used the same resources to produce more sales.

If a crankshaft outside the tolerance is assembled into the engine, and the engine is assembled into a car that is then sold to a customer, it can have an effect on the functioning of the car: excessive noise, higher gas consumption, or even breakdown of the engine. When this happens during the warranty period, the producer has to pay the warranty costs. In the case of the crankshaft, the warranty costs can be several hundred times higher than if the crankshaft had been properly inspected before assembly. In this case, inspection can save much warranty money for the company.

When inspection screens out the bad from the good, a great many bad units may be prevented from being shipped out or passed on to the next operation within the factory. However, because of human error and inaccuracy in testing equipment, inspection itself is not infallible. Thus, even inspecting 100 percent of the units still leaves a chance that bad units will be passed

along. Relying on inspection, there also can still be much variation between the tolerance limits, and thus we can expect variation in usage. Variation means lower durability or reliability. Therefore, we can still expect some warranty costs, although they will not be so high as when defective units are sold to the customer.

The initial step in improving quality is to prevent the occurrence of units outside the tolerance by bringing the manufacturing process within the tolerance (e.g., by adjusting the machine more frequently). Bringing the process itself under control so that the output of the process is within tolerance is a significant step in reducing variation. The benefits of this action are seen in reduced inspection costs, reduced warranty costs, higher reliability, and increased customer satisfaction.

At first glance it might seem that everything inside tolerance would be good and that inspection is a satisfactory method of control. But consider the engineer's thinking. The designing engineer has calculated that the *optimum* functioning of the shaft (reliability, durability, noise, etc.) requires the parameter—in this case, the diameter—to be at the specified value of 35 mm. Producing the shaft *at the specified value* rather than just somewhere between the tolerance limits is a way to reduce warranty costs and improve the reliability of the product. A part produced by processes with lower variation operates with less friction, runs more smoothly and more quietly, and requires less maintenance and repair, often leading to dramatically reduced warranty costs. That is the reason we strive both to ship products that are within the tolerances and to reduce the variation around the required parameters in the production process. The more we reduce the variation, the more we improve the interplay of the part with other parts in the engine. When we improve the critical components of the engine, we improve other parameters of the engine such as gas consumption, noise, durability, and reliability, and thus we increase customer satisfaction.

The rest of this chapter describes the most commonly used methods, tools, and techniques in quality improvement. (More details about these topics can be found in the references listed at the end of the chapter.) To follow a plan of quality improvement is to implement changes based on basic methods commonly used in modern industry worldwide. Some of the

tools can be used when gathering data (checklist, histogram), others when analyzing the data (normal distribution curve, Pareto, Ishikawa, process capability analysis, scatter diagram), another when planning improvement (flow chart), some for overviewing the product quality (acceptance sampling) or for monitoring the processes (statistical process control).

The tools work together. The data gathered in the checklist, for example, can be analyzed by the histogram and process capability analysis and then be plotted into the control chart. Pareto helps identify the vital problems that cause the greatest losses, and the Ishikawa diagram depicts the interrelation of possible causes. Some tools can be used at several phases of process improvement, from data gathering, through implementation, and finally to an overview of the improved process. An example is the flow chart, which can be used for description of the process before improvement, for comparing several options of process improvement, for outlining the steps to implementing changes, and finally for monitoring progress over time. In sum, the following quality tools are used to quantify potentials for improvement, to choose effective improvement actions, and to implement them.

Metrology

"Quality means conformance."[3] These are the words of the well-known quality expert P. B. Crosby. Conformance to the requirements is checked by measurement. The science of measurement—metrology—is an important tool for analysis and assessment in quality inspection and quality improvement. In ancient Egypt and Mesopotamia, measures and weights were controlled by the emperor to ensure standards in the trade of precious metals and oils.

Metrology is inevitable. Standardization is required when manufacturing uniform products in large quantities. Just imagine trying to use a battery that does not fit your Walkman or camera. Long ago, precision goods such as watches and rifles were produced without interchangeable parts. When rifles were handcrafted, the parts from one rifle would not fit another rifle. This was a hindrance to the army when repairing or maintaining rifles. By making standardization in manufacturing possible, metrology saves a tremendous amount of time and money. Such complex products as cars, with several thousand components, can be assembled at a very high daily rate from interchangeable parts manufactured throughout the world.

Today, international measurement standards are vital in manufacturing, not only for cars but for all goods (needles, screws and bolts, shirts, jackets, and shoes). Standardization is achieved by calibrating measuring and test instruments to international standards. When selecting a new supplier, a crucial quality question is whether the supplier's measuring and test equipment is regularly calibrated. The simple fact that the supplier inspects vigorously does not guarantee high-quality output. With poor tests, a poor product can be thought to be a good one and vice versa.

Checklist

Metrology provides us with various data to gather and document for analysis (See **Exhibit 13.3**). Data collection and processing are key elements of quality improvement. The checklist contains the collected data (for example, measurements of a monitored parameter) plus additional supporting data for identification such as date, time, location of measurement, and instrument used (see **Exhibit 13.4**). A checklist could be used for collecting data about the delivery problems of cars. Several categories of problems are listed, ranging from exterior or interior dirt, to paint problems and damaged or scratched plastic parts. The number of specific defects is documented each day (see **Exhibit 13.5**). This tool helps to document the data for further analysis by other quality improvement tools such as a Pareto diagram, histogram, scatter diagram, or control chart. In addition to recording the problems and their count, it is also important to record the date, time, model of car being checked, the number of cars checked, and the name of the person performing the checks.

Histogram

The collected data from a manufacturing process can be analyzed with a histogram. The histogram is a tool for presenting a large amount of measured data representing one phenomenon or parameter, for example, the age of employees or the diameter of a shaft produced on a turning machine (see **Exhibit 13.6**). The histogram depicts the distribution of the measured values and thus, in the case of the product parameter, depicts the results of the manufacturing process for that parameter (e.g., the machining or turning of the shaft) when the tolerances have been established.

Consider an example from mechanical engineering (See **Exhibit 13.7**). In designing a shaft, the engineer has set the tolerance limits for the diameter with an upper tolerance limit (UTL) of 18 mm and a lower tolerance limit (LTL) of 17.80 mm. This means that the tolerance for the diameter is 18 mm minus 17.80 mm, or 0.20 mm.

Exhibit 13.3: Organizational Data

Disorganized data...

...are hard to understand

Exhibit 13.4: Checklist: Example of Attributive Data

Checklist date: Sept. 3, 1995   Time: 12:30
Delivery problems

No.	Problem	Count
1	Dirt	ⅢⅡ ⅢⅡ
2	Paint	ⅢⅡ ⅢⅡ ⅢⅡ
3	Weak battery	ⅢⅡ ⅢⅡ
4	Engine noise	|||
5	Electro equipment	ⅢⅡ ⅢⅡ ⅢⅡ ||
6	Plastic parts	||
7	Others		

Exhibit 13.5: Checklist: Example of Measurement Data

CHECKLIST
Date: *Sept. 2, 1995*   **Time:** *10:32*
Part: *Shaft*   **Parameter:** *Diameter 18.0* $^{-0.2mm}$
Upper Tolerance Limit: *18.0mm*   **Upper Tolerance Limit:** *17.8mm*

Machine: *CM 2500 SX*   **Operation:** *Turning*
Measuring instrument: *Micrometer*   **Operator:** *Smith*

Note: Process capability study

No.	Values in: mm		
1.	17.95	No. of measurements	: 50
2.	17.9	No. defective	: 3
		% Defective	: 6
3.	17.85	Above tolerance	: 2
4.	18.05	% Above	: 4
5.	17.95	Below tolerance	: 1
6.	17.84	% Below	: 2
7.	17.97	Max: *18.05* Min: *17.78* Average: *17.92* Stand. dev.: *0.029* Range: *0.27*	

Exhibit 13.6: *Parameter Varies from One Unit to Another*

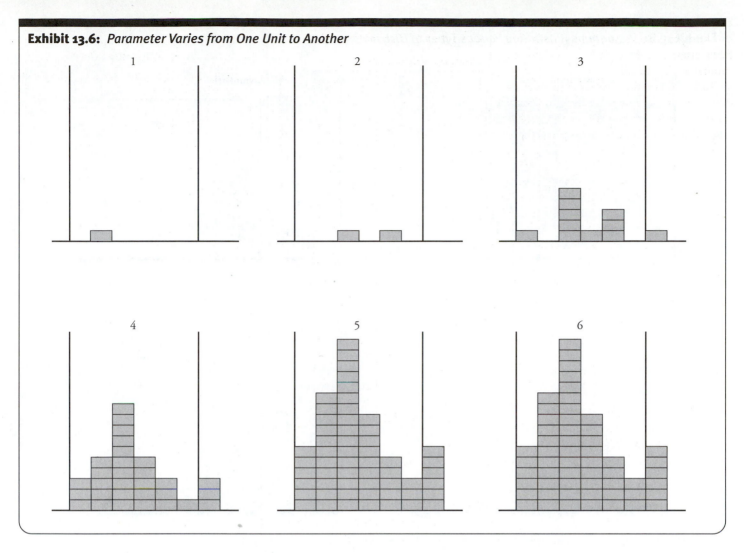

Exhibit 13.7: *Histogram*

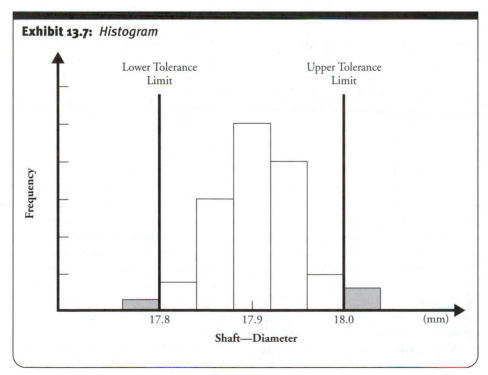

Anything produced outside the tolerance limits is unacceptable quality. In some cases, an unacceptable product can be reworked. When the diameter of the shaft is 18.10 mm, which is outside the tolerance, more material can be cut off. With this additional machining the quality of the product can be improved. However, as discussed in the crankshaft example earlier in the chapter, rework adds cost for extra inspection, transportation, manipulation, and machining of the shaft. Later, we will see that even when the parameters are within the tolerances, we can still improve the quality of the process to improve the quality of the product (See **Exhibits 13.8** and **13.9**).

The following is a simplified approach to constructing histograms:

1. Determine *k,* the number of intervals of the histogram. The number of intervals is computed from *n,* the number of plotted data, where *k* = square root of *n.* In most cases, the number of intervals will range from 5 to 20. There is no need to split the histogram into more

Exhibit 13.8: *Histograms Illustrating Various Types of Distribution*

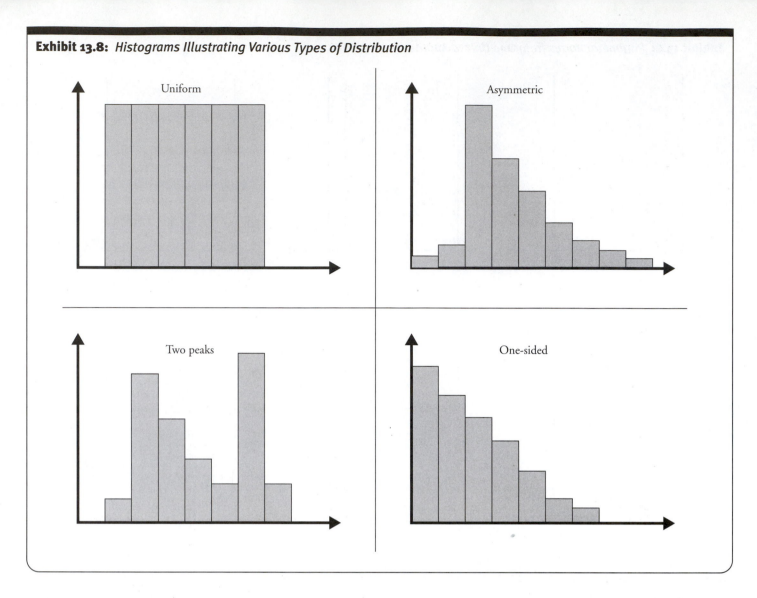

than 20 intervals. When *k* is below 5, which means there have been fewer than 25 measured values, there is little reason to present the data in a histogram.

2. Divide the range *R*, which is the difference between the maximum measured value and minimum measured value, into *k* intervals.

3. Plot the bar, with its height representing the number of measured values in that interval.

Normal Distribution

An additional step in analyzing the data in a histogram is to plot a curve that fits the data in the histogram (see **Exhibit 13.10**). Mathematical techniques are used to find the best curve for the measured and collected data. This curve is called the distribution curve.

One of history's most well-known mathematicians, K.F. Gauss (1777–1855), made

a significant contribution to applied statistics by introducing the normal distribution curve of a random variable as derived from his observations of nature. The model of normal distribution is one of the most frequently used models in statistical quality control (processing of measured values, statistical process control, acceptance sampling). A normal distribution curve has the peak at the middle value and is symmetric, with two inflection points creating a bell-shaped curve (see **Exhibit 13.11**). Values closer to the peak have a higher probability of occurrence than the more distant values. The area below the distribution curve expresses the probability that the given value comes from the given interval. For example the probability that the value comes from the interval $(-\sigma, +\sigma)$ is 1, meaning that 100 percent of all values are found in this interval. In practice the values in **Exhibit 13.12** are used. Refer to **Exhibit 13.13** for a graph of these figures. When

the distribution curve does not fit the histogram—as in **Exhibit 13.14**—another distribution model should be used.

Statistical Quality Control

The most important contribution of statistics to quality improvement was the method of control charts developed by W. A. Shewhart in 1924. He used statistics for mass and batch production. As mentioned earlier, at that time the lack of pressure from either customers or competition prevented quality improvement ideas from gaining any widespread attention. The most used methods of statistical quality control are acceptance sampling, process capability analysis, and statistical process control.

When units have already been produced and their quality needs to be checked, acceptance sampling might be used rather than 100 percent inspection, which can be

Exhibit 13.9: *Various Histograms (gray bars represent defective units)*

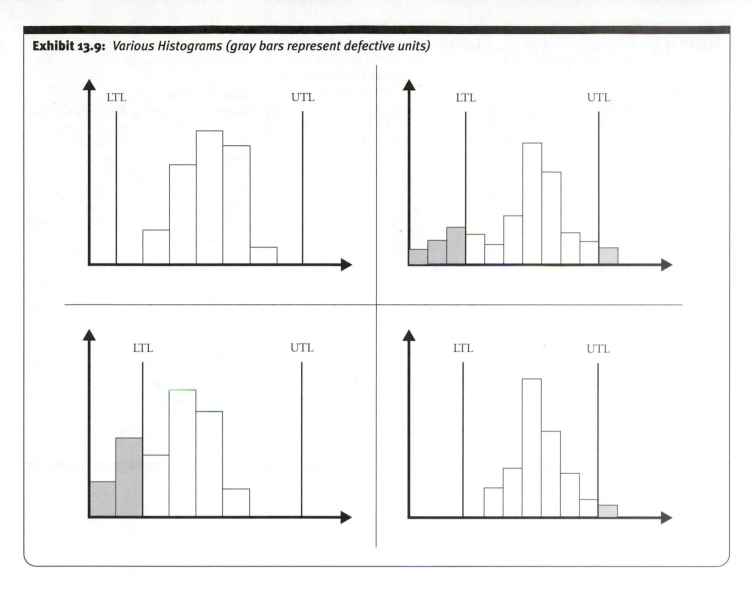

Exhibit 13.10: *Normal Distribution Curve (Model) That Fits the Real Sample (Histogram)*

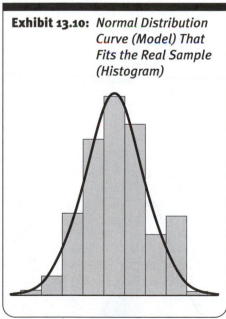

Exhibit 13.11: *Normal Distribution and Its Parameters*

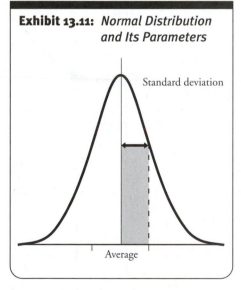

Exhibit 13.12: *Probability Values*

Interval	Probability	% of values
$\overline{X} \pm 1\sigma$	0.66	66
$\overline{X} \pm 2\sigma$	0.95	95
$\overline{X} \pm 3\sigma$	0.9973	99.73

toward process improvement by statistical process control.

Process capability analysis determines how capable the process itself is at bringing its output inside the tolerance (see **Exhibit 13.15**). Returning to the crankshaft example, we can consider whether the process is working within the tolerance. The answer is found by comparing the specified tolerances for a given parameter to the statistical characteristics of the process (process average, standard deviation, and so on). When analysis shows that the variation is very low compared to the tolerances and that the

expensive and time consuming. One of the uses of acceptance sampling is when one company buys components from another.

It might also be used between stages of a process within a plant. While acceptance sampling is considered an effective method of inspection, it does allow some poor quality to pass, so the emphasis today is more

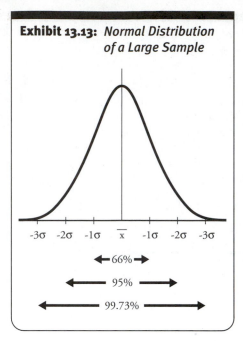

Exhibit 13.13: *Normal Distribution of a Large Sample*

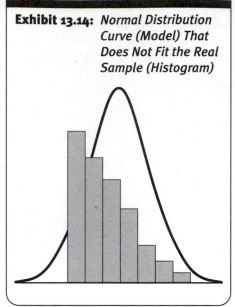

Exhibit 13.14: *Normal Distribution Curve (Model) That Does Not Fit the Real Sample (Histogram)*

process is well inside the limits and has low probability of defects, we can cease inspection. In addition, we often do not need to continue monitoring the process by statistical process control.

When the process generally works within the tolerances but there is still some certain probability of exceeding tolerance (for example, by wear of the grinding tool, breakage of the tool, temperature influences), statistical process control can be used. It warns us that we need to adopt some kind of corrective actions to tackle the problem (see Exhibit 13.15).

Acceptance Sampling

Consider the following situation: A company needs thousands of components to assemble products each day. Inspecting all of them will increase the inspection costs to a point that will make the product unsalable. Acceptance sampling helps to determine statistically what size of sample to select from an incoming lot and how many units from the sample have to pass the inspection to accept the whole lot (for example, a lot of 5,000 units, select 253 units; 251 of them must pass inspection to accept the whole lot). This is called the *acceptable quality level,* or AQL (2 of the units, 253–251, can be defective, and still the whole lot will be accepted; see **Exhibit 13.16**).

Some acceptance procedures may yield a decision to accept a lot with a specified number of defective units in the sample. Despite the defects, the whole lot is accepted. Other procedures require that all units

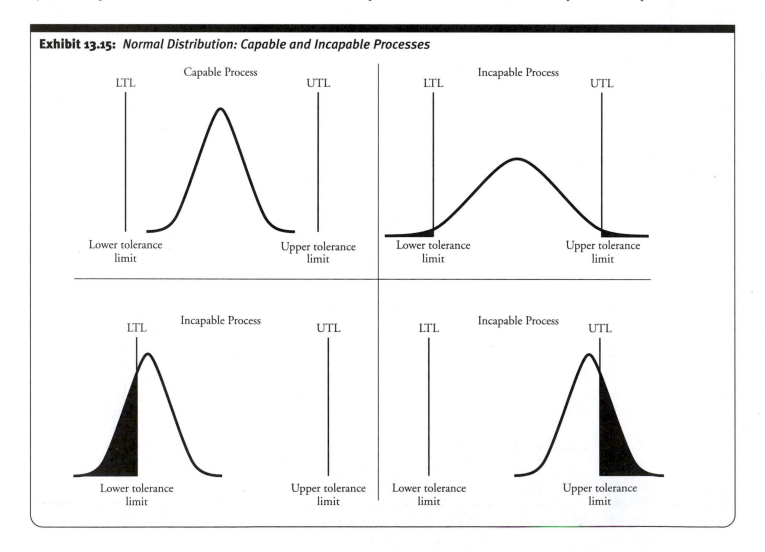

Exhibit 13.15: *Normal Distribution: Capable and Incapable Processes*

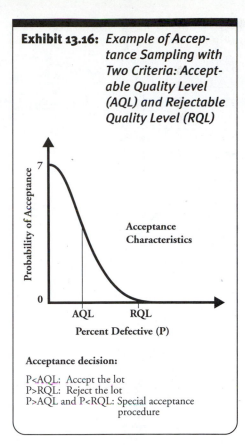

Exhibit 13.16: *Example of Acceptance Sampling with Two Criteria: Acceptable Quality Level (AQL) and Rejectable Quality Level (RQL)*

Acceptance decision:

P<AQL: Accept the lot
P>RQL: Reject the lot
P>AQL and P<RQL: Special acceptance procedure

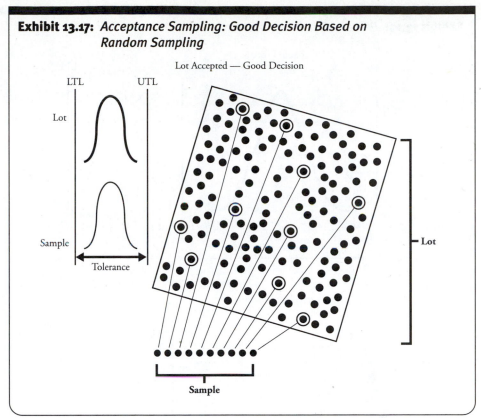

Exhibit 13.17: *Acceptance Sampling: Good Decision Based on Random Sampling*

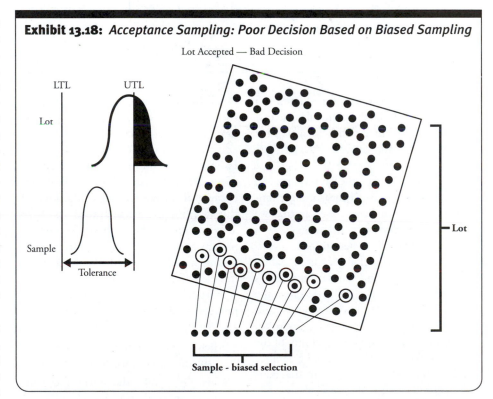

Exhibit 13.18: *Acceptance Sampling: Poor Decision Based on Biased Sampling*

from the sample pass the inspection before the whole lot is accepted. A major drawback in acceptance sampling is that the sample on which the decision is based could be biased, intentionally or unintentionally (see **Exhibit 13.17**). This might occur if there are practical reasons for the sample to consist of units that do not represent a truly random sample of the shipment, for example, if the inspected portion happens to be from the first cartons taken from the truck and those cartons happened to contain parts produced by one factory shift when there is a difference in results from shift to shift. In this case, a lot that does not meet requirements might be accepted based on the biased sample that could result in further costs down the line in manufacturing or later in warranty claims (see **Exhibit 13.18**).

Generally there is a tendency today not to tolerate *any* defects in the sample and, moreover, not to allow the philosophy that there can *be* any defective units in the incoming lot. For this reason, modern companies may reduce or discontinue acceptance sampling of incoming material, having the philosophy that the extra costs (inspecting the products or improving the process) should be covered by the supplier. The preferred philosophy today is to strive for "zero defects,"[4] which calls for fault-free production without scrap or rework.

Process Capability Analysis

Process capability analysis (PCA) determines how well the process is able to meet the required characteristics. For example, when machining a shaft, how well can the turning machine meet the required tolerances for the shaft's diameter?

The tolerance of a characteristic is defined by its limits (upper and lower) around the parameter. For example, the diameter of the crankshaft from our earlier example has the parameter (or nominal value) of 35 mm, a lower tolerance limit (LTL) of 34.95 mm, and an upper tolerance limit (UTL) of

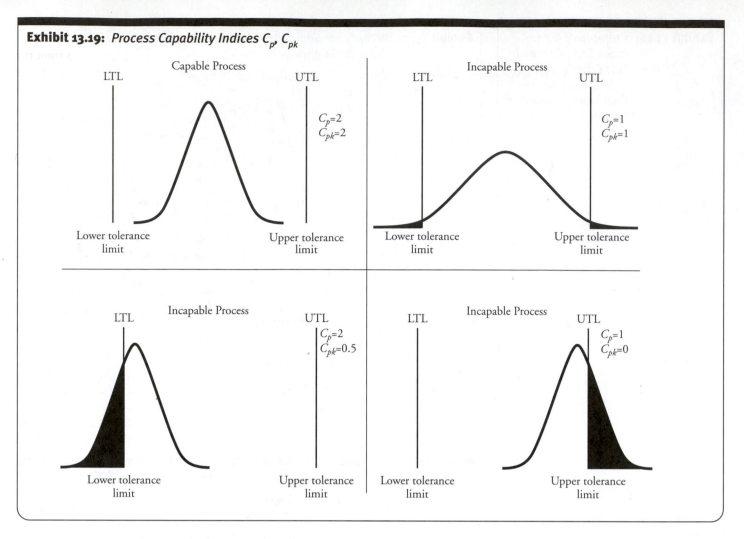

Exhibit 13.19: *Process Capability Indices C_p, C_{pk}*

35.05 mm. The tolerances for filling a soft drink bottle might be the nominal value of 1 liter, LTL of 0.95 liter, and UTL 1.05 liter. We can see that the characteristics of these parameters are measurable (i.e., there are instruments to measure the values expressed in numbers and units of measure like millimeters, grams, or liters). We say that we quantify the parameter by measuring it.

Process capability is determined statistically by evaluating the measured values where the averages and standard deviations (process variance) are computed against the tolerance. The smaller the variance is, and the better the process average fits the tolerance center, the greater the capability of the process to work within specified tolerance limits. Thus, the chance that defective products will occur is also smaller.

Two measures, C_p and C_{pk}, are commonly used. C_{pk} simply compares the standard deviation (the mathematical expression for process variation) and the average with the tolerance. When the index C_{pk} is greater than 1.33, we say that the process is capable of working within tolerances. When the value is above 2.00, the process is extremely

good. In simple terms, when the width of the curve that represents the process (the normal distribution curve) is within the tolerance limits, the process is *capable*. However, this condition might be satisfied without the process being within tolerance because of the positioning of the curve. In this case, we say that the process is *shifted*. The shift creates the difference between the process average (the peak of normal distribution curve) and the tolerance center (the middle point of the tolerance).

The index C_{pk} is used to evaluate the process in the following way (see **Exhibit 13.19**):

- When $C_{pk} < 1.33$, the process is not capable of working within tolerances.

- When $C_{pk} > 1.33$, the process is capable of working within tolerances.

- When $C_{pk} > 1.67$, there is no scrap or rework, and the costs of screening for defective units can be avoided.

One of the well-known applications of this index is the Six Sigma approach, a quality improvement philosophy from Motorola, which has the goal of achieving zero

defects. At this process capability there are only 3.4 ppm (parts per million) defective.[5] (See **Exhibit 13.20**.)

In practice the formulas and the criteria can vary slightly, and some additional measures can be used in implementation according to needs, habits, and computational possibilities. Process capability analysis should precede statistical process control. Generally speaking, the only processes that can be monitored and brought under control when disruptions occur (e.g., a broken tool, untrained operator) are those that have the capability of working within the tolerances.

Capability analysis is usually done so that the parameter is measured for several units (for example, 50 units). Based on a mathematical formula, the number of units needing to be measured per time period in order for the results to represent a given process is determined. The statistical characteristics are computed from measured values using a normal distribution. This is a common model for most processes such as machining parts, filling bottles, or packaging frozen pizza. The statistical char-

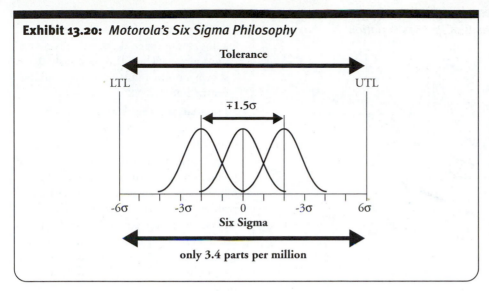

Exhibit 13.20: *Motorola's Six Sigma Philosophy*

Tolerance

LTL   UTL

$\mp 1.5\sigma$

-6σ   -3σ   0   -3σ   6σ

Six Sigma

only 3.4 parts per million

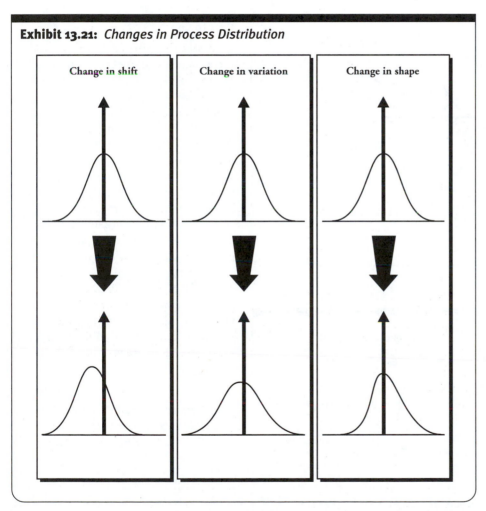

Exhibit 13.21: *Changes in Process Distribution*

Change in shift   Change in variation   Change in shape

acteristics are described by the standard deviation, which represents the process variation or the variance (square root of the process variation), and the average. For our purposes, it is important to know how far the average has shifted from the tolerance center. That is the reason we use the term "shift" in the Global *Marketplace* software (see **Exhibits 13.21** and **13.22**).

Statistical Process Control

Statistical process control (SPC) uses control charts to monitor processes and to indicate corrective actions (such as adjusting the machine or changing a tool) to reduce the defect rate (see **Exhibit 13.23**).

The control chart plots a statistical characteristic of a measurable parameter for a sample (for example, the average of

the shaft diameter; see **Exhibit 13.24**). One of the advantages of control charts is that only a small sample selected from the process (such as five products per hour) needs to be checked. Using mathematical formulas, it can be determined how large the sample size should be and how often the sampling should be done in order to monitor and control the process. Even small samples can uncover disruptions in the process and departures from the required nominal value set for the given parameter. This results in a considerable savings in inspection costs.

Control limits, which are tighter than tolerance limits (the engineering specifications), are used. The engineer specifies not only the diameter of the shaft, expressed by one number (e.g., 35 mm) but also the tolerance for the vital parameters. Tolerance expresses the range (i.e., 0.1 mm) that is an interval for the parameter acceptable for its proper functioning. The control limits are generally computed from the nominal value of the parameter (or from the tolerance limits) and statistical characteristics of the process (average, standard deviation). Before computing the control limits, process capability must be determined from information about past performance of the process. The control limits usually lie inside tolerance limits so they can warn us before defective product is produced. The purpose of setting control limits is to signal when the process may be out of control. This could be when the statistical characteristic falls outside the control limits or when some specific patterns within the control limits are observed. In simple terms, the tolerance limits are the specifications for the product (i.e., to fulfill a certain function—a shaft fitting into a hole or liquid filling a bottle to a given volume), and the control limits are specifications for the process that lead to fulfilling the requirement. However, it is important not only that the process does not exceed these limits but also how the process flows within control limits.

Examples of non-normal patterns (illustrated in **Exhibit 13.25**) that predict the occurrence of defective products are:

• **Trends.** The measurements of a characteristic are gradually increasing or decreasing and approaching in the direction of one of the control limits. There is a risk that the control limit, and then the tolerance limit, will be exceeded, indicating the risk of defective products.

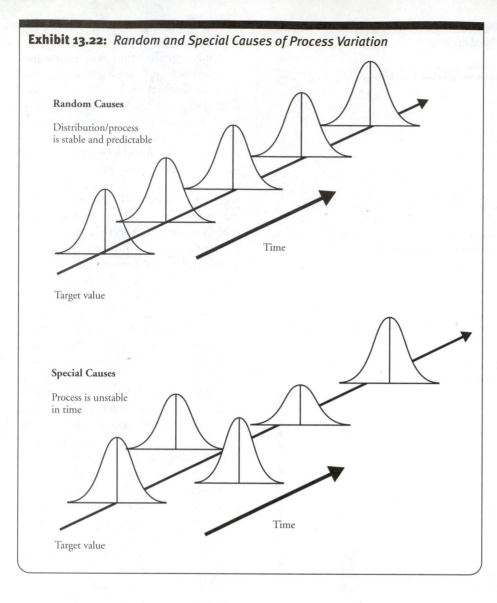

Exhibit 13.22: *Random and Special Causes of Process Variation*

Random Causes

Distribution/process
is stable and predictable

Time

Target value

Special Causes

Process is unstable
in time

Time

Target value

• **Runs.** Five or more values are in the same half of the control zone. This represents a nonrandom special cause that is changing a process which had previously shown a normal distribution around the central line.

• **Fluctuation.** The characteristic skips from one control limit to another and is close to the control limits.

These patterns help us to look for causes of quality problems, such as the wear of a tool, a broken tool, incorrect temperature control, or poor machine maintenance, and will allow corrective action to be taken, often even before the defective product appears. These patterns help us to be proactive, rather than reactive, to anticipate and prevent problems.

Pareto Chart

Even when improving a simple product, there is the question of where to start. The Pareto chart is a simple tool for setting priorities for selecting the most significant problems to address. Each bar of the graph represents one group or category of problem (e.g., electrical, mechanical, noise, dirt), and its height can express the number of problems or the financial losses caused by the specific problem. The categories are sorted in descending order, and there is also an increasing cumulative line, which represents the cumulative percentage of problems (see **Exhibit 13.26**).

Often 80 percent of all losses are caused by just 20 percent of all categories. This is called the *80/20 rule*. For quality improvement, this rule means that by focusing on just a few categories, significant improvement can be achieved. The chart can be

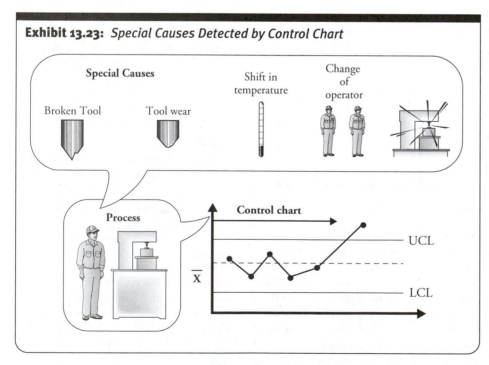

Exhibit 13.23: *Special Causes Detected by Control Chart*

Special Causes

Broken Tool   Tool wear   Shift in temperature   Change of operator

Process

Control chart

$\overline{X}$

UCL

LCL

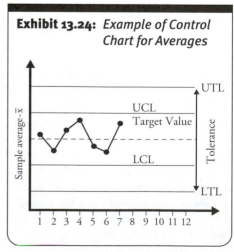

Exhibit 13.24: *Example of Control Chart for Averages*

Sample average-$\overline{x}$

UTL
UCL
Target Value
LCL
LTL

Tolerance

1 2 3 4 5 6 7 8 9 10 11 12

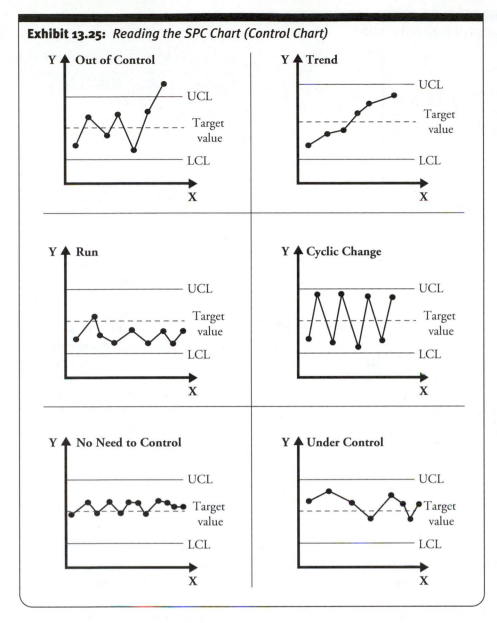

Exhibit 13.25: *Reading the SPC Chart (Control Chart)*

used to prioritize customer complaints from the field, defective components, problems with suppliers, defects on manufacturing equipment, and so on (see **Exhibit 13.27**).

A Pareto chart can be used to determine which critical components require the improvement. We can plot the warranty costs per component in descending order and clearly see which components' poor quality contributes to the burden of warranty costs.

Ishikawa Diagram

The Ishikawa Diagram is named for one of the pioneers of Japanese quality improvement, Dr. Kaoru Ishikawa. It is also called a *fishbone* or *cause-and-effect diagram* (see **Exhibit 13.28**). This tool analyzes the causes of a problem by organizing details into categories in a format that resembles fishbones. Only verbal descriptions of causes are used, and the implementation of the diagram can be for technical as well as nontechnical applications (service, administration, etc.). To be an effective tool, the diagram should be created by the individuals working in the process who have insight on factors affecting quality.

The Ishikawa diagram can be used when analyzing sources of variation. Let's return to the crankshaft example and consider the factors for improving the process of grinding the crankshaft. The problem of variation in the shaft's diameter might be due to various causes (pictured later in Exhibit 13.37), such as:

- Machine—excessive vibration of the machine.
- Man—different operators use different ways of adjusting the machine, resulting in variation of machine parameters.
- Material—use of the wrong grinding tool.
- Method—a poorly designed manufacturing process so that too much material is ground off in one operation, causing variation in the shaft's diameter.
- Miscellaneous—environmental influences such as fluctuation of temperature can cause variation in the grinding process.

In the Global *Marketplace* simulation, teams will find it useful to use the Ishikawa diagram for depicting the most vital actions for improving the variations of critical parameters, which lead to extra warranty or inspection costs.

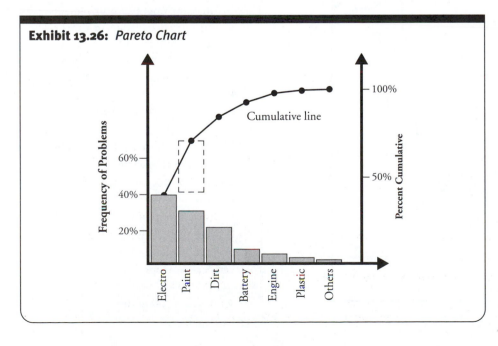

Exhibit 13.26: *Pareto Chart*

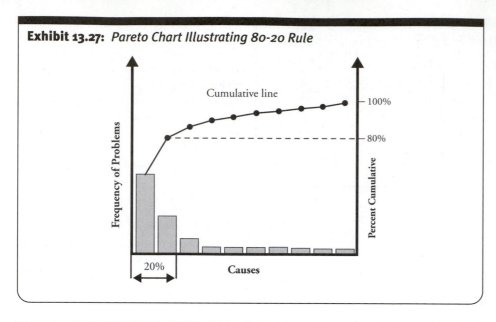

Exhibit 13.27: *Pareto Chart Illustrating 80-20 Rule*

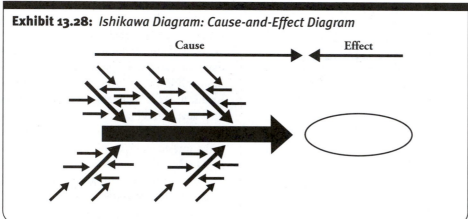

Exhibit 13.28: *Ishikawa Diagram: Cause-and-Effect Diagram*

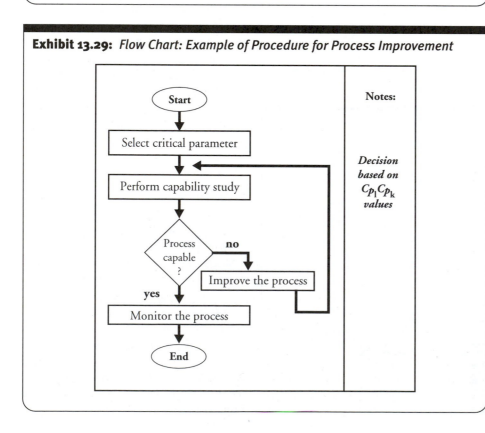

Exhibit 13.29: *Flow Chart: Example of Procedure for Process Improvement*

Flow Chart

A flow chart (**Exhibit 13.29**) clearly depicts the steps of a complex procedure, including the decision points. Such a chart is useful in programming as well as analyzing current processes, work descriptions, inspection procedures, quality manuals, maintenance manuals, error detection, and training of new personnel.

Scatter Diagram

Loose tolerances of fitting the crankshaft with other parts of the engine can cause excessive noise in the engine. When the processes leading to the shaft's parameters show less variation, there will also be less noise. The scatter diagram can depict the relationship of real measured data (e.g., the shafts coming from different processes with different variation and the noise of these shafts when built into the engine). The result of this diagram is the curve, which represents how the decreased variation helps to reduce noise. The experience from one parameter or one part can then be used when deciding how to improve the noise of another component.

This tool is also used to analyze the relationship between two variables such as dimension and temperature, truckload and gas consumption, or time of treatment and hardness of the coating. The relationship of the two variables, which is also called *correlation*, can be linear or nonlinear. There can also be little or no relationship between the variables (see **Exhibit 13.30**).

Quality Circles

This idea for quality improvement teams was introduced in Japan in the 1950s by Dr. Kaoru Ishikawa.[6] Quality circles (QCs) can be implemented at each workplace in the organization; 3 to 15 people gather and tackle issues such as:

- Defect reduction and quality improvement.
- Motivation and effective teamwork.
- Use of problem-solving techniques.
- Creation of an environment for problem prevention.
- Improved communication.
- Harmonized relationship between management and workers.
- Personal development and empowerment.
- Work safety and health.
- Cost savings.

Exhibit 13.30: *Scatter Diagram: Understanding the Correlation between Two Variables*

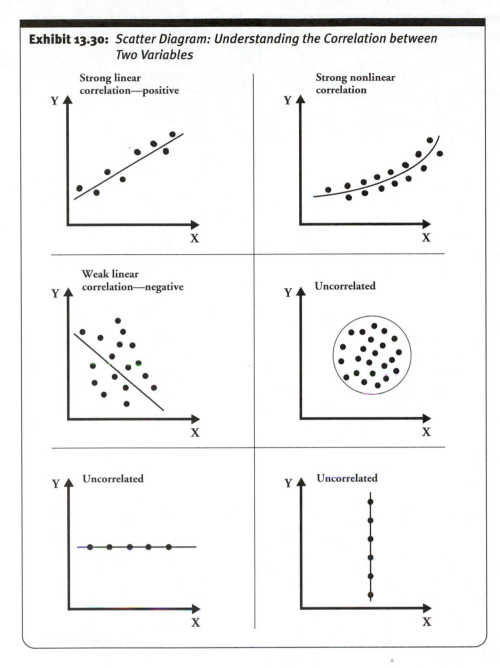

Quality circles use simple tools such as the Ishikawa diagram, Pareto charts, and histograms within the working process of:

• Problem identification.

• Problem selection.

• Problem analysis.

• Proposal and implementation of action.

• Presentation to the management.

Increased employee involvement is considered an important benefit of the QC. The Washino Machine Company in Japan had an average of 0.1 suggestions per employee per year in 1959. The QC activities started in 1983 resulted in 33.8 suggestions per employee and benefits of approximately $2,853 per person. Prizes were paid to the QC participants, averaging $92 per person.

Quality circles can be implemented on the shop floor level in manufacturing when quality improvement (variation reduction) is needed. Because the quality circle should deal with the problem from the perspective of the team's workplace, let us consider a case in the machine shop where the critical parameters of the crankshaft are being determined. The problem of high defect costs per crankshaft has been identified and has been attributed to the machine shop. The first step will be to build a team from the machine operators, inspectors, maintenance staff, and supervisors to improve the process. The goal of the team is to implement actions that lead to variation reductions so that the defect rate will fall. The team will first gather the data, which will show in a checklist what the defect rate is for each machine (or type of machine) in the shop. Then the data are presented in a Pareto chart so that the machines that cause the most problems can be determined. The 80-20 rule of Pareto charts says that often 80 percent of problems are caused by 20 percent of the factors. In this case, from 21 types of machines, 3 machines are causing 78 percent of the defect costs. An Ishikawa diagram is then used to pinpoint the causes of the high defect rate on those machines.

The team analyzes the causes and decides on a course of action (e.g., training operators in preventive maintenance or implementing statistical process control). The recommendations are then presented to management and responsible staff, along with the action plan, implementation dates, and the budget needed. The management proceeds cautiously to change practices with just one type of machine, approving a pilot project based in part on cost benefit analysis. After demonstrating benefits first from the most critical machine, the managers then decide to use the experience from the pilot project, assigning the members of the pilot team to start the project also for other critical machines. The teams are given the responsibility to implement the proposed actions as well as to monitor the installation of new machines. This helps ensure that when implementing a new technology, the old problems will not be repeated and preventive actions can take place. All new personnel are trained in the quality improvement tools and included in the quality circle activities. Specific follow-up dates are set when the best teams present their results to the management and are commended by the top management. The daily task of the teams then becomes not only manufacturing the planned units but also finding ways to reduce the variation of all processes—those not only of machining but also of logistics, waste disposal, storage, and so on.

QUALITY IMPROVEMENT STEPS

The ultimate goal of improving quality is to achieve higher customer satisfaction. Thus, quality improvement today goes far beyond inspecting the product; it seeks to detect the possibilities for improvement of processes. Moreover, the term "customer" no longer means just the end user of the product; it now includes any other external

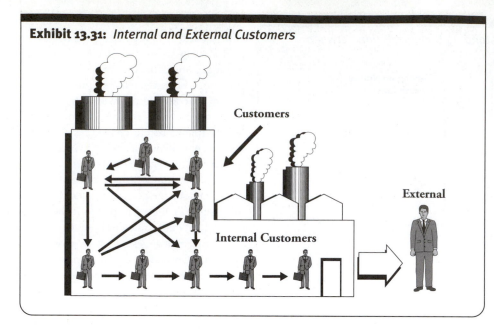

Exhibit 13.31: *Internal and External Customers*

Customers

External

Internal Customers

Exhibit 13.32: *Quality Improvement Steps*

- Analyze nonconformity
- Develop theories
- Test theories
- Identify cause
- Implement corrective action
- Evaluate effectiveness
- Monitor process

Exhibit 13.33: *PDCA Cycle*

Plan	Plan improvement: What is to be improved? Why improve it? How can it be improved? The steps of this stage are: • Problem definition • Problem analysis • Cause analysis • Planning of corrections This step uses the various quality improvement tools such as checklists, Pareto diagrams, histograms, Ishikawa diagrams, flow charts, scatter diagrams, etc.
Do	Select an action from the number of possible actions and implement it.
Check	Monitor to what extent the improvement leads to desired results. In this step control charts and statistics can be used. The good and bad side effects are listed.
Act	Develop preventive action so that the status before the improvement will not occur again. Action includes education, training, and review of the improvement process.

customers (such as dealers, salespeople, or service providers) and internal customers (the internal company departments) who are customers to each other. For example, manufacturing is the customer of the design department (see **Exhibit 13.31**). Thus, when we speak of quality improvement, we mean the improvement of all processes within the company—those that contribute directly to product quality such as design or manufacturing, as well as those contributing indirectly such as administration, training, or finance. This philosophy is generally described by the terms *continuous improvement* and *total quality management,* which mean that there is always room for improvement and for enhancing customer satisfaction, and that this improvement effort needs to extend to every process of the business.

Quality improvement is not just a random attempt to improve everything, regardless of importance. It is a thorough approach starting with analysis, proceeding to implementation, continuing with the evaluation of results, and becoming a continuous monitoring of processes (see **Exhibit 13.32**). This is why some companies speak of continuous improvement instead of quality improvement.

Let us discuss two approaches to quality improvement: the PDCA cycle[7] from the United States and the Japanese approach called *kaizen.*[8]

PDCA Cycle

This tool, also called the *Shewhart cycle,* represents the four steps of quality improvement. PDCA stands for plan, do, check,

and act, a never-ending process of improvement where action is followed by new planning (see **Exhibits 13.33** and **13.34**). To illustrate the PDCA cycle, let us look back to our quality circle example and see how the process was followed.

Plan

The problem of high defect costs per crankshaft was identified and attributed to the machine shop. The goal was established for the team to implement actions leading to variation reductions so that the defect rate would fall. The team gathered the data and made a checklist showing the defect rate for each machine in the shop. The data were presented in a Pareto chart, pointing out the machines that caused the most problems. An Ishikawa diagram pinpointed causes of the high defect rate on problem machines. The team analyzed the causes, decided which actions were the most important, and presented their recommendations to management.

Do

The pilot project was implemented.

Check

The results, including cost benefit analysis, were presented to management. Managers decided to use the experience from the pilot project and had the pilot team start the project for other critical machines.

Act

The teams were given the responsibility of implementing proposed actions and monitoring the installation of new machines,

helping to ensure that the old problems would not be repeated. New personnel were trained in the quality improvement tools and brought into quality circle activities. Follow-up dates were set. The best teams presented results to management and were commended. The daily task became manufacturing the planned units as well as finding ways to reduce the variation of all processes.

Kaizen

Kaizen is a Japanese word meaning continuous improvement with the involvement of

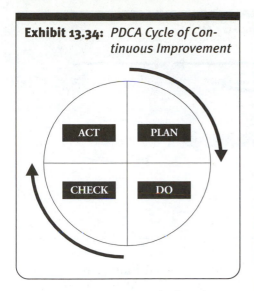

Exhibit 13.34: *PDCA Cycle of Continuous Improvement*

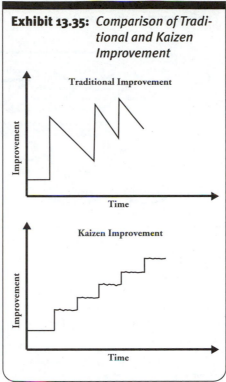

Exhibit 13.35: *Comparison of Traditional and Kaizen Improvement*

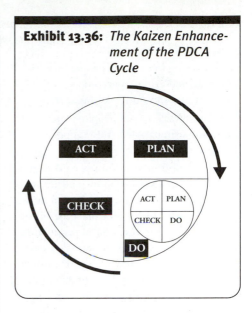

Exhibit 13.36: *The Kaizen Enhancement of the PDCA Cycle*

everyone in the company: the board, managers, and all employees. It is a synonym for process-oriented thinking. By contrast, results-oriented Western approaches to improvement proceed in big steps with big results, which usually do not last very long.

The philosophy of kaizen is that improvement of product quality can come only from improved processes, and thus the legacy is "No day without any improvement in the company." Improvement is done in small steps on a continuing basis, as contrasted to the Western rush for dramatic improvements based on big investments (see **Exhibit 13.35**). Japanese companies try to build quality into their processes. The process orientation of managers can be seen in areas such as discipline, time utilization, work morale, and communication.

The philosophy of kaizen is connected with the approach of total quality management, where the interests of other quality related issues can be seen:

- Quality assurance
- Cost reduction
- Delivery times
- Work safety
- Design of new products
- Improvement of productivity
- Relations with suppliers

Kaizen is based on the PDCA cycle, but it improves on the cycle by including another cycle inside the Do step. This means that the worker who performs the Do step is capable of improvement within this step by adopting the PDCA cycle within the step. The workers are empowered to make their own decisions and not to wait for management orders on how to do it. In other words, the goals are compulsory, but the methods are optional. When management decides on methods and implementation needed for daily improvement, it is then also responsible for the results, and the motivation of the workers falls considerably. In the Do step, which can be aimed toward improvement of the workplace layout, the worker performs planned activities and tries to analyze the workplace, devising her own ideas on how to better maintain the place and the machine for quality work. This speeds up the feedback for improvement in the workplace because generally the Plan and Act steps are performed by management, the Check step by management, and inspection and the Do step by the worker.

For improving in small steps using kaizen, the so-called SDCA cycle (where "S" stands for standardize) is implemented. This is a step where the attained quality, procedures, and new processes are stabilized and become the base for the next improvement. The role of management is then to harmonize the interaction of PDCA and SDCA cycles (see **Exhibit 13.36**).

In order to be able to proceed without waiting for a check from management, workers are empowered to both decide and set a standard by which they will perform the daily maintenance of the manufacturing equipment and to determine what kind of tools they will use. They record this on checklists that help them perform quick checks of how well the workplace is prepared to achieve the defined goals. An example of this could be a checklist that helps to monitor the cleanliness of the work area where subassembly of the car braking system takes place. The checklist covers the specific requirements for the protection of parts during transportation, cleanliness of storage boxes, cleanliness of the place when the subassembly is complete, environmental influences such as dust and air ventilation, cleanliness of the rework areas, and so on. When the requirements for the specific processes are standardized by putting them on paper (by defining criteria for each critical process step), then progress can be monitored on a regular basis and data for future improvement can be obtained.

The kaizen approach is based on five principles:

- **Order (*seiri*).** Identify the important issues and get rid of the unimportant.
- **Each tool at the right place (*seiton*).** In order not to waste time looking for the tools, documents, parts, and materials needed for the work.
- **Cleanliness (*seiso*).** Keep the workplace clean.
- **Individual order (*seiketsu*).** Start with yourself, with cleanliness and order.
- **Discipline (*shitsuke*).** Keep to the procedures prescribed for the workplace.

Kaizen activities are supported by teaching thorough questioning of six basic sets of questions— Who? What? Where? When? Why? How?—and by a simple checklist by which all people in the company can improve their processes. The aim of the kaizen approach is to identify

- Waste (*muda*)—of people, materials, machines, time, space, tools, opportunities, product volumes, etc.
- Overloading (*muri*)—of people, materials, machines, time, space, tools, opportunities, product volumes, etc.
- Deviation (*mura*)—of people, materials, machines, time, space, opportunities, product volumes, etc.

A great deal of attention is paid to discovering special signs—abnormalities such as oil leaks, excessive vibration, or loose bolts—in order to prevent machine breakdown and thus interruption of production, capacity loss, and other unnecessary costs. During the training of the machine operators, the relationships among failures, improper operating procedures, and poor maintenance are stressed. Contrast this philosophy to the practice and the commonly used slogan in U.S. companies: "Operators make it, maintenance fixes it."

Kaizen Example from Toyota

The improvement program at Toyota[9] focuses on seven categories of waste:

1. Overproduction.
2. Waiting imposed by an inefficient work sequence.
3. Conveyance inessential to a smooth, direct workflow.
4. Processing workpieces more than they require.
5. Inventory in excess of immediate needs.
6. Motion that does not contribute to work.
7. Correction necessitated by defects.

Employees on assembly lines were spending much time reaching for screws to insert in multiple holes in their workpieces. Toyota devised a simple dispenser that deposits exactly the needed number of screws into an employee's hand when he pulls upward on a release at the bottom of the dispenser.

And the Final Joke about Kaizen

Three businessmen—French, Japanese, and American—find themselves in the midst of a revolution. The revolutionaries sentence them to a firing squad but give each of them one last wish. The Frenchman asks that he be allowed to sing a final chorus of "La Marseillaise." The Japanese asks to give a final lecture on kaizen. That proves too much for the American, who breaks down and pleads, "Please, please,

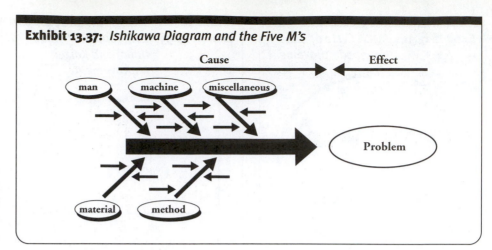

Exhibit 13.37: *Ishikawa Diagram and the Five M's*

shoot me first! I can't stand to hear another lecture on kaizen."

This is just a joke; the real experience from Japanese companies is that where there is not enough kaizen, there is not enough improvement.[10]

OUTCOMES IN THE BUSINESS ENVIRONMENT

Product quality can be jeopardized during almost any manufacturing stage. Therefore, resource allocation is a must in any quality improvement program. This section illustrates (1) how some quality improvement tools can be used to identify possibilities for improvement of poor quality and (2) the necessity to pay attention to the details, which can be crucial for success or failure in the market. Also following are arguments for the process orientation to developing quality products. An overview of quality-related costs is presented, followed by two stories illustrating how quality improvement makes money and strengthens the company's position in the market.

Origin of Poor Quality

Where does poor quality come from? In one approach to quality improvement (known as the *Juran trilogy*),[11] poor quality is tracked to the quality planning stage, where poor planning causes chronic waste in scrap and rework. (Juran described the interrelatedness of quality planning, quality control, and quality improvement.) The Juran approach asserts that nonoptimal processes are planned (e.g., machines are utilized outside optimal capacities due to planned scrap and rework, extra costs for inspection, and rework due to the high variations in processes). This

waste is a potential for quality improvement, which should be reviewed on a continuing basis.

One of the tools for describing the origin of poor quality is the Ishikawa diagram, illustrating what is known as the Five M's: material, machine, man, method, and miscellaneous (see **Exhibit 13.37**):

- Material—incoming material or parts from suppliers, material flow.
- Machine—breakdown of a machine, maintenance of a machine, adjustment of the machine.
- Man—skills, knowledge, training, personality, health, motivation.
- Method—manufacturing procedures, inspection, design, organization of the company.
- Miscellaneous—environmental influences, competition, costs.

This approach can help in the search for sources of variation in manufacturing. One source of variation can be use of product in different environments, such as driving a car in different weather or environmental conditions. Deterioration of a product can also cause the quality of the product to vary significantly—tire wear influences the car's drivability and maneuverability and can cause the car to become unsafe.

In the past, poor quality was looked for in manufacturing. Today, poor quality is looked for more upstream, in the design phase, where the products, the parameters of the products, and the appropriate manufacturing processes are designed. In the past, workers were blamed for poor quality. Now more and more companies understand that poor quality is the result of poor processes. Poor quality is a sign that the systems that create the processes must be changed.

Interrelatedness of Elements

A product is the sum of its components and the relationships among them. Sometimes poor quality, even of one component, can influence a customer's decision about buying the product. An example of such an influence in a purchase decision could be a personal computer in which a faulty capacitor in the power adapter makes the entire computer useless for the customer.

There may be other deficiencies in components that are critical in some way. Supplier shortages can cause inadequate quantities of material being delivered, thus creating a temptation to utilize inferior material rather than halt the manufacture of products that can be immediately sold.

Recalls are nightmares in the car industry. One small defective screw in a safety part such as an airbag can cause a huge product recall action. All airbags would need to be checked to replace a part that costs only a small fraction of what the product recall would cost. Customers have to be located, rework from the dealer is much more costly than at the plant, and usually the customers are offered additional services, such as free gasoline, a car wash, or a replacement car. On the other hand, not doing a recall because of some "small problem" can lead to loss of image and lawsuits.

Mechanical parts, such as instrument controls or the wheels and gears of feeding mechanisms in copiers, scanners, printers, or fax machines, are prone to wear out. Worn parts increase the usage variation of the product until finally the machine cannot be turned on or the paper jams in the copier. The mechanical parts then need to be replaced during maintenance. Another approach, however, is to anticipate this deterioration due to usage and prevent the usage variation by designing the parts from better materials or to tighten the tolerances of mechanical parts so that the parts work and cause less wear. In fact, reducing tolerances is synonymous with improving the manufacturing process. Products coming from those processes have lower variation, fit better, and last longer.

Products can also be designed in such a way that they are cost effective for production—that is, they might be easy to assemble but very difficult to disassemble when rework is needed. Bad design in a home appliance might involve one simple part, such as a fuse, being located at an inaccessible spot. Just the regular cleaning of the machine or appliance can mean complicated disassembly and reassembly of the product. This is, of course, not a customer-friendly product.

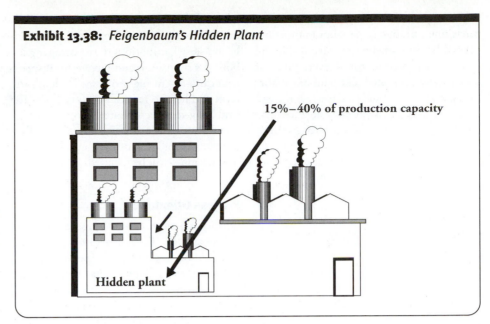

Exhibit 13.38: *Feigenbaum's Hidden Plant*

15%–40% of production capacity

Hidden plant

Manufacturing

Inferior manufacturing and failure to keep up with proper operations procedures can lead to problems such as weak batteries or dirt in the gas tank and eventually to product failure, when the customer is faced with a dead car on the road. Using old lubricants can cause excessive noise in a machine; a change in the glue concentration could result in window seals not surviving a hot summer or next winter's freezing weather.

Absenteeism in manufacturing can be devastating for a company, not only because of capacity loss but also because of quality problems introduced by untrained temporary employees. In the United States, the resulting faulty cars are called "FM cars"—made on Fridays or Mondays. The defect rate is often correlated with the absenteeism rate.

The poor quality of one component, or even of one parameter of that component, often does not stay isolated but influences other components or operations during manufacturing; then the losses due to one inferior operation, if not quickly detected and reworked, can be multiplied by another operation. Even rework that has been done well can negatively influence the quality of the whole product. Poor paint on a car might be attributed to bad logistics. If the edges of the metal sheet have been damaged during handling on the shop floor, then when the sheet goes to the press, chips from sheet edges damage the press die, causing surface defects on the car body. After the press shop and welding, the car body is reworked because of poor surface quality. The rework is done at high cost by paying a skilled staff to smooth and grind the car body. The results could look smooth until the coated car body comes through the paint shop oven, where the reworked surface changes its structure under the heat. Paint rework follows, this time requiring special materials and processes. Even after successful paint rework, customers might later experience differences in fading of colors in the car body. During an especially cold winter, the reworked paint may chip off when the car doors are being closed.

In Japanese car plants metal sheets in the press shop are stored in plastic tents after the first cutting operation to keep the metal free of dust and dirt that may cause poor quality in the next operation. The operators who touch the sheets and pressed parts wear clean textile gloves, instead of the leather gloves typically used in plants.

The bottom line for deficiencies is that the company loses money. A. V. Feigenbaum, writing about the philosophy of total quality control, has said that if capacity losses of 15 to 40 percent are estimated, losses can be seen as the equivalent of having another plant hidden inside the real one.[12] (See **Exhibit 13.38**.) A big capacity loss occurs when poor products need to be scrapped. The money paid for the materials and labor producing this product is lost, and extra money is needed to scrap the product (storage, transportation, etc.). The scrapping of some parts can be a complicated procedure, which also costs extra money.

For example, when the car airbag module needs to be scrapped, special procedures are needed because of the explosive inside the module, which could cause severe injury if accidentally detonated. For temporary storage, special metal boxes are used, and these require storage in a segregated area to avoid incidental damage to good airbags. Even the rework of poor product is a complicated matter requiring special equipment and experienced, highly paid employees.

Resource Allocation

Where is the best place for a business to put its money when quality improvement is needed? Should it be invested in inspection, new equipment, or training? It is impossible to improve everything at once, especially when the business is just starting out. Improvement costs money, time, and resources. Buying sophisticated automatic instruments for inspecting 100 percent of incoming screws would be false economy, and it would not guarantee having no defective screws in assembly. The screws might arrive at the plant in good shape but collect dirt or be damaged in the plant. Inspection of 100 percent of incoming parts would be expensive; even in manufacturing a space shuttle, this money could always be put to better use.

If you are a manager or planning to become a manager, you might wonder if you will need to know how quality improvement works. Certainly, there are many consultants who will be glad to analyze quality problems for you. Often external consultants will charge a high fee to tell you what you and your staff already know. Ask, and you will see how many good ideas come from those who work on the line each day.

Even the training people from the best universities or training institutes can be counterproductive, or at least inefficient, in use of time and resources when there is no motivation for improvement and implementation, when the critical components of the product and their critical processes are not identified, or when problem solving and implementation do not follow the training.

The Japanese quality guru, Taguchi, compared quality improvement to buying real estate. When buying a house, realtors say there are three things to consider: location, location, and location. Taguchi says that when you are improving quality, there are also three important things to consider: cost, cost, and cost. By this he meant that

when allocating the resources for quality improvement, we should proceed cautiously and see what it brings to the company in both the short term and long term. Inspection can prevent big problems in the short term and help to reduce warranty costs. To find long-term economies, careful investment in variance reduction—analyzing the process capability and tackling the sources of variation—will be required.

Process Orientation

Quality is a must. It is no longer a differential advantage. Today, customers take for granted both the technical aspects of quality, safety, and reliability that they require and appreciate and the "soft" aspects of quality, like the handling of individual needs, prompt delivery of product, and after-sale service. Many of those activities were introduced not because of customer requirements but because of competition. Today the stimulus for quality improvement comes from the plans and strategic decisions of competition rather than directly from the customers.

Naturally, customers want the delivered product or service to satisfy their needs, and they also expect surprise, delight, and fulfillment of unexpected needs. Until very recently, quality activities have been oriented towards the *product*. The rules were simple: A product was good or it was bad. Today the orientation of quality improvement is more toward the *process*. Companies adopting a process orientation philosophy used to argue that there was some acceptable poor product from a good process rather than some good products from a poor process. If a process does not yield zero defects, it is now seen as a process with a potential for improvement. That is the reason in this chapter and in the *Marketplace* simulation there is emphasis on process variance as the important measure of quality. The reduction of variation in all processes (manufacturing processes, as well as design, marketing, after sale, and so on) is the basis that leads to the improvement of product quality.

The time management concept of discerning between *urgent* and *important* activities is similar to the difference between *product* and *process* orientation.[13] How can a company have good products when the managers are neglecting process improvement and working only on urgent problems—that is, fire fighting? In the long

run, the important thing is the process orientation.

According to renowned management consultants,[14] there are two things in the company to manage: the control of processes and the improvement of processes. This approach marks a shift of attention from the quality of a product to the performance of a process. Until there is an attempt to identify and eliminate the root causes of variation, the processes cannot improve. This approach, called *minimalism*, is concerned with eliminating disruptions to processes. For process improvement, information about departures from expected behavior is needed. This could be provided by tools such as checklists for gathering data, histograms, Pareto charts, Ishikawa diagrams, and control charts for presenting the data. Effort would then be focused on disruptions and things gone wrong. While we can, of course, start improving everything, it would be more pragmatic to start with Pareto charts to point out the most critical factors. Then more information would be gathered about the causes of those disruptions. We would not need to have complete information on what is already sufficient in our manufacturing because it would be a tremendous amount of data, but we would need to have precise information about those things we want to improve. Just fiddling with the process can make the process worse. As an example, there is a saying about using a thermostat: "Leave a window open and the thermostat will turn the furnace on more frequently. It will not, however, close the window, or even call attention to the fact that the window is open."[15]

An example of process orientation from the automobile industry is shown in the rework areas off the assembly line, where defective cars (because of missing parts, paint problems, poor fitting, or electrical and other functional problems) are repaired. Those areas require much space in manufacturing plants, a highly skilled work force, and complicated logistics. They have been viewed as a necessary evil. When a group of manufacturers from the United States visited the new plant of a Japanese manufacturer, they were surprised to find that the rework area was almost nonexistent. Clearly, the process orientation was contributing to process improvement from the early stages of product life (i.e., from the product and process design stages).[16]

The goal of improving processes is that every unit should be as close to its target, customer requirement, or specification as possible. In manufacturing, quality can deteriorate as a result of variation in materials or in process parameters such as grinding speed, pressing force, operator variation, and so on. Thus, process orientation has two primary objectives in terms of variation reduction: a stable process and a capable process.

- An unstable process changes in time—the average changes or the variation changes. The process is hard to predict and to control, and sporadic spikes may occur. For detecting poor quality, a sampling inspection is required.
- A stable process—the average variation does not change, and the process is predictable and easier to control than the unstable process. A stable process, however, does not necessarily mean a capable process (i.e., within the tolerances or specifications).
- A capable process does not change, is predictable, and works within the tolerances or specifications.

Role of Management

Managers too often do not support quality improvement, or they give it their half-hearted support. One of the reasons is that they see process capability analysis and other methods as additional demands for resources (that is, for money). There is a need to present quality improvement to management in terms of potential savings. How much are we losing when we pay suppliers and rework staff for defective products? How much could we lose if customers throughout the country file warranty claims? Quality improvement can also be presented in terms of its benefits for productivity, as in **Exhibit 13.39**; what is saved by decreasing internal defects, material costs, rework, logistics costs, and so forth when we reduce variation in the process? In one year, the Automotive Electrical Division of ITT Hancock Industries Group achieved a 70 percent reduction in quality costs in its Mexican plant while decreasing its scrap 79 percent.[17]

Quality improvement has to be expressed by financial data, but it means far more than reduced warranty costs, scrap, and rework. Quality improvement also improves human relations. When the people at the shop floor level feel that their ideas are appreciated and contributing to the success of the company, they unleash

Exhibit 13.39: *Deming Chain*

Improved quality

↓

Improved productivity

↓

Reduced costs

↓

Competitive price

↓

Increase market share

↓

Stay in business

↓

Provide more jobs

the tremendous reservoir within themselves that is the base of kaizen (or continuous improvement in small steps). Successful companies know that to improve quality, they need to provide a challenging workplace for all of their employees. They need to develop opportunities to match the abilities of each of their employees. When we consider the interrelatedness of defects or poor quality, such as in the example of damaged metal sheets ultimately influencing customer satisfaction, we can only agree with P. Crosby, who said, "Quality is free."[18] What is not free is scrap, rework, and dissatisfied or lost customers.

Quality improvement methods and tools are not limited to manufacturing. They are also useful for services such as banking, health care, and even the government.[19] These services all have customers, including many internal customers, and all processes are candidates for improvement.

Sometimes people say that only Japanese companies are capable of tremendous quality improvement, but there are many examples of quality improvement successes in non-Japanese companies, even in car manufacturing. When MIT studied quality and productivity among world car manufacturers, it found that knowledge is transferable and applicable outside Japan and Japanese plants.[20] An example of this is the Ford plant in Hermosillo, Mexico, where top results (even better than in the best Japanese plants) in lean manufacturing, quality, and productivity have been achieved.

The role of management in quality improvement can be judged by the philosophy of kaizen:[21] "If management is for total quality, poor quality is a sign of poor management." This is a new way of thinking that can engender resistance among clerical staff as well as management. The role of management here is to show which direction to go and to provide the vehicle for getting there. The vehicle is not only the money for the project but also training in modern quality improvement methods and tools, personal commitment when defining the quality improvement project, working at and taking care with the project, and showing interest in staff participation in quality improvement. Quality improvement should be a daily priority for management, not just a once or twice a year conference topic. Managers must see the danger of a hidden plant that steals capacity from the plant they are running and must see the proportion of resources needed for quality and customer satisfaction.

Quality Costs

Quality cost can be seen as the total cost attributed to poor quality, which burdens the end user or the manufacturer. In short, the cost of quality is the expense of doing things wrong. Production managers are misdirected if they complain that the expenses of quality management (costs of testing, training, and prevention) just increase the product price and delay delivery to the customer. This section of the chapter seeks to show that quality improvement and prevention are needed to reduce overall quality costs. Quality costs can be viewed as arising in three categories of activities: failures (external), appraisal, and prevention (internal) (see **Exhibit 13.40**).

Internal failure results in scrap, for example when a poor part or subassembly is detected in the company but cannot be reworked. Once the text of a book is printed with poor contrast and poor sharpness of characters, for example, the sheets of paper will have to be scrapped and new sheets ordered for reprinting the book. Only a tiny fraction of the cost of the scrapped paper can be offset by recycling the paper. Rework adds costs when extra effort is needed to achieve the required quality. When there is dirt in the car paint, it can be reworked by grinding off the old coatings and applying all the necessary layers again, treating the paint in the oven or

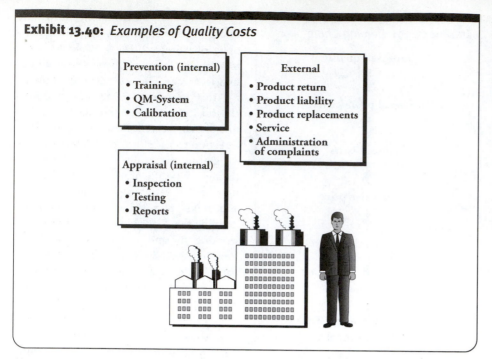

Exhibit 13.40: *Examples of Quality Costs*

Prevention (internal)
- Training
- QM-System
- Calibration

Appraisal (internal)
- Inspection
- Testing
- Reports

External
- Product return
- Product liability
- Product replacements
- Service
- Administration of complaints

with special rework heating equipment. All in all, rework requires more money than the original process because of extra time, material, equipment, staff, and special skills. The same applies for services such as hair styling. Another cost is from lost production or lost capacity for production of goods that could be sold but were not because of poor material, parts, subassemblies, or services from other divisions or suppliers. The cost connected with internal failures and troubleshooting can be added to those for reinspection and repeated testing of reworked items.

External costs arise when poor quality is detected once the product or service is sold to the customer. Product liability costs include claims that the manufacturer is responsible for covering—such as the free repair or replacement of defective products and the costs for returned products. In order to stop the spread of repeated defects, the product should be recalled, adding extra costs, including the cost of complaints to customer service staff and management. A recall action, which is necessary for safety or health reasons, can bring financial disaster to the company.

Appraisal costs to stop the delivery of defective products and to minimize the processing of defective materials, parts, or subassemblies are also part of quality costs. These can be for inspection and testing equipment within the company or at the supplier's plant; staff for incoming inspection, manufacturing inspection, or final

inspection; and costs for data processing of inspection and test results. Appraisal must be independent. It must be able to select inferior quality regardless of the pressures of unmet demand or production targets.

Prevention costs are incurred for training people in quality improvement methods and to operate and maintain equipment. Performing quality system audits, building a quality system, writing manuals, and developing programs to reduce process variation using special methods in the design phase—all are seen as quality costs.

Inspection reduces the internal costs for scrap and rework and external costs for liability claims, but inspection has very limited capability. Prevention continues to reduce costs beyond the point where inspection cannot help.

Prevention costs, when effectively applied, reduce all other types of quality costs including appraisal costs. Some companies, especially new businesses, are reluctant to put money into prevention, but the successful executive shares a different experience. A classical approach to costs views spending money as a trade-off between failure costs on one side and appraisal and prevention costs on the other (see **Exhibit 13.41**). However, the philosophy of prevention better describes the model, which shows the trends of quality costs from the start of the company. Inspection plays its vital role in the beginning but with decreasing need as appraisal and prevention costs begin to rise (see **Exhibit 13.42**).

Improving Quality of IBM Computer Disk Drives

When IBM had problems with high quality and tight tolerances in one of its products, it used statistical process control methods for quality improvement. Nick Clason, advisory engineer in the section that dealt with read/write head components, explained the approach:

> Let's say you have five outside supplied parts and five that are produced in-house. If the in-house parts are good and any of those made outside are bad, when you put them together in the final assembly, what do you have? Five bad assemblies. . . . About four years ago we made a conscious decision that because we always had requirements for top quality—zero defects—we needed to look beyond the usual practices of using incoming inspection to catch problems. With the dollar volume and product quantities increasing as tolerances were getting tighter, we knew we could not wait until we got a shipment before we found out whether it was good.[22]

Up to this point the story is not too unusual. Many companies look to their suppliers to provide better quality control. In 1983 this IBM facility started with hand-collected statistical quality data and a few critical suppliers. The monitoring of process quality would normally be performed by staff from the quality control department, but IBM sought a big shift to give manufacturing more responsibility for producing, inspecting, monitoring, and the improvement of processes. Nick Clason said:

> We are not only monitoring the final product—that is not our entire purpose—we also must see to it that quality is being controlled at each step of the process by using statistics. We needed to look beyond the usual practice of using incoming inspection to catch problems. Reviewing a supplier's manufacturing process rather than waiting to start when the finished product is at receiving adds a slightly different dimension to the client/supplier relationship. It doesn't do us any good to get and then reject 10,000 parts. We have to know before the supplier finishes making the parts that they are good in critical parameters.[23]

Another supplier of IBM was spending 80 hours each week inspecting one parameter and still getting only about 62 percent acceptance. It would ship IBM parts it thought were good, and IBM would ship back 38 percent as defective for that para-

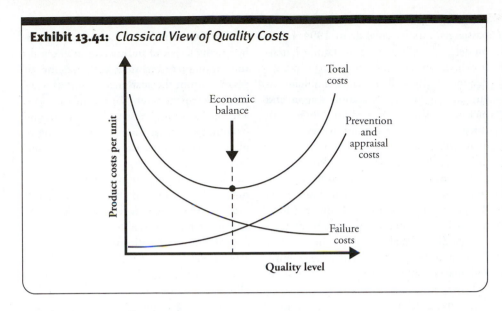

Exhibit 13.41: *Classical View of Quality Costs*

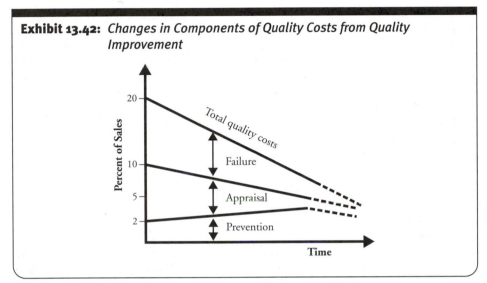

Exhibit 13.42: *Changes in Components of Quality Costs from Quality Improvement*

meter. Two months after IBM installed a statistical process control (SPC) system at that supplier, the inspection rate fell and the quality went up. By March 1983, IBM was not rejecting a single part for the monitored parameter, and the firm's inspection time was down to less than 10 hours per week—all because the supplier was paying more attention at the process level and making adjustments if the process started to drift out of its normal pattern.

IBM's suppliers also introduced several types of monitoring. In-process monitoring, while the part is being made, provides parameter measurements at key points. Critical parameters are measured as they become apparent on a product. Then, when the part is complete, a final inspection samples those same parameters again.

None of IBM's suppliers refused to go along with the SPC plan, but that does not mean that all embraced it wholeheartedly.

The degree of application and effort put into monitoring and controlling the process has varied widely. When you look at the charts on a particular process and find they are the same this year as they were last year—the process is acceptable, within specifications (tolerances), but it has not gotten any better—this is a sign of superficial application of the concepts. Training and motivation must be questioned. IBM must get it across to suppliers that SPC is a tool, not a panacea. Statistics will point out only what is wrong and where you should put your efforts. They will not make the effort for you, adjust the machine for you, improve your tooling, or change your process for you. SPC will tell you when, where, and how much effort is needed. If you have a 50-step process and 45 of those steps are in control, but the other five are widely scattered, where would you put your efforts? Without the charts you might never know.

IBM achieved impressive benefits from using SPC with its suppliers, including a $250,000 savings on hardware costs in a six-month period, by calling attention to one supplier's problem. The firm was sending IBM an electronic component with a defect rate that was higher than the firm indicated and higher than the guaranteed rate. IBM had been accepting the component and using it in assembly, resulting in a defect of greater magnitude. Once the inspection data were available, IBM was able to show the supplying facility and ask it to improve the manufacturing processes. It worked.

That was not the only saving this particular IBM facility could quantify. It documented $4.5 million in savings in 30 months. IBM technicians noticed a trend in control charts that were within limits but which if allowed to continue would have resulted in a warehouse filled with unusable parts. If IBM had used these parts to build assemblies, the assemblies would have to have been scrapped. If you add cost avoidance to the direct savings, the number is much, much larger than the $4.5 million documented saving.

Initially, IBM met with some reluctance to change. Some suppliers said that they cooperated only because they wanted to keep a good customer happy. In several companies, IBM installed expensive machinery and had process capabilities studies done. The IBM engineers told these companies that if they did not adjust certain parameters, they would have a high percentage of scrap. The suppliers' reactions? One company president said he was a good toolmaker and could tell more about his processes with a micrometer in hand, walking through the shop, than IBM could ever tell him with statistics.

IBM engineers told the president of that company that IBM would not accept his product unless he would make certain adjustments and screen for those parameters 100 percent. If he did not make the adjustments, he would get scrap rates of 13, 18, and 21 percent. He did not make changes, but he did screen 100 percent for two weeks and got scrap rates of 13, 18, and 21 percent. Monday morning the president told the IBM engineers that he now believed. That toolmaker was not the only one to become a believer. Another company that was highly resistant to installing the system turned around six weeks after implementing it and gave IBM a price break of one dollar per part. That was $1 on an $8 part! The supplier was still making more profit at the lower price than it did before using SPC.

"Our industry is changing; it's growing," Nick Clason concludes. "When you get into high-volume production of anything, you can't expect to do 100 percent inspection. You've got to apply statistics somehow. The marketplace is becoming very aware of that. This system has worked very well for us, and very well for our suppliers."[24]

Skoda Story: Quality Improvement as a Vital Part of Doing Business in New Markets

The following story shows the role of quality improvement when delivering a change during the creation of an international joint venture. The car manufacturer Skoda, in the Czech Republic, was founded in 1895 and is one of the oldest automotive producers in the world. During the period of central planning (1948–1989), Skoda was the most successful car manufacturer within the Eastern bloc. After the opening of Eastern and Central Europe in 1989, the marketplace changed in many ways: there were dramatic changes in exchange rates, the collapse of markets in the former Soviet Union and Yugoslavia, and the opening of domestic markets to other European and Japanese imports, as well as a flourishing market for cheap imported used cars.

Since early 1990 Skoda had been looking for a strong innovative partner with the manufacturing and financial capability to keep the company competitive in a changing market. After a decision of the Czech government (which was at that time the owner), the April 1991 affiliation agreement made Skoda the fourth brand of the multinational Volkswagen corporation. Volkswagen marketed the German brands (VW and Audi) and the Spanish Seat. The multinational created a joint venture with Skoda, obtaining 31 percent of joint venture shares, thus making Skoda the biggest joint venture in Eastern and Central Europe.

Skoda produced 172,000 small passenger cars and pick-ups in 1991, 200,000 in 1992, and 220,000 in 1993, most of which (60–70 percent) were exported to over 50 markets on five continents including Germany, the United Kingdom, France, Italy, and Israel. New markets have been opened in South America and Asia. In addition to its three production facilities—including the design center, engine and power train plant, tool plant, press, body and paint shop—as well as three assembly plants, the company expanded and began assembling passenger cars in Poland. In 1994 a new model, the Felicia (a small family hatchback), was introduced. The Felicia had been developed with Volkswagen in simultaneous engineering teams. A station wagon and pick-up version followed in 1995, with three types of engines and features such as dual airbags, anti-lock brakes, and air conditioning. New models, using Volkswagen platforms, are being developed for coming years, increasing both the product range and the production volume and thus reaching more customers in more than 60 markets.

The Skoda quality story is the equal of its dramatic success in increasing volume and market share. One of the first steps Volkswagen undertook after the joint venture agreement was to create a supplier qualification program with more than 250 domestic companies. The program included analyzing weaknesses, developing improvement strategies, improving training support, and monitoring processes. When suppliers' processes were improved, a dramatic reduction of incoming inspection at Skoda was possible, allowing increases of capacity and emphasis of Skoda quality engineers on prevention. The task was not only to analyze causes of problems but also to develop remedies for variation reduction, for process improvement, and for supporting implementation on the shop floor.

In manufacturing, the improvement of processes starts with factory workers being viewed as process managers (i.e., the people who have the best knowledge and skills for the improvement). The role of their managers is to support the workers so that the attitude toward improvement becomes the company culture. This was done by snowball training in improvement techniques for team supervisors, who then trained all the team members. The teams on the assembly lines, which assembled several hundred cars per shift, were another place to begin. Teams were fed back information from specific checkpoints, which addressed problems that the team could improve. Inspection still had a role at the shop floor level, but a big part of this activity was shifted to the teams that produced the products. Most traditional inspection ceased. The emphasis was also put on building a transparent quality system, and ISO 9000 certification was achieved in just one year. (The European Community required that all new models must have the ISO 9000 certificate of their quality systems by the beginning of January 1996.)

Quality was seen more and more from the customer's point of view, for example, by driving tests and audits. The audit checks the car or part of it, such as the engine, or gearbox, from the customer's point of view. Inspection parameters such as dimensions and surface roughness are checked, and parameters such as noise, rattles, fitting of plastic parts on the dashboard, or the cleanliness of door interior or trunk carpets are checked. At the beginning of the joint venture with Volkswagen in 1991, the audit index for the whole car (on the scale of 1 to 5) was 4.8 for Skoda models (i.e., at the low end of the scale). Within three years, the 1994 audit index showed a rank of 2.1, the most dramatic quality improvement in Skoda's history. Customer satisfaction increased as a result. In 1994, Skoda was ranked in the United Kingdom as 13–15 from 53 models by the market research company J. D. Power and received the score of 82 percent in customer satisfaction—a score equal to the BMW-3 series and well ahead of Ford, Volkswagen, or Citroen models.[25] Skoda was described as one of the surprises by the following text: "Who'd have thought that the butt of all those jokes would bring its owners as much satisfaction as the BMW-3 series? Skoda owners rate the warranties, service costs, and all-round performance of their cars very highly."[26]

Paralleling the J. D. Power results, the number of Skoda cars sold in the United Kingdom tripled. In 1995 the J. D. Power results in the United Kingdom were even better, with the Skoda ranked as 11–13 among 70 models and with a customer satisfaction score of 86 percent, equal to Nissan's Sunny and Micra and again leaving behind Ford, Volkswagen, Citroen, Subaru Legacy, and Nissan Primera models.[27] The survey analyst said: "Like last year, Skoda does remarkably well. The Favorit [model name] beat such illustrious models as the Mercedes 190, BMW-3 series, and Jaguar XJ6 for owner satisfaction. It's only slightly better than average for reliability, but scores very highly indeed for service costs and warranty provision."[28]

After the launch of the new Felicia model in 1995, another customer satisfaction survey was done in Germany, one of the most demanding markets in Europe. Customer complaints had dropped by approximately 50 percent as compared to the 1994 model. The press response was also very positive, which greatly benefited the brand image. In addition to ads in magazines, television spots, and billboards, the company started sponsoring the Czech

Olympic Team and the World Ice Hockey Championship and promoting the cars with a game at the fast growing chain of McDonald's in the Czech Republic. The Skoda cars also won the 1994 World Cup for cars with engines up to 2000 ccm., leaving behind Nissan, Ford, GM-Opel, and other well-known world brands.

In 1995 groundbreaking took place for a new Skoda plant designed on the lean manufacturing philosophy. This means possibilities for additional increases of production capacity, quality, shorter delivery times, and value for money. This was a new chapter in quality and productivity improvement of this European car manufacturer. In 1998 Skoda was the first European brand to be ranked first in the United Kingdom Customer Satisfaction Study conducted by J. D. Power.

SIMULATION IMPLICATIONS

By leading students along the path from detection to prevention in a process orientation, the *Marketplace* simulation will help you to understand and learn decision making about priorities and action plans for quality improvement. A vital element of process orientation is to understand variation, its sources, and the possibilities of its reduction. Understanding variation is all in the daily routine of company decision making. Such decisions must be based on facts, and the quality improvement techniques here can help you and others to interpret quality data, not only for improving the product, but also for improving the quality of the whole company and its management.

In the *Marketplace* simulation, the contribution of sources of variation is expressed in a scale from 0 to 100 percent, but in the real world we cannot eliminate all variation. There will always be some amount of variation in the company's processes. More important is the trend of the reduction of variation over time, the costs at which it can be achieved, and the benefits it will bring to the company. For the purpose of the simulation, it is predetermined that variation can be reduced by a maximum of 80 percent.

SUMMARY

Prevention is not hard to do—it is just hard to sell.[29]

This chapter has shown the basic ideas of modern quality management that can be characterized as reducing inspection by introducing more prevention—in other words, process improvement. The vital ideas of the chapter are as follows:

- **Inspection and warranty costs.** When the company is not paying attention to inspection and allows poor product to be delivered to the customer, costs are much higher than when the poor quality is discovered in manufacturing. In this way, wise allocation of inspection costs can prevent the disaster of rising warranty costs. If the inspection is necessary, it should be done as close as possible to the source of the problem. Disaster in warranty costs caused by poorly designed inspection processes can ruin the company.

- **Product improvement and process improvement.** Inspection itself does not improve the quality of product; it only sorts the poor from the good. Today the mere improvement of finished products cannot assure the company that it can be competitive in quality. To improve the product, first the processes should be improved.

When you sell a product in volume, such as packaged drinks, you set a price for a specific volume. The greater the variation is above the minimum volume, the more money you are losing. The same applies to delivery times and other parameters. When variation is reduced, the entire inspection process can often be discontinued.

Understanding the variation of processes is a vital step in quality improvement. The sources of variation are not only poor materials or machines, but also people, environment, and manufacturing methods. Quality improvement tools—checklists, histograms, Pareto diagrams, control charts, Ishikawa diagrams, flow charts, and so on—can be used to determine the sources of variation, to identify ways to reduce it, and to implement the desired changes in the processes.

Outcome for the Business

Modern quality improvement focuses resource allocation on improvement of processes rather than on "fire fighting" activities such as sorting out good from bad (see **Exhibit 13.43**). Quality cannot be sorted out; it must be designed and manufactured into the process. This is today's prerequisite for customer satisfaction. How much the product was inspected is not as important as how the quality was improved. Yes, this

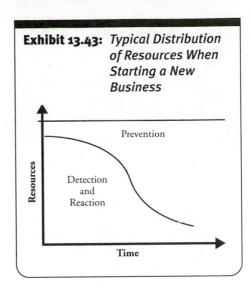

Exhibit 13.43: *Typical Distribution of Resources When Starting a New Business*

approach is really hard to sell, but as Dr. Deming used to say: "You do not need to do it. Survival is not compulsory."

Suggested Readings

Anderson, Bjørn, *Business Process Improvement Toolbox* (Milwaukee, WI: McGraw-Hill, 1999).

Deming, W. E., *Out of the Crisis* (Cambridge, MA: Massachusetts Institute of Technology, 1989).

Eureka, W., and N. E. Ryan, *The Customer-Driven Company* (Dearborn, MI: ASI Press, 1988).

Godfrey, A. Blanton, and J. M. Juran, *Juran's Quality Handbook* (New York: McGraw-Hill, 1999).

Imai, M., *Kaizen: The Key to Japan's Competitive Success* (New York: McGraw-Hill, 1986).

Levinson, William A., and Frank Tumbelty, *SPC Essentials and Productivity Improvement: A Manufacturing Approach* (Milwaukee, WI: OSQC Quality Press, 1997).

Ott, Ellis R., Edward G. Shilling, and Dean V. Neubauer, *Process Quality Control: Troubleshooting and Interpretation* (New York: McGraw-Hill, 1998).

Smith, Gerald M., *Statistical Process Control and Quality Improvement* (Upper Saddle River, NJ: Prentice Hall, 2001).

Taylor, W. A., *Optimization and Variation Reduction in Quality* (New York: McGraw-Hill, 1991).

Teladi, M., F. Scaglione, and V. Russcotti, *A Beginner's Guide to Quality in Manufacturing* (Milwaukee, WI: ASQC Quality Press, 1992).

Walton, M., *The Deming Management Method* (New York: Putman, 1986).

1. Asow was a town far away from the capital, where criminals, dissidents, and other undesirable persons were sent as punishment.

2. A. Blanton Godfrey and J. M. Juran, *Juran's Quality Handbook* (New York: McGraw-Hill, 1999).

3. P. B. Crosby, *Quality Is Free* (New York: McGraw-Hill, 1979).

4. Ibid.

5. Motorola won the Malcolm Baldrige National Quality Award in 1992, the highest acknowledgment of quality improvement in the United States. The savings of the Six Sigma approach during the previous five years were more than $2 billion worldwide.

6. W. E. Deming, *Out of the Crisis* (Boston, MA: Massachusetts Institute of Technology, 1989).

7. Godfrey and Juran, *Juran's Quality Handbook.*

8. M. Imai, *Kaizen: The Key to Japan's Competitive Success* (New York: McGraw-Hill, 1986).

9. The Toyota production system, Toyota Motor Corporation, Operations Management Consulting Division, 1992.

10. Ibid.

11. Ibid.

12. Godfrey and Juran, *Juran's Quality Handbook.*

13. A. V. Feigenbaum, *Total Quality Control* (New York: McGraw-Hill, 1993).

14. S. Covey, A. R. Merill, and R. R. Merill, *First Things First: To Live, to Love, to Learn, to Leave a Legacy* (New York: Simon and Schuster, 1994).

15. J. Ramchandran, "Minimalistic Manufacturing: Doing More, Better with Less," *Prism* (First Quarter 1995).

16. Ibid.

17. D. Halbestram, *The Reckoning* (New York: Avon Books, 1994).

18. Crosby wrote, "You can get rich by preventing defects," *Quality Is Free.*

19. At the IMPRO 1991 Conference of the Juran Institute held in Atlanta, the use of quality improvement techniques at U.S. Military Airlift Command during operations Desert Shield and Desert Storm was presented. The effort was described as an historic shift from Inspector General to top-down emphasis on total quality.

20. J. P. Womack, D. T. Jones, and D. Roos, *The Machine That Changed the World* (New York: Harper Perennial, 1991).

21. Imai, *Kaizen.*

22. This story was adapted from T. Inglesby, "IBM+SPC=Quality," *Manufacturing Systems* (July 1987).

23. Ibid.

24. Ibid.

25. "The 1994 JD Power Survey Results in Full: Who Wins and Who Loses and Why," *Top Gear* (May 1994).

26. Ibid.

27. Ibid.

28. Ibid.

29. Crosby, *Quality Is Free.*

Chapter 14

Kenneth C. Gilbert
University of Tennessee

The Lean Enterprise

The "lean enterprise"[1] refers to the coordination of the companies in a value stream as if they were a single entity focused on providing value for the consumer. The lean enterprise is a new model for making, distributing, and selling products that has evolved from a marriage of new capabilities in manufacturing, information technology, and logistics. The model is built around:

- Manufacturing systems that are responsive, making every product every day and flexing to respond to demand variation in order to replenish exactly what is consumed downstream.

- Distribution centers that act as switching stations rather than storage depots.

- Retailers that replenish frequently and supply point-of-sale (POS) data to the entire value chain.

- Frequent shipments between the stages of the value stream.

- An entire value stream that is coordinated by "pull" (replace what has been consumed) replenishment strategies.

Lean manufacturing, the manufacturing element of the lean enterprise, has resulted in a quantum leap in productivity over the traditional manufacturing model, or batch manufacturing. Lean manufacturing uses a fraction of the floor space, labor, and inventory of batch manufacturing and produces a better quality product. Three essential ingredients in the implementation of this new model are a focus on eliminating waste, improving flow, and achieving economies of scope rather than economies of scale.

"Eliminating waste" means eliminating, whenever possible, things that do not add value. Transporting, storing, counting, and inspecting inventory are all forms of waste. Other forms of waste are quality defects and processing transactions.

Learning Objectives

After reading this chapter the student should:

- Know the key elements of the lean enterprise model.

- Understand the primary differences between traditional batch manufacturing and lean manufacturing.

- Understand pipeline whiplash and know the key leverage points for eliminating it from the value stream.

- Understand the role of setup reduction in improving responsiveness to the value stream.

- Know how to determine the optimal frequency of changeovers.

"Improving flow" means keeping the parts moving at the rate of consumer demand. This requires eliminating the focus on maximizing the velocities of the flow at individual points in the value stream (measured as machine utilization and efficiencies). For example, large production batches and large order quantities may maximize the flow at certain points but create stagnant inventories, thus suboptimizing the flow of the value stream.

"Achieving economies of scope rather than economies of scale" means developing the capability to build and move a variety of products in small quantities as efficiently as building and moving a large quantity of one thing. For example, the reduction of setup times to enable production in smaller batches is aimed at achieving economies of scope. Combining inbound and outbound transportation into frequent repetitive mixed loads ("milk runs") is also aimed at achieving economies of scope.

SOME HISTORY

The lean enterprise has its roots in the Toyota Production System,[2] whose evolution dates to the early 1950s. Taiichi Ohno, the Toyota manager who led the development of this new system, cites Henry Ford as the inspiration for many of his ideas.

In 1915 Henry Ford's system captured many of the ideas of the lean enterprise. There was a constant focus on finding cheaper and better ways to produce the Model T. The flow time through the entire process from raw material to a finished care was a few hours. There was little work-in-progress inventory. The constant flow and low inventory were accomplished by a layout that followed the flow of the product. For example, the line fabricating a door ended at the point on the assembly line where the door was placed on the car. Therefore, the parts flowed like water from tributaries leading to the main river, which was the assembly line.

The business functions at Ford were also very simple. Scheduling was simple and required little or no paperwork. The production rate of the assembly line automatically determined the rate of all upstream processes. Accounting was simple, and the organizational chart was flat. Marketing consisted of setting up dealerships where customers could stand in line for the opportunity to spend $360 on the premier motorcar in America.

The Ford system was predicated on several constraints. First, there was no variety in the product and there were no model year changes. All of the cars were black and had no options. Second, the manufacturing process was insulated from demand variation. Manufacturing improvements drove periodic price reductions and ensured a constant backlog of orders. Third, the company was vertically integrated, with all processes at one location. Iron ore was brought into the massive River Rouge facility, where it was made into steel, which was made into car parts, which then were assembled into cars. Thus, coordination of material flows was simple because no geographical and organizational boundaries were crossed.

In the 1920s General Motors ended Ford's market dominance by offering the customer choices. GM offered the cars in different colors with different options and with model year changes. GM also segmented the market by price. It intended for young, first-time buyers to purchase a Chevrolet, then upgrade to Pontiac, Oldsmobile, Buick, and finally Cadillac, as the buyers became more affluent. The car became more than just a means of transportation. It also was also a reflection of the financial status and personal taste of the owner.

The variety offered by General Motors required that cars and components be made in batches. For example, if a car was offered in a two-door coupe, a four-door sedan, a convertible, and a station wagon, then only one of these models could be run on the assembly line at a given time. Changeovers between models were time consuming and costly. Hence, each of these models would be made only once a month and in a batch large enough to match the forecasted sales. Therefore, demand for parts used in making each model also occurred in batches. The variety in these parts (due to the different options) required even further batching.

This type of production, which became the standard for industry worldwide, is called *batch production*. It requires large inventories of finished goods and of component parts. The flow is sporadic because the inventory from a given batch sits in the warehouse until it is needed by the next operation. Many resources are devoted to moving, storing, and keeping track of inventory. Equipment is arranged by function. For example the stamping machines are located together, and the stamped parts do not go directly to the next operation but to the warehouse. Scheduling is complex because the many batch operations have to be coordinated to a centralized schedule. The organization chart has many layers. Understanding costs and profitability is difficult.

In an attempt to manage all of this complexity, General Motors was divided into profit centers. GM also introduced the concept of cost accounting to answer questions related to the cost and profitability of different products and different organizational units. Such questions were irrelevant to Henry Ford because he had only one product and one organizational unit.

The first goal of the lean enterprise is to deliver the variety of the General Motors value stream but with the simplicity, flow, low inventories, and absence of waste of the

Model T value stream. A second goal is to achieve this flow across organizational and geographic boundaries, allowing each organization to pursue its strengths, or core competencies. The lean enterprise requires manufacturing processes (1) that are quickly capable of changing between products, thus eliminating the need for large batches, (2) that are laid out according to the flow of the product, and (3) that use pull or replenishment scheduling, in which the production of parts is triggered by downstream consumption of the part rather than a centrally coordinated schedule.

Lean companies share several attributes. A lean company works closely with its customers, works closely with its suppliers, works well across functional boundaries, and has its people enthusiastically engaged in improving critical processes. Global competition has made constantly improving customer value a necessity for survival. Satisfying the customer is not solely the responsibility of one function but requires the cooperation of all functions. Vertical integration has been replaced by a focus on core competencies, so that cooperation along the value stream is vital. And without constant improvements in productivity, any company is soon left behind by the competition.

PUSH VERSUS PULL MANUFACTURING STRATEGIES

A fundamental difference between batch manufacturing and the lean manufacturing is the difference between "push" and "pull" manufacturing strategies. Batch manufacturing uses a push strategy, whereas a goal of lean manufacturing is to use a pull strategy to the extent possible. Push systems attempt to coordinate production rates centrally and to use inventories to absorb variation between production and downstream consumption. For example, a finished goods inventory acts as a buffer against variation in sales. In a push environment, manufacturing production measures tend to focus on the utilization of the equipment (the percent of available hours per day it is used) and the efficiency of equipment (the hourly production rate expressed as a percentage of the maximum).

Pull systems hold inventory constant and allow production to vary. In theory when a unit of product is sold, a replacement unit is built. The demand in the marketplace sets the drumbeat for the entire production process. To achieve this, the process must be so flexible that changing from one part to another requires little effort, and it must have sufficient capacity to respond quickly to variation in the quantity demanded. In a pull environment, the performance measures must measure the ability of the process to respond to demand rather than measure the utilization and efficiencies of the equipment.

THE BULLWHIP EFFECT: THE BEER GAME

To understand the fundamental principles of the lean enterprise, it is necessary to understand the role of demand variation and its impact on the value stream. Most value streams have large variation in inventory levels, orders, and shipments. This variation causes many problems, including high inventory holding costs and lost sales resulting from stockouts. But many companies have gained a competitive advantage by simultaneously reducing value stream inventories and achieving a high ability to meet customer demand. The central concept underlying the ability to gain such an advantage is this: *Most variation in the value stream is created by the value stream itself, not by the consumer.* As an illustrative example, consider the phenomenon known as the *bullwhip effect.*[3] The bullwhip effect describes how variation in demand can multiply as it passes through successive stages of a value stream. Thus, a small swing in consumer demand can produce huge swings in orders and inventories in the value stream, just as a small flick on the handle of a bullwhip can create a violent snap at the end of the whip.

To illustrate the bullwhip effect, we will describe a simulation called the *beer game,*[4] first developed in the 1960s by MIT's Sloan School of Management. The game uses a four-stage product delivery system to demonstrate the problems inherent in a traditional value stream.

The four parties in the simulation are a factory, a distributor, a wholesaler, and a retailer. The goal of each is to sell a single brand of beer to their customer, the next link in the value stream. A manager at each stage of the value stream manages an inventory while filling weekly orders from the downstream customer and placing orders with an upstream supplier, as shown in **Exhibit 14.1**. Each stage experiences a four-week lead time: Four weeks will lapse between the time that an order is placed to the upstream supplier and the time when the product arrives. Each week, the retailer's demand for that week from the consumer is revealed. The demand at each of the other locations is determined by orders placed downstream. At the beginning of the simulation the system is in a steady state, with the consumer buying four cases of beer per week, and each stage of the value stream is ordering and receiving four cases of beer per week. Each stage is also holding a constant inventory of 12 cases of beer. Therefore, each player's weekly order cycle is as follows:

- The player begins each week with 12 cases in stock.
- At the beginning of the week the player receives (based on an order placed four weeks earlier) 4 cases from the upstream supplier.
- During the week the player receives orders for 4 cases and ships them to the downstream customer.
- The player ends the week with 12 cases in inventory and then places an order with the upstream supplier for 4 more cases, to be delivered four weeks later.
- The player ends the week with four weeks of outstanding orders for four cases per week.

Then the equilibrium is disrupted. The consumer increases his weekly order to eight cases. Consider the impact on the retailer. The retailer will begin this week with 12 cases, receive 4 cases, but sell 8 cases, and end the week with only *8* cases in inventory. The retailer must now decide how many cases to order. Suppose that the

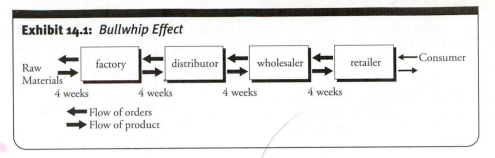

Exhibit 14.1: *Bullwhip Effect*

Raw Materials → factory (4 weeks) → distributor (4 weeks) → wholesaler (4 weeks) → retailer (4 weeks) → Consumer

← Flow of orders
→ Flow of product

player's ordering policies are based on two very simple but logical rules, the first a forecast rule and the second an order quantity rule:

1. **The forecast rule.** The forecast of the average weekly demand for the next four weeks is the average of the weekly demand over the most recent four weeks.

2. **The order quantity rule.** Using the forecast, order the amount needed to replenish the ending inventory (four weeks from now when the order arrives) to a target of 12 cases.

Based on rule 1, the retailer forecasts her weekly demand to be five cases per week:

$$\frac{4 + 4 + 4 + 8}{4} = 5$$

Rule 2 requires that the retailer's inventory on hand plus the inventory on order be sufficient to cover the forecasted demand for the next four weeks and still have 12 cases left in inventory. Therefore, the retailer must order the sum of the inventory target (12) plus the forecasted demand for the next four weeks minus the inventory that she already has on hand or on order:

Order = Inventory target +
Forecasted demand for next four weeks −
Current inventory − Orders already
placed for next three weeks.

$$= 12 + (5 + 5 + 5 + 5) - 8 -$$
$$(4 + 4 + 4) = 12 + 20 - 8 - 12 = 12$$

The retailer will order 12 cases.

A fundamental insight: The consumer demand increased by 100 percent (from 4 cases per week to 8 cases per week), but the retailer's order to the wholesaler increased by 200 percent (from 4 cases per week to 12 cases per week). *The retailer doubled the variation in demand.* This increase in variation is due to the four weeks that are required to react to the forecasted increase in demand.

Next consider the wholesaler. Assume that the wholesaler is identical to the retailer, except that the wholesaler's demand is created by the retailer's orders. Initially the wholesaler receives 4 cases per week, sells 4 cases per week, and ends each week with 12 cases. Then the wholesaler unexpectedly receives an order from the retailer for 12 cases. The wholesaler will begin the week with 12 cases, receive 4 cases, sell 12 cases, and end with an inventory of 4. The wholesaler uses the four-week average forecasting

Exhibit 14.2: *Reduction of Waste in Changeover Equation*

168	Usable hours in a week	
132	Hours needed for production	← Reduce Scrap
	2% scrap	
	5% downtime	
	1% obsolete	
36	Idle hours	← Eliminate Obsolete Products

rule and the inventory target of 12 cases. Thus the wholesaler's forecast will be: (4 + 4 + 4 + 12) / 4 = 6 cases per week. The wholesaler's order will be:

Order = Inventory target +
Forecasted demand for next four weeks −
Current inventory − Orders already
placed for next three weeks

$$= 12 + (6 + 6 + 6 + 6) - 4 -$$
$$(4 + 4 + 4) = 20.$$

Thus the wholesaler's order to the factory increases from four cases per week to twenty cases per week, an increase of *400 percent*.

Following the forecasting rule and order quantity rule, the distributor reacts to the wholesaler's order of 20 cases by ordering 36 cases, an increase of 800 percent. The factory responds to this order by ordering enough raw material for 68 cases, an increase of *1,600 percent* variation doubles at each stage. Of the 64-case increase in the factory's orders, only four cases were directly attributable to a change in consumer demand. *The value stream created 94 percent of the variation observed in the factory's orders.*

Reducing the Bullwhip Effect

By making changes in the beer game, we learn how to reduce the bullwhip effect:

- **Reducing lead time reduces the bullwhip effect.** Suppose that in the computations above, we shorten the lead time to one week. We would find that the variation in orders grows by a factor of 1.25 at each stage. With two-week lead times, the variation grows by a factor of 1.5, and for a three-week lead time the variation grows by a factor of 1.75. In general, the multiplier increases proportionally to the lead time.

- **Point of sale data reduces the bullwhip effect.** Suppose that each stage of the beer game is provided the consumer's orders (POS data), and each player uses the con-

sumer demand in the forecasting rule, so that all of the stages have the same forecast. Under this scenario, the variation grows additively at each stage, rather than multiplicatively. For example, with a four-week lead time the orders are as follows:

customer	8 cases
retailer	12 cases
wholesaler	16 cases
distributor	20 cases
factory	24 cases

- **The bullwhip effect is eliminated by a pure pull strategy.** (In a pure pull strategy each stage orders each week exactly what was sold that week.). However, pull strategies are feasible only when the lead time is short. For example, if demand were to increase permanently to eight cases per week, during the four-week lead time ,the retailer's inventory will drop to −4, a backlog of four cases. Under a pure pull strategy this backlog would be permanent.

- **A more stable forecast reduces the bullwhip effect.** The way to make the forecast more stable is to shorten the time buckets. For example, if the orders are placed daily instead of weekly, then the change in the forecast between orders would be much smaller.

The bullwhip effect can be reduced by shortening the lead time, by sharing POS data, and by increasing the frequency of orders. As the lead time becomes shorter and the forecast becomes more stable, the ordering policy converges more and more closely to a pure pull strategy, in which there is no variation added by the value stream.

Organizational Implications of the Bullwhip Effect

The changes needed to reduce the bullwhip effect require a perspective in which the value stream is seen as a single entity rather than separate pieces. For example, large production batches and large shipping quantities may appear to be economic when viewed strictly from the local perspective of production costs or transportation costs. But viewed from the perspective of the value stream, the long reaction times created by big batches and shipping quantities are very costly. Traditional measures of cost and other performance measures are incomplete and lead to suboptimal decisions.

The real leverage in improving the performance of the value stream comes from the lean enterprise, from an integrated management of the value stream. Optimizing the separate links of the value stream independently does not optimize the value stream. For an organization to be the best at what it does inside its own walls is no longer sufficient. It must also be in a cooperative mode of operation with partners up and down the value stream.

CUTTING REACTION TIMES BY INCREASING CHANGEOVERS

A&B Company

The bullwhip effect illustrates that quick reactions to changes in demand are very important to the performance of the value stream. One major determinant of reaction time is the frequency of changeovers. Suppose a company produces each individual product only once a month. Then the company has a slow reaction time because there is one opportunity per month to react to changes in demand. Making each product more frequently, say once per day, reduces the reaction time.

Let's look at another hypothetical production facility, A&B Company, which runs one production line around the clock, seven days a week. Meeting its current level of demand for its products requires 150 hours per week of time on this line. The remaining 18 hours are therefore the only time A&B can afford to have its machine down for changeovers, which are necessary to install the tooling required for different products. At the current rate of 9 hours per changeover, A&B can afford only two changeovers per week. Thus, in any single week of 168 usable hours of production, A&B could process only two different products on the line:

150	Hours needed
	5% scrap
	5% downtime
	10% obsolete
18	Idle

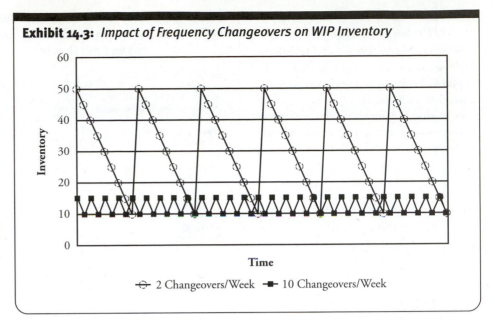

Exhibit 14.3: *Impact of Frequency Changeovers on WIP Inventory*

2 Changeovers/Week ⊶ 10 Changeovers/Week ▪

18 hours ÷ 9 hours per changeover = 2 changeovers per week

Because A&B can afford only two changeovers per week, it builds large quantities of Product A in the beginning of the week and large quantities of Product B in the last half of the week. The actual amounts it builds are based on forecasts of market demand. While A&B builds Product B, it watches the inventory of Product A nervously, hoping that its forecast is right and that it will actually have enough of Product A to last until its next production run. To remedy this problem and simplify the situation, A&B needs to reduce either the waste associated with the current production process or the time required to make changeovers.

The waste associated with production has three common components: downtime, scrap, and obsolescence. Downtime is often associated with the complexity of the plant's machinery and will be considered fixed for the purposes of this example. Scrap materials and components and obsolete products, however, are often related to the large inventories and long flow times that we are attempting to eliminate.

We can increase the number of changeovers quite dramatically (see **Exhibit 14.2**) if we can significantly reduce the waste in the changeover equation.

36 hours ÷ 9 hours per changeover = 4 changeovers per week

If we improve our quality control, we can reduce the amount of production time that results in scrap. Also, by finding a better balance between what is demanded by the market and the quantity being produced, it is possible to eliminate the production of obsolete products. With these improvements, the number of idle hours can be increased from 18 to 36. We can now increase the number of changeovers to four per week.

The benefits of the improvement have a positive cascading effect on the process. By increasing the frequency of changeovers, we decrease the amount of time between a problem with the batch and the detection of that problem at final inspection. Thus, the amount of scrap is reduced. Also, we decrease the likelihood that we will be building product that is not in demand by the market (obsolete product). In return, we gain extra time that can be used to make changeovers and increase our flexibility.

The second way to increase the number of affordable changeovers is to reduce the time required for each changeover. Lean manufacturing uses this tactic and has frequently been able to reduce changeover time by a factor of 10.

If we take the same example of A&B Company and reduce the time required for a changeover to three hours, we have increased the flexibility by allowing up to 12 changeovers per week. On the other hand, if we truly did not need this level of flexibility, we would have up to 36 additional productive hours available on the line every week.

168	Usable hours in a week
132	Hours needed for production
	2% scrap
	5% downtime
	1% obsolete
~~40~~ 36	Idle hours

$\frac{36}{368}$ hours ÷ $\frac{3}{30}$ hours per changeover = 12 changeovers per week

By increasing the number of times we can build any individual product, we reduce the amount of inventory required to support the demand during the time we are building other products. A comparison of the inventory needed to support the two different situations is shown in **Exhibit 14.3**.

This example demonstrates the effectiveness of changeovers on a plant's inventory. However, is the effort to reduce this inventory profitable for the company? In the next section, we will address the question of whether frequent changeovers are profitable for the plant.

PROFITABILITY OF CHANGEOVERS

Way Out Widgets

As mentioned earlier, Henry Ford's one-color strategy was originally quite profitable. Under this system, for example, Ford never had costs of changing the paint booth from one that produced only black cars to one that could produce a variety of colors. However, when General Motors offered consumers a choice of colors, Ford was eventually forced to adapt.

In today's business environment, customers expect a wide variety of product offerings. A trip to the grocery stores shows that shoppers looking for simple products such as bread, milk, or butter will find an array of choices for each. This environment creates complicated manufacturing decisions; for example, how long should the plant produce a particular model before switching over to another, how much inventory should be kept for each stock keeping unit (SKU), and is there sufficient production capacity to produce all that is needed?

This section will illustrate how companies can become more flexible and achieve greater profitability when they modify their operations to allow frequent changeovers, smaller lot sizes, and smaller inventories. You will also discover how the utilization of capacity can affect the success of these modifications.

Way Out Widgets is a company that produces two types of widgets: green widgets and blue widgets. The company's plant operates 260 days per year (5 days × 52 weeks). The demand for blue widgets is 100 units a day, and the demand for green widgets is also

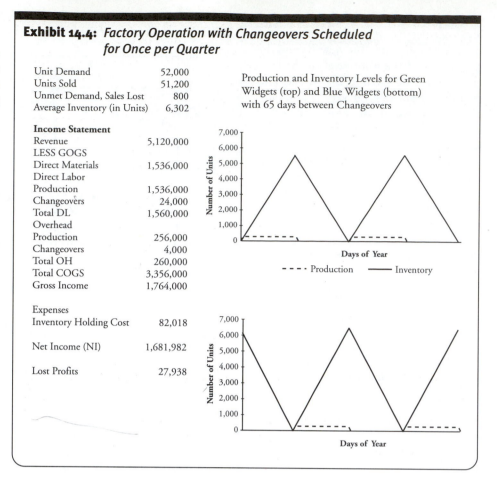

Exhibit 14.4: *Factory Operation with Changeovers Scheduled for Once per Quarter*

Unit Demand	52,000	
Units Sold	51,200	
Unmet Demand, Sales Lost	800	
Average Inventory (in Units)	6,302	
Income Statement		
Revenue	5,120,000	
LESS GOGS		
Direct Materials	1,536,000	
Direct Labor		
Production	1,536,000	
Changeovers	24,000	
Total DL	1,560,000	
Overhead		
Production	256,000	
Changeovers	4,000	
Total OH	260,000	
Total COGS	3,356,000	
Gross Income	1,764,000	
Expenses		
Inventory Holding Cost	82,018	
Net Income (NI)	1,681,982	
Lost Profits	27,938	

Production and Inventory Levels for Green Widgets (top) and Blue Widgets (bottom) with 65 days between Changeovers

100 units a day; therefore the total demand is 200 units per day. The annual demand for this company is 52,000 widgets. If the company is unable to meet demand on any given day, the customers will buy their widgets elsewhere. The company's plant has one production line, which can produce 200 units per day. The company can produce blue widgets for a period of time, build inventory, and then change over to start making green widgets. It takes a whole day to modify the machinery to switch from blue to green, or vice versa. Thus, the company cannot produce on changeover days.

Several costs go into producing widgets, and they are identical for green and blue widgets. The three main costs are direct materials, direct labor, and overhead. The direct materials cost is $30 per unit, and direct labor is $30 per unit. Overhead is derived from taking all of the plant's overhead expenses, which are $1,000 per day, and dividing this number by the number of widgets produced. For example if the company produced 200 units on a given day, the overhead cost per unit would be $5 ($1,000 ÷ 200 units). If the company produced only 100 units per day, the over-

head cost would be $10 per unit. The company sells each widget for $100 per unit. Gross profit is the difference between $100 and the sum of direct materials, labor, and overhead.

If the company is making 200 green widgets on a given day, it would sell half to satisfy daily demand and place the other half in inventory to sell after the company changes over to blue widgets. As a result, the company has an additional expense in inventory holding cost. Inventory holding cost is 20 percent of the value of the average inventory held per year. Way Out Widgets has no other costs. When inventory-holding costs are subtracted from gross income, the balance remaining is the company's net income.

Current Operations

Let's now take a look at how Way Out is currently running its business. Later we will modify the way the factory is run in order to increase changeovers, thereby reducing lot sizes and inventory. We will then see if these changes improve the performance of the firm.

Exhibit 14.5: *Changeovers Scheduled Once Every Three Weeks*

Unit Demand	52,000
Units Sold	48,600
Unmet Demand, Sales Lost	3,400
Average Inventory (in Units)	1,307

Income Statement

Revenue	4,860,000
LESS GOGS	
Direct Materials	1,458,000
Direct Labor	
Production	1,485,000
Changeovers	102,000
Total DL	1,560,000
Overhead	
Production	243,000
Changeovers	17,000
Total OH	260,000
Total COGS	3,278,000
Gross Income	1,582,000
Expenses	
Inventory Holding Cost	17,076
Net Income (NI)	1,564,924
Lost Profits	117,811

Production and Inventory Levels for Green
Widgets (top) and Blue Widgets (bottom)
with 15 days between Changeovers

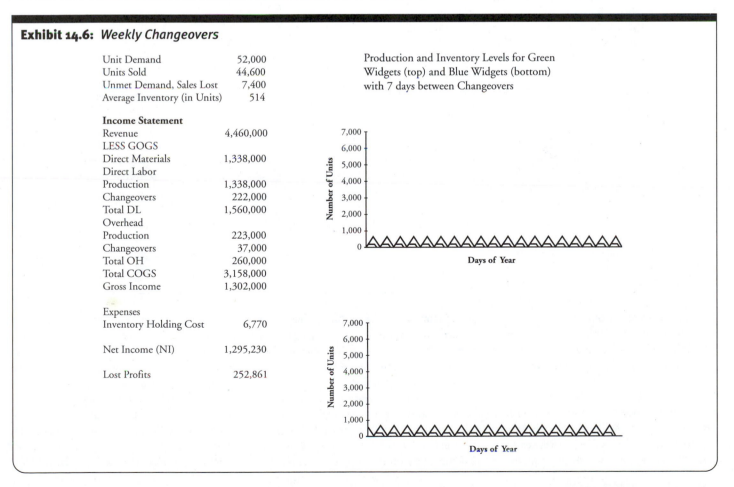

Exhibit 14.6: *Weekly Changeovers*

Unit Demand	52,000
Units Sold	44,600
Unmet Demand, Sales Lost	7,400
Average Inventory (in Units)	514

Income Statement

Revenue	4,460,000
LESS GOGS	
Direct Materials	1,338,000
Direct Labor	
Production	1,338,000
Changeovers	222,000
Total DL	1,560,000
Overhead	
Production	223,000
Changeovers	37,000
Total OH	260,000
Total COGS	3,158,000
Gross Income	1,302,000
Expenses	
Inventory Holding Cost	6,770
Net Income (NI)	1,295,230
Lost Profits	252,861

Production and Inventory Levels for Green
Widgets (top) and Blue Widgets (bottom)
with 7 days between Changeovers

Exhibit 14.4 illustrates how Way Out is currently operating the factory. The graphs show that Way Out produces widgets of one color, blue, for 65 days, and then switches over to green and produces that color for 65 days. The large production lot size of 13,000 units (65 days × 200 units per day) results in a tremendous amount of inventory. As one color increases in inventory, the other declines. On average there will be 6,300 units of each brand in inventory. (Note that half of 13,000 is 6,500 units rather than 6,300. During the year the company stocks out of inventory during the days of changeover when one brand's inventory is depleted, thereby reducing the average inventory figure.)

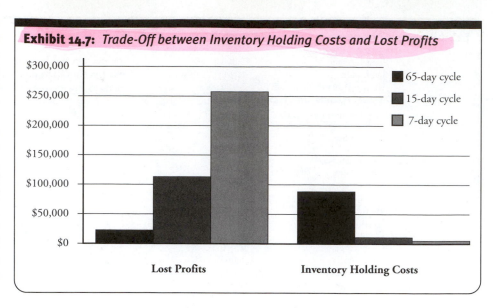

Exhibit 14.7: Trade-Off between Inventory Holding Costs and Lost Profits

- 65-day cycle
- 15-day cycle
- 7-day cycle

Lost Profits · Inventory Holding Costs

Way Out's Income Statement

Is Widget's inventory level a problem? Exhibit 14.4 provides an income statement to illustrate how profitable Way Out is from its operating activities. Let's briefly examine the income statement.

The top of the statement gives the demand and units sold. The number of units lost is the number of units that Way Out could have sold if they had not had stockouts during the year. Note that the sum of units sold and units lost equals demand. Finally, the average inventory in units is the average of the company's inventory at the end of every day of the year. These four numbers are used in the generation of the company's income statement.

The first line of the income statement is revenue, which is equal to the number of units sold times the selling price of $100. Cost of goods sold consists of the direct materials, direct labor, and overhead. Cost of goods sold is $30 per unit. Direct labor is divided into two subcategories: production direct labor (number of units sold × $30 per unit), and changeover direct labor (cost of labor during changeovers). The changeover cost for a day is calculated as the labor cost that would have been spent on production (200 units × $30 per unit) multiplied by the number of changeovers in a year. In this case there were four changeovers.

The overhead cost is also separated into two subcategories. Production overhead costs are $1000 per day times 256 days of production. Changeover overhead is $1,000 per day times the days spend in

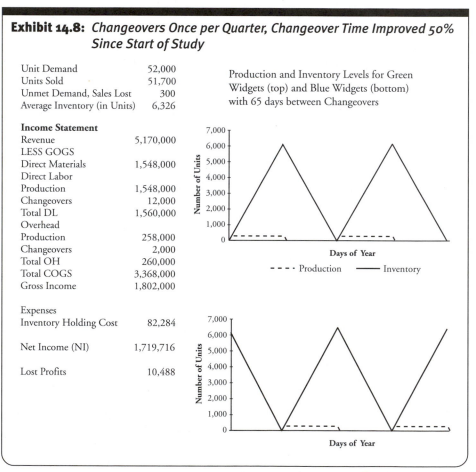

Exhibit 14.8: *Changeovers Once per Quarter, Changeover Time Improved 50% Since Start of Study*

Unit Demand	52,000
Units Sold	51,700
Unmet Demand, Sales Lost	300
Average Inventory (in Units)	6,326

Income Statement	
Revenue	5,170,000
LESS GOGS	
Direct Materials	1,548,000
Direct Labor	
Production	1,548,000
Changeovers	12,000
Total DL	1,560,000
Overhead	
Production	258,000
Changeovers	2,000
Total OH	260,000
Total COGS	3,368,000
Gross Income	1,802,000
Expenses	
Inventory Holding Cost	82,284
Net Income (NI)	1,719,716
Lost Profits	10,488

Production and Inventory Levels for Green Widgets (top) and Blue Widgets (bottom) with 65 days between Changeovers

- - - - Production · —— Inventory

doing changeovers. The importance of separating direct labor and overhead into production and changeover subcategories will become clearer as we begin to modify the company's operations.

Gross income is revenue minus the cost of goods sold. The only expense in this simple example is the inventory holding cost for the 6,302 units of inventory. This cost is calculated by multiplying the average daily inventory times the sum of its costs (direct materials, direct labor, overhead), and then multiplying the total by 20 percent. Net income is equal to gross income minus inventory holding costs.

The last section of the income statement shows lost profits. Lost profits are what the company would have made if it had been able to meet the total demand (no stockouts). In this case, the company would have

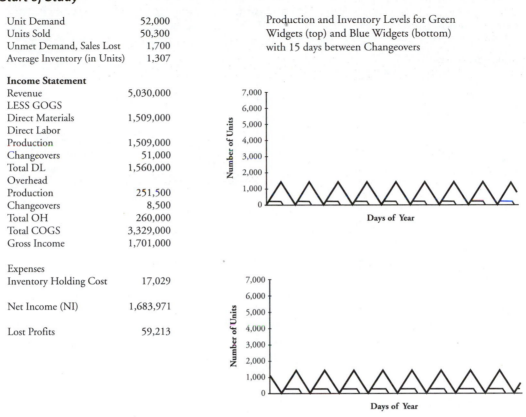

Unit Demand	52,000
Units Sold	50,300
Unmet Demand, Sales Lost	1,700
Average Inventory (in Units)	1,307

Income Statement

Revenue	5,030,000
LESS GOGS	
Direct Materials	1,509,000
Direct Labor	
Production	1,509,000
Changeovers	51,000
Total DL	1,560,000
Overhead	
Production	251,500
Changeovers	8,500
Total OH	260,000
Total COGS	3,329,000
Gross Income	1,701,000
Expenses	
Inventory Holding Cost	17,029
Net Income (NI)	1,683,971
Lost Profits	59,213

Production and Inventory Levels for Green Widgets (top) and Blue Widgets (bottom) with 15 days between Changeovers

Days of Year

Days of Year

made almost $28,000 if it had sold the additional 800 units.

Reengineering Way Out Widgets

Let's now reexamine Exhibit 14.4 and see what improvements might be made to Way Out's operations. Way Out is currently achieving $1,681,982 profit. The company sold 51,200 units, which satisfied 98.4 percent of the market's demand. However, the largest expense is the inventory holding cost of $82,018 resulting from 65-day production cycles and 13,000-unit lot sizes.

Suppose we increase the frequency of changeovers to that of every three weeks (every 15 days). Under this system, Way Out will produce blue widgets for 14 days, take a day for changeovers, and then produce green widgets for 14 days. This system will result in a lot size of 2,800 units (200 units a day × 14 days).

Exhibit 14.5 depicts this system. As you can see, the inventory holding cost has been reduced from $82,018 to $17,076. However, net income has actually decreased

because revenues dropped from $5,120,000 to $4,860,000. Why did revenues fall? The number of units lost jumped from 800 to 3,400 units. So, while inventory holding costs were reduced by $64,942, lost profits increased by $89,873.

Now let's try reducing the production cycle to six days with a changeover on the seventh day. This strategy results in a lot size of 1,200 units. In this scenario (see **Exhibit 14.6**), inventory holding cost is reduced to $6,770, but net income has continued to drop.

The trade-offs between inventory holding costs and lost profits are illustrated in **Exhibit 14.7**. As you can see from the graph, the relationship between inventory holding cost and lost profits is inversely correlated. A reduction in production cycle time (and the reduction of the production lot sizes) results in more lost profits and inventory holding costs savings.

Why has this happened? The answer is that the company is operating at full capacity. The line can only produce 200 units a day, and demand is equal to 200 units

a day. Each time the company does a changeover, it loses 200 units of production, which translates to about $7,000 of lost profit. Therefore, the more changeovers, the less profit. Under this scenario, the most profitable decision for Way Out would be to maintain the 65-day production cycles.

Improve Changeover Time

If Way Out is operating at capacity, how can we improve the bottom line? The answer is to improve the rate at which changeovers are accomplished. Under the current system, it takes a whole day to do a changeover. But suppose that through redesign of the production line, automation, the elimination of waste, or other improvements, changeovers could be accomplished in less than a day. The faster changeovers would result in less lost demand per day during changeover days. Increasing sales would result in higher profits.

Let's look again at the 65-, 15-, and 7-day production cycles. However, suppose the company has worked on changeovers

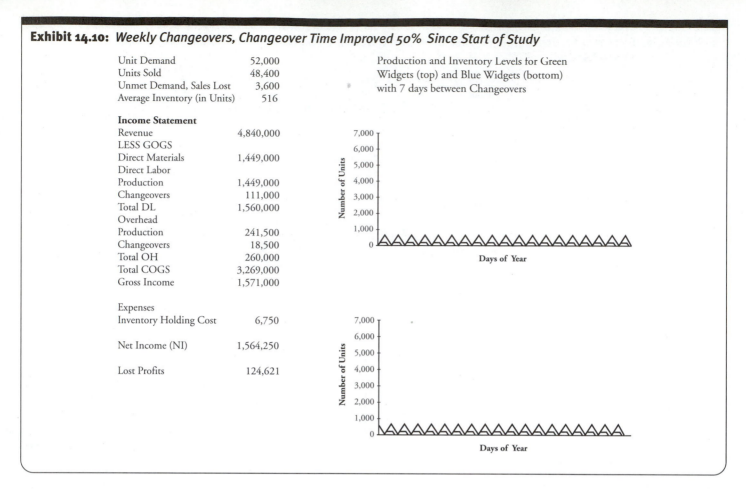

Exhibit 14.10: *Weekly Changeovers, Changeover Time Improved 50% Since Start of Study*

Unit Demand	52,000
Units Sold	48,400
Unmet Demand, Sales Lost	3,600
Average Inventory (in Units)	516

Production and Inventory Levels for Green Widgets (top) and Blue Widgets (bottom) with 7 days between Changeovers

Income Statement

Revenue	4,840,000
LESS GOGS	
Direct Materials	1,449,000
Direct Labor	
Production	1,449,000
Changeovers	111,000
Total DL	1,560,000
Overhead	
Production	241,500
Changeovers	18,500
Total OH	260,000
Total COGS	3,269,000
Gross Income	1,571,000
Expenses	
Inventory Holding Cost	6,750
Net Income (NI)	1,564,250
Lost Profits	124,621

and achieved a 50 percent improvement in changeover time. **Exhibit 14.8** illustrates the 65-day cycle. In comparison to the income statement for the original 65-day cycle (Exhibit 14.4), we find that net income has increased by $37,734. Way Out was able to sell 500 more units per year as a result of producing 100 units on changeover days.

Note also that the changeover accounts under both direct labor and overhead have decreased. These reductions are because the accounts are being credited for only half a day of changeover expenses per changeover. Finally, this scenario has a slightly higher inventory holding cost than the original 65-day cycle. This higher inventory cost of $266 is due to the holding costs of the 500 additional units produced during the year.

Exhibits 14.9 and **14.10** show similar improvements when we reduce the changeover time by 50 percent for 15-day and 7-day cycles. In each case, additional units are sold, resulting in greater profits compared to the same scenario with one-day changeovers. A reduction in changeover time improves profitability. The 65-day cycle is still the most profitable.

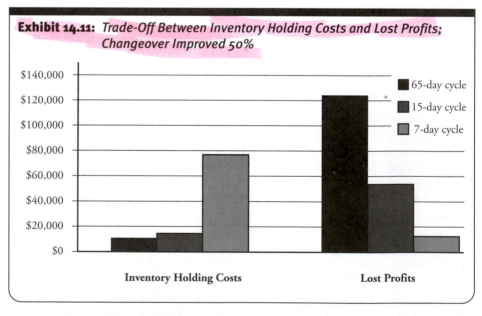

Exhibit 14.11: *Trade-Off Between Inventory Holding Costs and Lost Profits; Changeover Improved 50%*

The trade-offs between inventory holding costs and lost profits for the 50 percent improvement in changeovers are shown in **Exhibit 14.11**. Compare this to Exhibit 14.7. Note that the magnitude of the lost profits is less dramatic for all cycle times with the improved changeover time.

Since we were successful in increasing profitability by improving changeover time

by 50 percent, let's see what happens if we are able to improve it by 90 percent, or 99 percent. **Exhibit 14.12** summarizes the results. Compare net income from the original 65-day production cycle with net income after 90 percent and 99 percent improvements in changeover time.

Exhibit 14.13 shows the impact of changeover efficiency on the manufactur-

Exhibit 14.12: *Summary of Changes to Net Income as a Result of Changeover Improvements*

Way Out Widgets, Net Income

Changeover Improvement	65-day Cycle	15-day Cycle	7-day Cycle
None	$1,681,982	$1,564,924	$1,295,230
50%	1,719,716	1,683,971	1,564,250
90	1,725,882	1,778,940	1,761,456
99	1,725,178	1,789,355	1,799,005

Exhibit 14.13: *Cycle Time versus Changeover Efficiency*

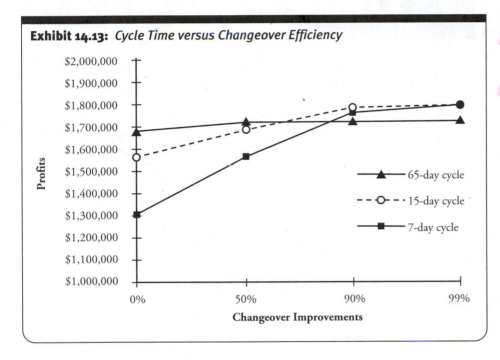

Exhibit 14.14: *Trade-Off between Inventory Holding Costs and Lost Profits: Changeover Improved 90%*

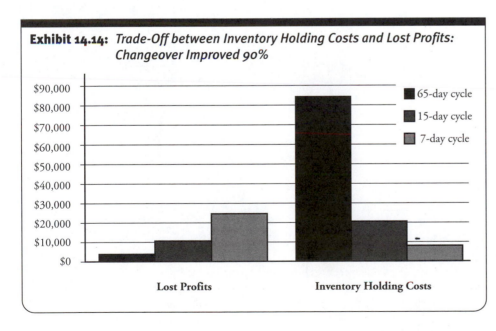

ing cycle time. **Exhibits 14.14** and **14.15** show the changing correlation of inventory holding costs to lost profits as changeover times are improved by 90 percent and 99 percent respectively. With a 90 percent improvement, the differences for lost profits decrease for all cycle times, and become less noticeable with each improvement in changeover time. Comparing these figures to the early scenarios (Exhibits 14.8 and 14.9), you will notice that the shape of inventory holding costs is similar for all four scenarios. The important difference is that lost profits continue to drop as changeover efficiency is increased. This demonstrates that the firm receives maximum profits as its actual production approaches demand, or its capacity.

LESSONS LEARNED

So far we have examined two kinds of production facilities: one operating below capacity and one operating at capacity. These two examples illustrate both how to increase changeovers and how to do it without sacrificing profitability.

The first production facility, A&B Company (which produced products A and B) was operating below capacity. This firm increased its flexibility and lowered its inventory by using its excess capacity for changeovers. When the firm eliminated wastefulness and increased its changeover speed, it created additional excess capacity. The additional excess capacity meant that the firm could increase changeovers, therefore further reducing inventory and further increasing flexibility.

The number of changeovers that A&B Company could accomplish was a simple function of how much excess capacity the firm has at any one time. As long as the firm uses the following equation, it will not sacrifice profits:

Number of changeovers = Excess capacity (in units) ÷ Capacity required for changeovers

The second firm, Way Out Widgets, was operating at capacity. Since it had no excess capacity, the number of changeovers could not be figured using the above formula. In order for Way Out to increase changeovers, reduce inventory, and become more flexible, it had to sacrifice sales. Increasing the frequency of changeovers resulted in trade-offs between

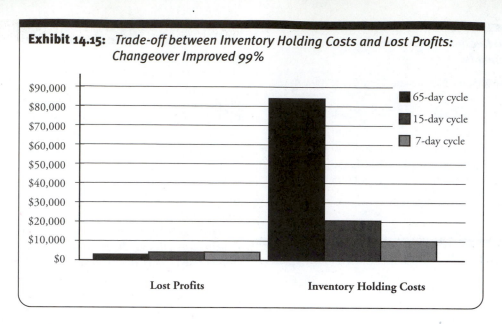

Exhibit 14.15: *Trade-off between Inventory Holding Costs and Lost Profits: Changeover Improved 99%*

benefits of lower inventory holding costs and drawbacks of decreases profits. A comparison of the profitability of each of the four scenarios is graphed in Exhibit 14.13. The graph shows that the shorter production cycles are not as profitable until a certain level of changeover efficiency has been achieved. Specifically, the 15-day production cycle becomes profitable only after changeover time is cut by 75 percent. It is at this point that the savings in inventory holding costs exceed the lost sales from changeover time. Similarly, the 7-day production cycle becomes profitable following an improvement of about 85 percent in changeover time. In summary, changeover frequency can be calculated by the following trade-off rule: *If the sum of inventory holding cost savings from an addition changeover is greater than the profits lost from that same changeover, then the firm can afford an additional changeover.*

The focus here has been profitability. The Way Out example illustrates that the right combination of changeovers combined with reduced changeover time will result in higher profitability for the firm. Another important reason for improving changeover time is that it allows the firm to be more flexible in adjusting production levels to meet fluctuations in demand. Just as important, improving changeover time enables the firm to discover defective batches quickly before large quantities are produced, as well as providing protection against loss due to inventory obsolescence.

Unlike the examples of A&B Company and Way Out Widgets, demand in the real world will never be perfectly predictable. To survive and thrive, a firm must become flexible enough to respond quickly to sudden changes in demand.

1. James P. Womack and Daniel T. Jones, *Lean Thinking: Banish Waste and Create Wealth in Your Corporation* (New York: Simon & Schuster, 1996).

2. Yasuhiro Monden, *Toyota Production System: An Integrated Approach to Just-In-Time, Instituteof Industrial Engineers* (Norcross, GA: Engineering and Management Press, 1998).

3. Hau L. Lee, V. Padmanabhan, and Seungjin Whang, "The Bullwhip Effect in Supply Chains," *Sloan Management Review* (Spring 1997).

4. Peter M. Senge, *The Fifth Discipline: The Art and Practice of the Learning Organization* (New York: Currency/Doubleday, 1994).

Chapter 15

Profit Management

James M. Reeve
*Deloitte & Touche
Professor of Accounting
University of Tennessee*

Assume you are deciding whether or not to purchase a car. There are many issues to be considered in the decision, but one of the most important is determining whether you can afford the purchase. If you were to evaluate the financial impact of purchasing a car, you would naturally begin by considering the purchase price. However, the costs do not end with the purchase price. In addition to the purchase price, there are the additional annual expenses associated with automobile ownership: interest on a car loan, maintenance expenses, insurance expense, gas, parking fees for work or school, and annual registration, to name the most obvious. On the plus side, however, automobile ownership may have some financial benefits. These benefits would include the obvious, such as savings from avoiding public transportation. The benefits also would include some items that would be not so obvious. A car might provide you greater flexibility in shopping, thus providing you the ability to seek lower costs for food and clothing. A car would allow you to drive to relatives instead of taking a bus or flying, thus saving fare costs. A car might give you greater flexibility in locating a job, thus providing you the ability to seek a higher income. The net benefit of car ownership (benefits less costs) must be compared to your financial resources. This comparison will provide you insight as to whether you should get a car—and if you do, how much you can spend on it.

Just as you should evaluate the relative financial impact of various choices, such as purchasing a car, so must a company evaluate the financial impact of its choices. Companies need financial information to guide decisions such as:

1. How many units must be sold in order to earn a specified amount of profit?

2. Will additional advertising, promotion, or salesperson effort be profitable?

3. Should a product be discontinued?

4. What will be the profit impact from changing the sales price?

5. Should a new region be opened, or should the investment go to expanding an existing region?

6. Will offering a rebate be profitable?

7. Should a new salesperson be hired?

8. Should the company invest in improving quality?

In this chapter we will discuss how companies use financial information to make decisions.

BASIC COST TERMS AND RELATIONSHIPS

What is meant by the term "cost"? The term may refer to the *cost* of a new machine, the *cost* of goods sold, the *cost* of land, the *cost* of salaries. **Exhibit 15.1** illustrates the nature of cost. A *cost* is a payment of cash or other asset in return for a benefit. The benefit may either be immediately realized by the firm or be deferred (delayed) into future periods. Benefits that are realized immediately are termed *expenses*, while benefits that are deferred into the future are termed *assets*. For example, a company will pay salaries to receive the immediate benefit of employee services. This type of cost is termed salary expense. In contrast, a company may purchase a truck. The benefits to be received by the truck are deferred over a future period of time. Thus, this type of cost is an asset. As the benefits of the truck are received, it will be depreciated over time. The depreciation represents the realization of truck benefits over the truck's useful life, and is treated as an annual

BEST-USE CORRELATIONS

This chapter addresses the mental and financial discipline of profit management and activity-based costing, which are critical to your *Marketplace* decisions in Q5 and beyond.

Incremental Analysis

With incremental analysis, firms capture the value of working on the margin to improve profitability of activities that have the greatest marginal contribution.

Activity-Based Costing (ABC)

ABC is helpful in evaluating the financial contribution of each business activity, product, or sales territory. As a starter, each product you produce is charged with the relevant costs to create it (direct materials, labor, changeover costs, and overhead) so that you know the true cost of goods sold.

In addition you are given an ABC profit report for each product and sales channel. For example, all relevant advertising and marketing expenses are charged against each brand and sales outlet. Teams use these profit reports to learn the relative profitability of each product and channel so that they can allocate their resources effectively.

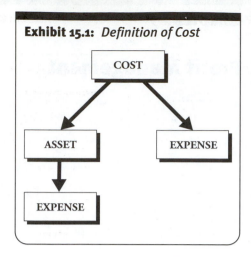

Exhibit 15.1: *Definition of Cost*

expense over the truck's useful life. Thus, all costs eventually become expenses.[1] Some costs become expenses immediately, as in the case of salaries, while other costs become expenses over a future period of time, such as with truck depreciation.

Basic Cost Terms

Companies find it useful to categorize costs according to many different criteria. One of the most important ways to categorize cost is by their source. **Exhibit 15.2** provides an overview of commonly used cost terms categorized by source.

The total costs to make a product can be divided into three distinct categories, manufacturing, distribution, and administrative costs. The manufacturing costs are commonly divided into three separate types of cost: direct material, direct labor, and factory overhead. *Direct material* is the cost of the purchased parts and materials that are used in the product. A color TV, for example, would have direct materials in electronic components, a picture tube, and a cabinet. In contrast, *indirect materials* are manufacturing materials not used in the product or are incidental to the product. For example, the cost of solder for the printed circuit boards assembled in a TV or cleaning supplies used to clean the factory floor would be considered indirect materials.

The *direct labor* includes the wages of workers involved in making the product. For a color TV, direct labor would include the wages of assembly workers who assemble the electrical components of the TV. In contrast, *indirect labor* consists of labor used in the factory to manage and support the manufacturing process. For example, the salary costs of factory engineers, accountants, supervisors, and management would all be considered indirect labor.

Factory overhead is essentially all the remaining factory costs other than direct labor and direct materials. For example, factory overhead consists of indirect material, indirect labor, depreciation of factory equipment, process engineering, cost of quality improvement, cost of product changeovers, factory utilities, and factory property taxes.

The sum of the factory overhead and direct labor costs is called *conversion cost*. Conversion costs are the costs needed to convert raw materials into finished products. Some companies simplify reports by reporting only conversion costs rather than reporting direct labor and factory overhead as separate items.

The distribution costs consist of the costs to distribute the product, including both warehousing and freight costs. Selling costs represent the cost to sell the product, including advertising, sales office expenses, promotional costs, and sales force compensation. The administrative costs are all the other costs of the business and include corporate office expenses, executive salaries, and corporate support costs, such as computer costs.

Product Costs

The manufacturing costs are termed *product costs* because these costs are required to make the product. For financial reporting purposes, product costs are first treated as inventory until the product is sold. This treatment is consistent with the matching principle, which requires expenses to be matched against their associated revenues. Product cost flows are illustrated in **Exhibit 15.3**.

Direct labor, direct materials, and factory overhead are first assigned to products that are in the manufacturing process. This is termed *work in process inventory*. As the product is completed, the work in process becomes *finished goods inventory*. When the product is sold, the cost is transferred from the finished goods inventory to cost of goods sold. Thus, it would not be unusual to spend money for production costs in one period and have these same costs become cost of goods sold on the income statement at a later period.

Period Costs

The distribution and administrative expenses are called *period costs* for financial reporting purposes. *Period costs* are costs that are associated with a period of time, rather than a

Exhibit 15.2: *Costs Categorized by Source*

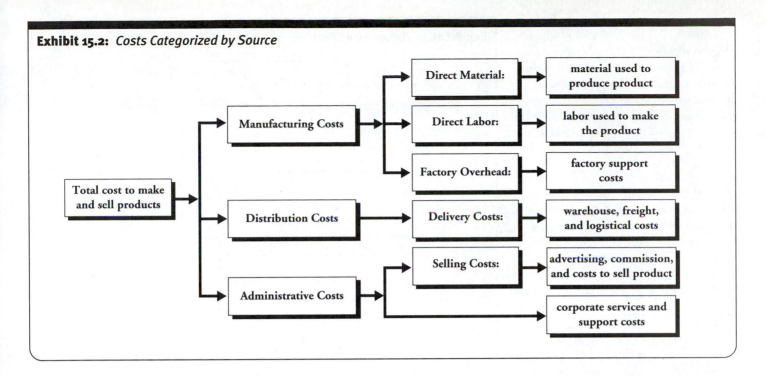

Exhibit 15.3: *Product Cost Flows*

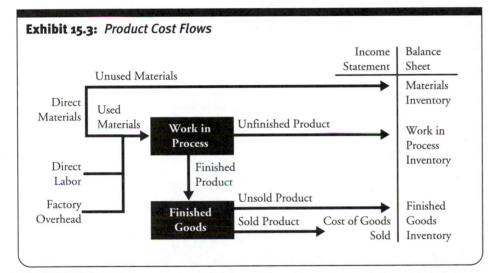

Exhibit 15.4: *Activity Bases*

Type of Business	Cost Category	Activity Base
University	Faculty salaries	Number of classes
Passenger airline	Fuel	Number of miles flown
Manufacturing	Direct materials	Number of units produced
Hospital	Nurse wages	Number of patients
Hotel	Housekeeping wages	Number of guests
Bank	Teller wages	Number of banking transactions
Insurance	Claim processing salaries	Number of claims

product. These costs are not inventoried but are expensed on the income statement when they are incurred. Thus, unlike product costs, period costs are recognized as an expense in the period the cash is spent.

Service companies have much less uniformity in the use of cost terms, but generally a service company would have operating costs instead of manufacturing; marketing costs instead of distribution; and administrative costs. Many service companies do not use inventory accounts since there is no manufactured product.

Cost Behavior

Profit management is strongly influenced by the behavior of costs. *Cost behavior* describes how cost changes relative to changes in an associated activity base. An *activity base* is a measure of physical volume of activity. For example, the activity base associated with machining is machine hours.

There is a wide variety of activity bases used by managers for evaluating cost behavior. See **Exhibit 15.4** for some examples of these bases, along with their related cost categories, for a variety of businesses.

There are two basic cost behaviors: fixed and variable. A *fixed cost* is one that does not change with changes in the underlying activity base. A *variable cost* changes proportionately to changes in an underlying activity base. To illustrate, consider the annual operating costs of an automobile. The activity base for automobile expenses is the number of miles driven. The annual registration and insurance costs are fixed relative to the number of miles driven in a year. However, the fuel and maintenance costs are variable to the number of miles driven during the year.

Incremental Analysis

It is important to understand the impact of a decision on expected costs. For example, assume you were considering a job as a pizza delivery person for the summer. Assume further that this job required you to use your own car. It would be important for you to evaluate how much your car expenses would increase as a result of delivering pizza. The fixed costs, such as the registration and insurance, should not change. However, the fuel and maintenance costs would increase with the increased driving from pizza delivery. Thus, at a minimum, you would need to be assured of receiving sufficient compensation to cover these variable expenses. In addition, if you were planning on a long-term pizza delivery career, you would probably want additional compensation to recover a portion of the original purchase price of car since you would need to replace the car more frequently.

Managers often must evaluate courses of future operations or choose among competing alternatives. This type of analysis is called *incremental analysis.* Incremental analysis must often focus on the revenues and costs that are relevant to the decision at hand. Costs that have been incurred in the past are not relevant to the decision. These are called *sunk costs.* To illustrate, assume a college is evaluating a decision to add a section of *Survey of Business.* Assume there is demand for this section by 30 additional students. The analysis should include the relevant revenues and costs as follows.

Differential revenues	
from 30 students	$9,000
Less differential expenses:	
Instructor salary	6,500
Supplies	500
Computer-related expenses	500
Differential profit	$1,500

The new section should be added because it will contribute an additional $1,500 profit to the school. Notice the fixed costs associated with the classroom were not included in the analysis. The ongoing classroom depreciation will be incurred regardless of whether the section is added or not; therefore, it is not relevant to this decision. The classroom depreciation is a sunk cost.

Break-Even Analysis

An important tool using variable and fixed costs is break-even analysis. A break-even analysis determines the sales volume that is sufficient to cover both fixed and variable expenses. To illustrate, assume the Griffin Company manufactures a product that has

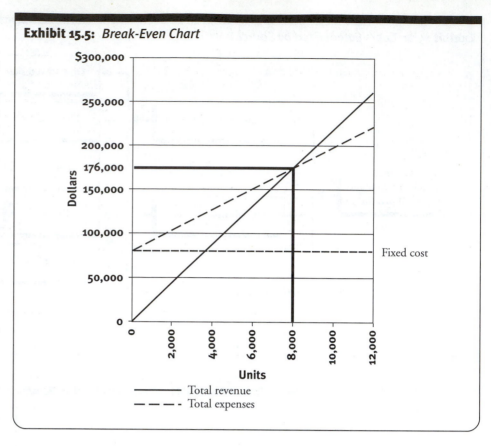

Exhibit 15.5: *Break-Even Chart*

— Total revenue
--- Total expenses

a sales price of $22 per unit, a variable cost of $12 per unit, and $80,000 of fixed cost. A chart could be constructed as shown in **Exhibit 15.5**. The sales volume line is drawn at a slope for $22 per unit. The total cost line is the sum of the fixed cost line at $80,000 plus the variable cost of $12 per unit. The total cost line intersects the sales line at a point representing $176,000 and 8,000 units. This point is the break-even point.

The break-even point can also be calculated mathematically by dividing the total fixed costs by the contribution margin per unit. The *contribution margin* per unit is the sales price less the variable cost per unit. The contribution margin per unit for Griffin is $10 ($22 − $12). The break-even volume of 8,000 units can be shown as follows:

$$\text{Break-even volume} = \frac{\text{Fixed costs}}{\text{Contribution margin per unit}}$$

$$\text{Break-even volume} = \frac{\$80,000}{\$22 - \$12}$$

$$\text{Break-even volume} = 8,000 \text{ units}$$

Managers can evaluate the impact of decisions or events on the break-even point. A summary of these decisions or events and their impact on breakeven follows (I is for increase, D for decrease).

Variable	Decision	Break-Even Impact
Sales price	I	D
	D	I
Variable cost per unit	I	I
	D	D
Fixed cost	I	I
	D	D

PLANNING

One of the ways management directs operations is by developing plans expressed in financial terms. Such a plan is termed a *budget.* A budget charts the course of future action for an enterprise and is useful for verifying that the plan is on track. A budget serves management in the same manner as an architect's blueprints aid a builder or a navigator's flight plan aids a pilot.

The budgeting process begins with management's strategy. The strategy is formulated in terms of planned events and outcomes. *Events* are planned actions, such as launching a new product, building a plant, or opening a new region. *Outcomes* are the result of events. An example of outcomes is increased planned sales levels that result from increased advertising or from opening a new region. The budgeting process translates planned events and outcomes into financial terms.

Exhibit 15.6: *Budgeting Process for the Gemini Company*

(a)

Income Statement for the Year Ended December 31, 20X1

Sales*	$500,000
Cost of goods sold**	300,000
Gross margin	$200,000
Selling expenses:	
Advertising	30,000
Sales salaries	50,000
Sales office expenses	20,000
General and administrative expenses:	
Research and development	40,000
Operating profit	$60,000
Taxes	24,000
Net income	$36,000

* 100,000 units × $5 price/unit

** (100,000 units × $2.00 variable cost/unit) + $100,000 fixed cost

(b)

Outcomes for 20X2 Planned Events

Planned Event	Estimated outcome
Increase advertising by $20,000	Increase sales by 10,000 units
Increase research and development by $10,000	Launch new product, increase sales by 3,000 units
Open new region, increase sales salaries by $30,000 and sales office expenses by $5,000	Increase sales by 14,000 units

(c)

Direct materials	$1.00
Direct labor	.60
Variable factory overhead	.40
Total variable production cost per unit	$2.00

(d)

Advertising expense	$50,000
Sales salaries	80,000
Sales office expenses	25,000
Research and development	50,000
Total	$205,000

(e)

Budgeted Income Statement for the Year Ended December 31, 20X2

Sales	$635,000
Cost of goods sold	354,000
Gross margin	$281,000
Selling expenses:	
Advertising	50,000
Sales salaries	80,000
Sales office expenses	25,000
General and administrative expenses:	
Research and development	50,000
Operating profit	$76,000
Taxes	30,400
Net income	$45,600

(f)

Gemini Company Projected Cash Position

Projected cash from operations:	
Source of cash from sales	
(127,000 units × $5.00 per unit)	$635,000
Use of cash for production	
(127,000 units × $2.00 per unit)	254,000
Use of cash for selling, general, and administrative expenses	205,000
Use of cash for taxes	30,400
Net cash from operations	$145,600

To illustrate the budgeting process, see **Exhibit 15.6(a)** for the Gemini Company's income statement for the year just ended and Exhibit 15.6(b) for the events and outcomes that are planned for the coming year, 20X2.

The budgeting process begins with estimating sales for the upcoming year. Planned sales are determined by multiplying the planned quantity of sales by the planned price. In estimating the quantity of sales, the historical sales volume is a useful starting point. The historical sales volume is adjusted by the planned events and other general economic and industry factors. The total estimated sales quantity is multiplied by the expected price to determine the total estimated sales. For Gemini Company, assume that only the planned events are expected to affect the projected sales volume. In addition, Gemini management expects a price of $5 per unit. Therefore, the planned sales are expected to increase by:

27,000 units × $5 per unit = $135,000

After the projected sales are determined, the production costs must be estimated. The *variable* production costs will increase with the increase in sales. The *fixed* production expenses will not increase, unless there has been a planned event to expand plant capacity. We assume that there is sufficient plant capacity to produce the planned sales volume. The variable production costs per unit for Gemini Co. are given in Exhibit 15.6(c).

Therefore, the estimated increase in production costs can be determined by multiplying the increase in sales unit volume by the variable production cost per unit as follows:

27,000 units × $2.00 = $54,000

Assuming no planned changes in inventory balances, the cost of goods sold on the income statement would be expected to increase by $54,000.

The sales, general, and administrative budgeted expenses would be determined next. This budget is determined using information from the planned events combined with the historical income statement information. Given the events noted above, Gemini would have the operating expense budget shown in Exhibit 15.6(d).

The complete budgeted income statement can now be developed; see Exhibit 15.6(e).

Management will also be interested in how projected events will affect the company's cash position. In Gemini's case its projected cash will increase by $145,600, shown in Exhibit 15.6(f). The change in cash is greater than the net income by $100,000. This is so because Gemini has $100,000 of depreciation expense, which is included in the cost of goods sold (part of factory overhead) on the income statement but is not a use of cash. Although Gemini had no projected investing and financing activities, the budgeted cash flows would be also be affected by such activities. Examples of such activities include expanding the plant, investing in a subsidiary, or issuing stock.

Evaluating the projected performance is the final step of the budgeting process. This is because the budget, requiring management to change assumptions, events, pricing, and estimated outcomes may not be acceptable. For Gemini, first consider the projected change in gross margin relative to the change in projected sales. Sales are estimated to increase by 27 percent ($135,000 ÷ $500,000). However, the gross margin increased by 40.5 percent ($81,000 ÷ 200,000). Why did gross margin increase more than sales? The reason is due to economies of scale. *Economies of scale* allow a company to produce more units at a declining cost per unit by spreading the fixed costs over a larger number of units. In Gemini's case the plant capacity did not change with the increase in production volume; thus, the cost per unit declined as production increased. This caused the cost of goods sold to increase at a slower rate than the increase in sales and, hence, caused the gross margin to increase at a faster rate than the sales volume increase.

Next, management should evaluate the change in operating profit relative to increases in sales volume. For Gemini, the operating profit is projected to increase by 26.7 percent ($16,000 ÷ $60,000), which is near the projected sales growth rate (27 percent). However, the operating profit grew at a slower rate than the growth in the gross margin. Why is this? The reason is that the sales, general, and administrative expenses are projected to grow at rate faster than the growth in sales (46.4% vs. 27%). Thus, the large increase in gross margin was lost by an equally large increase in sales, general, and administrative expenses. This could be a cause for concern, indicating that incremental sales effort is producing increasingly smaller amounts of sales. An example of this

occurs when incremental advertising or sales effort begins to generate diminishing returns. For example, the 45th salesperson in a sales office may actually cause confusion and add little to sales. A manager must be careful in interpreting such information, however. For example, alternative explanations may be that the company is incurring significant start-up, product launch, and research and development (R&D) expenses for which the sales volume has yet to materialize.

As the year progresses, actual results can be compared to the budget. Deviations from the budget can indicate changes in tactics or other "mid course corrections." For example, the Mattel Toy Company overestimated the demand for a particular type of Barbie® Doll during a recent Christmas season and had to reduce price on this particular type of Barbie to remove the inventory.

CONTROLLING

After the plan has been set, operations must be monitored or controlled. This is done by comparing the actual amount of money spent and earned against the amount budgeted. The differences between the budgeted amounts and the planned amounts are termed *variances*. For example, if Gemini had actual sales in 20X2 of $600,000, then this would be an unfavorable revenue variance of $35,000 ($635,000 − $600,000) from the budget. The actual cause of the variance could be analyzed further by determining the amount of the variance due to prices or quantities different than planned. Such variances can also be determined for the expense line items.

In addition to financial variances, companies also use a variety of measures to control operations along a number of dimensions. A popular approach for measuring performance is the *balanced scorecard*.[2] A common balanced scorecard design measures performance in the innovation and learning, customer, internal, and financial dimensions of a business. These four areas can be diagrammed, as shown in **Exhibit 15.7**.

The *innovation and learning* perspective measures the amount of innovation in an organization. For example, a drug company, such as Eli Lily, would measure the number of drugs in its Food and Drug Administration approval pipeline, the amount of R&D spending per period (as a percent of sales), and the length of time to turn ideas into marketable products. Man-

aging the R&D process is critical to Eli Lily's success as an organization, so innovation and learning measures are needed in additional to more traditional financial measures. The *customer perspective* measures customer satisfaction, loyalty, and perceptions. For example, Amazon.com measures the number of repeat visitors to its Web site as a measure of customer loyalty. Amazon.com needs repeat customers because the costs of acquiring new customers are very high. The *internal process* perspective measures the effectiveness and efficiency of internal business processes. For example, DaimlerChrysler measures quality by the average warranty claims per automobile and efficiency by the number of labor hours per automobile.

The *financial perspective* measures the economic performance of the business. Summary financial measures include return on investment (ROI) and residual income. The ROI can be calculated according to the DuPont formula as:

$$\text{Return on investment} = \text{Profit margin} \times \text{Asset utilization}$$

$$\frac{\text{Net income}}{\text{Total assets}} = \frac{\text{Net income}}{\text{Sales}} \times \frac{\text{Sales}}{\text{Total assets}}$$

Thus, the return on investment is the product of the profit margin and the asset utilization. As an illustration, the DuPont formula can be pictured as a pasta machine. The dough (revenue) goes in at the top of the machine. The speed of the crank is the asset utilization, and the size of the opening is the profit margin. When the crank is turned fast and the opening is large, then much "spaghetti" (profit) is made. For example, Microsoft's DuPont analysis reveals:

$$\text{Return on investment} = \text{Profit margin} \times \text{Asset utilization}$$

$$18\% = 41\% \times 0.44$$

Microsoft has an exceptional profit margin, which is the primary contributor to its return on investment. In contrast, Dell Computer Corp's DuPont analysis reveals,

$$16.2\% = 6.8\% \times 2.4$$

Dell's return on assets is obtained by smaller profit margins but higher asset utilization in comparison to Microsoft. Overall, the DuPont analysis shows a company where ROI can be improved.

The residual income (or economic value added—EVA) of a business is related to the ROA but calculated as an absolute dollar

Exhibit 15.7: *Balanced Scorecard*

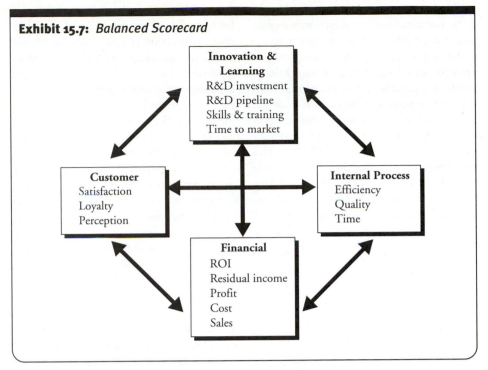

UNIT PRODUCT COST AND FULL COST REPORTING

When costs are associated with an element of the business, that element is said to be a *cost object*. A *cost object* is a cost accumulation point. Examples of cost objects are departments, products, customers, regions, and plants. Costs are associated with objects to support decision making about the object. For example, controlling the costs of a department requires the department to be treated as a cost object. Likewise, determining the profit of a product or customer requires costs and revenues to be attached to the products or customers.

One of the responsibilities of management is to price products to achieve a profit. What price should be used? Often the price is determined using a variety of factors, including the prices set by competition and the cost. The full cost of the product establishes the pricing floor below which the product is sold at a loss. The product cost requires manufacturing costs to be attached to the product cost object.

The product cost is determined from the three manufacturing costs. Direct materials are direct to the product; thus, this assignment is usually not difficult. Direct labor is also direct to the product. Again, the accounting system tracks the amount of labor used in making a product, so this cost can be identified with the product easily. For example, Sony knows how much material cost and labor goes into its various color TV models because its accounting and manufacturing systems track these items.

In contrast to direct labor and direct materials, the factory overhead is not direct to the products. As a result, the factory overhead must be allocated, or assigned, to the product. The method of allocation should trace the factory overhead to the product, or other cost object, using an activity base that is associated with the overhead cost. Often the factory overhead is divided into separate activity cost pools. *Activity cost pools* are factory overhead cost accumulations that are associated with a given activity, such as machine usage, inspections, moving, production set ups, and engineering activities. An activity base for each activity cost pool is used to assign the activity cost to the product. For example, the number of inspections would be an appropriate activity base for the inspecting activity, while the number of machine

figure rather than as a ratio. The residual income is the excess of income from operations over a minimum acceptable income from operations. The minimum acceptable income from operations is normally computed by multiplying a minimum rate of return by the amount of business total assets. Often, the minimum rate of return is the cost of capital for the firm. To illustrate, assume that Dell Computer Corp.'s minimum cost of capital was 10 percent. Dell's residual income would be calculated as:

Residual income = Operating income −
(Total assets × Minimum rate of return),

$$\$1,320 =$$
$$\$2,663 − (\$13,435 × 10\%)$$

In words, Dell returned $1,320,000,000 to shareholders' beyond the minimum cost of capital.

CAPITAL BUDGETING

Organizations must not only plan and control their annual operations through an operating budget but also plan their capital budget. The capital budget is the budget for new fixed assets, such as property, plant, and equipment. The money spent on capital is money that is placed at risk for a future return. Future returns are often uncertain; thus, care must be taken in analyzing capital projects. Fixed asset investments can be justified if the cash flows from the investment exceed the original cost of the investment.

One method of evaluating a capital project is the cash payback period. The *cash payback period* is the number of years required to return the original cost of the investment. Companies will often set a minimum cash payback period for approving an investment.

To illustrate such an analysis, assume Maddox Company is considering a $1,000,000 plant expansion. Assume further that Maddox has a minimum cash payback period of three years. That is, an investment must provide a cash payback of three years or less to be accepted. The $1,000,000 plant expansion will allow Maddox to launch a new product. The new product is expected to sell 10,000 units per year at a price of $65 per unit. The variable manufacturing cost is $20 and the selling cost is $5 per unit. In this simple example, the new product launch is expected to generate $400,000 per year in positive cash flows (10,000 units × [$65 − $20 − $5]). The cash payback period for this investment would be:

$$\text{Cash payback period} = \frac{\text{Investment amount}}{\text{Equal annual cash flow}}$$

$$\text{Cash payback period} = \frac{\$1,000,000}{\$400,000} = 2.5 \text{ years}$$

Thus, the investment would meet Maddox's minimum payback threshold (≤ 3 years) and would be accepted.

hours would be an activity base for machine related costs. The activity base is divided into the activity cost pool to determine the activity rate used for allocating factory overhead to cost objects. When activities are used to trace costs to a cost object, it is termed *activity-based costing* (ABC). John Deere & Co. uses ABC to determine the cost of machined parts. In its system, activity pools and rates are determined for purchasing, setup, materials handling, supervision, part administration, and machining.

To illustrate, assume that Jenkins Company manufactures two products, a 19" color TV and a 27" color TV. The company plans to manufacture and sell 5,000 units of each color TV. The factory overhead for Jenkins Company is divided into three activity pools: variable factory overhead (includes supplies, power, supervision), changeover overhead, and fixed factory overhead (includes plant and equipment depreciation and plant management salaries). The activity base associated with *variable* factory overhead is determined to be direct labor hours. The 19" TV requires one direct labor hour per unit, while the 27" TV requires 1.5 direct labor hours per unit. The total amount of direct labor hours to produce both products is 12,500 direct labor hours (DLH), as shown below:

TV	Units/Hour	DLH
19"	5,000 × 1.0 =	5,000
27"	5,000 units × 1.5 =	47,500
Total		12,500

Assume that the variable factory overhead for Jenkins Company is $125,000. The variable factory overhead rate can be determined by dividing the variable factory overhead by the activity base to get a rate of $10 per direct labor hour as follows:

$$\text{Variable factory overhead rate} = \frac{\$125,000}{12,500 \text{ direct labor hours}}$$

Variable factory overhead rate = $10 per direct labor hour

The amount of variable factory overhead assigned to each unit of product can now be determined by multiplying the direct labor hours (DLH) per unit by the variable factory overhead rate as follows:

TV	Units/Cost/ Hour	Variable Factory Overhead/ Unit
19"	1 × $10	$10 per unit
27"	1.5 × $10	$15 per unit

The *changeover* activity is related to the costs associated with changing the production line from producing one type of product to another. In Jenkins Company, changeover is related to changing the production process from producing one color TV size to producing the other color TV size. Assume the direct labor, machine depreciation, and other overhead costs associated with a changeover are $150,000. This changeover cost is related to the number of changeovers that occur in the production line. The number of changeovers associated with each product is as follows:

TV	Changeovers
19"	100
27"	200
Total	300

Therefore, the $500 rate per changeover could then be determined as shown below:

$$\text{Changeover rate} = \frac{\$150,000}{300 \text{ changeovers}}$$

Changeover rate = $500 per changeover.

The changeover cost associated with each type of color TV can be determined by multiplying the changeover rate times the number of changeovers for each product. Therefore, the changeover cost associated with 19" TVs is $50,000 ($500 × 100 changeovers). Since there were 5,000 units of the 19" TV, the changeover cost would translate to $10 per unit ($50,000 ÷ 5,000 units). The changeover cost associated with 27" TVs is $100,000 ($500 × 200 changeovers), or $20 per unit.

A rate for the *fixed* factory overhead can also be calculated. To illustrate, assume Jenkins Company had plant and equipment depreciation for the year (a fixed cost) of $800,000. In addition, assume the practical capacity of the factory equipment is 40,000 machine hours. The practical capacity represents the total available capacity of plant and equipment in normal operating use. Dividing the practical capacity into the fixed factory overhead yields a fixed factory overhead rate of $20 per machine hour, shown as follows:

$$\text{Fixed factory overhead rate} = \frac{\$800,000}{40,000 \text{ machine hours}}$$

Fixed factory overhead rate = $20 per machine hour

Now assume the 19" TV required 2 machine hours per unit and the 27" TV required 4 machine hours per unit. To pro-

duce 5,000 units for each TV, there would be 30,000 total estimated machine hours. Notice that this is less than the 40,000 hours of practical capacity. The Jenkins Company has 10,000 hours of excess capacity in its fixed overhead. The cost of this excess capacity can be determined by multiplying the fixed factory overhead rate by the number of hours in excess capacity, or $20,000 (10,000 hours × $20). The cost of excess capacity can be displayed on the income statement below the gross profit line in order to highlight the cost of underutilized assets.

The remaining fixed factory overhead would be allocated to the units produced. The fixed factory overhead allocated to each unit of product would be determined by multiplying the machine hours per unit by the fixed factory overhead rate. Therefore, the 19" TV would have a fixed factory overhead of $40 per unit (2 machine hours per unit × $20), while the 27" TV would be $80 per unit (4 machine hours per unit × $20).

The unit cost for each TV can now be determined by adding the three overhead unit costs from above with the direct material and direct labor per unit given in the table below. The 19" TV has a unit cost of $160, and the 27" TV has a unit cost of $295, as shown below:

Item/Unit	19"	27"
Direct material	$ 80	$150
Direct labor	20	30
Variable factory overhead	10	15
Changeover cost	10	20
Fixed factory overhead	40	80
Total	$160	$295

These amounts are termed the *full* product cost per unit. The per unit product cost can be used by Jenkins Company to guide their pricing strategies. The price must be set high enough to cover the full product cost, distribution, administrative, and excess capacity cost, as well as ensure a long-term profit. Assume Jenkins sets prices on the 19" TV at $210, and the 27" TV at $320. If Jenkins sells 5,000 units of each type of TV and the distribution and administrative expenses total $150,000, then the income statement would appear as shown in **Exhibit 15.8**.

As you can see from the income statement, the sales price is sufficient to cover all the costs of the business and still generate an operating profit of $80,000. The method for determining the operating profit illustrated above is termed *full-cost*

Exhibit 15.8: Income Statement— Jenkins Company

Jenkins Company
Income Statement
For the Year
Ended 20XX

Revenue	$2,650,000[1]
Cost of goods sold	2,275,000[2]
Gross profit	$ 250,000
Selling and administration	150,000
Excess capacity cost	20,000
Operating profit	$ 80,000

[1] (5,000 units × $210 per unit) + (5,000 units × $320 per unit)

[2] (5,000 units × $160 per unit) + (5,000 units × $295 per unit)

Exhibit 15.9: Ipso and Facto Selling and Administrative Activity

Selling and Administrative Activities	Ipso	Facto
Post-sale technical support	The product is easy to use by the customer	Product requires specialized training in order to be used by the customer
Order writing	Product requires no technical information from the customer	Product requires detailed technical information from customer
Promotional support	Product requires no promotional effort	Product requires extensive promotional effort
Order entry	Product is purchased in large volumes per order	Product is purchased in small volumes per order
Customer return processing	Product has few customer returns	Product has many customer returns
Shipping document preparation	Product is shipped domestically	Product is shipped internationally, requiring customs and export documents
Shipping and handling	Product is not hazardous	Product is hazardous, requiring specialized shipping and handling
Field service	Product has few warranty claims	Product has many warranty claims

accounting. This is so because all of the manufacturing costs, both direct and indirect, are included in the cost of goods sold. The full cost approach is required by GAAP in preparing financial reports to external users, such as owners and creditors.

ACTIVITY-BASED COSTING FOR SELLING AND ADMINISTRATIVE EXPENSES

Generally accepted accounting principles also require that selling and administrative expenses be treated as period expenses on the income statement prepared for external users. However, accountants may allocate selling and administrative expenses to products in preparing product profitability reports for management. A traditional method is to allocate selling and administrative expenses to the products based on the relative product sales volumes. However, products may consume activities in proportions that are unrelated to their sales volumes. When this occurs, activity-based costing may provide a more accurate allocation approach.

To illustrate, assume the Abacus Company has two products, Ipso and Facto. Both products have the same total sales volume. However, both products are not the same in terms of how they consume selling and administrative activities. **Exhibit 15.9.** identifies some of these differences.

If the selling and administrative expenses of Abacus Company were allocated on the basis of sales volumes, both products would be allocated the same amount since they both had the same sales volume. Does this seem correct? Should both products have

the same selling and administrative expense? No, they should not. Ipso is much less complex and hence less expensive than Facto. The activity-based costing approach would allocate the selling and administrative activities to each product based on its individual differences in consuming these activities. For example, field service could be allocated on the basis of the number of warranty claims. Since Facto has more claims than Ipso, more of this activity would be allocated to Facto and less to Ipso. As a result, allocating selling and administrative expenses using activity-based costing would result in more accurate product profitability reports for Abacus Company management.

Managers often use activity-based costing principles to determine the profit of various segments of the business. Segment profit reporting will be discussed in the next section.

SEGMENT PROFIT REPORTING

General business managers use profit information to evaluate the performance of business segments. A *business segment* is a portion of business that can be managed for profit. Examples of business segments include sales regions, products, distribution channels, and customers. For example, a business segment for Procter & Gamble is

Ivory Soap® because the Ivory Soap product line is managed for profit in Procter & Gamble.

Under segment profit reporting, the direct costs are separated from the indirect costs. This is done to eliminate the impact of indirect costs from the decision. Recall that we stated earlier that sunk costs are not relevant to future decisions. Separating the direct costs from the indirect costs in this way is termed *direct costing*. To illustrate, we will begin with product segments.

Product Profit Reporting

We will first illustrate profit reporting for product segments. The basic structure of such a report is as follows:

Revenues
Less:
    Direct materials
    Direct labor
    Direct manufacturing activities
    Other nonmanufacturing direct expenses and activities
Product margin

Determining product profit begins with identifying the revenues associated with a particular product. Normally, this process is not difficult. Next, the direct costs must be assigned to the product. The direct costs consist of the direct material and direct labor.

Additional direct costs include manufacturing activity costs, such as those associated with changeover, inspection, moving, or scheduling activity. In addition, as stated in the previous section, product direct costs may consist of nonmanufacturing expenses that are considered period costs for financial reporting purposes. For example, product-specific advertising, warranty expenses, and shipping expenses may be direct costs for product profit reporting, even though they normally are considered period costs for financial reporting. The *product margin* is the revenue less the direct expenses and activities associated with the product.

Costs that are not direct to the product, including fixed factory overhead, are not included in the product profit report. This is so because the indirect costs are not relevant to decisions regarding the product line, except pricing as shown above. For example, if the product manager decided to increase advertising for the product line, we would expect sales volume to increase along with the additional promotional expenses. However, the manager would not expect costs unrelated to the product line to be influenced by the promotion decision; therefore, these indirect costs should not be included in the report. To do so could hinder break-even and incremental analysis.

The calculations and implications of these profit numbers will be illustrated with the following example. The Denver Company manufactures two varieties of sporting equipment, golf equipment and snow skis. The sporting equipment is distributed and sold to retailers in the Northern and Southern sales regions. The product profit report shown in **Exhibit 15.10** is prepared for Denver Company.

Why did the golf club product line have a better product margin percentage of sales than the snow ski product line? The report indicates that the snow skis had higher warranty, advertising, changeover, and sales commissions as a percentage of sales than did the golf club line. These higher costs more than offset the more favorable direct material costs as a percentage of sales experienced by the snow ski line, resulting in lower profitability compared to the golf equipment.

Region Profit Reporting

Once products are manufactured, they must be sold in the marketplace. Additional distribution, sales, and administrative costs are incurred at this stage. These costs are often direct to sales regions. For example, the salaries of the salespersons in the Northern Region may not be direct to the golf equipment because the salespersons may sell both golf equipment and ski equipment. However, the salesperson's salaries are direct to the region, since they are incurred for the sole benefit of the region.

The region profit report for the Denver Company is illustrated in **Exhibit 15.11**.

The region profit report begins with the revenues earned in the region. These revenues are from product sales of golf equipment and snow skis in the region. The direct product costs associated with these sales are then subtracted from the revenues to create the product margin. The total product margin of $1,190,000 in Exhibit 15.11 will equal the total product margin in the product profit report in Exhibit 15.10.

After deducting the direct product costs, the direct region costs that are common to all products sold in the region are subtracted in order to determine the region margin. The direct region costs are incurred as the result of decisions made by the region manager but are not direct to the products. An example of such an expenditure is the lease expense associated with a sales office (office expense). The lease expense is direct to the region; however, all products benefit from this expenditure.

The resulting region margin can be used to evaluate the relative profit performance of the regions. For Denver Company, the Southern Region has a slightly higher region margin as a percent of sales than the Northern Region. A close examination of Exhibit 15.11 indicates that, except for local advertising, the region direct costs are

all higher as a percentage of sales. How, then, is the final performance better? Apparently, the Southern Region is able to sell a more profitable mix of products and generate a higher product margin than the Northern Region. The product margin is high enough to offset the higher region direct costs, so that overall the Southern Region has slightly better performance than the Northern Region.

After the region margin is determined, the costs common to all products and regions are then subtracted from the total region margin to determine the total operating profit. These common costs cannot be directly associated with either regions or products. These costs are not influenced by decisions made with respect to products in the regions and so should be excluded in determining the profit performance of these segments. Such common costs include factory depreciation, the cost of excess capacity (as described earlier), general research and development, corporate administrative expenses, and other factory overhead that benefits all the products in the plant. The resulting operating profit will be the same as found on the financial statements prepared for external users.

Managers of regions and products must be careful to price their products so that all costs are covered, not just the direct costs associated with their segment responsibilities. For example, the management of Denver Company must price the golf equipment and snow skis to cover an additional $349,000 of common costs, beyond the product and region direct costs. As can be seen, the Denver Company generates sufficient profit to cover common profit and generate an 8 percent return on sales.

Exhibit 15.10: *Product Profit Report*

Denver Company Product Profit Report
For the Quarter Ended March 31

	Golf Equipment	Percent of Sales	Snow Skis	Percent of Sales
Revenue	$3,360,000	100.00%	$3,500,000	100.00%
Direct material	1,400,000	41.67	1,190,000	34.00
Direct labor	70,000	2.08	70,000	2.00
Changeover cost	490,000	14.58	560,000	16.00
Warranty	70,000	2.08	350,000	10.00
Advertising	280,000	8.33	700,000	20.00
Sales commissions	140,000	4.17	210,000	6.00
Shipping	70,000	2.08	70,000	2.00
Product margin	$840,000	25.00%	$350,000	10.00%

Exhibit 15.11: *Region Profit Report*

Denver Company Region Profit Report
For the Quarter Ended March 31

	Northern		Southern		Total	
Revenues	$3,940,000	100.00%	$2,920,000	100.00%	$6,860,000	100.00%
Direct product costs	3,330,000	84.52	2,340,000	80.14	5,670,000	82.65
Product margin	$ 610,000	15.48%	$ 580,000	19.86%	$1,190,000	17.35%
Direct region costs:						
Promotions—sales force incentives (all sales)	25,000	0.63	30,000	1.03	55,000	0.80
Local advertising—all products	25,000	0.63	5,000	0.17	30,000	0.44
Office expenses—leases	45,000	1.14	80,000	2.74	125,000	1.82
Sales force training	30,000	0.76	50,000	1.71	80,000	1.17
Region margin	$ 485,000	12.31%	$ 415,000	14.21%	$ 900,000	13.12%
Company common expenses:						
Research and development					24,000	0.35
Depreciation					50,000	0.73
Quality expenses					75,000	2.92
Excess capacity					200,000	1.09
Operating profit					$ 551,000	8.03%

Exhibit 15.12: *Region by Product Profit Report*

Denver Company
Region Product Profit Report—Northern Region
For the Quarter Ended March 31

	Golf Equipment		Snow Skis		Northern Region Total	
Revenues	$1,440,000	100.00%	$2,500,000	100.00%	$3,940,000	100.00%
Direct material	600,000	41.67	850,000	34.00	1,450,000	
Direct labor	30,000	2.08	50,000	2.00	80,000	
Changeover cost	210,000	14.58	400,000	16.00	610,000	
Warranty	50,000	3.47	230,000	9.20	280,000	
Advertising	170,000	11.81	450,000	18.00	620,000	
Sales commissions	70,000	4.86	140,000	5.60	210,000	
Shipping	30,000	2.08	50,000	2.00	80,000	
Direct product costs	$1,160,000	80.56%	$2,170,000	86.80%	$3,330,000	84.52%
Product margin	$ 280,000	19.44%	$ 330,000	13.20%	$ 610,000	15.48%
Direct region costs						
Promotions—sales force incentives (all sales)					25,000	0.63
Local advertising—all products					25,000	0.63
Office expenses—leases					45,000	1.14
Sales force training					30,000	0.76
Region margin					$ 485,000	12.31%

As stated earlier, often the full product costs per unit are used to help set pricing levels. However, incremental business can contribute profits to the business at prices less the full cost but greater than the contribution margin per unit. Such aggressive pricing can be a successful short-term tactic to improve profit. However, this tactic can lead to downward pressure in prices in the long term, so it should be used carefully and sparingly.

Region by Product Profit Reporting

Assume the manager of the Northern Region wished to have more specific information about the product performance in the region. The product manager could request a region by product profit report. Such a report would allow the manager to "drill down" to the product profit incurred inside a particular region. An example of a region by product report for Denver Company is shown in **Exhibit 15.12**.

The total Northern Region margin of $485,000 is the same as the Northern Region margin reported in Exhibit 15.11. However, in Exhibit 15.12 we are able to see how the various products contribute to the overall region margin. First, the revenues are identified for the two products. Apparently, snow skis have a larger percent of the total region sales than do golf equipment. Next, the direct manufacturing costs (direct materials, direct labor, and changeover) are subtracted from the revenues. The percentage of sales for the manufacturing direct expenses is the same as shown in the product profit report in Exhibit 15.11. This is so because these expenses are factory expenses and are not influenced by the region of sale.

The nonmanufacturing direct product costs (warranty, advertising, sales commissions, and shipping) may be specific to both a product and a particular region. For example, in Exhibit 15.12 the advertising is direct to the product. In addition, this advertising may be initiated from decisions made by a regional manager. Therefore, the advertising is also direct to a given region. The region by product profit report should segment the advertising dollars spent to support products from the region. In a sense, the region by product profit report discloses the intersection between product and region direct costs. As a result, the advertising costs as a percent of sales shown in Exhibit 15.12 may not be the same as those shown in the product profit report in Exhibit 15.10. This is because the percentage of nonmanufacturing direct product costs in Exhibit 15.10 is an average across all regions. The specific regional decisions about advertising in each product line are reflected in the region by product profit report, thus the percentages are unique to the region. The same would be true for the other direct product expenses incurred in the region, such as warranty, sales commissions, and shipping.

Lastly, the direct costs to the region are subtracted from the total product margin in order to determine the region margin. These costs, as discussed, are common to all the products sold in the region, so are not included in determining the product margin.

SUMMARY

In this chapter we have reviewed various cost terms used by industry and examined how these costs are used to improve management decisions. We differentiated between variable and fixed costs and showed how this distinction could be used for break-even and incremental analyses. We saw how businesses use financial and nonfinancial information to plan and control operations. We introduced capital budgeting analysis. We illustrated how companies determine the full cost per unit of product and use this information to support pricing decisions and develop financial statements for external users. One method of developing an accurate full product cost is through activity-based costing. The financial statements used by external users, however, may be insufficient for guiding the strategies of the firm. Therefore, we demonstrated how distinguishing between direct and indirect expenses can be used by firms to develop segment profit reports. These reports can be used to determine the profit earned by products, regions, channels, cities, customers, and other strategic segments of the business. Unlike full costing, only the direct costs of a segment are included in determining segment profit in order to remove the distortions that can arise from allocating common costs.

1. The one exception to this general rule is the cost of land. Land is not depreciated; thus, this cost remains an asset until it is sold.
2. The balanced scorecard was developed by R. S Kaplan and D. P. Norton and explained in *The Balanced Scorecard: Translating Strategy into Action* (Cambridge, MA: Harvard Business School Press, 1966).

Chapter 16

John T. Mentzer
University of Tennessee

Supply Chain Management in a Global Economy

The term *supply chain management* (SCM) has risen to prominence over the past 10 years.[1] For example, at the 1995 Annual Conference of the Council of Logistics Management, 13.5 percent of the concurrent session titles contained the words "supply chain." At the 1997 conference, just two years later, the number of sessions containing the term rose to 22.4 percent. In fact, when I chaired the 1997 conference, I joked with the conference committee that one of my goals was to have at least one track at the conference that did *not* contain the words "supply chain management!" SCM has become such a hot topic that it is difficult to pick up a periodical on manufacturing, distribution, marketing, customer management, or transportation without seeing an article about SCM or SCM-related topics.[2]

There are many reasons for the popularity of the concept.[3] Specific drivers may be traced to trends in global sourcing, an emphasis on time and quality-based competition and their respective contributions to greater environmental uncertainty. Corporations have turned increasingly to global sources for their supplies. We need only turn over the products each of us uses each day and look for the country of origin to see how global the world economy has become. You will find that a small minority of your favorite products actually originated in your own country. This globalization of supply has forced companies to look for more effective ways to coordinate the flow of materials into and out of the company. Key to such coordination is an orientation toward closer relationships with suppliers.

Further, companies in particular and supply chains in general compete more today on the basis of time and quality. Getting a defect-free product to the customer faster and more reliably than the competition is no longer seen as a competitive advantage but simply a requirement to be in the market. Customers are demanding products consistently delivered faster, exactly on time, and with no damage. Each of these necessitates closer coordination with suppliers and distributors. This global orientation and increased performance-based competition, combined with rapidly changing technology and economic conditions, all contribute to marketplace uncertainty. This uncertainty requires greater flexibility on the part of individual companies and supply chains, which in turn demands more flexibility in supply chain relationships.

WHAT IS SUPPLY CHAIN MANAGEMENT?

So, given this growing popularity of supply chain management, what is it? Mentzer and others have defined two terms that are relevant to this question.[4]

- A *supply chain* is a set of three or more entities (organizations or individuals) directly involved in the upstream and downstream flows of products, services, finances, and/or information from a source to a customer.

- *Supply chain management* (SCM) is the systemic, strategic coordination of the traditional business functions and of the tactics across these business functions within a particular company and across businesses within the supply chain, for the purposes of improving the long-term performance of the individual companies and the supply chain as a whole.

Much is implied by these definitions. First, there is a definite distinction between *supply chains* as phenomena that exist in

BEST-USE CORRELATIONS

The globalization of supply, the demand for defect-free products, and the need for reliable, on-time, and damage-free delivery require close coordination and cooperation between suppliers and distributors. This chapter explores supply chain management, and the mechanisms *Marketplace* firms can use to elicit channel cooperation in an uncertain global marketplace.

Outsourcing

The choice of either outsourcing or becoming the source of production, a decision *Marketplace* teams face in the second year of operations, presents a number of new challenges. Figuring out how to move products, information, and money between channel partners and eliminating channel conflict is a key concern.

Working Together Is Not Easy

Will you outsource production or become a third-party supplier? The challenges of working out supply arrangements with channel partners is not easy. Your channel partner may be seen as an opponent with whom you must negotiate vigorously for the best contract.

After a few of these short-term contracts, you will hopefully conclude that the system is not working as smoothly and efficiently as you imagined, and it requires a lot of energy to negotiate each quarterly contract. There has to be a better way.

Logistics Leverage

The better way is to follow the advice and examples set out in this chapter. Firms that treat the supply chain as a single distribution system and find ways to make it more efficient and effective achieve logistics leverage. They gain a competitive advantage over firms that have not taken the initiative to think and act as one.

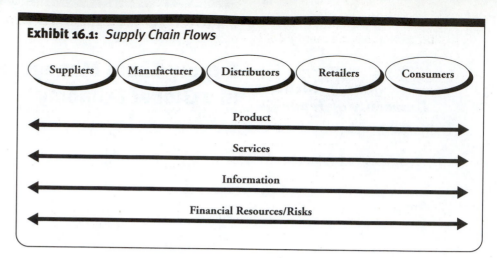

Exhibit 16.1: *Supply Chain Flows*

Suppliers — Manufacturer — Distributors — Retailers — Consumers

Product

Services

Information

Financial Resources/Risks

business and the *management of those supply chains*. The former are simply something that exists, while the latter requires overt management efforts by the organizations within the supply chain. Mentzer and others use the analogy of a river to describe this difference.[5] A river exists whether anyone manages the flow of water from the mountains to the ocean or not. When an individual state uses (and often pollutes) the river without consideration of the other states along the river, it is acting much like the independent, arm's-length method that companies traditionally used to manage their relationships with suppliers and customers in the supply chain. Such behavior by states in the United States has actually led to lawsuits, in which one state sues a state further up river to release more water for its use and/or clean up the water before sending it on down the water basin. The analogy to supply chain management comes when the states work together to keep the water basin clean and to flow enough water so that each state receives what it needs. In other words, the states take a *systemic, strategic* view of the water basin.

Second, SCM must include four upstream and downstream flows (products, services, finances, and/or information) coordinated through three or more companies. **Exhibit 16.1** provides an illustration of the type of companies that might be involved in a supply chain and their potential bidirectional flows. This straightforward, linear flow does not entirely capture the complexity that supply chains can exhibit. A major manufacturer of computer printers, for example, does not actually make or distribute any printers. This company sees its strength in designing and marketing the printers. It develops a new model of printer, develops the market-

ing plan (based upon market research information provided by partner companies that do their market research in various countries), and estimates demand in various markets around the world for this printer based upon the marketing plan. The company has five partner manufacturers in Southeast Asia that contract to produce each model in the worldwide quantities needed by the company. The output of the production plants is then turned over to another partner company whose job is to transport and store the printers in anticipation of the demand (this type of company is called a *third-party logistics provider*, or *3PL*). Financing for the production and distribution of the printers is provided by an international consortium of partner banks. Thus, the only thing the printer company does is printer design and marketing; the production, distribution, financing, and market research information flows are handled by companies working in *systemic, strategic* coordination with the printer company. This situation leads to a much more complex supply chain, as illustrated in **Exhibit 16.2**.

Third, given the potential for countless alternative supply chain configurations, any one organization can be part of numerous supply chains. Wal-Mart can be part of the supply chain for candy, clothing, hardware, and many other products. This multiple supply chain phenomenon explains the network nature that many supply chains possess. For example, AT&T might find Motorola a customer in one supply chain, a partner in another, a supplier in a third, and a competitor in still a fourth supply chain.

Fourth, the final consumer is considered a member of the supply chain. This point is important because it recognizes that retail-

Exhibit 16.2: *Ultimate Supply Chain: Computer Printers*

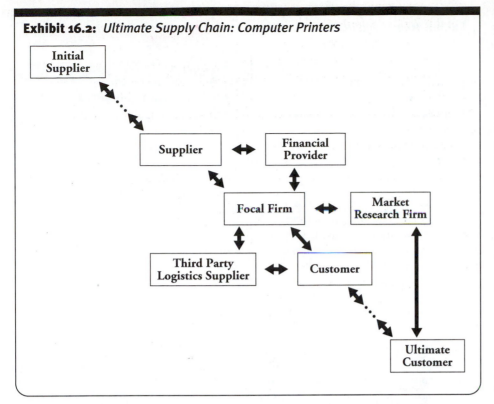

- Integrated Behavior
- Mutually Sharing Information
- Mutually Sharing Risks and Rewards
- Cooperation
- Same Goal and Same Focus on Serving Customers
- Integration of Processes
- Partners to Build and Maintain Long-Term Relationships

ers such as Wal-Mart are part of the upstream and downstream flows that constitute a supply chain.

Fifth, since SCM refers to the combination of a particular set of functions to get a specific output, all of the traditional business functions are included in the process of SCM. Notice, in our printer example, the traditional business functions of product development, production, marketing, sales, finance, forecasting, and logistics all had to be coordinated—not only within the printer company but also across numerous companies as well—for the entire supply chain to work. It is this intracompany and intercompany cross-functional coordination that leads to the emphasis on *systemic, strategic* management.

Last, this implementation of SCM must include the systemic, strategic management of the activities listed in **Exhibit 16.3**. As we discussed in the computer printer example, *integrated behavior* means coordinating all the traditional business functions (product development, marketing, sales, finance, production, forecasting, and logistics) between the supply chain partners (suppliers, carriers, customers, and manufacturers) to respond dynamically to the needs of the end customer. *Mutually sharing information* (such as production schedules, inventory levels, forecasts, sales promotion strategies, and marketing strategies) reduces the uncertainty between supply partners and results in enhanced SCM performance. *Mutually sharing risks and rewards* across the supply chain over the long term yields a competitive advantage.[6] The former means sharing such risks as carrying inventory and developing and producing products with uncertain future demand. The latter means sharing the rewards of such risk taking fairly across supply chain partners. For example, one manufacturer of cloth formed a partnership with its thread supplier, the pants manufacturer, and the retailer to coordinate inventory and demand flow throughout the entire supply chain. The result of the partnership was increased revenue and inventory savings for all four companies except the thread manufacturer. As a result, the cloth manufacturer did something that would be unheard of if it had not been looking at the supply chain strategically over the entire system—the cloth manufacturer went to the thread supplier and told it to raise its price! This was a recognition that without sharing in the rewards of the managed supply chain, the thread manufacturer had no long-term motivation to continue to share in the risks.

Clearly, neither this example (nor any of the first three activities just discussed) can be accomplished without *cooperation* among the supply chain members. *Cooperation* refers to similar, or complementary, coordinated activities performed by firms in a business relationship to produce superior mutual outcomes or singular outcomes that are mutually expected over time.[7] Cooperation is not limited to the needs of the current transaction and happens at several management levels (e.g., both top and operational managers) involving cross-functional coordination across the supply chain members.[8] The cloth example involved cooperation from the CEOs of the four companies all the way down to coordination between production, transportation, and inventory managers across the companies.

The motivation for supply chain cooperation comes from all members of the supply chain having *the same goal and the same focus on serving customers*. In the cloth supply chain example, this common goal was inventory risk reduction and was set jointly by the four CEOs. All of these activities go for little if the goals cannot be implemented, and the implementation of SCM needs the *integration of processes* from sourcing, to manufacturing, to distribution across the supply chain. This integration is made up of a series of partnerships, and SCM thus requires *partners to build and maintain long-term relationships*.

THE ROLE OF LOGISTICS IN SCM

In the previous section, we referred to SCM as including all traditional business functions. This is true, and the roles of many of these functions in SCM are discussed in other chapters in this book. However, the motivation for many supply chain management initiatives is the reduction of such logistics costs as inventory, transportation, facilities, or purchasing. It should come as no surprise, then, that the supply chain concept originated in the logistics literature, and logistics has continued to have a significant impact on the SCM concept. This does not mean logistics and SCM are the same thing—there exist important differences between the definition of supply chain management and logistics.

The Council of Logistics Management's (CLM) definition of logistics reinforces this difference, as well as the fact that logistics is *a part of* supply chain management:[9]

> Logistics is *that part of the supply chain process* that plans, implements, and controls the efficient flow and storage of goods, services, and related information from the point of origin to the point of consumption in order to meet customers' requirements. [emphasis added]

Thus, CLM has also distinguished between logistics and supply chain management, and acknowledged that logistics is *one of the functions* contained within supply chain management. If this is the case, what is the role of logistics in SCM?

Stated succinctly, the role of logistics in SCM is to provide logistics service quality to customers. This is not as simple as it sounds because providing this service quality means coordinating complex logistics performance dimensions (**Exhibit 16.4**) with customers and suppliers (i.e., SCM) to give customers what may be a complex array of desired logistics services (**Exhibit 16.5**).

PERFORMANCE DIMENSIONS OF LOGISTICS

As **Exhibit 16.6** illustrates, two of the logistics performance dimensions, transportation and inventory, are major components of our annual gross domestic product (GDP).[10] The largest of these logistics performance dimensions is *transportation*. Logistics service providers make transportation decisions so as to match the mode of transportation to the products being moved (**Exhibit 16.7**). Different products exhibit different characteristics with respect to their value and ability to be damaged or stolen (fragility)—which translates to product risk. For example, coal is not a very risky product; it is low value for the amount of tonnage that must be moved, so it is seldom stolen, and it is not easily damaged. Contrast this to diamonds (made from the same elements as coal), which are very valuable by weight, easily stolen, and easily damaged. It should not be surprising that coal is typically moved by rail and water (low cost, slow modes that are prone to product damage), while dia-

Exhibit 16.4: *Logistics Performance Dimensions*

- Transportation
- Facility Management
- Inventory Management
- Purchasing/Order Management
- Packaging
- Asset Management
- Systems

monds are almost always moved by air (high cost, fast, and not prone to product damage). In addition, the distance and volume of the products to be shipped will affect the transportation mode selection.

As the example illustrates, transportation modes exhibit different characteristics with respect to cost structure, speed, reliability, and safety. Cost structure means the relative degree of fixed costs (FC) versus variable costs (VC) of operation. A higher fixed cost means the mode is only cost effective if the fixed cost is spread over a larger volume, longer distance shipment. Thus, larger shipments traveling longer distances tend to use higher fixed cost, lower variable cost modes. Speed and reliability mean how consistently fast the mode can deliver products. A fast, unreliable mode (i.e., varying delivery times) may be less desirable than a slower, but reliable mode. Finally, easily damaged products should not be shipped on modes that are less safe (i.e., more prone to damage products). **Exhibit 16.8** provides a summary of the modal characteristics. Often, logistics managers use a combination of modes (called intermodal shipping) to achieve the advantages of several modes of transportation.

Logistics managers also must make decisions on *facility management*, or the number and location of manufacturing locations and distribution centers. Each new facility has a fixed cost component (investment in building and equipment, and the annual cost of keeping the facility open) and a variable cost component (the costs associated with moving each product into and out of the facility), but each new facility also affects the overall costs of the logistics system. Adding facilities tends to increase systemwide inventory levels (because more safety stock is carried at each location) but decrease transportation costs (because cheaper, volume-load shipments can be made to the facilities instead of more expensive less-than-volume-load shipments directly to many customers).

16.5: *Customer Desired Logistics Services*

- Personnel Contact Quality
- Order Release Quantities
- Information Quality
- Ordering Procedures
- Order Accuracy
- Order Condition
- Order Quality
- Order Discrepancy Handling
- Timeliness

Inventory management is a simple decision of when to order (called the *reorder point*) and how much to order (called the *order quantity*). The reorder point is determined by the base stock (the amount of inventory that is forecast to be needed until the next order arrives) and the safety stock (the amount of inventory carried in case the forecast is wrong). The complication in inventory management comes from how often this simple decision has to be made. Since, in logistics, each nuance and feature that the customer may want represents a different product (having the wrong version of the product available for the customer will not create logistics value in the mind of the customer), each variation of the product is called a *stock keeping unit* (or SKU). For example, Whirlpool makes refrigerators, a consumer durable found in most homes in developed economies. However, this one product line becomes thousands of SKUs when we consider that customers want different colors, different storage capacity, and different features (freezer on the side versus freezer on the bottom, water and ice dispensers in the door, etc.) and will not buy the product if the wrong SKU is available. Further, every place where an SKU is carried in inventory (called a *stock keeping unit by location,* or SKUL) represents a unique inventory management decision. For example, suppose the average Wal-Mart store carries 50,000 SKUs (actually a rather conservative estimate, since each separate size of a particular style of jeans, for example, represents a separate SKU) and Wal-Mart has 2,000 stores worldwide. Wal-Mart makes inventory management decisions by store on a daily basis. This means Wal-Mart must make this simple inventory management decision of when to order and how much to order 100,000,000 times every day! Clearly, computer systems will be needed to help with this logistics activity.

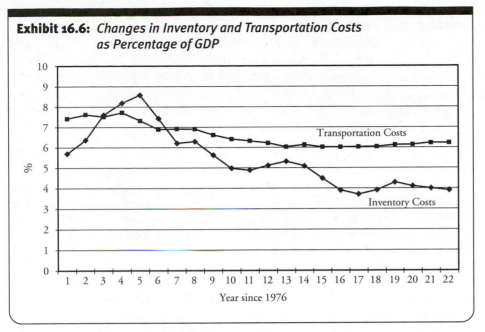

Exhibit 16.6: *Changes in Inventory and Transportation Costs as Percentage of GDP*

Transportation Costs

Inventory Costs

Year since 1976

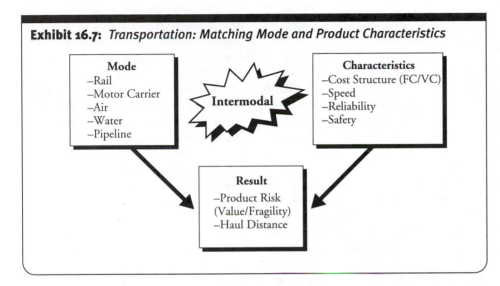

Exhibit 16.7: *Transportation: Matching Mode and Product Characteristics*

Mode
- Rail
- Motor Carrier
- Air
- Water
- Pipeline

Intermodal

Characteristics
- Cost Structure (FC/VC)
- Speed
- Reliability
- Safety

Result
- Product Risk (Value/Fragility)
- Haul Distance

Exhibit 16.8: *Transportation Mode Characteristics*

Mode/Characteristics	Cost Structure	Speed	Reliability	Safety
Rail	High FC Low VC	Slow	Reliable	Low
Motor Carrier	Low FC High VC	Faster	Less Reliable	Higher
Air	High FC High VC	Fastest	Affected by Weather	High
Water	High FC Low VC	Very Slow	Low Reliability	Very Low
Pipeline	Very High FC Very Low VC	Very Slow	Very Reliable	Very High

Closely coordinated with inventory management are the areas of *purchasing/ order management*. When inventory management decides what and how much to order, purchasing must have a previously selected vendor in place to provide the product, and order management establishes the processes by which orders are issued and tracked. Purchasing can profoundly affect both the unit cost of items purchased (whether raw materials or components for the company's production processes, or finished goods for resale) and the terms of purchase and payment. Order management controls the costs of placing individual orders and provides feedback to purchasing on the timeliness and condition of orders so purchasing can assess the future viability of each vendor.

Packaging is not only a means to promote the product; effective packaging also provides product protection that allows for flexibility in logistics decisions. As we discussed earlier, cheaper modes of transportation are often less safe, so a better-packaged product that is more resistant to damage may lower transportation costs. The trade-off decision between lower transportation costs and higher packaging costs is a common logistics management area, where coordinating this decision across the company, its vendors, and transportation providers is a key area of supply chain management.

All of the areas just discussed involve investment in assets: transportation means equipment, facilities means buildings and materials handling equipment, inventory in itself is an investment, and order management often entails considerable investment in communications equipment. Assets always imply fixed costs, which (as we discussed earlier) means we want high volumes of products using the assets to write off the investment (called *economies of scale*). When high product volume cannot be achieved, effective asset management looks for ways to transfer the asset base to a supply chain partner that has the product volume to make the investment work. Third-party logistics providers (3PLs) often invest in the transportation equipment and/or facilities to provide several supply chain customers with the service (thus combining the product volume of several customers). Similar arrangements also exist for consolidating orders and/or the purchasing function. The point of asset management is to keep the cost for each unit of product moved through a supply chain to a minimum, and the key to this is consolidating volume through fixed assets (whether owned by the company or outsourced to 3PLs) to achieve economies of scale.

Finally, computer systems are the templates companies lay over their supply chain processes. Once a supply chain process has been defined, the communication, data capture, and analysis functions are performed by computer systems. Effective computer systems aid the logistics manager in making cost effective, customer preference driven decisions.

CUSTOMER-DESIRED LOGISTICS SERVICES

Logistics managers often fall into the trap of concentrating so hard on improving the logistics performance dimensions (i.e., the operational aspects of logistics) that they forget to concentrate on what the customers actually want to result from the logistics system (i.e., the marketing aspects of logistics). Mentzer, Flint, and Hult found that customers desire a number of logistics services from their supply chain partners: personnel contact quality, order release quantities, information quality, ordering procedures, order accuracy, order condition, order quality, order discrepancy handling, and timeliness.[11]

Personnel contact quality refers to the customer orientation of the supplier's logistics contact people. Specifically, customers care about whether customer service personnel are knowledgeable, empathize with their situation, and help them resolve their problems. This is the "face" of the company, and it often establishes the customers' perceptions of (and loyalty to) the company. Many companies in the consumer products goods industry, for example, have found that retail store managers' perceptions of the manufacturer are not just determined by the company's advertising campaigns and salespeople but rather are largely influenced by the attitude, appearance, and knowledge of the delivery people. Thus, the "truck drivers" influence how loyal the store managers are to their manufacturers.

Order release quantities is related to the concept of product availability. Customers should be the most satisfied when they are able to obtain the quantities they desire. The importance of product availability has long been realized as a key component of logistics excellence, and telling a customer "we can fill your order, but we cannot send

you all that you wanted" is not logistics excellence and will not satisfy the customer.

Information quality refers to customers' perceptions of the information provided by the supplier regarding products from which customers may choose, such as information contained in catalogs, on Web sites, and so on. If the information is available and of adequate quality, customers are able to utilize the information to make decisions and, as a result, will be more satisfied.

Ordering procedures refers to the efficiency and effectiveness of the procedures followed by the supplier. Unfortunately, some companies make it difficult to do business with them. One manufacturer of personal computers was extremely proud of the efficiency of its 800-number customer ordering system—the system drastically lowered the company costs of receiving and processing orders by forcing customers to follow a set of telephone touch-tone protocols to place orders. The company was proud of this system until it found that a large number of potential customers wanted to talk to a real person when making this large purchase, and when the caller did not pick one of the preprogrammed selections, the phone system hung up on them! Although efficient from a logistics perspective, the system lost the company untold customers to the competition.

Order accuracy refers to how closely shipments match customers' orders when they arrive. This includes having the right items in the order, the correct number of items, and the lack of substitutions for items ordered.

Order condition refers to the lack of damage to orders. If products are damaged, customers cannot use them and must engage in correction procedures with supply chain partners, depending on the source of the damage.

Order quality refers to how well the products work. This includes how well they conform to product specifications and customers' needs. As compared to order accuracy, which addresses the complete set of products in the order (i.e., the accuracy of the kinds and quantities of the products in the order), or order condition, which addresses damage levels of those items due to handling, order quality addresses manufacturing of products. It is interesting that supply chain partners often attribute a portion of their perceptions of the quality of logistics services to the quality of the products being delivered.

Order discrepancy handling refers to how well supply chain partners address any dis-

crepancies in orders once the orders arrive. If customers receive orders that are not accurate, in poor condition, or of poor quality, they seek corrections from their supply chain partners. How well these partners handle these issues contributes to customers' perceptions of the quality of their services. One of the greatest challenges for the business-to-consumer (B2C) e-commerce industry has been that it is easy to place orders, and it is easy to receive the orders placed, but if there is anything wrong with the order, there is no conveniently located retail store where the consumer can return the order. Thus, consumer dissatisfaction is created not from the logistics of ordering and receiving the product but from the logistics of returning orders that did not meet customer expectations.

Timeliness refers to whether or not orders arrive at the customer location when promised. More broadly, timeliness also refers to the length of time between placing orders and receiving them. This delivery time can be affected by transportation time, as well as backorder time when products are unavailable. It is a particularly important component of desired logistics customer services in the business-to-business (B2B) supply chains and in the mail order and B2C e-commerce supply chains.

If we look at logistics as a process from the customer's point of view, we see that customers place orders (involving personnel contact quality, order release quantities, information quality, and ordering procedures), orders are processed and shipped (resulting in order accuracy, order condition, and order quality), and orders are received (resulting in perceptions of timeliness). Customers have contact with this process when placing orders and upon order receipt. When order receipt is not as expected, customers stay engaged in the logistics process via order discrepancy handling.

The key to logistics management is the matching of these logistics performance dimensions with the customer-desired services. This involves the creation of logistics value through logistics customer service trade-offs. Companies that do this effectively across their supply chains create a competitive advantage called *logistics leverage*.

CREATION OF LOGISTICS VALUE

Exhibit 16.9 illustrates this process of matching logistics performance dimensions with customer-desired services. *Inefficient* supply chains are the result of companies deciding what logistics services they can best provide to customers and concentrating on those internally determined foci of excellence. Inevitably, the result is that companies spend vast amounts of money attaining high levels of performance on many logistics dimensions that are unimportant, or even unnoticed, by customers. *Ineffective* supply chains are the result of just the opposite—companies not performing well on logistics dimensions that customers consider important.

An example of inefficient supply chains is a company that prided itself on 100 percent product availability—whenever its customers ordered a certain class of product, the company had it available and in stock. The company invested millions of dollars in maintaining this exceptional level of inventory availability. However, a little customer research revealed that customers not only did not need this level of service (company competitors did not provide such service levels, so customer processes were designed to deal with a supplier stockout rate of 7 percent), but they were unaware that the company's service level was that high.

An example of ineffective service comes from the same company, whose customers told it what they really wanted was order status information—something the company had never bothered to provide.

The key to creating logistics value is to start with the customers and ask them which desired services they consider important and then manage the dimensions of logistics performance in a manner that delivers that level of performance. The result is low levels of performance on dimensions that *do not* matter to customers (adequate service) and high levels of performance on dimensions that *do* matter (resulting in satisfied customers). This approach to logistics value creation entails taking wasted resources (i.e., those applied to creating inefficient service—the unnecessarily high inventory levels in our example) and reapplying those resources to areas where the company is underperforming in the eyes of the customer (i.e., ineffective service—in our example, development of an order status information system for customers).

LOGISTICS CUSTOMER SERVICE TRADE-OFFS

If we think of the failure to match logistics performance dimensions with customer-

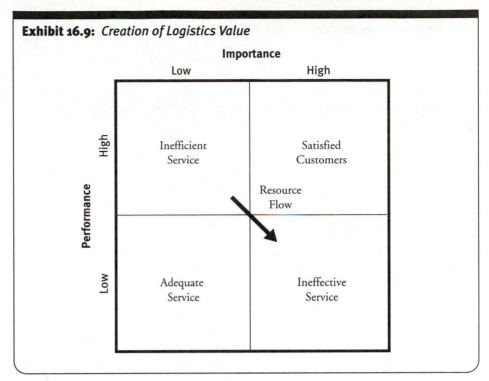

Exhibit 16.9: *Creation of Logistics Value*

desired services as the cost of lost sales, we can view the delivery of logistics customer service as a series of cost trade-offs (**Exhibit 16.10**). The costs of all the logistics performance dimensions discussed earlier increase at an increasing rate when we try to improve customer service (i.e., lower the cost of lost sales). As you can see from Exhibit 16.10, where the two lines intersect is the optimal combination of logistics performance dimensions and cost of lost sales, or where the costs of the logistics component of the supply chain are optimized.

However, the innovative logistics manager can overcome these trade-offs by shifting the performance dimensions line to the right, thus keeping logistics costs at the same (or lower) level, while increasing customer service. The key to this is viewing the supply chain from an overall system perspective (i.e., supply chain management) and looking for innovative ways to accomplish the logistics function.

When we combine innovative, customer-driven logistics with the ability to market that superior performance to customers, we attain a source of competitive advantage called *logistics leverage*.[12]

LOGISTICS LEVERAGE

Many companies competing in global markets have decreased prices,[13] improved products,[14] and reduced design-to-shelf cycle times,[15] only to find these strategies

quickly copied by competitors.[16] Companies are actively searching for ways to build a sustainable advantage in the marketplace for their supply chains.[17] In the 1980s, many firms turned to quality improvements in product design and internal processes to achieve competitive advantage.[18] Today, however, organizations have focused on delivering customer value to remain competitive.[19]

In the current environment, it is difficult to maintain differential advantages that accrue from supply chain changes in product, promotion, or price. Many of today's products, albeit manufactured in different global locations, have become homogenized and indistinguishable to the customer.[20] Given the ever-shortening technology cycle, companies trying to create or maintain differentiation in the marketplace often find product changes quickly greeted by a countermove from competitors. Likewise, changes in promotion and price may be quickly duplicated. A particular challenge for supply chain strategy today is determining how to promote products whose features are perceived as homogenous by customers. Because for many companies any change in product, promotion, or price has only a temporary impact in their markets, the way to *sustainable* competitive advantage may lie not in changing the product, promotion, or pricing strategies of the supply chain but rather in improving ancillary supply chain services, such as logistics.[21] For

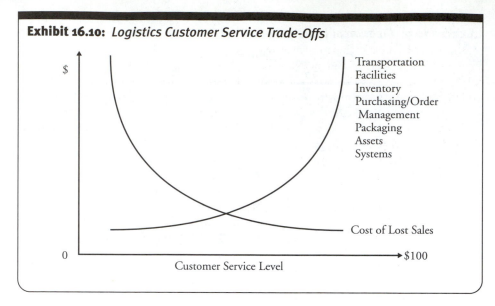

Exhibit 16.10: *Logistics Customer Service Trade-Offs*

Transportation
Facilities
Inventory
Purchasing/Order
 Management
Packaging
Assets
Systems

Cost of Lost Sales

$

0

$100

Customer Service Level

this reason, logistics has been suggested as the strategic "battleground . . . displacing manufacturing, marketing, and quality as the focus of top management."[22] Many firms now stress logistics capabilities as a means of creating differentiation.[23]

Such service improvements are most likely to yield a sustainable positional advantage in the market when implemented through changes in the supply chain infrastructure—people, technology, facilities, and/or strategic supply chain relationships.[24] Thus, a key supply chain strategy that can potentially create and maintain this positional advantage is termed *logistics leverage*.[25]

Logistics leverage is the achievement of excellent and superior, infrastructure-based logistics performance, which—when implemented through a successful marketing strategy—creates recognizable value for customers. As such, logistics leverage represents a maintainable "positional advantage" for the company and the supply chain—value-added services that the customer recognizes as important, and (since logistics leverage requires changes in the supply chain infrastructure) that competition cannot readily match.

Changes in supply chain infrastructure are the keys to the sustainability of logistics leverage. For example, strategic supply chain relationships can lead to an alliance that the competition cannot readily match. A logistics alliance is an extension of the superior skills of each partner to do value-added activities within the supply chain. For example, McDonald's has outsourced its entire logistics function, allowing it to concentrate on its core business.[26] Such an

alliance can also lead to innovative new products and processes that become valuable resources in the overall supply chain strategy. For example, Robin Transport designed trailers in which auto parts could be loaded and unloaded in places where standard trailers could not go, thus allowing General Motors to set up its production assembly process to benefit from more efficient materials handling.[27]

Examples of Logistics Leverage

Mentzer and Williams provide detailed examples of three companies that achieved competitive advantage through logistics leverage.[28]

Commodity Products versus Commodity Business

Company F is in the auto aftermarket, a supply chain that provides replacement parts to auto repair shops through a network of distributors—called *warehouse distributors* or *WD*s. Company F held approximately 30 percent market share in this channel, about the same as its two major competitors, with the remaining 10 percent divided among minor competitors.

The product in this supply chain eventually is installed by a mechanic as part of an auto repair for the owner of the car. As a result, there is virtually no brand recognition in this process—the owner of the car simply wants the car repaired and seldom asks for a specific brand. In fact, market research revealed that car owners valued only three things in this process:

- They wanted their car back the same day they took it in for repair.

- They wanted the problem fixed (i.e., they did not want the replacement part to fail again as long as they owned the car).
- They were sensitive to the price of the parts.

This led the auto mechanics to value the same three things:

- They needed the parts within 24 hours of ordering them from the WD so they could be ready for scheduled repair appointments.
- They were very concerned about product quality.
- The lower their price on the parts, the higher their margin.

This led one Company F executive to describe the industry as a "commodity business"—there is no difference between the competitors in the market with respect to promotional programs, or product quality or features, so the only basis on which to compete is price. However, since the major competitors had identical types of manufacturing plants, identical suppliers, and identical supply chains (the same supplier delivery systems to the plants and the same WDs to distribute the products to the same auto mechanics), their cost structures were very similar, and any reduction in price was immediately matched by the competition.

In other words, Company F faced the typical profit erosion of a "kinked demand curve" from an oligopoly with identical competitive mixes. If any competitor raised its price, the competition would not follow the higher prices, and the competitor lost market share. If any competitor lowered its prices, the competition matched the new price, and all competitors had the same market share but with lower profit margins. The industry was a classic example of Porter's competitor-focused industry.[29]

The road to logistics leverage began when the new CEO of Company F formed a task force to implement his personal vision of the company—to change the corporate vision from the company as a "manufacturer of products in the auto aftermarket" to "a marketer and distributor of products in the auto aftermarket." In other words, to focus the attention of the company not on the product itself but on how it got to the customer (the supply chain).

This profound shift in focus of the company from competitor focused to customer centered and supply chain focused led to the realization that Company F did, in fact, make a commodity product. The company's ultimate customers saw no difference in product quality or features, and the promotional programs were largely ignored by all members of the supply chain. However, this did not mean the company could not come up with marketing and/or logistics services that would differentiate it from the competition within the supply chain. In other words, the CEO realized that having a commodity product does not mean you have a commodity business—there are always services that can be offered with a product that can differentiate it in the minds of the customer.

The important aspect of this point for logistics leverage is that logistics services offered with the product often hold the key to differentiating a commodity product from its competition. Company F realized this once its entire supply chain was analyzed. Since all the competitors in the industry used the same suppliers and had the same manufacturing processes, the upstream supply chain was deemed not to hold any sources of logistics leverage. Similarly, market research focused at car owners and auto mechanics revealed little in how to differentiate Company F from the competition. However, Company F found the WDs were the key to logistics leverage. In other words, the WDs were the customers in the supply chain that were most important to Company F in achieving logistics leverage.

At the time of this example, there were 2,000 warehouse distributors in the United States, which meant that virtually every county with an auto repair shop had at least one WD. Their function in the supply chain is to provide ready access to inventory for the auto mechanic, who carries little or no inventory. When a customer would call to schedule an auto repair, the mechanic would assess the likely parts needed to effect the repair, call the local WD to ascertain whether the parts were in stock, and, if available, would send someone over to pick up the parts.

The WD operation usually consisted of a reception area with a counter for waiting on pick-up customers and a huge warehouse out back to hold in inventory all the parts any auto mechanic would conceivably order. As a result, WDs were small operations with huge inventory levels. In fact, the average inventory turns ratio for a WD was less than 1.0, resulting in huge inventory carrying costs compared to sales levels. Not surprisingly, most WDs were marginally

profitable operations. Here lay the source of logistics leverage for Company F.

Company F embarked upon a three-year plan to develop a wide area network for inventory planning and accompanied this with a plan to stage fast-moving inventory at various locations in North America and pull slow movers back to a central distribution center. When these plans were implemented, Company F made the following offer to all WDs: Company F guaranteed that any order placed with it that was not *completely filled* within 24 hours would be free. In other words, if an order for 160 different parts was placed and even one of those parts was not delivered in 24 hours, there was no charge for the entire order. Further, each WD was given one year to try out the program, and when it was convinced that Company F never missed a 24-hour delivery, Company F would buy back from the WD its excess inventory. This offer was hard to resist because the WD would be turning a business liability (the cost of carrying excess inventory) into an asset (cash).

The logistics leverage for Company F came from the fact that once a WD sold its excess inventory to Company F, the WD no longer had the ability to buy from the competition. WDs were literally faced with the choice of placing an order with Company F and being guaranteed 24-hour delivery or ordering from the competition and having the order arrive in 7 to 14 days—all when the WD was now only carrying at most several days of inventory. Over a two-year period, Company F raised its prices 15 percent above the competition (an act that would have been unthinkable before its new program) and doubled its market share.

What we learn about logistics leverage from the Company F example is never to confuse a commodity *product* with a commodity *business*. Company F's new logistics system took several years to develop and implement, but once it was in place, the competition could not match the infrastructure changes. This provided sustainable differential advantage for Company F (i.e., logistics leverage) that was not based upon a change in its commodity product. It was based upon how that product was distributed, the marketing of that distribution innovation (notice this is within our definition of supply chain management as including the coordination of all business functions—in this case, logistics and marketing), and how hard it was

for the competition to match that superior logistics infrastructure once it was implemented.

We also learn that the key to successful logistics leverage often involves asking the question: Who is our customer? Company F conducted considerable market research to identify what the members of its downstream supply chain—WDs, auto mechanics, and car owners—wanted. It eventually focused on the WDs because therein lay a source for competitive advantage. Auto mechanics and car owners were still important as customers but did not provide the source from which Company F could differentiate itself from the competition.

Exceeding Customer Delivery Time Expectations

Company L is in the machine tool business, a supply chain whose principal product may cost as much as $15 million. In fact, the capital cost of these machines is so large that customers of Company L (manufacturers who use the machine tools in making their products) estimate the costs of machine tool downtime in thousands of dollars per hour. These machines are marketed and distributed by Company L worldwide, so Company L must maintain a downstream supply chain that can deliver the machines, and replacement parts, anywhere in the world.

Although the machines are expensive, capital items, Company L found (through market research) that the major source of customer dissatisfaction with Company L and its competitors was the delivery of replacement parts (parts that often cost less than $50). For example, when a customer in Singapore has a broken part on the machine, its satisfaction with the machine and the manufacturer of that machine is largely dependent on how fast it can obtain a replacement part and get the machine back in operation. This satisfaction, in turn, has a significant effect upon repeat sales and word-of-mouth reputation. To keep customer dissatisfaction from becoming a problem, Company L routinely shipped replacement parts to customers by overnight delivery—an international transportation service that often cost more than the actual value of the part.

As a result of this market research insight (and in an effort to turn a customer dissatisfaction problem into a customer satisfaction advantage), Company L embarked upon a four-year plan to implement a dramatic new logistics leverage strategy that was embodied in the phrase: "We guarantee we will deliver replacement parts to any customer worldwide *before* they order it." Notice that this zero-delivery-time strategy embodies two key elements of logistics leverage: (1) excellent logistics performance (in this case, the ability to meet this guarantee) and (2) the ability to market this performance to customers (in this case, the dramatic promotional statement that easily conveys the superiority of its performance over the competition).

To accomplish this strategy, Company L began installing a cellular phone in every machine it sold (a minor cost compared to the overall purchase price). No matter where the machine is in the world, every day each machine conducts a diagnostic analysis of its performance, calls the Company L home office, and transmits the results of these diagnostics. Company L computers analyze these diagnostics every night, determine whether any parts are beginning to fail, and, if they are, issue a shipment order to its distribution center. Within several days (usually at least a week before the part actually fails), the plant manager of the customer company receives a package from Company L containing the part with instructions that the part is about to fail and should be replaced in the next regular maintenance session. Thus, the customer receives the replacement part before they order it.

Notice that this system eliminates the need for Company L to stage inventory all over the world and employ high-cost expedited modes of transportation. Since the order is no longer a rush order and can, in fact, be sent far enough in advance by slower, less expensive modes of transportation, Company L has been able to lower its inventory and transportation costs substantially, simultaneously dramatically raising customer satisfaction levels. The higher customer service levels eventually resulted in dramatically increased market share; that is, customers could buy their machine tools from one of several equally competent manufacturers, but only one of these (Company L) had the logistics system to eliminate the unproductive downtime while waiting for replacement parts.

What we learn about logistics leverage in this case is that excellent logistics performance means nothing if the customer is not aware that it exists (again, the supply chain management concept of coordinating all

business functions). Company L lowered its logistics costs dramatically by implementing the logistics aspect of this strategy. However, the dramatic increases in customer satisfaction and market share came as a result only of properly marketing this performance—a marketing strategy that was built around the dramatic and catchy promotional phrase, "We guarantee we will deliver replacement parts to any customer worldwide *before* they order it."

It is also important to realize that an effective logistics leverage strategy comes from insightful market research. Rather than just asking customers about the product, Company L asked customers questions *the customers* thought should be asked. As a result, Company L discovered a source of positional advantage. Companies can only ask questions customers care about if they first conduct qualitative interviews with customers to determine what satisfies and dissatisfies them and only then can design customer satisfaction questionnaires. It is precisely this qualitative/quantitative market research approach that Company L followed—an approach that led it to develop a logistics leverage strategy based upon what the customers told them was important.

Finally, notice again that the positional advantage of logistics leverage came from the fact that Company L announced this strategy only after several years of installing cellular phones in its machines (something the competition was not doing) and several years of reconfiguring its logistics inventory, transportation, and information systems to accommodate this strategy (something the competition was also not doing). The result was that once Company L announced its new replacement parts guarantee, the competition was in no position to match it and was faced with several years of expensive changes in how they manufacture and distribute their product (i.e., their infrastructure) before they could match it.

Virtually Integrating the Value Chain: Dell Computers

In 1984, a University of Texas student who had been selling rebuilt PCs out of his dorm room pondered entering the emerging PC market. Ordinarily, entering a relatively established market would have been a ridiculous idea. It was conventional wisdom that Intel and Microsoft had taken all the margins out of the PC business and that all the products were viewed as commodities. In addition, all the key players in

the industry were using the "engineering-centric" view: They were building massive structures to produce everything a computer needed from disk drives to memory chips and applications software. Certainly, a new entrant could not compete.

The young college student, Michael Dell, decided to enter the market and, by doing so, totally revamped the industry. Dell applied customer focus, supplier partnerships, mass customization, and just-in-time delivery to implement the strategy of virtual supply chain integration; succinctly, virtual supply chain integration leverages logistics to create and sustain customer value.

By selling directly to customers via the Web, Dell Computers used e-commerce to communicate with customers, maintain low costs, and completely customize products according to customer specifications. Dell Computer was driven by the desire to create value for the customer. Michael Dell himself said, "looking for the [customer] value . . . is most important."[30]

Dell mastered virtual integration in the supply chain. Through the use of the Internet, Dell's customers gained access to the same product, service, and catalog information as Dell's employees. Tailor-made Internet sites called Premier Pages gave customers direct access to purchasing and technical information about the specific configurations they buy from Dell. Thus, customers could order, configure, and even gather technical advice online, thereby turning a commodity product into a totally customized product offering.

For those customers that wanted or needed more personalized assistance, Dell sent out one of more than 10,000 service technicians to their sites. However, only a small number are Dell employees. Most are "virtual employees" who dress like Dell employees, talk like Dell employees, and even cater to the customer like Dell employees but are actually contract employees. According to Michael Dell, this allows Dell's employees to focus on activities that create the most value for customers.

Activities such as coordination with its virtual manufacturing facilities and inventory velocity and reduction are of primary concern for Dell because they result in lower costs to customers. Dell has a virtual manufacturing arrangement with key suppliers such as Sony. Sony employees work in the Dell facility on joint planning and product development. Because of this close relationship and Sony's reputation for building reliable computer monitors, Dell decided not to perform quality checks on Sony monitors. Thus, it determined there was no reason to maintain inventory. So, Sony manufactures monitors just in time for Dell. When needed, Dell instructs UPS or Airborne Express to pick up 10,000 monitors from Sony's plant in Mexico and a corresponding 10,000 computers from Dell's facility in Texas. UPS or Airborne Express matches computers with monitors in the delivery process, eliminating the need for Dell to have an expensive distribution center to perform these functions.

Dell strives to implement virtual supply chain integration because it allows Dell to meet customer needs faster and more efficiently than any other PC maker. If customers want, Dell will install company-specific software before delivery. It will also put an asset tag with the company's logo on the machine and keep an electronic register of the customer's assets. This saves the customer the time and expense of having its employees place asset tags on the equipment. Dell also places technicians at major customers' sites. Thus, Dell becomes the customer's virtual IT Department instead of just a traditional supplier.

Logistics leverage is at the core of Dell's virtual supply chain integration strategy. Customer value is created and sustained in this highly competitive industry because no one can duplicate the customization, the logistics infrastructure, the employee infrastructure, and the unique supply chain partner relationships, all of which have resulted in decreased costs and increased customer service. Even when retailers aligned with Dell's competitors began charging higher rates for servicing and supporting Dell products, customers remained loyal.

Leveraging logistics allows Dell to have long-term special relationships with both suppliers and customers. Unique product offerings and cost reductions have resulted in loyal customers and supply chain partners, sustainable position, and high profits. Thus, Dell has used logistics to reduce cost and focus on creating value for customers and supply chain partners.

CONCLUSIONS

What we hope you learned from this chapter is that:

- Supply chains exist whether we manage them or not.

- Supply chain management requires strategic management of all the traditional business functions across the inbound and outbound system flows of three or more companies.
- The cooperative activities listed in Exhibit 16.3 are key to firms managing supply chains.
- Logistics is a core supply chain management process that manages the product, service, and related informational flows through the supply chain.
- Logistics leverage, a source of strategic advantage for supply chains, can be achieved only by matching the logistics performance dimensions in Exhibit 16.4 with the customer-desired logistics services in Exhibit 16.5.

Effective supply chain managers focus on developing cooperative, mutually beneficial relationships with their supply chain partners, relationships that coordinate the crucial function of logistics with the other business functions of marketing, finance, sales, demand planning, and production. Often the key to this coordination in logistics is focusing on the largest logistics components, transportation and inventory, *and* the logistics service dimensions that customers tell you are the most important. Notice in all three of our logistics leverage cases, the companies focused on key logistics service dimensions *and* reduced systemwide transportation and inventory costs. The focus on costs generates savings that impact the bottom line (profitability) of the company while the focus on customer-desired logistics services brings customer loyalty and increased market share that the competition cannot match (logistics leverage). Either or both are undeniable vehicles for success in our dynamic business marketplaces.

1. Martha C. Cooper, Douglas M. Lambert, and Janus D. Pagh, "Supply Chain Management: More Than a New Name for Logistics," *The International Journal of Logistics Management* 8, no. 1 (1997): 1–14.

2. David Frederick Ross, *Competing through Supply Chain Management* (New York: Chapman & Hall, 1988).

3. John T. Mentzer et al., "What Is Supply Chain Management?" *Supply Chain Management,* John T. Mentzer (ed.) (Thousand Oaks, CA: Sage Publications, Inc., 2001).

4. Ibid.

5. Ibid.

6. Martha C. Cooper and Lisa M. Ellram, "Characteristics of Supply Chain Management and the Implication for Purchasing and Logistics Strategy," *The International Journal of Logistics Management* 4, no. 2 (1993): 13–24.

7. Erin Anderson and James A. Narus, "A Model of Distributor Firm and Manufacturer Firm Working Relationships," *Journal of Marketing* (January 1990): 42–58.

8. Cooper, Lambert, and Pagh, "Supply Chain Management."

9. Council of Logistics Management, Oak Brook, IL: Council of Logistics Management, 1998.

10. Mentzer et al., *Supply Chain Management.*

11. John T. Mentzer, Daniel J. Flint, and G. Tomas M. Hult, "Logistics Service Quality as a Segment-Customized Process," *Journal of Marketing* (October 2001).

12. John T. Mentzer and Lisa R. Williams, "The Role of Logistics Leverage in Marketing Strategy," *Journal of Marketing Channels* 3–4 (2001): 29–48.

13. Craig Zarley, "The Channel Challenge," *Informationweek,* (June 1997): 43–46.

14. Robert Woodruff and Sarah F. Gardial, *Know Your Customer: New Approaches to Understanding Customer Value and Satisfaction* (Cambridge, MA: Blackwell Business, 1996).

15. Robert C. Camp, *Benchmarking* (Milwaukee, WI: American Society of Quality Control, 1989).

16. Michael E. Porter, *Competitive Strategy: Techniques for Analyzing Industries and Competitors* (New York: The Free Press, 1985).

17. George Day, "The Capabilities of Market-Driven Organizations," *Journal of Marketing* 4 (1994): 37–60; and Daniel Innis and Bernard LaLonde, "Customer Service: The Key to Customer Satisfaction, Customer Loyalty and Market Share," *Journal of Business Logistics* 15, no. 1, 1–27.

18. Michael J. Stahl, *Management: Total Quality in a Global Environment* (Cambridge, MA: Blackwell Publishers, 1994); and Michael J. Stahl (ed.), *Perspectives in Total Quality* (Boston, MA: Blackwell Publishers, 1999).

19. Woodruff and Gardial, *Know Your Customer.*

20. Patricia Daugherty, Theodore Stank, and Alexander Ellinger, "Leveraging Logistics/ Distribution Capabilities: The Effect of Logistics Service on Market Share," *Journal of Business Logistics* 2 (1998): 35–51.

21. Donald J. Bowersox, John T. Mentzer, and Thomas W. Speh, "Logistics Leverage," *Journal of Business Strategies* (Spring 1995): 36–49.

22. Lamont Woods, "The Myths and Realities of Customer Service," *Electronic Business* (1991): 156–158

23. James Anderson and James Narus, "Capturing the Value of Supplementary Services," *Harvard Business Review* (January–February 1995): 75–83

24. George Day and Robin Wensley, "Assessing Advantage: A Framework for Diagnosing Competitive Superiority," *Journal of Marketing* (Spring 1988): 1–19.

25. Mentzer and Williams, "Leverage."

26. Lisa M. Ellram and Martha C. Cooper, "Supply Chain Management, Partnerships, and the Shipper-Third Party Relationship," *The International Journal of Logistics Management* (1990): 1–10; and Lisa M. Ellram and Martha C. Cooper, "A Managerial Guideline for the Development and Implementation of Purchasing Partnerships," *International Journal of Purchasing and Materials Management,* 27, 3, 2–8.

27. Donald J. Bowersox, "The Strategic Benefits of Logistics Alliances," *Harvard Business Review* (1990), 36–45.

28. Mentzer and Williams, "Leverage."

29. Porter, *Competitive Strategy.*

30. Joan Magretta, "The Power of Virtual Integration: An Interview with Dell Computer's Michael Dell," *Harvard Business Review* (March–April 1998): 73–84.

Joyce E. A. Russell
University of Maryland

Lisa Dragoni
University of Maryland

Chapter 17

Managing Human Capital in Start-Up Firms

OVERVIEW

The fastest growing sector of businesses today is small and medium-size firms. In the United States, of the more than 5 million companies in 1995, 99.7 percent had fewer than 500 employees and 78.8 percent had fewer than 10 employees.[1] By 1999, small firms (less than 500 employees) employed 53 percent of private sector employees, contributed 47 percent of all sales, and were responsible for 51 percent of the private gross domestic product.[2] Small businesses have also been responsible for the majority of newly created jobs, and the very smallest businesses were the largest job creators.[3] Similar results are found in other parts of the world. Firms with 50 employees or fewer account for 56 percent of total employment in the private sector in Northern Ireland and 48 percent in the United Kingdom.[4] In fact, from 1970 to 2000, small manufacturing firms increased from 10 percent of all manufacturing units to 90 percent in Northern Ireland.[5] Thus, they are critical to a country's economy since they provide a large portion of the new jobs.

Despite the importance of small businesses to a country's economy, there has been little research on the human resource (HR) practices of these firms. In fact, most research has examined HR practices for large, well-established organizations.[6] In addition, even though there are hundreds of books that provide advice on starting new businesses, very few of those books contain information on managing people or human resources.[7]

The number of small firms continues to increase, yet many of them fail or go under within six years.[8] There are a number of reasons for their failures, including having to deal with excessive bureaucracy, financ-

ing, labor shortages, and other people concerns. One of the largest problems faced by small businesses is labor shortages. In fact, in a survey of 641 small business entrepreneurs, they identified this as their most pressing concern.[9] Often start-ups wait until their second wave of fund-raising to pay attention to HR issues, and by that time it may be too late and they have already gotten themselves into trouble.[10] The dot-com crash of 2000 revealed that many companies had not even put any HR policies into practice. As a result, they left themselves open to sexual harassment charges and employee lawsuits over unfair dismissals. As one consultant remarks, "Business owners used to regular dental and

BEST-USE CORRELATIONS

Managing the human resource capital of small entrepreneurial firms is a key competency of successful *Marketplace* enterprises. As this chapter forcefully shows, strategic use of your team's human resources not only can provide a competitive advantage, but also improve the financial performance of the firm.

Productivity and HR Decisions

In *Marketplace* firms compete for a limited number of employees whose quality is directly affected by the compensation packages offered. Employee satisfaction and productivity are also affected by the firm's handling of tough real world problems such as discrimination, termination, and employee appraisal. Your best course is to use the strategies provided in Chapter 17 to avoid common pitfalls and set effective precedents and policies.

You Will Be Measured

In *Marketplace*, you must actively manage human resources. Each quarter, employee satisfaction, productivity, and stability are measured and calculated as part of your team's overall BSC score. In short, HR cannot be ignored, though the preoccupation of new firms to generate revenue often jeopardizes their ability to perform HR functions well.

medical checkups would also benefit by giving their businesses periodic personnel checkups." This is true because each year thousands of unhappily terminated employees sue their former employers, and these complaints cost small business owners millions of dollars in legal fees, emotional distress, and lost productivity.[11]

The current chapter focuses on people issues, specifically how to manage a firm's human resource capital so that it will be successful. Human resource management is concerned with *staffing* the right people in the right jobs, *training* employees, *appraising* employee performance, and *rewarding* employees (STAR). Research indicates that the effective management of human resources is one of the most critical problems faced by small firms.[12] For a new start-up to succeed, it must handle all of the business functions (e.g., marketing, financing, technological issues, cash flows) and at the same time create a culture where individuals want to come to work, are motivated to give their best effort, and are committed to staying with the firm and increasing its value. As one CEO/founder stated, "How do you build a culture that people do not want to leave? The challenge is retention. Our culture has developed so that people believe I am really looking out for their well-being. I lose very few employees to my competitor."[13] Thus, managing a firm's employees and human resources is essential for the success of the organization. This has been shown to be true for firms all over the world.[14] Why is it so important to effectively manage the firm's HR capital? Because research indicates that firms with effective staffing, training procedures, reward systems, and increased employee involvement were associated with higher productivity, better financial performance, and lower levels of employee turnover.[15] In addition, strategic use of human resource management can improve the financial performance of the firm and, in some cases, provide a competitive advantage.[16]

HR CHALLENGES FACING NEW AND SMALL BUSINESSES

New and small businesses face unique HR challenges. From the onset, founders are focused on building a name and reputation and turning a profit. This single-mindedness and drive are necessary to succeed; and, therefore it becomes difficult for the founder to shift gears and devote her atten-

tion to internal management issues. Moreover, entrepreneurs may not have the management know-how to manage human resource issues effectively.

In addition, resources such as time, personnel, and money are much more limited in small businesses than in their larger counterparts. For this reason, human resource management issues tend to take a back seat to other more operational concerns until a crisis situation arises. At that point, often the issue may result in frustration, anger, or loss of personnel, or may undermine motivation and morale in some way. By this time, HRM, or the lack thereof, is negatively impacting performance rather than facilitating it.

HRM Practices in Family-Owned Businesses

Research indicates that family businesses lag behind their nonfamily counterparts in terms of implementing HRM practices. Often family firms use advertising in newspapers and recruiting internal candidates to fill managerial vacancies.[17] They are less likely than nonfamily firms to use formal appraisal systems to evaluate performance and to use merit-performance related pay to incentivize and motivate workers. Only 27 percent reported using a formal performance system to assess family members, and of that group only 38 percent stated that the remuneration of the family member was based on the appraisal. In addition, family firms spend less money on training their employees even though they rated training and development as one of their biggest HRM challenges for the future.[18] It will be critical for family-owned businesses to develop more professional HR systems and to institutionalize them as the business grows and expands.

Often, family-owned businesses do not have an HRM department and instead rely upon the founder or a family owner to handle HR issues. In addition, many of these businesses do not have an HR plan for the firm. Even those firms that do have an HR plan often do not involve the HR person in its development.[19] This may explain why family businesses have more difficulties managing their human resources, especially when it concerns staffing issues such as laying off employees. They have been criticized for having difficulties being objective with family members and for not providing enough training. Often, in companies dominated by the CEO, the involvement of line managers in HRM strategy is less likely. In addition, family firms are less likely than nonfamily firms to have mission statements.[20]

Whether a new or small business is family owned or not, unique HR challenges exist. The purpose of this chapter is to describe ways to best manage challenges so that a firm's HRM can become an asset instead of a liability.

IMPROVING FIRM PERFORMANCE THROUGH HUMAN RESOURCE MANAGEMENT

Firms can use their human resource management system to improve their performance by focusing on two key concepts: external fit and internal fit.

"External fit" refers to the alignment between a firm's strategy and its human resource management practices. In other words, human resource practices should help, not hinder, the firm in achieving its strategic vision. For example, firms with a strategy to maintain and improve their existing operations in a narrowly tailored domain are best served by a human resource system that emphasizes *building and developing human resources*.[21] This type of strategy demands employees to learn and grow with the firm. For this reason, the most effective practices are those directed toward hiring entry-level employees, promoting from within, providing formal training, evaluating how employees do their work (rather than just their outcomes), and compensating individuals based on their level in the firm or years with the firm.

On the other hand, an HR system focused on *acquiring human resources* best complements a firm seeking to create change and uncertainty in the market.[22] This type of strategy demands that employees have the most-up-to-date skills, regardless of what the current initiative is. Under this strategic focus, the firm needs flexibility in its skill base. Therefore, the most effective HR practices for this strategy are those geared toward recruiting the "best and the brightest" under a negotiated contract, using informal training on an as-needed basis, employing outcome-based performance appraisal, and implementing compensation systems that are competitive with other firms.

When firms complement their strategy with appropriate human resource practices, they may enjoy significant rewards.

Exhibit 17.1: Comparison of Staffing Practices

Example of Internal Fit		Example of a Lack of Internal Fit	
HR Functions	*Sample HR practices*	*HR Functions*	*Sample HR practices*
Staffing	Hire entry-level employees	Staffing	Hire contract and temporary employees
Training	Provide extensive training	Training	Provide extensive training
Appraisal	Provide developmentally focused appraisals	Appraisal	Provide developmentally focused appraisals
Rewards	Compensate based on years with firm	Rewards	Compensate based on years with the firm

Research shows that firms with an alignment between strategy and HRM may enjoy as high as 50 percent higher return on assets and equity.[23]

In addition, having an internally consistent system of HR practices is referred to as "internal fit." In other words, HR practices should convey a consistent message to employees to have beneficial effects. For example, consider a firm that is most concerned with maintaining a long-term relationship with its employees. In this case, the staffing, training, appraisal, and reward practices complement one another to convey a particular message, as illustrated by the left-hand side of **Exhibit 17.1**. The right-hand side of the exhibit shows a contradiction of HR practices. In this case, the staffing practice of hiring contract and temporary employees does not fit with the other practices. The training, appraisal, and reward practices communicate to employees that the firm invests in a long-term relationship with their employees while the staffing practice values short-term relationships. Research shows that having an internally consistent system of HR practices positively impacts the firm's bottom line.[24]

In sum, small firms can positively influence their financial performance by maximizing their external and internal fits. Moreover, small and new firms are uniquely positioned to achieve alignment between strategy and HRM—and consistency in their HR practices—if they begin by thinking strategically about their HRM system early in their founding and how it can help them achieve their operational mission.

LIFE CYCLE OF THE FIRM

To be successful in a global market, new firms or smaller companies need to have a highly motivated, skilled, and satisfied work force that can provide outstanding service or quality goods at low costs. To create this type of work force, the HR practices need to be developed in line with the strategy and growth of the company.[25] Thus, it is important to examine the life cycle of the firm when managing the human resource issues. As the organization grows and develops, its human resource management programs, practices, and procedures must change and develop to meet its needs. Each stage incorporates and builds upon the previous stages. **Exhibit 17.2** describes the important components to consider and the stage of growth.[26]

Stage I. Initiation

A new organization experiences issues such as starting up, the founder providing leadership, setting informal rules and expectations, and determining a limited array of products, markets, and services.[27] The HR functions that managers are primarily concerned with include hiring employees, determining salaries, and creating personnel policies (e.g., vacations, benefits, sick leave). At this time, the organization must develop individual files for each employee to keep records of days off, compensation, and training attended. Rather than simply "learn as you go," it would be beneficial for the owner/founder to develop a strategic HR plan that outlines how many people to hire and over what time period and how they will be trained, evaluated, and compensated. It is also important for the owner to create a vision for the firm. As one CEO/founder stated, "The vision incorporates the values of the founder and owner. Write down what you really believe and where you want to go and then find the people who have similar dreams and get excited about it."[28]

Exhibit 17.2: *The Human Resource Strategic Matrix*

Components	Stage I: Initiation	Stage II: Functional Growth	Stage III: Controlled Growth	Stage IV: Functional Integration	Stage V: Strategic Integration
Manager Awareness	Aware of function's administrative role	Aware of function's broad role but not committed	Aware; often frustrated at fragmentation	Cooperative and involved	Integrated
Management of the Personnel Function	Loose, informal; often none	Personnel manager; program orientation; manage conflicts among subfunctions	Personnel executive; business orientation; control, measurements, goals	Function orientation; department goals; planning, long-range direction, line/staff relations; collaborative	Company orientation; consistent and integrated with business strategic direction
Portfolio of Programs	Basic salary and benefits administration; basic record keeping; nonexempt hiring	Many new programs added responding to business needs in comp. benefits, training, etc.; revisiting basic programs	Management control programs; budgets, ROI; portfolio reevaluated in measurable and analytical terms; advanced compensation	Interdisciplinary programs; focus on department goals and direction; productivity; change management; succession planning	Cultural and environmental scanning; long-range planning; emphasis on effectiveness and efficiency in direct response to business needs
Information Technology	Manual employee profile; record keeping	Automated salary and basic profile; advance record keeping	Automate personnel work; mainly profiles, EEO, tracking; basic metrics	Utilize computer for projection; planning, analysis, and evaluation	Planning tools, research, and analysis; long-range issues and "what if" questions linked to the personnel and the organizational data base
Personnel Skills	Administrative routine and housekeeping	Functional specialists	Increased professionalism in function and managerial skills	Integrating activities; skills in systems, planning, and evaluation	High-level involvement in organization; skills dealing with macro issues
Awareness of Internal and External Environment	Not aware	Aware of environment and corporate culture but do not incorporate them into function's activities	Aware of risks and opportunities in environment; address some in programs	Aware of; react and incorporate into planning process; environmental changes identified	Systematically search for impact the environment has on organization; take an active role in making and shaping decisions

Source: L. Baird and I. Meshoulam, "Managing Two Fits of Strategic Human Resource Management," *Academy of Management Review* 13, no. 1 (1988): 116–128. Copyright © 1998 by ACAD of Mgmt. Reproduced with permission of ACAD of Mgmt. in the format Textbook via Copyright Clearance Center.

Issues to consider in the initiation stage follow:

- What is your vision for the firm (size, location, mission)?
- Will you hire an HR manager, outsource the HR issues, or make the decisions yourself? At this point, usually the founder or any managers typically make the early decisions about employees rather than hiring an HR manager. They could hire an HR person or outsource some of the HR issues (payroll, benefits management).
- What types of jobs are needed in the firm?
- How many people will you need to hire to meet your objectives for your firm? How many employees vs. managers?
- Over what time period will you need to hire them?
- Should they already have the skills required to do the job (a selection issue), or will you provide training to them (a training issue)?
- What initial benefits and salary packages will you use with employees and managers? Will any of them have partnership deals with the firm, or can they invest in the firm?

Stage II. Functional Growth

At this point, technical specialization, dynamic growth, expanded product lines and markets, and more formal marketing practices often characterize the firm.[29] The key jobs for a manager are to recruit, hire, and train the right people so that the firm can continue to be competitive. As the organization grows, managers must hire HR staff or other administrators to assist them in HR practices since they will probably not have the time to do everything themselves. They may have to formalize some of the HR practices, such as computerizing the payroll records or other employ-ee records.

These are issues to consider in the functional growth stage:

- Can you handle all of the personnel issues yourself, or do you need a business manager or HR manager to handle the people issues (hiring, training, evaluating)?
- Job descriptions should be prepared for each type of position. These should clarify job duties, major tasks, and required knowledge, skills, and abilities.
- How will you evaluate the performance of employees and managers? Performance expectations and the evaluation system should be designed and explained to employees.
- What type of benefits and incentives will you use to retain your valuable employees?
- What type of record keeping will you use to track employee training, payroll, and performance evaluations?

Stage III. Controlled Growth

The firm is now more concerned with new acquisitions, diversified product lines, scarce resources, and competition for resources. As the firm grows and employees become more diverse, issues of communication and control become more central as HR concerns. Often, more automation is needed and justifications must be given for HR programs.

Issues to consider in the controlled growth stage follow:

- If the number of employees increases (15 or more), records for Equal Employment Opportunity (EEO) purposes will be needed for all personnel decisions. These include hiring decisions, entry into training programs, promotions, demotions, and transfers. Are you prepared to make those decisions? Do you have an HR manager who is up-to-date on EEO?
- As the organization grows in size, do you have established career paths and ladders for employees (e.g., opportunities for sales employees to advance to new regions)? Is there an established succession planning system to train and develop managers?
- Formal training programs might be designed if they can show a clear return on investment. Smaller firms might use informal, on-the-job training and cross-training to make sure employees gain needed skills.

Stage IV. Functional Integration

Diversification in terms of products or divisions often occurs at this stage. The firm may need to engage in more coordination activities if they are highly decentralized. The HR staff will need to coordinate and integrate functions such as training, compensation, and recruiting.[30] The firm will want to ensure that various divisions are adhering to common practices yet at the same time, they should be careful not to micromanage what managers are doing.

Issues to consider in the functional integration stage include these:

- Will you have an HR manager and staff at each geographic location, or will a central corporate HR staff handle all HR activities?
- If HR staff are decentralized and located in different regions, will they periodically get together to coordinate activities and to reduce duplication?
- What change-management strategies will you establish (i.e., how will you ensure that the firm is adaptable and flexible enough for needed changes in strategy, that employees are receptive to changing the way they do business if necessary)?
- It will be important to periodically benchmark compensation and benefit plans with your competitors to make sure you are able to retain your employees.
- You should conduct an annual survey or focus groups with representative employees and managers to gauge their satisfaction with such things as the work, organization, supervision, pay, benefits, and co-workers. Smaller organizations may want to use informal methods (interviews, focus groups) to meet with employees to assess their satisfaction with the firm, while larger companies may use surveys in addition to interviews.

Stage V. Strategic Integration

At this stage, the focus by managers is on flexibility, adaptability, and integration across business functions. If done correctly, all staff members should see HR practices as their responsibility. HR programs should be integrated across locations as well as coordinated with other functional areas (e.g., accounting, finance, marketing).

These are issues to consider in the strategic integration stage:

- Managers of various functional areas should integrate HR issues with their overall business strategy.
- Long-range plans for personnel should be evaluated (e.g., hiring, retirements, training).
- HR information systems should be established to automate payroll and training received.
- An orientation program for new employees should be reviewed to ensure that it is consistent with the firm's strategic objectives (i.e., that the firm is attracting and hiring the type of personnel who best meet the company's goals).
- Performance management systems should be reviewed to ensure that they are rewarding the behaviors critical to the firm.

MANAGING THE FIRM'S HUMAN RESOURCE CAPITAL

Among small firms, HR management is seen as the second most important activity behind general management.[31] Yet often managers of small firms lack training in formal personnel management practices. Instead, they emphasize areas of accounting, finance, production, and marketing over HRM.[32] This has resulted in low productivity and in high dissatisfaction and turnover among employees. In one study, poor HRM practices were cited as the leading cause of small firms' failures.[33] Often, the small business owner or founder of the new firm handles HR practices, and yet many report frustration with their personnel practices. In some cases, they are not even aware of their own failure in dealing with personnel issues.[34]

In a recent survey of 173 CEO/founders of a variety of firms (e.g., manufacturing, services, retail, wholesale, financial/real estate, construction, and transportation), the HR issues seen as most important included recruitment/selection/retention, compensation and special pay programs, training, role of HR and strategy, benefits, motivating and rewarding employees, legal issues/EEO, and career development.[35] A survey of the Young Entrepreneurs Organization asked members to indicate the most important areas for which they and their organizations required more learning. The 156 entrepreneurs indicated that the most important areas in which they needed learning were in HR issues such as recruitment, retention, motivation, training, rewarding, compensation, and negotiation.[36]

In the following sections, we outline the key human resource areas that entrepreneurs should focus on when starting their new business. These include:

- Staffing
- Training
- Appraisal
- Rewarding
- Using communication and continuous improvement systems
- Understanding legal considerations

Staffing

The staffing function is concerned with *recruiting* potential employees and matching the right person with the right job (*selection*). When the firm is effective at staffing, it is able to attract top applicants and select the best people for their job.

Recruiting Employees

"Quality of life is important. If your industry does not provide this, it is more difficult to recruit people."[37]

In most cases, a new small business may work without any employees at all for a period of time and then decide it needs to hire one or two to start. Some small businesses might have ambitions to really grow the business and will need to hire many employees. Regardless of how many employees need to be hired, it is essential that the business bring in the best possible employees. Most owners feel that recruiting and retaining key staff is one of the major concerns for small firms[38] because skilled employees are often seduced by the attractions of larger firms or professions.[39] Thus, smaller firms need to develop plans that will attract talented employees. In addition, the wrong recruitment decision can be disastrous for a smaller firm since one "bad hire" can have a strong impact on the morale and productivity of the rest of the work force. In small businesses, it is critical to have "superstars" who can take on additional responsibilities, are loyal to the entrepreneur's vision, share the owner's ethics and principles, are creative in their area of expertise, add to the synergy of the team, and welcome positive change.[40]

Encouraging a diverse and talented work force is an important goal for small firms. Northern Arts, a regional arts board located in Newcastle, United Kingdom, employs 30 people and has offered programs to ensure equal opportunities for its employees, especially women. The chief executive noted that morale in the organization has significantly improved over four years, the work force is more productive, and women feel more encouraged to stay longer in the firm.[41]

Job Descriptions

Debbie Sotelo, an HR manager with True-San.com, reports that communication is a big problem for many start-ups. She points out that often in the interview process candidates get different job descriptions and instructions from different supervisors.[42] What is most important is to give candidates a "realistic job preview" of what is required on the job. This should include both positives and negatives about the job.

Written job descriptions are used to convey the major tasks and duties required on the job. They also convey management's expectations for the job (i.e., the most important or critical features of the job). Good applicants will usually want to know what the job involves and what is expected of them. Job descriptions are used for many purposes, including recruiting and selecting employees, training them, and evaluating their performance. As a start-up or new employer, you should make sure to include the major duties, time spent on various tasks, knowledge, skills and abilities required, performance expectations, expected salary range, bonuses and other perks or benefits, and any other responsibilities or unique aspects of the job context (e.g., requires extensive traveling, specialized equipment, use of a car). In addition, it is important to know what is done on the job in a typical day. An organizational chart indicating where the job fits is also useful. Some of the biggest problems firms have with the hiring process are due to having job descriptions that are not updated, are inflexible, or have unrealistic specifications.[43]

Small firms are just as likely as larger firms to rate certain work force characteristics as important. These include concern for the firm's success, ability to inspect employees' work, employee flexibility, ability to work in groups, self-disciplined problem-solving skills, multiskilled work force, communication skills, and quantitative skills.[44] If these or other characteristics are important on a job, the managers must make sure these are included in the job description for a position.

Methods Used for Recruiting Employees

Various methods are available for recruiting employees. Initially, founders and managers of new or small businesses rely on their social networks to fill positions with family and friends. Once they have exhausted these sources, they often look to "strangers" to fill jobs.[45] Research indicates that job postings, newspaper ads, employee referrals, and walk-ins are the most common method used when recruiting employees for smaller firms.[46] Usually, smaller firms fill vacancies from within the organization. They do not make much use of external sources of recruitment despite the fact that some of these techniques (e.g., educational institutions, personnel reference services) might prove useful. Employee referrals can yield good candidates if you offer incentives to your current employees to help you find the best candidates. Regardless of which method is used, the firm should periodically assess how effective the recruiting tools are for attracting the best or right people for the firm.

Recruiting tools can be used internally (to attract employees within the firm to make transfers or take promotions) or externally (to attract applicants from outside the firm). Some of the more popular recruiting methods include:

- Job postings (via the Internet such as http://www.monster.com or www. careerpath.com) or company Web sites or on bulletin boards.
- Advertisements in newspapers, direct mail, radio, television, magazines, or Web sites (e.g., http://www.careermag. com/ or http://www.careermosaic. com).
- Campus visits (to colleges, technical schools, etc.).
- Walk-ins (applicants who walk into the firm looking for a job).
- Employee referrals (employees in the firm refer others to apply).
- Job fairs.
- Employment agencies and search firms.

Selecting Employees

"The real challenge is how do you determine without hiring that person and having them there for six months who is really going to be an awesome person? How do you figure out if they are going to fit into your values and vision? Passion for the business is a real key. How can you tell in an interview somebody who has passion for the job?

"We spent the last four months turning the company around because of this one single hiring decision. The ramifications of that one hiring decision really had kind of global consequences for us."[47]

Methods for Selecting Employees

One of the most difficult problems for small firms has been finding competent workers.[48] While many different tools exist for selecting employees, research indicates that one-on-one interviews, written tests, and work samples are the methods often employed smaller firms.[49] Other techniques that can be used to select employees include:

- Application blanks and résumés (be sure to verify information).
- Letters of recommendation.
- Background investigations and security checks and clearances.
- Cognitive ability tests and intelligence tests.
- Emotional intelligence tests.
- Job knowledge tests.
- Work samples or performance tests.
- Interviews (structured interviews with specific questions are more effective than informal, unstructured interviews).
- Personality tests.
- Honesty tests.
- Drug tests (required in some jobs).

It is critical that the technique used for selecting employees be shown to be valid for hiring that type of employee. Smaller or new firms should be aware that using the same selection device for all different jobs would probably not yield the best employees. For example, you would need to tailor the interview questions for different types of jobs. In addition, if the firm has more than 15 employees it will need to adhere to the EEO laws (see http://www.eeoc.gov).

Typical Selection Procedure

A typical selection strategy for a new small business might go something like this. First, the applicant would turn in a résumé and application form to the firm. Then, the owner would interview the applicant (assuming the applicant has the minimum qualifications). Then following a "successful" interview, the applicant's résumé and background information would be checked. In addition, any references might be called. If all goes well, then you might set up some interviews with other key employees of the firm to get their perspective. Depending on the nature of the firm and the job, you might also have the applicant perform a work sample or take a test (e.g., honesty test, drug test).

Structured Interviews

Standard, structured questions should be asked of all applicants, and interviewers can compare notes regarding the applicant's answers to these questions. Some general interview questions might include:[50]

- What do you know about our firm, and why do you want to work here?
- What interests you about this job, and what skills can you bring to our firm?
- What is the number 1 trait that differentiates you from other applicants?
- What is your most significant business achievement?
- What was your biggest failure, and what did you learn from it?
- What are your weaknesses, and how have you learned to address them?
- What are your strengths?
- What are your goals for the next five years?

It is also a good idea to ask *behavioral interview questions* to get applicants to talk about things they have actually done. Past performance is often seen as one of the best predictors of future performance. Some of these questions might include:

- Tell me about a time when you demonstrated effective *leadership* skills. When was it? What did you do?
- Tell me about a time when you worked effectively in a *team*. What was your role and what did you do?
- Describe a situation when you had to resolve *conflict* with someone else. What was the conflict about? How did you resolve it?
- Describe a situation when you had to show that you were *adaptable or flexible*. What was involved? What did you do?
- Tell me about a time when you demonstrated effective *negotiating* skills. What was involved? What did you do?

Many additional questions could be asked depending on the nature of the job and the specific skills required on the job. The key is to get applicants to talk about how they have demonstrated the behaviors that are deemed critical for the job in question.

Applicants could also be asked *situational interview questions*. The interviewer would give the interviewees hypothetical situations and ask how they would handle them. For example:

- Suppose we want to increase sales by 40 percent in our software segment. What suggestions would you offer for doing this?

- If you were asked to lead a team of engineers in the design of a new product, how would you get started?
- Suppose you go to a client site and find the client to be extremely upset about our services. What would you do?

It is critical that all selection tools used with applicants (application blanks, interviews, honesty tests, work samples) be validated or shown to be related to successful performance on the job.[51] In addition, managers should be trained in conducting interviews so that they do not ask any illegal questions about the applicant's age, race, color, religion, national origin, disabilities, arrest records, or marital or parental status. (Refer to http://www.eeoc.gov for more details on legal and illegal questions.)

Training and Developing Employees

"We need people to care for our company at the very lowest levels and we can't treat them as a commodity and can't even think of them as a commodity. We need some consistency, we don't want to have huge turnover. We want people to build from the ground up. We want to continue to train and teach them.

"If you are constantly training your employees they pretty much stay awesome employees. No matter how much you grow a company, the fundamentals are there. If they are being trained they will stay that way (awesome) and it is your job to make sure they do. Most of the time you see a person fail inside the organization is because they are not challenged. They have lost the passion for the work they do every day."[52]

When new businesses begin to hire the first few people, they need to make sure that the new employees receive the training that they need to be successful. For example, if you hire salespeople and do not train them on the products, you will have continual problems if they do not understand how the business works and what you are counting on them to contribute. They might make bad sales or not follow the rules. Or they might complain about being unappreciated or underpaid because they do not know what is going on in the firm.[53]

Training is critical to help orient and develop new employees. They need to understand the firm's strategic goals and objectives so they know what to focus on. Despite the importance of training, it has been estimated that only 36 percent of small and medium-size firms (employing fewer than 25 employees) in the United Kingdom provided any training for their employees, compared with 78 percent of medium and large firms that did so.[54] Interestingly, small and medium-size firms express considerable enthusiasm for training even though they are less likely to engage in it.[55] In many cases, small business owners complain about the cost of training, and yet, if they do not provide training, many of their "superstars" might leave to go to other jobs.

A variety of techniques exist for training employees. These include:

• Classroom sessions and lectures.
• Television and film.
• Self-paced, independent studies (having employees take courses in a self-directed style).
• On-the-job training (most common method for new start-ups and smaller firms).
• Computer-assisted training.
• Equipment simulators.
• Games and simulations.
• Case studies.
• Role-plays.

Smaller firms often use on-the-job training (OJT), coaching, seminars, apprenticeships, and computer-assisted instruction.[56] For example, Quality Commercial Services in Westminster, Maryland, uses OJT with its staff and also encourages construction crews to learn a variety of skills or be cross-trained in order to secure new building contracts. Most small businesses rely on training from outside sources such as consultants, vendors, seminars or workshops, colleges and universities, books, and training classes on the Internet.[57]

In new businesses, it would seem important to provide the following types of training (at a minimum):

• Orientation program (to orient employees to the job, the firm, co-workers, and managers). It is very important for employees to get a realistic preview of what will be involved in the work. They also must learn which aspects of the job are most critical to the firm and the owners. They should be introduced to co-workers.
• A mentor or someone who can coach the new employee.
• Training for working in teams.
• Cross-training of various skills or job rotation to acquire an understanding of various jobs. For example, DELTA Dallas Staffing Companies continually cross-train employees to make sure that each

employee knows the functions of other jobs and is confident carrying out those assignments. Recruiters are trained in front-desk operations, and administrative employees receive sales training.[58]

As the organization grows, the HR manager might want to design various programs to help develop employees' careers. These would include career planning workshops, career counseling sessions, and career ladders and paths. In addition, some special programs could be developed depending on the issues employees face (e.g., work-family programs, preretirement programs, mentoring programs).

Appraising Employee Performance

"I think the thing that is required is communication with an employee on an ongoing consistent basis so that he or she has the chance to communicate and find out how he/she is doing and get that verbal reward back. That is the one thing we as entrepreneurs can do is show appreciation. If that is missing, all the bonuses and all the health care and everything in the world are meaningless. He (she) has got to feel appreciated."[59]

Once new employees are trained and educated on the critical aspects of their jobs, evaluating their performance becomes important for a number of reasons.[60] Performance appraisals can be used for administrative decisions such as who is deserving of a raise or promotion. Keeping track of top performers so that they can be rewarded assists in keeping morale high and sends the message that compensation decisions are merit based. In addition, performance appraisals provide structured opportunities to counsel and develop employees in an effort to improve their performance. Evaluation systems may also be used to determine future training needs. Lastly, appraisals provide documentation that the firm's human resources practices are in compliance with employment laws.

Today, many small businesses are setting up 360-degree appraisal systems similar to those used in larger firms. This means that employees provide a self-evaluation and are evaluated by their peers, higher-level managers, and perhaps clients or customers. One study of more than 300 small and medium-size businesses found that the performance management systems were comparable to or even more sophisticated than those used by large firms.[61] In another study, it was found that the most extensively used HR practice among small service firms was the performance appraisal system

that required evaluations of employees at least once a year.[62]

Establish Goals and Develop an Action Plan

Setting goals with employees is a good way to have them direct their attention to the most important aspects of the job. A well-known guideline for establishing goals is the SMART method:[63]

S Specific. Goals must be clear, direct, and definable.

M Measurable and meaningful. Goals must be aspects of the job that are measurable as well as meaningful to employees and employers.

A Appropriate. Goals should be appropriate to the employee's experience, training, potential, and responsibilities.

R Realistic. Goals should be realistic. This means not overly difficult or too easy.

T Time limit. A specific time limit should be agreed upon for when the goal should be met.

Get employees involved in discussing and setting goals with you. Your performance appraisal form could contain a section for goal setting. Write down the agreed-upon goals and give a copy to employees. Also, it is a good idea to measure progress toward goals and give feedback to employees quarterly. Hold them accountable for the goals. This is especially critical in new smaller firms since mistakes can be costly. Be willing to make changes in goals based on feedback from employees or clients. For example, if the new customer tracking system has not been implemented and employees are having difficulties meeting their sales goals, you might need to revisit and modify the goals. In addition, celebrate with employees when they reach their goals! Do not wait until they have reached the major milestones to reward employees. Give recognition when they accomplish minigoals in order to provide them with valuable information and to motivate them.

Procedure

To evaluate employee performance, first you will need to design a performance management instrument. What is most critical is to refer to the job description to see what the major tasks and job duties are for the job. You might design a tool that can be used by the employee (self-evaluation) or similar tools that can be used by the manager, peers, or clients. Some entrepreneurial firms do not have an established performance appraisal system. Instead, they establish a philosophy of shared responsibility for performance improvement with the employees and managers. This means that managers are responsible for working with employees to establish performance goals and for coaching them. Employees are responsible for soliciting feedback to grow and develop, for taking advantage of training opportunities, and for taking the initiative to learn about the business.[64] Either way, some type of plan or system is needed so employees are aware of how they are doing. Employees must be held accountable for goal achievement, and everyone from the CEO on down must be willing to communicate performance expectations and goals. Linda Crawford, CEO and president of DELTA Dallas Staffing Companies, states that she wants her staff to be independent and also accountable.[65]

Exhibit 17.3 illustrates comparisons between mature and entrepreneurial firms regarding performance management strategies. While smaller firms have the advantage of being more flexible, they must also be sure to treat employees fairly. Further, they must document and communicate expectations as well as establish systems that ensure consistency and compliance with employment laws.[66]

Whatever performance appraisal method is developed, it is important to provide training to *everyone* on the new system. Whoever will serve as raters (managers, peers, clients) should receive training on how to rate employee performance. In addition, employees must be educated on the features of the new system and how and when it will be used.

Example

Patapsco Valley Veterinary Hospital, in Ellicott City, Maryland, brought in a consultant to design a formal performance appraisal system for the veterinary technicians. To design the system, all employees were interviewed in order to conduct a thorough analysis of the job (major duties, knowledge, skills and abilities). In addition, in-depth discussions with the owners (veterinarians) were held to better understand the purpose for the system (what their intended purpose was for it) as well as how important each of the major job duties was for successful performance of the vet techs. A tool was designed and later reviewed by all employees. Once changes were made, the system was implemented. The first meetings the owners had with the vet techs were to clarify the rel-

---

Exhibit 17.3: *Typical Performance Management Strategies*

Mature Companies
✓ Emphasis on consistency, so that everyone is treated the same.
✓ Adherence to "one-size-fits-all" programs.
✓ Tightly controlled, inflexible salary-increase guidelines.
✓ Tendency to rely on published salary grades and ranges.
✓ Tendency to give everyone roughly the same percentage merit increase.
✓ Abdication of performance management responsibility by senior management.

Small, Entrepreneurial Firms
✓ Emphasis on inconsistency, so that people can earn what they deserve.
✓ Abundance of flexible programs and practices.
✓ Willingness to bend the rules as a matter of course when making salary decisions.
✓ Tendency to avoid relying on salary ranges and grades.
✓ Absence of formal performance appraisals. Instead, managers and employees work together to improve performance.
✓ Presence of real pay-for-performance.
✓ Direct management involvement in pay and performance decisions.

Source: C. J. Cantoni, "Learn to Manage Pay and Performance Like an Entrepreneur," *Compensation & Benefits Review* 29, no. 1: 52–58, copyright © 1997 by Sage Publications, Inc. Reprinted by permission of Sage Publications, Inc.

---

ative importance of various job duties and to explain the form and its purpose. Following this, employees completed self-appraisals. Then, staff held private meetings with each employee to discuss their performance over the past few months. They also discussed how the form would be linked to compensation over the next year. A portion of the form for the Patapsco Valley Veterinary Hospital (PVVH) is shown in **Exhibit 17.4**.

Generally, smaller firms or new start-ups will want to develop their own forms that can assess performance over the past as well as list goals and continuous improvement plans for the future. In many cases the forms will be used to provide developmental feedback to employees, although they can also be used to provide raises or promotions or other administrative decisions. This is a challenging job for new owners and managers. Often, managers are uncomfortable providing feedback to employees or are unsure what to do. (Some tips for handling the performance appraisal review sessions are given in the Chapter 17 Appendix.)

Using the Progressive Discipline System

While appraisals are necessary and valuable, they are not a substitute for continuous performance management initiatives. At times, employees do not meet expectations in terms of their performance and/or their conduct, and therefore disciplinary action is warranted. Progressive discipline proce-

dures include a progression of disciplinary action if the behavior continues. When implemented properly, these procedures are constructive and help clarify and reinforce the policies of the firm as well as promote organizational performance. Typically, progressive discipline includes the following:

1. An oral, informal warning or reprimand is given.
2. A written warning is issued to the employee and placed in his or her file.
3. Probation—the employee is given a specific amount of time to improve his or her performance.
4. Suspension—the employee is suspended without pay for a specified period of time.
5. Termination—the employee is fired.

Some guidelines for disciplinary systems are:

- Have clearly defined expectations for performance and consequences.
- Use early interventions to try to correct conduct or performance problems.
- Be consistent in applying discipline with employees (no favoritism).
- Match the punishment to the crime (do not be overly strict with minor violations and too lax with serious violations).
- Be timely in using discipline.
- Document all written warnings, probations, suspensions, and terminations and the conditions surrounding them.

> **Exhibit 17.4:** *Annual Performance Evaluation Form for Veterinary Technicians*
>
> **Directions:** For each of the following dimensions, rate yourself using the scale (Below Expectations, Meets Expectations, Exceeds Expectations). Circle one response for each dimension. Provide specific comments, especially for any ratings given of BE or EE.
>
> | | | | |
> |---|---|---|---|
> | **ATTENDANCE & PUNCTUALITY:** Regularly attends work. Gives advance notice if unable to come to work. Arrives at work on time. Returns from breaks in a prompt and timely fashion. Arrives at scheduled appointments and meetings on time. Does not abuse sick leave, lunch periods, breaks, or comp time. | BE | ME | EE |
> | **PROFESSIONAL APPEARANCE & WORK HABITS:** Appears neat, clean, and appropriately dressed. Regularly appears suitably dressed and fitting to the demands and expectations of the job. Minimizes idle conversations and the use of business phones for personal conversations. | BE | ME | EE |
> | **ETHICAL CONDUCT:** Complies with ethical principles established by relevant professional organizations. Adheres to ethical codes established by PVVH or others. Encourages ethical conduct by co-workers. Takes appropriate action on ethical violations. | BE | ME | EE |
> | **COOPERATION / TEAM BUILDING:** Provides help or assistance to co-workers in a timely manner in order to improve the performance of the PVVH. Shares tips with others for performing the job more efficiently. Fosters teamwork and cooperation. Encourages others to coordinate their activities. Instills pride and team spirit among co-workers. | BE | ME | EE |
> | **CLIENT RELATIONSHIPS:** Establishes and maintains polite and courteous interactions with clients. Interacts with clients to establish and maintain rapport. Elicits their ideas, views, and feelings as appropriate. Effectively deals with clients regardless of their status, position, or background. Represents a positive organizational image of PVVH to the public. Deals with clients with minimal conflict or difficulties. Responds effectively and quickly to requests by clients. | BE | ME | EE |
> | **ANIMAL RELATIONSHIPS:** Greets animals upon their arrival in a positive manner. Establishes and maintains effective interactions and relationships with animals. Effectively deals with animals regardless of the type of animal (e.g., canine, feline, bird, rodent). Responds to difficulties or challenging, stressful situations with animals in a professional and timely manner. | BE | ME | EE |
>
> Source: Excerpts from J. E. A. Russell, *Annual Employee Performance Evaluation Form* (Ellicott City, MD: Patapsco Valley Veterinary Hospital, 1999).

- Have the employee provide his or her signature that he or she received the warning. If he or she refuses to sign, bring in a witness to sign off that the employee was given the warning.

Firing Employees

Unless an employee is protected by an individual contract with the employer or a union, or is a civil service employee, the employee will fall under *employment-at-will* status. This means that an employee can quit working for a firm at any time. In addition, the employer has the right to terminate the service of the employee at any time, for any reason or for no reason as long as it complies with applicable laws (see http://www.eeoc.gov). For example, an employer cannot fire a person because she has joined a union or because of her race, age, sex, religion, national origin, or disability. Of course, the employer and employee could sign a contract indicating that the employee will work for a specified period of time. If the firm wants to maintain its "employment-at-will" status, then it should clearly state this in the employee manual.

Firing should be the last resort—when an employee has not improved his performance over the specified time period, or when he has violated a serious company policy (e.g., theft, harassment, drinking or drugs on the job, fighting, insubordination). Although it will always be difficult to fire employees, we offer some tips to make it more effective:[67]

- Make sure all managers are trained in the firm's discipline and termination procedures.
- Review the performance appraisal materials and make sure you have already documented and informed the employee about substandard performance. She should not be surprised when she is fired. In other words, she should have already received feedback on numerous occasions about her low level of performance as well as suggestions and goals for improvements. If the company manual indicates that a progressive discipline system is in place, then it should be followed. It should be clear to employees when they are suspended that the next step is termination (if their performance or conduct does not improve).

- Explore all the alternatives before deciding to fire an employee. These might include demotions, retraining, additional grace periods for performance improvements, or hiring the employee on a part-time basis for specific work.
- Inform and seek advice from your HR manager and attorney regarding the termination in case there may be possible litigation. Get their input *before* you fire the employee.
- Prepare a firing package when appropriate. This would include severance pay, continuance of health insurance, and duration of benefits and perks.
- Give dates for when the employee should return company assets (keys, ID cards, credit cards, tools, computers, cars, phones). Change computer passwords or change his access to company computers and intranet.
- If the employee has incurred expenses for the company that have not been reimbursed or has won monetary awards or trips that have not been paid, then make arrangements for quickly handling those.

- Arrange a time for the employee to clean out her desk, office, or locker.
- Arrange for forwarding of any mail that the employee would receive.
- Arrange for outplacement services to assist the employee in finding additional work. This would help him with résumé critiques and job counseling.
- Prepare for the termination meeting. Have your documentation available and treat the meeting as a professional business meeting (i.e., keep emotions out).
- State the facts of the case, but do not argue about them. Allow the employee the opportunity to express or vent her feelings in a controlled manner. Answer any questions the employee has.
- Have a witness present (e.g., the HR manager or another manager) at the termination meeting. This gives you an additional person who can testify (if necessary) regarding what was said and done in the meeting.

Keep in mind that under COBRA (Consolidated Omnibus Budget Reconciliation Act), if a firm has 20 or more employees, then a terminated employee is entitled to maintain his health-insurance coverage for 18 months after he leaves the company. This is true for termination unless it was for gross misconduct, in which case no continuation is mandated.[68]

Rewarding Employees

"We found that in the technology industry, people really want a good culture as well as really fun projects to work on. Money is just secondary to people.

"It is all about trust. If your employees don't trust you, it doesn't matter what pay plan you put into place, it's going to affect you."[69]

HR can create an attractive start-up environment by emphasizing more than just money. The money has to be fair, but it does not have to be everything. Providing learning opportunities, addressing individual needs, and creating meaningful work will also be important to employees. Employers must create a motivational environment for employees. A survey of 280 small business CEOs found that they spent more of their time on motivating employees rather than any other HR issue.[70]

Most small firms do not have a systematic or rational approach to their compensation practices. In fact, research indicates that the size of the firm is related to the sophistication of the methodology used to determine wages as well as the complexity of the benefits packages offered. For example, many smaller firms (1–50 employees) provide pension and disability programs, while larger small firms (51–150 employees) provide some type of health, life, and disability insurance.[71]

There are a number of issues to consider in a total compensation plan. One important consideration is whether you will be incentivizing employees to work individually or as part of teams. Some research has shown that smaller firms are less likely to understand the importance of incentives relative to larger firms. Other research indicates that entrepreneurial firms have better systems in place for rewarding and compensating employees. These start-up firms make significant pay distinctions based on performance (unlike larger firms) and deal aggressively with performance problems.[72] This may be because the firm's survival is at stake.

Some questions you will need to think about when designing your compensation system are:[73]

- Are you going to make your base salaries competitive with the going rate in the area, or higher, or lower?
- Are you going to establish a structured pay scale for specific jobs in your company, or are you going to set salaries on an individual basis?
- What combination of salary, bonuses, and benefits are you going to use?
- How will you determine salary increases—based on performance? Cost-of-living adjustments? Time with the firm?
- Will you award any bonuses? Will these be based on individual performance? Team performance? Organizationwide performance?

Some guidelines to make sure your compensation system works include:[74]

- Whatever system you decide to use, you should design it *before* you hire your first employee. This will ensure that you have a defined plan in place and will not set precedents for your first employee that you will later have to change.
- Determine what basis you will use to provide raises to employees (seniority, merit, cost-of-living-adjustments, bonuses, incentives).
- Once you use the system be sure employees understand it. Some firms establish complex incentive systems to motivate employees and then find out that employees do not even understand them. If employees do not understand the system, it is unlikely that it is motivating them.
- Make sure you can measure the aspects of performance for which you will be paying the employees.
- Make sure to be consistent and use the same system with all the employees in one job.
- If you use bonuses, tie them directly to performance and use them frequently (e.g., quarterly or monthly) so that employees can see the direct link between their performance and the bonus.
- Benchmark your salaries, hourly rate, bonuses, and benefits with your competitors to make sure you are in line with them. Otherwise, you might lose some of your employees! You can find out the going rate for salaries and other benefits from trade and professional associations, chambers of commerce, employment agencies, networking with colleagues, and the Internet.

Some of the issues to consider when rewarding employees deal with direct and indirect compensation and are described below.

- *Direct Compensation* or financial remuneration or cash:
  - Hourly pay
  - Salary
  - Overtime pay
  - Bonuses—could be annual, incentive bonuses, "on-the-spot" bonuses, or retention bonuses
  - Commissions
  - Profit-sharing plans
  - Signing bonus
- *Indirect Compensation* or benefits:
  - Government-mandated programs such as social security, unemployment insurance, workers' compensation, disability programs.
  - Employee welfare programs such as health care plans, dental plans, vision plans, life insurance, day care or elder care support, survivor benefits.
  - Pension plans including 401K plans, profit-sharing plans, other savings plans. Among firms with less than 25 employees, only 19 percent offer some type of retirement plan.[75]
  - Time-off programs such as vacation, personal days off, sick leave, family

leave, sabbaticals. Flexible schedules, job sharing, permanent part-time work, and telecommuting are also issues to consider and very important to today's workers. None of these benefits are legally required for an employer to give employees, although most firms do offer these benefits. Some firms offer rewards to employees who do not take any sick leave days or personal days.

- Employee services such as tuition reimbursement plans, child/family care, housing and relocation services, employee assistance programs, and employee recognition programs.
- Perks (e.g., parking spot, company car and mileage, spending account, dry cleaning, cafeteria, casual dress days, birthday celebrations at work, financial counseling, exercise and recreation rooms, memberships in professional associations, subsidized lunchrooms, memberships in social clubs).

Employee Recognition and Award Programs

In addition to direct and indirect compensation programs, a new firm might consider using some recognition and rewards to acknowledge and motivate employees. To be effective, it is important to consider compensation from a total rewards perspective.[76] This means owners should look at learning opportunities, recognition, and monetary rewards such as base pay and incentives. A great resource to help when determining creative reward programs is the bestseller book *1001 Ways to Reward Employees*.[77] Not only does it provide good ideas for financial rewards, but also it offers suggestions for nonfinancial or low-cost rewards, both of which might be more acceptable to start-up or smaller firms. Recognition can be given to individuals (e.g., employee of the month), work teams, and co-workers for performing tasks "above and beyond the call of duty."

Communication and Continuous Improvement Systems

Once HR practices are implemented dealing with each of the four HR functions (i.e., staffing, training, appraisal, and rewards), the next considerations deal with (1) how to communicate expectations to employees and (2) how to improve existing practices. The following section addresses each of these considerations.

Communicating Expectations to Employees

Certainly, managers can and do communicate their expectations; however, written policies and procedures help to ensure that these expectations are consistently conveyed to all employees, thereby protecting the firm. This manual should be clear and concise and not written in overly technical jargon. Employees should be asked to read the manual and provide their signatures indicating that they have read the manual and are willing to adhere to the guidelines. There should also be a statement indicating that the manual provides a general source of information. It is critical that someone in the firm (usually the HR manager) periodically review and update the manual. If changes are made, current employees should receive copies of those changes in a timely manner. They could even be asked to provide their signature indicating that they received the new changes.

Some of the key features that could be included in the manual are described below.[78] Before distributing the manual to employees, you should have an attorney or experienced HR manager review it.

- Welcome letter or statement from the founder, CEO, and/or president.
- Company mission statement, values, and goals.
- A statement indicating that the manual is not a contract for lifetime employment for the employee.
- Equal employment opportunity statements (including regulations regarding sexual and other forms of harassment).
- Benefits plans (e.g., health insurance, maternity/paternity leave, pensions, profit sharing, sick leave, company-reimbursed education policies, dental plans, vision plans, child or elder care systems).
- Policies concerning the workday and policies regarding overtime pay, time off, and breaks.
- Performance appraisal process, career opportunities and promotions, wage increases or bonuses.
- List of the paid holiday and vacation days and policies.
- Parking and transportation information, including maps.
- Drug and alcohol policy. Preemployment screening and postemployment testing.
- Standards of conduct, including professional dress, attendance, and punctuality.

- Progressive discipline system. List causes for disciplinary action and termination as well as severance pay policies.
- A page where the employee can provide his or her signature and date indicating that he or she has read the manual and agrees to adhere to it.

Employers can find many of the forms they will need to use in various personnel books or texts. One consulting firm, The Personnel Department, Inc., has created "The Personnel Department in a Box," which contains many of the policies and forms a company needs (e.g., warning letters, new-hire letters, personnel manual templates).[79] One survey of small service firms found that most did provide a handbook or written guidelines to employees.[80] While having policies and procedures manuals can clarify roles and issues for employees, the firm must still encourage employees to be creative and to show initiative on their jobs and not feel overly confined in what they can do.

Setting up Communication and Employee Suggestion Systems

One important feature of high commitment firms is to allow employees to provide suggestions for improvements in the firm. Employees should be encouraged to participate actively in the firm and to engage in two-way communication. In addition, at least once a year it would be useful to conduct one-on-one or group interviews with employees or use surveys if there are a large number of employees to ask them how they feel things are going in the firm. Some of the issues you might ask about include their satisfaction with the:

- Nature of the work
- Leadership team
- Pay, benefits, perks, hours
- Working relationships and co-workers

You should also ask employees what they like best about working there, what suggestions they have for improvements, how committed they are to the firm, and what the likelihood is that they will stay or leave the firm in the next year.

Conducting Exit Interviews

Every time an employee leaves your firm, it costs you money. This is due to the time and expense involved in recruiting, selecting, training, evaluating, and supervising the employee. Ideally, you would like to avoid having your good employees quit. If, however, you do have some employees who choose to leave your firm, it is a good idea to conduct an exit interview with them. You might conduct one interview at the time when they leave and another meeting as a follow-up six months later. Research indicates that conducting the exit interview at a later time often reveals more valuable information.[81] This information would help your firm continually improve. The HR manager could conduct this meeting. It is best not to have the person's immediate supervisor conduct the meeting so that the employee feels she can be more candid. Some of the questions the interviewer could ask the employee are:[82]

- What was the main factor in your decision to leave the firm? Often, the employee may say "personal" reasons, yet if you probe further, you might discover that there were also job-related reasons (e.g., the employee did not think the supervisor was fair, the employee wanted more recognition).

- Why are you leaving at this particular time?

- What did you like most about the firm?

- What did you like least? What suggestions would you offer to our firm to improve?

- When you first started working here, what impressed you most about the firm? In what way did this change?

- What would have made you stay longer at this firm?

- How would you rate the job, working conditions, supervisory relationships, relationships with co-workers, teamwork, morale, training, career opportunities, communication, and compensation?

- How fully was your job explained to you before you accepted it?

- If you could discuss with top management exactly how you feel about this company, what would you tell them?

- What does the job to which you are going offer you that you were not getting here?

Some firms never seek their employees' input about the job and organizational factors until employees are exiting the firm. While it is important to solicit their views at this time, it would be even better if you periodically asked employees about their opinions. This might enable you to make needed changes in the firm and avoid losing valuable employees in the first place!

Legal Considerations

Unlike larger firms, most small firms do not have a human resource staff or function and thus are often less familiar with equal employment opportunity legislation and laws. To avoid charges of unfair dismissals and discrimination lawsuits, it is critical that a firm hire a competent HR manager or someone who understands EEO and Affirmative Action laws and practices. For more detail on the laws, refer to current HR texts[83] or the Web site for the Society for Human Resource Management (http://www.shrm.org) or Equal Employment Opportunity Commission (http://www.eeoc.gov).

Some of the HR issues that involve legal concerns for a firm include:[84]

- Sexual harassment

- Discrimination (age, religion, sex, nationality, ethnicity)

- Hiring violations

- Workplace safety violations

- Working conditions violations

- Wage and hour violations

Business owners must be aware of relevant laws or have someone on staff who is. Some of the most important laws related to HR are described below. Unless otherwise indicated, most of these apply to employers with 15 or more employees who work 20 or more weeks per year. In addition, usually they also apply to labor unions, employment agencies, and state and local governments. (See the reference material at the end of the appendix to this chapter for sources to contact to learn more about each of these issues.)

- Age Discrimination in Employment Act (ADEA), applies to private sector employers with 20 or more employees working 20 or more weeks per year

- Americans with Disabilities Act (ADA) (1990)

- Civil Rights Act (CRA) of 1964, Title VII

- Civil Rights Act of 1991

- Consolidated Omnibus Budget Reconciliation Act (COBRA)

- Employee Retirement Income Security Act (ERISA)

- Equal Pay Act (EPA) (1963)

- Fair Labor Standards Act (FLSA)

- Family and Medical Leave Act (FMLA) (1993), applies to private employers with 50 or more employees

- Federal Unemployment Tax Act (FUTA)

- Occupational Safety and Health Act (OSHA)

- Pregnancy Discrimination Act (1978)

Addressing Employee Health and Safety Issues

There is an increasing emphasis on health and safety issues for employees. These include workplace injuries and illnesses, drugs in the workplace, smoking and alcohol abuse in the workplace, occupational stress, and workplace violence.

In the United States, the Occupational Safety and Health Administration (OSHA) was created in 1970 within the Department of Labor. Its purpose was to encourage employers and employees to reduce workplace hazards and to implement new or improve existing safety and health programs. OSHA also requires a reporting and record keeping system to monitor job-related injuries and illnesses. In addition, it establishes training programs and develops mandatory job safety and health standards. Employers with 11 or more employees must maintain records of occupational injuries and illnesses as they occur. OSHA also periodically inspects various workplaces for safety issues. (For more detail on OSHA, see http://www.osha.gov.) Some states also have similar laws whereby state inspectors enforce the safety laws.

As a start-up or new employer, it is your responsibility to be aware of OSHA and other related laws to ensure the health and safety of your employees. Some of the items covered by OSHA include:[85]

- Walking and working surfaces, ladders, housekeeping, power lifts, scaffolds

- Exits, emergency exits, fire prevention plans

- Ventilation, noise exposure, radiation, hazard signs

- Hazardous materials such as gases, flammables, explosives, waste

- Personal protective equipment such as protection of eyes, face, head, feet, and respiratory organs

- Fire protection—extinguishers, sprinkler systems, detection and alarm systems

- Materials handling and storage

- Operating machinery and handheld equipment

- Training and operation in welding, cutting, and glazing

- Electric wiring and electrical equipment

You should create a safe work environment by setting up safety awareness programs for your staff. In addition to safety issues, you should establish a healthy work environment for your employees. Be sensitive to employees' level of stress and burnout from the job and make needed changes. In addition, examine issues such as water and air pollution, exposure to chemicals, cigarette smoking, radiation effects from video display terminals, strains and stresses due to repetitive work, and excessive noise. You should also establish written policies regarding drugs and alcohol in the workplace, sexual or racial harassment, and workplace violence. To protect your work force, you should:[86]

- Establish and communicate to employees a strong zero-tolerance policy for harassment, illegal drug and alcohol use, and workplace violence.
- Screen out potentially violent or unstable employees during the recruiting and selection process.[87]
- Provide counseling through an Employee Assistance Program (or refer employees to counseling) for employees with personal, financial, or substance-abuse problems.
- Take precautions when difficult decisions are being made (terminations, layoffs) since many problems occur at these times.
- Be alert to employees who show evidence of substance abuse problems, engage in frequent displays of anger and threats of violence against co-workers or managers, bring weapons to work, or engage in other extreme behaviors (isolation, deteriorating hygiene).

SUMMARY

As noted earlier, research has shown that HRM practices are related to a firm's financial performance and are critical for the success of a firm. Many new start-ups, family-owned businesses, and other smaller companies are aware of the importance of HR issues, and some of them are using best HRM practices. Also, one benefit that smaller firms have is that they often establish HR programs that are more flexible and less bureaucratic than larger firms.

The current chapter illustrates some of the major issues that smaller firms or new start-ups should consider as the company becomes established and grows. While we recommend that smaller firms or new start-ups establish various types of HR programs, we also recognize that these programs do not have to be overly bureaucratic to be effective. Sometimes, informal plans and systems can work very effectively as long as

they are linked with the firm's overall strategic plan. What is important is that some type of system be developed and in line with the firm's strategy and have some internal consistency among its subparts so as to convey a clear message to employees. Managers must formalize their expectations for employees and at the same time encourage employees to take responsibility for their work lives. In addition, to make sure that their practices are in line with the law and are meeting their intended needs, it is critical for small business owners to periodically review and audit their personnel practices or call in a specialist to do this.

1. (USSBA) United States Small Business Administration Office of Advocacy, "Characteristics of Small Business Employers and Owners" (1997). http://www.sba.org

2. U.S. Small Business Administration, Office of Advocacy, "The Facts about Small Business" (1999). http://www.sba.gov/ADVO See also Society for Human Resource Management (SHRM), *Personnel/Human Resource Management in Smaller and Growing Organizations* (Valhalla, NY: Research Institute of America Group, 1997).

3. U.S. Small Business Administration, Office of Advocacy, "The Facts about Small Business."

4. R. Reid, T. Morrow, B. Kelly, J. Adams, and P. McCartan, "Human Resource Management Practices in SME's: A Comparative Analysis of Family and Nonfamily Businesses," *Journal of the Irish Academy of Management* 21, no. 2 (2000): 157–181. See also T. H. Wager, "Determinants of Human Resource Management Practices in Small Firms: Some Evidence from Atlantic Canada," *Journal of Small Business Management* 36, no. 2 (1998): 13–23.

5. Reid et al., "Human Resource."

6. H. G. Heneman and R. A. Berkley, "Applicant Attraction Practices and Outcomes among Small Businesses," *Journal of Small Business Management* 37, no. 1 (1999): 53–74. See also A. E. Barber, M. J. Wesson, Q. M. Roberson, and M. S. Taylor, "A Tale of Two Job Markets: Organizational Size and Its Effects on Hiring Practices and Job Search Behavior," *Personnel Psychology* 52, no. 4 (1999): 841–867. See also H. G. Heneman, R. L. Heneman, and T. A. Judge, *Staffing Organizations*, 2d ed. (New York: McGraw-Hill, 1997).

7. J. A. Katz et al., "Guest Editor's Comments Special Issue on Human Resource Management and the SME: Toward a New Synthesis," *Entrepreneurship Theory and Practice* (Fall 2000): 7–10.

8. M. Thatcher, "The Big Challenge Facing Small Firms," *People Management* 2, no. 15 (1996): 20-25.

9. National Federation of Independent Business, "Labor Shortages Top Taxes as Main Small Business Concern," December 16, 1998. http://www.nfibonline.com

10. V. Infante, "How dot-coms Learned to Value the Tried and True," *Workforce*, May 2001, p. 15.

11. J. Applegate, "Small Firms Need to Bone Up on Personnel Issues," *San Diego Business Journal* 18, no. 23 (1997): 12–13.

12. G. N. Chandler and G. M. McEvoy, "Human Resource Management, TQM, and Firm Performance in Small and Medium-Sized Enterprises," *Entrepreneurship Theory and Practice* (Fall 2000): 43–57.

13. R. L. Heneman, J. W. Tansky, and S. M. Camp, "Human Resource Management Practices in Small and Medium-Sized Enterprises: Unanswered Questions and Future Research Perspectives," *Entrepreneurship Theory and Practice* (Fall 2000): 11–26.

14. R. N. Lussier and S. Pfeifer, "A Comparison of Business Success versus Failure Variables between U.S. and Central Eastern Europe Croatian Entrepreneurs," *Entrepreneurship Theory and Practice* (Summer 2000): 59–67. See also J. Corman, R. N. Lussier, and K.G. Nolan, "Factors That Encourage Entrepreneurial Start-Ups and Existing Firm Expansion: A Longitudinal Study Comparing Recession and Expansion Periods," *Academy of Entrepreneurship Journal* 1, no. 2 (1996): 43–55; L. R. Gaskill, H. E. Van Auken, and R. A. Manning, "A Factor Analytic Study of the Perceived Causes of Small Business Failure," *Journal of Small Business Management* 31, no. 4 (1993): 18–31; R. N. Lussier, "A Nonfinancial Business Success versus Failure Prediction Model for Young Firms," *Journal of Small Business Management* 33, no. 1 (1995): 8–20. See also R. N. Lussier and J. Corman, "A Business Success versus Failure Prediction Model for Entrepreneurs with 0-10 Employees," *Journal of Small Business Strategy* 7, no. 1 (1996): 21–35.

15. J. Pfeffer, *The Human Equation* (Boston: Harvard Business School Press, 1998). See also M. A. Huselid, "The Impact of Human Resource Practices on Turnover, Productivity, and Corporate Financial Performance," *Academy of Management Journal* 38, no. 3 (1995): 635–672.

16. P. Bamberger and I. Meshoulam, *Human Resource Strategy: Formulation, Implementation, and Impact* (Thousand Oaks, CA: Sage Publications, 2000).

17. Reid et al., "Human Resource Management Practices in SME's."

18. Ibid.

19. Ibid.

20. J. H. Astrachan and T. A. Kolenko, "A Neglected Factor Explaining Family Business Success: Human Resource Practices," *Family Business Review* 7, no. 3 (1994): 251–262. See also S. W. King, G. T. Solomon, and L. W. Fernald, "Issues in Growing a Family Business: A Strategic Human Resource Model," *Journal of Small Business Management* 39, no. 1 (2001): 3–13.

21. R. E. Miles and C.C. Snow, "Designing Strategic Human Resource Systems," *Organizational Dynamics* 16 (1984): 36–52.

22. Ibid.

23. J. E. Delery and D. H. Doty, "Modes of Theorizing in Strategic Human Resource Management: Tests of Universalistic, Contingency, and Configurational Performance Predictions," *Academy of Management Journal* 36, no. 4(1996): 802–835. Also see P. M. Wright, D. L. Smart, and G. C. McMahan, "Matches between Human Resources and Strategy among NCAA Basketball Teams," *Academy of Management Journal* 38, no. 4 (1995): 1052–1074.

24. C. Ichniowski, K. Shaw, and G. Presnnushi, "The Effects of Human Resource Management Practices on Productivity: A Study of Steel Finishing Lines," *The American Economic Review* 3 (1997): 291–313.

25. A. Ardichvili et al., "The New Venture Growth: Functional Differentiation and the Need for Human Resource Development Interventions," *Human Resource Development Quarterly* 9, no. 1 (1998): 55–70.

26. L. Baird and I. Meshoulam, "Managing Two Fits of Strategic Human Resource Management," *Academy of Management Review* 13, no. 1 (1988): 116–128.

27. Ibid.

28. Heneman, Tansky, and Camp, "Human Resource Management,"19.

29. Baird and Meshoulam, "Managing Two Fits."

30. Ibid.

31. D. W. Hess, "Relevance of Small Business Courses to Management Needs," *Journal of Small Business Management* 1(1987): 26–34.

32. G. M. McEvoy, "Small Business Personnel Practices," *Journal of Small Business Management* 10 (1984): 1–8.

33. Ibid.

34. R. D. Gatewood and H. S. Field, "A Personnel Selection Program for Small Business," *Journal of Small Business Management* (October 1987): 16–24.

35. Heneman, Tansky, and Camp, "Human Resource Management."

36. Ibid.

37. Ibid.

38. I. O. Williamson, "Employer Legitimacy and Recruitment Success in Small Businesses," *Entrepreneurship Theory and Practice* (Fall 2000): 27–42. See also Heneman and Berkley, "Applicant Attraction Practices."

39. Thatcher, "The Big Challenge."

40. E. Tyson and J. Schell, *Small Business for Dummies* (Foster City, CA: IDG Books Worldwide, Inc., 2000).

41. Thatcher, "The Big Challange."

42. Infante, "How dot-coms Learned."

43. A. R. Pell, *The Complete Idiot's Guide to Human Resource Management* (Indianapolis, IN: Alpha Books/Pearson Education Company, 2001).

44. S. P. Deshpande and D. Y. Golhar, "HRM Practices in Large and Small Manufacturing Firms: A Comparative Study," *Journal of Small Business Management* 32, no. 2 (1994): 49–56.

45. Williamson, "Employer Legitimacy and Recruitment Success."

46. Deshpande and Golhar, "HRM Practices." See also J. S. Hornsby and D. F. Kuratko, "Human Resource Management in Small Business: Critical Issues for the 1990's," *Journal of Small Business Management* 28, no. 3 (1990): 9–18.

47. Heneman, Tansky, and Camp, "Human Resource Management."

48. Gatewood and Field, "A Personnel Selection Program."

49. Deshpande and Golhar, "HRM Practices."

50. Tyson and Schell, *Small Business for Dummies.* See also M. Messmer, *Human Resources Kit for Dummies* (New York, NY: Robert Half International, Inc., 1999).

51. H. J. Bernardin and J. E. A. Russell, *Human Resource Management: An Experiential Approach,* 2d ed. (New York: McGraw-Hill/Irwin, 1998).

52. Heneman, Tansky, and Camp, "Human Resource Management."

53. N. Brodsky, "The First Salesperson," *INC,* December 1998, pp. 33–34.

54. Department for Education and Employment. *Training Statistics* (London: The Stationery Office, 1996).

55. H. Matlay and T. Hyland, "NVQs in the Small Business Sector: A Critical Overview," *Education and Training* 39, no. 9 (1997): 325–332.

56. Hornsby and Kuratko, "Human Resource Management."

57. Tyson and Schell, *Small Business for Dummies.*

58. B. P. Sunoo, "Growing without an HR Department," *Workforce,* January 1998, pp. 16–17.

59. Heneman, Tansky, and Camp, "Human Resource Management."

60. K.R. Murphy and J. N. Cleveland, *Understanding Performance Appraisal: Social, Organizational, and Goal-Based Perspectives* (Thousand Oaks, CA: Sage Publications, 1995).

61. D. Lane, "People Management in Small and Medium-Sized Enterprises, IPD Research Department," cited in Thatcher, "The Big Challenge."

62. V. Kaman, A. M. McCarthy, R. D. Gulbro, and M. L. Tucker, "Bureaucratic and High Commitment Human Resource Practices in Small Service Firms," *Human Resource Planning* 24 (2001): 33–44.

63. Tyson and Schell, *Small Business for Dummies.*

64. C. J. Cantoni, "Learn to Manage Pay and Performance Like an Entrepreneur," *Compensation and Benefits Review,* 29, no. 1 (1997): 52–58.

65. Sunoo, "Growing."

66. Kaman et al., "Bureaucratic and High Commitment."

67. Pell, *The Complete Idiot's Guide.* See also Tyson and Schell, *Small Business for Dummies.*

68. Pell, *The Complete Idiot's Guide.*

69. Heneman, Tansky, and Camp, "Human Resource Management."

70. M. P. Cronin, "Motivation Inclination," *INC* 15, no. 8 (1993): 28.

71. Amba-Rao, S. C., and Pendse, D. (1985). "Human Resources Compensation and Maintenance Practices," *American Journal of Small Business* (Fall 1985): 19-29. See also Hornsby and Kuratko, "Human Resource Management."

72. Deshpande and Golhar, "HRM Practices." See also Cantoni, "Learn to Manage Pay," 52–58.

73. Messmer, *Human Resources Kit.*

74. Tyson and Schell, *Small Business for Dummies,* 279.

75. Ibid.

76. B. Parus, "Designing a Total Rewards Program to Retain Critical Talent in the New Millennium," *ACA News,* February 1999, 20–23.

77. B. Nelson, *1001 Ways to Reward Employees* (New York: Workman Publishing, 1994).

78. Messmer, *Human Resources Kit.* See also Tyson and Schell, *Small Business for Dummies.*

79. Applegate, "Small Firms." See also The Personnel Department, Inc. (212-818-0666).

80. McCarthy, Gulbro, and Tucker, "Bureaucratic and High Commitment," 33–44.

81. Pell, *The Complete Idiot's Guide.*

82. Pell, *The Complete Idiot's Guide.*

83. Bernardin and Russell, *Human Resource Management.*

84. Tyson and Schell, *Small Business for Dummies.*

85. Pell, *The Complete Idiot's Guide,* 218–219.

86. Messmer, *Human Resources Kit.*

87. Bernardin and Russell, *Human Resource Management.*

TIPS FOR CONDUCTING PERFORMANCE APPRAISAL REVIEW (PAR) SESSIONS

Note: The biggest problem with most PAR sessions is that managers feel uncomfortable with the process. This is primarily because they have not received training in how to conduct a PAR session. The tips below should help you make the session much more successful by helping you to be *prepared*. These tips assume that you are using a performance appraisal form and that there is an employee version and a manager version of the form. This will make you more comfortable and confident. This will also send the message to employees that you value their contribution to the company.

STAGE 1: BEFORE THE SESSION: PREPARATION

- *Select the right environment* to hold the session (quiet, no interruptions, comfortable setting).
- *Give the Employee Form to the employee and ask that she/he return it to you within one week.*
- *Complete your ratings of the employee on the Manager Form.* If other managers will also be evaluating the employee, have them complete the form as well.
- *Review the employee's self-appraisal form* and his/her self-ratings and comments.
- *Review your own ratings and comments for the employee on the Manager Form.* Make sure you have already completed your ratings for the employee, and have already thought about the employee's greatest strengths and greatest areas to work on. If you have given the employee any low ratings, be sure you have specific behavioral examples to share with him/her. The employee will ask for these examples.
- *If two managers will be meeting with the employee, be sure both managers have examined the employee's completed form prior to the meeting and are fully prepared.* Make sure the two managers agree on how they rate the employee and the employee's greatest strengths and areas for improvement. This is critical since you do not want two managers sending different messages to the employee in the PAR session. It will be confusing to the employee, and the managers will look incompetent. Make sure the two managers agree on what role they will each play during the meeting (that is, will they both offer comments, who will start the meeting, who will end the meeting, who will take notes).
- *Identify a few (2–3) critical areas for improvement that you want to address with the employee.* Perhaps you believe an employee has many areas for improvement. While you may want to talk about all of these areas for improvement with the employee, he/she cannot process all those suggestions in any one meeting. Thus, you need to prioritize her/his areas for improvement. Identify the 2–3 areas you want her/him to work on *now*. These 2-3 areas should be the focus of the current PAR session when you start discussing areas for improvement with her/him. Be sure that both managers agree on the 2–3 areas for immediate attention.
- *Schedule the PAR session with the employee* (allow at least one hour). Do not hold the meeting when you might be tired, angry, or too busy.
- *Prepare the room* that will be used for the meeting (put chairs in the room, have a clock that you can unobtrusively use to keep track of time, put tissues in the room).

STAGE 2: DURING THE SESSION: CONDUCTING THE PAR SESSION
Effective Nonverbal and Verbal Behaviors During the PAR Session

Remember that your nonverbal behaviors and how you act during the PAR session are often more important than what you say to the employee.

- Maintain eye contact with the employee at all times.
- Look interested by nodding your head appropriately as she/he speaks.
- Listen to the employee (do not interrupt her/him, do not finish her/his sentences).
- Body posture should be leaning forward to show interest (do not fold your arms over your chest).
- Avoid using sarcasm in tone or statements; do not be threatening or judgmental.
- Smile when appropriate.
- Be specific and use clear behavioral examples to illustrate your points. Explain to her/him the specific aspects of her/his performance that you find effective or ineffective.
- Be careful not to overwhelm the employee by providing too much information.
- Take notes to make sure you will remember key comments made by yourself or the employee.

Holding the Session

- *Bring all relevant materials to the PAR session* (the employee's self-appraisal form, your rating form, a notepad to take notes).

- *Meet the employee and greet her/him when she/he arrives.* Say hello, be sincere, and thank her/him for meeting with you at this time. ("I'm glad we are going to have an opportunity now to talk about your performance and the contributions you have made to the company.") It is critical to start off on a positive note—you need to smile and show comfort with the process. If you do not show comfort ("Well, I know we have to talk about your performance, but it isn't that critical" or "I really hate to do these appraisals"), you are discounting the whole process and sending a negative message to the employee.

- *Address the employee by her/his first name* ("Hi Karen, I'm glad we were able to schedule our meeting now").

- *Start off with some small talk* to warm things up ("How are your kids, ... that class you are taking").

- *Indicate the purpose for the PAR session.* ("Let me tell you what the purpose of this particular meeting is. This is an opportunity for us to talk and discuss your performance in the company. I am very interested in hearing your views, and in sharing my views with you.")

- *Reassure the employee right away* that you value her/his contribution to the firm ("First, let me tell you that we really value your contributions to this company and we feel very fortunate you are working with us").

- *Reassure the employee that anything you discuss will be kept in strictest confidence, and will not be shared with anyone else.* ("I just want you to know that anything we talk about in our PAR meeting will be kept between us, and not shared with anyone else").

- *Have the employee describe her/his performance* before *you provide your feedback*. The more you allow the employee to talk/vent, the more you will learn about what motivates her/him. ("Let's start out by having you talk about how you feel your work on the job is going. Maybe we can start by having you describe the dimensions you feel particularly strong or effective in.")

- *Start with the areas she/he feels strong in.* Listen to the employee's comments about each area in which she/he gave herself/himself a high rating. For each dimension, listen to her/his comments and then offer your own views. (" Okay, you believe you are exceptional in attendance. Can you help me understand why you feel that way?")

  If you disagree with the employee's rating (you gave her/him a lower rating, and the employee's self-rating was higher), after listening to the employee's views, you might either (1) change your mind since now you have learned some things you did not know before, or (2) explain to the employee why you rated him/her lower. ("I can see why you rated yourself high on that dimension, now let me explain why my rating was different. I agree that you attend work on time and do not abuse sick leave and that you are meeting our expectations for this. We are really happy about your performance on this dimension. For me to give an exceptional rating on this dimension, you would need to be arriving early or staying late to help in the transition, or coming back from breaks early—consistently doing something out of the ordinary on this dimension.")

  After addressing the areas where the employee gave herself/himself the highest ratings, if there are other areas that you gave her/him high ratings that were not mentioned, you can now mention those.

- *Next, discuss the areas you both agree that the employee deserves an acceptable rating in.* ("Okay, let's look at those areas where we both agree that you have met expectations and done a fine job.") Once again, allow the employee plenty of time to talk. Make sure the employee knows that you are pleased with her/his performance on these dimensions since she/he has met the expectations on the job.

- *Discuss the employee's areas for improvement* (areas where you or the employee gave him/her a low rating). It is better to refer to these as "areas of improvement" rather than as "weaknesses." Start with any areas she/he gave low self-ratings, and try to understand why the employee gave him/herself a low rating and what she/he feels can be done about the area. The employee may say he/she needs more training or assistance from co-workers.

  If the employee has not given any low self-ratings and you have, then you need to identify those areas with him/her. This is where many managers get nervous. Remember your goal is to get the employee to understand why you have given him/her a low rating (why you feel his/her performance is not acceptable), and to develop a mutually-agreed upon plan for how he/she can improve performance on this dimension (e.g., maybe he/she can attend training, maybe he/she needs to realize how important this dimension is to you as the manager).

  While you may have given the employee low ratings in many areas and will discuss all of the dimensions and ratings, for the current PAR session focus your attention on 2-3 key areas that you think are the most important for him/her to work on right now. ("While there may be several areas it would be good for you to work on, I want to have you focus on these 2-3 areas right now. We will come back to the other areas in our next meeting, and discuss strategies for dealing with those at that time.") If there are a number of improvement areas, you should schedule a follow-up meeting in the next several months to begin working on 1–2 additional areas.

- *Discuss a continuous improvement plan for the employee.* Most employees today want more career coaching by their managers. Spend at least 10–15 minutes discussing goals you and the employee agree he/she will work on during the next 6 months. Document these. Make sure that the employee agrees with the goals and the timetable.

- After the ratings and improvement plan have been discussed, *ask the employee if she/he has any questions about the PAR process or her/his ratings.* Listen to her/his comments. Maintain eye contact and be interested in what she/he has to say.
- *Ask if the employee has any additional questions or comments about* her/his job, duties, the work environment, the managers, co-workers, etc. Listen to her/his comments.

Reactions by Employees and Your Responses as the Manager

Sometimes, employees get upset during the PAR session. First, you have to get them to be calm. *Remember, you cannot get an employee to change her/his behavior if she/he is not calm, and does not listen to you.* Sometimes, it will be better to stop the meeting and reschedule to another time. There is no sense in pushing forward in a PAR session if the employee continues crying or screaming. Unless you can calm the employee down within 10 minutes, you should reschedule.

Crying

Sometimes employees become emotional because they are upset about the ratings or sometimes simply because they are overwhelmed with life in general (e.g., could be having marital or family problems, money problems). *If the employee becomes emotional (starts crying),* then be sympathetic, listen, allow her/him to cry. Maintain eye contact and nod to indicate you are sympathetic. Provide her/him with tissues. If she/he continues crying, you might tell her/him to feel free to go out and use the restroom. ("I can see you are very upset, do you need a few minutes to yourself?") You could also volunteer to leave for a few minutes. ("How about if I give you a few minutes to yourself? I can leave and come back in a few minutes if you'd like.") Usually, an employee does not like to cry in public and feels bad enough about crying or getting emotional. The employee usually does not want you to leave, but just to listen to him/her. *Do not offer unsolicited personal advice* since such employees usually do not want it. You could, however, say "I can see you are pretty upset; would you like any advice about this issue?" If the employee says yes, you can provide advice. If you are not trained as a psychologist, then refer the employee to get help rather than trying to provide serious life counseling. *The best thing you can do as a manager is to* listen *and be sympathetic.*

Anger

Sometimes employees get angry about the ratings or are upset about life in general or the working conditions, and they raise their voice, scream, or act obnoxious. When an employee reacts this way, maintain eye contact with her/him. State "I can see that you are upset; if you can lower your voice, I would be happy to listen to hear what you are concerned about." Do not allow the employee to scream at you. "I am interested to hear what you have to say, but we are going to have to reschedule our meeting to another time, when you feel you will be able to control your voice." *Do not get into a screaming match with an employee.*

Upset

If the employee is upset but is not screaming, then go ahead and hear him/her out. "I can see you are upset; would you like to share what is bothering you?" Listen to her/his concerns. Then, provide your own assessment of the situation. "I understand that you are upset about how this manager or co-worker is treating you. What do you think can be done about this?" It is always a good idea to get the employee's ideas about how to change the situation first. Remember, if you are not sure what can be done about the situation, then you can always say "I need to think about this issue, and I will get back to you about it." Then, you have to get back to the employee within one week; otherwise you will lose some credibility. If the issue is about her/his own performance (e.g., the employee gave himself/herself a higher rating than you did), and the employee disagrees and gets upset, you need to first hear why the employee is upset (why he/she disagrees). Then, you need to calmly explain what specific behaviors you saw to indicate a lower rating.

STAGE 3: ENDING THE SESSION

- *Repeat agreed-upon goals, objectives, and the timetable.* ("Okay, let's make sure we are in agreement about your developmental plan. Can you tell me what you got out of our session about the things you will be working on?" It is a good idea to have the employee state what she/he thinks the goals were, to make sure she/he really understands them and agrees with them. "And, you are comfortable with these goals and the timeframe for meeting them?"
- *Repeat her/his value to the organization.* ("I really appreciate all the work you do for our company. You bring a lot to this company.")
- *Thank the employee for his/ her help, time, and cooperation* in making the meeting effective. ("I am glad we had this opportunity to talk. I appreciate your time and cooperation in making it an effective session.")
- *Indicate the follow-up that will be done.* ("Okay, we will meet again in 6 months for our next review." Or, "Okay, I'll get back to you about the training opportunities in two weeks, and you will get back to me about the equipment needs in two weeks. Do you want to set up that meeting now?")

- *Ask for any final questions, concerns, or comments.* ("Is there anything else you want to bring up at this time?")
- *Get signatures for the manager's PA form.* ("Okay, now I need to have both of us sign my copy of the Manager's Form. Remember, your signature just indicates that we have actually had this meeting, not that you necessarily agree with all the ratings.") Get both signatures and date the form.
- *Indicate what will be done with the forms.* ("I will copy both your form and my form and will give you a copy of both. I will also keep a copy of both and put those in my employee files so we have a record of it.") Make sure to provide the employee with a copy of both forms within 3–5 days. This is important to the employee. You cannot add other comments on the form unless you show them to the employee and have her/him initial that she/he has seen those comments.
- *Thank the employee a final time* and escort her/him out of the meeting room. ("Thanks again. Have a good night, weekend.")

STAGE 4: AFTER THE SESSION

- *Make necessary copies of the forms.* Make one copy of the Manager Form and one copy of the Employee Form, and give these to the employee in an envelope within 3-5 days after the PAR session. Do not leave them lying around for anyone to see.
- *File your copies.* Put your copy of the Manager Form and the Employee Form in the employee file that you keep. Keep these confidential.
- *Future contact with the employee.* Maintain eye contact and a pleasant demeanor when seeing the employee, regardless of what happened during the session (e.g., the employee got upset, the employee had been crying).

ADDITIONAL REFERENCE MATERIALS
Professional Associations and Information on Laws and HR Issues

American Compensation Association (ACA)
http://www.acaonline.org

American Management Association (AMA)
http://www.amanet.org

American Psychological Association (APA)
http://www.apa.org

American Society for Training and Development (ASTD)
http://www.astd.org

American Staffing Association (ASA)
http://www.staffingtoday.net

Americans with Disabilities Act (ADA)
http://www.usdoj.gov/crt/ada/adahom1.htm

Bureau of Labor Statistics (BLS)
http://www.bls.gov

Employee Benefit Research Institute (EBRI)
http://www.ebri.org

Employers Council on Flexible Compensation
http://www.benefits.net

Employment Laws Assistance for Workers and Small Businesses (ELAWS)
http://www.dol.gov/elaws

Equal Employment Opportunity Commission (EEOC)
http://www.eeoc.gov

Human Resources Law Index
http://www.hrlawindex.com

National Association of Personnel Services (NAPS)
http://www.napsweb.org

Occupational Safety and Health Administration (OSHA)
http://www.osha.gov

Society for Advancement of Management (SAM)
http://www.enterprise.tamucc.edu/sam/default.htm

Society for Human Resource Management (SHRM)
http://www.shrm.org
http://www.shrm.org/hrnews

Workforce Online
http://www.workforceonline.com
World at Work
http://www.worldatwork.org

Career Web Sites (to advertise jobs or search for applicants)

http://www.monster.com
http://www.headhunter.net
http://www.jobsearch.org
http://www.hotjobs.com
http://www.dice.com
http://www.careerbuilder.com
http://www.nationjob.com
http://www.jobs.com

Relevant Journals and Publications for HR Issues

Business Week
http://www.businessweek.com
Fortune
http://www.fortune.com
Harvard Business Review
http://harvardbusinessonline.hbsp.harvard.edu
HR Magazine
http://www.shrm.org
INC
http://www.inc.com
Training
http://www.trainingsupersite.com
Training and Development Journal
http://www.astd.org

Appendix

Ernest R. Cadotte
University of Tennessee

Business Simulations
*The Next Step in Management Training**

It is said that Japanese entrepreneurs live and work according to an almost mythic tome, *A Book of Five Rings,* written in 1645 by the great samurai Miyamoto Musashi. Although he was considered virtually invincible, Musashi did not feel he had mastered strategy. At the age of 30 he decided to redirect his life and devote himself to a search for the principles of strategy. Near the end of his life, Musashi retired to a cave to write. He intended his book as a treatise that would apply not only to battle strategy but also to "any situation where plans and tactics are used."

Several of Musashi's principles on strategy have powerful applications in today's business world. To paraphrase Musashi, the mastery of strategy requires that one fulfill the following six directives: be honest; be familiar with every skill and profession of business management; know the difference between profitable and unprofitable activities; attend to detail; identify and work on only those activities that will have value in the future; and train continuously in order to develop an intuitive judgment and understanding of business situations and an ability to perceive things that others cannot see. Mastery of these elements, Musashi believed, occurs only through constant training and tireless practice.

Peter Senge makes a similar observation regarding the importance of training in his book *The Fifth Discipline: The Art and Practice of the Learning Organization.*[1] Senge states that training, not study alone, is what changes a person. Through purposeful training, an individual can learn to act and think in expanded ways and can thus be transformed into a new competitive force.

There are many methods of management training. Textbooks, lectures, and case studies represent forms of solitary training. Virtual business simulations represent a form of combative training in which students pit their business skills against those of formidable opponents under the watchful eye of a training coach. This article advocates the inclusion of large-scale, virtual-reality simulations in the training of future managers. Reality simulations have unique training capabilities that foster personal transformation in the manner advocated by Senge. Moreover, they can help students develop an almost intuitive understanding of business, including a seamless perspective of its functional elements and a knowledge of how these elements can be coordinated to achieve a strong and profitable position in the market. Another distinctive feature of simulations is their emphasis on management—of the firm, of its strategy, and of its resources.

The position taken in this article reflects my personal experiences as a developer and provider of business simulations in the classroom with MBA students, executives, undergraduates, and even high school students. The points made here also draw heavily on the experiences of a host of educators who have used a variety of business simulations, in a variety of learning contexts.[2]

BRIDGING GAPS IN BUSINESS SCHOOL EDUCATION

Are business schools doing their jobs? A critique by Behrman and Levin in the *Harvard Business Review* more than a decade ago suggested that the answer at that time was no.[3] According to the authors, critics were asserting that business schools place too much emphasis on quantitative analysis, tools, and

---

* This appendix originally appeared in the Autumn 1995 edition of *Selections, The Magazine of the Graduate Management Admission Council.*

models and too little emphasis on qualitative thinking, complex trade-offs, and creativity; too much on theory and not enough on execution; too much on short-term performance and not enough on long-term success; too much on career and corporate goals and too little on interpersonal relationships and social ethics; and too much on separate disciplines at the expense of integrative problem solving and management.

Part of the criticism of business education over the years has stemmed from our primary methods of teaching—lecture/textbook and case study. **Exhibit A.1** (pages 382–383) details the characteristics, advantages, and disadvantages of these methods and of reality simulations.[4]

The lecture/textbook format is very efficient for communicating a large number of concepts to a large number of students. However, this format does not do enough to encourage creativity, the integrating of functional material, problem solving, decision making, risk taking, or interpersonal skills.

Case analysis is a major step in the transition from the academic world to the business world. Students have the opportunity to analyze and solve complex problems, think in strategic ways, and integrate material across disciplines. The limitation is that students do not have to execute their decisions and live with the consequences. They are also not required to respond to competitive moves and countermoves or to deal with the decisions of others.

Simulations can go farther than traditional methods in bridging the gap between the classroom and the world of real-life business decision making. Simulations are self-contained. Further, the more sophisticated games offer a broad scope and provide students with substantial authority and responsibility. As with case analyses, with simulations students are required to analyze and solve complex problems, think in strategic ways, and integrate material across disciplines. In addition, they must act on their decisions and deal with the consequences; this includes adjusting strategies in response to changes in end-user needs or wants and to competitive moves or countermoves.

Business simulations have only lately begun to reach their full potential. Until recently, hardware constraints, software-design requirements, and student work-load considerations limited the depth and breadth of decision making that could be modeled. New developments in microcomputers and business software have greatly expanded the possibilities. Almost all of the published simulations are being upgraded as a result of advances in computer software and hardware and increased acceptance of simulations by educators. Currently, there is a limited number of large-scale simulations.[5]

SIMULATION METHOD OF ACTIVE LEARNING

A simulation is an experiential learning exercise in which students practice the design, implementation, and control of business strategies. They worry about the applications, not the definitions, of business concepts, principles, and methods. Decisions do not occur sequentially but simultaneously and interactively, just as they do in the business world. The paramount objective is to help students internalize business thought through the practice of business decision making.

The more sophisticated business simulations, which may be labeled reality simulations, are designed to capture the qualitative and quantitative dimensions of business decision making within the context of a total business enterprise. Students essentially run a business for 8 to 16 decision periods, depending upon course design. The problems and opportunities encountered require total immersion into the business enterprise.

In these simulations, students have the opportunity to work either as top managers or as entrepreneurs. They must survey the market, identify and evaluate market opportunities, design and execute a business program, monitor their own performance and that of the competition, and adjust their strategy and tactics as necessary. Decision making, which occurs at the tactical level, includes such business activities as brand design, research and development, capacity planning, production scheduling, inventory control, media planning, and sales-office management. Since all decisions are constrained by limited financial resources, the ability to manage the sources as well as the uses of cash is critical to success.

While the business is small enough that everyone involved can see and experience each aspect of the enterprise, the exercise is usually so complex that teamwork is required. Importantly, the active learning process is nourished by team interaction. Of particular value are the frequent discussions and debates that arise because of the complexity, interconnectedness, and novelty of the decision making. High-level thought processes are required to understand, inform, and persuade one's colleagues concerning a continuous stream of issues. These conditions help students to enhance their critical thinking skills and develop business language.

Creation of Virtual Business Reality

The simulation develops a living case in which participants create their own virtual business reality. The decision context is provided in the simulation software and manuals. The players provide the living details through their own deliberations, actions, and interactions with competitors and with the market.

Although the industry context does not change, the exercise actually represents a series of interconnected cases. In a sense, every decision period represents a new case and set of circumstances. It might begin as a team-building exercise that shifts to a market-opportunity analysis case, then moves into a test-marketing case, and finally becomes a market-development case. At a later point, the need to finance research and development as well as market expansion might shift attention to the raising of equity capital from outside investors. The need to develop an extended business plan and pro forma cash flows will pull together many related decisions.

As the industry and the firm mature, price and reliability become more important. At this point, the team's attention might shift to the improvement of factory operations via the use of common components, greater emphasis on product quality, reductions in line-changeover times, and the use of different techniques for production scheduling. And, of course, there is always the need to fend off aggressive competitors.

External market analysis further shapes the issues being addressed as team members try to understand how the market is altered by competitive moves, while at the same time assessing the impact of their own firm. Internal debates rage over an additional feature, a lower price, another salesperson, or a new media outlet, and the effects of these on consumer preference, competitive advantage, cash-flow requirements, and profitability.

As case studies, simulations are much richer than the decision outline found in any template or manual. It is the imaginations and thought processes of the students that fill in the details; the computer program becomes simply a tool for organizing the work and recording the team's decisions.

Students do not need to role-play because the situation they are dealing with is, in part, of their own doing. The process of thinking strategically forces students to go beyond the immediate problem to consider their firm's future and how they want to shape it.

Role of the Instructor

With simulations, the instructor's role departs from the traditional format. Although lectures on strategy, competitive analysis, or cash flow may be warranted, the instructor's major responsibility is to serve the dual role of devil's advocate and coach.

As devil's advocate, the instructor should challenge the team to thoroughly understand the dynamics of the market and the decision-making environment. During regularly scheduled executive briefings, team members should present their analyses of the market, the decisions they have made, and their justifications for those decisions. The instructor's role is not to provide solutions to the team's problems but rather to raise questions and issues that have not yet been addressed.

As coach, the instructor's role is to help students develop critical thinking skills. At the very least, the questions instructors ask during executive briefings should stimulate students to consider additional dimensions in their strategic thinking. Also, students come into meetings with the faculty with pointed questions based upon a need to know, much like their executive counterparts. The current situation can thus be used to illustrate concepts, principles, and theories concerning innumerable topics.

The instructional assistance comes at a highly relevant time and within a context that is germane for and unique to each student. From a pedagogical point of view, this approach is highly effective. The students' involvement in a business makes them highly receptive to ideas, techniques, and thought processes that might help them to resolve difficulties or better shape their firm's future. The approach is also very efficient: Techniques that are clearly understood do not require elaboration by the professor.

MANAGERIAL SKILLS PRACTICED IN SIMULATIONS

A simulation exercise serves as a reasonably intact organization in which disciplinary content is reinforced and the linkages among disciplines are obvious. In addition, the more sophisticated simulations offer students the opportunity to practice a number of important skills, including strategic planning and thinking; strategy management; leadership, teamwork, and interpersonal skills; budgeting and cash-flow management; and understanding and delivering of customer value.

Strategic Planning and Thinking

Strategic planning, which gives purpose and direction to the firm's future actions, requires the setting of objectives and the development of a detailed plan of activities that are interconnected, time phased, and financially sustainable. Strategy emerges with the understanding of market opportunities and corporate capabilities. Preoccupation with short-term goals may cause long-term problems.

In some sense, strategic planning is a mechanical task of organizing activities over time. While strategic planning is necessary, it is not sufficient for success. The more critical component, strategic thinking, requires an understanding of tactical options and of how one can skillfully select and coordinate these in order to achieve a desired objective. Further, strategic thinking requires the ability to project into the future both the possible ramifications of a particular tactical maneuver and its potential interactions with present and possible future tactics.

The skills of strategic planning and thinking are not easy to develop; a great deal of practice, feedback, and coaching is needed. An advantage of simulations is that they provide a variety of interconnected business situations in which participants repetitively analyze circumstances, establish objectives, and lay out plans of coordinated activities that extend several planning periods into the future. Unlike the situation with a case study, with a simulation the planning does not end with a formal, long-term strategic plan. Rather, the plan must vie for prominence in an evolving, competitive environment. Consequently, with each day students encounter a new set of circumstances that calls for a reevaluation of yesterday's plan.

Strategy Management

To borrow from Thomas Edison, we might say that the management of strategy involves 1 percent inspiration and 99 percent perspiration. Strategy management requires on-your-feet thinkers who are skillful adjusters. Part of management

education's task is to enhance the decision-making skills of future managers, who are likely to be called on to dynamically adjust strategies as new information comes to light and unexpected events unfold.

To succeed, the manager of a strategy must be focused, flexible, and fast, as well as capable of recognizing fundamental shifts in business conditions. It is also essential that the manager explore new possibilities by developing and testing ideas in both the company and the market, and that he or she be ready and able to reallocate resources when conditions require the firm to move in new directions.

The "correctness" of a decision will depend upon the circumstances at the particular point in time. With each success or failure, the manager and the competition create new conditions, which often require still newer strategies and tactics.

A simulation experience is unique in its ability to provide training in strategy management; no other learning tool can give students experience in the execution and constant adjustment of a strategy. Further, simulations allow students to personally observe the interconnectedness of business functions. With firms everywhere downsizing or eliminating their strategic business units, the manager of a strategy cannot count on functional specialists to fill in the knowledge gaps between functional areas. He or she must have a solid cross-functional understanding of the business enterprise.

Simulations forcefully illustrate the management challenges facing organizations, and they provide a more holistic and deeper understanding of strategy implementation than is possible using traditional teaching methods alone.

Leadership, Teamwork, and Interpersonal Skills

In a business simulation, a group of individuals is brought together to form a team. The manager of the strategy is also the manager of the team. He or she must assess the team's skills, organize the work, manage the work in process, and reorganize as needed. This individual must be a leader with team-building and interpersonal skills. It is his or her job to help the team become more cohesive, to create a sense of mutual commitment and trust, to nurture the talents and capabilities of team members, and to help participants develop team skills. Managing a team is far more difficult than

Exhibit A.1: *Comparison of Lecture/Textbook, Case Study, and Simulation Methods*

	Lectures/Textbook	Case Studies	Reality Simulations
Emphasis	language tools of business	situation analysis problem diagnosis problem solving strategic thinking	business process execution of strategy/solutions management of tactics team work
Content	concepts principles theory analytical tools	decision situations diverse scenarios and contexts complex problems	business processes interdependent decisions time-phased implementation continual adjustment
Method of learning	knowledge acquisition sequential presentation of information cognitively passive listening reading memorization highly structured classroom low ambiguity right and wrong determined by definition	critical thinking sequential analysis of typical/important decisions cognitively active analysis debate semi-structured classroom circumscribed problems and opportunities high ambiguity right and wrong determined by logic	decision making and management simultaneous treatment of interdependent decisions cognitively and emotionally active must take calculated risks responsibility for decisions unstructured classroom undefined, unanticipated problems and opportunities complexity makes it difficult to perceive cause and effect very high ambiguity right and wrong determined by outcome; vary with business conditions financial performance market performance no ambiguity in performance measurement
Advantages	efficient large number of ideas large number of students minimum prep for faculty standardized across faculty common text text-based lectures multiple-choice exams work pace set by tests study can be delayed	closer to real life actual decision situations sorting out information problem identification problem solving cross-functional issues interpersonal relations (group cases) leadership organization analysis esprit de corp team work division of task responsibility need for cooperation exposure to diversity of decision contexts industries work pace set by assignments regular progression of cases steady, frequent workload opportunity for mini-tutorials case studies illustrate key decisions, relevant issues and tradeoffs	closest to real-life manager's role focus on execution authority and responsibility to act work with budgets and cash flows continuous skillful adjustment necessary interpersonal relations leadership vision initiative coordination over time team work division of functional responsibility functional accountability extended interdependence (10–15 weeks) work out bad decisions resolve points of tension deal with decision nuances due to overlapping decisions time-phased implementation cash-flow constraints work pace set by decision deadlines current decisions demand attention decisions affecting future can be delayed

Lectures/Textbook	Case Studies	Reality Simulations
Advantages (*continued*)		
	intellectually challenging	opportunity for mini-tutorials
		familiar with decision context
		receptive due to involvement
		understanding enriched by personal relevance
	builds confidence due to practice in communication and persuasion	captivating
	problem solving	personal stake
	logical thinking	competitive spirit
		students assume the role as simulation becomes reality
		living in microcosm helps students to see interconnectedness of business decisions
		builds confidence due to practice in decision making
		risk taking
		management of operation
Disadvantages		
limited development of	staff or consultant type training	limited variety of experiences
knowledge integration	focus on problem identification	single industry scenario
strategic/critical thinking	no responsibility for execution	confined set of tactical and strategic decisions
creativity	no management of team members	development of large-scale simulations very expensive
interpersonal relations	no risk taking required	length of exercise limits practical number of simulation experiences
problem solving	can reinforce functional silo thinking	anxiety-producing for students
risk taking	more quantitative, less qualitative	immediate total immersion
decision making	individual case preparation leads to competitive and not cooperative behavior	everything needs attention
management skills	anxiety-producing for students	clues to problems not well structured
repetitive for faculty	unstructured problems	must take initiative
	attention to detail	must live with mistakes
	no right answer	success (grade) measured by outcome, dependent upon team members
	skills and knowledge exposed in class	competition
	thinking always challenged	information not yet available
	success (grade) measured by analysis of detail	changes with changing condition
	logic	time intensive; always more to do
	communication skills	challenges for faculty
	preparation is hard work	lengthy learning process
	challenging for faculty	difficult to stay in touch
	extensive preparation	complexity of game
	less structure in classroom	dynamic environment
	must think on feet	need to manage student discomfort
	must offer credible analysis	other faculty not supportive
		not familiar with method or value
		limited classroom work
		reduced student contact
		simulation competes with other classes for students' attention and time
		time consuming—competes with research, publishing

managing materials, an advertising campaign, or some other mechanical activity. It is very important for the team manager to regularly assess and improve his or her role and effectiveness.

In large, complex simulations, teamwork is essential for success. There is simply too much information to process and there are too many decisions to make for any one or two individuals to do it all. Each member of the team must determine how he or she can actively contribute, and each must depend upon the others to do their jobs.

A simulation experience is a more complete team-building experience than cases and other group projects because the team must live with its decisions. When a poor decision by an individual or by the team makes adjustment necessary, long-term stress is added to the team-dynamics equation. Team members do not forget whose ideas were accepted and whose were not. They also remember whose ideas helped the organization, as well as whose held it back or even damaged its potential.

A number of people on the team will have good ideas, but only a limited number of those ideas can be accepted and implemented. Students must fight for their ideas, and at the same time they must listen and respond to the ideas of their colleagues. All team members must develop communication skills and learn the arts of negotiation and confrontation, which are necessary parts of the decision-making process.

The team experience can provide all participants with an understanding of the role of leadership within a micro setting, and it can illustrate how work gets done in the face of financial and time constraints and the presence of multiple viewpoints. Members also see firsthand how personal factors can color rational decision making.

A particularly attractive feature of simulations is that participants can pause at strategic points from the routine of business and focus on interpersonal skills and team dynamics. The case studies are the experiences of the team and of its individual members. Team facilitators can step into these situations and manage the process of self-diagnosis and adjustment. Working like personal trainers or coaches, they can offer students specific suggestions on how to work with others to accomplish organizational and personal goals. At the end of the exercise, facilitators can lead the team through a final review of its progress and process and encourage team members to develop personal plans of action for contributing to and managing future teams.

Budgeting and Cash-Flow Management

The management of resources usually translates into the management of money. Strategic planning and execution require strong skills in budgeting and cash-flow management. All participants must anticipate the timing of disbursements and receipts relative to the execution of the plan. During the planning phase, there are often adjustments to both the plan and the budget as the team integrates tactics with cash-flow requirements. During the execution phase, the adjustments become even more critical as resources are reallocated in response to evolving and unexpected events and information.

Cash-flow management is perhaps the most difficult technical skill to master. The manager of the strategy must understand the differences between cash-flow management and profit management, and he or she must realize the constraints of financing growth from sales revenue.

One of the advantages of a simulation is that all decisions are tied in to the income statement, balance sheet, and cash-flow statement. Students can immediately see how their decisions impact the firm's various accounts and its profitability. By living with their own company, team members develop an almost intuitive understanding of financial statements and cash flows. They learn to carefully manage receipts and disbursements and to project their cash-flow requirements several quarters into the future.

A simulation also helps students to understand financial accountability. The exercise can be structured so that the team presents its business plan and funding needs to outside investors. Because investors want to maximize the returns on their investments, they demand high performance from a venture firm. Every managerial student must come to grips with the harsh reality that the bottom line is the ultimate driving force behind any business enterprise.

Understanding and Delivery of Customer Value

To deliver customer value, the manager must first know what customers want and need. Because many customers have difficulty articulating exactly what this is, it is the manager's task to sort out all the data and to infer customer wants and needs.

To accomplish delivery of customer value, managers must understand how a particular component or service translates into a benefit for the customer. They must then determine how to combine components and services to achieve the value desired, and with a profit. Management students must understand that even when firms are able to find and deliver the right assortment of features and services, the work is still not over. Good products are imitated, and customer expectations shift upward. Like it or not, the manager will be caught in an upward spiral of innovation and imitation.

The understanding and delivery of customer value is a very difficult aspect of management to master; again, a great deal of practice is required. In a simulation, the learning process parallels the experience in business—that is, clues are introduced intermittently and without explicit directions for how to capitalize on them. Students must listen to what customers say and watch how they react, infer priorities and preferences, and engage in trial-and-error decision making. Under the watchful eye of the instructor, this evolving experience will help students become proficient in understanding the market and responding to and anticipating market needs.

Other Skills Developed through Simulations

Simulations can help students enhance a number of skills beyond those described above. In preparing and presenting business plans, students enhance their skills in oral and written communication, as well as in time management.

In addition, by the time students complete a comprehensive simulation, the decision process of analysis, planning, execution, and control should have become very natural for them. Many students adopt the decision process naturally; most discover it out of necessity.

Students can also learn a great deal about themselves through a simulation exercise. Can they succeed, and possibly thrive, within a highly unstructured venture environment? Can they deal with the ambiguity that is inherent in any new venture? Are they able to take calculated risks when there is very limited information available? As they gain experience and an understanding of what it takes to succeed in an ever-changing business environment, students will usually find that their ability to make good decisions is enhanced. In turn, this realization enhances self-confidence.

ISSUES FOR STUDENTS

At first, many students are uncomfortable with business simulations. This discomfort comes in many forms and may be different for different students. Management faculty who are regular users of simulations report the following general reasons for students' initial unease:

- The learning format is highly demanding, with students needing to learn a vast amount in the first week alone.
- Students must take more initiative in structuring the learning process than is the case with other pedagogies.
- The old formula for getting good grades is not effective; the dynamic application of knowledge is totally different from the acquisition of information.
- An individual student cannot completely control his or her own destiny. The decisions and actions of other team members and of the competition interfere.
- There are few right or wrong answers; rather, the answers change as the market changes.
- A decision cannot be judged good or bad until the outcome is known.
- Simulations are very time consuming, and there is always more work that could be done to gain the competitive advantage.
- Some students do not like to be graded on market or financial performance because these are moving targets. Such students prefer to be evaluated strictly on their skills in analysis, writing, and oral presentation, as well as on the amount of effort they put into the simulation exercise.
- The instructor cannot tell the students what to do, even though the students do not know what to do.

Most of these sources of discomfort actually derive from the strengths of simulations. Once students are past their initial discomfort, most find that they do like simulation exercises. Faculty who conduct simulations report that students frequently describe the experience as challenging, motivating, and fun. Students say, too, that simulation exercises give them a sense of ownership.

ISSUES FOR THE INSTRUCTOR

In most cases, instructors face a learning curve in using simulations. With large-scale simulations, an instructor may need a semester or two before he or she feels completely comfortable with the use of this device as a learning tool.

There is also a need for the instructor to stay in touch with the events of the simulation exercise. This is of particular importance with complex, large-scale simulations, where an instructor who does not stay in constant touch will quickly be left out of the action.

The fact that some students do not like simulations is also a very real issue. A small number of vocal students can make it uncomfortable for an instructor, especially during the first run or two of the exercise. Also, these negative opinions can pull down teaching evaluations. Without administrative support, junior faculty members must carefully assess the use of simulations despite the tremendous learning potential of such exercises.

Simulation users find that other faculty may not share their enthusiasm for this pedagogical method. Where a simulation is the dominant element of the course, the instructor may spend less than half the normal time in the classroom. Most of the instructor's contact with students occurs during weekly or biweekly executive briefings. The students set their own schedule and run the simulated firm as they would their own company. Other faculty members may feel that this setup provides too much freedom and too little structure.

Finally, the mechanics of the simulation can add several hours to the instructor's work load each week. Also, if the simulation is used with a large number of students, the instructor might need a dedicated computer and a graduate student (game administrator) to help with the processing of team decisions.

FUTURE OF MANAGEMENT EDUCATION

No single pedagogy can fulfill all the needs of management students. Simulation exercises represent one advance in our methods of management training. In light of all that is possible with new computer technologies, we have barely scratched the surface. Innovative technological tools can be used to refine and advance management education, giving us greater freedom to help students visualize, experience, comprehend, and retain what we want them to learn. There is almost nothing we cannot simulate or present in close to living detail.

Maximum business preparedness will be achieved through a combination of traditional methods with such new methods as the reality simulation. New learning methodologies can build upon, reinforce, and fill in the gaps of current ones. The challenge is to evaluate and adapt new technologies to our current and evolving needs and in so doing to move management education forward into the next century.

Acknowledgments

I would like to thank the following educators for many of the ideas presented in this article: Frank Alpert, University of Missouri, St. Louis; Mary Jane Burns, Florida International University; Jerry Conover, Northern Arizona University; Jim Dupre, Grove City College; Ron Decker, University of Wisconsin, Eau Claire; Alan Flaschner, University of Toledo; Jonathan Freeman, University of Toronto; Lois E. Graff, George Washington University; Greg Gundlach, University of Notre Dame; Lance Masters, California State University, Hayward; John Nichols, Florida International University; Marty Roth, Boston College; Steve Thrasher, Pacific Lutheran University; Linda Van Esch, St. Mary's University, Halifax, Canada; Keith Wilson, University of Manitoba, Winnipeg, Canada.

1. Peter M. Senge, *The Fifth Discipline: The Art and Practice of the Learning Organization* (New York: Bantam, Doubleday, and Dale, 1990).

2. For this article, 15 faculty were interviewed regarding their opinions of the value of simulations. These faculty have used an assortment of simulations over the years, including the following:
   - Ernest R. Cadotte, *Global Corporate Management in the Marketplace* (Cincinnati, OH: South-Western Publishing, 2003).
   - Ernest R. Cadotte, *Strategic Management in the Marketplace* (Cincinnati, OH: South-Western Publishing, 2003).
   - Jean-Claude Larreche and Hubert Gatignon, *Markstrat 3* (Cincinnati, OH: South-Western Publishing, 1998).
   - Charlotte H. Mason and William D. Perreault, *The Marketing Game,* 2nd ed. (Homewood, IL: Richard D. Irwin, Inc., 1992).
   - Anthony J. Faria, Ray O. Nelson, and Dean Roussos, *Compete* (Homewood, IL: Richard D. Irwin, Inc., 1994).
   - Hans B. Thorelli, *International Operations Simulation/INTOPIA* (Englewood Cliffs, NJ: Prentice Hall, 1995).

3. Jack N. Behrman and Richard I. Levin, "Are Business Schools Doing Their Job?" *Harvard Business Review* 62, no. 1 (January–February 1984): 140–147.

4. For an excellent discussion of the advantages of the case method, see Thomas V. Bonoma, "Learning with Cases," Boston: Harvard Business School, 1989.

5. See Frank Alpert, "Large-Scale Simulation in Marketing Education," *Journal of Marketing Education* (1993): 30–35; and Alvin C. Burns and James W. Gentry, "Simulations in Marketing: Past, Present, and Future," *Marketing Education Review* (1992): 3–13.

Index

quality control 307–308; quality improvement 312–313; simultaneous engineering teams (SETs) 178–179; teams, use of 52

cash and marketable securities 193–194

cash flow 122

cause-and-effect diagram. *See* Ishikawa Diagram

census data 116, 125

Centennial Technologies Inc. 256–257

CEO (Chief Executive Officer) as board chairman 253; board of directors, seduction of 243; on boards of directors 246; hiring and firing 248–249; informal governance by board of directors 250; and outside board members 245–246; pay, setting 252; removal 253–258

CFO (Chief Financial Officer) 253

chain of command, boards violating 247–248

chairperson, board of directors 253

changeovers profitability 320–325; reaction times, cutting by increasing 319–320

channel customers 112, 123

channel partners key competitors, competitive analysis 111–112; strategy in selecting 170

channel profile kinds, why so many 117–118; market opportunity analysis 207

Chem-Pro 110, 111

choice evaluation 114–115

Chrysler 35, 38, 241

Churchill, Winston 27

Clason, Nick 310, 312

classes, financial assets 215–218

CLM. *See* Council of Logistics Managements

clutter, advertising 169

Coca-Cola 105–106

coherence, principle of 83

cohesiveness, high-performance teams 265–266

collective-action problem 239

collectivism 58–59

colleges lack of teaching about leadership 17–21; leadership development grants 32

committee meetings 251

commodity products 350–351

common size statements 217–218

common stock 197

communication high-performance teams, characteristics of 266; human resource management (HRM) 366–367

comparable company approach, equity valuation 230–232

comparisons, use evaluation 115

compensation boards of directors 243; executives 252

competition assessing, quality function deployment (QFD) 186–187; forecasting 125–126; identifying in market opportunity analysis (MOA) 105–106; pricing 159–160

competitive advantage 93–94, 96

competitor profiles capabilities of competing products or services 110; firms within markets 108–109; industry sales trends 108; key competitors 109; market opportunity analysis (MOA) 108–112; select key competitors 109–110

components, estimating value 230–232

composition of groups 271–272

compromising or accommodating strategy 64

computer industry behavior patterns 113; competition 106; distribution channels, analysis of 111; emerging products and firms 110; logistics leverage 352–353; Microsoft Works 2001, improving 185–186; operating profit 199; pointing device, design characteristics 182–183; product costs and changeover 155

conflict management style 73–74; in teams 61, 63–64

consensus decisions 59, 60–61

consequences customer value 114, 134–136; of product use 131–132

consulting contracts 243

consumer magazines 111

consumption goals 131

contingency plans 96–97

continuous improvement systems 366–367

control limits 299

controls business strategy, implementing 87–88; profit management 334–335

conversion cost 330

cooperation 265

corporate governance boards of directors, composition 240–250; businesses versus corporations 238–239; CEO removal, reaching consensus about 253–258; Enron collapse 237; global economy 240–241; growth bonus for corporations 239; history 236, 238; joint-stock companies and "limited liability" 236; legal issues 244–250; management, power, and accountability issues 235–240; mergers and boards of directors 236, 238; monopolies 238; shareholder disenfranchisement 239–240; trends and issues 245–246

costs advertising 162, 164; of capital, determining 224–225; changeovers, profitability 320, 336; of goods sold, income statement 198; logistical trade-offs 349; low-cost provider 172; pricing 121–122, 161–162; profit management 329–332; quality 309–313; reducing with use of teams 53; transportation 346, 347

Council of Logistics Managements (CLM) 346

Covey, Stephen 29–30, 30, 33

credit ratings 215, 216

Crest toothpaste 130

CRM. *See* customer relationship management

Crosby, Philip 22

Csikszentmihalyi, Mihaly 30

current liabilities 195–196

customer ads, scoring 168; base, quantifying 115–116; channel profiles 117; delivery time expectations, exceeding 351–352; end user profiles 112, 113; loyalty 108; market opportunity analysis 206–207; needs satisfaction, maximizing 107; number of, estimating 124–125; product quality, test of 290; quality function deployment (QFD) 181–184; response functions to product design 154–155; satisfaction, creating in product design 150

customer relationship management (CRM) 144

customer value consequences of product use 131–132; consumption goals 131; data, using for strategic advantage 143–145; defined 130–133; end user profiles 113–114; hierarchy 133–137; reasons to study 129–130; use situation, importance of 132–133

D

data, strategic customer relationship management (CRM) 144; logistics and transportation 144–145; pricing decisions 144; products, developing new 144; promotion 144; quality function deployment 144; target markets, identifying and serving 143

Day, George S. and Wensley, Robin 94

deadlines, handling changing 267–268

deal, negotiating 211

debt bank 223; cost of capital 224

decision-making orientation, customer value hierarchy 140

decomposition analysis 215–217

defects 296–297

Dell Computer 199, 334, 335, 352–353

Delphi technique 61

demand distribution and sales management 170–172; distribution points 170; as function of potential, forecasting 124; macroeconomic analysis 104; price elasticity 158–159; purchase pattern, discovering 113; variation, impact on value stream (bullwhip effect) 317–319

Deming, W. E. 177–178, 289

democratic team decisions 59

DeMott, Benjamin 32

Denver Company 338–339

deployment 89

depreciation 195, 196

descriptive schools of business strategy 79

design, product advantage, losing differential 154; brand loyalty 157–158; competing and response functions to benefits 153; customer preference for benefits over components 149–150; customer response functions, deducing 154–155; customer satisfaction, creating 150; interactions effects 152; market response functions 151–152; minimum performance requirements 156; more is not always better (elasticity of peanut) 150–151; multiple products in a segment 157; overdoing benefits 153–154; product costs and change over time 155–156; quality control